Families Today

Families Today

Second Edition

Connie R. Sasse, CFCS

GLENCOE
McGraw-Hill

New York, New York
Columbus, Ohio
Mission Hills, California
Peoria, Illinois

Reviewers

Loretta Pryor Bruce
Vocational Department Chairman
Home Economics and Cooperative
   Education Teacher
Burleson High School
Burleson, Texas

Peggy Morrison-Thurston
Coordinator of Alternative Education
   Programs
South Broward High School
Hollywood, Florida

Sheila Stender Sartin, CFCS
F.H.A. Advisor and Home Economics
   Teacher
Hamburg High School
Hamburg, Arkansas

Barbara Snodgrass
Chairman of Home Economics Department
Pendleton Heights High School
Pendleton, Indiana

Ruth Thomas, Ph.D.
Associate Professor
Home Economics Education
University of Minnesota
St. Paul, Minnesota

Elizabeth Trinkle
Home Economics Teacher
Pendleton Heights High School
Pendleton, Indiana

Contributors

Mark Bregman

Kay Chadbourne

Sharon Thompson

Glencoe/McGraw-Hill

A Division of The McGraw-Hill Companies

Printed in the United States of America

Send all inquiries to:
Glencoe/McGraw-Hill
3008 W. Willow Knolls Drive
Peoria, IL 61614-1083

ISBN 0-02-642926-8 (Student's Edition)
ISBN 0-02-642929-2 (Teacher's Wraparound Edition)

Printed in the United States of America

3 4 5 6 7 8 9 10 11 12 QPH 02 01 00 99 98 97

Table of Contents

The Family Foundation

"When Grandpa Riley moved in with us, Mom said, 'He needs us.' My grandmother had died, and Grandpa wasn't doing very well. The first few weeks weren't easy. I don't think my grandfather felt like this was his home. He hadn't lived on a farm since he was a kid. Having him here all the time was kind of different. Then one day we started looking at an old photograph album. Grandpa started telling me stories about what he used to do on the farm when he was my age. The world sure has changed a lot — and so has my life since Grandpa Riley moved in. Like I told my mother just last night, 'I really need him.' "

DAVID

15

Families Make A Difference

IMAGINE THAT ...

you have been asked to plan a society without families. You may wonder how people would get along if they didn't have what families provide. Is there anything that can replace the family? Why are families so important? As you can see, your assignment is a difficult one. Even with imagination, you may not be able to picture the world without families of some type.

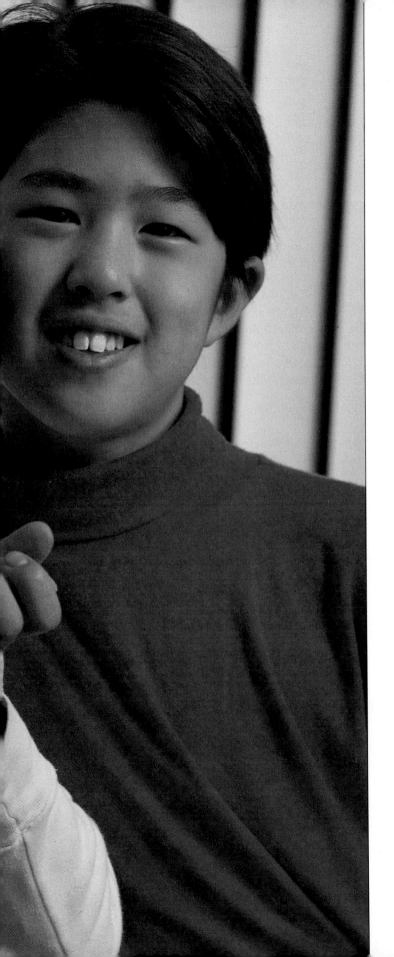

SECTION 1

WHY STUDY FAMILIES?

THINK AHEAD

About These Terms
functions
conflict resolution

About These Objectives
After studying this section, you should be able to:
♦ Explain what you can gain by studying about families.
♦ Describe a helpful attitude to have when learning about families.

ow much do you know about families? Simply living in a family does not make anyone an expert on them. When asked to name what means the most to them in their lives, people often respond, "My family." Obviously, the care of families is too important to be left to chance. Turning to the expertise, knowledge, and experience of others makes good sense.

♦ ♦ ♦

WHAT CAN YOU GAIN?

You may be surprised to discover all that you can learn and put to good use in your life after studying about families. Take a look.

An Appreciation of Families

Sometimes the most important things in life are taken for granted — families, for example. Can you think of reasons why this might be true? Families are an everyday part of life for most people. Sometimes it's easy to lose sight of the importance of anything that is simply there all the time.

By studying about families, you can learn why they are so important. Families

Families are important — to society and to individuals. What can you learn about families that will help you take good care of the family you belong to?

When you are very close to people, it can be easy to take them for granted. Family members need to care about each other — and show it.

provide many **functions**, or purposes, yet their job is not always easy. So much can interfere as families work to fulfill their functions. You might never have thought about all that families provide.

As you read this text, you will have new insights into what it means to be a family. You will see that many different kinds of families exist. You will see that both similarities and differences in families can be valued. As your understanding of families increases, your appreciation for them is likely to also. When you value something, you are more likely to take good care of it. Families are supposed to last for a long time. Taking good care of them is a worthwhile goal.

"The family is one of nature's masterpieces."

GEORGE SANTAYANA

Knowledge About You

What you learn about families will give you a better understanding of yourself. In a sense the family is a mini version of the world. As you relate to family members, you learn what it takes to get along with other people. The more you understand about family relationships, the better equipped you are to make them work. The knowledge and skills you gain transfer to the larger world. In time you will be able to take all that you have learned about relationships and use it when you are on your own.

Within the family you grow and develop. You discover the kind of person that you are and that you want and need to be. As you study families, you will see the important link between families and individuals. You may even look inward to find ways to strengthen that link in your own life.

Knowledge About Skills

Any study of the family would not be complete without learning and practicing skills that families need. Successful family living depends on these skills.

Communication heads the list. Without good communication families can easily have problems. Misunderstandings can occur as feelings are not made clear. Learning to communicate well can be a key to family harmony.

Learning to make good decisions is another basic skill. Good decision making can help you as an individual and as a family member. Families must decide how to raise children, how to spend their time, and how to relate to each other. Their ability to make good decisions can make life smoother within the family.

Other skills are also needed in families. The ability to manage is one. Everything from managing finances to household schedules depends on this skill. Learning to manage well helps bring order to family life.

Conflict resolution is still another important skill that families need. **Conflict resolution**, which you will learn more about in a later chapter, is an approach to solving disagreements. Since disagreements are normal, appropriate methods for solving them are useful. Too often arguments get out of hand when people react with their feelings rather than their minds. Practicing good conflict resolution skills helps family members get along better with each other.

As you study the family, you will learn about all of these skills — and others. You will see why they are important to families, but even better, you will discover ways to put them into practical use in your life.

People in a family get along with each other better when they have good communication skills. Do your communication skills need any improvement?

How To Build Family Strength

Your study of the family can serve another purpose. It can help you make the family you live in stronger.

Families today face many challenges. Some are more complicated than others. Work schedules may have to be meshed with family time. Many families must cope with economic difficulties, death, drug problems, abuse, and crime. Some families may face the challenges that divorce and remarriage present. Even a changing world with scientific advances and new patterns of living must be handled. All of these affect families. Any of these could affect you in some way.

Few, if any, families can say that they are problem-free. Having problems is nor-

mal. Families can be strong and still have problems. They cannot be strong, however, if they can't find ways to manage and solve their problems.

What, then, do families need to realize? They need to know:

- That problems can be solved.
- That change is possible.
- How to solve problems.
- Where to get help.
- That a commitment to family comes first.
- That every family member is a contributor.

As a family member, the strength of your family now depends, in part, on you. This course will increase your knowledge about what happens in relationships, both inside and outside the family. You will read not just about the problems families have but about

All families have problems at times. Strong families look for ways to solve them.

solutions as well. What you learn can encourage you to participate in strengthening your own family. Great or small, your contributions can make a difference.

An Interest in Families

Studying the family can give you a foundation for life. Whether you form a family of your own someday or not, you will always be part of a family. You have the ability to make the family of your future what you want it to be. The knowledge you gain now will be useful. It can help you prevent mistakes before they happen.

You may even find that your interest in families will extend beyond your own personal life. Some people find careers that enable them to work with families. Others use political avenues to influence public policies and laws that affect families. Many people simply become volunteers who give their time to provide services for families. You will read more about all of these possibilities in this course.

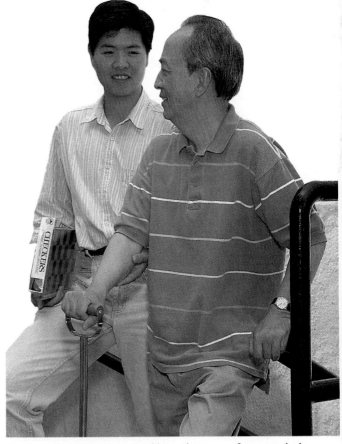

An interest in families can extend beyond your own. Some people do volunteer work that helps other families in the community.

GETTING STARTED

When Jennifer began a course on relationships and family living, reading about families made her think about those that she knew. Some were similar to hers in certain ways, but many were quite different. Her thoughts were closely linked to something her teacher said as the course began.

As Mrs. Ashley put it, "During your study of the family, you must show respect. In other words, you must speak and act with thoughtful regard for all families. Just as your family is important to you, the same is true of others. Families do not all look the same, nor do they act alike. Still, they have some very strong similarities. As you will learn, families tend to strive for many of the same things for their members. The methods they use and the obstacles they face may be different. Despite their differences, the value of all families to people and society can't be denied."

Like Jennifer, you are about to study the family. Her teacher's words are just as significant for you.

SECTION 1 REVIEW

1. Why are families sometimes taken for granted?
2. How can studying about families give you a better understanding of yourself?
3. List three skills needed for successful family living.
4. What six things do families need to realize about solving problems?
5. Identify two ways in which your interest in families can extend beyond your personal life.
6. What does respect have to do with studying families?

FAMILIES MEET EMOTIONAL NEEDS

THINK AHEAD

About These Terms

emotions   *self-esteem*
emotional support   *personality*
self-concept

About These Objectives
After studying this section, you should be able to:
- Define and give examples of emotional support.
- Express the relationship between emotional support, self–concept, and self–esteem.
- Compare ways that families give emotional support to their members.

he American poet Ralph Waldo Emerson once said, "Make yourself necessary to someone." What better place is there to see this thought in action than in the family? As you will learn throughout this chapter, families provide so much. Nothing that families do, however, quite compares to taking care of emotional needs.

◆ ◆ ◆

Family members provide for each other in many ways, but nothing is quite as important as meeting emotional needs.

WHAT ARE EMOTIONS?

When someone says something nice to you, what is your reaction? Like most people, you probably have a good feeling that lifts your spirits. You may want to return the good feeling or pass it along to someone else.

All the feelings you have in response to thoughts, remarks, and events are called **emotions**. Emotions can be positive or negative, depending on the way they make you feel. In general, positive emotions, such as amusement, joy, and love, are thought to be good feelings; negative emotions, such as frustration, anger, and fear, tend to be unpleasant ones.

Feeling a negative emotion is not wrong. After all, people can't help the way they feel. When negative emotions are felt too often, however, the resulting pain can complicate lives. Even worse, sometimes people react to negative emotions in harmful ways that affect not only themselves but others as well. Often it's others in their own families who are hurt.

In any family it is normal for each person to feel many different emotions. For the well-being of the family, however, the key is to promote positive emotions and manage negative ones. Later you will read about how individuals can understand and manage negative emotions. For now the focus is on promoting positive emotions in the family through emotional support.

People in a family feel all sorts of emotions at different times. Even though some emotions don't feel good, they are still normal.

THE IMPORTANCE OF EMOTIONAL SUPPORT

Everything that families do to help meet the emotional needs of each member is part of giving **emotional support**. Any time you do or say something that gives another person a good feeling, you contribute to that person's emotional health. Something as simple as giving a sincere compliment is valuable. So is listening to someone who is trying to solve a problem. When you help ease the concerns of others, you are giving emotional support.

What happens when people receive emotional support from their families? You can probably think of many benefits. Emotional support does everything from helping people feel good about themselves to making life more enjoyable.

Expressions of Emotional Support

Families give emotional support with words and actions. Here are some examples. Can you add to these lists?

WORDS
- "I'll do that for you."
- "Thanks for listening."
- "That's a nice color on you."
- "You did a good job."
- "You are a special person."
- "I love you."

ACTIONS
- Smiling.
- Giving someone a hug.
- Listening to someone's problem.
- Offering to help.
- Sharing time together.
- Taking care of a family member.

Forming A Self-Concept

Growing up and becoming a well-adjusted person is a complex process. Families need to make children feel secure and loved. Children should feel accepted for who they are. When they grow up with plenty of emotional support from family, they are much better equipped to recognize good qualities in themselves.

The picture you have of yourself is called **self-concept**. Like everyone else, you

The picture you have of yourself is called self-concept. Families do much to contribute to the formation of self-concepts.

began to form this view as a young child. By combining the experiences you have had and the things people have said to you, you develop a self-concept. Over time, your self-concept can change. New experiences can cause you to revise the view you have of yourself throughout life.

All sorts of descriptive words are used to explain self-concept. When Jeff tried to describe himself, he thought of these terms first: athletic, thoughtful, disorganized, opinionated, and strong. His list was not limited to just these words, however. All the qualities that Jeff sees in himself combine to make his self-concept.

How do you think Jeff formed his list? Jeff's family helped him develop a self-concept. Looking at one of the qualities that Jeff has will show you how. Jeff sees himself as thoughtful because he has always followed the example set by his parents. The quality he respected in them has now become his own. Jeff's family helped him learn to be considerate of others by rewarding his thoughtfulness. They praised him and often returned the favors he did for others. As a result, Jeff is a thoughtful person, and he sees this quality in himself.

Building Self-Esteem

How you *see* yourself is one thing, but how you *feel* about that image is another. The way you feel about yourself is called **self-esteem**. People with high self-esteem feel good about themselves. When self-esteem is low, however, people do not feel good about themselves. They may lack confidence and believe that they have too many flaws.

Normally, people do not feel the same way about themselves all the time. Self-esteem can be higher on some days than on others. In general, however, most people can identify the average level of their self-esteem.

BALANCING WORK AND FAMILY

A "Can-Do" Approach

When it comes to balancing the demands of home and workplace, having a high level of self-esteem gives you a definite advantage. When you feel positive toward yourself, you look on demanding situations as challenges to be met, not as obstacles that might defeat your plans.

With high self-esteem, you become more creative in finding solutions, since you believe that more options are within your doing. Even when your attempts to balance work and family obligations are less successful than you had hoped, you remain confident in your abilities. Your feelings of self-worth are too deeply rooted to be shaken by disappointment.

High self-esteem also gives you confidence in other people's abilities to manage. You know that you need not be all things to all people. You don't expect it in others, and you don't demand it of yourself.

Families need to promote self-esteem. The emotional support they give leads to good feelings. When families make people feel secure and accepted, self-esteem can soar. Children who develop high self-esteem grow up believing they can be successful. They are willing and eager to try. They also relate well to other people because they are comfortable with themselves. Adults in a family need self-esteem boosters, too. A teen who clearly expresses appreciation for a parent helps build the parent's self-esteem. People want to be successful and happy. By giving emotional support to each other, families can have a great impact on self-esteem.

Your family is important. Sometimes it's easy to lose track of this thought. You can find ways to show family members that you value them. Here are some suggestions to get you started:

- Offer to do a job that you don't normally do.

- Give a sincere compliment.

- Turn off the television and have a conversation with a family member. Ask questions about something that concerns him or her.

- Suggest that your family do something together.

- Say "thanks."

Handling Difficult Times

Families also provide emotional support to help people get through tough times. Handling problems is easier if you don't have to deal with them alone. Family members are usually the first to be there when something goes wrong.

Shortly after Kim began driving, she was involved in a minor traffic accident. Although there were no injuries, she was extremely shaken by the experience. Since the car had to be towed, Kim's mother was called to the scene to pick her up. Admitting to her mother that she had made a costly mistake was not easy for Kim, but her mother's presence and reassuring arm around the shoulders were welcome.

In emotionally supportive families, shelter is offered from the outside world. Sometimes it feels good to get away from the pressures and responsibilities of work and school. People usually feel that they can be themselves. They have a sense of belonging. Even when problems are only the day-to-day ones that people routinely face, families can provide a supportive place to be.

Sharing the Good Times

Good times are often better when they are shared. Family members offer recognition, pride, and warmth when good things happen. When Enrico's grandparents celebrated their fiftieth wedding anniversary, he was there to enjoy the occasion with them. In fact, the whole family turned out. Even simple experiences are more enjoyable when family members support each other in positive ways.

CREATING A FAMILY BOND

Emotional links in a family are usually lasting. As other relationships come and go, family ties remain. A sense of belonging exists. Family members are likely to keep their interest in your life, just as you do in theirs.

Within the family people receive affection from each other simply because they are family, not because of talents and skills they have. Ideally, family members accept and love each other without conditions. This does not mean that you will always get along perfectly with other family members. It means that underneath the day-to-day problems of living, there is love and affection.

As Beau put it, "I can't say that I always like my sister; she can be a nuisance at times. Still, when she was cut from the basketball team, she was really hurt, and I hurt for her. It made me realize just how much I do love her, even though we have our disagreements."

TAKING THE FIRST STEP

Providing emotional support is a two-way street. One person cannot always be the giver and someone else always the receiver. Adults need emotional support as much as children and teens do. Think about the actions you take in your family. Do you often have something positive to say? Do you offer to help before you are asked? By taking the first step some of the time, you can be the one who gets the cycle of good feelings rolling.

Who took the first step in the Johnson household in this situation? When Maggie Johnson arrived home after working the evening shift, she found a note from her seventeen-year-old daughter. It read:

"I fixed some spaghetti for dinner. There's a plate for you in the refrigerator. Love you, Mom. Tonya."

As Maggie ate the spaghetti, she wrote a return note to her daughter: "The spaghetti was super. You're the best! How about a movie this weekend? We've earned a break. Love, Mom."

For Maggie and Tonya emotional support comes in many ways. Even though their time together is limited, they still find ways to show they care. They have discovered that good feelings come with giving emotional support as well as receiving it.

SHAPING LIVES IN THE FAMILY

Whether people eat steak or hamburger at home doesn't really have much impact on their lives. What they experience emotionally, however, does.

Within the family personalities are shaped. All the characteristics that make a person unique are called **personality**. You might

A pleasing personality is more likely to develop when a family gives emotional support.

describe a classmate as fun-loving, outgoing, and caring. These are part of his or her personality. In a later chapter you will learn more about personality development.

Many factors combine to create personality, but the family influence is strongly felt. Often the traits acquired throughout the developing years are kept for life. With positive emotional support from the family, people are more likely to develop personality traits that serve them well. This in itself is reason enough to make emotional support a priority of family life.

SECTION 2 REVIEW

1. What is one of the most important functions a family can provide?
2. Define emotions.
3. Explain the difference between self-concept and self-esteem.
4. In what way does a family bond often differ from other relationships?
5. Explain this statement from the text: "Providing emotional support is a two-way street."
6. What is personality?

FAMILIES TEACH VALUES

THINK AHEAD

About These Terms
values *moral code*
value system

About These Objectives
After studying this section, you should be able to:
* Explain what values are.
* Compare ways that families teach values.
* Determine the connection between values and behavior.

ave you ever made paper airplanes? Although some sail smoothly through the air, others spin immediately to the ground. Successful flight, like life, depends to a great extent on the rudder. On an airplane the rudder is a movable part at the back of the plane. It controls the direction of flight. What is the rudder in life that controls a person's direction? Values are probably at the top of the list.

◆ ◆ ◆

The flight of an airplane depends on the rudder. What controls the directions that families take in life?

You choose clothes and words that reveal your attitudes about what is important. You adopt qualities that you admire and feel are right for you. Together, all of these make up your value system.

Families have value systems, too. A family's value system is usually a blend of what family members believe. The adults in a family provide the foundation for the value system. Sometimes they have to reach agreement on certain issues in order to build a reliable value system. Without agreement, confusion can result.

Kinds of Values

Some values are a matter of preference. That is, they are not necessarily right for everyone. A person who likes to spend time alone may value privacy, while someone who values companionship may want to be with people. A person who takes on a difficult job values a challenge, yet someone who prefers a job without risk values

WHAT ARE VALUES?

Values are beliefs and feelings about what is important. They are based on ideas about what is right, good, and desirable. Giving a child fruit for a snack shows that the parent values good health. Families that speak kindly to each other value courtesy. Teaching a child to share a toy with a playmate shows that friendship is valued. As you think about the values people have, you may find that the list is a long one.

The set of values that you have is called your **value system**. How you spend your time, energy, and money indicates your values. You choose certain activities over others. You enjoy some people more than others. You may feel that some principles are worth standing up for, even fighting for, yet others do not interest you at all.

A value system includes principles that are worth standing up for. Do you have any causes that would drive you to take action?

security. Because values like these are not appropriate for everyone, you choose those that are fitting for you.

Many values, on the other hand, are generally accepted as right for all. Values like these come from society. That is, the people in a society have reached agreement on what is most important for the good of the people. Many of these values are reflected in documents and laws. For example, the Declaration of Independence, the Constitution, and the Bill of Rights all set forth certain values that were important to those who wrote them. Values like freedom and equality have formed a basis for creating many of the laws that people live by.

Religious teachings have also produced values that are widely accepted. Some basic philosophies are simply understood as correct. The idea that people are valuable and worthy of respect, for example, says that the way you treat others should reflect the way you want to be treated. This concept, handed down over the years, is recognized by people as right. Values like compassion, courtesy, acceptance, and tolerance are an outgrowth of this principle, making these values, and others like them, appropriate for all people.

LEARNING VALUES

Values are first learned within the family. The values that families teach are used every day. They are passed along to children, who eventually pass them along to their children. Even when a value is not adopted right away, it often is in later years.

Families teach children how to treat people and what to believe. They do this in several ways:

EXAMPLE Older family members demonstrate values to younger ones by their own actions. For instance, a parent who shovels snow for a neighbor who is sick gives a lesson without words. The young person sees that caring for others in need is the right thing to do.

DIRECT TEACHING Often lessons are taught by simply telling younger family members what is right. A parent teaches a direct lesson by holding a child's hand and saying, "You may not hit people. It hurts them."

RELIGIOUS TRAINING In many families religion provides principles to live by. The principles learned can be carried over to all aspects of life.

A Moral Code

Many values are part of a person's **moral code**. These are the principles of right and wrong that you live by. Families fulfill the moral needs of their members by teaching values that belong in a person's moral code.

Adults in a family need to express what their values are, so that young people can grow up with a sense of what is right and good for them and others. This training gives a feeling of security. Guiding principles are always there and ready for use. Otherwise young people may have an unsure feeling about what to do, especially when problems occur.

The "Right" Values

Families teach values, but how do they know what is "right"? As you just read, there is agreement on the "rightness" of certain values. Still, not all answers are clearcut. For example, a family that is vegetarian believes that it's better not to eat meat. In another family, however, eating meat is perfectly acceptable. You can probably think of many values that differ from

Are all values absolute, or unquestionable? For example, people kill during wars. What reasons are given to defend as well as deplore killing under such circumstances?

one family to the next. Religious and ethnic backgrounds, as well as personal preferences, can account for many of these differences.

Some values cause debate. For example, most people accept the belief that killing is wrong. In times of war, however, this value is viewed differently by some. Although many people believe killing in defense of country is permissible, others say that there is never justification to kill. Reaching agreement on controversies like these is not easy. Indeed, it may even be impossible.

Sometimes you may feel that you don't know what is right. You may think of reasons that support both sides of an issue. You may even question why some people believe as they do when your opinion is just the opposite. All of these feelings are normal. What is most important is to work at discovering what you do believe. Turning to family values for guidance can help. When tackling new issues, look for logic and reason in your attitude and then act accordingly.

INFLUENCES ON VALUES

Value systems are subject to change and challenge. Over the years, new interests and concerns can cause some of your values to change. You will routinely find them challenged in many ways. It pays to be cautious as you absorb other ideas into your thinking.

Friends have a strong effect on a person's values. This is especially true during the teen years when values are being tried and tested. Although you can learn from friends, sometimes there are pressures to go against what you value.

Your values are tested every day in many other ways. The media — movies, television, magazines, and newspapers — suggest all sorts of values, not all good ones. Smoking and drinking are made to look appealing. Beauty and good looks are emphasized. Violence is a common theme. Your own good sense and a strong value system can help you resist such influences.

Families, friends, and the media are not the only influence on values. Schools and teachers have an effect, too. Neighbors, community contacts, and religious training are other influences. Many of these can have a positive impact on your thinking.

THE IMPORTANCE OF A VALUE SYSTEM

A strong value system can be a useful tool. Here are some of the ways it can be helpful to you:

- A *value system helps you make decisions.* The more difficult the decision, the more you need values to guide you. Values can reduce confusion in your life. When you know what is important to you, making choices is easier. For example, when Maria turned down a ride with friends who had been drinking, she made a quick value decision. Later, an accident not only resulted in injuries but also legal troubles for her friends. Maria avoided this by making a decision based on values she had been taught in her family.
- *Values provide motivation.* When something is important to you, you are likely to go after it. Knowing what you want can cause you to take action. You are much more likely to focus rather than drift in life. For example, Curt values financial security. Because of this he is getting the education he needs for a good job someday.
- *Values control behavior.* Positive values keep people from doing what they shouldn't do. They place limits on behavior.
- *Clear values provide confidence and strength.* If you have ever been in a situation in which you didn't know what to do, you know that this brings a feeling of insecurity. When you have values that steer you, however, you feel confident and secure.
- *Values bring consistency to your outlook and actions.* People know what to expect from you. Behavior that is reliable is more readily accepted by others.
- *Positive values enable you to focus on others, not just yourself.* When Matt saw a small child walking along the street, he was concerned. Taking the child in hand, he walked her to the closest house, which turned out to be the little girl's home. The mother was unaware that the child had wandered outdoors. Because of Matt's concern for others, he affected two lives in a positive way. In return he felt good about his actions.

DEVELOPING A VALUE SYSTEM

Your value system has developed with the help of your family. Because you are increasingly influenced by people and events outside your family, however, values may seem to conflict at times. For this reason, you need to be prepared to preserve, defend, adjust, and strengthen your value system. Good judgment will help you. Here are some guidelines to use as you develop a value system that will serve you well throughout life:

- *Follow the rules of society.* Rules and laws were created from the experiences of those who have discovered that without order there is destruction. The rules of society are based on values that respect life, property, and truth. Thus, such acts as killing, stealing, and cheating are not allowed. Taking the laws of the land seriously contributes to the strength of society. It also makes you a stronger person. People who follow the laws gain respect and opportunity in society.

  Laws, of course, are changed when it is necessary. Challenges to the law can be made, but not by breaking them. Speaking out, legal demonstrations, and writing to legislators are all ways that people use to bring about legal change.
- *Choose right over wrong.* Even though answers are not always clearcut, you will often know deep inside what is right. Often it is tempting to push an important value to the side. Take time to think about what is really best for you and others. Challenge what you see and hear before you accept it. If you are not sure, ask yourself these questions: "Is it illegal? Will it be harmful to me or anyone else? Will I regret it later?"
- *Learn from others.* Observe what goes on around you. The mistakes and experiences of others can be helpful as you

Identifying Cause and Effect

Recognizing what causes things to happen can be helpful to you in life. You can prevent problems from occurring and work toward positive effects.

EVA PEREZ *"I couldn't be prouder of my son. I raised him in a neighborhood where there was trouble around every corner. He could have gotten in with a gang, but he didn't. When other kids were involved with drugs, my Terrance stayed clean. I'll have to admit there were a few tears when I watched him walk up for his diploma. I believe he's got a future ahead of him, and getting a scholarship to the junior college is going to help him get off to a good start."*

TERRANCE *"Sometimes my mother did things that made me mad — and sometimes even scared — but I always knew that I had to play by her rules. If I didn't, she would find a way to make me pay. I had curfews, but many of my friends didn't. She made me study hard, even when I tried everything I could think of to get out of it. My mother wants something better for me, better than what's ahead for some people I know. Mom says education is the way. For a long time I didn't believe her. I'm not sure why it took me so long to see that she's right."*

CAN YOU IDENTIFY CAUSE AND EFFECT?

- In this family scene, you can identify several *causes and effects*, some that happened and some that didn't.
- What could have caused Terrance to head for a lifetime of trouble?
- As he was growing up, was Terrance able to see what might happen to him (the effects) if he didn't follow his mother's rules? Explain why or why not.
- What do you think caused Eva Perez to handle her son as she did?
- Why did Terrance sometimes resent his mother's actions? Was Terrance responsible enough for his own actions?
- Explain what caused Terrance to succeed.
- How can you prevent negative things from happening to you in life?

decide what to include in your value system. Talking to an adult you trust — a family member, teacher, or counselor, for example — can also help you clarify your principles.

- *Become aware of your values.* When you know clearly what your values are, they will be there when you need them.

- *Contribute to the family value system.* When Becca took a family living course at school, she learned that sharing leisure time is good for a family. She began to think about how often the people in her family went separate directions to follow their own interests. At Becca's suggestion, the family planned an evening of games and popcorn. Her idea helped the family renew a value that had been recently overlooked.

ACTING ON VALUES

Values mean nothing without action. That's the way it is with values. First you learn them, and then you live by them. You are only honest if you act that way, even when no one is watching. You are only thoughtful if you pay attention to the feelings of others. No matter what you say, people will soon see your real values through your behavior. As you examine your value system, ask yourself if your actions match your beliefs. If not, why? What can you do to act on what you believe is important?

The same principle is true of a family value system. People in a family can say that they believe in togetherness, but unless they find ways to share time, then it isn't true. If a family values cooperation, then they must use it to solve problems. If they value education, they must show it by helping younger members learn and encouraging them to stay in school and do well. A family value system can help keep the family and its members moving in the right direction. It will only be as strong as family members make it. A family has the responsibility to teach positive values. You have the responsibility to help put those values into action.

SECTION 3 REVIEW

1. What is a value system?
2. Give two examples of values that are a matter of preference and two examples of those that are accepted as right for all.
3. What is a person's moral code?
4. Explain how values can be influenced.
5. Describe the relationship between values and decisions.
6. What three questions could you ask yourself in order to help figure out what is right and wrong?

Values are shown through actions. What values do you think this family is showing?

SECTION 4

FAMILIES PRESERVE CULTURE

THINK AHEAD

About These Terms

culture
enculturation
culture shock
assimilation

subculture
ethnic identity
cultural heritage
ethnocentrism

About These Objectives

After studying this section, you should be able to:

* Define culture and give examples of cultural qualities, similarities, and differences.
* Describe and tell how to avoid the dangers of ethnocentrism.

The customs of any culture seem normal to the people who live within that culture. To people from other cultures, the customs may seem unusual.

hen you sit down to eat a meal, do you sit on the floor? A chair? A mat? What utensils do you use? A fork? Chopsticks? Your fingers? Some of these options may seem unusual and others normal. Your family has shown you what is customary in your culture and given you knowledge that helps you get along in your community.

◆ ◆ ◆

WHAT IS CULTURE?

Everything about the way a group of people live is called **culture**. Culture can be seen in what people believe as well as how they act. Economic conditions, as well as knowledge, art, and technology, affect what a culture is like. As members of a society, people develop a culture that is shared by the group.

If you had the opportunity to travel around the world, you would see cultures of many different kinds. What qualities would make each culture unique? Language could be one. Styles of dress could be another. Attitudes, customs, and

CHAPTER 1 • FAMILIES MAKE A DIFFERENCE **35**

daily routines might also be different. Even within a country, you might see evidence of different cultures.

Cultures are complex. When social scientists talk about cultures, they describe the simple qualities that make up the whole culture. These are called cultural traits. A common gesture, such as a handshake, is one trait. A custom, such as a ritual followed when someone dies, is another.

Several traits combine to make a cultural pattern. For example, all the customs that are followed when a couple marries make up a pattern that is characteristic of their culture. If you have ever attended a wedding of people from another culture, you have observed how cultural patterns can differ.

Many qualities make up culture. Some are visible. What evidence do you see of this Thai teen's culture?

CULTURAL SIMILARITIES

When describing cultures, it is easy to focus on the obvious differences. Actually there are many similarities. Regardless of where they live or how they live, people all around the world have the same basic needs.

First of all, people need a place to live and food to eat. In any culture, these are priorities. Living in society means that some system of order must be developed. People need methods for settling differences. In some cultures a system of police, courts, and prisons is set up. Power and responsibility must also be assigned. Leadership comes in many forms, a president, prime minister, queen, or king, for example. Decisions are also made about who will make the laws and how they will do so.

As you look at different cultures of the world, you will see still other examples of similarities. People need ways to protect themselves. They establish and practice religion in some form. Through artistic methods, they seek ways to express themselves. Can you think of any other similar needs that different cultures have?

Wherever you go around the world, you will find another similarity. Each society has a family system of some type. Although the people may live together in different patterns and styles, families are the foundation of each society. Families around the world serve their members in the same basic ways. In addition, they are important to each society because they help preserve the culture as well as make the society strong.

CULTURAL DIFFERENCES

What makes various cultures interesting is their differences. The differences come in the ways that people meet their basic needs. People are not necessarily able to choose the methods they use. Many come about simply because of necessity. For example, people who live in tropical climates wear lighter weight clothing and less of it than those who live where it is cold. Often they use fibers that are readily available to make the clothes.

What people eat is also determined by what is available. If rice grows well in a wet climate, then rice is likely to become a staple in the diet of people who live where it rains heavily. In another climate rice may not grow well, but wheat and corn do. These, then, become the basis for foods and eating habits in another culture.

Cultural differences have come about naturally. When people live together in one society but separate from other societies, they develop their own individual ways of doing things. The patterns and beliefs become ingrained in the society and carry on through the society's history.

Families teach culture to their young. Such knowledge enables people like these men to know how to function in their society.

FAMILIES TEACH CULTURE

The key to passing along culture is the family. Families are the main teachers of culture in any society. Each generation passes along what it has learned to the next as the culture carries on. This process is called **enculturation** (in-KUL-chur-A-shun). Without it people would have a hard time functioning in society. They would not know what behavior is acceptable and what is not.

BLENDING CULTURES

Have you ever seen a movie in which one of the characters was brought into a culture that was extremely different from

anything he or she had ever known? What happened? Probably, **culture shock**, the difficulties and feelings of uneasiness that people have when they are exposed to another culture. In general, people are most comfortable with what is familiar to them. In your own culture, you know what behavior is expected and approved. You might not be so sure in another culture.

The boundaries between cultures today are not as distinct as they once were. With advanced methods of communication, travel, and doing business, people of different cultures are finding more opportunities and reasons for getting together. Often people move from one culture to live in another. As they adopt the culture of the new environment, they may put aside many of the habits, customs, and patterns that they knew before. This is called **assimilation** (uh-SIM-uh-LAY-shun).

PRESERVING CULTURE

You live in a country that has a culture of its own. You may have grown up hardly aware that you were learning the ways of a particular culture, but you were.

Your country also has many subcultures, which you may or may not be linked to. A **subculture** is a culture shared by a group of people who live within a larger, different culture. For example, a child of Chinese parents, who grows up in the United States, might live as an American but also learn and practice many customs and traditions of the Chinese culture.

Because the ethnic identity of people in your country is so varied, there are numerous subcultures. A group of people who

MULTICULTURAL PERSPECTIVES

FAMILIES

AROUND THE WORLD

Keeping Tradition Alive

For many families around the world culture is preserved through traditions. In Jewish families, Passover is a traditional celebration of freedom. It recalls the time 3,000 years ago when thousands of Jewish people escaped from Egypt where they were slaves.

Passover lasts for eight days in the spring. During this time, Jewish people do not eat regular baked goods. They eat only unleavened bread called *matzo* (MAHT-suh), because this is what the Jewish people took with them long ago when they left Egypt.

On the first night of Passover, a special meal, called a *seder* (SAY der), is served. The seder lasts several hours as guests talk, sing, ask questions, and have fun. At the seder, guests eat special foods in remembrance of the flight from Egypt.

The seder includes foods of special significance. There are bitter herbs (usually horseradish), representing the bitterness of slavery. A combination of apples, nuts, and cinnamon represents the sweet taste of freedom. Fresh greens, such as celery, symbolize spring and the new life of the Jewish people. The celery is dipped in salt water for the tears the Jewish people cried in slavery. Some families include hard cooked eggs in the seder meal to represent the Jewish people—the worse the Egyptians treated them, the stronger they got.

Each person at the seder has a book, a *Haggadah* (huh-GAHD-uh), on his or her plate. This includes the history of Passover, legends, folk tales, and songs. Sometimes families make their own Haggadah. The family spends many weeks planning what parts of the Haggadah they will use at the seder.

Passover is a family celebration. People always try to be home for it. Passover is a time when older members of the family teach children the customs and the history of their people.

share a common set of traits and customs, or culture, have an **ethnic identity** (ETH-nick). For some, ethnic identity is linked to ancestors who lived in other countries. For others, a link to a certain race or religion gives ethnic identity.

Cultural Pride

Culture is a source of pride for many families. It is part of history. For this reason families want to preserve culture, not lose it. Many families take pride in teaching young members about the beliefs, customs, and traits that have been important to their ancestors and continue to be for them. Called **cultural heritage**, this set of information about a group of people is often carefully preserved within families.

Feelings about cultural heritage are often very special. Some people carry their feelings too far, however, thinking that their own culture is the best, or the most natural. This attitude, called **ethnocentrism** (eth-no-SEN-triz-um), is dangerous, because it can lead to acts of hatred and violence. Nothing excuses such behavior. As you have just read, different cultures developed because of circumstances and environments. Each one came about naturally in its time and place.

Every family's heritage, regardless of what it is, can be valued. Cultural heritage is a source of pride but never a reason to look down on others. You can feel good about your own heritage while appreciating the heritage of others at the same time. Families are responsible for teaching their own culture to their young, but they must also teach respect for other cultures as well. When people of different cultural backgrounds live side by side, the society cannot be strong without understanding and tolerance for each other.

Families Teach Respect for Other Cultures

Attitudes in families are often passed from one generation to another. As children grow up, what they learn from their families about other people is likely to become part of their thinking. Families can help children learn respect for other cultures in many ways. Here are a few:

- By watching what they say. Comments and labels that ridicule others are easily picked up by children — just as easily as positive ones.
- By including people of other cultures in their lives. Friendship is one of the quickest ways to understanding.
- By experiencing other cultures — the food, the clothing, the customs — either at home or by visiting events that have cultural themes.
- By giving children toys and books that represent other cultures, a doll or a storybook, for example.

SECTION 4 REVIEW

1. Name three qualities that make cultures unique.
2. Why are cultures different from each other?
3. Why is enculturation important?
4. How are cultures preserved in society?
5. What is a subculture?
6. What is ethnocentrism?

Families teach children how to get along with one another and with other people.

FAMILIES PROVIDE BASIC NEEDS

THINK AHEAD

About These Terms

socialization   needs

independence   wants

About These Objectives

After studying this section, you should be able to:

- List and describe components of the socialization process.
- Compare the ways families meet intellectual needs and physical needs.
- Differentiate between needs and wants.
- Explain Maslow's theory on needs and its implications for families.

y this time you should have a greater understanding of what families provide — but there is more. Although emotional needs rank high and teaching values and culture are important, certain other needs must be met by families, too. These are social, intellectual, and physical.

◆ ◆ ◆

Families provide so much for their members. What needs do you think are being met in this family?

MEETING SOCIAL NEEDS

Have you ever seen the child's toy that has pegs of different shapes that must be placed in the matching holes? In a sense people are like these pegs, all searching for a place in life. Families help people learn how to fit into society. This process is called **socialization**.

Many small lessons are part of the socialization process. Through socialization, you learn:

*   *How to get along with others.* Learning to share a toy was one of your early lessons in getting along with others. Cooperating while playing a game was another. People who learn simple lessons like these from family members later find that getting along with friends and the people they work with is easier.

Through the socialization process, children learn how to get along with others. As they play together, they discover that having good relationships with others means both give and take. In what ways do you show that you have learned this lesson in life?

- *What behavior is acceptable where you live.* As families teach culture, people learn behavior that enables them to get along with others and function well in society.
- *How to be independent.* Two early lessons about **independence**, the ability to take care of yourself, came when you learned how to put on your own clothes and how to cross streets alone. As a teen, you are learning how to make decisions that are in your best interest. The goal is that eventually you will be able to manage successfully on your own.

- *What responsibilities you have to your world.* Responsibilities are first learned as children clean up after themselves and help others in little ways. These lessons are gradually broadened to include the world outside the family. Concerns for such issues as protecting the environment and preventing crime begin in the family. Families have a responsibility to look beyond their own interests and instill a community spirit in their members.

When families prepare people for life, getting along is easier. Through the socialization process, people find that, like the pegs of varied shapes, they have a place where they fit.

Family members often develop intellectually together. A parent who explores nature with a child, for example, may be inspired to learn more in order to teach the child.

MEETING INTELLECTUAL NEEDS

Throughout life, people develop their minds. They not only gain knowledge, but they also learn ways to improve their thinking skills. Over time, wisdom, in the form of good sense and insight, may grow as well. Families contribute to the intellectual development of all family members, but their impact on children is especially important.

The family is a child's first teacher. Many of your first lessons in life were probably learned from members of your family. With a good start, children have a better chance of doing well in school and throughout life.

If you happen to have a younger brother or sister, you may have helped him or her grow intellectually. All family members can help in this area. For example, Eva influenced her brother's intellectual development without even realizing it. By playing with him and talking to him when he was still just an infant, she promoted Alonzo's language development. As he grew older, she read stories to him and took him to the park where he could see people and activi-

Meeting basic physical needs is important in families. All the physical provisions in the world mean very little, however, without love and caring.

In the Gowren family, everyone contributes financially in order to make ends meet. Even the younger members of the family pay for some of their own expenses by working. Mrs. Gowren works in an appliance store. Mrs. Gowren's mother, Mrs. Olney, lives with them. She is a teacher's aide. Fifteen-year-old Will has an after-school job at a fast food restaurant. Jana, who is eleven, earns money by babysitting and mowing lawns.

ties. Eva's efforts, combined with those of the rest of her family, were very important to Alonzo.

Families need to be involved in a child's formal education. Any teacher will tell you that students are more likely to do well when adult family members take an interest in education. This means going to conferences, talking or writing to teachers and administrators, supporting teachers in their efforts, monitoring schoolwork, and attending special events.

MEETING PHYSICAL NEEDS

People need food, shelter, and clothing in order to survive. These are physical needs.

Providing the basics is a struggle for some families today. Most families do the best they can. When family members see this, they value the caring and the effort that is made. What they have or don't have seems less important.

Usually certain family members earn money for what the family needs by working. When jobs are not available, families may seek outside help through friends, relatives, and government programs.

Protecting Family Members

Physical needs include more than just providing food, housing, and clothing. Family members also protect each other.

Health care is one example of this. Simple health care is usually handled at home. This is where illness and minor injuries are treated. For more serious problems and for routine checkups, family members go to doctors and other health care workers. Eric takes his daughter Chauncey to the well-baby clinic every three months. By doing this, he can be sure that Chauncey has the protection she needs against diseases and also that no undetected health problems exist.

Families protect in other ways, too. The rules that families set help protect children from dangerous situations and ones that they may not be able to handle. One of the first rules that Josh learned was that he was not supposed to touch the range. Later, he learned not to leave the apartment without another family member. Rules were made to keep him safe in and around his home.

As a teen, you probably have other kinds of rules to follow. For example, rules about curfews and telling your family where you will be while away from home are aimed at keeping you safe. Caring families set rules. Remembering this makes following rules easier.

NEEDS AND WANTS IN THE FAMILY

Throughout this chapter you have been reading about how families fulfill the needs of their members. This is a good time to distinguish between needs and wants. **Needs** are required for a person's survival and proper development. **Wants**, on the other hand, are desired but not essential. The people in your family need food to survive. If you get a craving for ice cream, however, this is only a want. You can survive without it.

All the needs that families provide can be met in different ways. For example, think of how a family could fulfill a child's intellectual needs. Everything from reading a story, to talking about a school assignment, to visiting the country's finest museums could serve this purpose, but which of these are essential for meeting intellectual needs? Although traveling to museums would be a wonderful experience, not all families can do so. A family that recognizes the needs they must meet and then looks for their own best ways to meet them is doing the right thing.

Maslow's Theory on Needs

Some of the needs that families provide are more basic than others. Psychologist Abraham Maslow looked at needs in order to understand human motivation. He believed that the level of a person's motivation is related to the level at which needs are met.

Maslow illustrated this principle by identifying the five human needs shown in the pyramid on this page. He placed the needs in order, from the lowest level need, physical, to the highest, self-actualization. By placing them in this order, he illustrated how each need must be met before the next higher need on the pyramid can be met.

According to Maslow's theory, the lowest level of unmet need is what motivates behavior. It commands a person's attention and effort until it is filled. For example, when children go to school hungry and tired, they are unable to concentrate on school subjects until they meet their physical needs for food and sleep. When lower needs are met, people can then concentrate on the higher needs in the pyramid.

Self-actualization is the need for personal growth and the need to realize your own potential. While Maslow believed that each person has an inborn need for self-actualization, few people ever achieve it. This is because only when all the other needs are met can people truly begin to develop their potential talents and abilities.

Maslow's Hierarchy of Human Needs

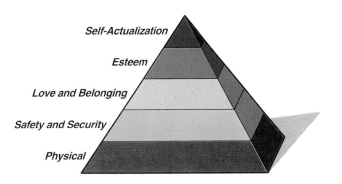

Self-Actualization—the need for personal growth and the need to realize potential

Esteem—the need to be considered as adequate, worthy, and deserving of respect

Love and Belonging—the need for acceptance, warmth, affection, and approval from others

Safety and Security—the need for protection from harm or injury and for security from threats

Physical—the needs of the body, such as food, sleep, and activity

Maslow's theory seems to make common sense; however, there are any number of exceptions that can be listed. What about writers, artists, or inventors who become so wrapped up in work that they forget to eat or sleep? It is difficult to know just how much of a lower level need must be fulfilled before the higher level need begins to motivate behavior. Like many theories about human behavior, the idea is more clearcut than real life. At the same time, Maslow's theory offers one way to look at human needs and how they motivate behavior.

Maslow's theory does have strong implications for families. The interrelationship of the needs becomes evident by looking at the pyramid. If families neglect the needs at the lower levels, the journey to the top is hindered, perhaps even blocked. Families want their members to reach the highest level of the pyramid. Clearly, they have responsibilities to meet in order to make this happen.

MEETING ALL NEEDS

Suppose Carlos helped his younger sister write the alphabet on index cards. Then he used them as flashcards to help her learn the letters. Which function of the family was served? Most people would say "intellectual." This is true, but is there more? Both Carlos and Rosa are likely to benefit emotionally, too. Carlos feels rewarded as Rosa learns. She feels his concern for her. If she gives him a hug or thanks him, he feels appreciated.

As you can see, the functions of the family are linked. The O'Day family became involved in a recycling project together. The project increased their knowledge, gave them a good feeling, and provided a service to the community. In this way, intellectual, emotional, and social functions were served, all at the same time.

Families provide for the needs of their members in so many ways. One way is not necessarily better than another. When love and consideration provide the backdrop, the methods are far less significant.

MAKING A DIFFERENCE

The family has been important for thousands of years. Many times throughout history, critics have said that the family was in trouble and would soon vanish. Despite this, families have continued to exist. The reason is that families are needed to serve very important functions in the lives of their members, as you have seen throughout this chapter. No replacement has yet been found that could fulfill this purpose.

Because families are the foundation of society, there is little reason to think they will disappear. They may change as society changes, but they will remain, nevertheless. Without a doubt, families have the power to make a difference — to individuals and society. It is this power that must be preserved and strengthened, and you can play a part in this effort.

SECTION 5 REVIEW

1. Why is the socialization process important?
2. Where do people usually begin their intellectual development?
3. Name two ways in which families protect their members.
4. What is the difference between a need and a want?
5. According to Maslow's theory, what happens if a lower-level need is not met?
6. Why have families continued to exist throughout history?

Chapter 1 Review

Chapter Summary

- Studying families is important. It gives you a better understanding of yourself and a greater appreciation of how families meet needs of their members.
- Families provide for many needs: social, intellectual, physical, moral, and cultural. Perhaps most important, however, is meeting emotional needs.
- Values are beliefs about what is important. Some values in society are generally accepted as right for all people.
- Strong families build strong communities by teaching positive values.
- Culture includes everything about how a group of people live. Circumstances make cultures different, but no one culture is better than another.
- Families pass along culture to each generation through enculturation.
- Families meet social needs by teaching family members how to fit into society.
- Families meet intellectual needs by providing a stimulating home environment and by taking an interest in a child's education.
- Families meet many physical needs, such as food, housing, and clothing.
- Maslow's theory on needs states that basic needs must be met before higher ones can be fulfilled.
- Families meet needs in many different ways. The method is less important than the love and consideration that is shown.

Chapter Review

1. Identify five things you can gain from studying about families.
2. What should you keep in mind as you study families?
3. What is emotional support? Give three examples of giving emotional support.
4. How do families help family members develop a positive self-concept and high self-esteem?
5. Explain why emotional support is important in good and bad times for a family.
6. What effect does emotional support have on personalities within the family?
7. What are values?
8. How are values learned?
9. List four guidelines to follow when developing your value system.
10. Give five ways in which a value system can be helpful.
11. What is culture?
12. Explain how cultures are alike and different.
13. Explain why ethnocentrism is dangerous. What attitude is helpful in combatting it?
14. Identify four things that are learned through the socialization process.
15. Why must families meet the intellectual and physical needs of family members?
16. Explain the implications of Maslow's theory for families.

Chapter 1 Review

Critical Thinking

1. Of all the needs a family meets, choose one that you think is most important and explain why.
2. What different needs are met when a family shares a meal?
3. What do you think is meant by the saying, "Actions speak louder than words"?
4. Which is more important when people of different cultures live in a community together, blending the cultures or preserving them? Defend your answer.
5. What might happen to a person who is not brought through the socialization process?

Activities

1. **Researching publications.** In newspapers and magazines, find articles about careers involving families, or about laws affecting family life. Summarize these for your classmates. (*Acquiring and evaluating information, summarizing*)
2. **Your value system.** Write a short essay describing a time when your value system helped you make a difficult decision. (*Writing, integrity/honesty*)
3. **Explaining cultural items.** If you have items with cultural significance at home, bring them to class and explain their meaning to your classmates. (*Interpreting and communicating information*)
4. **Identifying the key point.** Write down what you think the most important point was in Chapter 1. Compare your conclusions with the rest of the class. (*Analyzing, writing, comparing*)

STRENGTHENING VALUES

Aim For Closeness

Closeness means sharing living space – and more. It means family members can trust each other with their thoughts, dreams, and fears. They are ready to help when someone has a problem. Joshua feels family closeness when:

- He sends a card to his sister in college because he misses having her around.
- His stepfather listens to his concerns about a math grade and helps him study for the next test.
- His family talks about the day's events as they fix a meal together.
- He and his family cheer for his younger brother at a baseball game.
- All the family members get together for a picnic, with relatives coming from many miles away.

How does your family show closeness? What can you do to bring the members of your family closer together?

What Families Are Like

IMAGINE THAT ...

a company is producing a video on families. Your family has been chosen as one of five to be taped. When the tape is completed, you all sit down to watch it together. The first thing you notice is how different the families are. Your family is not like any of the other four that appear in the video. Each family has individual traits and qualities. You begin to think about other families that you know. They also have unique characteristics. Toward the end of the video, a question is raised: "What is a family today?" No simple answer comes to mind. In fact, no simple answer exists.

FAMILY PATTERNS

THINK AHEAD

About These Terms
images
ideal
legal guardian

About These Objectives
After studying this section, you should be able to:
- Explain why the images people often have of family are not always realistic.
- Describe the different family patterns and the advantages and concerns of each.

s you think about families, you may see certain **images**, the mental pictures of what you believe something is like. Can you create a description of what a family is? If you are having trouble coming up with an answer, don't think you are alone! This is difficult, even for the experts.

◆ ◆ ◆

Does the word *family* bring any particular image to mind for you? What you see might be quite different from the images that other people have.

IMAGES AND REALITY

Where do your images of what a family is come from? Some come from television. Other images come from the real families you see around you.

Television Families

On television, you can see families portrayed every day. Some television families solve complex problems in a half hour. Some family members are incredibly witty, including the two-year-old. Some families are unusually attractive. Some are simply ridiculous. Still others show an **ideal**, or perfect, image.

A family on television can have a flawless holiday — with the relatives, food, decorations, gifts, and sharing all coming together at just the right musical moment. The realities of a messy kitchen, an overcooked turkey, a tired cook or two, and a cranky Uncle Ned may not be shown.

Program writers aim to entertain you. They need a storyline and an ending. Time puts limits on what they can do. In real life, the storyline is long, complicated, and sometimes even boring. Conclusions are not reached every half hour.

Television can influence your thinking more than you realize. What you see on the screen begins to seem like the way real life is for others. You may begin to feel that your life and your family don't measure up. It's important to guard against such feelings. Real families are very different, from each other and from the television images. When you understand this, it becomes much easier to accept reality.

Real-Life Families

You may have heard the saying, "The grass is always greener on the other side of the fence." This means that what others have may look better to you than what you have. Even the real families you know, however, may not be what you think they are. Most families don't show "real" life to outsiders. What you see may look good, but the picture you have is incomplete. You may wish you had a family similar to a friend's. You might be surprised to discover the friend longs for one that has some of the qualities of yours. Given the opportunity to live in the other family, you might change your mind.

A REALISTIC APPROACH

Change seldom comes without first having a feeling of dissatisfaction. There is nothing wrong with looking for ways to improve your family life. In fact, you should do this. On the other hand, trying to live up to images that are false or out of reach will never work. This is both pointless and frustrating.

Obviously, your family is not on television. Moreover, it is not like the rest of the families you know, yet something special is there if you will look for it. The reality is that different doesn't necessarily mean better or worse. It simply means different.

LEARNING ABOUT FAMILY PATTERNS

A look at the families in any community will tell you one thing for sure: families come in all shapes and sizes. Think about the families you know. How many different family patterns, or forms, can you describe?

As you think about families, you will see that family patterns are not the same. Even though families have different patterns, however, they are still families. Learning more about family patterns can give you a better understanding of the special concerns and benefits that come with each situation.

In the rest of this section you will read about different family patterns and how members function within them. You will be learning still more about some of these patterns in other chapters of the text.

Single People

Even though single people often live alone or with one or more roommates, they are usually still part of a family. Most single adults maintain family bonds with their parents, brothers and sisters, and other relatives. A single person who has little or no close family can turn to friends to meet the needs that a family normally provides.

Single people often have freedoms that are not found in other family situations. Many of those who live alone can come and go as they please without having to coordinate with anyone else's schedule or needs. Time to devote to a career and interests, as well as community involvement, may be more readily available. A feeling of independence is commonly enjoyed by many singles.

Many singles need to link with other people. Such contact is fulfilling. By making an effort to include friends in their lives, singles can add to their feeling of contentment.

Couples

Couples have no children in the home. One advantage they have over other family types is a greater opportunity to focus on each other. With just the two of them, a close bond may be easier to develop. They look to friends, relatives, and community for added fulfillment.

Income for a couple can also be an advantage. With only two people in the family, money does not have to spread as far to meet needs. They may be lucky enough to have money for special activities and interests, such as travel.

Recognizing Assumptions

When you don't know the whole story, it is often easy to make **assumptions**.

LUCAS *"Sometimes I think I'd rather live at Matt's house. His mother works nights at a restaurant, so she's never around telling Matt what to do. He's lucky that he can eat whatever he wants for dinner and do whatever he feels like in the evening. Besides that, the people in his family never fight. I've been there a few times on weekends, and I've never seen them have an argument."*

MATT *"Even once in awhile it would be nice to have Mom around at night. Sometimes I can't decide what I want for dinner and I don't feel like fixing anything, so I just heat up a frozen dinner. My mother works hard, and I appreciate that, but we don't have much time to talk anymore, not even on the weekends."*

CAN YOU RECOGNIZE ASSUMPTIONS?

- An **assumption** is a conclusion reached without knowing all the facts. What assumptions has Lucas made? On what were his assumptions based?
- How can making these assumptions cause Lucas problems?
- Could Matt make any assumptions about Lucas? What might they be?
- How can a person avoid assuming things that are not true?

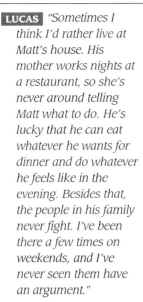

One of the problems couples can have involves careers. When both partners are employed, careers can conflict. For example, what do Cliff and Janelle do if one of them is offered a job in another town? Will the other one stay behind, look for a new job, or quit working? This is not an easy decision to make.

Nuclear Families

A nuclear family consists of a mother, father, and their children. The nuclear family is what many people imagine when they think of a typical family.

One of the advantages of a nuclear family is that the responsibility of raising children can be shared. Although fathers used to spend less time with their children, today many are actively involved. It is not uncommon to see fathers changing diapers and pushing strollers along the street. They also attend school conferences and go to school events that involve their children. Fathers have learned that they have much to gain by close interaction with their children, and the children do, too.

Two incomes are often needed to make ends meet in nuclear families today. When both parents are employed, the family may need child care of some type. Finding good caregivers isn't always easy. Parents need quality care for their children. Sometimes the parents can arrange work schedules so that at least one parent is home at all times. If not, they may turn to outside help. Even though providers are seldom high-paid, the expense is still a burden for most families.

Sometimes one parent is not employed outside the home. For these families, child care may not be a problem. Although mothers have commonly stayed at home with children in the past, some fathers do so today.

In a nuclear family, household as well as child-raising responsibilities can be shared. Families need to work out a fair way of doing this.

Certain advantages exist for children in a nuclear family. With both parents present, children can learn what it means to be a father and a mother firsthand. Parents who share responsibilities can also share the time they have to spend with their children. They may have more energy for this, too, than a single parent might.

For the partners in a nuclear family, simply having another adult around is an advantage at times. Good times are often more enjoyable when they are shared, and bad times are easier to get through when you have someone readily available to help.

Sharing the responsibility of raising children is common in nuclear families today.

Single-Parent Families

A single-parent family consists of one parent and his or her children. Many single-parent families result from divorce. Others form when a parent dies or leaves home. Some people who head single-parent families have never married.

Single parenting can be rewarding as well as challenging. The greatest challenge perhaps is in juggling all the responsibilities. Many single parents must provide and manage all the income for the family. Unless the children are old enough to help, the parent must take care of all household tasks. The parent must also give guidance and love to children. Finding the time and energy to do all of this may not be easy. Sometimes relatives and friends help out.

Like other busy parents, single parents must regularly set aside some special time for children. The relationship between parent and child is strengthened in this way. Single parents also need contact with other adults. Some communities have single-parent organizations where people can socialize and share their common concerns.

Children need contact with other adults, too, so they can learn the roles of both men and women. An uncle, for example, can help take the place of a missing father. The Big Brothers-Big Sisters organization has volunteers who can serve as this link.

Not everyone agrees on how children fare in single-parent families. In all likelihood, it depends on the situation. Sometimes children learn to be more independent. As Angelia put it, "Although it took some years for me to recognize it, I now know how hard my mother had to work to make everything okay for us. Because of the way I've lived, I feel very self-sufficient. I'm not afraid to tackle anything. My mother always says she's proud of me. Well, I feel the same way about her."

Blended Families

A blended family consists of a husband and wife, at least one of whom has children from a previous relationship. A blended family can include the children of both spouses.

When blended families form, family members become stepmothers, stepfathers, stepsisters, and stepbrothers. They are related by the marriage rather than by birth. Any new children who are born into the family are half-brothers or half-sisters to the existing children. That means the children share one, but not both, birth parents.

Growing up in the same family is different from suddenly being part of a new one. Adjustments are needed by both adults and children. They need to make an effort to make new routines and relationships work. Patience and understanding help. In a later chapter, you will read more about how blended families manage together.

Extended Families

An extended family includes relatives other than the parents and children. Grandparents, aunts, uncles, and cousins are all part of an extended family. Such relatives are part of your extended family whether you live with them or not.

Extended family members, regardless of where they live, can be an important resource for each other. Most relatives expect to be there for each other when they are needed. It's just part of being a family.

While friends can be selected, families cannot. A family can be a real mixture of different personality types. For this reason, getting along with relatives may be a challenge at times. You may know of families in which disagreements have kept people apart for years. Everyone loses in such a situation. Working together to keep the bonds close is worthwhile. Most people feel that nothing can replace family ties.

Taking advantage of family ties, however, can be a problem. After Paul and Denise had their first child, they expected her parents to take care of the baby for part of nearly every weekend. Having already raised their own children, Denise's parents were ready to relax and enjoy their leisure time. Although they loved their grandson, they did not want this kind of routine responsibility. Denise and Paul had to learn that this was going beyond the limits of family duty — at least in their family.

Adoptive Families

Adopted children are not biologically linked to their parents. That is, they were not born to them. Instead, the parents have gone through a legal process to make the children part of the family, creating an adoptive family. Sometimes families have both

Navajo Clan Kinship

FAMILIES

AROUND

THE

WORLD

The Navajos of the American Southwest have a broad concept of extended family. It is called the clan.

Navajo society is *matriarchal*. That means that children belong to their mother's clan, not their father's. When a woman marries, her husband, according to tradition, comes to live in her home.

In the past, a Navajo's extended family often lived literally within shouting distance of each other. The group was usually made up of an older woman, her husband, and their unmarried children. The woman's married daughters were there, too, with their husbands and children. Married sons moved away to join their wives' families.

The mother's clan bond is very close. A woman's sisters are like additional mothers to her children. The sisters are even called "mother." A woman's brother is like a second father to her sons.

Because the father's sisters belong to a different clan, his children address them as "aunt." Navajos never marry members of their mother's or father's clans.

Today, Navajos still honor clan kinship, no matter how distant. Even if they have never met a particular clan member before, they may go out of their way to do him or her a favor.

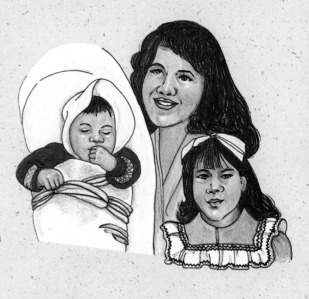

birth and adopted children. The adopted child usually takes the family's last name and is legally protected by all the same rights that a birth child has.

People adopt children for many reasons. Often they do so because they cannot have children of their own, yet they wish to raise a child. Some people want children, but they prefer to take care of those with a need rather than bring additional children into the world. Sometimes children are adopted by a relative.

When an infant is adopted, much of the adjustment is by the parents, who are often thrust into the parenting role almost overnight. This can be awesome, although exciting. If the child is older, adjustment comes on both sides. Whatever memories and experiences the child has will be brought along. Fear and insecurity may also be present. Patience and understanding can help. Acceptance can come in time if family members make the child feel safe and secure.

Legal Guardians

Sometimes parents die or can no longer take care of a child for some reason. A relative or close friend of the family may wish to take care of the child. The courts can make this person a **legal guardian**, one who has financial and legal responsibility for taking care of the child. The child's last name is not changed when this occurs.

Foster Families

A foster family takes care of children on a temporary basis. A child might stay in the home for as little as a few days or as long as several years. Foster homes are used when children need a place to stay for a while, for whatever reason. The children may be waiting for an adoption to take place. They may need a place to live while family problems are solved.

Foster parents are usually licensed by the state. They are screened by social workers and often provided with some training. They receive a small amount of money from the state to help pay the child's expenses.

Foster parenting is rewarding for many people. It can be trying, however, if a child has difficult problems. Becoming attached to children who will eventually leave is a special concern for foster families. They learn to accept the idea that the arrangement is temporary. They must give love but be willing to let go when the time comes.

MANY VARIATIONS

As you can see, families are as varied as the people who live in them. Even the patterns that you have just read about are not always distinct. Some patterns may be combined.

What truly counts in any family is not its form. It is what goes on inside that is important. It is within the family that people gain the skills, strength, and knowledge that enable them to cope in society and build new families to carry on.

A foster parent must be willing to give love but also to let go when the time comes

---

SECTION 1 REVIEW

1. How do television families differ from real families?
2. Identify two freedoms often enjoyed by single people.
3. What advantages do couples sometimes have over other family types?
4. How do nuclear families differ from blended families?
5. What is an extended family?
6. Explain the difference between adoptive families and foster families.

FAMILY PERSONALITIES

THINK AHEAD

About These Terms

autocratic style interdependence
democratic style goal
dependent

About These Objectives

- Describe characteristics that contribute to a family's personality.
- Explain the difference between the autocratic and democratic styles of family management.
- Discuss the place of dependence and independence in healthy families.

or a long time I felt uncomfortable when visiting at my friend Kate's house. The people in her family were always hugging each other, but at my house no one does that." What have you noticed about families? Like Emily, you might feel more comfortable with some than with others. You may be surprised to discover how differently families operate.

◆ ◆ ◆

The personality of a family is a composite of the people within.

WHAT IS FAMILY PERSONALITY?

Just as you have a personality, a family does, too. All the characteristics that combine to make a family unique give the family a personality. The atmosphere in the home, the way the family manages, the dependence level of members, and the family's values and goals are all part of its personality.

Learning about family personalities makes you more understanding of all families, including your own. This section will help you analyze some of the characteristics that are part of a family's personality.

Different Atmospheres

After spending some time in a family's home, you become aware of the atmosphere. Because people are all so different, family atmospheres are, too. The pace may be relaxed and organized, or it may be fast and furious. The attitude may be casual and friendly or formal and distant.

The Bartolo family is loud. They laugh as easily as they cry. Displays of affection are common. Family members like to tease, and each has learned to give as well as take in this kind of exchange. Emotions are quickly revealed by everyone. Arguments are frequent, but short. When they are over, they are forgotten.

The Williams family is quiet. They share conversation, but joking is not their style. Although they care about each other, they don't openly show much affection. Family members are more likely to display how they feel by doing things for each other without talking about it. Arguments, if they take place at all, are in the form of discussions. Family members are uncomfortable with anything that sounds angry, so they settle disagreements gently.

Your family may not be like either the Bartolo or Williams family. Yours may be a combination or something different altogether. It depends on the characteristics of the people in your family. As long as people feel loved and secure, the atmosphere doesn't matter. In healthy families, the atmosphere allows people to make the best of themselves and each other.

Family Management Styles

A family's personality is linked to how they manage together. Not all families manage in the same way. Management styles show in the way people make decisions.

The Autocratic Style

In some families one person makes most of the decisions for the family. Decisions about spending money, routines within the household, and activities are controlled by one individual. Some minor decisions may be handled by others, but the responsibility for major decisions is in one person's hands. This is the **autocratic style** of operating.

Rachel Simon's family, for example, uses the autocratic style. Her father makes most of the major decisions for the family. Rachel's mother has no interest in taking this kind of responsibility. If Mrs. Simon did want to be involved in more of the decisions, they would have to talk about how to manage in a different way.

Every family's personality and atmosphere is different. In this loud, emotional family, everyone enjoys a good argument or a good joke.

The Democratic Style

Another method of managing is common in many families. With the **democratic style**, decision making is distributed. Decisions are made by more than one person. Opinions and abilities are taken into consideration when deciding who will take care of what.

Leon's family is an example of the democratic style of operating. Because his mother is a good money manager, she pays the bills each month. Both of his parents participate in making major decisions. They purchased a car and planned their budget together. Although everyone in the family helps prepare meals, Leon's father does more than the rest because he enjoys cooking and is good at it. When a vacation is planned, everyone helps make the decision. They also worked together to set up a schedule of household duties to share. As you can see, in Leon's family, rights and responsibilities belong to everyone. They take advantage of personal strengths and interests when deciding what each person will contribute. Everyone feels included and valued.

In a family that operates democratically, the opinions and feelings of children are important. That doesn't mean that children will necessarily get a vote in all matters. Parents are responsible for using adult judgment. They must use their experience and knowledge to make sure that good decisions are made. This is in the best interest of the whole family.

Dependence and Independence

An aim of most families is to help members become independent. As you read in Chapter 1, independence means the ability to take care of yourself. Along with independence comes an increasing confidence in your own opinions and abilities. **Dependent** people, on the other hand, rely greatly on others. With little trust in themselves, they need to have decisions made for them, and they avoid taking action on their own.

Children, of course, are dependent from the start. They need support of all kinds from family members. When they eventually become independent, however, they can take care of themselves and make the most of what life has to offer.

Too much dependence can be a problem. It feels confining and limits people. Some families are dependent in nature. In a very dependent family, members rely too heavily on each other. They do everything together. Their needs blend, making them

When families operate democratically, decision making is shared. Does this mean that every family member gets an equal vote on every issue?

less aware of their own individuality. They may shy away from the outside world, which increases their dependence on each other. Children do not learn to be independent as easily in situations like this.

Occasionally one person encourages, or even forces, another to be dependent. A husband may feel better about himself if he feels that his wife cannot get along without him. A mother may fulfill her own desire to be needed by keeping her child dependent on her. Dependence is promoted when one person does not allow another to make decisions, especially important ones, and experience the outside world. Dependence is also promoted when one person says things that destroy the other's self-confidence.

Dependence should not be confused with family closeness. Closeness feels good; it is not limiting. Family members need to feel that they can rely on each other. They need to know that people are there when needed, although not for everything. Called **interdependence**, this feeling of mutual reliance is healthy. Family members need to spend time together, sharing feelings and activities. Family closeness makes people feel secure without holding them back.

In families that function well, independence is promoted but not carried to an extreme. Family members are encouraged to become decision makers and explore relationships with others. Although family closeness is still critical, each member is open to the outside world. The family provides a link to many opportunities and experiences.

"A single arrow is easily broken, but not ten in a bundle."

JAPANESE PROVERB

Family Goals

All families, as well as individuals, have hopes and dreams. Many of these become goals. A **goal** is something you plan to be, do, or have, and you are willing to work for it. The goals that drive your family are not usually the same as those that other families have.

Jackson's family would like to move to another part of the country. They want to live closer to his grandfather, who is ill and needs their support. They are making plans that will take them in this direction.

As children grow within the family, they are allowed and encouraged to do more and more on their own. They gradually move from a state of total dependence to one of independence as young adults.

Elizabeth's family would like to buy a house of their own someday. For this they are willing to make sacrifices along the way. Goals affect what goes on in each of these families.

Goals are based on the unique values and needs of every family. Families make value decisions every day. Many are casual. They aren't particularly harmful or helpful. For example, a family can choose an afternoon of softball, picnicking, biking, or watching a video. Different families will make different choices. It doesn't really matter what they decide.

Other kinds of value choices, however, have greater impact. Will the family spend money on vacations or save for a child's education? Will they spend free time on community work or an extra job? Will they spend leisure time together or apart? Will they be honest or dishonest with each other? Will they solve disagreements by fighting or by talking it out? As you can see, value decisions are made on many levels, from simple to complex. In other words, some have a much greater impact on the family than others do.

PUTTING IT ALL TOGETHER

A family is like a puzzle with hundreds of pieces. So many different factors come together to make the whole. Each person in a family brings a personality of his or her own to the group. The combination creates a very special result. Family personalities are as interesting as they are complex.

SECTION 2 REVIEW

1. Identify four characteristics of family personality.
2. Describe the atmosphere in a healthy family.
3. How do families manage using the autocratic style of operating?
4. Explain how interdependence is helpful in families.
5. Why do goals vary among different families?

The goals that families set are based on values, needs, and wants. When a major goal is set, a family takes steps to meet it.

THE FAMILY LIFE CYCLE

THINK AHEAD

About These Terms
family life cycle   *empty nest*
launching

About These Objectives
- Describe the family life cycle pattern common to many families.
- Identify the concerns and challenges of each stage in the family life cycle.
- Identify exceptions to the cycle.

One generation overlaps another as the family life cycle pattern continues.

Social scientists have identified a basic family pattern in society called the **family life cycle**. A family that follows the cycle moves from life as a couple to parenting. The children grow up and eventually leave home. The parents find new interests in their middle years. Their pace slows as they age. In the meantime a new generation has already begun the same pattern. Because this pattern is a general one, many exceptions exist.

♦ ♦ ♦

THE STAGES

Not everyone labels the stages of the family life cycle in exactly the same way. Nevertheless, the basic pattern is still the same.

The Beginning Stage

The family life cycle begins with a couple. Having grown up in different settings, two young people have adjustments to make in their early years together. They are moving into uncharted territory with each other. Because these years can set the stage for life, young couples need to walk carefully.

Many couples find that having some time to themselves — without children — is helpful. They can get to know each other better before another person shares their life.

As a couple, two people must learn to think and act as a team. Daily routines must consider two people, not just one. They learn to rely on each other and yet maintain their individuality. As they make plans, their ability to work together and communicate is tested. All of this is a hefty assignment for two people. Allowing some time to build a solid foundation for life is a good idea.

Adjusting to their own relationship is only part of the picture. A young couple must work out relationships with others, too. Each has an extended family. Learning how to get along with them and include them may take some effort. The same is true of friends. Would you, as a young wife or husband, share former friends or make new ones? How might you involve friends in your life?

Making Decisions as a Couple

Many decisions face a couple in the beginning stage of the family life cycle. Decisions that could be made alone before must now involve another person.

Where to live is one of the first questions to answer. How close to live to other family members must be decided. Living too close may increase dependency. Living too far away may be uncomfortable. Each couple must work this out for themselves. Because people are very mobile today, decisions about where to live may come up often.

Part of getting established means gathering all the furnishings and equipment needed in a household. Doing so can be expensive, especially when you have very little to start with. Many young couples use items donated by family members. They also find bargains at garage sales and discount stores to help them get going.

Stages of the Family Life Cycle

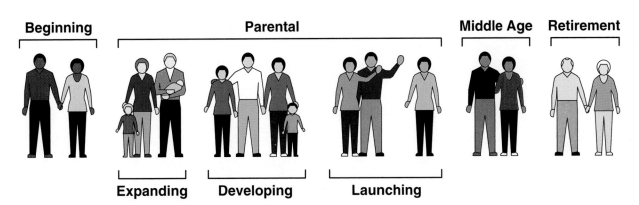

Career plans are often a major concern at the beginning stage of the cycle. Careers have a direct impact on finances. Any decisions made about education and careers will affect the family for many years.

Career decisions can be complicated. Early decisions can have long-term effects. For example, while her young husband was in medical school, Marta worked in a clerical job to support them. They agreed on this. When Dave began his medical practice, they had their first child. Marta stayed at home to raise the family. A divorce took place nine years later, leaving Marta with no education or training to support herself. Marta went into the marriage thinking she would be taken care of for life. In the real world, this doesn't always happen.

Deciding how to manage the finances is important in the beginning stage. Because many couples struggle financially today, two incomes can make a difference. Decisions that couples must make include these: What will they spend money on? Will they have separate checking accounts or one in both names? If one, who will manage it? Who will pay the bills? If they have two incomes, will they put the income together or each be responsible for certain expenses? As you can imagine, money can be a source of problems if decisions are not made carefully, with the wishes of both people considered.

The beginning stage of the family life cycle is an exciting one. A new relationship with promise for the future exists. Because what lies ahead is unknown, an almost pioneering spirit can take hold at this point in life.

The Parental Stage

A society needs children in order to survive. Families that follow the family life cycle supply this need. A decision about having children, however, should not be made lightly. Discussions about children take place during the beginning stage of the family life cycle and even before marriage. Some couples remain childless, either by choice or circumstance. Therefore, the life stages they go through are somewhat different from the standard family life cycle.

When children do enter the picture, however, the couple moves into the parental stage of the cycle. In this stage families are raising children to be productive, independent adults. The parental stage lasts until children are financially on their own. This stage is a long one in the life of a family and has three parts: the expanding years, the developmental years, and launching.

Young couples are in the beginning stage of the family life cycle. What decisions might they have to make?

The Expanding Years

During the first part of the parental stage, sometimes called the expanding years, new members are added to the family. While children are small, most families are very focused on home and family life. Young children require a great deal of time and attention from parents. Parents may feel tied down at times. The number of activities that the couple can share alone together usually drops drastically.

As Cassie put it, "Jason and I used to enjoy all kinds of activities together. We'd bowl, play tennis, ride our bikes on overnight trips, and go to the movies at least once a week. Our children, who are two and four, have brought such joy into our lives, but our lifestyle sure has changed. Now we go to the park, rent videos, and ride our bikes around the block with the children in their special seats. We can't afford a sitter very often, so Jason and I don't get away together much. We love doing things as a family, but sometimes we have to make an effort to find a few moments just for us."

Children add a definite financial obligation to a family. Everything from the basic food and clothing needs to medical, education, and entertainment expenses must be met. If child care is needed, this adds another expense to the budget.

The Developmental Years

As children grow older, the developmental years of the parental stage are entered. Children are in school, and more activities focus outside the home. As children move into their teens, this period becomes very different from the earlier years. Teens are gradually getting ready to leave the family, learning the skills they need to be independent. As they test their independence, they spend more time with their friends. They are looking toward the community and the world to explore new interests.

While raising children, the family pace is often a busy one. The time needed to get everything done is limited. People need to share duties and manage well to prevent pressures from building. Sometimes they also have to realize that not getting every job done — and done perfectly — is okay.

Launching

The end of the parental stage is marked by the exit of children from the family home. Called **launching**, this process sends children out on their own.

In some families the parental stage lengthens when adult children return home. Often the reasons are economic. The adult child may be saving money to buy a house or paying off a college loan, for example. In the Ortega family, Raul returned home at age twenty-three when he decided to enter a training program to become an electrician. Over half of young adults age twenty to twenty-four live with their parents.

The Middle-Age Stage

When the children have grown up and left home, the family becomes a couple again. A new stage, middle age, is entered. It can bring a mixture of feelings. Not all are positive. This can be a time for questioning. The **empty nest** (the home with children gone) can leave parents without a purpose. If the nest fills again with children who return home, adjustments may be needed. A career that has already peaked may feel less challenging. The couple may question their own relationship if it has been neglected. Most couples work through these feelings by finding new goals and new purposes in life. If time is available for volunteering, this can be meaningful. Simply having time to enjoy hobbies can be a pleasure that was missed for many years.

Income pressures often decrease during this stage of the cycle. As people hit their career peaks, their incomes are probably at an all-time high. If children are independent, they are no longer an expense. Therefore, couples may have more money to spend as they wish and to save for retirement. A return to each other is also possible. They can renew the companionship and sharing that they enjoyed when they were first starting out.

Becoming grandparents is a special pleasure for many people in this stage. They can enjoy grandchildren in a way that they never had time to enjoy their own children. Sometimes they take care of grandchildren on a regular basis. Two common reasons for taking on this responsibility are family problems and parents who are employed full time. Grandparents are fulfilling this need for child care more and more today. Some are providing a safety net for children who might otherwise have difficult times.

The middle years may also find people caring for aging parents. Since women have traditionally been caregivers, this responsibility often falls upon their shoulders. If they still have younger family members to care for too, balancing all the family responsibilities may be quite difficult.

The Retirement Stage

The family life cycle is completed with the retirement stage. Not everyone views retirement in the same way. Some people eagerly look forward to the time when they can travel, enjoy hobbies, or just relax. If they have planned for retirement, making themselves financially secure, it is much easier for them to be positive about this period in life.

Other people fear retirement. They may wonder what they will do with themselves. These are usually people who have never developed interests outside of their jobs. The end of the career means the end of everything.

The retirement years can be good ones. Although health problems are more likely at this time than in any other, people who have taken good care of themselves have a better chance of enjoying life. Continuing to exercise and eat right can help them maintain health and wellness.

Many retired people continue to work. They may retire from their careers, but they move on to something else. Part-time work can help ease the shock of lost income. It also helps some retired people keep busy, giving them a purpose and direction in life. Volunteer work is another option. Making a contribution to society gives the retired person a good feeling.

Loss is a part of the aging process. People lose partners and friends through death. They lose mobility. They may need to move from their home of many years. They need the comfort and support of family when these things happen.

Retirement means different things to different people. Can you describe why?

People who have led a full life are usually prepared for their later years. They adjust to aging and slowing down and discover simple pleasures that they never noticed before. They reflect on the past and are willing to share the wisdom that life has given them.

TAKING ACTION

You and the members of your extended family are experiencing different stages of the family life cycle. For each person there are problems and adjustments that go along with the stage. What strengths and skills do you have to offer that could support family members as they manage at each stage? Here are a few ideas to get you started:

- Reading and writing letters for an elderly relative could help him or her keep in touch with others.

- Spending some time with young children might give relief to a harried parent within your family.

- Calling to talk with a relative who lives alone could boost his or her spirits.

- Taking a half hour to help a younger brother or sister with homework could improve a grade as well as an attitude.

EXCEPTIONS TO THE PATTERN

Not every family fits neatly into the family life cycle pattern. You may be able to think of many reasons why people follow different patterns. Divorce is one. Remaining childless is another. Becoming a couple at an older age is one more.

The stages of the family life cycle may be different lengths in various families. For example, one family may have two children, raise them to the teen years, and then have another child. Obviously, the parental stage for this family is especially long. The stages may even overlap in certain ways. A family with children still at home could have a retired parent. A retired couple might take in a foster child. A grandparent may rear a grandchild. Many possibilities for variation exist.

Despite the many exceptions, the basic cycle continues in society. Children grow up in families and then raise families of their own. This is the way it has been, and will continue to be, for a long time.

SECTION 3 REVIEW

1. Identify the four stages of the family life cycle.
2. Name three types of decisions that young couples must make as they begin life together.
3. What does launching mean as it relates to the family life cycle?
4. What is meant by the "empty nest"?
5. Why do income pressures often decrease in the middle-age stage?
6. Explain two concerns that some people have at retirement.
7. Is the family life cycle the only family pattern that people follow? Explain your answer.

Chapter 2 Review

Chapter Summary

- Real families differ from each other and from those shown on television.
- Families take many different forms, each with special concerns and benefits.
- Single people often have freedoms not found in other family situations, but they still need to link with other family members and friends.
- Since couples have no children, their income can be used in other ways. They also have the opportunity to focus on each other.
- Parents and children in nuclear families can benefit from having two parents to share child-raising responsibilities.
- Children and parents in single-parent families face many challenges and rewards. They can benefit from support from other adults.
- Members of blended families must make adjustments together.
- Extended family members can offer additional support.
- Some families are formed legally, through adoption, legal guardianship, and foster care.

Chapter Review

1. Why are the images that people have of families not necessarily realistic?
2. How can comparing your family to television families cause problems? What is a more realistic approach?
3. List five family patterns that can be found in society.
4. Describe how the atmosphere in families can differ.
5. Distinguish between the autocratic and democratic styles of family management.
6. Explain why too much dependence can be a problem in a family.
7. Identify the stages of the family life cycle.
8. Explain this statement from the text: "As a couple, two people must learn to think and act as a team."
9. How does the family focus change from the expanding years to the developmental years? What causes this change?
10. Identify three ways in which the middle-age stage can be one of questioning for a couple.
11. Identify three ways in which people can prepare for an enjoyable retirement.
12. List three exceptions to the family life cycle pattern.

Critical Thinking

1. What pattern does your family fit? How has it changed in the past? How might it change in the future?
2. What advantages and disadvantages can you identify for children in single-parent families? How might single-parent families deal with the disadvantages you have identified?
3. How do you think decisions should be made in a family, with the autocratic or democratic style of family management? Why?
4. What do you think adult life might be like for a person who never learns to be independent?

Chapter 2 Review

5. Why doesn't the entire family life cycle fit every person?
6. Which stage of the family life cycle do you think would be the most difficult for people? Why? Explain which one you think would be the easiest.

Activities

1. **Defining family forms.** Look up the word "family" in the dictionary. Working with a partner, decide which definitions, if any, would cover all family forms. (*Teamwork, interpreting information*)
2. **The family life cycle.** Think of an exception to the family life cycle pattern that might occur for a person. Then write a short paper explaining how that person's life cycle is different from the expected life cycle pattern. (*Visualizing, interpreting and communicating information*)
3. **Identifying family patterns.** As a class, make a list of popular television shows that portray family life. For each, identify the prominent family pattern and describe the characters and situations portrayed. Do you find a wide variety of families and characters on television? If not, what types are most popular? (*Teamwork, interpreting information*)
4. **Performing a skit.** In small groups, write and perform a skit portraying a possible situation in one stage of the family life cycle. Have the rest of the class identify the stage portrayed. (*Teamwork, interpreting and communicating information*)

STRENGTHENING VALUES

Aim For Unity

Unity means oneness. When families have unity, they are more than just a group of individuals. The unity of the Mendoza family shows because:

- They often do things together.
- When one family member needs help, the others are standing by to offer support.
- They don't let differences in personality and opinion pull them apart.

No matter what form your family takes, you can have unity. In what specific ways could you make your family more unified?

Families in a Changing World

IMAGINE THAT ...

a time machine has carried you many years into the future. Your host takes you to visit the factory where he works. All the people at the factory are working at computers. The physical work is done by computer-controlled robots. Because you are to visit your host's home, you ride on the commuter hovercraft with him. When you get off the hovercraft, you board a people-mover that will take you to his home. As you move along, you think about all the changes that have occurred in society. You begin to wonder what the families you meet in this world of the future will be like.

SECTION 1

TRENDS AFFECT FAMILIES

THINK AHEAD

About These Terms
trend
service industries

About These Objectives
After studying this section, you should be able to:
- Identify trends that affect families.
- Explain the effects of trends on families.

ooking into the future isn't easy. People who study changes in society use statistics and other facts about the past to identify patterns of change. When they see a general direction of change over a period of time, they have identified a **trend**. Just as things are not the same as they were in the past, they will not be quite the same in the years ahead.

♦ ♦ ♦

YESTERDAY'S FAMILIES

In the 1700s living on a farm in North America was common. There was much hard, physical labor involved in running a home and farm. Food was raised and prepared, buildings were constructed by families and friends, clothing was made and washed by hand, and crops were often hand-planted and harvested. Families were usually large, and everyone pitched in to get the work done.

From your study of history, you know that many families began to move to urban areas during the 1800s. Farming declined as industry flourished. Life in urban areas was not easy either. In many families, every member, even small children, worked at a job so there would be enough money for the family to survive.

Although the lifestyles of yesterday's families were different in many ways from those of today, there were certain similarities. Families have always worked to provide for their members. The basic needs of families are not much different than they were years ago. The primary difference is in what people and society are doing to meet these needs.

Families today live in a rapidly changing world. Change, of course, took place in past years, but the pace has increased with time. Families are touched by a growing number of outside influences, some of which have increased the challenges that they face.

"Life belongs to the living, and he who lives must be prepared for changes."

JOHANN WOLFGANG VON GOETHE

How have families changed over the years? In what ways are they similar?

LOOKING AT THE TRENDS

Trends affect you, your family, and your family life, and they will continue to in the future. Knowing about them can be helpful. You can move into the future with confidence. Since you know what to expect, you can be better prepared for what's ahead.

Family Patterns

In an earlier chapter you read about the different family types. Certain trends have become apparent regarding some of these:

SINGLE PEOPLE The number of single-person households is growing. Such households form in many ways. Some people remain single or choose single living over marriage. Waiting to marry at older ages contributes to the number of singles. Divorce and death can also leave people alone.

COUPLES Couples who live on their own make up a large segment of households today. More couples than in the past postpone having children, have fewer of them, or have none at all. Many couples have already raised and launched their children.

NUCLEAR FAMILIES Fewer than half of all American families fit this form today. Divorce has had an effect on this number. Typically the nuclear family of the middle 1900s had a stay-at-home mother and an employed father. As more and more women have entered the workforce over the years, this pattern has changed.

BLENDED FAMILIES Many marriages today end in divorce. Although the rate has gone down in recent years, it has increased overall since the 1970s. Many divorced people with children remarry, producing a growing number of blended families.

In the middle 1900s nuclear families commonly had a stay-at-home mother and an employed father. If you have ever watched old movies or situation comedies on television, you have probably seen examples of this pattern.

SINGLE-PARENT FAMILIES The fastest growing household category is that of single-parent families. Divorce and the rise in births to women who are not married account for many of the single-parent families today.

EXTENDED FAMILIES In previous centuries extended families commonly lived together under the same roof. With smaller homes and greater mobility, people have drifted away from this pattern. As you have read, however, many extended families are living together today. Adult children, alone or with their own children, often move in with parents. Older relatives may move in with younger ones to provide child care or because they need care themselves.

The Aging Population

On the whole, people are living longer than they used to. This trend is having a strong impact on society.

Medical advances and improvements in nutrition have contributed to the longer lifespans. For example, Greta's grandfather has had heart bypass surgery. The doctor said that without the surgery, her grandfather would have probably died of a heart attack within a year. Instead, he can now look forward to living up to twenty years longer.

Another cause of the aging population is the change in birth rates. After World War II, there was a baby boom. Many babies were born and families were large. Your parents may have been born during the baby boom, from 1945 to 1965. After 1965, the birth rate started dropping and fewer children were born. The sheer numbers of people in the baby boom years means the average age of the population increases as the baby boomers get older.

With a larger population of aging people, new concerns arise. More medical and health services are needed for the aging.

Homes may need to be specially equipped for them. Better transportation services must be provided. Support services are needed for the elderly who live at home and for those who take care of them in their homes. What other needs can you think of?

The aging population has a strong impact on families and the way they function. Many families have older members who need care and attention. These older family members may need financial support as well. As aging family members are brought into the homes of their children, the families must make adjustments.

Damon's grandmother lived by herself for many years. When the rent on her small apartment was raised again, she could no longer afford to live there. She moved in with Damon's family. They turned the dining room into a bedroom for her. Situations like this one are common today and will continue to be in the future.

The Changing Workplace

During your lifetime, you may hold a job that doesn't even exist now. Whereas people often had one job for a lifetime in the past, they might now have several.

As the population ages, families have an increasing responsibility to help care for older family members.

For many years jobs were available in manufacturing. People were needed to make goods, such as cars, trucks, appliances, and equipment. Far fewer workers are needed for these jobs today. With advanced technology, computers and robots can now do tasks that people used to do. Computer technology has also increased the ability to process and distribute information.

For these reasons, the workplace is changing. An increasing number of jobs now involve processing information with the aid of computers and providing services to others. Such jobs make up what is known as **service industries**.

Service Industries

Over three-fourths of employed Americans now work in service industries. Many services have resulted from the changes in society. Catalog shopping, house cleaning, food catering, and home maintenance are all service areas that have expanded in recent years. Creative people continually think of new services to fit people's needs.

Many people provide services from their homes. Working at home can be convenient for families who need a parent at home to care for children. The drawback is that working while watching children at the same time can be difficult. Parents may still need some child care.

Many people who have lost manufacturing jobs have been able to retrain for other types of positions in service industries; however, learning new skills after many years of doing the same type of work can be difficult. Family support is needed when a person is going through a job change.

When the meat packing plant where Allie worked closed, she started doing home repair jobs. Although she feels that her work is more interesting now, she has to put in longer hours for less pay. The change has been difficult for Allie and her family.

People who, like this bakery worker, provide services for others, now make up the majority of the American work force.

Declining Family Income

Family incomes are lower than they were in the past. Among the reasons is the move to a service economy. On the whole, service jobs do not pay as well as those in manufacturing.

For whatever reasons, many families today struggle financially to make ends meet. They may no longer be able to afford items they once expected to purchase. Many are not able to buy a home of their own. The soaring cost of college means that families who expected to send their children to college may not be able to. Many students must rely on financial aid and work income rather than family help in order to receive advanced education or training.

In general, females have had a particularly difficult time earning an equitable wage in the workforce over the years. Although their earnings have increased overall, change is still needed. Many women who make a living wage now do so because they have received the education and training they need to get a good job. Unfortunately, many women are not in this category.

Women who are single parents are particularly at economic risk. Many of them have no jobs or ones with very low pay. Often they receive little or no financial support from the fathers of their children. An increasing number of single women and their children live in poverty, a trend called the feminization of poverty. Women who have prepared themselves to be independent wage earners, on the other hand, fare much better as single parents.

Dual-Income Families

An increasing number of households now have two wage earners. Both parents may have careers that they wish to pursue, or they may need the income from two jobs. As you have already read, families with two wage earners often have special needs related to child care and management. They may also need additional services because they have less time for routine household tasks.

One common trend today is the increasing number of dual-income families. When both partners are employed, what special needs might they have?

A Global Workplace

The workplace has become global rather than local. Products and services developed in your area may be sold in other countries. Stores in your community carry many products from other countries. Can you think of any products you frequently buy that are grown or made in another country?

Some businesses in your area may be owned by people or companies from other countries. Therefore, decisions about the workplace in your community may actually be made on the other side of the world.

As the world becomes smaller, through improved communication and transportation technology, links with other countries will continue to increase. Families are likely to live and work close to people of all ethnic backgrounds. Learning to understand and get along with people of different nationalities will be increasingly important.

Lifelong Education

Another trend in today's society is the move toward lifelong education. Formal education is no longer just for the young. People of all ages are attending college or getting other types of training.

As you have already read, many people need retraining when jobs are eliminated. Others need new skills in order to enter the workplace. Trudy, for example, got married right out of high school, so she had no work skills. When she needed a job to help support her two children, she decided that the health care field was what she wanted. She went to a community college, taking their program in medical records administration. Now she has a hospital job that she loves. Going back to school enabled her to get a job that pays better than many others she might have taken without an education.

MULTICULTURAL PERSPECTIVES

FAMILIES

AROUND THE WORLD

More than 100,000 Amish people live in the United States and the Canadian province of Ontario. Most make their living by farming. For the Amish, the family is the center of life. They avoid anything that would break up their families and their communities. After careful thought, Amish leaders have included much modern technology in that category.

Electricity, televisions, computers, radios, stereos, and VCRs separate the family, the Amish believe. Instead the Amish spend evenings together talking, sewing, telling stories, and receiving visits from neighbors. The atmosphere is quiet, without the interruptions of news, movies, and cassette tapes that could disturb them.

The phone is avoided for much the same reason. Calls would interrupt the normal flow of work around the farm and family time together. Phones also reduce the desire for families to visit each other. Visiting is a social activity among the Amish that helps establish their sense of community.

The Amish do not drive or own cars, since doing so might encourage Amish children to move away from the family. They use horses and buggies and stay within their community.

The Amish do not use tractors either. All heavy farm work in an Amish community is done by horse. "The horse reproduces itself," say the Amish, "but the tractor produces only debts."

The Amish farms take more hand labor, but that is okay because there are a lot of hands on an Amish farm. Grandparents, parents, and children all live on the same farm. All family members work. Amish farmers retire young, often in their late forties, and let their children take over the farm. They then take on a second career such as equipment repair, carpentry, or gardening.

Some people obtain more education because they want to upgrade their position on the career ladder or because they simply want a career change. The latter happened to Jose. As he said, "I've always enjoyed selling, but the last couple of years haven't been as satisfying to me, so I decided to make a change. I'm going to school to learn to be a real estate appraiser. There's a lot of variety in that kind of work, and I think I'll really enjoy it."

Many retired people find they have the time for more education. Community colleges often offer special classes and activities for older adults. What opportunities for lifelong education are available in your area?

A person who returns to school often puts in long hours, perhaps combining work, classes, family life, and study time. Returning to school can mean that families must make adjustments. Family members may need to get by on a reduced income.

They may also need to contribute extra time and energy to household jobs. On the plus side, when someone in a family is stimulated by a return to school, the rest of the family may share the good feelings.

HANDLING CHANGE

Sometimes change is not easy to handle. You probably know someone who is resistent to change and, therefore, frustrated by it. You may also know of families or communities that practice a lifestyle similar to that of many years ago. They have chosen to avoid the changes in society. Not everyone, however, can easily make this choice.

Most people have to live with the societal changes going on around them. What happens is largely out of their control. As you will read in the rest of this chapter, change is inevitable and ongoing. Recognizing how society is changing can help families prepare better for the future. Understanding the effects of change can provide clues for coping.

SECTION 1 REVIEW

1. What is a trend? How can information about trends be used?
2. What is the fastest growing household category?
3. Identify two reasons for the aging population.
4. What has happened to many of the people who formerly worked in manufacturing industries?
5. What economic trends affect individuals and families?
6. In what way is the world becoming smaller?
7. Explain the importance to families of recognizing social change and understanding its effects.

SECTION 2

THE IMPACT OF TECHNOLOGY

THINK AHEAD

About These Terms
technology
intrusive

About These Objectives
After studying this section, you should be able to:
- List and describe the benefits of technology.
- Contrast with the benefits the drawbacks associated with technology.
- Recommend ways of dealing with new technology.

o much of the change that families and individuals encounter involves technology. In a general sense, **technology** is using scientific knowledge for practical purposes. Through technology people make new discoveries. They create new products and devise better techniques for getting things done. Families must learn to manage technology in positive ways.

◆ ◆ ◆

Technology is all around you. You see it in new products and better methods for getting jobs done.

THE BENEFITS

Taking technology for granted is easy to do. You live in a world where technology in one form or another touches you every day. The television brings you and your family news from around the world. Chances are you listen to music with a radio, tape player, or compact disk player. These are just a few common forms of technology that may be part of your life. How else do you use technology?

Technology enriches lives in many ways. As you think about what has been done with technology, you can see the benefits.

Convenience

A walk through the appliance sections of any department store will show you examples of convenience. So much of what family members used to do by hand can now be done in seconds with the right tool.

Appliances can be bought to make dough, clean the air, make pasta, and compress garbage. With modern conveniences, jobs can be done quickly and more efficiently.

Meals can be prepared in record time today. Supermarkets sell all kinds of foods that are ready for almost instant use. The microwave oven enables people to have food ready for eating in seconds. The dishwasher simplifies and speeds the cleanup process.

Handling finances is also more convenient than it has ever been. With the use of automatic teller machines, you can get cash at any time of the day or week. Busy families find this flexibility helpful. Such machines also allow other kinds of financial transactions. Convenience for some families means paying bills without ever having to write a check. A bill can be automatically deducted from a family's bank account if the arrangements are made to do so. Paychecks can also be automatically deposited in a person's account.

Improved Communication

When a major event occurs in the world, you know about it almost immediately. With media coverage, you can be right there, even experiencing it as it happens. This is far different from those times when families had to wait weeks and even months to get a message from a relative.

The telephone is often used as a quicker and more personal form of communication than letter writing. If you don't want to miss a call, an answering machine will record messages. People no longer talk on the phone just at home or work. Mobile phones make it possible to converse outdoors and in automobiles. Still other forms of quick communication include fax machines, electronic mail, and computer modems.

Health and Medical Advances

Technology in the health field enables lives to be saved, lengthened, and enriched. Pacemakers help regulate the heartbeat. Dialysis machines rid the body of wastes when kidneys no longer function. Laser surgery uses a highly focused beam of light rather than the traditional scalpel. Organ transplants, such as heart or liver transplants, allow many people to lead longer lives. Joint replacements let people regain lost movement. Medical research continually provides new information and techniques for treating diseases, illnesses, and injuries.

Health concerns are also met by new ways of preparing foods for consumers. Synthetic ingredients, which are produced by chemical means, are used in foods. For example, artificial sweeteners reduce calories, and artificial fats can help people lower their intake of fat. Beef is leaner, and low-cholesterol eggs are available. Special preservation, shipping, and handling techniques make fresh fruits and vegetables accessible year-round in most parts of the country.

Entertainment

Technology has certainly brought new forms of entertainment into families' lives. The television has been around for a long time, but now with the addition of a VCR, you watch whatever you want whenever you want. Cable networks and satellite dishes increase the viewing choices you can make. Computer games are available for home use, or you can go to an arcade to find eye-catching video displays to test your skills.

Those who create entertainment are challenged to make it increasingly spectacular. People go to amusement parks that have bigger and better rides every year. Water parks duplicate ocean waves. Fireworks displays are awesome, artistic creations, sometimes even set to music. Special effects bring lifelike qualities to the movie screen and the theatre stage. Can you think of other examples of how technology provides dazzling entertainment?

Safety Factors

As the world becomes more complex, new ways of helping people feel safe and secure are introduced. Security systems can be installed in homes and businesses as well as automobiles. Elderly people can carry communication devices that enable them to call for help if they should fall while home alone. Protective equipment, such as air bags and children's car seats, make travel safer. In the event of an emergency, such as an auto accident or fire, equipment and techniques are readily available. They are used to rescue people and get them the

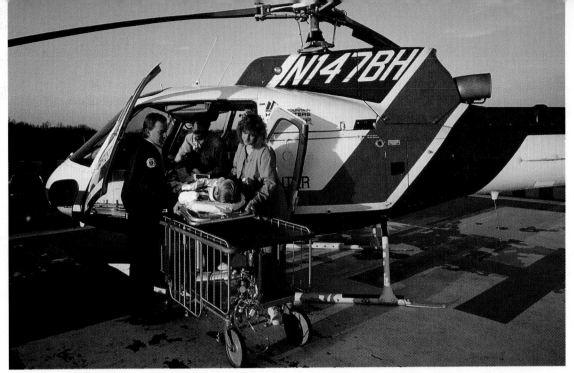

Technology helps save lives. Specially equipped rescue helicopters help ensure that accident victims receive immediate attention and get to a hospital as quickly as possible

care they need as quickly as possible. As you can see, technology plays an important role in protecting people.

Providing Jobs

Progress is not made without work. Because of technology, many people have jobs. Bankers, teachers, technicians, scientists, engineers, and many others help design and produce the products and services of technology. Without a doubt, technology needs people as much as people need technology.

THE DRAWBACKS

Just as you and your family have been touched by the benefits of technology, you have probably also been troubled by it at times. There is a downside to technology, but it is one that can be handled. Tech-

nology will not go away. All the positives that you have read about are worth keeping. Understanding the related difficulties, however, can help you and your family learn how to work with technology.

The Pace of Change

As noted ealier, technological change occurs at a much faster pace today than ever before. Think about your world. What choices do you have when you buy a product at the store? Right after you buy one model, is it made obsolete by a new model? This can be frustrating to people and families. Constantly having to make decisions and adapt to what is new is not easy.

People who don't like to make decisions have a harder time in today's world than they used to. The options you have are greater than ever before. Just looking at all the products that line store shelves will show you how true this is. Having to make so many choices can be confusing, even stressful. People who handle this easily have learned to stay informed and not become overly concerned with small decisions. They also understand and use the decision-making process that you will study later in this text.

Pressures

New products are intended to help make life easier. In some ways they complicate life. Families can feel pressure to have what others have. Advertisements are designed to make people want to buy a product or service. Families have to weigh the advantages and disadvantages of owning each item. Appliances will do almost anything for you that you once did by hand, yet each one costs money, takes up space, and uses up scarce resources to manufacture, distribute, run, repair, and replace.

Families need to weigh the possible benefits of new purchases before buying them. Too many kitchen appliences might make life more difficult instead of easier.

Health Concerns

Even though many technological advances promote health, health can also be hindered. Technology can lead to a sedentary lifestyle. In other words, many people sit rather than exercise. See for yourself by analyzing how these examples of technology affect physical activity levels: riding lawnmowers, television, computers, automobiles, and garage door openers. Can you think of other examples?

Interest in exercise has grown over the years, as evidenced by the development of exercise equipment for use at home and in health clubs. People recognize that they must make an effort to include physical activity in their lives. Families need to get children started early so the habit and the interest are there. Planning regular activities that can be done together, such as walking, biking, playing ball, and swimming, is also a good idea.

Good nutrition requires good decision making in a technological world. Fast food, both at home and in restaurants, is readily available. Often such food is high in calories, fat, and salt. Families need to choose a variety of healthful foods both at home and in restaurants. Many restaurants now offer low-calorie, low-fat, and low-salt meals.

Although speedy and simplified meal preparation is handy, the drawback is that often family members follow separate schedules. Family members may miss out on sharing time as they prepare and eat meals. Scheduling certain meals together each week may be the answer for some families.

The lure to the television set is ever present. Where once people were limited to what the networks provided, they can now also choose from cable programming as well as hundreds of rental videos. What problems might be linked to excessive television watching?

Cost and Value

Much technology comes with a high cost, especially in the medical field. Advanced techniques and equipment are extremely expensive. Families that have no insurance can be devastated by the cost of a serious illness. In the quest to save lives, huge bills can mount up. How the costs of new types of medical care will be covered is an issue that has not been solved.

Not all technology is useful. An appliance that gets used once or twice and then cast aside means the money spent was wasted.

Sometimes technology needs to be controlled to be useful to a family. Many of Ted's friends complain about the poor quality of the television programs their children watch. Ted has a solution. In his words, "I agree that there are some pretty bad programs out there, but you don't have to let your children watch them. Ours are limited in how long they can watch each week. Some programs are off limits. To balance that, we've found wonderful educational and nature programs that are great. We also use our VCR for old movie classics and how-to tapes that we all enjoy."

Teens who have easy access to automobiles are often tempted to spend considerable time away from home. What effect might this have on family life?

Making Things Too Easy

Technology can even be too simple. Easy access to cash and credit is a problem for some families. For Peter and Trish, credit cards complicated their lives when overspending was so easy. They soon realized that they had to control the cards instead of letting the cards control them. Now they don't charge anything they can't pay for each month. By paying the bills in full every month, they avoid paying the high interest on the accounts.

The Environment

Technology has had a negative effect on the environment. You see examples of this all around you. Chemical wastes enter the water, earth, and air. Garbage fills dump sites. The more products people create, the more they throw away. Technology uses up energy and natural resources. The dangers are apparent, but the solutions are slow in coming. Modern approaches call for using technology to cure its own problems. For example, waste disposal is safer with modern techniques. More efforts along this line can reduce the negative impact.

You need to think carefully about how technology affects the environment. As you help look for solutions and participate in them, you contribute to making a better world for your family and future generations.

Family Life

Within the family, technology has caused some changes. Togetherness and communication are threatened. Can you think why? Here are some ideas to get you started. Automobiles enable teens and adults to go off in different directions. Televisions and computers capture attention for hours at a time. All kinds of entertainment lure family members away from the home.

BALANCING WORK AND FAMILY

Families can use technology at home and at work to help build closeness. In the home, labor–saving devices such as automatic dishwashers and self–cleaning ovens give people more time and energy for family activities. With a VCR, people can record programs or rent videos that the entire family can enjoy for an evening's entertainment. A hand-held video camera allows families to preserve traditions, special events, or simply good times together, which they can relive, share, and pass on to younger members.

On the work front, technology in the form of computers, fax machines, e-mail, and so on makes it possible for many people to do some work at home or to establish a home office. Not only does this make these people more accessible to family members, but it also allows others in the home to see what they do for a living. Knowing how someone spends the working day helps build understanding and appreciation. Family members may even be able to help with some work tasks, such as copying or faxing papers. Working at home has the added advantage of saving workers the time they would spend commuting—time that they can spend with family instead.

At times, of course, it may be more desirable to avoid technology and to do things "the old-fashioned way." Activities such as baking homemade bread or building a log fire offer fine opportunities for strengthening family bonds.

Controversy and Technology

Controversy comes with technology. Think about the following questions:

- Have people become so saturated with entertainment that it takes more and more to impress them? For example, does a teacher's lecture pale in comparison to computer games and music videos?
- Do children's toys allow them to be creative?
- Has medical technology gone too far? For example, how should the use of life-support systems be handled?

Technology poses many questions. Not all are easily answered. Only by sharing ideas and careful thought can reasonable solutions be found.

Doing things together and talking can improve family relationships. If technology starts to get in the way, families need to look at schedules and make some changes. They may need to set limits on automobile use, television, and time spent away from the family. A good balance is the answer.

Intrusiveness

Technology can be **intrusive** (in-TROO-siv). That is, it enters your life without your invitation or willingness. For example, has a computer ever dialed your telephone number and given you a recorded message? When technology demands your time or is out of your control, you may feel annoyed, yet you do have choices. You can hang up the phone and forget it. You can also register a complaint with whoever made the computerized call. Simple solutions can sometimes cure the frustrations that people feel.

SINCE technology has a dramatic effect on families

HOW can people stay informed about the latest developments?

Newspapers, magazines, and television programs are quick to report on new consumer products and trends. Many schools and community centers offer classes that teach people about new technology, using computers for example. Talking to adults in related job areas is always a good source of current information.

JOINING THE TEAM

+ What products can you name that have been developed in recent years?
+ How have these products affected families?
+ How did you learn about these products?
+ In what ways can it help people to stay informed about technology?

MANAGING WITH TECHNOLOGY

As you can see, technology has both rewards and hazards. Most people prefer learning to work with technology to sacrificing the benefits. As you and your family learn to make technology work for you, keep the following thoughts in mind:

+ Have a sense of humor. Devices fail and strange things happen. Laughing is better than getting upset.
+ Make time for activities that don't involve technology. Your family can enjoy simple pleasures in life, too.
+ Use what you need and want to and don't worry about the rest. You may find some real benefits in a more relaxed approach.
+ Stay informed. Technology is fascinating. Knowing something about it can make you feel more comfortable.

+ Realize the many benefits of technology. Doing this puts the negative side in perspective. Remember that technology can improve life and help solve problems. As you think about the benefits, you will discover that you and your family have much to gain.

SECTION 2 REVIEW

1. What is technology? How is it used?
2. Name four products of technology that have improved communication.
3. Identify three ways in which technology has helped save and lengthen lives.
4. Give three examples of how technology helps people feel safe.
5. Describe four drawbacks associated with technology.
6. How can staying informed about technology be helpful?

SECTION 3

THE NEED FOR STRONG FAMILIES

THINK AHEAD

About These Terms
pessimist
optimist

About These Objectives
After studying this section, you should be able to:
- Explain why society needs and has an interest in strong families.
- Identify who is responsible for making families strong.

veryone thinks of changing the world, but no one thinks of changing himself." These words from the Russian writer Leo Tolstoy provide food for thought when thinking about change. Society cannot correct every problem that comes along. Families must look inward for some of their own solutions. Simply longing to change the world, or expecting it to change, is not enough.

• • •

You can wait for the world to change, or you can do something to make it change yourself. It's your choice.

THE SITUATION IN SOCIETY

Society is much more complex now than it has ever been. Many communities are struggling to find ways to help families and individuals with their problems. Where society and families are concerned today, the news is both good and bad. Although looking at the negative side may not be pleasant, it is necessary. Problems can't be fixed if they are ignored. Solutions aren't likely to come if you and others in your generation do not give some thought to identifying what needs improvement and then take steps to make things better. When you accept the responsibility for making your family's life better, you help make a better society.

Statistics Are Revealing

Statistics show that many families today face some tough situations. Take a look:

- Over half of all first marriages end in divorce. Over a million children must deal with divorce every year.

The problems of society are the problems of families. Who will solve them?

- More than 20 percent of children live in poverty. Children who live in poverty are at a disadvantage compared to children whose basic needs are met.
- Children in single-parent families have less than one-third the median per person income of those from two-parent families. Although some single-parent families function well, many others do not.
- The 1990 census reported that more than one-quarter of all first-time mothers are unwed.
- Over 1,400 teen girls become mothers every day. Two-thirds of them are unmarried.
- More than three children die every day due to parental abuse.
- More than 20 percent of today's sixth grade children will drop out of school before graduating if the present rate continues.
- Approximately 1.3 million children between the ages of five and fourteen take care of themselves for some portion of the day while parents are working.
- One child in eight has an alcoholic parent. Over 1,000 children between ages ten and fourteen start drinking alcohol every day.
- One of the leading causes of death among young people ages fifteen to nineteen is killing by firearms.

All of these statistics point to problems in society today. Although some of these problems have existed for a long time, they have increased over the years. What you see in your life and in your community may or may not be part of this picture. Chances are, however, that at least some of these situations are apparent to you.

The Plus Side

There is a positive side to the situation of families in society today. It can be seen in several ways. Not only is there a growing desire for society to address family problems in a more active way, but there is also an awareness that families and individuals can do much to help themselves if they are willing to try. Just as important is an increasing recognition of the many strengths that families have.

An Interest in Families

A surge of interest and concern for families is apparent today. You can find examples in newspapers and magazines as well as other media. People want changes in society that will benefit families, easing their problems and worries.

FAMILY LAW Laws of all types have an effect on families. Policies and laws that concern families are continually under scrutiny. As society changes, the laws that people live by change, too. New problems and situations arise that must be addressed. For example, a society that includes a large aging population may need new laws designed to meet the needs of these people. Laws must be passed and revised in order to protect individuals and families.

Laws deal with all aspects of family life. Some control the circumstances for marriage and divorce. Others that deal with taxes and interest rates influence how much money a family has to spend. Even state and federal laws affect the education that children receive. Laws regarding Social Security affect older family members. The poor and unemployed are affected by laws that set up and control programs designed to help them.

Some laws relate to specific situations that occur in families. Child support and paternity laws help make sure that both parents support the children they bear. For example, people want the legal system that requires an absent parent to supply financial support for a child to be streamlined. Financial responsibility must accompany parenthood, and those people who do not recognize this must be identified and held accountable. Some laws deal with child, spouse, and elder abuse and neglect. Children who get in trouble with the authorities are dealt with under special laws for juveniles.

The responsibility for laws lies not just with legislators. People have to remember that laws are made and changed under public pressure. You owe it to yourself,

Laws affect all aspects of family life.

your family, and all families to take an interest in the legal process and make your opinion known. Letters and phone calls to legislators can make a difference.

BUSINESS AND INDUSTRY People are also urging business and industry to look at their family policies. Family and work lives affect each other. When one is strained, so is the other. Business leaders are recognizing that they have much to gain by addressing family needs. For example, how can employed parents take care of all the needs of children — health, school, and otherwise — unless they have some flexibility and the cooperation of employers? When employers work with employees on family policies, both sides benefit.

COMMUNITY INTEREST Many agencies have been created to help families with their concerns. Even the course you are taking now is an indication that family life is worth examining. People are realizing more and more that families need support from all corners of society in order to function well.

Because society cannot solve all of the problems that families have, families must recognize and develop their own abilities to help themselves.

TAKING RESPONSIBILITY

In many ways society works hard to help families with their needs and their problems. Schools do more than just teach the basics. They handle discipline problems, deal with hunger, and provide additional knowledge — about the hazards of drug use, for example. Police forces deal with family arguments and young people who run away or become involved in dangerous and illegal activities. Social agencies give support to families who have needs of all types.

Although these and other resources are helpful and necessary, many families need to take a more active role themselves. Society cannot be expected to do it all. By recognizing their own power and strengths and taking on more responsibility, families can relieve some of the pressure on a society that is already overburdened.

RECOGNIZING STRENGTHS

If you pour water into a glass to the halfway point, is the glass half empty or half full? Someone with a negative point of view, the **pessimist**, might say "half empty." In contrast, the **optimist**, a person who looks at the positive side of an issue, might say "half full." People do look at situations in different ways. The positive view of families today takes the focus off weaknesses and puts it on strengths.

Healthy families have many good qualities, or strengths, that work for them. They communicate by listening and sharing feelings. They support each other. They spend time together. They care. These are some of the qualities that are characteristic of strong families.

Describing strong families is not easy. There is no magic line that is crossed when a family becomes strong. Instead, families are at all levels of strength. Because no family is perfect, each can find ways to improve upon the strengths it has.

A family's strength lies not so much in how well it provides as it does in how well the family tries. When the father of one large family became ill, everyone pulled together to make the best of a bad situation. Without his income, they struggled, but the spirit of family pulled them through. The measure of this family's success did not depend on what they had. Instead, it relied on the support they gave each other. The family looked for strengths — and found them.

Often you will hear strong families described as healthy families. In general, these are the families that fulfill the needs of their members to the best of their ability. They identify the strengths they have and need, and they work to develop them. When problems arise, large or small, they look for ways to cope and try to find solutions. If this means getting help from people outside the family, they are willing to do so.

Society needs strong families. When families are functioning well, they are a buffer against many of life's problems. Their strength combines with that of other families to make society strong, too.

When people are asked to describe or talk about themselves, they often point out all their flaws first. For some reason, they forget to look for the good in themselves. People can just as easily overlook what is good about families. From the optimist's point of view, however, the family bag of strengths is more likely half full than half empty, and with effort it can fill even more.

SECTION 3 REVIEW

1. Give four statistics that reveal the tough situations many families face today.
2. Give three examples of laws that deal with family life.
3. Why should business and industry be interested in families?
4. Describe three ways that society helps families.
5. Who besides society is responsible for family strength?
6. What is the optimist's view of families?

Chapter 3 Review

Chapter Summary

- Many trends affect family life.
- The nuclear family is less common today. The numbers of single-person households, couples, blended families, and single-parent families are growing.
- The population is aging. This brings new concerns and adjustments for families.
- The workplace has seen a rise in lower-paying, service industry jobs. These and other factors have lead to an increase in dual-income families.
- The workplace has become global, leading to a need for better understanding among people of different nationalities.
- Lifelong education is another trend in today's society.
- Technology affects families in positive and negative ways.
- There is a growing concern for the well-being of families.
- Families must take responsibility for staying strong and healthy. They must recognize their strengths to get through tough times.

Chapter Review

1. Identify four trends that affect families.
2. Choose three family patterns and describe the trend associated with each one.
3. Identify three needs or concerns that have arisen from the aging of the population.
4. Define service industries and give two examples of service industry jobs. Name one advantage and one disadvantage of the increase in these jobs.
5. In general, how do women fare in the workplace? How can they improve their situation?
6. Give three reasons for the trend toward lifelong education.
7. Give one specific example of how technology is helpful in each of the following areas: convenience, communication, health and medicine, entertainment, and safety.
8. Identify three ways in which technology and the pace of technological pace can cause stress for families. How can they handle this problem?
9. Identify three ways in which technology has made food preparation easier, and two drawbacks to this convenience.
10. Give three examples of how technology has hurt the environment. What is one approach to curing the problem?
11. Give four tips for managing with technology.
12. How do people know that problems exist in society? What are three problems society faces today?
13. List three general aspects of society in which an interest in families is shown.
14. Give a general description of what strong families do.
15. Why does society need strong families?

Critical Thinking

1. What skills will become more important as the number of service industry jobs grow?
2. Why do you think some people have trouble coping with change? What attitudes or skills can help overcome this problem?

3. Have people grown too dependent on technology for convenience, health care, or medical treatment? Explain your answer.
4. Is technological change the same thing as technological progress? Explain your answer.
5. Why do you think focusing on family strengths is more important than concentrating on weaknesses?

Activities

1. **The global workplace.** In magazines or newspapers, find examples that show how the workplace has become global. List the positive and negative aspects of this trend. (*Interpreting and communicating information*)
2. **Viewpoint on technology.** Interview a grandparent or someone in that age range to determine his or her feelings about technology. Find out what technological advancements the person has seen over the years. How receptive is he or she to the different kinds of change? (*Speaking, listening*)
3. **The cost of technology.** Choose one aspect of technology, such as a particular medical treatment or a specific product, and investigate how the cost to the public has changed since it was developed. Graph your results. (*Interpreting and communicating information, mathematics*)
4. **Equipment demonstration.** Select a piece of technological equipment that some members of your class may not know how to hook up or operate. Demonstrate how to do so. (*Applying technology, teaching skills*)

STRENGTHENING VALUES

Aim For Adaptability

When you can alter your habits or priorities to fit a change in situation, you have adaptability. Franklin showed his adaptability by:

- Sharing his bedroom with his younger brother Isaac when their grandfather came to live with their family.
- Learning to do the family laundry when his mother went back to college.
- Learning some helpful phrases in Spanish when several students from Mexico City transferred to his class.
- Changing his weekend plans so that he could be home when relatives came for a visit.

What changes have you had to adapt to? What personality traits make it easier to adapt to new situations?

Strengthening Relationships

"The first time I saw Troy he was playing soccer with a bunch of kids from my neighborhood. I thought he had a good pass — for an 'old' guy. Whenever Troy wasn't working, he would spend time with me and my friends. Troy has always been a hard worker. He wants kids to see that you have to work hard to make a good life for yourself. The day that Troy became my step-dad was the best one in my life. I still share him with the neighborhood, but knowing that he's there every day — to listen to me and just joke around with — makes me feel good. When I'm older, I know I'll be a lot like him."

MARCUS

95

Roles and Relationships

IMAGINE THAT ...

you are in a large park. Painted on the grass of the park is a huge target shaped like a bull's-eye. You are standing in the center of the target. Surrounding you are three circles, each one larger than the one closer to the center. Imagine that your family members are standing and sitting in the circle closest to you. In the next circle out are your friends. In the largest outer circle are all the other people that you know or have met. As you look through the crowd, you can see neighbors, your teachers, a friend who moved away in grade school, and many others. How does it feel to be the center of the target for so many people?

RELATIONSHIPS COUNT

THINK AHEAD

About These Terms

relationship
mutuality
trust
self-disclosure
rapport

empathy
social exchange
theory
exploitation

About These Objectives

After studying this section, you should be able to:

- Identify the kinds of relationships and tell why they are important.
- Describe good relationships.
- Describe how relationships work.
- Identify danger signals in relationships.

robably no part of your life has more effect on you than your relationships with other people. Relationships can be frustrating, disappointing, and painful. On the other hand, they can be satisfying, fulfilling, and a source of pleasure and growth. They are what you make of them.

♦ ♦ ♦

KINDS OF RELATIONSHIPS

Every time you make a connection with another person, a **relationship** forms. Some relationships are *voluntary*. That is, you choose them. Others, such as those with most family members and people on the job, are *involuntary*. They are not chosen.

Family relationships will likely be among the most important ones you ever have. Few bonds are stronger than those between family members.

Most people have relationships that extend beyond the family. They need friends, too. *Friendships* include people of all ages and backgrounds. Some are much closer than others.

Beyond family and friends, people have many *casual relationships*. You may know students from other schools and people that you have met through your activities. They are people you know but are not particularly close to.

TAKING ACTION

Did you ever wish you could be treated more like company in your own home? Coax your family to try an experiment.

First, take the time to figure out what marks the difference between "regular family behavior" and "company behavior." (Consider tone of voice, attentiveness, eye contact, neatness of appearance, and the withholding of criticism, among others.)

Next, schedule at least an hour with your family (during a meal or fun night) when everyone treats each other like company.

Finally, discuss with your family their feelings during the experiment. What family behavior changes would they be willing to try? You might initiate a new level of respect!

Family relationships usually last for a lifetime. Most friendships and casual relationships do not.

A NEED FOR OTHERS

Some people need more relationships in life than others do. A person who is very social may want a wide circle of friends. Another person may need fewer relationships to be happy. More important than quantity is quality. Relationships should be satisfying. A pleasant encounter with a store clerk can set the tone for the rest of your day. Pleasant encounters with those who are close to you can set the stage for life.

When relationships are positive, they serve some important functions in your life. First, your emotional needs are met. Through family and friends, you feel loved and accepted. Relationships also enrich lives as people share experiences, feelings, and ideas. Not only do others contribute to your life, but you contribute to theirs as well. Finally, relationships help you get things done. What you accomplish is often related to the help and support you have from others.

"*We must learn to live together as brothers or perish together as fools.*"

♦

MARTIN LUTHER KING, JR.

RELATIONSHIP QUALITIES

What makes a relationship a good one? Several qualities can be singled out as keys to good relationships, especially those with family and friends.

Through positive relationships you learn more about yourself and about others. They enrich your life.

MUTUALITY A good relationship is mutual. **Mutuality** (myoo-chu-WAL-ut-ee) means both people contribute to the feelings and actions that support the relationship. They know and understand what they want from each other. A balance in the exchange between the partners exists, even though it is not always equal. That is, a person might give more to the relationship at some times than others. The closer the relationship, the more willing people are to give without expecting something back right away.

TRUST The belief that others will not reject, betray, or hurt you is called **trust**. Acceptance and support are part of trusting. Trust is needed in all relationships, regardless of how close they are. Friends and family members trust each other not to reveal confidential information. Cast members of a school play trust each other to attend practices and learn their lines. In what other relationships do you see trust?

SELF-DISCLOSURE To build close relationships, people have to learn to share themselves with others. **Self-disclosure** means telling about yourself. The ability to disclose information about you to at least one other person is important for good mental health.

How much information a person discloses is significant. Most relationships begin cautiously. People normally reveal more about themselves as the relationship becomes closer. People who never self-disclose may find it hard to build close relationships with others. In general, people tend to reveal the same type and amount of information that they receive.

In the strongest, closest relationships, partners feel free to talk about their fears, angers, hopes, joys, and sorrows. For Marcy, this kind of relationship developed when she became friends with Heidi. At first they talked about simple things — their interests and facts about their lives. Eventually, they began to share thoughts and feelings. Marcy told Heidi about a very frightening experience she had a year ago. Because Marcy trusted Heidi, she could confide in her.

RAPPORT   In good relationships, people have rapport with each other. **Rapport** (ra-POR) is a feeling of ease and harmony with another person. As one teen put it, "No matter what we're doing, I'm comfortable with Ty. We can talk or be quiet; it doesn't matter. Even when we disagree, there's no tension. He's my friend because he's so easy to be with."

EMPATHY   When you have the ability to put yourself in another person's situation, you have **empathy** (EM-puh-thee). You try to set aside your own ideas and understand the other point of view. People who have empathy are particularly tuned in to feelings. When someone else is hurting, they know it and they want to help.

SHARED INTERESTS   Relationships survive better when at least some interests are shared. You probably know the feeling. With someone who has no interests like yours, you have little to talk about or do together. When you meet someone who shares a special interest with you, however, the bond is there. You have a strong base for building a relationship.

HOW DO RELATIONSHIPS WORK?

People who study relationships are interested in what makes them work. They analyze why some relationships thrive and prosper, yet others wither and die. The social exchange theory is one explanation.

Social Exchange Theory

The social exchange theory takes an economic approach to explaining relationships. The premise is that in relationships, just as in life, you don't get something for nothing. Relationships have rewards and costs.

Empathy helps you see a situation through someone else's eyes and find ways to help.

Rewards are anything that brings pleasure or satisfaction in a relationship. People look for different kinds of rewards from their contacts with others. Some look for support or stability, and others for excitement, love, or material benefits.

People commonly meet their needs through relationships. Everything from physical needs to emotional ones are fulfilled as they interact with others. When needs are met, relationships are rewarding.

Costs in a relationship are the physical, mental, and emotional contributions that are made. Some costs are taken for granted; they are expected in the relationship. For example, when Kendall fixes a sack lunch for his young son to take to school every day, the cost is the time and energy it takes to do so. Some costs are painful, even punishing. When Megan's friends didn't show up after she had made plans with them, Megan was hurt. This was a painful cost paid in the relationship with her friends.

The idea that people trade rewards and costs in their relationships is called the **social exchange theory**. In any relationship with others, there is some kind of exchange. For example, love is given and returned. A favor is extended and gratitude is expressed. You can probably think of many other examples.

Every relationship has rewards and costs. The example above described how Kendall packs a lunch for his son every day. Despite the costs to him, Kendall has the rewards of knowing his son will eat well and also feeling good when Danny calls out, "Thanks, Dad!" as he runs for the school bus.

Critics of the social exchange theory say it is too mechanical. Some people feel economic principles of cost and reward are not suited for the emotional content of relationships; however, there is no doubt that when relationships are pleasurable to both parties, they continue. When exchanges are painful, the relationship suffers.

Remembering to express your appreciation to your parents can help strengthen your relationship.

DANGER SIGNALS

Just as good relationships have qualities in common, poor relationships have recognizable danger signals. Knowing them can help you repair and improve those relationships you value.

Imbalance of Costs and Rewards

When the exchange of costs and rewards is too lopsided, a relationship suffers. Few people are willing to pay cost after cost in a relationship and never receive any rewards in return. Any cost, if it is too painful, may be cause to end a relationship. When a person receives rewards that are equal to or greater than the costs, the relationship is likely to continue. Survival hinges on the willingness of each party to give rewards as well as take them.

In some relationships, especially involuntary ones, a balance may not be possible. For example, Stan works in the Shipping Department of a plumbing and heating supply house. The man he works most closely with is difficult to be around. Stan has discovered ways to deal with Jake, but he finds that he must give more than he receives in the relationship. Since Stan has little choice about who he works with, he makes the best of the imbalance.

Sometimes the only way to deal with a relationship is to change your expectations, as Stan did. If you recognize that the other person is not going to change, you can try to accept that. You can prepare yourself for the lack of support and appreciation. The relationship, while it may always be difficult, can be more manageable with this attitude.

Exploitation

Exploitation, or using another person unfairly for personal benefit, is a danger signal in a relationship. On occasion everyone uses other people. Continually doing so, however, poisons a relationship.

Exploiters tend to be self-centered, with little trust in others. They often have little feeling for fairness and feel no guilt when they don't fill commitments. Exploiters believe that everyone is out to get the maximum, so they use others before others use them.

Shelly is an example of an exploiter. She always acts as though people are there for her convenience. She has no regard for other people's feelings. She borrows her sister's clothes without asking. She talks often but seldom listens. She even makes plans and then cancels at the last minute in order to do something more fun. Shelly exploits people for her own benefit and can't understand why she is not liked by others.

What are some ways your friends influence your life? Are any of them a negative influence?

Predicting Results

Predicting results means guessing in advance how something will turn out. To make good predictions, a person must evaluate a situation carefully.

SHAWN *"I don't care if Alex is my older brother; he's got no right to tell me what to do. I can hang around with anybody I want to. So what if Beau is older than I am. He likes me, and I like his gang of friends. I feel like I belong when I'm with them. Nobody crosses Beau's gang. They get respect. I used to be afraid of them, but not anymore. If I go along with them, I can be one of them. That's what I want."*

ALEX *"Shawn's my brother and he's only fourteen years old. I've seen Beau and his friends in action, and it's not a pretty sight. Most of them aren't even in school anymore. They just spend their time on street corners. I stay away from them, and I think Shawn should, too. He gets mad when I say something, so I just keep quiet until I feel like I have to put in my two cents worth. I don't want to ruin my relationship with Shawn, but how does a brother just stand by and do nothing?"*

CAN YOU PREDICT RESULTS?

When you *predict results*, you examine the facts and decide what may happen. Doing this can help you plan a course of action.

- What do you think Alex believes may happen to Shawn?
- What predictions can you make about Shawn's future? About Alex's?
- Why do you think Alex and Shawn feel as they do? How is their relationship threatened?
- What should Alex do at this point?
- Do you ever think about how your actions can affect your future? Have you ever changed your plans because you saw that trouble was ahead? Explain what happened.

Change in Quality

When any of the qualities of a good relationship that you just read about weaken, the relationship is threatened. Unless repairs are made, the relationship may not continue.

An end to *trust*, for example, can mean the end of a relationship. What happened to Victoria and Margarita is an example. Their problem began with a disagreement. Later, Margarita walked into the college dorm room they shared and found Victoria reading Margarita's mail. Margarita never regained a sense of trust in Victoria, eventually causing their relationship to end.

If you will think about the other qualities of good relationships, you will see that problems with any can be a sign that the relationship is in trouble.

WALKING AWAY

Not every relationship is meant to be. Many can help you, but others are just the opposite. Some people just let relationships "happen." They forget that voluntary relationships are chosen ones. You don't need people in your life who use you, intimidate you, cause problems, or hurt you in some way. Your job is to decide when it is in your best interest to walk away from a relationship.

Because they are involuntary, most family and work relationships are kept. Efforts are made to maintain them. Still, exceptions exist. One teen, who had been sexually abused by a relative, sought counseling and then ended the relationship. Sometimes it takes courage to take action against a destructive relationship, but it may be necessary.

BUILDING RELATIONSHIPS

Building and keeping good relationships isn't easy. So much can get in the way. One teen quit trying to make close friends, because every time he did, his family moved away. He felt less pain when he had no close friends to leave behind. Another teen filled his life with video games rather than friends. He managed with technology more easily than he did with the people around him. Another teen was simply frustrated with her relationships. Hardly any were satisfying to her. She wondered if something was wrong with her. Like everyone else, these teens need relationships in their lives.

How can you build quality relationships? You will find many ideas throughout this text. Relationship skills can be developed. Everything from learning to communicate well, to resolving conflicts appropriately, to reaching out to others can help. In addition, you can watch people who get along well. What do they do to make their relationships work? You can find magazine articles and books that will give you ideas. You can even talk to adults and counselors who have knowledge and experience. Above all, look beyond yourself. When you focus on others and understand their point of view, your relationships are much more likely to thrive.

SECTION 1 REVIEW

1. What are relationships?
2. Explain why people need good relationships.
3. Why is mutuality essential in a good relationship?
4. Describe why trust and self-disclosure are important in good relationships.
5. Give an example showing how the social exchange theory works in relationships.
6. Identify three danger signals that are characteristic of poor relationships.

SECTION 2

EXAMINING ROLES

THINK AHEAD

About These Terms

role   *role expectation*
given role   *stereotype*
chosen role   *role conflict*
role models

About These Objectives

After studying this section, you should be able to:

* Explain what roles are and how they are learned.
* Recognize the inaccuracy and harmful effects of stereotypes.
* Explain the relationship between role expectations and role conflict.

ometimes I just don't get it. When Angie and I are alone, she is a totally different person than she is when we're with Deanne and her friends." As you can see by Lynn's comment, people do not act the same way in every situation. As you read on, you will see why.

◆ ◆ ◆

WHAT ARE ROLES?

People who study relationships have noticed that roles have a strong effect on relationships. A **role** is an expected pattern of behavior associated with a person's position in society. No one has just one role; each person has many.

Roles help people know how to act in different situations. When you're with friends, do you talk and act the same way that you do when you're with your family? Chances are, you don't, at least not all the time. As you think about it, you'll realize that you change your behavior to suit many different situations. In other words, you take on different roles.

You may be surprised at the number of roles you have if you try listing them. Family roles are probably the most obvious ones. A person can have several roles within the family. A woman, for example, could be a wife, daughter, mother, sister, aunt, and cousin. What roles might a teen have in a family?

Many other roles occur outside the family. Erving is a student at school and an employee on his part-time job. Because he plays baseball, he is a team member. In society Erving is a citizen and a consumer. He is also a friend to many different people.

ACQUIRING ROLES

Roles are either given or chosen. A **given role** is one that is automatically acquired. At birth a person becomes a son or daughter. The role of brother or sister occurs if there are other children in the family. Many other roles are automatic, too. Your roles as student, consumer, and citizen are all given ones.

A **chosen role** is one that is deliberately selected. People choose to marry and become husbands and wives. They may choose to become parents by having children. They become employees when they decide to take jobs.

LEARNING ROLES

What you know about roles you have learned. Families provide much of this information. Sabrina, for example, learned about her role as a volleyball team member in several ways. First, her family taught her some of the responsibilities a person has when working with others. As a youngster in a Little League program, she learned more. She even read in books and magazines about athletes she admired. Now she is prepared to be a good team member.

Role Models

Sabrina also learned about her role as an athlete by watching those who had gone before her. Mandy, a senior setter on the volleyball team, was someone Sabrina looked up to. Sabrina admired her and hoped to follow in Mandy's footsteps.

Sabrina was using a common way to learn a role — by observing others. Children learn what it means to be a father or mother by watching their parents. They also develop ideas about the roles of husbands and wives. They look up to older sisters and brothers in order to follow their example. Outside the family people look to others for role information. You might watch a student leader, a fellow employee, or a friend to learn about behavior that goes along with different roles. The people you learn from are called **role models**.

What roles does this young man have?

They shape your thinking, giving you examples of behavior to copy. In turn, you serve as a role model for others.

Not all role models are good ones. Just as positive qualities can be mirrored, negative ones can be, too. People need to make good decisions about what behavior is worth imitating.

Role Expectations

When you learn about roles, you decide how you want to behave in different situations. You also develop ideas about what other people should be like and how they should behave. The behavior you anticipate is called a **role expectation**. For example, you expect a person whose role is doctor to be and do what you believe is right for that role. If she doesn't do what you expect, you may not be comfortable.

Stereotypes

Sometimes ideas about roles and role behavior are inaccurate. They turn into generalities that don't apply to all people. A **stereotype** is a standardized idea about the qualities or behavior of a particular category of people. Stereotypes are often linked to physical features or ethnic backgrounds. Terrance, for example, at 6'6", wishes he had a quarter for every time someone has asked him if he played basketball in high school. He didn't. He doesn't even like basketball, but because of his height, the question that he gets tired of answering always comes up.

Stereotypes can be annoying, but they can also be destructive. The stereotype of the "wicked stepmother" and the "spoiled, only child," for example, can prevent stepmothers and only children from being seen as individuals. If you judge someone on the

Changing Role Expectations

Changes in working patterns have led to changes in role expectations for family members. When few married women worked, for example, they were primarily expected to run the home and take care of the children. As the family's sole breadwinner, the husband had a primary role in deciding how the money should be spent. Now most married women work outside the home. Wives and mothers are as involved in a family's financial planning as are husbands and fathers. Men are playing a more active role in housework and child care.

Changes in adult roles also affect teens. Teens' household responsibilities were once limited to caring for their own belongings and occasionally watching younger siblings. Today, doing the family's laundry, preparing meals, and regularly caring for siblings may all be part of a teen's "job description."

Likewise, changing attitudes about family roles have influenced how people work. For instance, as fathers become more involved in raising their children, more fathers are asking for—and receiving—family leave from their jobs.

Changes in role expectations can be unsettling if they occur suddenly. When a change in circumstances causes a sudden change in roles, all family members need to show extra patience as they adjust to the new expectations.

basis of a stereotype, you are very likely to be wrong. If you go one step further and talk about or mistreat that person, you are hurting the individual, and that's definitely wrong.

Getting Personal in Sweden

Americans are very informal. At home, at school, and in business, they tend to use people's first names when conversing. Rarely are titles used as forms of address.

Things are different in Sweden. What a person does for a living is a vital part of his or her identity. It is so important that, for many years, a person's occupation was included in the phone book listing. The listings were also alphabetical according to occupation. Ingmar Bergquist, attorney, for example, was listed before Ingmar Bergquist, professor. Swedes who did not include their titles were listed after everyone else.

The Swedish use titles when they talk to each other as well. They say, "Yes, School Superintendent," or "No, Mrs. Professor." The Swedish almost have to use titles as a form of address. The formal word for "you," ni, is considered rude or condescending.

Some who write about Sweden say the formality of titles and the lack of a formal "you" helps make the Swedish lonely. One way they break through the barrier between them is by using the word du. Du is the informal version of "you." The Swedish do not use it carelessly. Only within the family or with close friends do they relax and use first names and the informal du.

Americans use first names even when people are not good friends. In Sweden, however, first-name friends are chosen carefully. It may take years before some people will permit you to address them as du, but when that happens, you are friends for life.

ROLE CONFLICT

Because people learn roles from so many different sources, each person's view is not always the same. Suppose a young man grew up in a household where all the cooking and cleaning was done by his mother and sisters. He never did this kind of work. Eventually, he marries a woman who believes partners should share household tasks. He doesn't see the work as his job. The two obviously have different attitudes about the roles of husband and wife. Their disagreement over role expectations is called **role conflict**.

Ideas about who has what role have changed over the years.

One of the reasons that people view roles differently is that roles change over time. The image of what a father should be, for example, has slowly changed over the years. Fathers are more involved with their children than they used to be. People don't see and accept role changes like this at the same rate. Therefore, any two people could view a role differently at any point in time.

UNDERSTANDING ROLES

Strong relationships are built with understanding. When role conflicts occur, people need to examine the expectations on both sides and reach some conclusions. To do so, they must turn to such skills as communication and conflict resolution. You will study both of these in the next two chapters of this text.

SECTION 2 REVIEW

1. Define role.
2. What is the difference between a given role and a chosen role?
3. Explain how role models help shape your thinking about roles.
4. What is a role expectation?
5. Why are stereotypes inaccurate and often destructive?
6. Give an example of role conflict in a relationship.

Chapter 4 Review

Chapter Summary

- A relationship is a connection with another person. Some relationships are voluntary, and some are involuntary.
- People need positive relationships to meet emotional needs, to feel accepted, to be enriched, to get things done, and to contribute to the lives of others.
- Mutuality is a quality of good relationships.
- Trust is an important element in all relationships, regardless of how close they are.
- Self-disclosure plays a significant role in developing strong, close relationships.
- Rapport, empathy, and shared interests help build common bonds in good relationships.
- Paying attention to the danger signals in relationships can help you repair, improve, or walk away from poor relationships.
- Every person plays a number of roles in relationships, either chosen or given.
- People learn about roles primarily through role models, who provide examples that shape thinking.
- Stereotypes unfairly categorize people according to standard ideas about qualities or behavior.
- Role conflict occurs when those involved in a relationship have differing role expectations.

Chapter Review

1. Give an example of a voluntary and involuntary relationship.
2. Why is quality more important than the quantity of relationships?
3. How does mutuality strengthen relationships?
4. Explain the role trust plays in self-disclosure.
5. Define empathy. Give an example showing how empathy may be put into action in relationships.
6. What are rewards and costs in relationships? Give an example of each.
7. Name two ways to cope with an imbalance of rewards and costs in a relationship.
8. Explain how exploitation can weaken a relationship.
9. Give an example of a given role and a chosen role.
10. How do people learn roles?
11. What is a stereotype? Give an example of a stereotype that you find destructive in society.
12. How can role expectations cause conflict?

Critical Thinking

1. What advantages and disadvantages do you associate with different kinds of relationships?
2. Think about all the qualities essential to a good relationship (mutuality, trust, self-disclosure, rapport, empathy, and shared interests). Which do you think are the most challenging to work at? Explain your reasoning.

Chapter 4 Review

3. Do you agree or disagree with the idea that the social exchange theory approach to relationships is too mechanical? Defend your position.
4. Describe two people you think show the qualities of a positive role model. Why are they positive role models?
5. What kinds of role expectations do you think others have of you? How might this affect your role expectations of others?

Activities

1. **Describing a good relationship.** Create a "word picture" describing your response to the following statement: "My idea of a good relationship is . . ." (*Visualizing, speaking*)
2. **Empathy skit.** With a partner, write a skit that demonstrates the concept of empathy between two friends. Perform your skit for the class. (*Teamwork, writing, sociability*)
3. **Expectations of relationships.** Interview your parents and grandparents (or other adults of a similar age that you know) about their role expectations for marriage and family relationships. Compare their expectations to your own expectations for marriage and family relationships. What are the similarities and differences between the generations? (*Interviewing, comparing*)
4. **Ideas for eliminating stereotypes.** As a class, create a list of ideas that will help eliminate stereotypes. (*Teamwork, creative thinking*)

STRENGTHENING VALUES

Aim For Loyalty

Loyalty means being faithful to a cause or person. It means offering support even when things go wrong. People who are loyal don't let misunderstandings and pressures from other people sway them from their faithfulness. Danielle shows her loyalty:

* To her family, by going with them to a family reunion even though one of her friends wants her to spend the day with her at the State Fair.
* To her friend Julie, by walking away when a group of people start talking about Julie in a negative way.
* To her country, by standing and singing the National Anthem before the school assembly begins.
* To her employer, by making the effort to get to work even when bad weather has kept many employees at home.

Is loyalty to a cause right or wrong if the cause is wrong? Explain your point of view. Can a person be loyal to himself or herself? If so, in what ways? To whom or what do you show loyalty? How do you show it?

Improving Communication

IMAGINE THAT ...

today is your birthday. During the day, several members of your family wish you a happy birthday and let you know that they care about you. You enjoy receiving their messages. One person in your family says, "I love you. Have a happy birthday!" Another gives you a hug. You get birthday cards in the mail from some relatives and a friend. For dinner your family fixes your favorite foods. Someone else even does one of your household jobs for you. As you start to open your gifts, you think of all the different kinds of loving messages you've received from your family and friends. They are messages that make you feel good.

SECTION 1

THE PROCESS

THINK AHEAD

About These Terms
communication
communication channel
verbal communication
nonverbal communication

About These Objectives
After studying this section, you should be able to:
- Define communication.
- Explain the importance of communication in relationships.
- Name and describe the four basic elements of communication.

People often take communication for granted. It seems like a simple, natural part of everyday life. Like everyone else, however, you have probably had trouble communicating at times. Communication is a skill that can be learned and improved.

◆ ◆ ◆

AN IMPORTANT SKILL

Communication is the process of creating and sending messages and of receiving and evaluating messages from others. The messages communicate information, thoughts, and feelings.

Communication is basic to good relationships. It is the energy that sparks caring, giving, and sharing. It fosters understanding among people. In today's world, when everyone is busy with work, school, or activities, communication is vital in keeping track of what family and friends are doing and in building relationships.

THE ELEMENTS

The four basic elements in the communication process are communication channels, participants, timing, and the use of space. These elements are important in successful communication.

Communication Channels

A **communication channel** is the way in which a message is passed. One of the main channels of communication is speech. You use spoken words, or **verbal communication**, as you go about your daily life. Speech, however, is only a small part of the communication that occurs. **Nonverbal communication**, communication without words, is also a primary means of communicating with others.

"Speak clearly, if you speak at all; carve every word before you let it fall."

OLIVER WENDELL HOLMES

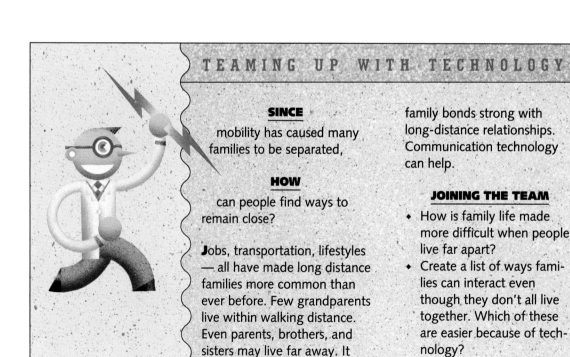

TEAMING UP WITH TECHNOLOGY

SINCE

mobility has caused many families to be separated,

HOW

can people find ways to remain close?

Jobs, transportation, lifestyles — all have made long distance families more common than ever before. Few grandparents live within walking distance. Even parents, brothers, and sisters may live far away. It takes more effort to keep

family bonds strong with long-distance relationships. Communication technology can help.

JOINING THE TEAM

* How is family life made more difficult when people live far apart?
* Create a list of ways families can interact even though they don't all live together. Which of these are easier because of technology?

Nonverbal communication has many formats. Facial expressions, gestures, and posture all send messages. For example, when Reba frowns, slumps against the counter in the kitchen, sighs, and rubs her forehead, her family knows that she has a headache. Jason's big smile and confident strut as he comes into the family room tell everyone that something good has happened to him.

Sometimes actions send negative messages. When Les was 30 minutes late to pick up his sister from dance class, his behavior showed that picking her up on time wasn't as important as what he was doing. Ginny sent a nonverbal message to the others about how she was feeling by slamming the front door as she left the house.

Actions can also send positive messages. Without being asked, Ivana helped her brother Misha trim the yard because she knew he was going to have trouble getting it done before going to work. Doing someone else a favor or helping do a job communicates concern and support for others.

Another kind of nonverbal communication uses others as a means of communication. At the supper table, Lindsey said, "Bill, please ask Grant to pass the meat." Bill obliged by saying, "Grant, please pass the meat to Lindsey." Grant responded, "Tell her to reach over and get it herself." Although words were used in these messages, the main message was nonverbal — that neither Grant nor Lindsey was willing to speak to the other.

Participants

Who participates in communication? In the family, do all members participate in sending and receiving messages? Do all the members communicate with all the others? The flow of messages is important.

Verbal communication is what you say. Nonverbal is what you communicate through body language. Most messages combine both.

Whether you are at home, at work, at school, or somewhere just having fun, better communication results when everyone is involved in exchanging messages.

Some people dominate conversation, not allowing others a chance to speak. The balance between participants is missing. One participant misses out on the other's thoughts when this happens.

Timing

Knowing the appropriate time to send a message can affect how the message is received. For example, Janine is not a morning person. She avoids talking to anyone in the family before she leaves for school. When her sister Joyce tried to talk to her one morning about borrowing a sweater, Janine snapped that she was tired of Joyce borrowing her clothes all the time. Because Janine tends to be grumpy in the morning, it was not a good time for Joyce to ask a favor.

Choosing a time when the receiver will be ready and willing to listen to the message you send is not always easy. True communication occurs only when the timing is right and both sender and receiver can focus on the exchange of messages.

Use of Space

How space is used can affect communication. How close do you get to others when you are communicating with them? The closer together you are, the more casual and intimate communication usually is. Family members seated around the kitchen table will probably talk more easily and freely than if they are scattered around the living room.

How does this father use space to improve communication with his child?

Family Communication

Family discussions can be an opportunity to improve relationships. How families communicate during these discussions is important. A positive approach is always best. When people feel put down or criticized, they may stop participating, and the family discussion will lose its meaning.

To keep discussions positive, you may wish to develop a list of rules with your family. Encourage suggestions from everyone. Keep those rules to which everyone agrees. The following list of "dos" and "don'ts" may help you develop your own list of rules.

DO:
- Treat everyone with respect.
- Encourage others to share their ideas.
- Compliment others for good ideas and suggestions.
- Keep an open mind to other points of view.
- Share your thoughts and feelings.
- Consider how others feel.
- Be tactful.

DON'T:
- Interrupt others.
- Put down ideas.
- Criticize or make fun of someone personally.
- Call people names.
- Take over the discussion.
- Be disruptive.

Do you sometimes feel that people in your family don't listen to you? Many conversations are not only ineffective, they are boring. Have some fun and stop being taken for granted by putting some playfulness and surprise in your interactions. Here are some possibilities:

- Try hamming it up like a "high-powered" salesperson when you're trying to win over a family member to your viewpoint.

- If a young sibling is tuning you out, put your hand in a sock and let your "puppet" express your ideas or feelings.

- If you have normally hollered to express strong feelings, try whispering instead.

Easy? Hardly! Through conscious, rather than automatic, reactions, however, you will enliven and enrich your conversations and relationships.

Have you ever had a conversation in which the other person seemed to be closing in on you? When you moved back, the other person moved closer. For conversation to be most effective, both people have to be comfortable with the distance between them.

Physical viewpoint makes a difference. For example, parent-child communication often occurs with the child looking up at the parent. This use of space puts the child in a weak position. When the parent sits or squats down and is on the same level as the child, communication is more effective.

USING THE PROCESS EFFECTIVELY

Good communication occurs when all four elements of the communication process are handled well. That is, the same message is sent on all the channels used, the flow of communication involves everyone present, and good timing and good use of space aid the exchange of messages.

SECTION 1 REVIEW

1. What is communication?
2. Why is communication important in relationships?
3. List the four basic elements in the communication process.
4. What type of communication channel is speech?
5. What type of communication channel is communication without words?
6. Describe what occurs when the communication process is used effectively.

SKILLS AND PROBLEMS

People who communicate well have a better chance to be successful in life.

THINK AHEAD

About These Terms

passive listening *feedback*
active listening *assertive*

About These Objectives

After studying this section, you should be able to:

◆ Explain the importance of listening in good communication.
◆ Identify and describe three skills besides listening that can be used to improve communication.
◆ Identify and describe problems in communication.

eople thrive on positive communication. Negative communication hurts relationships and interferes with creating strong ties between people. One good way to improve your communication with others is to learn to recognize what works against you and make some changes.

◆ ◆ ◆

COMMUNICATION SKILLS

Are you a good communicator? Find out by evaluating each of the skills described here and deciding where you need to improve.

Listening

Listening is one of the most important communication skills. A good listener receives messages accurately. The most difficult communication problem in families is that family members don't listen and respond to each other.

If you are a typical teen, you spend more of your waking hours listening than doing any other activity. One study showed that people spend almost three-fourths of their waking hours in communication. About one-fourth of the time spent communicating is spent reading and writing. Talking takes a little more than one-fourth of the time, while listening is almost one-half of the time. Just on the basis of the amount of time involved, it makes good sense to become a good listener.

Listening well means focusing on the other person. You need to understand both the words that are spoken and the feelings behind the words. You feel empathy.

As you can see in this example, Gloria's foster mother knows how to be a good listener. Gloria was really down when she got home. Her cash register drawer had been $30 off at the end of her work shift, and she didn't know why. She'd gotten a "D" on a test at school and had a disagreement with her best friend. Her foster mother said, "It sounds like you've had the kind of day that always makes me wonder why I ever got out of bed. Why don't you come tell me about it while we fix supper."

There are two types of listening skills that are useful in communicating with others — passive and active listening.

Passive Listening

Passive listening provides responses that invite the speaker to share feelings and ideas. The listener's ideas and judgments are put aside.

As Heather was telling her father about a fire in the chemistry class, he responded with such comments as: "Well, I'll bet that

How well do you think this family handles listening?

was exciting," "Umm," "Tell me more about what happened," and "Did everyone get evacuated?" These passive listening comments invited Heather to continue telling about what happened.

Active Listening

With **active listening** you try to understand what the speaker is feeling or what the message really means. The listener participates more in the message exchange, making comments that are designed to clarify what the message sender means.

For example, as Belle listened to her son Craig talk about the first day of basketball practice, her comments included: "I can see you were disappointed because Vince was selected to the blue team and you weren't," "It sounds as though you're going to like your new coach," and "Did that make you nervous?" Belle was listening to what Craig had to say and trying to find out exactly what he meant and how he felt about what happened.

Being a Good Listener

When you are truly listening, your body reflects your attention to the other person's message. When you lean toward the speaker, maintain eye contact, and make encouraging gestures, you use body language to say that you are indeed hearing what is said.

I-Messages

One skill in communicating is the ability to send messages that accurately reflect what you think, believe, and feel. These messages are called "I-messages" because they tell how a situation makes the speaker feel. When you use I-messages, you give facts about you.

Note the I-messages that Quinn's mother used when he missed supper without letting anyone know he would be gone. She said, "Quinn, I am really upset that I didn't know you would miss supper tonight. I worry that something has happened to you when you aren't here. I would be much more comfortable if I just knew that you weren't going to be here."

In contrast, "you-messages" blame and accuse other people. You-messages are common in all types of relationships. In the previous example, Quinn's mother could have said, "You're just impossible, Quinn! You make me so mad. You should have let us know you weren't going to be here. Can't you ever be where you're supposed to be? When are you going to learn to be responsible?"

You-messages are a direct attack on the other person and his or her actions. In contrast, I-messages state how you have

Good listening skills can help you build strong relationships.

Japanese is a Language of Participation

Language to most westerners is for communication, pure and simple. For the Japanese, however, language has an important social function.

In Japanese, it takes two to talk. In many other languages, one person waits for another to finish before speaking. Japanese people, however, often interject comments such as: "Yes, yes," "That's true, isn't it," and "Really?"

To keep two-way communication going, the Japanese may leave sentences dangling. The second speaker is expected to finish the sentence or make another statement.

The Japanese avoid words that are rude or that could embarrass someone. They do not say "How are you?" to friends on the street. Usually only close friends and family ask about health. Instead, acquaintances ask, "Where are you going?"

The words "about," "around," and "approximately" prevent embarrassment. If a friend cannot lend you *"about five dollars,"* he or she can lend you four without embarrassment.

The Japanese language reinforces or defines social relationships. Certain words and phrases are used only with family. Others are used with social superiors, such as an employer, supervisor, or teacher. To speak informally to a superior is insulting. To speak formally to friends is cold and can be rude.

The Japanese use as few words as possible. They often rely on gestures to fill in the blanks. Westerners might ask a

visitor to "Please sit down on the sofa." A Japanese might say only, "Please...." and gesture to a floor cushion.

The spare use of words is common between friends and co-workers. It is, however, particularly common in families. A husband might say to his wife, simply, "Hand me that," and she will know what he means.

---

reacted to those actions. Generally, I-messages are less threatening and cause more positive responses.

Sending I-messages is not easy for most people. When upset or hurt, people tend to lash out. It takes self-control to say exactly how you feel rather than expressing your feelings by attacking the other person.

Feedback

Feedback is a response to a message that indicates whether the message was understood correctly. Asking for feedback helps the sender know whether the correct message has been received. The receiver may ask for feedback to be sure that the correct message was heard.

If you don't understand what someone has told you, ask for feedback.

To illustrate this point, see what was said when Jack and his son Sal talked about what Sal was supposed to get at the grocery store. Sal asked, "You said I should get potatoes. Are you talking about fresh potatoes or do you want canned or dry ones?" Jack explained that Sal was supposed to get baking potatoes. Then he said, "You do know that we use skim milk, don't you?" Sal used feedback to find out more about the potatoes he was to buy, while Jack clarified his message to make sure that Sal knew the kind of milk to get.

Being Assertive

When you are **assertive** (uh-SURT-iv), you communicate your ideas and feelings firmly and positively. You speak up without being rude or offending others. You respect others' opinions, but you don't let them overpower you. You are not afraid to tell your ideas, and you are willing to let others express theirs.

With assertiveness, you take responsibility for yourself and for what you see and feel. You don't verbally attack others. Simply describing how you feel is correct. An assertive person gives both positive and negative points in a way that does not hurt others.

How would you describe Eva's ability to be assertive in this example? Betty called her sister Eva at the last minute on Saturday night. "Eva," she said, "my sitter just called and told me she's sick. Rob and I have tickets to a play tonight. Could you stay with the kids?" Eva often stayed with the children, but she already had a commitment for the evening. Although she hated to say no to Betty, Eva explained that she wouldn't be able to help out this time.

COMMUNICATION PROBLEMS

Communicating well with others is not always easy. By learning to recognize what can interfere, you can find ways to deal with such problems.

Mind Reading

With mind reading, people assume they know what another is thinking. Sometimes they mind read when they know each other well. Often, people try to read minds because they are too impatient. They don't want to listen to everything others have to say. Sometimes mind reading is a way to dominate the conversation and the other person. Mind readers often reach the wrong conclusion about what another person thinks. Mind readers need to pay more attention to others and make an effort to find out what is really on their minds.

How would you evaluate Joe's attempt at mind reading in this example? After dinner, Lonnie curled up in the corner and quietly watched the television, not participating in the spirited discussion going on in the room. His brother Joe watched him and thought, "Lonnie must be mad at somebody. I hope it isn't me. I think I'll stay out of his way tonight." Without feedback from Lonnie, there was no way to know whether the mind reading was accurate, yet it led Joe to avoid his brother for the whole evening.

Avoiding Subjects

Some subjects are off limits; that is, they aren't discussed. Very sensitive topics may be hard to handle. Family problems, such as a death or divorce, are not easy to talk about. A subject like sexuality may be conveniently avoided. Ironically, these are the topics that often need discussion the most.

You can approach these topics if you try. You might make it easier by including more than two people in the conversation. Open the conversation by referring to something similar that happened to someone else, a friend or a person on television, perhaps. Start with an I-message — handwritten, if that's easier.

Mixed Messages

Sometimes when messages go over more than one channel, the same message isn't sent on all channels. The result is a mixed message. For example, Spencer was talking to his dad about the classes he wanted to take next semester. His dad, however, kept checking his watch. Spencer finally asked, "Would you rather I talked to you later about this?" His dad turned on the television and said, "No, this is a good time to get this settled." What his dad did, turn on the television, contradicted what he said — that it was a good time to talk about Spencer's classes. Generally speaking, when a mixed message is sent, the nonverbal message expresses the sender's true feelings.

Avoiding Family Roadblocks

Of all the issues that families need to communicate on, those concerning potential conflicts between work, school, and home life are among the most important— and the most challenging. If communicating with one other person is a two-way street, then keeping track of all family members' needs, wants, and expectations can be an interstate highway with merging traffic.

One potential communication roadblock is differing levels of understanding. While parents and teens in a family may comprehend a situation, a preschooler may not. Experience also affects understanding. A parent might see aspects of a situation that a teen does not, simply because the adult has had more experience. In such cases, clear explanations are needed.

Another, related, difficulty that can stall communication is the tendency of some people in authority to overlook the feelings of others when reaching a decision. Family relationships do involve authority: parents have authority over children; older siblings over younger ones. It can be easy then to take an "I– know-what's-best" attitude regarding younger members' opinions and desires. Of course, parents generally do know what's best for their children. However, younger people's feelings need to be respected. Decisions about work and home affect the entire family. Everyone deserves a say, even if some ideas are not realistic. No one is too young to be shown respect.

Virginia Satir and Communication

Virginia Satir is a well-known family therapist. She was one of the first people to recognize the importance of communication in family life. She believes that communication is the main factor affecting peoples' health and their relationships with others. In her work, she stresses that every person communicates — the question is how they communicate and what happens as a result.

Satir has identified four common patterns of poor communication. These patterns are used in response to stress when people do not feel able to communicate directly about an issue.

- *Placating*. Placating means agreeing only because you want to please the other. The person who placates apologizes, never disagrees, and seeks the approval of the other. People placate so others won't get mad at them over the issue.
- *Blaming*. Blaming means finding fault and attacking the other. The blamer doesn't look for answers or responses, just disagrees with the other person. Blamers want the other person to see them as strong and as having a solution to the problem at hand.

- *Computing*. Computing involves being very reasonable and logical. The person who is computing doesn't show any emotion and stays calm and cool. Computers are showing that they aren't threatened by the stress or issues that exist.
- *Distracting*. Distracting is irrelevant communication. The words make no sense and are not to the point. The distracter ignores what others have said and changes the subject. Distracters behave as though stress or problems do not exist.

These unhealthy patterns involve sending mixed messages. The verbal messages usually do not match the nonverbal ones.

In contrast to these patterns of communication, Satir identifies leveling as a healthy pattern. In leveling, the message is straightforward and honest. Speakers tell what they believe and feel. The words, facial expression, tone of voice, and body position all match. Leveling provides the best chance to solve problems and build relationships.

Interference

Interference can disrupt all forms of communication. A persistent noise, such as a leaky faucet, may take your mind off the theme you are writing. Loud music can interfere with conversation. Watching television is one common source of interference, especially in family communication. People who want to communicate well with each other should not try to communicate when interference is present.

Silence

Silence is often a communication problem. Silence can send a strong message to others. It can mean disinterest, hostility, boredom, or outright "war."

Sometimes, though, silence means that people are afraid. They may think that if they talk, they will make mistakes and be laughed at or labeled a failure. Silence is also the most common response in youth and children experiencing family conflict .

When you have something serious to discuss, choose a place where you won't be distracted.

If a member of your family or someone else you know is silent much of the time, talk to that person and try to get him or her to talk to you. Encouraging the flow of messages may help the silent person begin to communicate again.

Different Outlooks

Sometimes communication problems occur because people don't have the same outlook on life or the same definitions for terms. This often happens in families. For example, Linda had been told that she had to clean her room before she could go shopping with her friends. She cleaned it, and then got ready to go. When her mother came in to check on the room, she said, "Linda, this room isn't clean! You haven't put away all the clothes and you didn't run the vacuum cleaner. You aren't going anywhere yet." Linda and her mother had not communicated clearly. They had different ideas about what "clean enough to go

shopping" was. To be useful, messages need to be specific and clear.

Because each person is different, each sees the world a little bit differently. To help deal with communication problems, people should always keep another's point of view in mind as they send and receive messages.

SECTION 2 REVIEW

1. Briefly explain why listening is one of the most important communication skills.
2. Name the two types of listening skills.
3. Compare sending "I-messages" with sending "you-messages."
4. What is meant by being assertive?
5. Name six problems in communication.

Chapter 5 Review

Chapter Summary

- Communication is a skill that can be learned and improved.
- Communication is basic to good relationships.
- The four basic elements in the communication process are communication channels, participants, timing, and use of space.
- Listening is one of the most important communication skills.
- "I-messages" and "you-messages" need to be controlled when communicating.
- Assertiveness is part of communicating well.
- Mind readers believe they know what others think without listening to what they say.
- When what someone does disagrees with what he or she says, the result is a mixed message.
- Communication problems can occur because people don't have the same outlook on life or the same definition of terms.

Chapter Review

1. What is exchanged when people communicate?
2. How does communication affect relationships?
3. Briefly describe the four basic elements in the communication process.
4. What is nonverbal communication? Give two examples.
5. What does effective listening involve?
6. Name and describe the two types of listening skills.
7. What is an "I-message"? How is it different from a "you-message"?
8. Define feedback.
9. Describe what is meant by being assertive.
10. List two reasons why people sometimes try to "mind read."
11. Give an example of a mixed message.
12. Explain why silence can be a communication problem.

Critical Thinking

1. What relationship does appearance have to communication?
2. How effective is gossip as a form of communication?
3. Do you think males and females communicate differently? Explain your reasoning.
4. How do you feel when someone you are talking to keeps looking away from you to see what is going on around you both? How would you rate this person's communication skills?
5. Some people fail to keep their end of a conversation going, and the conversation ends quickly. What can a person do to prevent this?

Activities

1. **Conveying messages.** Try saying these sentences in ways that convey different meanings: "You sure are a good friend." "Did you say that you're going to the football game with Josh?" Explain how people convey messages with more than words. (*Interpreting and communicating information*)

2. **I–messages.** Working with a partner, write ten you–messages. Then change them to I–messages. (*Teamwork, creative thinking, writing*)

3. **Communication cartoon.** Draw a cartoon that depicts a communication problem. (*Visualizing, creative thinking, drawing*)

4. **Body language.** With your class make two lists of body language, one negative and the other positive. Explain the usefulness, or lack of, for each. (*Teamwork, interpreting and communicating information*)

STRENGTHENING VALUES

Aim For Tact

Tact is the ability to say things in a way that won't hurt people's feelings or turn them off to your message. Mel shows tact when he:

- Asks his parents if they can talk about a curfew that he finds unfair.
- Waits until he and Scott are alone to tell Scott that he wasn't on the list of students who made the jazz band.
- Asks his teacher if he can come in at a convenient time to talk about a test that didn't go well for him.
- Tells a girl who wants to date him that he likes her just as a friend, and he hopes they can keep their friendship.

How did Mel show tact in each of these situations? How can you tell whether something you say is tactful? Describe a time when you had to handle a situation tactfully.

Resolving Conflicts

IMAGINE THAT ...

you are having an argument with someone in your family. You are very angry! Because you know the person you are arguing with so well, you know just what to say to hurt him or her the most, so you say it. As you expect, the person with whom you are arguing explodes in fury. Unfortunately, the person knows how to hurt you, too. Pretty soon you are both out of control. When you think back on the argument later, you realize that all the sound and fury accomplished nothing. The issue you were quarreling over never got resolved.

SECTION 1

THE PROCESS

THINK AHEAD

About These Terms
    conflict   *negotiate*
    power   *compromise*

About These Objectives
After studying this section, you should
be able to:

- Define conflict and describe what
  causes it.
- Explain the difference between constructive and destructive conflict.
- Name and describe the five stages of
  conflict resolution.
- Explain what is meant by negotiation
  and compromise.

rguments often
get very heated, and hurtful things are
said. The hostility and anger that may
occur during fights can lead people to
think that keeping out of arguments is
best. Disagreements and arguments,
however, are a normal part of any close
relationship. Problems arise because
people don't know how to deal with
conflict effectively.

◆ ◆ ◆

WHAT IS CONFLICT?

Conflict is a disagreement or struggle between two or more people. The stronger the emotions and intimacy between the people involved, the stronger any conflict is likely to be. Thus, you are apt to have the most conflict with your family and friends.

Resolving conflict is like any other skill you use in relationships. It can be learned and practiced. Learning to fight is somewhat like learning to dance. In the long run, people get the most satisfaction out of performing together.

CAUSES OF CONFLICT

Conflicts occur for many reasons. Whith good communication skills, though, most conflicts can be resolved.

What causes you to have conflicts with others? Each person is unique, and what you and your family members and friends argue about differs from what others argue about. There are, however, some common factors that cause conflict in relationships. They are the situations that people are in, the personalities of the people, and a desire for power.

Situational Factors

Situational factors arise out of daily life. Any aspect of living, working, or playing together contains the seeds of situational conflict. Conflicts over situational factors can occur in all kinds of relationships — between family members, friends, or acquaintances.

Note how a situation caused conflict for Rena and her mother. Rena said to her mother, "Mom, I need $5 for safety goggles for biology tomorrow."

"I'm not sure I've got enough to give you," her mother replied. "Adam's insurance for football is due tomorrow, and I've only got $10 to last until payday on Friday."

"But Mrs. Shurtz says we have to have the money tomorrow," said Rena. "Biology is required, and I've got to have the goggles. Football's just for fun. I need the money more than Adam does. He always comes first in this family."

With that, Rena and her mother were in the middle of a fight. Do you see any possibilities for a solution?

Situational conflict may be intense, but it is often short-lived. People usually deal with these common problems and move on.

Personality Factors

Personality factors come from the differences in people. Each person has a unique combination of values, characteristics, and style. Differences add pleasure and richness to life. They also create conflict. If a parent, for example, values order and neatness, but the children do not, conflict may occur.

Often conflict over personality factors is over small matters. The habits and mannerisms of one person may get on the nerves of another. Sometimes these small personality quirks can lead to major battles.

Bobby, for example, bought a cassette and played the music repeatedly. Finally, his sister marched into his bedroom and said, "I've had it with that tape. It's driving me crazy! If you play it one more time, I'm going to put it where you'll never see it again." In defense, Bobby retorted that he could play the tape whenever he wanted. What do you think happened next?

Power Factors

Power is the ability to influence another person. Power factors come into play in conflict when the issues are important to both people. Using power is one way to get the other to agree with your position.

Many arguments in families with teenagers are about power issues. Who has the power to decide on certain issues? Conflict over curfew is typically a power concern. Sometimes a teen's choice of friends leads to a power struggle.

CONSTRUCTIVE OR DESTRUCTIVE?

Conflict can have either positive or negative outcomes. *Constructive conflict* occurs when people work together to solve a problem, and they come to a better understanding of each other. They are likely to feel good about the decision and each other. With *destructive conflict* people attack each other, not the problem. Relationships may well weaken or end.

If you don't have the skills already, you can learn to settle differences constructively. Success can come with understanding the conflict resolution process.

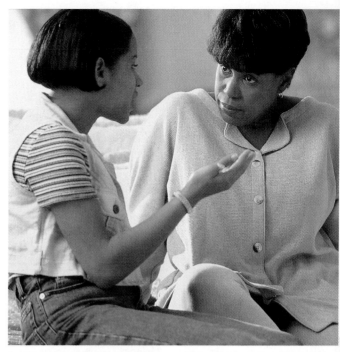

Families with teens may experience conflict as the teens learn to assert themselves.

THE RESOLUTION PROCESS

Conflict resolution is a process that occurs in five stages. First, you must be aware of the conflict. Setting limits is next. Argument is followed by negotiation. Once the conflict is settled, follow-up is needed.

Awareness

Most conflict is based on differences among people. In close relationships, these differences turn into disagreements. "Hot" emotions, such as anger, irritation, and exasperation, can turn disagreements into outright battles.

When a conflict is brewing, people become aware that there is a problem. The earlier the recognition, the better the chance for a simpler solution.

Recognizing Points of View

People have different points of view. That is, they see the same situation in different ways. This often leads to conflict and gets in the way of understanding.

YOKO *"Mom works long hours, so I take care of my seven-year-old brother after school. Since I have to stay home with him, I can't get a part-time job. Sometimes I wish I had some money of my own to manage. Any time I need money for something, I have to ask for it, and I never know what my mother's answer will be. If she has enough to spare, she might give it to me. I feel like I'm always asking for money."*

MRS. NOZAKI *"My job doesn't pay very much, so I'm never sure if I'll be able to make ends meet. I give Yoko as much spending money as I can, but by the time I pay bills and deal with unexpected expenses, there isn't much left. Sometimes she doesn't understand why I can't give in to her all the time."*

CAN YOU RECOGNIZE POINTS OF VIEW?

- Explain the two different points of view held by Yoko and her mother and tell why they might lead to conflict.
- How do you think Yoko and her mother should deal with the issue of money?
- Give an example of a recent conflict in which you and another person had different points of view. How would you benefit from understanding each other's point of view?

Setting Limits

In this stage of conflict resolution, the point or points to be argued are established. These are the limits of the conflict. Going beyond these to argue other issues is not allowed. Dragging in the fight from last week does not help solve today's problem.

At this point the people in conflict stake out their positions for the upcoming argument. For the conflict to be constructive, the opponents need to recognize each other's positions. Otherwise, they may get bogged down in mutual complaining.

When you are getting ready to fight, you can appreciate the other's point of view, even if it doesn't make sense to you. In other words, you validate the other person's position. You acknowledge and respect his or her viewpoint.

Juliette was arguing with her ten-year-old sister, who wanted to go to the mall with Juliette that afternoon. Juliette said, "You're right, I did say that I would take you to the mall to shop sometime. I know you need to buy Dad a birthday present before we spend the weekend with him. Going to the mall is important to you, isn't it?"

Juliette acknowledged that her sister had valid points and then went on to explain her own position. "This just isn't a good day for you to go with me. I'm only going to be there a little while, and then I have to go to work. There probably wouldn't be enough time for you to get your shopping done, and I won't have time to bring you home, either. We'll have to figure out another plan."

If people resort to stubbornness while arguing, they may not be able to settle the disagreement.

Arguing

During the arguing stage of conflict resolution, all the disagreements are brought to the surface. The goal of arguing is to understand each other's position better. This stage consists of a series of verbal and nonverbal messages. Each person tends to have some type of "game plan," or strategy, that will convince the other. If this stage of the conflict is fairly short, it's usually easy to move to the next stage. No personal attacks should be allowed. If they are, the fighters can get stuck arguing.

Negotiating

To **negotiate** is to deal or bargain with another. Although negotiations are common in business and government, people don't usually think of negotiating as part of family life or friendships. Negotiations are important, however, in settling conflict.

During negotiation, suggestions for possible solutions are made. Points of agreement are sought. More suggestions can lead to more agreement, eventually resulting in a solution to the problem.

"Better bend than break."

SCOTTISH PROVERB

Conflict can be solved successfully when the fighters arrive at a solution that is satisfying to both. Compromise may be part of the process. **Compromise** means giving in on some points of disagreement and having your way on others. You give a little to get a little.

In negotiating and compromise, the focus is on ways for both sides to "win." Total victory is usually impossible in ongoing relationships. Both sides can feel like winners, however, if the solution is a good one.

In successful negotiations, both parties feel that they have a fair deal. They believe that what they've gotten meets their concerns and needs.

Negotiation is not always successful. It can be destructive and disappointing. A solution may be reached that doesn't really please everyone. When solutions don't meet the concerns and needs of those involved, the quarrel is apt to appear again at a later time.

Following Up

The final stage in the conflict resolution process is following up. Solutions are put into action, and any emotional problems are resolved. Did the conflict lead to increased closeness between the fighters? Any grudges or hurt feelings may fester until they flare up into conflict again. Proper follow-up means putting the disagreement behind you so that the relationship can be strong again.

Disagreements can be settled with compromise. In this way, both parties wind up as winners.

SECTION 1 REVIEW

1. What is conflict?
2. List three common factors that cause conflict in relationships.
3. Explain the difference between constructive and destructive conflict.
4. Name the five stages of the conflict resolution process.
5. What does it mean to negotiate?
6. When both sides in a conflict give in a little to reach a solution, what are they doing?

SKILLS AND BARRIERS

THINK AHEAD

About These Terms

respect   tolerance
competition   mediator
control

About These Objectives

After studying this section, you should be able to:

• Describe ways in which you can use communication skills to help resolve conflicts.

• Name and describe five skills important in resolving conflicts.

• Name and describe four barriers to resolving conflict.

• Describe ways in which conflict can be reduced.

esolving conflicts fairly can improve the quality of your life with your family and friends. You have learned the process. Now you need to practice certain skills and avoid the barriers that get in the way of successful conflict resolution.

◆ ◆ ◆

USING SKILLS

To use the conflict resolution process successfully, you need several specific skills. When these skills are developed, conflict is more apt to be resolved in a constructive manner.

Communicate

Conflicts cannot be settled without communication skills. You learned about the communication process in the last chapter. Now take a look at how communication relates specifically to conflict resolution.

Listening

The key to good conflict resolution is to listen. Listening during conflict is not easy. Have you ever been so emotionally upset that you actually could not hear? It's especially hard to hear and receive a negative message without becoming more upset and being negative in return.

Try to listen with empathy during conflict. If you can understand and appreciate the position of the other person, you have a head start on a solution to your problem. If all you can think about is *your* position and *your* hurt feelings, it's much harder to work toward a solution.

Getting and giving feedback is important while you are listening. If you don't understand the messages you are receiving, ask questions. Just making the effort to understand helps smooth the way for cooperation.

When the person you are fighting with is saying one thing but using body language to "say" something else, what do you do? Generally, body language is a more accurate reflection of real feelings. Ask for feedback on the situation. Also be sure that you are not the one sending mixed messages.

When two people refuse to listen during an argument, neither one can understand what the other is thinking and feeling. What will the outcome be?

Here's how Shanna handled a mixed message from her father. She said, "Dad, you told me I can go to Carrie's party, but you don't look or sound happy about it. I want to go, but I don't want you to be mad at me if I do. Do you mean I can go or not?"

Talking

Use I-messages to state your position in a conflict. These allow you to express how you feel without attacking the other person. As you know, you-messages focus more on the person than on the issue.

Keep communication going. Using the silent treatment ends verbal communication. The nonverbal messages sent through the silent treatment don't help. When the fighters aren't talking, no negotiation or compromise is possible.

Control Emotions

Any conflict produces a number of emotions, most of them "hot." Keeping emotions "cool" and the emotional level low can help you focus on the issue. When the emotional level rises, the natural inclination is to attack. Unfortunately, this most often means attacking the other person, not the issue or problem.

When emotions get out of control, it is wise to take a "time out" from fighting. A short cooling-off period can help the fighters stay focused on the problem.

That's what Luke and his brother Howie did when they were arguing over who would get to use the car they shared on Friday night. Luke finally said, "Look Howie, we aren't getting anywhere. I'm so mad I could spit. Let's take a break and maybe if we calm down, we can figure out what to do."

Pick Your Time

Skill in picking the right time for resolving a conflict is important. Arguments can spring up at any time. A serious conflict requires time to settle. Time is needed to discuss, argue, and negotiate. When issues arise that can't be resolved quickly, it's best to set a time to meet about the problem.

Controlling Your Temper

Counting to ten before you react in anger is a good idea. You may decide not to be angry after all. Should you literally count to ten? You may if you want, but maybe thinking about some of these questions would be even more effective

- Is this issue important enough to risk the relationship?
- Are you sure of all the facts?
- Will this problem seem just as big tomorrow as it does today?
- Is your reaction going to be a mature one?
- Are you likely to say something you might regret?
- Have you searched for a peaceful solution?
- Will this episode help matters, or will it only serve as an outlet for tension?
- Is there any humor in the situation, which might help to relieve the stress?
- Is quarreling becoming a bad habit in this relationship?
- Is there a better way for you to settle your differences?

Sometimes a disagreement cannot be settled right away because you are too angry. Letting off a little steam by working out or some other physical activity can help you calm down.

Problems can't be solved if one or both parties are in a hurry and aren't able to concentrate on the issue at hand.

Mealtime and bedtime are not good times for conflict resolution. Self-control tends to be poor when people are hungry or tired. Emotions can get out of hand too easily.

Respect Others

All people have the right to their own opinions. They also have the right to defend their opinions to others. In the heat of battle, however, it's easy to belittle someone whose opinions differ from yours.

To **respect** is to hold someone in high regard. The language used during an argument reflects the amount of respect each person has for the other. Swearing and using negative names, such as "liar," "idiot," and "scum," show little respect for the other. Such language raises the emotional level of the quarrel and reduces the chance for a constructive solution to the problem.

Showing respect for others also means that you don't deliberately hurt them. When a relationship is close, people know how to aggravate each other. Doing so during a fight often means attacking others where they are most sensitive or vulnerable. This shows a lack of respect for them and their weaknesses.

Chad, for example, has always had a stutter. He has been to speech therapy and, in most situations, has overcome it. Under stress, however, he begins to stutter. His two brothers know that if they make fun of him during a fight, he will become upset.

His anger means that any hope for resolving the current conflict is gone. By taunting Chad, his brothers show lack of respect for him.

Overcoming Barriers

You can't resolve conflicts when barriers get in the way. You need to recognize and eliminate them.

Physical Reactions

People who try to settle conflicts with physical reactions are making a mistake. Think of all the negative outcomes. Lashing out physically — hitting, kicking, and scratching, for example — hurts people. Physical reactions get in the way of finding a solution. They damage, and sometimes end, relationships. The violence may even lead to more violence. People who fight physically are admired by few and disliked by many.

In a conflict, many people commonly feel like reacting physically. Emotions are so strong that they want to strike out at the other person. Children routinely react this way until they are taught better methods. Those who never learn to control their emotions continue to react in childish ways as adults.

Physical reactions to anger are common with children. They should not be once you grow older.

The Line in the Forest

FAMILIES

AROUND

THE

WORLD

Conflicts can be large and have effects on families. There is a snake-like clearing in the rainforest of Ecuador in South America. It is 150 miles long and 30 to 45 feet wide. This long clearing is called the *manga,* and it marks the border of the land of the Awa people.

There are about 7000 Awa — 2200 living in Ecuador and another 5000 across the border in Colombia. These people live in harmony with the rainforest, taking only what they need for food, shelter, and fiber. They carefully conserve the forest's resources for their children. For example, once they trap an animal in a certain place, they do not set traps there again for several months. This ensures that the area is not overhunted.

Others are not as careful with the land as the Awa. Cattle ranchers cut down the forest and convert it into grassland for their cattle. Loggers strip valuable woods from the land for sale overseas. Plantation owners replace the rainforest with palm trees, which are processed for their oil. These people ignore the Awa claim to the land. They overhunt, overfish, and destroy the way of life of Awa fami-

lies. The Awa had almost no way to fight the trespassers until a Peace Corps volunteer recommended the *manga.*

The *manga* says clearly that the land belongs to the Awa. Intruders cannot ignore it. The Awa can patrol the *manga* to prevent trespassing. In addition, they use the clearing to plant food crops and trees, which they then sell for cash. They improve their living conditions without changing their traditional way of life.

Keeping the *manga* clear requires a lot of work. However, the existence of the clearing proves to everyone that the Awa have the right to the land. The *manga* protects the Awa's part of the rainforest and the future of their families.

Competition

Another barrier to constructive conflicts is competition. **Competition** is a struggle for superiority or victory. The competition involved in a disagreement means going all out to "win" the fight. For competitive fighters, the sports mentality takes over. They don't see that compromise doesn't help you win a tennis match, but it helps you win in life.

Control

Directing the behavior of another person is called **control**. When power is the cause of conflict, the desire for control may get in the way of a solution. For example, a parent's wish to control a child could interfere with true negotiation and bargaining that could solve problems.

Experience shows that some situations are out of your hands, yet it's hard to get on with life while still feeling helpless to make a change. Create a ceremony to help put a conflict to rest. Here are some ideas:

- **Write the issues on balloons and pop the balloons.**

- **Write the issues on paper and ceremonially shred the paper.**

- **Write the issues on leaves and set the leaves adrift in a stream.**

- **Let a seed cluster (such as a dandelion) represent the conflict and blow it away.**

Letting go is not giving in. It is a choice to accept peace of mind in situations you cannot change.

REDUCING CONFLICT

Because of the nature of human beings and relationships, it's not possible to prevent conflict entirely. Too much conflict, however, is disturbing. Looking for ways to keep conflict to a minimum is worthwhile.

Looking for common ground with others helps reduce conflict. When people share common values and aims, there is less likely to be conflict among them. Because friends tend to choose each other for common interests and experiences, there may be less stress in friendships than in family and work relationships. Still, you can look for what you have in common with anyone and focus on that in your relationship.

Learning tolerance can also reduce conflict in your life. **Tolerance** (TAHL-uh-runts) is the ability to accept people and situations as they are. When you are tolerant, you can overlook much that is really not worth fighting about.

SETTING AN EXAMPLE

You can help others learn how to resolve conflict by leading the way. Younger siblings can learn by watching the methods you use to solve your conflicts. Friends can learn from you, too. You can even help others settle differences by acting as a **mediator**, the unbiased person in the middle who leads others in conflict to solutions. A proud feeling comes to those who not only settle their own differences successfully but help others as well.

You can use a mediator to help you solve disagreements, and you can be one yourself. Have you ever served this function?

Defusing Conflict

You can take the spark out of a potential conflict. A conflict that never develops is one that you don't have to worry about handling. Here are some techniques to try:

- *Don't let others irritate you.* Sometimes they are just trying to get a reaction.
- *Focus on the positive.* You might not even see what could be bothersome if you are looking for what is good.
- *Change the subject.* If you feel that things are getting tense, lighten up. Push the conversation in a totally different direction.
- *Take a personal stand against serious conflict, especially the kind that turns physical.* By recognizing the possible consequences of violent reactions, you and your friends can work together to reject such conflict.
- *Don't let people intimidate you or bully you into fighting.* Show your strength by doing what *you* want to do, not what *others* want you to.
- *Simply walk away.* Do so with confidence, saying, "I don't think this is worth fighting about."

SECTION 2 REVIEW

1. How can you use communication skills to help resolve conflicts?
2. Name five skills you need to develop and use to help you resolve conflicts.
3. Why are physical reactions a poor way to solve conflicts?
4. Why is competition a barrier to resolving a conflict?
5. What are some ways in which conflict can be reduced?

Chapter Summary

- Learning to handle disagreements can help strengthen relationships.
- Situational factors, personality factors, and power factors commonly cause conflict in relationships.
- Conflict can have either positive or negative outcomes.
- Conflict is a process that occurs in these five stages: becoming aware of the conflict, setting the conflict limits, arguing, negotiating, and following up.
- Skills for resolving conflict can be learned.
- Good communication is crucial in resolving conflict.
- Emotions need to be kept under control during conflict.
- Time is needed to discuss, argue, and negotiate.
- Issues must be addressed separately.
- Showing a lack of respect for others reduces chances for constructive solutions to problems.
- Confrontation, competition, comparison, and control are barriers to resolving conflict.
- Conflict cannot be prevented, but there are ways to reduce it.

Chapter Review

1. Define conflict.
2. Briefly describe three factors that cause conflict in relationships.
3. What happens when a problem is handled constructively?
4. Briefly describe the five stages of the conflict resolution process.
5. What is meant by compromise?
6. Why is listening important when trying to resolve a conflict?
7. Which is probably the more accurate reflection of how a person really feels, the words spoken or the body language?
8. Why isn't silence a constructive way to solve problems?
9. Why should you keep your emotions under control during a conflict?
10. What is respect? Give two examples of behavior that shows a lack of respect for another person.
11. Describe three barriers to resolving conflict.
12. Describe how tolerance can help reduce conflict in a person's life.

Critical Thinking

1. Do you think people have different levels of tolerance for conflict in their lives? Explain your reasoning.
2. What might happen if a person continually suppresses, or holds back, his or her anger?
3. Can you walk away from a conflict? Explain why this could be to your advantage at times.
4. What might cause a little disagreement to become a major conflict?
5. Describe a conflict that you have had and tell how it was resolved.
6. Why do you think some people feel compelled to win an argument?

Chapter 6 Review

Activities

1. **Conflict resolution skills.** Bring to class comic strips that illustrate conflicts. Evaluate the resolution skills depicted in the comics for the class. (*Acquiring and evaluating information*)

2. **A conflict questionnaire.** With a group of classmates, create a questionnaire that will reveal how well a person is able to handle conflict. Exchange questionnaires with another group and try them out. (*Teamwork, interpreting and communicating information*)

3. **Writing a script.** Write a script that shows how a conflict develops and how it is resolved. (*Creative thinking, problem solving, writing*)

4. **Mediating a disagreement.** Watch for an opportunity to mediate a disagreement between two people. Report to the class on your level of success. (*Problem solving, communicating information*)

STRENGTHENING VALUES

Aim For Cooperation

Cooperation is working together to get something done. It enables people to accomplish more together than they could working alone. Through cooperation people look for ways to work smoothly together in order to avoid conflict. Emily cooperates by:

- Vacuuming the carpet once a week to help keep her family's home clean.
- Doing her share of the research and preparation for her role on the debate team.
- Agreeing to take a short dinner break at work when her boss has a scheduling problem.
- Going along with her family's weekend plans even though she would prefer something different.

What conflicts did Emily avoid by being cooperative? What adjectives might be the opposite of cooperative? Do you enjoy people who might be described with these adjectives? How have you demonstrated a cooperative spirit in the past week?

CHAPTER 7

Building Family Relationships

SECTION 1

TRAITS OF STRONG FAMILIES

SECTION 2

GETTING ALONG IN FAMILIES

IMAGINE THAT ...

your English teacher has asked you to write an essay on what makes a family strong. You think about some famous families you have read about. With plenty of money and beautiful homes, they live in luxury. They have power and influence. Surely they are strong. A closer look, however, proves this thought wrong. You see evidence that the members of some of these families are struggling to get along with each other. Often their actions and their words show that they are not happy. True family strength doesn't seem to be there. These families have some of the same problems that many others have. You are about to write an essay on family strength. What will you say?

SECTION 1

TRAITS OF STRONG FAMILIES

THINK AHEAD

About These Terms
affirmation
commitment
traditions

About These Objectives
After studying this section, you should be able to:
♦ Describe traits of strong families.

n this unit you have studied relationships and relationship skills. Now explore how this knowledge applies to some very special relationships — those with family members.

♦   ♦   ♦

SIGNS OF STRENGTH

Families are strong because of what they *are*, not because of what they *have*. In studying strong families, social scientists have identified traits that characterize them. Some of these are described on the following pages. Remember that not every family has all the traits, but the more they have, the better the chance that family relationships can be what people want them to be.

Affirmation

Sometimes people like and love each other, but they forget to say it. They forget to show it. Taking such feelings for granted doesn't work. You can't just assume that people in your family know you love them. You need to give verbal messages that make your feelings clear. People can say, "I love you." They can also say, "You did that well." They can give a hug or do a favor. There are many ways to say and show that you have good feelings about someone. When you do any of these, you are giving **affirmation** (AF-ur-MAY-shun). You are providing positive input that helps others feel appreciated and supported.

Affirmation brings a good mood to family life. When her dad says, "You're sure doing a good job on that driveway," Tina is apt to finish her sweeping job in a good frame of mind. She may even pass the feeling along by affirming someone else in the family.

Trust

Trust is as important in family relationships as it is in any other. Both parents and children earn trust. Children learn to trust parents at an early age when their basic needs are met. Trust builds when parents are caring and true to their word.

Children have to learn how to be trustworthy. In strong families, children are given responsibilities suitable for their ages and experience. When ten-year-old Gerard arrived home on time for lunch, his grandmother felt confident about letting him play at his friend's house again sometime. Gerard earned her trust. As he grows older, he will be given additional freedoms and opportunities.

The road to trust can be a bumpy one. Sometimes people make mistakes. In strong families people have second chances. They also learn to do better when they are given a second chance.

Permission to drive shows parents' trust in a teen's driving skills and good judgment.

Commitment

A **commitment** is a pledge to support something of value. When people value the family, they accept responsibility for the way it functions. Family members are willing to work together and sacrifice for the benefit of the whole family. They have a genuine interest in the happiness and welfare of each family member.

Time Together

Happy families spend time together. They share interests and activities that bind them as a family. Time together is a base from which families develop the traits that keep them strong.

Lack of time may be the worst enemy for a family. Time spent on personal activities and organizations takes away from family time. Although people need time away from the family, too, a balance is best. Strong families try to share at least one leisure activity a week. They also spend time one-on-one with other family members.

Traditions

Strong families have traditions that give members a firm sense of family. **Traditions** are customs that are followed over time and often passed from one generation to another. Doing activities in the same way time after time lends stability to a family's way of living and strengthens the links between family members. Traditions also build a bank of common family memories. Traditions come in all sizes. They can be as simple as taking a walk together on Saturday afternoon or as elaborate as an annual reunion campout.

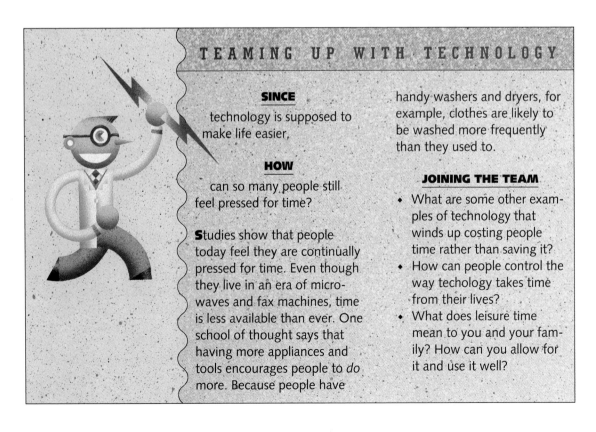

TEAMING UP WITH TECHNOLOGY

SINCE

technology is supposed to make life easier,

HOW

can so many people still feel pressed for time?

Studies show that people today feel they are continually pressed for time. Even though they live in an era of microwaves and fax machines, time is less available than ever. One school of thought says that having more appliances and tools encourages people to *do* more. Because people have handy washers and dryers, for example, clothes are likely to be washed more frequently than they used to.

JOINING THE TEAM

• What are some other examples of technology that winds up costing people time rather than saving it?

• How can people control the way techology takes time from their lives?

• What does leisure time mean to you and your family? How can you allow for it and use it well?

Family traditions bind a family together. They also create good memories.

Every family has characters and stories about them. Strong families treasure these family stories that get told and retold. As one teen described, "I always enjoy hearing my mom tell about her great grandmother, especially the story about when she was courted in the late 1890s. One time when my great grandfather came to see her before they were married, she went out to talk to him without any shoes on! That was as shocking in those days as going out in your underwear would be today."

Older family members are honored in strong families, and babies are welcomed. These families respect and love members of all ages. The age variety helps the family view itself as ongoing. Raul expressed this idea when he said, "I know this sounds funny, but my dad and I like to go to the cemetery where my grandparents are buried. That's where I get a sense that our family has lasted a long time already and will go on in the future. Family members who lived over 100 years ago are buried there. It's peaceful, and you begin to feel like your problems don't mean that much."

Communication

Good communication is one of the most important traits of strong families. Family communication helps fill the hunger for intimacy that all people feel. It helps prevent problems as well as solve them. The give-and-take of a family discussion allows all opinions to be expressed, both positive and negative.

One barrier to communication in some families is the television. When people become wrapped up in soap operas, sports events, cartoons, and comedies, there's little interaction with each other.

The television became a problem in Wanda's family until they made some changes. For a long time, they ate supper with the television news on and then continued to watch until bedtime. The family began weaning themselves from the television by having supper after the news with the television off. They also put a limit on the number of hours each person could watch television during the week. They were surprised to discover the pleasure of talking. Now Wanda's family controls the television; it no longer controls them.

Shared Beliefs

Strong families share beliefs about the meaning of life. They believe in a higher power that gives the family hope and sustains it in times of trouble. The core of beliefs also gives the family stability and a shared outlook on life.

Religious beliefs are a source of support for many families. Religious families are often better able to affirm and support each other. They often participate in organized religious activities.

In some cases, shared beliefs may not be religious in nature. Instead, they are a commitment to some ideal beyond the individual or family. Nathan's family shares an interest in the environment. Nathan's mother started and runs a recycling center. His father teaches biology classes, where he stresses the importance of a clean environment for all living things. Family vacations are spent backpacking in national parks. They all share a deeply felt sense of concern for the world around them.

Religious beliefs are often passed on within the family.

Respect

One of the marks of a strong family is respect for each other. Family members realize that each individual is different — and that's okay. They take pride in their unique traits and abilities.

Opinions

Respect for other opinions requires sensitivity. Family members who respect each other as people know that individuals draw their own conclusions about issues. Parents and children may not agree on every issue, but they need to respect the different points of view. Respect means listening to each other's opinions, trying to understand them, and having tolerance for them.

Privacy

Everyone has a need for privacy at times. Each person needs a safe place for private possessions and time to be alone. When someone needs privacy, the rest of the family should step back and make room. Even if the living space is small, family members can move aside for a while.

Strong Families Survive in Wartime

FAMILIES

AROUND

THE

WORLD

Strong families in Asia are usually built around respect for parents. Their decisions are law. After the parents, elder siblings — especially older brothers — are obeyed. In Vietnam, this hierarchy of respect has held families together during critical times. It has even maintained families that were split up.

During Vietnam's many wars, parents commonly sent their children away — usually to the United States. Older sons may have been urged to go to avoid serving in the army. These young men, sometimes little more than children themselves, sometimes had the responsibility of taking younger siblings with them. Often parents stayed in Vietnam in case the children were caught and returned to their village.

The flight to freedom was not easy. The fugitives left at night and were in constant danger. Once on the boat, they might be crowded into the hold with as many as 70 other refugees. They were subject to capture by pirates who might attack, rob, and kill them. Food and water were usually scarce. Once in a safe haven, such as Malaysia or Japan, the refugees might spend as much as a year waiting for entry into the U.S. During all this time, the one in charge of a group of siblings was the eldest brother.

In the absence of parents, the eldest not only had authority, but he also had the responsibility for his siblings' well-being. It was up to him to see that the younger children went to school in their new country. He had to find a job to feed and house them all. Things were easier if he had relatives in the U.S. to help. Often, however, they were on their own. Many of these refugee children are still waiting to see their parents, who remained in Vietnam.

Responsibility

Strong families practice and teach responsibility. A sense of responsibility shows when people say things like "I'll take care of it," "That's my job," or "Let me help." Responsible people do not need reminders or pressure. They simply do what should be done.

People show responsiblity in the family by carrying out the jobs that they are supposed to do. A parent may go to work or provide transportation. A child may put away toys. A teen might fix dinner or do homework. Family members also show responsibility by caring for each other. They step in with support whenever they sense that someone is in need.

Problems

Strong families develop ways to approach and solve problems. They know that problems can occur, so they try to identify them early — before they become harder to solve. If a problem does become serious, strong families pull together. They rely on each other, because they know that they are stronger together than they are apart. When problems go beyond their own ability to solve, a strong family will look outside the family for the help they need.

WHAT'S IMPORTANT

While reading about the traits of strong families, you may have recognized some that your family has. You may have also identified some weaknesses. Knowing what qualities need improvement can point you in the direction of positive change.

Willingly taking responsibility for some family tasks is a sign of maturity. It also eliminates a common source of family friction.

Morality

You read in Unit 1 that one of the functions of a family is to teach a moral code, the principles of right and wrong. Strong families present this code clearly. When parents agree on basic issues, they are more likely to teach morals. The parents talk about their beliefs so they can support each other in what they teach their children.

SECTION 1 REVIEW

1. How do people affirm each other?
2. What is a commitment?
3. Give three examples of traditions a family might follow.
4. What is one common barrier to communication in families? How can it be controlled?
5. Describe two ways that family members need to show respect for each other.
6. How do people show responsibility within the family?

SECTION 2

GETTING ALONG IN FAMILIES

How many individual relationships are part of this family system?

THINK AHEAD

About These Terms

family system   *environment*
siblings   *sibling rivalry*
heredity

About These Objectives

After studying this section, you should be able to:

* Explain what a family system is.
* Describe how relationships with parents can be understood and managed.
* Describe how sibling relationships can be understood and managed.

eople in families want to get along with each other. When things are not going smoothly, however, they often make a common mistake — they do nothing. Wishing for change doesn't accomplish anything. Only when people take action do things get better, but who will take the first steps? Couldn't it be you?

◆ ◆ ◆

The Family System

Together, family members, with different roles and personalities, make up the **family system**. A family system ties members together. Whatever any person in the system does affects others. Your actions affect every other part of your family system, just as theirs affect you. Suppose you come to dinner with a smile on your face. How will your smile affect the family system? What if you come to the table with a frown or in tears? What would happen then? Your actions can create very different reactions in the family system.

In any family system, getting along can be a challenge. When people make an effort, however, they can make the family system function well.

Looking at family relationships usually means first studying what goes on between any two people in the family system. Each child has a relationship with each parent and with each other child. If there are stepparents or extended family members, relationships become more complex. The variety of relationships involved provides the spark that can cause family relationships to shift and change.

As a teen, you are probably most interested in two types of family relationships — the ones you have with parents and those you have with brothers and sisters. Understanding and making these work can make life within the family system better.

Relating to Parents

Some teens, of course, do not live with their parents. Nevertheless, they probably have one or more relationships with adults who take on the parenting role with them. If you are in this situation, you will find that the principles described here about parents still apply to you.

Most relationships between parents and teens are loving ones. Surveys of teenagers show that most get along well with their parents and generally have good relationships with them. As with any close relationship, however, problems can occur.

Understanding

Before you can get along with parents, you must understand them. They, of course, must do their best to understand you, too. Since this text is for you and not them, however, the focus here is on what you can do to make the relationship work well.

When it comes to understanding, nothing works better than putting yourself in someone else's shoes. Have you ever thought about the job of parenting? Try writing a job description. Few jobs of such length and responsibility are undertaken with so little training. Parents are human. They want to do a good job, but they can make mistakes. Then they have to live with them. Realizing this can put you far along the road to understanding.

When you get wrapped up in your own concerns, you tend to forget what is on the minds of others. Parents have plenty to think about. They may be concerned with:

- *Making a living.* Do they have a job? Are they happy with their work? What pressures come with the job?
- *Providing for you.* Do they want to give you more than they are able to?
- *Family situations.* Do they have older family members to care for? Are there problems in the family?
- *Health.* Are they in good health? Has mere age made them a little slower and more tired than you are?
- *The future.* Do they worry about how they will manage as they get older?
- *You.* Are they unsure about whether they have prepared you well enough to make

your own decisions? Do they worry about how society's current problems will affect you? Have you been such an important part of their lives for so long that they are afraid to let you go?

Any of these concerns, and others, can affect a parent's behavior. Preoccupation and moodiness, when they happen, may have nothing to do with you. Perhaps a parent just has something on his or her mind.

Understanding parents also hinges on knowing what motivates them. They don't always see things the same way you do — for good reasons. Parents were raised in a different era. Their experiences and background are different from yours. One parent and teen, for example, battled over hairstyles until they happened to be looking at old family photos one day. The laughs they had over the hairstyles of 25 years ago helped them put their disagreement in a new light.

Although it comes as a surprise to some teens, many parents do know something. Just as you have knowledge that can be helpful to a young child, parents have experience and wisdom that can be helpful to you. Listening and asking for help and information makes parents feel good. They feel useful and special to you. When you respect their opinions as adults, they see that you are moving closer to adulthood yourself.

A parent who cares for older relatives has extra pressures and responsibilities.

> "*When I was a boy of fourteen, my father was so ignorant I could hardly stand to have the old man around. But when I got to be twenty-one, I was astonished at how much the old man had learned in seven years.*"
>
> — MARK TWAIN

Limits and Rules

Parents don't set limits and rules for the fun of it. Enforcing rules is far from fun, but it is necessary — for several reasons. Parents set limits and rules in order to direct family life. They want to be sure that the family's values are carried out. Protection is another reason for setting rules. Rules about crossing streets and coming home on time are set with safety in mind. Parents also set rules to develop certain qualities, such as honesty and truthfulness, in their children.

Limits and rules can be a source of conflict for families. Some teens feel that family rules are too restrictive. As teens become more independent, they feel ready for more freedom. Parents let go of rules or loosen them at a pace that they are comfortable with. Teens who have earned trust and show they are responsible are usually rewarded with additional privileges. Talking calmly with parents about your feelings and wishes is probably the best way to reach agreement on this subject.

Talking to Parents

Have you ever heard a parent say something like, "I can't believe it; it seems like only yesterday that Adrian was just a baby, and now she's almost grown"? Time flies for adults. You have only known your parents as adults, but they have watched you change dramatically from an infant to a teen. They have had to adapt all along the way. Sometimes parents aren't quite sure where you are in your development. Are you an adult yet, or do you still need their guidance? You have changed so fast, and sometimes without them even realizing that another stage has arrived. Can you understand why they might not always say and do just what you think they should?

As you can see, parents and teens can easily be on very different wavelengths. By talking with each other, they can know each other better. Parents and teens need to talk together. They want conversation that is pleasant and helpful, not argumentative. Here are some suggestions for improving conversation with your parents:

- *Take time to get to know your parents.* Simple questions about their lives pave the way for more involved conversation.
- *Bring along the right attitude.* So often it's not what you say, but how you say it. A short, snippy response to a question sets a negative tone. It may even end the conversation.
- *Look for easy approaches to difficult topics.* Talking about a television show, a movie, a book, or something that happened to a friend can ease you into touchy subjects. Often parents are just as uncomfortable as you are about some topics.
- *Use humor.* When things get heavy or could get heavy, look for ways to lighten up. Sometimes serious points can be made in humorous ways.

Introducing . . . Your Parents

In an episode of a television show a teen boy senses a gap growing between himself and his father. He realizes that he doesn't even know exactly what his father does for a living. Sharing one day at work proves to be a revelation.

How much do you know about your parents' jobs? Knowing how parents spend their working day can give you insights that might help improve family relationships. You might ask:

- Is the work environment indoors or outdoors? Pressure-filled or low-keyed?
- Do parents work as part of a team or separately? Are coworkers friendly? Demanding?
- What are your parents' duties? What skills do they use at work?
- What are their professional goals? Are they satisfied with their jobs? Actively working toward a promotion? Looking for a different job entirely?

In an age when society places such importance on a person's job it's important that you see your parents as separate individuals with their own goals and abilities. You may find that you and your parents have more in common than you thought.

Why Bother?

You have so much going on in your life. You have your own concerns and pressures, so why bother to make an extra effort to get along with your parents? The answer is simple. You need each other and will continue to, probably for a long time. If you let destructive patterns and habits go on, they become more and more difficult to break over the years. Someone has to be responsible for taking the first steps.

Sometimes first steps aren't easy ones, but when you look back, you'll know they were worthwhile.

RELATING TO SIBLINGS

Relationships with **siblings**, brothers and sisters, tend to be the longest of all family relationships. They often last for 70 or more years. People have long observed that brothers and sisters in a family are usually very different. Wondering why, psychologists have looked for explanations.

Adler's View

In the 1930s a German psychologist named Alfred Adler developed a theory for understanding personality. It was called Adlerian psychology.

Adler proposed that the nature, character, and actions of people are determined by the experiences they have while growing up. Adler believed that the family was a major influence on personality. He felt that birth order, or the order in which each child was born, was an important factor in shaping a child's personality.

In Adler's view, each child is born into a somewhat different family. A first child often comes to inexperienced parents. The first child, however, usually has the complete attention of parents. When second and later children are born, parents have experience with child rearing. The new baby enters a family where parents and older children have already built relationships.

Adler believed that parents tend to expect a great deal of their first child. The oldest child tends to grow up responsible, independent, and ambitious. First-born children are often leaders and achievers.

According to Adler, second-born children are less involved with parents than first-born ones were. Often cheerful and

Do you enjoy recognition and attention? Schools, employers, and communities give awards for outstanding contributions and performance. Families, however, often fail to recognize the strengths of their members.

How about creating awards and planning a presentation ceremony to affirm the people with whom you live? You (perhaps with another family member) could create low-cost certificates, badges, or ribbons that recognize your family members' strong traits, such as encouraging, peacemaking, dependable, hard working, cheerful, or entertaining.

Be sure to include awards for everyone, even if someone chooses not to participate. Sincere recognition shows appreciation!

practical, they are apt to get great pleasure from social activities and friendships. They tend to be good at peacemaking.

Youngest children are likely to be popular and fun loving. Often whimsical and generous, they learn early in life to get along with others. Youngest children, however, can be selfish and uncooperative. They sometimes have trouble finding out who they are after growing up in the shadows of older siblings.

"Only" children usually get a lot of attention from their parents. They may try harder to please their parents than children with siblings do. Only children tend to be fast learners, getting good grades and achieving much. They lead busy, productive lives. They are usually watched more closely, however, than children in larger families. They may be more at ease with adults than with other children.

Other Research

Although birth order is considered a major factor in personality development in Adlerian psychology, not all psychologists agree that it is that important. Other psychologists have studied how **heredity** (huh-RED-uht-ee), traits received from parents at birth, and **environment** (in-VY-run-munt), or experiences, make siblings alike and different.

Over the last 20 years, researchers have studied twins who were raised apart in order to see how heredity affects people. Research psychologist Thomas Bouchard at the University of Minnesota and Pennsylvania State University child psychologists Robert Plomin and Judy Dunn are some of those who have conducted such studies. They found that, although the twins they studied were raised in very different environments, they showed striking similarities that could be linked to their common heritage. Through studies like these, most psychologists have come to agree that heredity is a strong influence in shaping human personality.

Even more interesting, however, is the question of environment. Just how much does experience contribute to personality?

Studies have shown that even if identical twins were raised apart, they often have striking similarities as adults. What characteristics might be linked to heredity?

Studies have shown that parents, in general, are fairly consistent in how they treat their children at specific ages, yet they have little control over how their children perceive what they do.

Sibling Rivalry

Few families with more than one child escape the challenge of sibling rivalry. **Sibling rivalry** is competition between brothers and sisters. Every sibling wants recognition and love from parents. Each wants to be treated "fairly." In an attempt to reach these goals, they try hard to keep track of any mistreatment and oversights. Finding them causes complaints, fights, and even low self-esteem. If you are one who falls into the sibling rivalry trap, ask yourself these questions:

- *Do you keep track of the "rights" that come your way as carefully as you keep track of the "wrongs"?* Often the privileges and special treatment that come to people are too easily taken for granted and dismissed. You may have your special moment on one day, while a sibling has one at a different time.
- *Are all the members of your family together all the time?* Unless they are, you can't know how every individual is treated. Some things will be missed.
- *Do parents ever have reasons for their actions even though they are not clear to you?* Often they do, and even when they don't, they aren't deliberately trying to slight you.
- *Do parents have the time and ability to keep track of everything they say and do for their children all the time?* Even someone with the best memory would have trouble with this.
- *Are you exactly like your siblings?* Differences can account for different treatment.

According to Plomin and Dunn, environment has an effect, but the process is not what might be expected. Each child experiences the family environment in his or her own way. Everything that happens to a child is subject to the child's personality and perceptions. Thus, similar treatment and experiences in the family can give very different results in different siblings.

One of Dunn's studies revealed that siblings have one strong quality in common. They constantly compare how they are treated in the family. Their perception of treatment, however, is not always accurate. One parent, for example, might hug and kiss her one-year-old more than her three-year-old. She does this because the older child is becoming more independent, not because she loves him less. Even though the three-year-old, when he was age one, had the same treatment as his sibling, he sees this as a difference in treatment now, and his self-esteem is negatively affected.

- *Would you really want equal treatment with siblings?* You could stand to lose some things.
- *Do your siblings feel that you are favored?* If so, then who is right?
- *Is life "fair"?* Wherever you go in life, you will find inequities. Part of growing up means learning to accept some of these.

What To Do

Even though sibling rivalry can cause problems in a family, the feelings are still normal ones. Finding ways to handle such situations can make family life smoother. If you need to learn some techniques for getting along better with siblings, try these ideas:

- *Work on settling disagreements with your siblings yourself.* Parents may have trouble determining who's right and who's wrong. Any decision they make may be held against them.
- *Talk about your feelings.* Sometimes parents are not aware of what is going on inside you unless you say something.

Showing support and giving praise are two sure ways to minimize sibling rivalry.

- *Look for your own strengths instead of comparing yourself to siblings.* Siblings are as different from you as friends are, so why compare?
- *Make it a point to settle, or avoid, differences with your siblings.* They will be important people in your life for many years to come. It makes sense to take good care of the relationships.

YOUR FAMILY ROLE

Some members of families are reluctant or nonparticipating members. They may be very busy. They may put friends and outside activities first. Talking and spending time with family might not seem important. Unfortunately, they may not even realize what they are missing — until it is too late.

Does this description sound at all like you? If so, it may be time for a fresh start. Your role in the family can be "new and improved." How you get along with the people in your family affects how everyone gets along. You can set an example for others to follow. Begin now with a personal commitment to family strength and a pledge for action.

SECTION 2 REVIEW

1. What is a family system?
2. Why do parents often see things differently from their children?
3. List three reasons why parents set rules and limits.
4. Give four suggestions for improving conversation with parents.
5. What is the basis for Adlerian psychology?
6. What quality do many siblings have in common?
7. What is sibling rivalry?

Chapter 7 Review

Chapter Summary

- The more traits of strength a family has, the better the chance that family relationships are healthy.
- People use affirmation to show support and love for each other.
- Trust is a trait that is learned in families.
- Families need to make a commitment to spend time together. Traditions can make time together occur automatically.
- Good communication is a key element in strong families.
- Shared beliefs in a family can be religious in nature, or they may focus on some ideal.
- When people respect each other, they show that they understand and accept the differences between them.
- Families teach responsibility and morality.
- Family systems function well when all members make an effort to get along and contribute to family strength.
- Parents have many concerns that affect what they do within the family.
- Rules and limits can be a source of conflict in the family, but talking about them helps create understanding.
- Siblings have different personalities that affect how they get along with people in the family.
- By examining other points of view, siblings can improve their relationships.

Chapter Review

1. Give two examples of how you might affirm someone.
2. How do children learn trust?
3. Explain how time can be a problem in families.
4. What is a tradition?
5. What benefits come to families when they share strong beliefs about something like religious principles?
6. Must family members have the same opinions about issues in order to get along? Explain your answer.
7. Give two examples of how people show responsibility in the family.
8. What effect do individuals have on the family system?
9. What is the key to getting along with parents?
10. List four concerns parents have that can affect their actions in the family.
11. How can a teen best approach a disagreement about rules with parents?
12. What effect does attitude have when talking to parents?
13. Briefly describe Adler's theory.
14. List five questions a person should consider when sibling rivalry is a problem.

Critical Thinking

1. Do you think a parent can be a friend? Explain your reasoning. How would such a friendship differ from others a teen might have?
2. Which relationships would be more difficult to manage, those with parents who live apart or those with parents who live together? Explain your reasoning.

3. How do you feel when friends want you to take sides in a disagreement? How do you think parents feel when they are expected to do the same with their children?
4. Which would you rather be, an only child, a child with one or two siblings, or a child with several siblings? Explain the advantages and disadvantages of each.
5. Why do you think siblings often battle at home but present a united front to the outside world?

Activities

1. **Listing limits and rules.** Working with a group, create a list of limits and rules that you would establish if you were the parents of teenagers. Share your list with the class. (*Teamwork, interpreting and communicating information*)
2. **The perfect sibling.** Working with partners, write descriptions of the "perfect" sibling. Read these for the class and discuss how realistic they are. (*Teamwork, interpreting and communicating information, evaluating*)
3. **Television relationships.** As a class, make a list of television programs that depict parent–child and sibling relationships. Evaluate the reality and the quality of these relationships. (*Teamwork, interpreting and communicating information, evaluating*)
4. **Studying twins.** In your library find information on psychological studies of twins. Report your findings to the class. (*Acquiring and evaluating information, communicating information*)

STRENGTHENING VALUES

Aim For Humor

Humor is the ability to see the positive side of a situation and to laugh at mistakes. Humor can help pave the way to better relationships with others. It is laughing with others, not at them. Jonathan's good humor helped him when:

* The cake he was in charge of making for a family dinner flopped, but he put on the frosting anyway and called it a volcano cake.
* He put a cartoon that poked fun at older brothers on his younger sister's bedroom door.
* Someone shrank his favorite sweater in the wash, so he gave it to the family's dog to wear.
* One of his teachers repeatedly called him by his older brother's name, so, with a smile, he made a large nametag to wear to class.

What do you think can get in the way of having a good sense of humor? How would you rate your sense of humor, needs improvement, average, or very good? How have you used humor to your benefit recently?

Managing with Insight

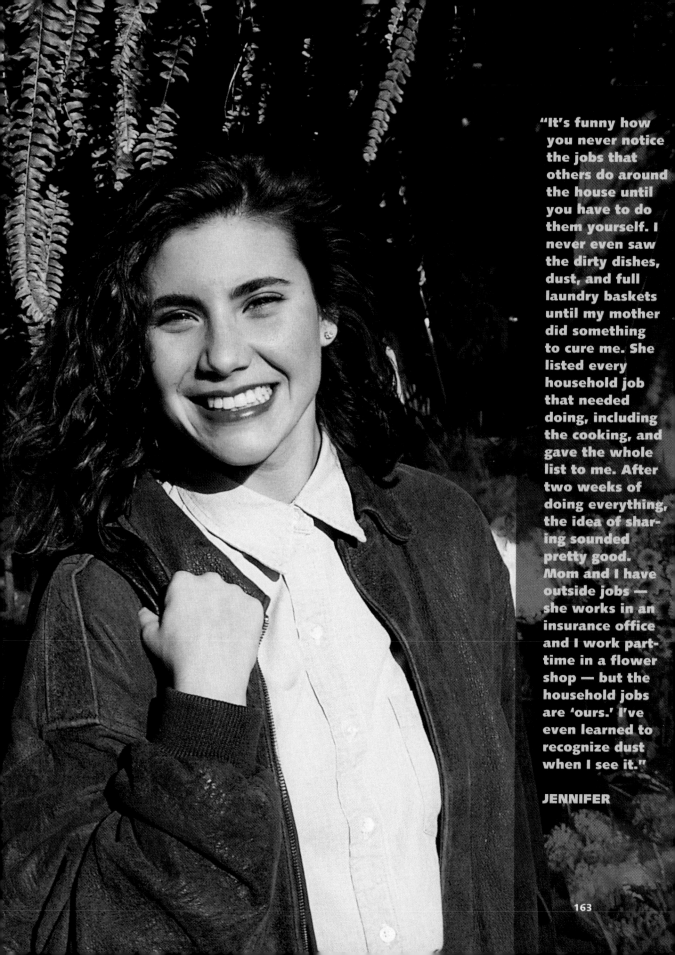

"It's funny how you never notice the jobs that others do around the house until you have to do them yourself. I never even saw the dirty dishes, dust, and full laundry baskets until my mother did something to cure me. She listed every household job that needed doing, including the cooking, and gave the whole list to me. After two weeks of doing everything, the idea of sharing sounded pretty good. Mom and I have outside jobs — she works in an insurance office and I work part-time in a flower shop — but the household jobs are 'ours.' I've even learned to recognize dust when I see it."

JENNIFER

163

Handling Decisions and Problems

IMAGINE THAT ...

a genie appears to you in a dream and says, "I will grant you three wishes." In your dream, you think about those wishes. What should they be? Your first thoughts are about things you want. Then your attention turns to your family and friends. You have an opportunity to help them — but how, with only three wishes? Finally, you focus on the world. A cooperative genie could help you make the world a better place. What an awesome thought! As you struggle to make a decision, the realism of your dream world makes you uncomfortable. Making decisions is not easy. You awake with mixed feelings. The pressure is gone, but so is the opportunity that teased your imagination.

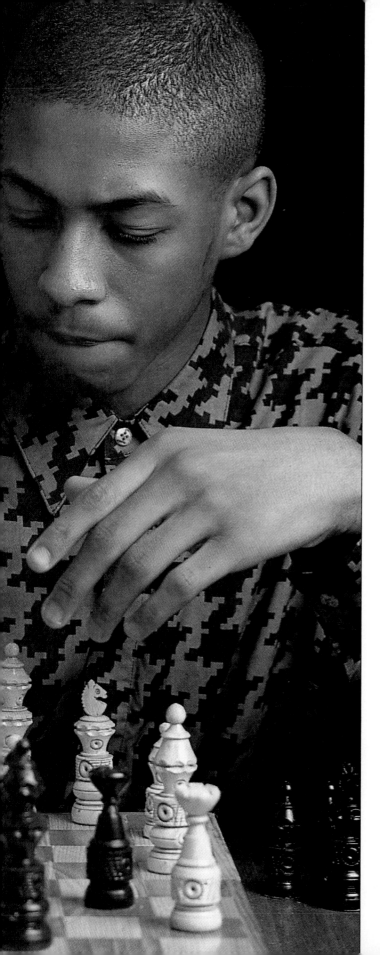

UNDERSTANDING DECISIONS

THINK AHEAD

About These Terms

decisions	*consequences*
impact	*risk*
moral decisions	*procrastination*
resources	*impulse decisions*

About These Objectives

After studying this section, you should be able to:

* Describe the kinds of decisions people make.
* Explain what affects decisions and what effects decisions have.
* Describe some poor approaches to decision making.

t's true. Even in real life, decision making is not always easy. Although people make **decisions**, or choices, every day, many give little thought to the methods used to make them. Mistakes can be costly. Common sense calls for learning about decisions and how to make them skillfully.

♦ ♦ ♦

WHAT ARE DECISIONS?

Daily living includes making hundreds of decisions. The small ones are most common. Many are so simple that they are made routinely, with little or no effort by the deciders. Your family must decide everything from what to eat, to who drives the car, to where you sit while watching television. These, and many other decisions like them, are so minor that it doesn't really matter how they are made.

Despite their simplicity, small decisions can cause problems. Have you ever heard anyone say, "Don't make a mountain out of a mole hill"? The message is, "Don't make more of something than what it really is." When people spend too much time worrying about small decisions, they may overlook the bigger decisions that need to be made.

How do you know whether or not a decision is an important one? The answer is impact. Some decisions have a greater **impact**, or effect, on your life than others do. Because some decisions have little or no impact and others have a great deal, not every decision can be handled with the same level of care. The greater the impact, the more need to spend time, thought, and energy in making the decision. For example, choosing a hair stylist or barber affects your appearance for awhile, but choosing a marriage partner has an impact on your life. The wise person puts more effort into one choice than the other.

As you sharpen your decision-making skills, learn to recognize what's important and what isn't. How would you rank the decisions in the following list: little or no impact, moderate impact, or high impact?

- Choosing a career
- Deciding what to wear to school
- Choosing a friend
- Deciding what to eat for lunch
- Deciding what courses to take in high school
- Choosing a book to read
- Deciding how much time to spend with family
- Deciding whether or not to use drugs

Moral Decisions

Some decisions have a special dimension. They deal with matters of right and wrong. Called **moral decisions**, these can have a strong impact on your life.

In your earlier study of values, you learned that certain values make up your moral code. Turning to these can help when you are faced with a moral decision.

As Francesca learned, moral decisions are easier to make when you have some principles to go by. While she was house sitting for a neighbor family, Francesca faced a decision of this type. Her job was to check the neighbors' house, water their plants, and make sure everything was all right for a month. One hot Sunday afternoon, Francesca's sister asked if she could go swimming in the neighbor family's pool.

Daily decisions can have a long-lasting impact. How do daily food choices, for instance, affect overall health?

A strong sense of values helps you make moral decisions. What values will this teen use to decide what to do with a lost wallet?

The neighbors had told Francesca specifically that no one was to swim in their pool while they were gone. Francesca's sister insisted that she would be careful and that the neighbors need never find out. Francesca turned down her sister's request. Would you have done the same?

WHAT AFFECTS DECISIONS?

Suppose you were a hermit, living all alone on a deserted island. Could your decisions be made without anything affecting them? The answer is "no." So many things affect decisions that you may often be unaware of what they are. Understanding what affects decisions can help you recognize those factors that sway your thinking. You can be better prepared to control them instead of letting them control you. Here are some influences on decisions. Can you think of any others?

- *Feelings About Yourself.* Good feelings about yourself give you the confidence to tackle decisions. They also help you take an optimistic view of what is possible. On the other hand, when you feel down, you may avoid decision making and believe that the possibilities are limited. Striving to increase the good feel-

ings you have about yourself can contribute to making better decisions.
- *Resources.* **Resources** are everything available to you for use in managing your life. They may be anything from skills that you have to people, money, and tools. Often the decisions you make are affected by what resources you have and how well you recognize and make use of them.
- *Pressure.* Sometimes people try to take decisions away from you. They may use many different methods to influence your thinking. You need to be aware of the pressures that come your way and make your decisions your own.
- *Needs and Wants.* Many decisions are based on an evaluation of needs and wants. In general, needs must be fulfilled before wants. Better decisions are made when you know the difference between the two and choose accordingly.
- *Values.* One of the most useful tools in decision making is a value system. People commonly turn to values to help them decide. Ignoring appropriate values is a mistake.

WHAT ARE THE EFFECTS OF DECISIONS?

Two trains are on the same track. One is headed east and the other west. They are headed toward each other, coming closer and closer. Someone made an error. What might the result be?

Unless quick action is taken, a consequence will occur. **Consequences** (KAHN-suh-KWEN-sez) are the results of decisions. Some are good. Some are not. The train derailments in life need to be avoided. Making good decisions is the place to start.

You can think about consequences before they ever occur. On the one hand, think about what can happen to *you*, but don't stop there. The decisions you make do affect your own life in many ways, but they also affect *others*. How will your family and friends be affected by a decision you make? What will the impact on society be? These are important questions to ask. The answers must be a factor in how you handle the decision.

Sometimes consequences are not clear. You may not know for sure what will happen. For example, when people start a new business, they have no guarantees that it will be a success. There is risk involved. **Risk** is the possibility of loss or injury. People must often weigh risks into the decision-making process. Some people are more willing to take risks than others. Some risks are more worth taking than others. Many great successes — and failures as well as tragedies — have followed risk taking. Risk may be okay, but it might not. When you don't know exactly what will happen, think carefully about what could.

HOW ARE DECISIONS OFTEN HANDLED?

Since people vary greatly, so do their reactions to the call for any kind of decision. Some people tackle decisions with careful confidence. Others, however, avoid making a decision or make them recklessly.

Procrastination

Sometimes people simply procrastinate when faced with decisions. **Procrastination** (pruh-KRASS-tuh-NAY-shun) means putting off. People who procrastinate recognize the need for decisions, but they choose to ignore them for now and handle them later. People with poor management skills often put decisions aside. Sometimes people who procrastinate feel uncomfortable with making decisions. They may not have the confidence to face even small decisions head-on. Eventually, when a decision must be handled, problems can occur.

For example, Wes wanted to take his girlfriend out for her birthday. He thought about the occasion a month in advance but put off making the arrangements. On the day, Wes called several restaurants for a reservation. The restaurant that was his third choice had an open time, but it was later than Wes had hoped for. Plans for the rest of the evening had to change. The restaurant was also more expensive than Wes wanted. Procrastination created problems that Wes could have avoided.

Denial

Failing to see that the need for a decision exists is another way of avoiding a decision. Even when strong evidence shows that something needs to be done, the indications are ignored or even denied.

Families and Education in Japan

FAMILIES

AROUND

THE

WORLD

Families in Japan make decisions about education with great care. For Japanese students the choice of college affects which companies will hire them. It may even affect who will marry them. Education is so important that preparation for college often begins very early — even as early as kindergarten. The right kindergarten enables the child to get into the right elementary school. The grade school determines which junior high the student will attend, and so on.

Families in Japan expect young people to do well in school. The value they place on education affects many day-to-day decisions. Everyone in the family makes sacrifices to give the student the best opportunity. The student gives up free time to study and attend *juku*. These special cram schools help students prepare for the entrance exams they must take for every school — often including kindergarten.

Fathers work hard to provide the money for *juku* and special tutors in all subjects. Mothers stay up late, listen to lessons, and prepare snacks and tea for the studying student. Parents want the best for their children. Because of this, they urge them and encourage them to study hard. Students feel a strong responsibility to succeed.

The pressure to do well is often difficult for young people in Japan. Sometimes there are consequences that go along with the decisions made regarding education. The health and well-being of young people may be affected. Slipping from first place in the class can be devastating. Even a reprimand from a teacher can be cause for great disappointment. A failed college entrance exam is also extremely hard to take. When these things happen, young people feel they have failed in their responsibilities and let their families down. Despite these concerns, students in Japan are admired for their discipline and high achievement.

What happened in Maria's family illustrates this point. Maria's grandmother lived in an apartment on a different floor of the building. Maria noticed that her grandmother was having trouble walking. She seemed shaky and often had to hang on to furniture in order to get around the room. Maria mentioned her concerns to her mother, who agreed that there was a problem. Every time they talked to Grandma Torres about moving, however, she wouldn't listen. Maria's mother didn't like to think about Grandma Torres' declining health. It wasn't until the day that Grandma Torres fell and broke her hip that the family took action.

Sometimes decisions are difficult to face. Confronting them may mean handling emotions and situations that are unpleasant. A serious look at the possible consequences of avoiding the decision can often give people the strength to do what needs to be done.

Transference

Allowing others to make decisions for you is another type of avoidance. In these instances the decision is transferred to someone else, and you must live with the results. Such decision making can be dangerous, especially if the decision has high impact on your life. If the person who controls the decision is unreliable, you are even more at risk. What might the outcome be for the people in the following situations:

* While making plans to see a movie, Deena's friends chose what they would all see. Although Deena had seen the movie and wanted to see a different one, she said nothing.
* Charlotte's parents were setting up a schedule of household responsibilities. They asked Charlotte what her preferences were, but she never gave them an answer.
* Salvador stopped at a house with several of his high school friends on a Saturday night. Although he did not want to drink alcohol, he accepted the bottle handed to him by one of his friends.

Impulse Decisions

Making a decision too fast can be just as troublesome as not making one at all. **Impulse decisions** are made quickly, without enough thought.

Impulse decisions are usually more connected to wants than to needs. They are often guided by emotions instead of reason. In such situations, people may fail to think about what can happen. For example, very serious consequences are possible for a person who chooses to be sexually active when the time and circumstances are not right. The prospects of pregnancy and sexually transmitted disease may be overlooked when impulse overrules good judgment.

There is a fine line between making decisions with authority and making them too hastily. Often people who can make quick, confident decisions are admired. The secret they have learned is knowing how to evaluate impact. Lateeka knows how to do this. When a decision has low impact, she thinks quickly about what needs to be done and she takes a stand. For high-impact decisions, however, she is the first to say, "I'll have to think about it."

EXAMINING YOUR SKILLS

What kind of decision maker are you? You have read about all kinds of decisions and some related problems. Did you recognize yourself in any of this? If so, you may need to work on your decision-making skills. At the very least, you can make some improvements. The next section will give you a practical approach to decision making.

SECTION 1 REVIEW

1. How can small decisions cause problems?
2. How can you tell whether or not a decision is an important one?
3. What is a moral decision?
4. Can you make decisions without anything influencing you? Explain your answer.
5. What is the relationship between consequences and risk?
6. Describe three ways in which people avoid making decisions.
7. What is an impulse decision?

SECTION 2

EFFECTIVE DECISION MAKING

THINK AHEAD

About These Terms

decision-making process
options
reasoning
evaluating

About These Objectives

After studying this section, you should be able to:

- List and explain the steps in the decision-making process.
- Tell why it is important to take responsibility for your decisions.
- Describe how the decision-making process can help people solve problems.

ould you attempt to build a model airplane without a plan? The trial-and-error approach to life can be disappointing. Often people need a system or technique that increases their likelihood of success. This principle is as true about making decisions as it is about any other task you might tackle.

◆ ◆ ◆

Some tasks require a certain technique in order to be done successfully. What is your technique for making decisions?

THE DECISION-MAKING PROCESS

To manage decisions well, you need a system. A good one already exists, and you can learn to use it. This is the **decision-making process**, a series of steps that are followed in order to make effective decisions.

Identify the Decision

You can't make an effective decision until you know exactly what you need to decide. You must first recognize the need to make a decision. Then you must be clear about what it is. Be as specific as possible. Identify the decision to be made precisely. You may wish to write it down.

As you think about the decision, evaluate the impact. A decision that will have little impact on your life can usually be made with less effort. A decision with higher impact, on the other hand, usually requires a careful approach. You may need to wait until you are less emotional, more rested, can do research, or simply have some time to think things through.

As you approach a decision, think positive. Knowing that you have a system for finding a solution can give you the confidence you need to move forward.

Identify the Options

Whenever a decision needs to be made, there are always **options** to choose from. This is the nature of decision making — choosing among possible courses of action.

The more options you can identify, the better prepared you will be to make an effective decision. Therefore, it pays to focus carefully on the question at hand and write down ideas that occur to you as possible answers. You may very well start by listing the most obvious options, but don't stop there. Sometimes the best solutions aren't apparent at first. They come when you are creative in looking for ways to approach a decision.

What do people mean when they say, "Two heads are better than one"? This statement says that sharing ideas and looking for solutions together is a good idea. Sometimes what you don't think of, someone else will. As you look for options, you may need to involve friends you can trust, family members, or people with expertise. Ask yourself whose help will be most valuable. Then turn to them.

Study the Options

Once you have identified possible courses of action, review each one on your list thoroughly. Get all the information you can about each option. You might read to get more facts. You might also ask for advice.

As you go over the possibilities, keep the following questions in mind. They will help you see the merits of each option:

- What are this option's strengths as a solution? What are its weaknesses?
- Is this option a realistic course of action for you and your family at this time?
- What will the consequences be if this option is chosen? What positive results might occur? Might anything negative happen? What will the effects be on you, your family, and society?
- Would this particular option meet your needs and wants or your family's needs and wants?

You may need advice from a more experienced person to identify all your options.

Analyzing Decisions

By analyzing decisions, you learn the difference between choices that work for you and choices that work against you. That helps you make better decisions in the future.

ELLEN *"Tricia and I work for Dad in his convenience store on weekends. Last Saturday an elderly woman came in and picked out a few items she needed. At the cash register she went through her purse and got upset when she realized she'd left her money at home. I told her to take the items and pay us the next time she came to town. Tricia stopped me and said I had to obey Dad's hard-and-fast rule about not giving customers purchases without payment."*

TRICIA *"I told Ellen and the customer very politely that Dad has an unbroken rule about being paid for store items. I even offered to have someone drop the items off at her house after work, but the lady said she needed them now. I wanted to help out, but I felt I couldn't ignore Dad's orders when he wasn't there. She left upset, and Ellen and I argued about it afterwards. We have different attitudes about the situation and disagree with each other on this decision."*

CAN YOU ANALYZE DECISIONS?

When you *analyze decisions,* you review your options in a situation to discover how they help or hinder you.

- Would you call the choice Ellen and Tricia had to make one of little or no impact, moderate impact, or high impact? Was it a moral decision? Explain your answer.
- What might the consequences connected with each teen's decision be?
- With whom do you agree, Ellen or Tricia? Why?
- Think of someone you know who made a decision that you believe was a mistake. What steps could the person take to avoid repeating the mistake in the future?
- What is the most recent important decision you have had to make? Was it the right one?

◆ What values are reflected by this option? Is this course of action right or wrong? Does it agree with your personal values and those of your family?

Make a Decision

Once you have gathered the information and opinions you need, you are ready to make a decision. Sometimes the right choice becomes clear to you as you review options. If the decision is a difficult one, however, you may need to eliminate options gradually until you have only the best one remaining.

Your ability to reason will be challenged as you eliminate options from the list.

Reasoning means thinking logically in order to reach a conclusion. The reasoning process involves collecting evidence, analyzing information, identifying facts, and making predictions. People who know how to reason have learned how to look at a situation from all angles. They look for why things happen the way they do and see what may happen if certain action is taken. They rely on careful thought rather than emotion to find answers.

Remember that whatever your decision, it is personal. The right choice is the one that will work best for you and your family. What you decide should reflect your values while meeting your needs and wants. An effective decision is one that you feel good about.

Changing Your Mind

Have you ever heard of a bride or groom whose mind changed at the altar? Sometimes changing your mind isn't easy, but it may be the wise thing to do. New evidence and additional thought may suggest a different path of action. It is far better to admit that you made the wrong choice and face any connected problems than to live with the long-term effects of a bad decision. Knowing that it's okay to change your mind can give you the courage to do so.

Act On Your Decision

Deciding what to do isn't the end of the decision-making process. A decision cannot serve its purpose unless it is put into action. Sometimes acting simply means stating your decision to others. If you are offered a job that you decide you want, you accept it. If you are offered a substance that you know will be harmful to you, you find words to turn the offer down. Other times, acting requires taking charge of your decision by following through in an organized

TAKING ACTION

The next time you feel "stuck" on a two-option decision, give this technique a try. If both possibilities seem to rate equally with you, flip a coin, using "heads" for one option and "tails" for the other. The object of this exercise is to see how you feel about the results you get.

If you're happy with the choice that the coin brings up, it's evidently acceptable to you. Go with that choice. If, on the other hand, you're uneasy with the results, consider your feelings to be a red flag. Perhaps the options weren't as equal to you as you originally thought. Your "gut reaction" is telling you to choose the option that you feel best about and are most comfortable with.

manner. You may have to plan and work to carry out the decision.

Evaluate the Decision

You can learn from the decisions you make by **evaluating** them. You study the results of your decision in order to determine how effective it was.

To evaluate a decision, first look at the outcome. Was it good, bad, or perhaps both? What did you like or dislike about the results of your decision?

Next, go back to the process for clues about why your decision turned out as it did. In going through the process, did you skip any steps or do any steps out of order? Was there information that you ignored or input you neglected to get? As you look back, would you eliminate certain options or add others that you now realize you left out? When you made your decision, did you pay enough attention to your values? Did you act promptly on your decision? Did you do everything necessary to activate your decision?

By reviewing decisions this way, you can improve your decision-making skills. Learn from your successes and mistakes. Both can show you how to make more effective decisions in the future.

Sometimes it is difficult to accept responsibility when things go wrong. What can you learn from assuming responsibility for your mistakes?

TAKING RESPONSIBILITY

You are responsible for the decisions you make — but why should you be? Wouldn't it be easier to let someone else take the blame when things go wrong? Wouldn't it feel better to look for excuses if you made a mistake? Here are the problems with this kind of thinking:

- Making mistakes is normal. By denying yours, you give the impression that you believe you are above making mistakes, and really no one is.
- People don't respect you when you make excuses. They see excuses as a sign of weakness.
- Others don't want to be blamed for your mistakes. This is a quick way to lose friends.
- Logically, if you take credit for what goes right, you have to take responsibility for what goes wrong.
- You can learn from your mistakes if you accept responsibility for them. Denying them may cause you to skip the evaluation step and make similar mistakes again.

When decisions turn out well, taking credit for the outcome is a pleasure. Owning your decision means saying, "This is what I decided, and I am responsible for the results." You show your strength when you take this kind of approach to decision making.

"*The taste of defeat has richness of experience all its own.*"

BILL BRADLEY

Some decisions must be made quickly. How can becoming skilled in the decision-making process make this easier?

USING THE PROCESS

How will you use the decision-making process in your life? Choosing what socks to wear in the morning hardly requires a written list of options and consequences. You can choose a pair in seconds and live with the results if they don't match. This is decision making in its simplest form. The process is barely needed, if at all.

On another level, you are aware of the process, and you use it quickly to make decisions. For example, suppose you were asked to sell popcorn during basketball games at school. If you said "yes," without considering other obligations, you could wind up with time conflicts. By using the decision-making process, however, you quickly think over the options, plus the advantages and disadvantages, in order to make a good decision.

Some decisions that you face need careful thought. For these the decision-making process is most helpful when it is used systematically. If you were making education plans, for example, you would want to explore all your options and write them down. Each option could then be examined carefully before making the decision.

Solving Problems

At still another level, the decision-making process can be very useful in your life. Both as an individual and as a family member, you will sometimes face problems in life. Some are more serious than others.

Usually they have one thing in common: they require you to make multiple decisions in order to find a solution.

Strangely enough, people are usually willing to deal with simple decisions, but often they let the big problems in life go. There are several possible reasons for this. Take a look at some:

• *The situation may not be recognized as a problem.* How do you know when you have a problem? You know because of the way you feel. If you feel confused, concerned, upset, or oppressed, you need to examine why. When such feelings are lasting and they are linked to a specific situation, a problem may need to be faced. Amy, for example, spent many months feeling down about herself and her life until she and her family acknowledged her father's drinking problem and took steps to deal with it.

• *Ignoring the problem may seem to be easier than tackling it.* Tony became a drug user at a very young age. Over time he saw how it was destroying his life, but trying to change things seemed impossible. Not until he faced the fact that his problem would only get worse did he decide that the difficult steps he needed to take were worthwhile.

- *The problem may seem overwhelming.* No problem is too big to handle. You may need to do two things: one, break the problem down into manageable pieces and, two, get help. For Sam's family, financial difficulties were the problem. Both of his parents lost jobs when the company where they worked closed. Their problem was not one that could be handled by making one decision. It required many. They broke the problem down into many decisions that had to be made and approached them one at a time. They also accepted temporary help from family and friends. Although the problem was a big one, the family survived because they looked at the pieces instead of the whole.
- *Options may not be apparent or may seem to be out of reach.* Beth and the members of her family were always fighting. Sometimes they hit each other. Although Beth was upset by this, she didn't realize that things could be different. For a long time she accepted the mistaken notion that the way they lived was the way it had to be. When Beth and her mother finally spoke to their minister about what was happening, they took their first step toward identifying ways to make things better for all of them. They discovered that situations can change.

The problems you face may not be as difficult as these. On the other hand, they might be. Simple or complex, problems involve decisions. Although the decision-making process is used every day in many routine ways, its greatest value comes when it helps you solve problems. Having a method to turn to when you have a problem to solve can make a difference in your life.

SECTION 2 REVIEW

1. Why is it important to think about impact when identifying a decision to be made?
2. What are options?
3. List three questions to ask about any option you are considering when making a decision.
4. How can reasoning help you make a decision?
5. What purpose does evaluation serve in the decision-making process?
6. What might be happening when a person says, "But it wasn't my fault"?
7. How does the use of the decision-making process vary with different decisions?
8. Describe a technique for handling a problem that seems overwhelming.

Negative emotions are one signal of a problem. What else can tell you that something is a problem in your life?

Chapter 8 Review

Chapter Summary

- Making good decisions can help prevent mistakes in life.
- Some decisions have a greater effect on your life than others do. That's why some require more time, thought, and energy to make.
- Your decisions affect not only you, but others as well. Before acting on a decision, you need to think about what it will do to others.
- Sometimes people approach decision making in ways that are not helpful. They may not make decisions that should be made or make them in haste.
- By learning and using the decision-making process, you can have greater confidence when you tackle decisions. Six basic steps are involved.
- Only you are responsible for the decisions you make.
- Problems can be solved by using the decision-making process.

Chapter Review

1. Explain what impact has to do with decision making.
2. What is a moral decision?
3. List four things that influence decisions.
4. What are consequences?
5. Briefly describe four inappropriate ways that people sometimes handle decisions.
6. List the six steps in the decision-making process.
7. Should a list of options be limited to only the best possible choices? Explain your answer.
8. List three skills that are part of the reasoning process.
9. How can you make a decision serve its purpose?
10. What is the primary benefit of the evaluation step in decision making?
11. Give three reasons why you should take responsibility for your decisions.
12. Why is the decision-making process more useful for some decisions than others?
13. Explain three reasons why people sometimes fail to solve problems that they have in life.

Critical Thinking

1. Some people prefer handling big decisions rather than small ones. Why might this be true?
2. What are your feelings about taking risks? When is risk taking appropriate? At what point does it become foolhardy? Do different people have different attitudes toward risk? Why?
3. Could there ever be good reason to procrastinate when making a decision? Explain your answer.
4. Making decisions impulsively is usually thought to be bad. Are there ever times when quick decisions are necessary? Explain your answer.
5. Some people "dare to dream" when they think about their options. What are the advantages and disadvantages of this?
6. Often people ignore serious problems that they have. Describe a problem that a person or a family could have that might get worse if ignored.

Chapter 8 Review

Activities

1. **Emotions and decision making.** Make a list of emotions that might interfere with decision making. With your class discuss ways to prevent these emotions from being a problem. (*Organizing information, problem solving*)

2. **The worst and best decisions.** Complete these sentences in writing: "The worst decision I ever made was . . ." and "The best decision I ever made was . . ." (*Decision making, writing*)

3. **The impact of decisions.** Search in newspapers and magazines for examples of decisions that are made by people in society. Explain the impact of these decisions. (*Acquiring and evaluating information, communicating information*)

4. **Analyzing approaches.** Working with a group of classmates, describe in writing a situation involving a difficult decision that needs to be made. Use any topic, such as a family problem or a problem with a friend. Present the situation to at least six people, asking them what they would do. If possible, record their answers. Then analyze the decision–making approach taken by each, considering their use of options, consequences, reasoning, values, time, and confidence. (*Teamwork, creative thinking, interpreting information*)

STRENGTHENING VALUES

Aim For Logic

Logic is sound, orderly thinking. It is the kind of reasoning that allows you to make wise decisions. Maria uses logic when she:

- **Considers her goals and talents in planning a career.**
- **Decides whether an activity that her friends like is right for her.**
- **Steps in and helps her brother and sister see both sides when they have a disagreement.**
- **Looks for reasons and facts to support an argument in a class discussion at school.**
- **Evaluates the accuracy of what others say, especially when they are trying to persuade her to do something.**

Some things can get in the way of logical thinking — emotions, for example. Can you explain how? In what ways can logic help individuals and families make decisions?

Managing Goals and Resources

IMAGINE THAT ...

your mother's birthday is in a few days, and you want to do something special for her. You decide to surprise her by making a nice dinner. You must find the recipes, buy the ingredients, prepare the food, and set the table — all without your mother's knowledge. You begin to work on your plan. Although you need to have dinner ready by 6:00 p.m. on her birthday, you realize that you won't be home until 4:30. You start to have second thoughts. With determination, however, you think about ways to make it work. You are reminded of something you once heard that gives you encouragement: "Where there's a will, there's a way."

LEARNING ABOUT GOALS AND RESOURCES

THINK AHEAD

About These Terms
long-term goals
short-term goals
motivate
human resources
material resources
facilities

About These Objectives
After studying this section, you should be able to:
- Describe the main types of goals that individuals and families have.
- List advantages of setting goals.
- Name the categories of resources and give examples of each.

Everyone has goals in life, but not everyone achieves them. Reaching a goal is sometimes a matter of identifying the goal, deciding what resources are needed, and learning how to manage these resources in order to attain your goal.

◆ ◆ ◆

181

WHAT ARE GOALS?

Accomplishing any goal in life is much like winning. Good feelings come when you set out to do, be, or accomplish something, and you succeed. You have that winning feeling.

You are probably familiar with goals in sports. The members of an athletic team may have several goals. They may want to stay physically fit, make friends, and learn to be disciplined. Such goals are important in sports, although they are often not as noticeable as the basic goal of making points in some way. For example, a softball team aims to score runs. By advancing players around the bases, they move toward that traditional sporting goal — winning. There is a major difference, however, between sports and real life. In sports, the rules of the game determine the goals. In daily living, *you* decide what your goals will be.

Some goals are much easier to achieve than others. Reading a book is a short-term goal that might be accomplished in a matter of days.

Types of Goals

Any one person can have a wide variety of different goals. A goal might be something simple, such as deciding to read a book over the weekend. It may also be something much more complex — improving your health or choosing a career, for example. Goals differ from person to person and from family to family. Only you can decide what specific goals are right for you.

Someone who decides to become a plumber has to realize that such a goal cannot be accomplished quickly. It may take months or even years. Because goals of this type require much time to be achieved, they are called **long-term goals**. Career goals are usually long-term ones. So are educational goals. Other kinds of long-term goals include marriage, children, large purchases, such as homes or cars, and plans for retirement.

By contrast, other goals involve the immediate future. **Short-term goals** require only short periods to achieve. In the time it takes to accomplish one of your long-term goals, you may reach hundreds, or even thousands, of short-term goals. Whenever you make a list of things to do in a day or week, you are setting short-term goals. Sometimes these shorter goals are necessary steps toward reaching one of your long-term goals.

Toshiro's approach to completing a research paper shows how small goals contribute to reaching larger ones. Toshiro had a month to work on his paper. He decided to read and take notes on one magazine article related to his topic every day for one week. During the next week, he tried different ways of arranging his note cards until he created an outline that worked. The third week, he wrote his rough draft. He wrote the final draft three days before the paper was due. Breaking up his long-term goal into short-term goals made Toshiro's project easier to complete.

WHY HAVE GOALS?

Setting both long- and short-term goals has many advantages for both you and your family. Here are a few of the ways goals add to life:

- *Goals give individuals and families a sense of direction in their lives.* When you set goals, you give a purpose to your activities. There is meaning to the way you spend your time. Having goals gives direction to your life. Goals can help you decide how to use your resources to get what you want.

See if you can identify how goals began to give Travis direction in this example. Travis loved to draw. He was always doodling on his notebooks and making sketches of his favorite subjects — cars and horses. Most of his drawings wound up in the wastebasket. An art teacher, who recognized Travis's talent, suggested that he enter a community art contest. Travis decided to do so. He had a goal. With interest and enthusiasm Travis spent several weeks on his entry.

The third place he took in the contest encouraged him to look for other contests he might enter. He started thinking about additional ways that he could use his talent. Career possibilities even entered his mind.

> "*If you don't know where you are going, you will probably end up somewhere else.*"
>
> — LAURENCE J. PETER

- *Goals motivate people.* To **motivate** simply means to cause people to act. While people without goals might procrastinate, people with goals tend to get moving. A teen who wants to improve her health, for example, might be motivated to start an exercise program. Sometimes people are inspired to learn new skills or change old habits in order to reach goals.

Goals are motivating. Sometimes they cause you to learn new skills. Joining the marching band, for example, means learning to play an instrument.

• *Goals promote positive feelings.* These feelings make life more enjoyable and fulfilling. People who set goals and work to achieve them feel good about their goals, their accomplishments, and themselves. Reaching a goal proves that you can take charge and do what you set out to do. This builds confidence, which leads to further goal setting and further accomplishments in the future.

The town where the Santines live sponsored a walkathon to raise money for the community's homeless. The Santine family wanted to help, so they made it their goal to participate as a group. The family walked together, rested together, and encouraged each other through the full five miles. When they made it to the end, they had raised almost $100 for the homeless. The Santines also received an award for being the largest family to have every member complete the walkathon. They felt terrific about themselves, each other, and their achievement.

WHAT ARE RESOURCES?

Goals are of little use without resources. Resources are what enable people to turn goals into reality.

Everyone talks about the resources of the planet. These are the natural substances and features of the earth that can be used for different purposes. When the subject is goals, however, the term resources has a more specialized meaning. You read earlier that resources are all those things that you use to help manage your life. Now take a closer look at what those resources are.

Resources can be divided into three main groups: human, material, and community. Knowing all the resources available to you is an important part of achieving goals.

Beat the Procrastination Trap

Even after you have set your goal, procrastination can still be a problem, especially if the goal is a large one. It can interfere with any stage of setting or reaching your goal. Here are some ways to overcome procrastination:

• Begin by deciding on the smaller details. Write down when and where you will start the project, as well as what tools and information you will need.
• Make a list of short, easy tasks that are related to achieving your goal and begin with them. This might be making a phone call or clearing a work area.
• Do least favorite jobs before easier ones. Sometimes the hardest tasks are the most important ones in achieving your goals. Getting them out of the way will make the rest of the load seem lighter. Also, if you put off unpleasant jobs, you might "accidently" run out of time for them.
• Join with others who are pursuing the same goal. If you are putting off studying for a math test, form a study group. Meeting regularly will not only force you to meet your goal, but also give you the added support of others along the way.
• Promise yourself an appropriate reward after you've reached your goal. Give yourself a little treat for achieving short-term goals. Save larger rewards for meeting major goals.

Human Resources

Human resources include the qualities that people have, such as knowledge, skills, talents, and energy. They also include the time you have available. People themselves can be resources. Many have information and skills to share that can help you reach your goals. They may also offer you their own time and energy.

Note how the Krauses used human resources to achieve a goal. Last spring, they decided to turn part of their basement into a room the whole family could enjoy. Mr. Krause's brother Lou, who is a carpenter, put up paneling and built cabinets for them. Mrs. Krause made attractive but inexpensive curtains and cushions for the room. The whole family pitched in to plan, lay tile, and paint walls. Without the efforts of all, the room would never have become a reality.

Material Resources

Material resources consist of money and possessions. Money allows you to purchase what you want or need to reach certain goals. You might buy a ticket to a ballgame, purchase a new fishing rod, or even enroll in a karate class. What goals might be associated with each of these purchases? Money can also be used to buy services that will help you reach your goals. If your family wanted to move, for instance, they could pay a moving company to transport furniture from one location to another, or they could rent a moving van. For other goals, such as having a certain career, money buys training, books, uniforms, and the tools of the trade.

Possessions are also resources used in achieving goals. If your goal is a trip to visit relatives, an automobile is a valuable resource. Other possessions can be equipment or supplies needed for performing specific tasks. If your goal is cleaning the house, a broom, mop, vacuum cleaner, sponges, and cleaning solutions are handy resources.

Community Resources

Being aware of *all* your resources means looking beyond self, family, and friends to the community. Every community has **facilities** that are useful for reaching goals.

Facilities are places designed for a particular purpose, such as schools, libraries, museums, and parks. You meet many of your educational and recreational goals with these facilities.

Community resources include services as well as facilities. Community services can help you achieve goals. The Cornwells, for example, wanted to be sure that Mrs. Cornwell's elderly father had lunch every day. He lived with the family, but no one was home at lunchtime to prepare his meal. The community's senior center turned out to be an excellent resource. Mrs. Cornwell's father could ride a senior's bus to the center where he was provided with a hot lunch. Added bonuses were companionship and recreation.

Other community services include government programs that supply everything from food stamps to health care. When Martin lost his job, he used the county job service to find a new one. His eight-year-old daughter Tanya benefits from Head Start, a national program that provides nutritious breakfasts for school-age children.

USING RESOURCES

Knowing what your resources are is one thing. Knowing how to use them is another. In the next section, you will discover how to set goals and manage resources to accomplish what you want to do.

SECTION 1 REVIEW

1. What is the major difference between goals in sports and goals in daily living?
2. Give four examples of long-term goals.
3. List three advantages of setting goals.
4. Identify three ways of overcoming procrastination.
5. Name the three main types of resources.

TEAMING UP WITH TECHNOLOGY

SINCE family members are part of a community,

HOW can they take advantage of community technology to meet family goals?

Families can use community services to meet personal goals. One person might use a public library's data base system to research family vacation plans. Another might view the community-access cable television channel to find out what's going on that might be of interest. Keeping up to date on community technology can help families plan their leisure time.

JOINING THE TEAM
- How do you use your community's technology? What other services are available that could benefit you?
- If you could invent a community service to meet people's personal needs, what would it be?

USING THE MANAGEMENT PROCESS

THINK AHEAD

About These Terms
management process
goal setting
resourceful
prioritize

About These Objectives
After studying this section, you should be able to:
* List and describe the steps in the management process.
* Explain why good management is so important.

ome people believe that if you have something that needs to be done, you should give it to the person who already has the most to do. Although this attitude may have some flaws, do you see the point? Often the busiest people are the ones who are the most capable, the ones who accomplish the most. An ability to manage their lives is surely part of their secret to success.

♦ ♦ ♦

WHAT IS THE MANAGEMENT PROCESS?

Most life situations can be managed more smoothly if you are organized. Reaching goals is a good example. You are more likely to succeed if you follow an organized plan. You may also get more done.

The **management process** is a system for managing goals and resources to get what you want in life. You can learn this system and make it part of your routine. The process includes four basic steps that must be followed in the right order.

Setting a Goal

Goal setting is the act of establishing a goal for yourself or your family. You decide what your goal will be and make it official so you will know what you are aiming for. The goals you choose to set will depend on your needs, wants, values, and interests. You may have several goals that apply to different parts of your life. Some may be short-term and some long-term.

When you set each goal, try to be realistic. Ask yourself if you will be able to reach this goal with the resources available to you. If you set goals that you can't possibly reach, you will likely become discouraged

---

The Management Process

1. Set a goal.
2. Make a plan to achieve your goal based on the resources you have.
3. Carry out your plan for reaching your goal.
4. Evaluate what happened in Steps 1, 2, and 3 in order to learn from your experience.

and frustrated. Sam's family, for example, wanted to have dinner together every night. The family valued time spent together, and Sam's mother thought that the dinner hour should be family time. It was a good idea, but one that just didn't always work for them. Sam's mother often worked late at the shop she managed. His sister Toni had a night class at college twice a week. Sam had debate practice from 5:00 to 6:00 p.m. on Tuesdays. The time available to the family made their goal unrealistic. Sam's mother was discouraged by the situation until she realized that they could find other times and ways to spend time together as a family. As a result, the family revised their goal.

Although a realistic approach is usually best, sometimes challenging goals can be set. After all, dreams can come true. Don't be afraid to go after what you want. By working hard and gathering all possible resources, you may be surprised at what you can accomplish.

Daring to dream when you set goals is okay. You risk disappointment, but you never know until you try. You can be realistic and optimistic at the same time. Often the greatest accomplishments begin with a dream.

When you set goals, set only as many as you can handle. Consider the amount of time and energy you have. Think about the money you have available. Will it cover all your goal-related expenses? If not, what are your options? You may need to limit or refine your current goals and save the rest for a time when you will have the resources to succeed.

Once you have set a goal, write it down. Be as specific and detailed as possible. This will give you a clearer focus on exactly what you must do to attain it.

Planning to Reach Your Goal

Once a goal is set, you can begin to work toward achieving it. This requires planning, or deciding how you will reach your goal. Planning is a way of getting organized and seeing the whole picture before you start to act.

When you plan, you look at all your resources and determine which ones you will use and how. If one resource is in short supply, you may be able to use a different resource instead. When you recognize and make good use of your resources, you are a **resourceful** person. This quality is valuable in helping you reach goals.

The Weisses, for example, had to be resourceful when they invited friends over. The friends had recently taken the Weisses out for dinner, so the Weisses wanted to do something in return. Money was short for the family; however, they didn't let this stop them from reaching their goal. They decided to prepare a nice but inexpensive meal at home. They rented a movie that everyone would enjoy and played it on a VCR borrowed from Mrs. Weiss's sister. What available resources did the Weiss family use instead of money to achieve their goal?

For the Weisses, planning meant thinking things through and coming up with the

Time Management Tips

Managing your time is an important part of planning to achieve your goal. Using your time efficiently allows you to accomplish your goals more quickly. Try these suggestions for getting the most from your time:

- *List and prioritize.* To **prioritize** (pry-OR-uh-tize) means to rank something according to its importance. Make a list of things you need to do today and number each item according to how important it is. Cross off each item as you accomplish it.
- *Schedule your week.* Get a daily planner and divide each day into one-hour blocks of time. Begin by filling them in with activities you know you will have, such as school and work. Fill in other activities as you learn of them. Don't forget to leave time for things that you enjoy. Leave some time unplanned, to finish up projects or just to relax.
- *Use time "scraps" and "leftovers."* Take advantage of short periods of time you might otherwise think of as wasted. Decide on your next day's outfit while waiting in the checkout line. Start writing a letter while waiting for a class to begin.
- *Double up on activities.* When possible, do two things at once. Sew on a button while talking on the phone. Read the newspaper while cooking spaghetti for dinner.
- *Organize your space.* Keep all the things you need for a certain activity together. Keep paper, pens, and textbooks in your study area. Arrange your kitchen so that items are near the places they are used.

BALANCING WORK AND FAMILY

Managing for Time Together

Use the management process to balance family life with other commitments:

- Set a goal that is realistic for your family, such as eating together once a week.
- Identify resources for reaching the goal—a daily planner, a park for family walks.
- Give everyone a part in reaching the goal. Including everyone helps ensure success.
- Encourage each other to follow through with the plan. "Family time" is best when the whole family is involved.
- Reevaluate periodically. Decide if everyone is satisfied with the arrangements. If not, agree on a new goal. Remember, the goal is to enjoy each other's company.

best method for getting what they wanted — an enjoyable evening with their friends. As you plan to reach your goals, use the following questions as a guide:

- What steps need to be taken toward reaching this goal?
- In what order should the steps be taken?
- What resources will be used in each step?
- Who will take each step?
- How long will each step take?
- When should each step be carried out to be sure the goal will be reached?

When you determine the answers to these and other questions, write them down. By writing down the steps of your plan, you will be less likely to leave out the important ones. You will also be able to check your progress when you start actively working to achieve your goal.

Management in the Ituri Forest

FAMILIES

AROUND THE WORLD

The Efe are a group of people who live in the Ituri Forest of northeastern Zaire. Historically, they have been nomads. That is, they traveled constantly in search of food; however, the fruit, roots, and animals that the Efe gathered and hunted weren't always easy to find. Also, the plants often contained poisons. It took days to process them so that they were safe to eat.

In order to reach their goal of improving their food situation, the Efe began trading with the Lese. These farmers needed help with planting, weeding, and harvesting peanuts, corn, a root crop called cassava (kuh-SAH-vuh), and a banana-like fruit called the plantain. A plan was agreed upon. The Efe began to supply the Lese with help in exchange for part of their crops. The Efe also traded game, fish, honey, and medicinal plants for other items that they needed.

According to the plan, one Efe family trades with one family of Lese. These trading partnerships are passed on from generation to generation. Evaluation shows that the system works out pretty well, though the Efe have suffered some losses. There is less game to hunt near the Lese villages than where the Efe used to travel. Also, the Efe no longer use their own language. They speak the language of the Lese, which makes trade easier.

Carrying Out Your Plan

After the planning is done, it is time to set your plan in motion. Keeping your goal in mind, go through your plan, using the necessary resources to act on each step. Stick to your plan as closely as you can, but remember to be flexible. Sometimes outside events require that you make adjustments.

Flexibility worked for Ray and his eight-year-old son when their original plans didn't work out. Ray had planned a special Saturday with Brendon — a baseball game in a distant city and pizza afterwards. Unfortunately, Ray's car broke down and couldn't be repaired until Monday. Putting

If things don't work out the way you planned, you need the flexibility to make some changes. What other personal qualities might be helpful in such situations?

their disappointment aside, Ray and Brendon devised a new plan. They rode their bicycles to a nearby park, where a baseball team was playing. They made their own pizzas at Ray's apartment and later walked to an ice cream store for sundaes. The day didn't go exactly as planned, but Ray still achieved his main goal of spending time and having fun with his son.

Evaluating What Happened

In the same way that you learned to evaluate decisions, you should also evaluate what happened when you worked toward a goal.

- *Think about your goal.* Was it realistic? Was it something you really wanted?
- *Review your plan.* Was it detailed enough? Did it make good use of resources? How could it have been improved?
- *Consider the way you carried out your plan.* Did you follow the steps in order? Did you skip any steps?
- *Look at the outcome.* Did you reach your goal? Were you pleased with the results? Why or why not?

Evaluating gives you the chance to see what works for you as a manager of goals and resources. By evaluating, you can teach yourself to improve your management skills. You may also learn something about your own personality.

BECOMING A GOOD MANAGER

As a teen, you have more opportunities to set goals of your own than you have ever had before. Sometimes teens are discouraged by situations they face. They may have family problems or believe they lack the resources they need for a better future. One teen who felt this way made a decision. She said, "I can't change what happened yesterday, and today is not particularly good, but I can make tomorrow different." By setting goals, digging for resources, learning to make good decisions, and putting management skills into action, she set out to make a better future for herself — and she did.

No matter what you face, you can do the same. Now is the time to start asking yourself what you want for your future. You have a choice. You can think, plan, and act, or you can let circumstances take charge of your life. What will you choose?

SECTION 2 REVIEW

1. Define the management process.
2. On what do the goals you choose depend?
3. Why is it helpful to write down your goal?
4. List four questions that can guide your plan to reach your goal.
5. List the four parts of evaluating your plan to reach your goal.

Chapter 9 Review

Chapter Summary

- The time needed to achieve a goal determines whether it is a long-term goal or a short-term goal. People need to set both kinds.
- Without goals people are not as likely to achieve what they want to in life.
- Achieving a goal can pave the way to setting and accomplishing others.
- Different types of resources are used to help people reach their goals.
- The management process can help you reach your goals.
- It is important to plan when working toward a goal.
- Sometimes plans have to be changed when a goal is sought.
- Improving your management skills can help you build a better future for yourself.

Chapter Review

1. How can setting short-term goals help you achieve long-term goals?
2. Explain how goals give life a sense of direction.
3. How do goals promote positive feelings?
4. Define human resources and give three examples.
5. Identify two ways in which money can help you reach a goal.
6. Define facilities and give two examples.
7. Identify the four steps of the management process in order.
8. Identify two things to remember when being realistic about setting goals.
9. Give two reasons for writing down the steps of your plan.
10. Name three things you can learn by evaluating your plan for reaching a goal.

Critical Thinking

1. Which do you think is a greater problem when most people set goals — trying to achieve too much or too little?
2. Debate the following statement: "It is impossible to live without goals. Everyone has goals, whether they are aware of them or not."
3. Why do you think some people are highly successful even though they had very few resources as they grew up?
4. Which do you think is more important in helping a person achieve goals, human or material resources? Explain your answer.
5. Why is resourcefulness important in achieving goals?
6. Is procrastination always negative? When might it be a good idea to delay taking action?

Activities

1. **How values influence goals.** Using examples from personal experience, write a paragraph or short essay explaining how values influence the goals people choose. (*Reasoning, writing*)
2. **Setting short–term goals.** Make a list of five to ten short–term goals that you want to achieve today. Then describe how you will reach each one. (*Self–management, communicating information*)
3. **Resources for goals.** As a class or in small groups, make a list of helpful resources for each of these goals: learning a foreign language; building a birdhouse; deciding on a career. Identify each resource as a human, material, or community resource. (*Teamwork, organizing information*)
4. **The management process.** Carlton's goal is to run a mile in under six minutes. Write a short essay explaining how he can work toward this goal using the four–step management process. Identify each step and tell what specific things he might do at each one. (*Visualizing, decision making, writing*)

STRENGTHENING VALUES

Aim For Efficiency

Efficiency is getting the most out of your resources with the least waste. Jay practices efficiency when he:

- Puts aways his possessions when he is done using them. Then he doesn't lose things and have a mess to clean up later on.
- Asks his boss questions about an assignment to make sure he understands exactly what is expected.
- Makes a weekly schedule for schoolwork, leisure activities, and a part-time job. By sticking to his schedule, he makes good use of his time.
- Organizes an area of his room for his texts, papers, pens, and other study materials. This way, he doesn't waste energy looking for these things when he needs them.

How could you improve your efficiency in the use of money? What could you do to make more efficient use of the time and energy that other people give you?

Managing Work and Family Life

SECTION 1
WORK AND FAMILIES

SECTION 2
FINDING WAYS TO MANAGE

IMAGINE THAT …

you are a parent of three children. You have a full-time job that keeps you out of the house from about 7:30 a.m. to 5:00 p.m. each day. Your spouse is employed in a job that requires extensive travel. Often your mate is gone all week, sometimes over weekends, too. Your children are ages three, five, and nine, each with very different care needs. Since your spouse is gone so often, cooking and cleaning are primarily your responsibility. Sometimes you wonder how you will get everything done. You are struggling with some difficult emotions.

SECTION 1

WORK AND FAMILIES

THINK AHEAD

About These Terms
work ethic
household work
income-producing work

About These Objectives
After studying this section, you should be able to:

- Describe two kinds of work that families do.
- Explain how attitudes about who does the work in a family have changed over the years.
- List ways in which jobs affect family life, and vice versa.

erhaps without even realizing it, most individuals and families are looking for some kind of balance in their lives. People need time for both work and play. When one pushes the other aside, people don't feel right. They sense that something is missing. The search for balance is tricky, but it is a search worth making.

◆ ◆ ◆

THE VALUE OF WORK

Every day after school Molly used to come home and sit in front of the television set. After a couple hours, she felt more tired than when she first sat down. She knew her family expected her to start supper, but getting to it was always difficult. Molly felt bored and unhappy with herself. It wasn't until Molly took an after-school job that her attitude changed. Having something to do gave her a new outlook. She liked relating to people on the job. She liked being busy. She liked earning some money. Most of all, she liked her new energized personality.

For many people like Molly, work is a valuable part of life. Work brings purpose to life. It not only provides something to do, but it also brings rewards. You saw some of the rewards that Molly reaped from work. Are there others? You might also point to pride in a job well done and satisfaction in making a contribution. People often talk about the "work ethic." The **work ethic** is an attitude toward work that says, "I value work, and I want to work hard in order to make my life better." Some say that the work ethic is what has made this country strong.

TYPES OF WORK

Families need work for the same reasons that Molly did — and more. Two basic kinds of work exist for families. One is the work that keeps the household going. The other is the work that produces their income.

Household Work

Not all work, of course, brings monetary reward. Some work must be done simply for the well-being of people. The work a family does in the home in order to keep up with day-to-day living is **household work**. Although people seldom get paid for household work, such work is worthy of value and appreciation.

Have you ever tried to list the jobs that must be done in a household? Some are very obvious, but others are not. Feeding the family is one responsibility that would probably appear on anyone's list of household jobs. Meals must be planned and food purchased and prepared. Clean-up follows. Straightening a closet and cleaning the oven, on the other hand, are jobs that need doing, but they are not as apparent as many others.

Some people never see or think about many of the jobs that are done in a household. If someone else cleans off a counter, puts away the dishes, and wipes up the dust, you may not even be aware that these jobs were accomplished. Nevertheless, such tasks, and many others like them, are handled in families every day — by someone.

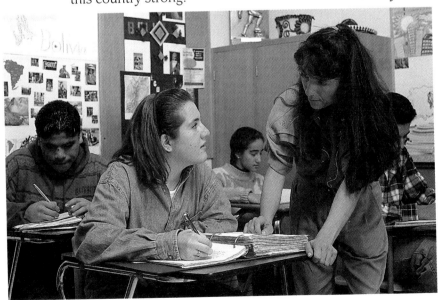

Work can provide great satisfaction. How is your "job" as a student rewarding?

Basic Family Management Tasks

Here you see the main jobs involved in running a household. Which ones can be broken down into separate tasks? How long does each take? How often must each be done? Think about how your family handles these tasks.

THE HOME
Decorating
Housecleaning
Home repairs
Yard work
Shopping for household supplies

FOOD
Meal planning
Grocery shopping
Cooking
Table setting
Kitchen cleanup
Dishwashing

CLOTHING
Shopping for clothes
Laundry
Ironing
Mending
Trips to drop off or pick up dry
   cleaning

TRANSPORTATION
Shopping for vehicles
Vehicle registration
Selection of vehicle insurance
Transportation of family members
Vehicle repairs
Cleaning/washing/polishing of
   vehicles

FINANCES
Financial planning
Earning of wages
Paying of bills
Banking

CHILD CARE
Feeding
Bathing
Dressing
Supervision
Training and early education
Miscellaneous support

Family members sometimes fail to appreciate what jobs others do — until they have to do the jobs themselves.

Not all household jobs are related only to cooking and cleaning. Many families have yard and maintenance work to be done. Errands may need running. A car may need to be serviced. All of these jobs are also important in families.

Household jobs differ in several ways. For one thing, some are done more frequently than others. Mowing the lawn may be a once-a-week job during the summer, but the job is no longer needed in the winter. In contrast, the family would have a problem if the laundry were only done during the summer. Most household jobs can be categorized according to how often they need to be done. Daily, weekly, and monthly are common time frames.

Jobs also differ in the amount of time they take. Doing the laundry may take several hours overall, but you can do other things while the clothes are washing and drying. You can't clean the bathroom, however, by setting out the cleaning supplies and walking away.

Some jobs are simpler — even more fun — than others, but you might not get people to agree. While one person may love to cook, another may hate it. If everyone dislikes it, then what?

Families have different approaches to household work. What they want and are able to get done depends on their attitudes and the time they have available. The willingness of family members to share the load is also a factor.

Income-Producing Work

The other type of work that families do is **income-producing work**. Such work provides money for needs. The amount of time that people must devote to this type of work varies. Most often the work is connected to a job that requires a commitment of time during the week. The amount of time is not the same for everyone. While one person may put in a forty-hour week, another may have to spend far more than this. Some may have fewer hours with a part-time job. In some families one person provides all the income. In many families today, however, multiple family members contribute income.

WHO DOES THE WORK?

Who does the work in a family? This is a question that could cause debate in almost any household.

In the traditional approach to family management, daily care of the home and family were the mother's responsibility.

Some family members enjoy certain jobs more than others do. What are the advantages and disadvantages of assigning household work according to preferences?

She cleaned the home, washed the clothing, prepared the meals, and helped the children with homework and school activities. If she worked before marriage, she was expected to stop when the first child was born. For the most part, household work was hers.

The father's responsibility consisted of providing financially for the family. His was the income-producing work. Not only did he earn the money, but he also made the primary decisions about how the money was used, including making major purchases, investing the money, and buying life insurance. He also had the final word in most other major decisions concerning the family. His work at home tended toward less routine jobs, such as repairing the car and installing appliances.

FAMILIES

AROUND

THE

WORLD

Caste in the Same Role

Among the Toucouleur, one of Senegal's many ethnic groups, family has a special influence on a person's future. Family background and marriage determine what job a person will have.

Toucouleur society is divided into 12 castes, or social levels. The seven middle castes are made up of artisans. They are weavers, potters, leatherworkers, woodworkers, and two castes of entertainers.

When both parents work in the same trade, their children follow in their footsteps. For example, the children of weavers become weavers. Only women in the potter caste make pottery, however. Their men do not have a particular occupation. At the age of ten or twelve, the children begin to learn the skills they will need in their careers.

Caste lines also determine who young people marry. Although all artists are considered of equal social status, and may intermarry, they usually marry within their caste. Women in Toucouleur society may also acquire an occupation through marriage. A woman who marries a leatherworker, for example, will become a dyer.

Children's responsibilities were usually limited to school and related activities. Older children were expected to help with some household tasks, but those remained largely the mother's job.

At one time many household tasks were more likely to be done by women than men. Is this true today?

Changing Tradition

Over the years the way people have handled work has changed. Yesterday's division of work responsibilities is not reasonable in many families today. You can easily see why. Many women now hold income-producing jobs. Just as women are sharing more of the responsibility for securing an income, men are sharing more of the the household responsibilities. Even children and teens make contributions.

Because "old habits die hard," however, sharing the workload has not been an easy adjustment in all families. Sometimes people feel that certain household work belongs only to women. Even when a woman has an income-producing job, she may still assume many of the household duties as well.

Studies have shown that women who are married, have two children, and are employed work an average of about 75-80 hours a week. Even when husbands share the household work, there are differences in how jobs are assigned. Women still do about two-thirds of the everyday jobs at home. They tend to do the repetitive daily jobs like cooking, cleaning, laundry, and mending. Men work on cars, do yardwork and home repair, pay bills, and do household errands. Their work tends to be more flexible. Men often have more control over when they do household work and how much of it they do.

Men are more apt to share child care than routine household tasks. Again, however, there are some differences in what men and women do. Men tend to play with, educate, and watch the children. Women are more likely to be in charge of feeding them, taking them to the doctor, washing their clothes, and other more routine tasks.

Change is often slow. As young men and women build their families today, however, a new attitude is developing. More and more people see work of whatever kind as something that a family must accomplish together. They choose fair methods that work the best for them.

THE RELATIONSHIP BETWEEN JOB AND FAMILY LIFE

A job that produces a family's income is usually a big commitment of time and energy. Household work is too. Combining both can be like having two full-time jobs. Problems come when one person bears too much of the burden. Even when work loads are shared equitably, managing life at home and on the job can still be a challenge.

People once believed that you could separate job and home life. Now they know that what happens at home affects the job, and vice versa. There is a definite interrelationship between job and family life, as you will soon see.

Men are taking a greater role in child care than they used to. They need and enjoy close interaction with their children as much as the children do.

Family Life Affects Jobs

Suppose you own a business with several employees. You notice that some of your employees have problems. What has happened to them at home is affecting their job performance. Take a look:

- *Lack of family training*. Cal has a poor attitude. He doesn't get along with fellow employees and can't take responsibility for getting his job done. Certain qualities that Cal should have learned in the family setting were never gained.
- *Home pressures*. Allyson is a single parent with two children. She is often up very late trying to get everything done at home after taking care of her children's needs. Allyson's family life is so busy that she feels pressured in trying to manage. She is tired and not very alert at work.
- *Family problems*. Trevor's wife recently moved out of the family home, taking their son with her. Trevor is depressed, and his emotional state is fragile. He is distracted at work.

As you can see, the job performance of each of these employees is threatened. Employers, who are concerned about their businesses, need employees whose personal lives are healthy and in order.

Jobs Affect Family Life

Just as jobs are affected by family life, family life is also affected by what happens on the job. You can see how in the following examples:

- *No Job*. Pete lost his job, leaving his family with little income. He is trying to find another one, but he feels frustrated and concerned, which is apparent to his family.
- *Relocation*. Karen has been offered a job transfer. She and her family must decide whether they want to move.

- *Job Challenges*. Corbin is an emergency medical technician. Although the work is rewarding, the emotional strain he is under is often felt by his family.
- *Work Schedules*. Rebecca is a minister who is called to duty at all hours of the day and night. Her family never knows for sure when she will be around.
- *Job Frustrations*. Tamika works with very tight deadlines on her job. She often takes out her frustrations at home.

Families are heavily influenced by what happens to people on their jobs. For families to function well, they need cooperation from employers who care about them.

LOOKING FOR ANSWERS

Work is an important part of life. When you know how to manage work, it can be very satisfying. Families and employers are making progress in finding ways to help people manage. The next section of this chapter will show you how.

SECTION 1 REVIEW

1. What is meant by the term "work ethic"?
2. Describe three ways in which household tasks differ.
3. How were household work responsibilities generally divided in the past?
4. Why do many families need to share household work today?
5. Explain what is meant by the phrase "the interrelationship between job and family." Give two examples to support your explanation.

Employers and families need to work together to be sure that society has strong families and a strong work force. In many ways each depends on the other for strength.

THINK AHEAD

About These Terms
   reimbursements
   leave of absence
   family management system
   strategy
   delegating
   support system

About These Objectives
After studying this section, you should be able to:

* Describe how employers help employees and their families.
* Explain how families can manage their lives effectively.

ociety needs a strong work force. When people work hard and well, the products and services they provide are good ones. The society prospers. To have a strong work force, a society needs strong families. Both employers and families can make a contribution.

◆ ◆ ◆

WHAT EMPLOYERS CAN DO

Employers are growing more aware of, and concerned about, the difficulty of balancing family life with life on the job. They are finding numerous ways to offer support to employees and their families.

Schedules

The traditional job schedule, where a person works a set eight-hour time frame for five days of the week, does not work for every family today. People have all sorts of activities that demand time. Medical appointments, personal business, community involvement, and family responsibilities are some. Often these needs must be met at times that conflict with job schedules. People who cannot do what needs to be done may feel stress in addition to other negative emotions.

Although employers have business needs of their own, most want employees to feel in control of their lives. With creative thinking, employers are learning how to provide work schedules that ease the lives of their employees. The benefit is a happier, more productive work force.

Flexible Work Hours

Some companies have flexible working hours, allowing employees a little control over the time period that they work. For example, a company might let employees choose an eight-hour work period that falls within 6:00 a.m. and 8:00 p.m. The late riser may decide to come in at 9:00 a.m. A person who needs to care for children after school might come in at 6:00 a.m. This choice means that people with different needs and personalities do not all have to live and work by the same schedule.

Flexibility has advantages. When employees can manage their lives better, they feel better about their jobs and are usually better workers. Less absenteeism is likely. Although employers must deal with the complications of scheduling, they often find the effort is worthwhile.

Compressed Work Week

Having a three-day weekend is another option. An employee who works a compressed work week might work four ten-hour days for this opportunity. The days can be long, but under the right circumstances, such schedules can be helpful.

Job Sharing

Two people who divide the time and responsibilities of one job are job sharing. They may each work four hours a day, sharing the salary and the benefits that go along with the full-time job. For people who need time to do other things, this approach can be very satisfying.

Flexible work hours are an advantage for many employees. For example, why might some people prefer to work in the evening?

Some businesses provide child care for their employees. How does this benefit both the workers and their children?

Parents have other concerns that involve children. What do you do when a child is ill? Some parents find it very difficult to tend to this need. They may send sick children to school or a child care facility if they are not allowed time off from work to be with the child. Addressing this problem is not easy, but some employers work out ways for employees to have the flexibility and time they need to care for children.

Support Benefits

Another type of support by employers directly addresses the problems that workers and their families face. One company, for example, supplies information about smoking, incentives to quit, and programs that can help. Another company provides counseling to employees who have addictions to alcohol and other drugs. An employee may be more likely to get help and solve problems when the assistance is within easy reach. If possible, concerned employers want to help, rather than let the problem or the employee go.

Leaves of Absence

A **leave of absence** provides time off from work to use for some purpose. Many employers grant leaves of absence when a child is born or adopted or when a family member is ill. Although these leaves are usually without pay, they do offer workers some job security. Employees know they will not lose their jobs for attending to family management responsibilities.

Child Care

Another way in which employers help workers meet family needs is by helping with child care. This is a major concern of working parents who can't be at home to care for children themselves. Some companies have child-care facilities at the place of business. Others offer **reimbursements** (re-im-BERS-ments), or money paid back, to families, so they can afford child care of their own choosing.

Limited Transfers

At one time many corporations commonly moved people on a regular basis. The realization that this was disruptive to families caused second thoughts. Today many businesses limit job transfers or at least give employees options.

WHAT FAMILIES CAN DO

While employers offer some kinds of help, families are still in charge of managing their lives. To do so, they need a **family management system**, a method of operating that distributes the household work fairly, allowing time for leisure activities, family togetherness, and community involvement.

Ideally no individual should have to carry an excessive amount of the work load when others are available to help. Sharing is supportive, and people who feel supported are happier and more willing to return the support. They feel less stress and carry fewer problems over to their jobs.

"*Many hands make light work.*"

◆

JOHN HEYWOOD, 1497-1580

Successful family management depends on a systematic, organized approach. Specific techniques make up a **strategy** (STRAT-uh-jee), or basic plan, for operating.

Understanding Family Values and Goals

People can't manage well when they don't agree on their goals. For example, if one person wants everything in perfect order all the time and the rest don't care, working toward such a goal becomes difficult. If one person enjoys lots of overtime work on the job and the rest of the family wants him or her to spend more time at home, how do they manage?

Before families can approach management techniques at all, they need to agree on what they value. They start by communicating.

Communicating

Open communication is the best way of gathering input and keeping family members informed. It is important to communicate well and frequently about the following:

- What people think needs to be done in the home as opposed to what they want to be done.
- People's time commitments.
- People's feelings and suggestions about their part in the family management plan.
- Support needed by individual family members and the group.
- Any problems that arise.
- Possible solutions to problems.
- Suggestions for improving the coordination, timing, and efficiency of family management.
- Household tasks and other family management jobs that need to be performed.
- Supplies needed to keep the family home and the family itself running smoothly.

Communication about family management is most often spoken. Therefore, it is useful to establish a time for talking about managing the family. In some households dinner time is set aside for family discussions. When this is not practical, setting a time for a weekly family meeting is a good alternative.

Written communication is also necessary for successful family management. Family members may leave notes for each other about their needs or about how to do particular tasks. Some families use the refrigerator door for posting lists of things to do. Your family might use a bulletin board for notes, lists, memos, and other written family communications.

Establishing Priorities

Communication helps a family set priorities. They must decide what is most important to them, putting some wants and needs ahead of others. Getting together to ask the right questions can help. For example:

- Which jobs should be done first and last?
- How often should a job be performed?
- Which tasks deserve the closest attention?
- Which jobs might be acceptably done with lower quality standards?
- Which tasks can be eliminated if time and energy resources are short?
- Which activities must be done regularly and promptly, even if this means relying on outside help?

Dividing the Labor

Once priorities have been set, the family can decide who does what. These techniques can be used:

- *Teamwork.* Have all family members work together on some or all tasks.
- *Separate Assignments.* Have different family members perform particular jobs on an ongoing basis.

Whether it is spoken or written, good communication is a must for successful family management.

Some families use a teamwork approach to the family management task of grocery shopping. They find they are more likely to get meals they enjoy this way. Also, sharing the work makes shopping much more pleasant. You might like to try this technique in your family.

To begin with, everyone gets involved ahead of time by preparing a grocery list as supplies run short. They also check newspaper ads for store specials, and they clip and organize coupons that they can use to save money. When they get to the store, each family member chooses a section and gathers needed items from that section. At home, they cooperate to put things away. Then they share a treat to celebrate a job well done.

• *Rotation* (ro-TAY-shun). Have people do certain tasks for a specified period. Then change assignments.

In dividing the labor, the age, skills, and strengths of each family member have to be taken into account. The existing responsibilities that each person has and their personal preferences should also be considered. Assignments can be made after discussing these factors.

Delegating, or assigning responsibilities to others, is not always easy. Usually parents delegate to children and teens. Sondra Taylor, for example, always made a list of jobs that her son Tom was supposed to do. For a long time he balked and complained about the work. Sometimes Sondra just did the work herself to save arguing. Tired and resentful, she wasn't very cooperative when Tom asked for her help or permission to do something. Eventually Tom learned that by accepting and performing the jobs that were delegated to him, he received cooperation in return. It made their lives run much more smoothly.

Everyone has abilities and qualities to contribute to family management. What are yours?

Scheduling Systems

Keeping track of where everyone is and what they have to do can be tricky. Families need a schedule for daily activities. They can use different techniques for making such information readily available.

One useful tool is the family calendar. An ordinary calendar can be used for this purpose, as long as it is large enough to write on. The family calendar should be posted in a prominent place, where everyone will remember to use it and check it daily.

Using a family calendar as an information source can be helpful in many ways. With it, a family can:

- Post the jobs that family members need to do.
- Arrange to get people where they need to go on time.
- Know where everyone is at all times, in case it is necessary to contact them.

- Know what times are available for family management activities, such as family meetings.
- Select the best times for family fun activities, such as recreation, outings, and vacations.
- Prevent schedule conflicts and time shortages.
- Avoid wasting valuable time.

Other scheduling tools may be used, too. The Stantons, for example, use a chart to show everyone's work and school hours. The Irvings keep a notebook that shows household jobs and who is responsible. These management aids are kept where family members can easily find them. They help the family operate efficiently by getting organized and staying that way.

Getting Support

A **support system** is a group of resources that provide help when a family needs it. Recognizing, developing, and using a support system can make life run more smoothly for a family. Common sources of support are family, neighbors, friends, and community services.

A typical management need for families today is child care. Young children certainly need care while parents are employed, but older children may also have needs. Supervision after school is a concern. Transportation to activities is another need. Many youngsters are unable to participate in activities because they simply have no way to get there.

At one time it was common for grandmothers to care for children while parents were employed. Today grandmother may be employed, too. If family members live far apart, support may not be possible. Neighbors and friends are a good alternative resource. Many families find ways to exchange with others in order to manage. One family, for example, formed a carpool with neighbors so that their daughters could get to Girl Scout meetings. Another family exchanged babysitting hours with friends so that the parents in each family could have some time away without the expense of a babysitter.

Although not every family can afford it, some pay to get the support services they need. A family might hire someone to do house cleaning or yard work. They might pay for a diaper service. They might also hire someone to sit with an elderly relative who needs companionship and health care.

A VIEW FROM ALL SIDES

If there's any time that you need to put yourself in someone else's shoes, it's when you think about managing family life. Often family members quietly harbor feelings that no one else is aware of. Do you know who *feels* the most burdened in your family? Do you know who *is* the most burdened in your family? Finding out may be the first step to better family management. It may also be the first step to a happier family life.

SECTION 2 REVIEW

1. Explain why employees are not all easily able to follow traditional job schedules.
2. List three scheduling methods that employers use to help employees manage better.
3. Why do some companies offer child care at their place of business?
4. What is a family management system?
5. Explain why communication is an important component in family management.
6. What does "delegate" mean? How does this term relate to family management?
7. Describe three benefits of using a family calendar.
8. What is a support system?

Friends and neighbors can be a valuable source of support for families.

Chapter 10 Review

Chapter Summary

- Work is a valuable part of life that brings rewards to people.
- Work serves different purposes for people.
- Attitudes about who does certain work in a household have changed over the years.
- There is an interrelationship between jobs and family life. Each has effects on the other.
- People need to learn how to manage so that all areas of their lives run smoothly.
- Employers can help employees and their families in many ways.
- Families can use a management system to make sure that household work gets done fairly. Several techniques contribute to this process.

Chapter Review

1. Explain why work is valuable.
2. Name and describe two basic kinds of work that families do.
3. How has the way families divide household work changed over the years?
4. List three ways that family life can affect a person's job.
5. List four ways in which a job can affect family life.
6. Describe two alternative ways of handling job schedules that can be helpful to employees.
7. What is a leave of absence?
8. Name one spoken and one written method for communicating about management in the family.
9. List three ways to divide the labor in a family.
10. Why should a calendar be put in a prominent place?
11. List two types of support that families can use to help them with family management.

Critical Thinking

1. Do you think the "work ethic" is alive and well in this country? Explain your answer.
2. Why do you think some people are unaware of many of the household tasks that need to be done?
3. Who should decide what jobs family members do? Defend your point of view.
4. Do you think standards of cleanliness need to be lowered for busy families? Whose standard should be followed in a home? Explain your answers.
5. What reasons might an employer have for not providing employees with flexible work hours and leaves of absence?

Chapter 10 Review

Activities

1. **The value of work.** Debate the value of work that provides income as opposed to work that does not. (*Reasoning, debating*)
2. **Listing housecleaning jobs.** As a class, make a list of housecleaning jobs that must be done throughout the weeks and months to keep a household in order. Compare ideas on how much time would be needed to carry out each responsibility. Assign a time to each task and calculate the average time needed for all housecleaning per week or month. (*Teamwork, organizing information, mathematics*)
3. **Dividing household responsibilities.** Write a letter to your imagined future mate, describing how you would like to divide household responsibilities. (*Visualizing, writing*)
4. **Household management rules.** With a partner create a set of five to ten rules for household management. Share your list with the class. (*Teamwork, organizing information, communicating information*)

STRENGTHENING VALUES

Aim For Thoroughness

Thoroughness (THUR-oh-ness) is doing things completely, giving them your full attention and care. Terry practices thoroughness whenever he:

- Double-checks to be sure he has done a job right.
- Listens carefully and makes suggestions during family management discussions.
- Records all his appointments, meetings, sports practices, and other time commitments on the family calendar.
- Follows through on all household tasks assigned to him, doing them promptly, completely, and well.
- Takes an active part in his family's support system, giving support to others and also asking for support when he needs it himself.

How could you be more thorough in your approach to family management? In what other parts of your life might thoroughness be a useful habit?

Supporting Family and Friends

"When they told me my younger brother had leukemia, I just couldn't accept it at first. We are real close. My family's been through a lot since then, especially Benji. I've felt everything — from sadness and resentment to frustration and anger. I guess we all have. Benji's in remission now and doing real well. If there's a good side to this all, it's that we've all grown closer. We've learned to make every day special, at least in some small way. I guess that's what really counts."

MIDORI

213

The Challenge of Change

IMAGINE THAT ...

your closest friend calls you on the phone with some news. Your friend's family is moving to another part of the country, many miles from where you both now live. You will not be able to see each other very often again. As you talk, you hear the concern in your friend's voice. A tight feeling forms in your throat. Having been close for many years, you are both struck by the thought of ending the relationship. You have always been so comfortable with each other — happy and reliant. Why does this change in your lives have to occur? How will you handle it?

THINK AHEAD

About These Terms
unemployment
identity
bankruptcy

About These Objectives
After studying this section, you should be able to:
* Explain what change means in people's lives.
* Describe how moving, unemployment, and financial problems affect the lives of individuals and families.
* Explain how people can cope when they are faced with a move, unemployment, and financial problems.

hange is a fact of life. All around you changes take place. Sometimes change is expected, and other times it is not. Change can bring gain or loss, excitement, uncertainty, or frustration. No matter what, you can count on change.

◆ ◆ ◆

215

THE IMPACT OF CHANGE

What changes do you have to handle in life? Some are small and routine. For example, if your dentist moves away, you have to find and get to know a new one. If the bus routes are altered, you have to find new ways to get around town. These are examples of simple changes that most people just take in stride.

Other changes have a greater impact on your life. Losing a job and experiencing a divorce, for example, are not simple changes. They alter life significantly. You will be reading about changes such as these throughout this unit.

In order to get along in life, you need to learn to cope with change. When not handled well, change can cause problems, sometimes serious ones. Knowing what to expect and how to react when change occurs can help you be prepared.

MOVING

You live in a very mobile society, in which people commonly move from one location to another. The process and the adjustment to moving is seldom easy. When a family moves to a new place, they enter an environment that is strange to them. They are likely to have feelings of uncertainty and anxiety. They also feel the strain of making all the arrangements that go along with moving.

Moving within the same neighborhood is usually less difficult than a distance move. Naturally, you have to go through the physical labors of packing and getting settled in a different residence, but that may be all. Moving to a new neighborhood or community involves much more. Not only must you adjust to a different home and neighborhood, but you must also adapt to changes in job, school, and friends.

Moving frequently is especially difficult. People who move often may be reluctant to settle in, because they believe it won't last. One teen stayed to herself at school and in the neighborhood each time she moved. She found it hard to connect with people that she would only know for a while. It always seemed pointless to her to get involved in any activities, since she would have to leave just when she started to belong.

One common change in life that people must handle is moving. What do you think is the most difficult part of moving?

Migrant Workers: Caught in the Middle

FAMILIES

AROUND

THE

WORLD

For some families of the world a move can mean going to a completely different culture. The effects of such a change in their lives can be very strong. Since World War I, North Africans have migrated to France in search of work and higher wages. They regularly send money to the families they have left behind. Migrant workers usually plan to return home once they have saved enough to provide their families with a better life.

Sometimes migrant workers (also called alien or guest workers) take their families with them to France. Working couples may have children while living in France. The children go to French schools and learn to speak French. Because of their close relationships with the French, both parents and children tend to develop a "French" attitude. If and when they return home, they may feel like foreigners in their native land.

Because of the changes they have experienced, migrant workers sometimes want to stay in France. They try to become more "French" in order to fit in better. They face prejudice in the French community, however, because their Arab-Muslim culture and their values are different. This can lead to confusion and a loss of identity. Children may have a poor image of themselves and their families because of their struggle to fit into the different culture.

Studies have shown that when these families maintain a strong cultural identity, they are better off. Their children do much better in school. Also, if they decide to return home, it's easier for them to fit into their native culture.

The best approach to moving frequently is to have the right attitude. Look at each move as an opportunity to learn and see more. Often people who have lived in many places have interesting stories to tell and observations to make. Some people keep and write to friends across the country. People who move frequently can learn to be experts at adjusting. They may discover that their ability to adapt to new situations serves them well throughout life.

Sometimes schooling is a problem when moves are frequent. School districts teach subjects on differing schedules, making it hard for a child to come in during the middle of the year and pick up from where he or she left off at the last school. Families need to keep a close eye on what might be missed and decide how any important concepts can be made up.

Preparing for a Move

When a move is ahead, families should discuss their plans together. Young children are better able to handle change when they understand what is happening and why. They can be allowed to make small decisions so they feel they have some control over what is happening. Letting children help pack and unpack and decide how furniture and possessions will be arranged involves them in the decisions the family must make.

If possible, family members should visit their destination before they move. It will seem less strange. Looking for points of interest in a new community can give you something to look forward to exploring when you arrive. The Chamber of Commerce in a city can provide information about the community. By studying the material ahead of time, you can have a head start on adjustment.

Children and teens might also visit their new school before the move. They will feel more comfortable about what to expect. Meeting a new friend or two also helps.

Many practical needs must be met for a move. Arrangements to end telephone and utility services and begin new ones must be made. Notification of a change of address must go to people, magazines, and businesses. Newspapers must be canceled. Bank accounts may need to be closed and opened. Families can decide together who will take care of each job.

Adjusting to a Move

No matter how well you prepare, new surroundings still seem strange for a while. You can't expect a place to feel like home at first. As strange becomes familiar, however, the feelings of insecurity go away and a sense of belonging takes over.

Making an effort is part of adjustment. People who have a job to go to are likely to adjust quickly. Others may need to look for ways to meet people. Community newcomer clubs are a good resource. Parents can help children make friends by locating other children in the neighborhood and making sure they meet.

Studies have shown that the wife and mother is the key person in a successful move. If she can get the family members pulling together to make a new home for themselves, the move is most apt to be successful. When a mother is not present, another family member can step in to serve this purpose.

Moving can be an exciting challenge for a family. It can draw family members closer together and provide new experiences that will help them grow as people.

Reaching Out to Others

Adjusting to a move is easier when people in the new area reach out. You can help people who move to your school or community in several ways:

- Greet a new person and make him or her feel welcome.
- Include someone new in an activity.
- Introduce yourself to a new neighbor. Some people take baked goods or some other item to new neighbors as a friendly gesture.
- Offer to help in some way. You might take care of a small child during the move in, provide a temporarily missing item, or give the person some needed information about the neighborhood.

When you know someone who has just moved to your school or neighborhood, you can help make him or her feel welcome. What can you do to reach out?

UNEMPLOYMENT

Work is very important to people. Through jobs they earn money that allows them to do, be, and have what they need and want in life — for themselves and their families. Not having a job is known as **unemployment**. When people are unemployed yet they need a job, life is not easy.

Financial Effects

Unemployment creates many problems for individuals and families. The first is financial. With the loss of income, family members have to manage with fewer financial resources. Unemployment insurance may pay a small amount, but it normally doesn't last longer than a year or so. People who have heavy debts and no savings are the most vulnerable to the problems of unemployment.

Other family members may take jobs to help boost income. Expenses often have to be cut severely. Conflict can occur in families as hard choices are made about what to do in order to survive.

Effects on the Unemployed

Work gives a person a feeling of self-respect and a sense of competence and ability. People who support themselves and others feel a sense of responsibility to have a job. Not having work when they need it can make people feel as though they have failed. Their **identity**, or view of themselves as people, may suffer. Often they see themselves as undesirable, and they doubt their own worth. They may feel anxious, depressed, and unhappy, having little confidence or faith in themselves. The longer unemployment lasts, the stronger the effects.

For many people the negative emotions produced by unemployment cause reactions. They commonly become irritable, sensitive to criticism, and sometimes even violent. Some make the mistake of turning to alcohol. They may also withdraw from others. If unemployment has caused severe financial problems for the family, the jobless person may feel guilty and react even more negatively.

An unemployed person often suffers health problems, such as ulcers, headaches, upset stomachs, and high blood pressure. If the health problems are severe, they can worsen an already strained financial situation.

Unfortunately, these physical and emotional changes can make it harder for an individual to find a new job. A job applicant who is unsure of his or her own worth, depressed, anxious, and ill is not apt to make a good impression on a prospective employer. He or she may even feel that looking for a job is pointless.

When a parent is unemployed, the best thing you can do is be understanding and supportive. Blame and accusations only make the situation worse. Encouragement helps. A parent already feels bad about the inability to provide. Care and love may help pull a parent through any rough times.

Effects on the Family

While the jobless person is suffering, the family is too. The financial and personal effects of unemployment can cause drastic changes in family life. The change in routine caused by the loss of a job can be unsettling for all family members.

In some families, members may at first become closer as they work together to overcome the problems that unemployment has caused. If the lack of a job lasts for a long time, however, the strains on family ties may become severe. Long unemployment is often a cause of family breakdown.

Young children of unemployed people tend to become sick more frequently than children of employed parents. Younger children are often more severely affected by the loss of a parent's job than older children. They are not likely to understand what is happening, and they have fewer outside friends and resources that can provide support.

The lives of teens can be affected when a parent loses a job. Frequently, they try to find part-time employment or to increase their hours if they already hold a job. They may be expected to help shoulder more responsibility for the family.

Teens often experience a loss of faith in the value of hard work. They see hard-working parents, who through no fault of their own, lose an important part of their identity. Teens are old enough to realize that the absence of work may be more damaging to the parent than the absence of money.

Coping With Unemployment

One of the first protections against the problem of unemployment is to plan ahead. If at all possible, save money in an

If one person in a family loses a job, others may need to pitch in to help financially. Even a teen who has a part-time job can make a difference in how the family is able to manage.

Recognizing Alternatives

The ability to recognize alternatives teaches you to see more than one side of a situation and to make positive choices. You consider various options before you make decisions.

HAKEEM *"When Dad got laid off, money was tight around the house. Dad wasn't sure how long the layoff would last, but after several weeks, he started to worry about whether they would call him back at all. We still owed some money on the new refrigerator, and the finance company sent a past-due notice. We were worried that they might try to repossess it. Every week Dad seemed to get further down in the dumps. My grandmother, who lives down the street, told me she was worried about him."*

ISSAN *"My uncle took me in when I was having some problems, so when he lost his job, I wanted to pitch in and help, along with the rest of the family. My cousin Hakeem said he would sell his car since he was still making car payments, but I said I didn't think he should do that because then he wouldn't have a way to get to his after-school job. I didn't have a job, because I always watched my younger cousin after school, and she was too young to stay alone."*

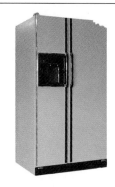

CAN YOU RECOGNIZE ALTERNATIVES?

- What are the financial problems facing this family? How can they be handled?
- What alternatives are possible for Hakeem's family? What are the advantages and disadvantages of each?
- Why does listing all the possible alternatives to a problem help you solve it successfully?
- Do you make it a habit to explore alternatives before solving a problem? Can you cite an example of a situation in which you did this? If so, describe what happened.

emergency fund. Families with savings that can cover up to three months of living expenses are much better able to handle the immediate stress of their income loss.

If unemployment is a problem, look at your resources. What personal resources can be used? Find out what community resources are available. Look for medical clinics and lawyers who provide sliding-scale or free services. Find out where to obtain public food, childcare, and financial advice.

Look at the entire family as a source of income. What services could each member provide? Who could work at what? Even young children can help by babysitting, running errands, housecleaning, or doing yard work for the family or others. Could the family exchange services or skills with other families?

Unemployment means taking a hard look at the family's financial status. Could any possessions be sold? Which expenses are absolutely necessary? All other expenditures should be postponed until the situation becomes stable again. Talking to creditors can help people find ways to manage bills.

The jobless person needs to be persistent in looking for a job. Something temporary might get the family by for a while, even when the job isn't a person's first choice. An employment agency or the state job service office might have job listings.

Finally, find a support system. Locate others who are unemployed or who live in families with an unemployed person. Get together to talk about your feelings. Having someone to talk to who understands can help ease some of the emotional problems of unemployment.

FINANCIAL PROBLEMS

Incomes increase and decrease throughout the family life cycle. What's more, the economy changes, making money management a challenge.

The loss of a job, of course, is not the only reason people have financial problems. Unexpected illness and overspending are others. Whatever the reason, people need ways to cope.

The first defense for financial difficulties is to economize, or find ways to save money. Some expenses stay the same each month, but others can be controlled. Here are some ways you can economize:

- ◆ Cut food expenses by eating at home instead of out. You can prepare food dishes from scratch instead of buying already prepared items. Watch the ads for bargains, and look for supermarkets that have the lowest prices. Buying in large quantities can also cut costs.
- ◆ Repair clothing instead of replacing. You might also look for "new" items in shops that sell used clothing at low prices.
- ◆ Skip costly entertainment and look for activities that involve little or no cost.
- ◆ Do yourself the tasks that you might normally pay to have done. Learning to make minor car repairs, for example, can save high costs.

When money is tight, you may not only have to *do* things differently, but you may also have to *think* differently. Sacrifice goes along with financial problems. As people focus only on basic needs, wants cannot be a priority. When family members are willing to put aside their own wants in favor of what others need, getting through tough times is much easier.

With today's technology, money is easily accessible. Many people have to be careful to keep spending under control in order to avoid financial problems.

If financial problems become unmanageable for a family, they may need outside help. Credit counselors are a good source of advice. Look in the Yellow Pages of the telephone directory under Credit Counseling Services. Be sure the firm is reliable. Some finance companies offer loans to consolidate bills into one payment, which costs you more in the end.

In extreme cases, **bankruptcy** (BANG-krupt-SEE) is chosen. This is a legal process that declares a person unable to pay debts. Any assets the person has are used to pay portions of what is owed. Bankruptcy should only be a last resort. Debt obligations are legally eliminated, but the effect on a person's credit record is serious.

Public assistance programs are available for people who face very serious financial problems. The Department of Public Aid in a state is a resource.

Emotional reactions to financial problems are similar to those described earlier about losing a job. People are quick to blame others in the family for financial problems. When it is apparent that one person is not a good money manager, steps taken early to help that person learn can prevent problems later on. Talking and working together in a nonthreatening way can help, before and after problems occur.

Financial problems often stem from the lack of a job. What do you think happens to a person's pride in a situation like this one?

Loss of Home

When financial problems are very serious, some people are no longer able to pay for a place to live. Homelessness is an increasing problem in society today. Many people become homeless for reasons that are out of their control. Difficult economic times that result in unforseen job losses can be the reason.

Many communities provide support for people in such situations. When families and friends are not able to help, shelters are provided that supply temporary housing until people can get on their feet again.

YOUR REACTION

How do you react to the changes that occur in your life? The nature of the change probably determines what you feel. Depending on what happens, reactions can be very strong, sometimes harmful. As you will see in the next section, such reactions need to be managed.

SECTION 1 REVIEW

1. Describe how change affects people's lives.
2. Give three suggestions that might help a family prepare for a move.
3. List four ways to make someone new feel welcome.
4. Describe what can happen to a person who is unemployed.
5. Give five suggestions for a family that must deal with the problem of unemployment.
6. List four suggestions for economizing.
7. What role does sacrifice play when families have financial problems?

SECTION 2

HANDLING STRESS

THINK AHEAD

About These Terms
stress
stress management

About These Objectives
After studying this section, you should be able to:
- Define stress and explain the link between stress and personality.
- Evaluate different methods of managing stress.
- Describe how stress can be helpful.

o keep a teapot from boiling over, what do you have to do? Turn down the heat? Let some steam escape? Remove the pot from the burner? Like the teapot, people have pressures inside, too. They need ways to get control before everything gets out of hand.

◆ ◆ ◆

FEELING STRESS

As you have seen, the changes that people experience can cause problems. A typical response to a difficult situation is stress. **Stress** is physical, mental, or emotional strain or tension.

People can feel stress in simple situations. Think about how you feel when you take a test. Do you and your friends all react the same way? Some may feel the stress of test taking more than others do. Many everyday situations can cause stress — crowds, noise, traffic jams, poor working conditions, waiting in lines, and strained relationships. Some people are less affected by situations like these than others are.

Stress accompanies trouble, but it can also occur when something positive happens. You may be happy about a change — a new baby in the family, for example — but you may still feel some stress.

The amount of stress a person feels is partly determined by personality. Some people seek out change, while others avoid it as long as possible. If you are the type of person who looks for new experiences and loves to learn new knowledge and skills, you are apt to be comfortable with change. On the other hand, if you prefer the old, familiar, and stable, change is likely to be more upsetting to you. If you are a patient person, you may be able to accept more that happens to you than someone else can.

Your feelings about control also affect your stress level. Do you feel in control or not? Situations over which you have some control tend to be less stressful than the ones that seem to be out of your hands.

Thomas Holmes and Stress

In the mid-1960s, research attention began to focus on identifying the causes of stress. Stress was identified as a major factor in both physical and mental illness. At the University of Washington in Seattle, psychologist Dr. Thomas Holmes studied events that create stress and looked at how much stress is too much.

As a result of his work, he created the Social Readjustment Rating Scale, a list of stressful events, each with a point value based on the degree of stress produced. Some events are negative and some positive. He then studied the lives of people who had serious illnesses. He discovered that 79 percent of these people had, in the past year, lived through stress-producing changes with point values totaling over 300. In other words, when major changes and stress occurred, the chances of a serious illness increased. How does the Holmes' list below relate to your life?

EVENT	POINTS	EVENT	POINTS
Divorce	73	Promotion at work	29
Death of a close family member	63	Outstanding personal	
Major injury or illness	53	achievement	28
Marriage	50	Beginning or ending schooling	26
Being fired from work	47	Change in residence	20
Pregnancy	40	Changing to a new school	20
Gaining a new family member	39	Major changes in eating habits	15
Major changes in financial state	38	Vacation	13
Death of a close friend	37	Minor violations of the law	11
Starting a new job	36		

Stress occurs in many settings — at home, at work, at school, and in all your relationships at times. Learning to manage stress can minimize the negative impact on your life.

Stress can accompany positive as well as negative events. Even the welcome addition of a new baby brings its share of stress. Can you describe how?

STRESS MANAGEMENT

Have you heard the old saying, "When life gives you lemons, make lemonade"? Learning to manage stress — or making lemonade — will help you respond to stress with as little wear and tear on yourself as possible. Accepting annoyances, conflicts, and worries as an unavoidable part of life makes them easier to handle. You can learn techniques that will help you cope responsibly and comfortably with the pressures of daily life. This is called **stress management**.

What Does Stress Feel Like?

Not everyone feels stress in exactly the same way. Stress strikes you where you are the weakest, and your weaknesses are not the same as everyone else's. Below are some of the signs of stress. Which ones are typical of you when you are under stress?

- Irritable or depressed
- Pounding heart
- Rash
- Dry throat and mouth
- Impulsive behavior
- Emotionally unstable
- Inability to make decisions
- Urge to cry or hide
- Unable to concentrate
- Weakness or dizziness
- Afraid but not sure why
- Tense
- Trembling; nervous tics
- Easily startled
- Nervous laughter
- Speech problems

- Grinding teeth
- Nail biting
- Hair pulling
- Tapping fingers and toes
- Can't sleep or sleeps too much
- Sweating
- Headaches
- Frequent urination
- Menstrual problems
- Neck and back pain
- Appetite loss or overeating
- Use of nicotine and drugs
- Nightmares
- Neurotic behavior
- Lost sense of reality
- Accident prone

Know Yourself

The first step in managing stress is to know yourself. Are you the kind of person who seeks challenges? Some people have the need to create stress and tension in their lives. They look for ways to make their lives more fast-paced and interesting.

Other people need a more relaxed, stable life. People who have come to know how much stress is enough can say "no" when they have reached their limit. When you have learned that, you can begin to control stressful events in your life.

Gina is an example of someone who had to discover the fine line between being busy enough and overwhelmed. Her fast-paced life included involvement in dance lessons, the cross country squad, Student Congress, and Computer Club. In addition, she did volunteer work at a home for autistic children and sang in the church choir. Although she loved to be busy, she learned that she couldn't do everything. Dropping a couple activities gave her some needed time to relax and carry out her other responsibilities well.

Take Care of Yourself

Health and fitness are directly related to your ability to cope with stress. Those people who are in good health are better able to handle stress well. A body that is flabby, overweight, underexercised, or ill is less apt to meet the challenge of stressful events.

A healthy diet that contains a balance of all types of foods is the basis for good health. Plenty of sleep and exercise are also important in keeping your body ready to meet problems. Regular physical checkups can catch any major problems early. Smoking and using drugs, including alcohol, are harmful and decrease your body's ability to handle tension and stress.

Manage Your Time

Lack of time is one common cause of stress. Managing your time well can help you work in the goals that are important.

To set priorities, you must know what you value. When you have the values that are most important to you in mind, you can spend your time on those. It takes self-control to manage your time by your priorities. People may encourage you to spend time on many activities that have little to do with your values. You can be self-disciplined enough to plan your time so you can make the most of it. Remember the time management skills you read about in Chapter 9? Use these to get control of activities.

Confront the Situation

If something is causing you a problem, take action. Be confident that you can find answers and solutions. Research shows that the body's production of epinephrine, a powerful stress hormone, lowers when people begin to take charge. Remind yourself of successes you have had before, and don't be afraid to make decisions. Often there are many ways to solve a problem, and you only need one.

"In the middle of difficulty lies opportunity."

ALBERT EINSTEIN

Develop Friendships

Having good friends is a wonderful source of support when you feel tense. Stress creates feelings you need to talk about. Sharing your problems and feelings can help lighten the burden you feel in coping with them.

Relax and Have Fun

Learning to relax and have a good time makes stress less likely. Life is a serious business, but it needs to be lightened with fun and recreation. Making time to do what you enjoy helps keep you mentally and physically healthy. Hobbies and entertainment can bring you back to your responsibilities with renewed interest and vigor. Some people play sports or listen to music to relax. You may have other activities that work for you.

What happens when you tell yourself to relax? You can't! Use your imagination to help. You can imagine that you are in a beautiful and safe place, such as on a beach or a mountain path. When you imagine that you are relaxing, your body cooperates. Often you can overcome sadness and tense feelings just by using your imagination to focus on the positive.

Let Yourself Cry

Humans are the only creatures that shed tears when under stress. Some people feel that crying is a poor way to cope with tension. People who cry to relieve their anxiety, however, seem to have fewer stress-related diseases than those who do not cry. Women tend to cry about five times a month, while men cry about once a month.

Emotional and stressful tears are chemically different than tears caused by irritations such as onions. Stress-related tears contain more protein and often have high levels of minerals or hormones in them. Some scientists feel that ridding the body of these chemicals is what causes the relief crying brings.

Tears should not be used, however, to manipulate others. They are an outlet for your emotions, not a means to get pity and favors from people.

Be Realistic

No one is perfect, including you. Good and bad things happen to everyone. A realistic attitude about what happens to you and what you are able to do can help you avoid stress.

All people carry on conversations with themselves. Such "self-talk" can be unrealistic and cause stress. Some people make disasters out of everyday experiences. Think about the message Emile gives to himself while working on a math assignment when he says: "You are so stupid,

Managing stress means including time for friendship and fun. What advantages do you think result from having a good balance between work and play in your life?

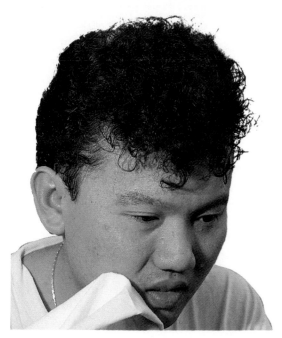
Holding back tears hurts. People who can cry let the tension out instead of forcing it to build on the inside.

Emile. You'll never learn this math. You know you'll flunk the next test. You'll probably never graduate."

Not every problem is overwhelming, and your "self-talk" should recognize that. Coming to terms with yourself and your abilities can help you understand what is realistic for you. Use "self-talk" to help yourself do the best job under the circumstances.

Plan Ahead

Stress is often the result of some unexpected event. If you can plan ahead to allow for something unexpected, you are less apt to be upset when it happens. Keeping up with your homework can help you be ready for a surprise test. Saving money will give you a financial cushion if you quit or lose your job or want to buy a special present or take a trip. By managing your resources and planning ahead, you can take changes in stride and reduce the stress they may bring.

Planning ahead can also help you control change. You may be able to avoid too many big changes at the same time. Deanne, for example, made arrangements to finish the school year at her old school even though she had moved to a new district. Her parents' divorce and the move itself seemed like a lot to handle. Postponing the change of schools helped control the stress Deanne felt.

You will react with less tension if you know the kinds of stress to expect than if you are unsure of what's ahead. You can't always figure out what's coming, but you can be prepared for the possibilities.

THE GOOD SIDE OF STRESS

What you have just read points out the negative side of stress. You might be surprised to know that there is a good side. While too much is harmful, some stress is necessary. Stress can spur you on to get things done. Some people even say they accomplish more under stress. Everyone, however, has a point where enough turns into too much. That's when good stress management becomes important.

SECTION 2 REVIEW

1. What is stress?
2. How can learning to say "no" help a person manage stress?
3. List three ways a person could relax in order to relieve stress.
4. Why is crying believed to be a good stress reliever?
5. How can "self-talk" help a person deal with stress?
6. Can people plan to prevent stress? Explain your answer.
7. When is stress helpful?

Chapter 11 Review

Chapter Summary

- Change is a fact of life. You may experience changes that are small and large.
- When people move, they have adjustments to make. Moving frequently is especially difficult.
- Planning for a move can help people handle it better.
- Moving can be an exciting challenge if people will view it that way.
- Unemployment has financial effects on families and individuals. It also has emotional effects on the jobless person and the family.
- If unemployment is a problem, families need to look for ways to cope.
- Financial problems occur for different reasons. Solutions depend on the severity of the problem.
- Homelessness can result when people have very serious financial problems.
- Stress is a common reaction to change and problems in life. It can cause physical and emotional reactions.
- People can use a number of techniques to manage the stress in their lives.

Chapter Review

1. How does attitude make a difference when people face a move?
2. What can be done to help children prepare for a move?
3. What can happen to the identity of a jobless person?
4. How can a teen best help a parent who is unemployed?
5. Is there anything a family can do to prepare for the possibility of unemployment? If so, what?
6. Why is filing for bankruptcy only a last resort when people have financial problems?
7. How does personality affect stress levels?
8. List six suggestions for stress management.
9. What does setting priorities have to do with managing stress?
10. Can people relax by telling themselves to do so? Explain your answer.
11. Are emotional tears the same as those produced by stress? Explain your answer.
12. Why do some people like a little stress?

Critical Thinking

1. Why would people who have a job adjust more easily after a move than those who do not?
2. Do you think anyone can find a job if he or she tries? Explain your answer.
3. Is any job better than no job? Explain your answer.
4. How can credit cards cause financial problems for people?
5. Describe situations that cause you the most stress. What could you do to reduce this stress?
6. Why do you think women cry more often than men do? Should they be more alike in their ability and willingness to cry? Explain your response.

Activities

1. **Making the best of a move.** Contact a moving company to obtain any literature they have about moving. Prepare a bulletin board display that shows how people can make the best of a move to a new area. (*Acquiring and evaluating information, communicating information*)

2. **The stress hormone.** Look up information on the stress hormone, epinephrine. Report your findings to the class. (*Acquiring and evaluating information, communicating information*)

3. **A stress test.** With a group of classmates, develop a stress test that people could take to find out how well they handle stress. Ask questions related to the principles of stress management. (*Teamwork, organizing information, communicating information*)

4. **Favorite stress relievers.** Many people have favorite stress relievers, such as playing the guitar, shooting baskets, and talking to a friend on the phone. With classmates, compile a list of these in a handout that can be distributed to students or placed in the school newspaper. (*Teamwork, acquiring information, organizing information*)

5. **Stress sources.** Using Holmes' list of stress sources, make a list of any that have been part of your life during the past year. Total the points. Compare totals with classmates to see how your stress level matches up with others. (*Mathematics, comparing*)

STRENGTHENING VALUES

Aim For Confidence

Confidence is having faith in yourself and your abilities. It is believing you can handle new or difficult situations. Kendra takes a confident approach to life when she:

- Stands up straight and looks people in the eye when she talks to them.
- Approaches new groups of people with the feeling that she can get to know them.
- Is willing to take on additional responsibilities, even though they are challenging, in her job.
- Believes she will do well in her schoolwork and takes action to make that happen.
- Approaches the changes that occur in her life with a positive attitude.

In what physical ways does confidence show in people? Do you think people sometimes appear more confident than they are? Are there any advantages in that? When do you lack confidence? When do you have it? What might you do to increase your level of confidence?

Divorce and Remarriage

SECTION 1

HOW MARRIAGES END

SECTION 2

BUILDING A NEW LIFE

IMAGINE THAT ...

you are married and have been for several years. The "honeymoon" has been over for quite a long time. Your children are still young, and you feel the responsibilities of caring for them. What is bothering you is that your relationship with your spouse is not what it used to be. You think about the problems you're having. On some days they seem serious, but are they serious enough? In your mind's eye that word looms boldly before you — divorce. Can that be the answer?

SECTION 1

HOW MARRIAGES END

THINK AHEAD

About These Terms

divorce	*adversarial*
invalidation	*divorce*
annulment	*grounds*
no-fault	*custody*
divorce	*alimony*

About These Objectives
After studying this section, you should be able to:

• Describe why marriages end and the stages that lead to divorce.
• Explain the methods for ending a marriage.
• Describe the decisions that must be made when a divorce occurs.

ivorce is a legal action that ends a marriage. It is a fact of family life today, producing major changes in the lives of family members. As many who have experienced a breakup will say, divorce can cause a great deal of pain, stress, and confusion. Few divorces can be called easy.

♦ ♦ ♦

233

WHY MARRIAGES END

The marriages that end seldom do so abruptly or unexpectedly. Most fall apart over a period of about two years. Couples who have problems in marriage often seek counseling for help in solving their problems. As you will read in Chapter 32, many efforts can be made to have, and rebuild, a strong marriage. When problems occur, many couples are able to get back on track, but some are not.

When marriages fail, the reasons are not all the same. Some couples grow apart and lose the shared interests that drew them together in the first place. The partners may not communicate well enough to maintain or rebuild the relationship. Other couples have specific problems that pull the marriage apart. Financial, sexual, and role problems are common causes of conflict and fights. Many women who file for divorce say problems come from mental or physical cruelty, a husband's neglect of home and children, financial problems, and drinking problems. Men often identify such problem areas as mental cruelty, neglect of home and children, and sexual problems.

Predictors

Marriages between all kinds of people end in divorce. Experts in divorce expect that about two-thirds of the new marriages in a year will end in some way other than the death of a spouse. Is there any way to tell which marriages will end? A few factors seem to play a role.

Age is one indicator. The younger a couple is when they marry, the more apt they are to divorce. The likelihood of divorce increases if the bride is pregnant. Teens and young adults often lack the maturity and experience to handle the responsibilities of marriage and parenthood. They may still be struggling to establish their own identities. Often they choose partners who will not be right for them when they are a little older.

Low income is also linked to divorce. Unemployment and financial problems relate strongly to the marital troubles that lead to divorce. One exception is that women who have high incomes are more apt to divorce than women with low or no incomes. A woman with no means of support may be more likely to stay in a difficult marriage.

Several other predictors have been identified. Those who have experienced the divorce of their parents are more apt to end their own marriages. Those who knew or dated their spouse for a long time are less likely to divorce. People who participate in religious activities are less likely to divorce than those who don't. Also, the greater the number of children in a family, the less likely the couple will divorce. Although you can certainly find exceptions to all of these, studies show that these conditions affect the likelihood of a divorce.

Marriages end for many different reasons. The one thing they have in common, however, is that the ending is seldom easy.

Pulling Apart in Stages

Whatever the specific problem areas before a divorce, the relationship generally unravels through three stages:

- *Isolation.* The couple becomes isolated, or separated, from each other. The partners withdraw and no longer share intimacy or closeness. They may act like strangers, holding polite conversations about neutral subjects.
- *Invalidation.* With **invalidation** (in-val-uh-DAY-shun), the partners respond negatively to each other. Instead of affirming, couples accuse and belittle. Negative feelings build up and feed on each other. Partners make each other feel small and worthless. For example, one partner might say to the other, "What kind of a parent are you? Can't you even keep that child in clean clothes?" Here, one partner invalidates the other's worth as a parent.
- *Betrayal.* Betrayal is the feeling that trust has been broken. The support each spouse expected from the other is no longer there.

The critical act in the breakdown of the marriage is the decision to separate and seek a divorce rather than the divorce itself. Emotions are the rawest and most painful at the time of separation. How families handle a divorce at this point has a strong effect on all family members, especially the children.

ENDING A MARRIAGE

When a marriage breaks down, there are three ways to end it legally — annulment, legal separation, and divorce. Sometimes a partner simply leaves, or deserts, the spouse. While desertion may, in fact, end the marriage relationship, it does not end the legal marriage.

Building up to a divorce can be very difficult for everyone in the family. Children are very sensitive to what is going on between parents.

Annulment

An **annulment** (uh-NULL-ment) decree states that a legal marriage never took place because of some prior condition at the time of the "marriage." In other words, the marriage did not legally exist.

Laws concerning annulment vary among the states. Some common causes of annulment include concealed or misrepresented pregnancy, insanity, bigamy (being married to more than one person), and forced marriage. An annulment is granted when it can be shown that fraud was involved. If one partner tried to cheat the other, the court may rule the marriage annulled.

Annulments are sometimes sought when a couple's religious beliefs ban divorce. If the partners divorce, they may be separated from their church. If the marriage can be annulled, however, they can continue in their faith.

Legal Separation

Some couples obtain a legal separation that allows them to live in separate homes but not to remarry. The partners make a legal agreement to live apart. They formally divide their property and provide for their children.

Legal separation can be a middle step between marriage and divorce. For some people, however, separation is permanent, especially for those whose religious beliefs forbid divorce and whose marriages cannot be annulled.

Divorce

By far the most common result of the breakdown of a marriage is divorce. Divorce rates soared during the 1970s, a period when divorce laws across the country changed dramatically. Divorces hit a peak in 1981 and have declined slightly since that time.

Divorce is regulated by state law, which may vary considerably from state to state. Some states no longer use the term divorce, instead calling the legal action the "dissolution of marriage."

There are two basic ways to file for divorce. One type of divorce, known as **no-fault divorce**, allows partners to simply claim that the marriage relationship has broken down, with neither one to blame. A separation may be all the proof needed of such a breakdown.

The other type of divorce is called an **adversarial divorce** (add-ver-SAIR-ee-uhl). For this type the spouses become legal opponents. One partner must accuse the other of some marital "crime." These crimes, such as mental or physical cruelty, desertion, adultery, and insanity, are called **grounds** for divorce. The grounds for divorce are set by state law. In this type of divorce, one partner is considered guilty, while the other is innocent.

Most couples file for no-fault divorces. No-fault is a much simpler legal procedure. The simpler procedure, however, does not solve the many problems couples face when they untangle their lives. It simply keeps from adding more burdens at a time when people are emotionally upset.

Four main decisions must be made during the time leading up to the divorce. The first is the type of divorce sought, whether no-fault or adversarial. The second decision is how the couple's property will be divided. The third issue is who will be legally responsible for any children. The final issue is what financial arrangements will be made. These decisions are made within the framework of state law.

Going separate ways is complicated by all the decisions that must be made. When two people can sit down and talk calmly about what should be done, divorce is more manageable.

Property Settlement

Most couples have some property to divide at the time of the divorce. Property can include a home, furnishings, cars, savings accounts, and investments.

Most no-fault divorce laws allow couples to split their property. A spouse who has been economically dependent in the marriage may have little power in bargaining for property.

If the spouses cannot agree to a settlement that seems fair to both, the judge can divide their property. Most judges take into account the contributions of each partner to the marriage. Women may be entitled to a portion of their husband's Social Security or pension, depending on the length of the marriage and other circumstances.

Child Custody

If a couple has children, the divorce decree will state who has responsibility for them. **Custody** is a legal decision about who has the right to make decisions that affect children and who has the physical responsibility of caring for them.

SINGLE-PARENT CUSTODY In single-parent custody, one parent has the legal right and the responsibility to care for the children and to make decisions concerning their lives. The other parent usually has the right to have visits with the children. Although more fathers are seeking and gaining custody of their children today, in most single-custody cases, the mother is the parent in charge.

Split custody means that each parent has single-parent custody of one or more of the children. Split custody may increase problems for children who want to be together. Older siblings often "parent" younger ones. Split custody may make it harder for siblings to help and comfort each other.

JOINT CUSTODY In joint legal custody, both parents share equally in making decisions about their children. Legally, the parents must work together for the good of the children. Joint custody can be arranged in several ways.

In some joint custody situations, children basically live with one parent. The child usually visits the other parent frequently. For example, Deon lives with his father, but often stays with his mother. Both of his parents are involved in decision making about his future.

In some families with joint custody, children split their time between the homes of their parents. In some cases, they spend one week in one home and the next week with the other parent.

Another arrangement is alternating custody. Children live with one parent for a long time, perhaps a year, then switch to the other parent. Each parent has decision-making power during the time that the children are there.

Joint custody is a fairly new legal arrangement. It grew out of research showing that children did the best after divorce when both parents stayed involved in their lives. Most states allow joint custody. In some states, it is the preferred arrangement.

Obviously, for joint custody to be successful, the divorcing parents have to be able to work together for the good of the children. Not all parents are able to do this, so joint custody is not a good choice for everyone.

THIRD-PARTY CUSTODY Another type of custody arrangement is third-party custody. This is when neither parent is able or willing to have custody of the children. The divorce judge appoints someone else as the children's legal guardian. The children may be put in the custody of a relative or placed in a foster home.

Assessing Outcomes

Learning to assess outcomes is a way to examine the results of your decisions. When you assess an outcome, you examine the results and consequences of a situation or event. If you're pleased with the outcome, you know your decision was positive.

LU *"A few years ago my parents divorced. I lived with my father for awhile, but we had a hard time getting along. I know I was bitter after the divorce, and I showed it. I started hanging around with the wrong people and doing things I had never done before. School didn't mean much to me anymore, so I dropped out. My mother had remarried and moved to another state. I guess I could have gone to live with her, but I didn't feel like I belonged in her new family. I left home a couple times. Then my grandmother asked me to live with her."*

MRS. CHANG *"I never thought I'd have to go back to raising a child again, but Lu needed something that I could give. I didn't want to replace his parents, but I thought maybe I could help him through a tough time. Lu and I had always gotten along well, so I had some influence with him. I offered him a place to stay, and he decided to take me up on it. He had to follow my rules, though, and one was getting back in school. That was two years ago. Now Lu is back with his father, and they're doing well. He even goes to see his mother when he can."*

CAN YOU ASSESS OUTCOMES?

- Describe the decisions that Lu made following his parents' divorce.
- Which decisions had negative outcomes? Which had a positive outcome? Explain your answer.
- How could someone who knows Lu be helped by assessing the outcomes of Lu's decisions?
- When you make decisions, do you reflect on what happened? Why is it a good idea to do so?

Financial Matters

The final legal agreement included in divorce concerns financial matters. These arrangements are for child support and spouse support.

CHILD SUPPORT How child support is structured depends on the custody arrangement. In single-parent custody, the non-custodial parent usually must pay a certain amount each month to help support the children. In joint custody, financial arrangements vary, depending on living situations and other factors.

Because most children live with their mothers, child support payments are usually made by fathers. Over three-fourths of divorced fathers have court orders to pay child support. Only about one-fourth of these fathers always pay on time and in full. Even full child support is usually less than half the cost of raising a child.

Not all fathers take their responsibility to pay child support seriously. Fathers who were involved in raising their children before the divorce are more likely to pay than fathers who had little to do with their children. Those who have money are more apt to pay than those who have few resources.

Fathers who live far away from their children, who have little influence over how mothers spend child support money, and who do not spend time with their children are less apt to pay. In addition, the longer since the divorce, the less apt a father is to provide child support.

The problem of unpaid child support is not an easy one to solve. The government has established several programs to locate those who aren't paying and force them to make payments. The divorce judge can jail a parent for not making child support payments. When offenders are in jail, however, they are not earning wages, so they do not make their payments then either. Many mothers do not feel it is worth the effort to jail a father for lack of child support.

SPOUSE SUPPORT Financial support of an ex-spouse is called **alimony** (al-uh-MOH-nee) or maintenance payments. The spouse with the most financial resources helps support the other. Very little long-term spouse support is awarded. Sometimes women receive spouse support briefly until they find a job or until they finish job training.

Coming To Agreement

The final authority in making the divorce decisions rests with the divorce judge. If the couple can agree, the judge usually just legalizes their agreement. If the partners cannot agree, the judge has the power to make the decisions for them.

Most children live with their mothers after a divorce. Many of the mothers do not receive regular child support payments from their ex-husbands.

Getting a couple to agree on the major divorce decisions is not always easy. Couples without children and with little property usually find these decisions easier to make. When a couple has children and their financial affairs are more complex, they may need help in making choices.

Often couples negotiate, or bargain, through their lawyers. In this case, the spouse who has the better lawyer may end up with the better agreement.

About half the states have established a procedure called *divorce mediation*, in which an impartial third person helps couples work out a solution. In some states a couple must see a mediator before going to court. In other states, mediation is an option.

Not all couples can benefit from mediation, since it depends on a spirit of cooperation. Couples who are able to work successfully with a mediator usually are happier with the outcome than couples who rely on the judge to make decisions for them.

Some couples cannot settle their differences alone. They may need a third party, a divorce mediator, to help them find solutions.

MIXED ATTITUDES

Attitudes toward divorce have changed over the years. When divorce was less common, people often felt shame and shock when it occurred. Now that divorce happens so frequently, such feelings are less likely. Still, some believe that divorce is taken too lightly these days, that people should try harder to work out their problems. On the other hand, when people live in very troublesome, even dangerous, situations, divorce can be a welcome solution. In either case, divorce is not easy, but people can learn to manage and adjust if they make an effort.

SECTION 1 REVIEW

1. List four possible predictors of divorce.
2. Describe the three stages that often lead up to divorce.
3. Briefly describe the three methods for ending a marriage.
4. Describe three types of child custody.
5. How does society deal with people who do not pay child support?
6. What is divorce mediation?
7. How have attitudes toward divorce changed over the years?

SECTION 2

BUILDING A NEW LIFE

THINK AHEAD

About These Terms
adjustment
stability

About These Objectives
After studying this section, you should be able to:
+ Explain how people adjust to divorce.
+ Summarize the effects of divorce on couples and on their children.
+ Compare and contrast blended families with nuclear families.

ven if you have not experienced divorce in your family, you probably know people who have. Attitude makes a big difference in how divorce is handled. Sometimes people have to accept what happens and get on with life. They go through a period of **adjustment**, working to change routines and feelings until everything feels normal again.

◆ ◆ ◆

ADJUSTING TO DIVORCE

Divorce is not easy for any of the people involved in it. The divorcing couple, their children, parents, and friends can all be affected when a family splits up.

The Divorced Couple

Both people have to put their lives back together again following a divorce. Each is usually a victim of loneliness, anger, depression, guilt, and feelings of failure.

People with more resources usually adjust to their new lives more easily than those with few resources. These include financial as well as emotional and social resources. Even with resources and social support from others, it takes from two to four years to get over the breakdown of a marriage. Those who tend to withdraw from others, who are not confident of their abilities, and who get panicked or depressed easily have a harder time adjusting.

Parents who have to deal with the everyday realities of caring for children may have a harder time. Their resources may be stretched farther. In addition, they may have to put aside their grief and sorrow at the end of the marriage to deal with their children's emotions.

As time passes, people learn to deal with their feelings and make new lives for themselves. Learning to be single again, to handle problems on their own, and to make new friends and build new relationships means that some of the wounds of divorce are starting to heal.

Children

Conflicting information describes the effects of divorce on children. Without a doubt divorce creates major changes for children. If your parents have divorced, you know how divorce can disrupt lives.

The period just before, during, and after the separation is when children have the hardest time adjusting. Some children feel rage and frustration. Others grieve for the loss of their intact family. Some children feel guilty, rejected, helpless, and lonely. In general, it takes up to a year for children to cope with their feelings and adjust to a new way of living. Emotional problems tend to lessen with time.

Change and Stability

Children who have few changes in their lives, or **stability**, handle divorce more easily than those who have major changes. With stability comes the comfortable, secure feeling that some things will stay the same. The stability of living in the same home, going to the same school, and keeping the same friends helps counteract other changes from the divorce.

Children need to know that the divorce will not interfere with their ties with either parent. Children who maintain loving relationships with both parents adjust best to divorce. A loyalty struggle is perhaps the most stressful part of divorce for children. When children know it's alright to love both parents, they are less often caught in the middle of the parents' conflict.

Separated by War

In Vietnam today, there are thousands of young Amerasians. These children, born during the Vietnam War, have Vietnamese mothers and American fathers. When American forces left Vietnam in 1975, these Vietnamese families were left behind.

Life has not been easy for these young people, who were not easily accepted by the Vietnamese people. Often the children were not allowed in school. Some were abandoned by their mothers. Others were harrassed by police and military. Many have been homeless.

These children have grown up thinking of themselves as Americans. They struggle to learn English and dream of coming to the United States.

Many young Amerasians hope to find their fathers when they reach America. Only a few of them do. Most simply have too little information about their American fathers. There is hope, however. Often, returning soldiers registered their Vietnamese families with the Red Cross. The Veteran's Administration also helps Amerasians find their fathers.

Some fathers, through letters, have searched Vietnam for years trying to find their sons and daughters. Once they found the children, however, it often took years of paperwork to get them out.

In 1987, the United States Congress passed the Amerasian Homecoming Act, which created a special category for Amerasian immigrants and their Vietnamese families. This made it easier for young Amerasians to come to the United States. After many years and with a certain amount of luck, many of these families have come together.

Parents who can overcome their own bitterness to establish a businesslike relationship for dealing with the children can help their children cope. They can show their children the benefits of having two homes with a loving parent in each.

How Children View Divorce

Children often imagine that they or their behavior created the split between the parents. For example, ten-year-old Wesley was sure his poor behavior was the cause of his parents' divorce. Before the divorce, he often came home from school with notes about his rowdy behavior. Because he had overheard his parents argue about how to deal with him, he believed that he caused the divorce. His guilt made the divorce especially hard for him to handle. When parents make it clear that the children did not cause the divorce, the children tend to cope better.

Children often see and react to the divorce in the same way as their parents. If the parents see the divorce as the best way for all family members to have a better life, children are apt to agree. If parents are bitter toward each other and continue to be angry, children often feel caught in the middle. The negative feelings interfere with both the parents' and the children's adjustment to their new lives.

Effects of Divorce

Research studies of children of divorced parents have generally found that children can handle divorce. When both parents are loving and attentive, the effects are minimal. Some studies show no differences in school achievement, intelligence, or self-esteem between children from divorced and nuclear families.

Children from divorced homes often are better adjusted than children from two-parent homes where conflict is severe. Recent studies have found that children who successfully cope with divorce seem able to function on two levels. The children experience unhappiness and yet are able to go on with daily life. Children who are most poorly adjusted after divorce usually come from families with severe financial problems.

Sometimes children who have lived through divorce experience long-term consequences. Often they are hesitant about deciding whether to marry. They may be more careful in choosing a marriage partner. On the other hand, if their marriages falter, they are more apt to divorce.

REMARRIAGE

Most divorced people eventually remarry. They want companionship and the emotional intimacy of the marriage relationship. Divorced men remarry sooner and in greater numbers than women.

Coping With Change

After a divorce, parents who have custody of children may need to ask the children to take on more responsibility around the home. Without a partner to share the tasks, the parent needs help. He or she cannot do everything that two people used to do.

Caring family members learn what responsibilities they can assume in order to divide duties more fairly—even when it means giving up some of their own school and social activities. Teens discover they can prepare entire meals; younger children learn to do laundry.

Contributing to the family's well-being in this way not only eases the burden on custodial parents, but also builds self-esteem and competence in teens and children. A united effort strengthens the family while ensuring that each member has some time for family, work, and personal activities.

About one-fourth of divorced people remarry within one year, with one-half marrying within three years. The younger a person is at divorce, the greater the chance of remarriage.

Most experts suggest that people not marry for at least four years after a divorce. This allows time to heal the hurt resulting from the divorce. People who remarry quickly to try to solve their problems rarely are successful.

In general, remarriages are happy marriages. The couple is older when the marriage occurs, which increases the chance for stability in the marriage. Partners are more likely to understand what they want and need in a spouse. The couple usually has different expectations and more tolerance in the second marriage. They are often more tolerant of issues like housework and money, which may have caused major conflicts in the first marriage.

It takes time and effort for members of a blended family to adjust to one another.

BLENDED FAMILIES

Over half of all remarriages create blended families. Estimates say that a majority of children born in the 1980s will live in a blended family at some point in their lives.

How Blended Families Differ

Blended families differ in many ways from nuclear families. In a blended family, all members have lost an important relationship in the past. The spouses have lost former marriage partners, and the children no longer have both birth parents in the home.

Important people in the lives of blended family members live elsewhere. The children have a parent somewhere else. Some step-parents have children of their own who live elsewhere. These people can either support or interfere with the life of the new family.

In nuclear families, the couple relationship is the longest, oldest one. In blended families, the parent-child relationship is the longer term one. For a while, the new

n the past, people often had a negative opinion of blended families, which were known as stepfamilies. For example, the story "Cinderella" is a classic stepfamily tale. Not only was Dad eliminated from Cinderella's new home, but her new mom and sisters were labeled "wicked."

Negative feelings about "stepfamilies" still exist today, but these can be overcome. One way is to use positive talk. Instead of saying "broken home," talk about having two homes. Instead of "visiting" the other parent like a guest, simply "go there." "Dad's wife" and "new sister" can replace "stepmother" and "stepsister." Try letting your language about a divorce situation set a positive tone!

spouse may feel excluded. Sometimes the children feel left out of the love and affection between the remarried couple. Jealousy and competing for attention are normal emotions and behaviors in a blended family.

Roles in blended families are not well defined. What is a stepparent supposed to be and do? How are stepchildren supposed to act? Trying to establish roles that fit the situation and people involved is not easy.

The Problems

Conflict takes place in all kinds of families. Certain issues, however, occur with frequency in blended families.

- *Favoritism.* In a blended family, favoritism usually occurs between the birth parent and his or her children. Sometimes, however, parents are harder on their own children than on their stepchildren. Understanding how difficult it is to achieve "fairness" can help everyone get along.
- *Discipline.* The rules that children were used to may be altered in the new family, requiring adjustment. Decisions have to be made about who disciplines which children.
- *Resources.* Child support payments may come into and go out of blended families. Decisions about which family members need scarce resources can be tricky in order to avoid resentment.
- *Values.* Rarely do all members of a blended family share the same values. They must learn to tolerate and understand each other's viewpoints.

Getting Along in a Blended Family

People who live happily in blended families have learned what it takes to get along. Here are some of their tips:

- Accept the new situation and do your part in making it work. Resistance only makes everyone unhappy.
- Respect relationships in the family. Some will be closer than others.
- Be flexible. You need to try new ways of managing space and time.
- Talk to each other, using I-messages. That's the best route to understanding.
- Spend time alone with stepparents and stepsiblings in order to get to know them better. Allow relationships to grow into something positive. Whether that turns out to be friendship or love doesn't really matter.
- Realize that family life is not always happy. Difficult moments are typical and occur in any family.
- Keep a sense of humor. Many situations have a humorous side if you just look for it.

Successful Blending

Just like nuclear families, blended families have to work at maintaining relationships. First, the couple must be committed to each other and the marriage. Children should not stand in the way. Because it sometimes takes three to five years to adjust to life in a blended family, patience is a key factor. Love takes time to grow. Successful blending can come to those who are patient and make the effort.

SECTION 2 REVIEW

1. How long does it commonly take people to recover from a divorce?
2. What is meant by the term "stability"? How is it helpful to children during divorce?
3. If parents are bitter and angry during a divorce, how will children feel?
4. What long-term consequences might children of divorce experience?
5. Why are remarriages generally happy?
6. Briefly describe two problems a blended family can have.
7. Should blended families expect to adjust in a few months? Explain.

Chapter 12 Review

Chapter Summary

- Marriages end for many different reasons.
- Certain factors have been identified that make divorce more likely.
- When a marriage is in trouble, the relationship usually falls apart in stages.
- There are three legal ways to end a marriage. The method chosen depends on the circumstances and wishes of the couple.
- A divorce, or dissolution of marriage, is the most common way of ending a marriage. The process is determined and regulated by state law.
- In a divorce, decisions must be made regarding the type of divorce, division of property, child custody, and financial matters.
- Several options are possible for taking care of children. The family and the court must decide what is best for all.
- Child support is more often assigned to fathers since mothers are more likely to have custody of any children.
- Partners may reach agreement between themselves on issues involved in a divorce, or they may receive outside help through the processes of negotiation and/or mediation.
- During a court appearance, final arrangements are made, and the marriage contract is terminated when the divorce is granted.
- At the end of a marriage, people must adjust emotionally and in practical ways.
- People who have ended a marriage tend to marry again. More than half of these remarriages create blended families.
- To adjust to life in a blended family, the members must find ways to mesh parts of different families into a new family group.

Chapter Review

1. Explain how age at the time of marriage can affect the chance for divorce.
2. List three stages that commonly lead a couple to divorce.
3. What is an annulment?
4. What is the difference between a no-fault divorce and an adversarial one?
5. Explain the difference between single-parent custody and joint custody.
6. Explain the problems that surround the child support issue.
7. What is alimony?
8. What is divorce mediation?
9. What can help a divorced person recover?
10. What can help children recover from a divorce?
11. How long should a person wait before marrying again after a divorce? Why is this time period recommended?
12. Explain the role of time in helping a blending family adjust.
13. List three suggestions for getting along in a blended family.

Critical Thinking

1. Do you think a couple should stay together for the sake of the children? Explain your answer.

2. What are the advantages and disadvantages of a joint custody arrangement for parents and children of divorce?
3. What do you think happens to children when fathers do not pay the child support that they are supposed to?
4. Do you think divorce was more difficult for couples and children when it was viewed as shameful and shocking? Do you think such attitudes prevented some divorces from happening? Explain your answers.
5. Are there any situations in which divorce is extremely necessary? If so, what are they?
6. Do you think divorce is taken too casually today? Why or why not?
7. Describe some advantages of living in a blended family.

Activities

1. **Divorce debate.** Debate this issue: Divorce should not be allowed. (*Reasoning, debating*)
2. **Justifying divorce.** With your class, make a list of reasons that justify divorce. Are you able to agree on the list? Why or why not? (*Teamwork, decision making, evaluating*)
3. **Custody battle.** Imagine that you are a ten–year–old child whose parents are in a custody battle over you. Write a letter to your parents explaining how you feel. (*Visualizing, writing*)
4. **Blended family.** Complete this sentence, "Living in a blended family is (would be) . . . ." Join a group of fellow students and discuss your responses. (*Visualizing, communicating information*)

STRENGTHENING VALUES

Aim For Optimism

Optimism is having a hopeful outlook on the future and believing things will work out well. Jameel practices optimism by:

- Looking at his mother's remarriage as a chance to build a larger family support system than he has ever had before.
- Telling a friend that he and his new stepbrother are having some problems, but he knows they can work them out.
- Helping a friend whose parents are getting a divorce see that everything can be okay again.
- Managing to make his friends laugh when they feel worried or discouraged.
- Pointing out the positive side of an issue in conversations with others.
- Believing in himself.

In what ways will Jameel's optimism be helpful to him and to his family? Which type of person do you think is more enjoyable to be around, an optimist or a pessimist? Why? Do you think a person can ever be too optimistic? Explain your answer. In what ways have you recently shown optimism?

Handling Crises

SECTION 1

UNDERSTANDING CRISIS

SECTION 2

THE CRISES PEOPLE FACE

IMAGINE THAT ...

you're listening to the radio as you get ready for school, and you hear about a hurricane that hit during the night in another part of the country. Some close relatives live in that area, and your heart jumps as you hear the announcer talk about the devastation. Many homes and buildings have been severely damaged, some completely destroyed. Lives have been lost, but it is too soon to know exactly how many. You feel an urgent need to know if your relatives have been affected. You hurry to talk to someone else in your family about what happened. Nothing else will seem important to you until you find out more — until you know what you have to face, if anything.

UNDERSTANDING CRISIS

THINK AHEAD

About These Terms

crisis   shelters

adaptation   intervention

About These Objectives

After studying this section, you should be able to:

* Describe what a crisis is and how a crisis situation can be identified.
* List and describe the stages in reacting to a crisis.
* List resources useful in a crisis.
* Explain what intervention is.

ew people escape serious problems sometime in life. Difficulties can strike directly or close enough to be deeply felt. Often pain, both mental and physical, accompany these situations, which are unwelcome but sometimes unavoidable. Coping isn't always easy, yet it is possible.

◆ ◆ ◆

RECOGNIZING CRISES

Difficulties in a person's life can result in a **crisis** (CRY-suss). When a situation is so unstable or critical that the outcome will make a decisive difference for better or worse, a crisis state has been reached.

Crises come in many ways. Some, such as the devastation from a hurricane, hit quickly. Others, such as the effects of alcoholism, may build slowly. Some crises result from a series of events. In one family, for example, a child was diagnosed with a life-threatening illness. This came after the family had recently lost their income and medical insurance through a job layoff. The stress and struggles that resulted from both events caused a crisis for the family.

When Is It Crisis?

Crises can best be identified by their overwhelming nature. They are much more demanding than everyday problems. Three elements help determine whether a situation is overwhelming enough to be a crisis:

- *Hardship.* Certain events create hardships. A serious house fire, for, example, causes loss of possessions as well as a place to live. Lives are seriously disrupted in such situations.
- *Resources.* Handling any problem effectively requires resources. If you have what you need, you may avoid crisis.
- *Attitude.* With the right attitude, some problems can be solved before they become overwhelming. On the other hand, with a negative approach, many situations can appear to be a crisis. For example, a parent whose grown son moves away from home can feel good about moving into a new stage of life or be devasted by a feeling of loss. Attitude makes the difference.

Reuben Hill and Crisis

Reuben Hill, a sociologist at the University of Minnesota, was one of the first researchers to study crisis and build theories to explain it. He developed a formula, ABC=X to explain what makes a family crisis. A is the event that occurs. B represents the resources the family has to meet crisis. C is how the family defines the event. X is the resulting crisis. A, B, and C interact to create X.

According to Hill, some people are crisis prone; they have many crises in their lives. Families who have many crises often have inadequate resources to solve their problems (B). They also often lack self-confidence and are likely to suffer from anxiety and fear. They are, therefore, more likely to define events as crises (C).

Dr. Hill was also the first person to classify crises. He saw three general kinds of events that create crises:

- *Loss of family members.* Such crises could be the death of a child, spouse, or parent; separation due to war; or hospitalization of a family member.
- *Addition of an unprepared-for family member.* This type of crisis could include an unwanted pregnancy or the addition of stepparents, stepsiblings, or aged grandparents to a family.
- *Loss of family unity.* Examples are nonsupport of the family, abuse, addictions, delinquency, and events that bring disgrace.

Suicide, divorce, desertion, runaways, and mental illness can be crises that involve combinations of these three factors.

REACTING TO CRISIS

Reactions to crisis follow a typical pattern. People go through a process that includes four stages. Time spent in each stage may vary, but the process is generally the same.

Stage 1: Impact

In this first stage, impact, people experience the shock of the crisis. Whatever it is that has happened hits them hard. They may feel numb or blank. Fear and helplessness are not uncommon emotions in the impact stage. For some period of time, usually a matter of hours or days, people are so overwhelmed that they can't, or don't, really function.

The first reaction a person normally has when diagnosed with a serious illness is an example of this stage. For Bud, a cancer diagnosis stunned him. He felt as though he had no control over anything.

In the first stage of crisis, a person may have trouble functioning. The impact of the crisis is so strong that time is needed to adjust.

How do you cope with problems? Some people pull into their shells as turtles do; some people run away. You can "get away from it all," however, without leaving.

Try experiencing calm by getting into nature. No, you don't need a forest or ocean to do it, either!

- Lie on your back and observe the trees and birds.

- Lie on your stomach and study the insects.

- Take a walk and use as many of your senses as possible to explore flowers, plants, rocks, animals, or an evening sky.

You can take that scene's spirit of wonder and calm with you afterwards.

Stage 2: Withdrawal and Confusion

In this stage, people pull back from the crisis situation. They may deny that a crisis even exists. They may also withdraw their feelings and not care about things around them. Some people in Stage 2 don't do much of anything, because nothing matters to them. Others hurry around but accomplish little. They get confused and have trouble focusing on what they are doing.

The latter describes how Danielle felt after her boyfriend was killed in a car accident. She refused to believe what had happened. In fact, she kept insisting that her boyfriend would be home soon. Everything seemed unreal and unimportant to her.

Stage 3: Focus

This stage involves focusing on the reality of the situation. People admit that a crisis has occurred and that action needs to be taken to deal with it. Some sense of control is regained over emotions and over the problem at hand. Seeing more clearly allows for exploring options and for making plans to take charge of the crisis.

A good example is Mrs. Jordan's behavior after she faced the fact that her son was an alcoholic. Once numbness and confusion left her, she attacked the problem head on by exploring community resources for treatment. Mrs. Jordan put together a list of potential treatment programs for her son. She also checked with her insurance company to see if it would help pay for treatment and, if so, how much.

Stage 4: Adaptation

The final stage in responding to a crisis is actually dealing with it. The plans made in Stage 3 are put into action. Through **adaptation** (ADD-ap-TAY-shun), people make changes that are practical and appropriate. In this manner, the crisis can be resolved, and life can go on in a normal, though changed, way.

Adaptation was important for Greg's family after a diving accident left him paralyzed. He and his family went through all the stages of crisis reaction. As part of the last stage, his family built a ramp into the house so that Greg could get in and out easily in his wheelchair. They turned the family room, which was downstairs, into a bedroom to replace Greg's upstairs room. Greg, himself, made arrangements for transportation to and from school. These changes helped Greg and his whole family get on with their lives.

HELP IN A CRISIS

If there is any time that people need people, it is during a crisis. Few crises can be handled alone. People in crisis need to recognize that they need support and go after it.

The family unit is a major source of help as people go through any crisis. Friends are another possibility for emotional support and for some kinds of direct assistance. Never be afraid to admit that you need assistance. Everyone does when crisis hits.

In times of trouble, help is only a phone call away. Even when you don't know someone to call, a hotline may give you the support you need.

Many people avoid telling coworkers or employers when they are experiencing a personal crisis. Some fear that coworkers will avoid them or that their employer will doubt their ability to concentrate on work. Others fear the opposite reaction: that people will pity them or try to protect them from the normal duties of the job, just when they need to show competence and control.

These people may be overlooking a valuable resource. Many businesses today are taking a more active role in helping employees deal with personal problems. They feel this approach benefits the company and the worker alike, since people are more productive when they are not distracted by troubles.

Some companies have generous family leave policies. Workers may take an unpaid leave of absence to deal with a family crisis without worrying about being fired or demoted. Free from that concern, they can concentrate better on resolving the situation at home.

In cases of substance abuse, companies may help pay treatment costs as part of an insurance or benefits package. In certain high-stress jobs, counselors are kept on staff to help employees deal with the pressure.

Some businesses offer other benefits which, while not expressly designed to ease crises, can help employees avoid them. They may offer health club membership at reduced rates. Their insurance plan may offer lower premiums to nonsmokers or nondrinkers. Some even sponsor company sports teams—a good way to relieve stress and to strengthen relationships with coworkers.

Help comes in many forms:

- *School.* A trusted teacher, school counselor, or school psychologist can help students cope with personal and family crises.
- *Religious Organizations.* Religious officials and group members can provide counseling, information, and assistance.
- *Health-Care Professionals.* Doctors, nurses, psychologists, psychiatrists, and social workers all have specific skills to offer people in a crisis. Most areas have clinics or health centers that treat physical, mental, and emotional conditions.
- *Hotlines.* Hotlines are telephone numbers you can call for advice and support. Some specialize in one type of crisis, such as suicide, partner abuse, or elder abuse. Others deal with many different kinds of crises. Hotlines usually operate twenty-four hours a day. They are staffed by trained volunteers.
- *Shelters.* **Shelters** offer a safe place to go if you experience physical violence or sexual abuse. These are places where victims of violence can stay to get away from their abusers and consider their options. A shelter can be located by calling a hospital emergency room, the police station, or an abuse hotline in your area.
- *Support Groups.* These groups are usually made up of people who have experienced, or are going through, a similar crisis in their lives. There are groups for alcoholics, child abusers, victims of specific diseases, and victims of sexual abuse. The principle behind these groups is to give and get support.

◆ *Agencies and Organizations.* Most communities have social service agencies and organizations that help people. Some are run by city, county, or state governments. Others are operated privately. The Yellow Pages of the telephone directory contains listings of such groups. Look under Social Service Organizations.

INTERVENTION

Intervention means taking direct action to cause change when someone else is in a crisis state. Why is intervention needed? Sometimes a crisis is beyond the ability of the person in crisis to handle or control. For example, a child could be in danger or a person might not be thinking clearly. Only the caring action of another person can bring about a solution.

Intervening is not always easy. It requires courage and resourcefulness. You have to be the kind of person who cares enough to try. You have to be bold enough to risk interference when the need is great. Friends and family members can begin the process of intervention. Additional steps may then be taken by the people and organizations named above. Intervention forces change that might not otherwise occur. As you will see in the next section, intervention can be critical.

SECTION 1 REVIEW

1. What is a crisis?
2. Describe three elements that help identify a crisis.
3. Describe the four stages of reaction to a crisis.
4. Describe seven resources that can be helpful in a crisis.
5. What is intervention?

THINK AHEAD

About These Terms

addiction	*co-dependency*
drugs	*violence*
alcoholism	*incest*

About These Objectives
After studying this section, you should be able to:
◆ Predict the likely effects of certain kinds of health problems.
◆ Recommend actions to take in cases of addiction, violence, and threats of suicide.

he situations that cause crisis are not easy to think about or talk about. Since they do happen to people, however, it makes good sense to be prepared. By reading, thinking, and talking about the crises that challenge people, you build your understanding. You will be better able to handle a crisis if it occurs.

◆ ◆ ◆

HEALTH PROBLEMS

Health problems come in many forms. They can be physical or mental. They can be short-term or long-range. They can come on suddenly or slowly. Whatever the characteristics, families need ways to cope.

Physical Problems

You know what it's like to deal with simple illnesses. When someone has the flu for a week, the household just doesn't operate normally. If illnesses, injuries, and disabilities are more serious, however, the impact is much greater. Family life changes. In addition to financial pressures, emotional strain can take its toll on people.

Effects on Family Life

As you may have noticed in your own life, people are usually most comfortable when they follow a fairly standard routine. When routines are disrupted, people feel unsettled. Routines and schedules can be turned upside down when health problems hit someone in a family.

Depending on the nature of the problem, adjustments must be made. For every family and every health problem, the adjustments will be different. For example, who transports a young child to school if the person who normally does is ill? How will meals be prepared for those at home when the ones who cook spend extra time at the hospital? Who will care for the ill person during the hours that no one is usually home? Through communication and cooperation, families work out problems like these. They often turn to extended family members and friends for help.

Sometimes an ill or disabled person feels guilty for causing disruption in a family. Reassurances and a cheerful attitude from family members can ease these feelings.

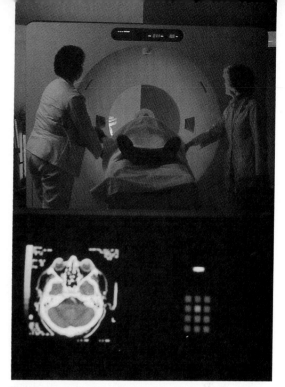

High technology makes the treatment of illnesses easier and more effective. The drawback is that the cost can be devastating to families who face a serious, or long-term, medical problem.

Financial Effects

Families commonly have financial problems when a serious illness or disability strikes. Income may be lost. Medical bills are usually high — and sometimes unbelievably so. If a family does not have insurance, they may have no means to pay. Even medication can be very costly, putting a heavy burden on the budget.

For these reasons, it is vital to think ahead about medical insurance needs. Even when health is good, a person never knows what is around the corner. If not provided through employment, medical coverage can be purchased independently.

People who are faced with unmanageable medical bills can talk to hospital personnel who counsel about such situations. A financial counseling service can help, too, as long as the firm is reputable. Some social service agencies and religious organizations also provide financial assistance.

Emotional Effects

When a family member is ill or disabled, all family members are likely to have an emotional response. After Phillip's father had a serious heart attack, the family was plunged into chaos. Strong emotions, such as fear and anger, were felt. As Mr. Atherton recovered, stressful feelings continued. His family was worried about him but had to carry on at the same time.

Each family member responds to illness individually. One who must take over a spouse's duties can feel bewildered and pressured. Often many decisions must be made. Hospital visits may be the highest priority for a while. Combined with worry about the illness, stress and tiredness can make this family member act in ways that don't seem normal.

Children can be confused by illness, depending on their age. A young child may not understand what is going on and be frightened by the reactions of others and the changes that take place. Even though older children and teens understand what is happening, feelings of fear and uncertainty are common. They may wonder what is going to happen and how it will affect them. Sometimes a normal, although troubling, feeling of resentment occurs. For example, a young person might see that a sick sibling is getting more attention and feel hurt and left out.

What To Do

When physical health problems challenge people, understanding helps them get by. By thinking about what the other person might be feeling, you can see what's behind their reactions. In addition, family members may need any, or all, of the following, from each other and outsiders:

- *A touch or hug.* Physical closeness is comforting to many people. Sometimes this is better than words.
- *Offers to take responsibility for what needs doing.* Family members can share the extra responsibilities rather than letting everything fall on one person's shoulders. People outside the family can stay in touch. Offers of help should take specific forms. In other words, avoid saying, "Call me if you need anything." Instead, say something like, "May I take the children to the park for the afternoon?"
- *Explanations.* Children need reassurances. They need love and attention more than ever. Saying things that are not true is not helpful. Usually simple, but honest, explanations are enough.
- *Knowledge.* Teens and adults often need to learn about an illness or disability. Knowledge can prevent unnecessary fear and allow a person to face the situation.
- *Openness.* Some people have a tendency to close up when someone is hurt or ill. Saying what you feel is good for you. It is an outlet that lets others know your needs and you know theirs.

An illness in the family affects members in different ways. How might a child react to a parent's illness?

Mental Problems

Recognizing mental problems is not always easy to do. Anyone can have negative emotions and lose the ability to think clearly at times. Sometimes people get so used to a person's instability that they might not recognize a problem. Two questions can point to the possibility of mental illness: Does the person function normally on a daily basis? Do the person's actions hurt or routinely trouble others? If the answers are "no" to the first question and "yes" to the second, the problem may be a real one that needs attention.

Mental illness can be very hard on family and friends. The ill person may be unpredictable. Expecting normal reactions, but getting unexpected ones, can be difficult. Sometimes people are embarrassed by mental illness. They think that physical illness is not controllable, but mental illness is. This is not so. Mental illnesses are just that — illnesses. Psychologists and psychiatrists can help people — and their families — deal with mental problems.

Help for mental problems can be located by looking in the Yellow Pages of the telephone directory under Mental Health Services. Even when problems are not severe, counselors can give assistance that might get control of a problem before it becomes serious. A mentally ill person may decide to take action on his or her own. If not, family and friends may choose to intervene by taking steps to force the person into treatment. State laws vary on what they are allowed to do.

ADDICTIONS

Addictions pose a strong threat to families, some types more than others. An **addiction** (uh-DICK-shun), is a person's dependence on a particular substance or action. People feel compelled to have the

Mental illness should be taken as seriously as physical illness. Getting the help of a counselor or treatment program can put a person's life back on track. The family as well as the individual stand to benefit.

substance or repeat the behavior in order to function. People form addictions to nicotine, drugs (including alcohol), and compulsive actions like overeating. Although addictions to nicotine and compulsive actions can cause problems in families, addictions to drugs more often reach crisis proportions.

Alcoholism

Drugs are chemical substances, other than food, that change the way the body or mind functions. Alcohol is one type of drug. Few forces are as destructive to individuals and families as alcohol is.

Problems with alcohol begin with that first drink. Because alcohol has a way of slowly taking control of people, many do not even realize what is happening to them. They don't know when their addiction to alcohol, or **alcoholism**, began. They even deny that they are dependent on the drug. The people around them know, however, because they have watched the gradual changes in behavior. They may even be victims of that behavior.

Some alcoholics are identified by certain characteristics. They drink frequently, sometimes alone and sometimes in the morning. Their drinking has increased over time, and some use alcohol to face particular situations. Drinking, or the aftereffects, may cause them to miss obligations, such as going to work or attending a family outing. Some alcoholics have blackouts. During a blackout, an alcoholic is conscious and functioning but later cannot remember what was said or done for a period of time. Blackouts can be a sign that the disease is moving into more serious stages.

One alcoholic's behavior may not be the same as another's. For one thing, the stage of the disease is a factor. Even though the characteristics above can help identify an alcoholic, some alcoholics may not have some or all of them.

Families know when alcohol is causing a problem. They are embarassed by what the alcoholic says and does. They worry about how the person's health will be affected. Often they are frustrated by unpredictable behavior. They may even be frightened or hurt by violent actions. Alcoholism causes many families to break apart. Emotional barriers build between family members, and divorce often occurs.

Family members react in different ways to alcoholism. Sometimes children blame themselves. They may neglect their studies and feel abandoned and resentful toward an alcoholic parent.

Co-dependency

In families where someone has a compulsive disorder, such as alcoholism, other family members can develop a condition known as **co-dependency**. Co-dependents become wrapped up in the dependent person's problems. They take on responsibilities that the other person should be fulfilling, which may even help the alcoholic hide the problem. They enable the alcoholic to continue drinking. Co-dependents try to control because they feel that everything is out of control. In trying to care for others, they neglect their own concerns.

Taking Action

People who are close to alcoholics have to take action — for their own sake as well as the alcoholic's. If you ever need to know what to do, here are some suggestions:

- *Become knowledgeable.* Read about alcoholism and talk to those who have good information.
- *Be thoughtful, not threatening.* An alcoholic will not stop drinking or seek help until he or she is ready to. Nagging does not help. A caring approach is best.
- *Be direct.* Use the term "alcoholism," and describe what is happening to the person and others because of the problem.
- *Seek help yourself, even when the alcoholic is not ready to.* Organizations like Alateen and Families Anonymous have advice and support. Look in the telephone directory under Alcoholism for listings. When the alcoholic is ready for help, Alcoholics Anonymous (AA) can

Knowledge can be your ally in a time of crisis. Learning about a disease like alcoholism, for example, can give you understanding as well as practical information about what to do.

help. This is an organization of people who have been through alcoholism. They know, firsthand, what the disease is like and what the person can do to move toward recovery. In some states alcoholics can be legally compelled to enter a treatment program. Many employers offer assistance programs for employees with drinking problems.

- *Be optimistic.* Many families face tough situations brought on by alcoholism every day. If they let fear and embarrassment rule, they may never find a solution. If they believe, however, that help is available and they go after it with determination, a better life is ahead.

Other Drug Addictions

Many drugs besides alcohol cause serious problems for individuals and families. Both medicinal drugs and illegal ones are addictive. Chances are, you have already learned in a health class or drug education program about the dangers of drugs. They affect health. Over time, they do serious damage to organs and systems of the body. They also cause changes in mental and emotional states, which, in turn, can lead to all sorts of other problems.

People with drug addictions may neglect their responsibilities to their employers, their schoolwork, and their families. They may develop behavior problems that make trouble at home, at school, at work, or in the community. Violent behavior is often linked to drug use. There may be legal problems connected with illegal drug use and with the unpredictable behavior of drug users. All these things place enormous strain on the family group. So do the costs of drugs and treatment for drug problems.

How do you know if someone has a drug problem? You may see some common signs. The person may miss school or work often and perform poorly when there. The

People who lose control of their own behavior through drug use need outside help. Why is intervention often critical in such situations?

person's behavior may not seem normal, marked by sudden mood changes. Attention seeking, aggression, and a poor attention span are other possibilities. You might also notice some physical signs, such as poor or changed appearance, slurred speech, and poor coordination. Low self-esteem is another indicator. Of course, the discovery of drugs and drug paraphernalia is an obvious sign.

The same techniques used to help an alcoholic can be used to confront and help people with other drug problems. Intervention is critical. Many of the same programs that treat alcoholism handle other drug addictions as well. Talking to the doctor can cut off access to prescription drugs if that is the problem. If illegal drugs are used, the police must be notified.

FAMILY VIOLENCE

People who react violently are always looking for reasons to excuse their behavior. They might say "The kid wouldn't stop crying," "I had to make him behave," and "She needs to know who's boss." They are wrong. The only excuse for violence is self-defense, and even that one can be controversial.

Violence is physical force used to harm someone or something. Violent actions may result in damage to property or in injury to people. Even death may result. Trying to explain why people act violently isn't easy. It isn't even clear. Stress might be labeled the cause for one person, yet another person with even more stress remains calm under the same circumstances.

Some violence occurs in one out of every two family homes each year. The police consider family violence calls among the most dangerous they must answer.

Violent behavior is often learned. When people grow up with violence, they begin to copy the same actions. Unless they learn ways to cope with stress and negative emotions, violence is passed along to another generation, and the cycle continues.

Violence hurts people, both physically and psychologically. Most people don't really want to hurt others. They may want to behave differently, but they don't know how. They might not even recognize that better ways exist. Whatever the case, they need to be stopped and reeducated.

Partner Abuse

One-fourth of all families experience some violence between the marriage partners. Abusive language may be part of the attack. Sometimes violence results in the breakup of a marriage. Other times, it becomes a repeated, destructive way of life.

Although some women are physically abusive toward men, the more common occurrence is violence directed by men against women. Men who batter women tend not to share their problems with others. They bottle their stresses inside until they explode. They often view women as possessions rather than partners. Abusers usually have traditional views of gender roles. Excessive drinking is often related to partner abuse.

Why do women stay in abusive relationships? Sometimes they don't want to admit abuse occurs. If they have low self-esteems, they may think they deserve the abuse, especially if they were abused as children. Women whose parents hit them are more apt to accept blows from partners.

Sometimes victims of abuse think they have no place to go. Relatives are not always willing or able to help. A woman may not believe she can support herself and her children alone. A feeling of commitment to the relationship can also cause her to stay.

Family violence is a serious problem in many homes. A counselor can show people how to get control of a situation before it gets out of hand.

Women who allow an abusive relationship to continue are making a mistake. Abusive relationships are likely to get worse, with children suffering, too. As you read earlier, many communities have shelters where women and children can go. Trained counselors can suggest further steps for these women. They can also provide ideas about help for the abuser.

Child Abuse

Abusive treatment of children takes several forms:

NEGLECT When people fail to provide adequate food, clothing, shelter, or medical care for children, this is neglect. Young children, especially, cannot be left alone to care for themselves under any circumstances.

EMOTIONAL ABUSE The National Committee for Prevention of Child Abuse defines emotional abuse as a "pattern of behavior that attacks a child's emotional development and sense of self-worth." Often the behavior is verbal attacks. The abuser may lash out with statements like, "You're no good" and "I wish you'd never been born." Name-calling can also be part of emotional abuse. Any parent under stress can verbally insult or withhold love from a child at times. A regular pattern of such behavior, however, indicates abuse. The emotional scars can last a lifetime.

PHYSICAL ABUSE Children who are physically abused are subjected to hitting and anything else that leaves an injury or scar. Burns, bruises, and cuts that are deliberately given mark this kind of abuse.

SEXUAL ABUSE This abuse takes place when someone subjects a child, male or female, to fondling, incest, or rape, or lures the child to be part of some sexual activity.

Incest is sexual activity between people who are closely related. Usually, the child knows the molester, who might be a parent, a stepparent, a sibling, or some other person present in the home. Often, the abuser convinces the victim that secrecy is necessary. Threats may be used. Children who are sexually abused need to understand that they did nothing to encourage the activity. The abuser is totally responsible for the actions and must be stopped.

Breaking the Cycle

Child abuse of any kind may continue regularly for years, leaving children in a state of daily fear, with lasting emotional scars. What's more, growing up with abuse may cause them to repeat the patterns with their own children someday.

No child or teen should have to live with any kind of abuse. There are laws against it. When you know that abuse is going on, either directed at you or someone you know, you have to get help. Talk to trusted people until you get someone to listen. Family members, friends, even a teacher can help.

Sometimes a family member doesn't want to listen to accusations of sexual abuse. A mother, for example, may not be able to believe, or face the fact, that her spouse could be sexually abusing a child. She may not realize that sexual abuse is not something children lie about. Turning to someone else who is willing to listen may be the only solution.

Intervention is critical in abuse situations. Without it, some children face a lifetime of anguish, or even death. People who suspect child abuse can call the police department or the national abuse hotline. The local child welfare office, usually listed under the Department of Children and Family Services in the telephone directory, is another resource. Sometimes family members must be separated from each other for awhile after abuse is reported.

Grandmothers of the Disappeared

FAMILIES

AROUND

THE

WORLD

Family ties and strength are important when a crisis hits. In 1976, the military overthrew the government of Argentina. At least 210 children were kidnapped, along with their parents, or were later born in captivity.

Not long after the coup, a group called *Abuelas de Plaza de Mayo*, or Grandmothers of the Plaza of May, formed. The women were the mothers and grandmothers of those who had disappeared. Every Thursday afternoon these women stood outside military headquarters to protest the kidnappings. They also gathered all the information they could about the disappeared. They questioned neighbors, prison janitors, released prisoners, and women who delivered the babies in jail.

Most of the disappeared adults were killed, but the grandmothers were determined to find their grandchildren. It was not easy. The captors sold the children on the black market and gave them away as gifts, bribes, or payment for services. With persistence, the grandmothers kept track of many of the children.

In 1983 the government began to listen to the grandmothers' pleas that the children be returned to their natural families, but the grandmothers had to prove the children really belonged to them. With the help of an American geneticist, they began to match the blood of the children with the blood of the grandparents.

More than 48 children have been returned to their grandparents on the basis of the blood test. The grandmothers continue to search for the rest, still determined to resolve a crisis that began many years ago.

Although this can be difficult, it is in the best interest of everyone. An abuser who learns how to control problem behavior may be reunited with the family later. The strain of confronting the problem is worth the effort when the result is a happier life.

People who are abusive, or fear they might become so, can be helped by Parents Anonymous, a national organization that sponsors support groups for parents throughout the country. This organization is listed in telephone directories.

SUICIDE

For everyone, life has its ups and downs. Sometimes people feel that a low point in life is overwhelming. Choosing suicide, however, is a permanent reaction to a temporary problem. Solving problems and letting strong negative emotions fade is a better answer. Down times eventually turn up when given a chance. There is no second chance with suicide.

Reaching Out

If someone you know reaches the point of considering suicide, he or she needs your help. How will you know if you need to respond? Take these signs seriously:

- Verbal comments, such as: "No one understands," "You'd be better off without me," and "There's no hope; it'll always be this way."
- Increasing depression.
- Avoidance of, and withdrawal from, people and activities.
- Substance abuse.
- Problems in school.
- Themes of death in artwork, poetry, essays, etc.
- Purchase of a weapon, object, or substance that could be used harmfully.
- Giving away special possessions.
- Saying goodbyes.
- Uncharacteristic behavior changes.
- Extreme emotions involving such feelings as anger and despair.
- Sudden happiness, perhaps indicating that a decision has been reached.
- Threats and/or suicide attempts.

A person who is suicidal wants help. Your response can make a difference. Don't be afraid to intervene. Action is essential. Talk to the person, expressing your concern. Say directly, "Are you thinking about suicide?" Don't act shocked or ask why. Instead, ask questions and listen rather than being judgmental and offering "empty" reassurances. Suggest people and places that can help the person, including the Suicide Prevention center listed in the telephone directory. Help the person see that there are alternatives, that you care, and that you know he or she can work things out. Stay with the person if necessary and remove anything that might be used harmfully. As soon as you can, seek help from family, friends, and agencies that handle crisis intervention.

A POSITIVE NOTE

The material you have just read is sobering, but there is a positive note. Often a crisis brings out the best in people. A community might rally around a family's problem, raising money and giving support. One person might find inner strength that he or she never knew was there when faced with a struggle. People reach out and pull together during a crisis. That's what makes the world a better place.

" . . . as we wake or sleep, we grow strong or we grow weak, and at last some crisis shows us what we have become."

— BISHOP WESTCOTT

SECTION 2 REVIEW

1. Explain how a serious illness can affect family life, finances, and the emotions of family members.
2. Why are mental problems often difficult to recognize?
3. Describe common symptoms of alcoholism.
4. Describe common indicators that someone has a problem with a drug addiction other than alcohol.
5. Why do many women make the mistake of staying in an abusive relationship?
6. Describe four types of child abuse.
7. List ten signs that a person might be thinking about suicide.

Chapter 13 Review

Chapter Summary

- When a crisis occurs, action must be taken in order to prevent serious consequences.
- People usually go through four stages when they react to a crisis. The early stages allow time to think before action is taken.
- Many resources are available to people in times of crisis if they will admit that they need help and seek it.
- Sometimes people need to step in to help someone else who is in a crisis state but cannot act alone.
- Health problems, either physical or mental, can cause a crisis for families.
- Alcoholism is a serious problem for individuals and families today. Without appropriate action and treatment, relationships can be destroyed.
- Family violence takes the forms of spouse abuse, child abuse, and elder abuse. None of these can be tolerated. Help is available.
- Suicide is a permanent reaction to a temporary problem. A person who has thoughts of suicide can be helped by someone who has the confidence to step in.

Chapter Review

1. List three elements that indicate a situation is a crisis.
2. List the four stages of reaction to a crisis.
3. Explain what a hotline is.
4. How can shelters help people who are victims of abuse?
5. Why is intervention important?
6. List four suggestions that people faced with a serious illness in the family might do.
7. How might a person find help for a mental illness?
8. What is an addiction?
9. What is co-dependency?
10. List four suggestions that the family of an alcoholic could follow.
11. What can a woman who is experiencing abuse from her spouse do?
12. Why is intervention particularly important in situations of child abuse?
13. Why is suicide the wrong choice for someone who has problems?
14. How can a person help someone who is thinking about suicide?

Critical Thinking

1. Why do you think some people are reluctant to seek help in times of crisis?
2. Why is intervention sometimes difficult?
3. How does a woman's financial situation relate to her willingness to leave an abusive relationship?
4. Suppose you took your child to the hospital emergency room to be treated for an injury. Hospital personnel begin to ask questions that make you feel like they are trying to determine if you are responsible for the injury. How would you feel? Why do they ask such questions? Is such an attitude toward you reasonable? Explain your answer.

Chapter 13 Review

Activities

1. **Handling a crisis.** Working with a partner, think of a movie you have both seen that deals with one of the crises discussed in this chapter. Write a few paragraphs that describe and evaluate how the characters handled the crises. (*Teamwork, interpreting and communicating information*)

2. **Child abuse intervention.** Search newspapers and magazines for articles on child abuse. Report to the class on how intervention did or did not play a role in specific incidents. (*Acquiring and evaluating information, communicating information*)

3. **A guide to crisis situations.** Working with a group, choose one of the following crisis situations: family illness or disability; mental illness; alcoholism; other drug addiction; spouse abuse; child abuse; or suicidal signs in a friend. Write a guide (perhaps a list) of what to do when faced with such a crisis. Compile group lists into a handout or pamphlet to share. (*Teamwork, organizing information, communicating information*)

Understanding Death

SECTION 1

BEFORE DEATH OCCURS

SECTION 2

HANDLING GRIEF

IMAGINE THAT ...

while driving through the country one afternoon, you notice a tiny graveyard beside the road. You stop the car and get out to take a look. The gravestones are old, some a bit on tilt, but the grass is well-kept and flowers have been lovingly planted and cared for. You notice dates from the early 1900s. One stone marks the grave of an infant, another, a young child. One stone is so old that you can't read the inscription. On others special thoughts have been carved. For a moment, you are struck by the thought that life, unlike death, is very fleeting. You pause by the last stone that catches your attention — a teen who died over 70 years ago. As you walk slowly back to the car, there are many things on your mind.

BEFORE DEATH OCCURS

THINK AHEAD

About These Terms
denial
isolation
hospice programs

About These Objectives
After studying this section, you should be able to:
- Explain how different circumstances affect attitudes toward death.
- Describe Elisabeth Kubler-Ross's stages of adjustment to death.
- Explain how people can give support to those who are dying.
- Describe how the hospice program helps people.

ou live in a society that tries to deny death. Death happens. It is a normal part of the life cycle that takes a person from birth, through life, to death. The more people avoid thoughts and discussions of death, the harder it is to handle it.

◆ ◆ ◆

A Natural Step

When Charla's grandfather died, he was living with her family. He was in his eighties, and Charla was by his side when he died. Charla learned so much from him about death in the weeks before. They talked often. He told about his life, but as he grew weaker, he often just wanted to hear Charla's thoughts. He would squeeze her hand and pat it gently as he drifted off to sleep for a while. One day he whispered to her, "I'm not afraid," and he smiled. Not long after that, he died.

Death came to Charla's grandfather in a natural way. He had lived a long life, and his time had come. For Charla the death was a loss, as any death is. She wanted to hang on to her grandfather and keep him with her, but that was not possible. His serenity and acceptance helped Charla see that death was the next natural step for him — and for everyone — in life.

Different Circumstances

The death of Charla's grandfather followed a normal pattern. He lived a long life and died when his body grew old. People who live a long life have time, little by little, to adjust to the idea of death. Often they are ready and comfortable when the time finally comes. They may have been able to prepare for death by putting their lives in order. One grandmother gave special keepsakes to her grandchildren and sorted through drawers, throwing away what was of no value to anyone else. Another person made his own funeral arrangements and purchased a burial site so that his family would not have to make such decisions. Having gone through all the stages of life, these people were ready for death when it occurred.

Often older people are comfortable with the thought of completing the natural life cycle that goes from birth, through life, and to death.

Sometimes death comes early *without* warning. People lose their lives in accidents, wars, and by violence. A person who dies in one of these ways usually has little or no time to think about death, let alone prepare for it. Whatever was unresolved in life remains that way.

Sometimes death comes early but *with* warning. Serious illness may force a person to deal with the knowledge that death is coming sooner than expected. Knowing can allow a person time to do and say things that might not otherwise be taken care of. Knowing also forces the person to adjust to the idea of death without the experience of a long life.

Coping in Stages

When illness forces people to face death before they are ready, they feel certain emotions that are fairly typical. Psychiatrist Elisabeth Kübler-Ross has spent a major part of her career working with patients and families who face death. Her experience shows that people go through five stages of adjustment.

Spending the Day with the Dead

FAMILIES

AROUND

THE

WORLD

In Mexico, the line between the living and the dead is blurred. After people have died, they are still considered part of the family. They even have their own day, *El Día de los Muertos*, the Day of the Dead.

Celebration of the Day of the Dead takes place on November 2nd each year, a day also known as All Souls' Day. Celebrations and preparations, however, actually start two days before. The women in the family clean house, make candles, and prepare food. They bake bread in animal shapes. The men build a small altar on which they put food and toys for the ghosts of children who have died. Those children, the *angelitos*, are thought to visit that night at midnight to enjoy their gifts.

November 1st, All Saints' Day, is used to prepare for the adult dead who are believed to visit at dawn on November 2nd. The women shop for bones and skulls made of marzipan (almond paste) and bread. Some of these have a space on the skull in which they write the name of the deceased person.

November 1st is also filled with music and carnivals. People visit family, neighbors, and friends. They talk about the dead and remember them. The visits and the remembering go on far into the night.

In the morning, on November 2nd, a mass is said for the spirits. The families then take food, candles, and music to the cemeteries. There they spread cloth over the graves of their relatives and share another day with their loved ones. Again, they may talk and celebrate until far into the night.

DENIAL AND ISOLATION In the first stage people who are dying deny that death is approaching. **Denial** (dih-NEYE-uhl) is refusing to believe the facts and, therefore, thinking and acting as if those facts don't exist. For example, given the news of a terminal illness, a person in denial might say, "No, I'm *not* going to die!" He or she might even go from one doctor to another, convinced that one will "tell the truth." People in denial block out reality because that reality is too shocking and painful to handle right away. Denial is a common reaction to any major loss.

After a while, people realize that death will occur. Then **isolation** (EYE-suh-LAY-shun) is common. This is the feeling of being set apart from others and completely alone. Since death is so personal, they feel that no one can understand, and no one shares in the loss. They may pull back from others who truly care.

When faced with a terminal illness, people often go through stages of adjustment. During the isolation stage, they feel very alone as they try to come to grips with the idea of dying.

ANGER When the fact of death is no longer denied, people go through a stage of very angry emotions. They are enraged by the thought of death, but the anger gets taken out on everyone and everything. The doctor may be confronted with angry outbursts, as may family and close friends. Sometimes religious beliefs are the target. People may be furious at a higher power, such as God, for allowing death to happen. In this stage of adjusting to death, people are usually difficult to get along with. By understanding the anger and not taking it personally, family and friends can stay supportive.

BARGAINING At some point people who face death may try to gain more living time. Bargaining, or "making deals", is used to offer something in exchange for continued life. For example, they may promise to get rid of bad habits or take up new good ones. Religious bargaining might focus on promises to pray more. Those who have not been involved in a religion before may promise to become so now. Through bargaining, people try to gain control over the situation. Though death has been acknowledged, bargaining expresses the hope of doing something to postpone death — even for a brief time.

DEPRESSION The depression stage occurs when people realize that attempts to bargain for a longer life will not work. It becomes evident that death can't be avoided. A person's condition may have worsened, or he or she may feel weaker. Depression can be aggravated by financial problems resulting from the cost of care, causing guilt feelings. More than anything else, people feel the upcoming loss of everyone and everything held dear. This stage, filled with heavy emotions, may seem almost unbearable to family and friends. Understanding and sympathy are the most useful tools in helping people get through this stage.

ACCEPTANCE In this final stage, people accept death. They are able to look back over life and acknowledge what was good but realize that it will soon end. The strong emotions of the first four stages of adjustment are gone in this last stage. The person has come to terms with the situation and is ready to face what lies ahead peacefully.

SUPPORT FROM OTHERS

As dying people go through the stages described above, they need support and love. Sometimes people who are dying want to spend time with their friends; others do not. Family members and close friends may be needed on a continual basis. Other friends can keep in touch and follow the advise of family regarding visits.

All the way along, don't be afraid to be there and to listen. Turning away because *you* don't want to face the truth may be hard on the dying person. If you don't know what to say, take your cues from him or her. Is the person looking for hope?

TEAMING UP WITH TECHNOLOGY

SINCE

technology allows medical professionals to prolong life,

HOW

can people decide when to let death occur naturally?

Much controversy surrounds the issue of prolonging life through extraordinary medical technology. With very advanced abilities and equipment, medical professionals can save lives of infants that are born with serious health problems. People who suffer severe injuries in accidents can be kept on life-support systems that keep them alive even though they are unable to function. How much medical intervention should be allowed to keep people alive? This is a question without a simple answer.

JOINING THE TEAM

- Have you ever read about anyone who was kept on a life-support system? What happened? How were decisions made?
- How should decisions about using technology this way be made?

Then listen and be hopeful, too. Has he or she accepted death? Then don't give reassurances that everything will be okay. Talk about simple, everyday things. Doing so can be helpful, a relief from the heavy thoughts that are often there. Touch instead of talk when that seems right.

As the person becomes accepting of death, he or she may want to talk about it. Concerns about death and about those that will be left behind may need expression. Loved ones often find this conversation the most difficult. They may want to deny death when the dying person has reached the point of accepting it. When you know that the dying person may say something like, "I wonder what it will feel like to die," you can be prepared to respond simply and calmly.

When people know that death is coming, they have an opportunity that not everyone has. They can say whatever needs saying. Things that seemed important before may not seem so now. Relationships can be mended and reinforced for all time. As a result, remembering can be filled with warm thoughts, not regrets.

HOSPICE

Families that need help before death occurs often turn to hospice programs. **Hospice programs** provide support and care for people who face death.

Some hospice organizations have facilities where people with terminal illnesses can spend their final days. While such hospices provide medical care, they are more homelike and comfortable than hospitals or nursing homes. Patients at a hospice receive personal care, good nursing, and emotional support, so they can live out their days in comfort and with some enjoyment. Doctors, nurses, physical therapists,

The final days and weeks in a terminally ill person's life can be enriched by the care and aid of hospice workers. These people are trained to help people and their families make the best of the time that is left.

psychiatrists, counselors, and chaplains work with the dying and their families.

Families are actively involved in the patient's life at the hospice. Family members help with the patient's care and also receive counseling.

Even when a hospice facility is not available or cannot be used, staff and trained volunteers are on call to give support and help. The patient often remains at home and the hospice team provides needed care there.

SECTION 1 REVIEW

1. Why are aging people often able to accept death peacefully?
2. When death comes with warning, what does this allow a person to do?
3. What is denial?
4. What is isolation?
5. Which of the stages of dying is often the most difficult? Why?
6. How can a person give support to someone who is dying?
7. What is the hospice program?

HANDLING GRIEF

THINK AHEAD

About These Terms
grief   *will*
cremation

About These Objectives
After studying this section, you should be able to:

- Predict the stages that a person will go through when grieving.
- Summarize the practical decisions that must be made at the time of someone's death.
- Recommend ways to help children deal with death.
- Describe appropriate ways of comforting a grieving person.

he death of a friend or relative is not an ending for the people who survive. When a person dies, the impact he or she had on others continues to be felt. In memory and often with deep emotion, people live on in the hearts and minds of those they leave behind.

◆ ◆ ◆

GRIEVING

The loss of a special person through death leaves people with emotional and physical feelings that can be very painful. These feelings are known as **grief**. Grief is a difficult emotion that needs to be expressed.

Because grief is so painful, some people try to avoid grieving. They may push the hurt deep inside, trying not to feel it. They may think they should be strong, yet even people who are strong still feel pain.

Blocking out grief is a short-term solution to pain. The pain inside does not disappear. Therefore, when people refuse to grieve, they often experience other problems later on. Some studies have shown that drug addiction, delinquency, illness, and even death can result from unresolved grief. Although it isn't easy, facing grief and experiencing its pain are necessary.

By expressing grief, people release tension that would otherwise be locked inside. Grieving acknowledges the loss, which helps a person deal with it.

"Sorrow is a fruit; God does not allow it to grow on a branch that is too weak to bear it."

— VICTOR HUGO

Stages of Grieving

Sometimes the grief process is called "grief work" or mourning. Three stages make up the process:

STAGE ONE The first stage of grieving is *shock and numbness*, often coupled with denial. People may busy themselves with a flurry of purposeless activity. This stage helps the bereaved, those in mourning, screen out the reality of what is happening.

STAGE TWO The *reality* of the situation sinks in during this stage. People feel a cutting sense of loss. Waves of sadness often overwhelm them. Depression and anxiety are common in this phase of grief.

STAGE THREE The final step in the grief process is called *recovery*. Recovery means facing and bearing the loss. The grieving person recognizes that the loss is final. Hopes, dreams, and plans shared with the person who has died are given up. The bereaved person makes the changes and adjustments needed to return to a normal routine.

How Long?

The time for mourning varies, but getting through the whole process normally takes a long time. As you might expect, the age of the person who died and the cause of death can affect how long. The relationship to the person who has died also makes a difference. The closer the relationship, the longer it may take to recover.

number of white blood cells that work in the body to fight disease drops dramatically, making it more likely that a grieving person will become ill.

Grief produces a whole range of emotions. Mixed feelings are common. Sadness and loss are usually the primary feelings. Anger and fear, however, also occur. Sometimes death brings relief and gladness. Relief is most common when the person suffered through a long, painful illness before dying. Because relief and gladness are not expected emotions at the time of death, they may also produce feelings of guilt. Resentment may be felt, too. A person may resent the dead person for dying and leaving him or her behind. Emotions like these soon disappear, and people should not worry about feeling them.

DECISION MAKING

Although difficult, in the period right after death, when grief is the strongest, many practical decisions have to be made. The first decision is what will happen to the body of the deceased. Families usually choose between burial and cremation.

Estimates say that grieving may take two years after the death of a parent and from four to six years after the death of a spouse. The process sometimes continues as long as eight to ten years when the survivor has lost a child to death.

Symptoms of Grief

Most people are not prepared for the severe physical and emotional reactions they feel in grief. They are unaware that grief can affect all aspects of the body and mind.

Physically, the first reaction is numbness. A painful tightness in the throat is common. People may experience a sense of unreality. Sleep patterns are often disturbed. Some people begin sleeping for extended periods of time, while others are unable to sleep well. Lack of interest in food can be a problem. Finally, the stress of grief often causes illness. During grief, the

The grief process can last a very long time. When people know this, they are better able to understand the feelings they have months and even years after experiencing the death of a loved one.

Funerals can range from simple to very elaborate. Before they die, some people participate in the planning of their own funeral.

Cremation (kree-MAY-shun) is the reduction of a body to ashes through intense heat. Whichever option is chosen, arrangements must be made.

People also make decisions about the funeral. This ritual honors the memory of the deceased, but perhaps more important, it gives the bereaved a chance to mourn and say goodbye. For many, a funeral is a necessary part of grieving.

Funerals can be very expensive. They may be the third largest purchase in a person's life — after a home and car. Family members can work together to plan a ceremony that honors the deceased without causing financial problems. Reputable funeral directors will not apply pressure to spend more than the family is comfortable with. Often they are a source of help with many questions and concerns that survivors have.

Discussing funeral arrangements in advance is helpful. Although such discussions may not be pleasant, decisions can be made more easily.

Often many financial details must be taken care of in the weeks following a death. Bills, including medical ones, and insurance forms from the deceased's last illness often need to be handled. Sometimes there are benefits, such as life insurance or Social Security, to apply for. Notification of the death may need to go to people and businesses.

The deceased's property must be taken care of. Often this is handled through a will. A **will** is a legal document that states how a person's property is to be distributed after death. If there is no will, the deceased's property is distributed according to state law.

Even if there is not much property, often car titles and bank accounts need to have the names changed on them. The deceased's clothes and personal items may be given to family, friends, or charity.

Although all of this may sound insensitive, it is necessary. Facing the practical side of death helps put the emotional side in place.

Adults have much on their minds when a death occurs. The feelings and reactions of children, however, cannot be ignored. Children need help at their level of understanding as they observe what is going on around them.

Supporting Children

Children need special help in dealing with death. They can be confused by what happens if they are left out or given inappropriate information.

Young children have an incomplete concept of death. Up to age four, they are not able to understand loss through death. They do, however, understand feelings of separation and rejection. Therefore, helping very young children deal with death means making sure they feel loved and secure.

Between the ages of four and seven, children usually think death is temporary and reversible. At about age seven, death is seen as permanent, but children may believe the deceased keeps some body functions. They also believe death is something that happens to other people and families.

At some point in the preteen years, the child understands that death is final and comes to all people. Children who have had experience with death, through pets, peers, parents, or grandparents, understand it better than those who have not.

Many families are open with their children about death. Such families first consider each child's age and ability to understand. They talk to the child about death in a simple, straightforward way. They give honest and clear answers to the children's questions about death.

When three-year-old Laine's mother died, this is what her father told her: "I have to tell you something very, very sad. Let me hold you on my lap while we talk. Mommy was hurt. She was hurt too badly to live. Now her body has stopped working. Mommy has died, and she won't be coming back. We'll miss her so much, but Daddy is here. I love you a lot, and I'll take care of you."

Simple, clear answers about the cause of death are reassuring to children. Especially confusing are the once-common practices of telling children a dead person is asleep or on a journey. Sometimes parents tell a child the deceased is now in heaven. This can lead children to believe they should be able to visit there.

Shortly after Casey's father died, he started refusing to stay in bed. Instead, he hid in places around the house, insisting that he didn't need to sleep. It turned out that an aunt had told Casey that his father was sleeping. Casey thought that if he went to sleep, he would die, too.

Some families try to shelter their children from death. The parents may be unable to face death or have poor communication skills. This is unfortunate, because children need to to have their questions answered. When children are given no answers, or incomplete ones, they often imagine things that are worse than the truth. They may grow up with fears about death.

Emotions can be affected by the lyrics of popular music. Try listening to your favorite radio station for a half hour. Imagine how someone who is grieving might feel after listening to the same music. What effects do you think the lyrics would have on the person?

Do you know music or lyrics that give you hope when you're down or feeling a sense of loss? If you have the equipment, you could create a therapeutic musical tape that helps you deal with these feelings. Take it a step further by sharing it with a friend who needs a lift.

Children can be helped to see that death is a part of the cycle that all living things go through. Although death is a sad time, new beginnings and growth lie ahead.

SUPPORTING FRIENDS

When someone you know is grieving, the easiest thing to do is turn away. Often people feel they don't know what to say or do when a friend has lost a loved one. This may be the time, however, when a friend needs you the most.

Friends send cards and very simple notes of condolence. Sometimes they bring food to the family. When talking to a grieving person, a hug or handshake may be all that is needed. Saying something like "I'm sorry" or "I'm thinking about you" is appropriate, too.

Remember that a person's grief process goes on for a long time. Weeks and even months later your friend might like to talk about the person who died. Knowing that you haven't forgotten the deceased can be comforting. You might bring up a special memory that you have, and if your friend needs to talk, you have provided the opener.

A MESSAGE FOR YOU

So much that is positive can come from thinking and talking about death. You can realize that the reactions you have to death are normal ones. You can also be prepared to support others when they face death or grief. What is more, you can discover a new appreciation for life. Do you remember reading about Charla's grandfather at the beginning of this chapter? Several weeks before he died, he said something to her that she will always remember. He said, "Take time to smell the roses."

SECTION 2 REVIEW

1. Why is grieving important?
2. List five symptoms of grief.
3. Describe three practical decisions that must be made when a person dies.
4. How does age relate to what a child can be told about death?
5. How can you best respond to a friend who is grieving?

Chapter 14 Review

Chapter Summary

- Death is often accepted peacefully by those who have lived a long life.
- Death can come with or without warning. People who have warning can prepare for it.
- Elisabeth Kübler-Ross identified five stages that people go through when they know they are going to die.
- Sometimes people who are close to a dying person find it difficult to know what to do or say; however, they need to be there for the person.
- Special programs are available to help individuals and families deal with approaching death.
- Grief is a difficult but necessary emotion. The process of grieving takes place in stages.
- Certain practical decisions must be made at the time of a person's death. They are not usually easy to handle, but dealing with them can help people adjust to a death.
- Support is available for those who are grieving.
- Children have special needs when they must cope with death. These correspond to their age.
- Although it may not be easy, being there for a friend who is grieving is one of the most important things you can do.

Chapter Review

1. How does age relate to acceptance of death?

2. How do some older people show that they are getting ready for death?
3. Describe how a person in the denial stage might act.
4. During the anger stage, what should friends and family remember?
5. Give an example of what a person might do in the bargaining stage.
6. Why do some people turn away from a dying person?
7. List two suggestions for giving support to someone who is dying.
8. Why is a hospice program sometimes preferred to a regular hospital setting?
9. What is grief?
10. What can happen to people who refuse to grieve?
11. Describe the three stages in the grief process.
12. How long does the grief process normally last?
13. Is it okay to feel relief and gladness after a death? Explain your answer.
14. How can discussing funeral arrangements well before death be helpful?
15. Should you tell a six-year-old that a deceased family member has gone on a long trip? Why or why not?
16. Why is it sometimes helpful to a friend to bring up the memory of a loved one who died?

Critical Thinking

1. Why do you think people in this society want to deny death?
2. Which do you think would be better for a person, dying with or without warning? Explain your answer.

3. Some people refuse to go to funerals. Why do you think they feel this way? What is your attitude?

4. Do you think a funeral that is expensive does more to honor the deceased than a simple funeral does? Explain your answer.

5. Do you think children should come to funerals? Explain your answer.

6. What is meant by the statement, "Take time to smell the roses"?

Activities

1. **Dealing with dying.** Make a list of emotions that a person might feel at each of Elisabeth Kübler–Ross's stages of dealing with dying. (*Organizing information*)

2. **Funeral questions.** Working with a partner, write five to ten questions that you would ask a funeral director if you had to make funeral arrangements. (*Teamwork, organizing information*)

3. **Funeral costs.** Research the costs of funerals in your area and report back to the class. (*Acquiring and evaluating information, mathematics, communicating information*)

4. **Writing an epitaph.** An epitaph is a short inscription on a tombstone. Write what you would like to say on yours. (*Creative thinking*)

STRENGTHENING VALUES

Aim For Strength

Strength is needed for many purposes. You can confront difficulties without becoming discouraged. You can act despite your fears. You can get involved and help other people solve their problems. Strength has particular usefulness when you must deal with situations that involve death. Henry's inner strength allowed him to:

♦ Go to his friend Tyler and talk to him when Tyler's father died.

♦ Take his dog Shane, who was old and very sick, to the vet to be put to sleep.

♦ Go with several friends to the funeral of a classmate, who was killed in an auto accident.

♦ Become a teen counselor on a crisis hotline.

How does each of the actions above show Henry's strength? Is strength a trait of males, females, or both? Explain your answer. Can a person be strong and still let emotions show? Explain. Describe some ways that you have shown strength.

Extending Your Relationships

"I'll never forget my first couple of weeks at Jefferson High. It was midyear, so everybody already had friends that they hung out with. You know how uncomfortable it is when you're alone and no one else is? That's the way I felt. I really hated going to the cafeteria for lunch — until Carmen came along. She just sat down one day and started talking. We've been good friends ever since. We can tell each other anything, and we like the same things. She even talked me into joining the Marching Band, and I'm really glad she did. Through Carmen I've made some other friends, too, but no one is as special to me as she is."

SILVIA

281

CHAPTER 15

Working with Others

SECTION 1

WORKING RELATIONSHIPS

SECTION 2

GROUPS, LEADERS, AND FOLLOWERS

IMAGINE THAT ...

you have been working in a large cinema complex. Because you've done a good job, the boss has decided to give you a raise and more responsibility. He wants you to go on the evening shift and manage the crew. You have heard about them. People say that things get out of control at night. Rumors of people asleep on the job, popcorn wars, and hard feelings among employees are running rampant. You decide to accept the challenge. The first night you call a meeting of all employees. As you walk into the room, you feel the electricity in the air. A few faces look eager. Others are sullen. Some arms are crossed on bodies that slouch in the chairs. They are all waiting to hear what you have to say.

WORKING RELATIONSHIPS

THINK AHEAD

About These Terms
cooperation   *authority*
reciprocation

About These Objectives
After studying this section, you should be able to:
* Explain what a working relationship is.
* Describe keys to good working relationships.
* Explain how to understand and get along with those in authority.
* Describe different working relationships and how to handle them.

ach relationship has its own challenge. People are all so different that every combination of individuals brings together a new set of qualities that can mesh or clash. What you have learned already about relating to others will blend with the ideas in this unit to help you manage and improve the many different kinds of relationships in your life.

◆ ◆ ◆

WHAT ARE WORKING RELATIONSHIPS?

Much of what you have read so far in this text has centered around family relationships. In this unit, you will explore many other kinds of relationships. You will be looking at friendship, with people your own age as well as older adults. You will study male-female relationships, giving thought to love and sexuality. In this chapter, however, the focus is on more formal relationships. These are the ones that form in order to accomplish a task or goal, whether simple or complex. They are called working relationships.

Working relationships come in different settings. Two common ones are at school and on the job. You might also work with people in the community and in religious organizations. Even short encounters, such as those with an insurance representative or a store clerk, can be called working relationships.

Good working relationships are just as important to smooth living as any others are. You will see the benefits as you read on.

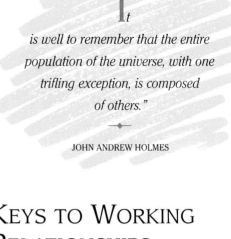

KEYS TO WORKING RELATIONSHIPS

Four keys to good working relationships are a friendly attitude, respect for others, cooperation, and reciprocation. Striving for these is a good idea.

A FRIENDLY ATTITUDE When Kirsten walks down the street in the small town where she lives, she is usually smiling. She looks people in the eye when she greets them and calls them by name when she can. Even the people she doesn't know well think favorably of her and feel good when they meet her. This, in turn, creates a positive response in others.

Of course, it isn't possible to be "up" all the time. Some days you may not feel like smiling. Sometimes you may have problems that make it difficult to be cheerful. Good relation-

Since people will spend much of life on the job, learning to get along well with others at work is an important skill to have.

When Everyone is Family

FAMILIES

AROUND

THE

WORLD

Cooperation is an important part of family, as well as work, relationships. The Omaha, a group of Native Americans in eastern Nebraska, have a view of family that at times seems to include cooperation from most of the community.

In the past, the brother of a man who died would marry that man's widow. Without the second marriage, there was no one to provide for her and her children. If a woman died, her sister would marry the widower, caring for him and his children. Because aunts and uncles might someday become a mother or father, children commonly addressed their parents' siblings as "mother" or "father."

The Omaha also made sure that children were always cared for. If a family fell on hard times and was unable to care for their children properly, the youngsters would be sent to a family that was better off. When times were better, they returned to their own family but kept the new family as well. Members of that second family were treated just like members of the natural family.

When an Omaha family adopts someone, that person becomes a true part of the family. Even adoptees who are not Omaha — or who are not even Native American — are addressed by the same titles and engage in the same ceremonies as someone born into the Omaha people.

ships often call for some acting ability. If you act cheerful, chances are good that you will begin to feel that way. Psychologists suggest that if you change your behavior, your feelings will follow.

RESPECT Have you ever given a speech before the class, only to find some of your classmates were talking, reading a book, or staring out the window? How did that make you feel? Respectful people do none of these things when someone is talking.

They listen. If another person has a problem, they show concern and a willingness to help.

COOPERATION The ability to work with others is called **cooperation**. Owen, for example, worked weekends as a hospital orderly. When he learned that he had been selected to attend a student government convention, Owen immediately went to his supervisor at work and asked her if he might take that weekend off. She agreed to schedule someone else if he would work two days of that person's shift at another time. Together they decided on the days and time that suited them both. Cooperation allowed them both to accomplish what they needed.

RECIPROCATION Finally, good working relationships are based on giving and getting in return. This is **reciprocation** (ri-SIP-ruh-KAY-shun). People tend to get what they give. If you approach others in a friendly way, they are more likely to be open to you. If you show that you respect others, they are more apt to regard you highly. If you show a willingness to cooperate with others, they are more likely to try to meet you halfway.

UNDERSTANDING AUTHORITY

In most working relationships, someone has authority. **Authority** is the right to give orders, make decisions, and enforce rules. Working well with others means learning to accept and get along with people in authority.

Generally, people with authority have earned it through qualities, knowledge, or skills that they have. They may have acquired positions that give them power. Teachers, bosses, and police officers are typical examples of people in authority. Anyone can be in a position of authority at one time or another. Have you ever taken taken care of young children? Then you were in authority.

Getting along with people in authority is easier for some people than it is for others. Remember that:

- *Authority is often connected to a job.* The person in authority is simply doing what he or she is supposed to.
- *Authority is assigned to people so that someone can keep order, promote safety,*

and make sure jobs get done. The purpose has nothing to do with making life difficult for anyone.
- *Like everyone else, people in authority have strengths and weaknesses.* Expecting them not to make mistakes just because they have authority is unfair.
- *Being in authority can be difficult.* Anyone who has cared for a five-year-old, for example, knows that managing the actions of others can be tricky.

Responding to Authority

Authority creates different responses in different people. When faced with authority, some people are pleasers. They do

Like other people in authority, teachers have a job to do. How many students do you think one teacher might be responsible for during the course of a day?

what the person in charge wants. These people usually have respect for tradition and work well under the direction of others. They don't "make waves."

On the other hand, some people rebel at authority. They tend to do the opposite of what is asked of them. They may create disturbances when they question those in charge.

Some type of balance between pleasing and rebelling is often the best way. Too much of one or the other may not make the best student or worker. There are times when it is better to follow orders and do your work. There are also times when questioning authority in an acceptable way helps people learn and creates changes that benefit everyone. Knowing which behavior is appropriate in which situation is an important life skill.

Channeling Rebelliousness

Nicole had always had a rebellious streak. Since she didn't understand the purpose of many of the sanitation rules at the diner where she worked, she decided that she didn't really need to follow them. This cost the restaurant a favorable rating when the health inspector made a surprise visit. Nicole nearly lost her job. From that experience, she learned to question rules she didn't understand rather than ignore them. She even turned her natural resistance into a positive quality when she found a different, more efficient, way of organizing the diner's supplies. Her rebelliousness, constructively channeled, became a force for improvement.

During adolescence, some teens feel the need to rebel against authority. Teens are in the process of forming their own identities, values, and goals. Part of this involves questioning the power and authority of others. In the long run, however, everyone must live and cope with authority. Too much rebelliousness hurts the rebel eventually.

Adults can help teens who have rebellious feelings. Talking with a trusted adult about why such feelings occur can help a teen get on the right track. What will be gained?

You can learn to meet your own needs while still complying with those who have power over you.

SPECIFIC WORK RELATIONSHIPS

Until you stop and think about it, you may not realize how many working relationships you have. Whether you work with others at school, on a job, or in a club, the right skills and attitudes can come in handy.

Relationships at School

Teens spend many hours of the day at school. There they relate to other students, some of them friends and acquaintances, as well as teachers, administrators, and support staff.

Schools are organized for efficient learning. To accomplish this, rules exist about student behavior and how things are done. Doing well in school often means learning how to follow the rules and behave appropriately. Therefore, pleasers may do better in school than rebels. Rebels should think about these questions: What happens when you break the rules? What happens when you follow the rules? Which behavior benefits you the most in the long run? It's your choice.

Joe is an example of someone who went from rebellion to cooperation at school. Low self-esteem caused Joe to want to be the center of attention. He got the attention he craved in negative ways, by rudeness in class and flaunting the rules at every opportunity. A few fellow students joined him and reinforced his behavior, but most found him annoying and troublesome. Those who wanted to learn and liked a calm atmosphere resented Joe's actions. He didn't care about them.

Joe's grades went downhill, along with his behavior. Then he began to talk with one particular teacher, who had an interest in Joe. Gradually, Mr. Abbott was able to help Joe see that nothing was good about the situation. Joe really wasn't happy. Hopes for his future were going down the drain. Joe had some personal problems, but he couldn't let that ruin his life. Joe decided to make some changes, small at first. He knew his friends and fellow classmates would be startled by the changes, but he decided not to worry about that. He had to save himself — and he did.

Joe began to see what school could do for him. Once in a while, a student can't see the advantages that school has to offer. Do you? Will you have the education you need to get a good job with a good income? Will you be one of those people who gets a job and then is embarrassed and held back because of poor writing and math skills? Will you be well rounded and confident in many settings because of your knowledge and abilities? When you have the foresight to see how today affects tomorrow, you are much more likely to make the most of your school relationships.

Relationships on the Job

Good relationship skills on the job are often as important as good work skills. Some estimates say that almost 85 percent of people who are fired lose their jobs because they can't get along with others. There are two basic relationships at work. One is with the boss, and the other is with co-workers.

Understanding Your Boss

A work supervisor generally has two jobs. The first is to get work done. The second is to take care of the needs of the workers. Often these responsibilities conflict.

As a construction worker, Heather understood her boss's conflict when she needed time off to take care of a personal problem. Her supervisor rescheduled her work so it could be done later. Heather knew, however, that if their project was held up because she couldn't finish her job on time, her supervisor would be held accountable. Heather appreciated her boss's flexibility and concern for her personal life. For her part, she took off no more time than she needed and worked especially hard to get her job done on time.

Although most bosses care about the personal lives of their employees, they still have a job to do. When work does not get done, businesses cannot survive and peo-

Did you ever notice how easy it is to be surrounded by people and yet remain unaware of them? An example of this might be on the highway where people are perceived as vehicles or traffic.

Try relating with someone in a new way this week. It might be a neighbor or someone in your apartment building you hardly know. It could be someone who offers you service — a bus driver, cafeteria worker, clerk, or maintenance person.

Smiles and greetings for acquaintances make life more enjoyable. Furthermore, using people's names and knowing their interests enriches relationships and may turn them into friendships!

Getting Along with Co-workers

How you relate to other workers affects how well you like your job. People who get along with their co-workers are more apt to be satisfied with their jobs. Good relationships can make unpleasant tasks more enjoyable and make difficult tasks easier to handle.

Eduardo discovered this principle when he began work at a small printing company. There, all the employees helped with all the work. Some jobs were more interesting than others. Because everyone got along so well, however, Eduardo didn't mind even the routine tasks. The first time he had to stay late to help take inventory, one person brought a tape player and another provided snacks. Good companionship turned a tedious job into an enjoyable evening.

As with all relationships, getting along with your co-workers takes some effort. Avoid talking about others. Be willing to help a co-worker. You will get cooperation in return. Do your part so that others don't have to do your work. Have a good attitude so that others enjoy having you around. Look for the positive qualities in people and make light of their weaknesses. Remember that you won't necessarily like all the people you work with, but you can get along with them if you try.

Everyday Encounters

Hardly a day goes by that you don't have to relate to someone you don't know well. The receptionist at a medical clinic and the clerk in a shoe store are two examples. Winning the cooperation of these people can be helpful to you. You need their help now, and you may need it again in the future. Your manner can affect the kind of day that another person has. What you do and say can also affect whether you walk away feeling low or high. A considerate response creates less stress in both of you.

ple can lose their jobs. Bosses have many responsibilities, and they count on employees to show up on time, keep absences to a minimum, and do the work as scheduled. Bosses appreciate and reward those who work hard and have a positive attitude about their work. Making a boss's job easier instead of harder makes you a winner in his or her eyes.

SINCE technology affects working relationships,

HOW can people adjust?

The effect of technology on working relationships is interesting. In many instances communication and cooperation between people has been eliminated. People work with technology instead of each other. For example, a video lecture might replace a teacher for a while. A boss might dictate a letter into a machine rather than to a secretary. Computerized messages rather than personal ones may be received and sent by businesses via the telephone. All of this can make work relationships more technical than personal.

JOINING THE TEAM

- What other examples can you describe of how technology has replaced personal exchanges?
- What are the disadvantages of this situation? The advantages?
- Do you think some people are more receptive to this kind of technology than others are? Explain your answer.
- How can a person who is bothered by the impersonal side of technology adjust?

Elena, for example, had been waiting almost an hour to see the doctor. When she was finally called, she wanted to say, "It's about time! I don't have all day to sit here and wait." Then she saw the nurse's tired smile. Elena realized that while she had been waiting, the nurse had been working hard. "You must be really busy today," she said. The nurse smiled, relieved that someone understood. Elena left with a good feeling inside.

YOUR INFLUENCE

The only person you can control in your working relationships is you. Although you cannot control others, you can influence their response. You can take the initiative to improve a relationship at whatever stage it may currently be. Some people let pride get in the way of taking action. They want others to approach them first. A strong, secure person, however, is willing to reach out — and enjoy the results.

SECTION 1 REVIEW

1. What is a working relationship?
2. Describe four keys to good working relationships.
3. What is authority?
4. Compare pleasers and rebels.
5. Why is getting along in school important?
6. List three things an employee can do to please a boss.
7. List three suggestions for getting along with co-workers.

SECTION 2

GROUPS, LEADERS, AND FOLLOWERS

THINK AHEAD

About These Terms

bylaws
parliamentary
  procedure

leader
diplomacy

About These Objectives

After studying this section, you should be able to:

* Explain how groups function.
* Describe the roles of leaders and followers in a group.

ooner or later you will probably work with others in a group. You might join a school or community club that interests you. You might be part of a school committee or one in a religious organization. Even working with others on a class project is group work. What group experiences have you already had? How well did they go?

◆ ◆ ◆

GROUPS

Groups organize for many different reasons. People may have a common interest they want to share, or they may have a goal to accomplish. Group relationships can be very formal. They can also be quite casual. A group may be ongoing or end when its goals are achieved.

Often the work of a group, especially a formal one, begins in meetings. Committees may be established and assignments made. People usually have responsibilities to take care of between meetings.

Before a group can function well, rules may need to be established. These are called **bylaws**. A set of bylaws is written and accepted by the group as their guiding force.

Rules of another type are needed in most groups. These are rules of order that describe how a meeting should be run so that everything goes smoothly and all points of view are heard. Rules of order are called **parliamentary procedure**. *Robert's Rules of Order* is one book that gives a detailed description of parliamentary procedure.

Many groups form for a purpose. What groups do you belong to? Why did they form?

As groups carry out their goals, they work best when they follow a specific procedure. Goals are best accomplished within the framework of the management process that you learned in Chapter 9. This process leads the group from goal setting, to making and carrying out a plan, to evaluating the results. Groups make decisions democratically, that is, by vote. A strong group has members who accept the group decisions even when they go against their own wishes.

The work of a group is accomplished with greater ease when the group has structure. Someone acts as the leader, or manager. Sometimes this person is called the president. Other officers may be assigned or elected, including someone to act as the recorder, one who keeps written records of the meeting activity. No group would be complete without team members, or followers. The right combination of leaders and followers is what makes a group effective.

LEADERS

A **leader** is someone who guides or influences others. Leaders may emerge from a group rather than being appointed or elected. When this occurs, the leader is usually someone who is highly involved with the group. A high contributor tends to be seen by others as a leader. By working hard for a group, you may find yourself as one of its leaders.

Cory did not start out with the goal of being a leader on his basketball squad. He loved basketball and never missed a practice. He often stayed late to work on his shooting. Because of his devotion to the team and the game, he was selected team captain his senior year.

Leadership can be practiced at many different levels. Very high levels of leadership are exemplified by the president of your country and the leaders of huge corporations. The student body president and the principal are leaders in your school. Leadership, of course, can be seen in countless other ways. Even in a simple friendship between two people, one may take a leadership role, setting an example for the other and giving direction to their activities.

Leadership Skills

The specific combination of traits needed in a leader often depends on the situation. There are, however, general types of skills that are useful to leaders.

People listen to a leader whom they respect. What does a leader do to earn respect?

Technical Skill

The first type of skill useful to leaders is technical skill. A technical skill is knowledge or ability. For example, Phillip had to know how to use a cash register and balance the cash drawer when he was put in charge of the volunteers who worked at the museum gift shop.

Katrina became the head coach of a softball team of seven-year-old girls when the other coach quit. Because she had played softball for many years, she had the skills to teach her players how to throw and hit the ball and run the bases.

People Skills

Leaders must be able to work effectively with people. They need to know how to motivate others. That is, leaders must be able to make people *want* to do things. They must also be able to communicate with them and to resolve conflict when it occurs.

Nanette is the glue that holds her group of friends together. It is her ability to help everyone get along, to make everyone feel an important part of the group, and to solve problems that makes her the group's informal leader. Her skill at working with people makes her a natural leader in other situations as well.

Thinking and Planning Skills

Good leaders must be able to think and make plans. Dealing with ideas is an important part of leadership. Timothy, for example, is president of the computer club at school. He always has suggestions about programs for club meetings and projects the club can do. His skill at creating good ideas for club activities has led members to think he's the best president they've ever had.

Leadership Tasks

Leaders of groups have two major tasks. The first is to accomplish the work of the group. The second is to promote good relationships among group members. Both of these tasks are important for a group to function well. Sometimes, however, it is not easy to do both.

Accomplishing the Work

To get a group to accomplish its work means the leader must motivate members to achieve the group's goals. A leader must be prepared to plan, schedule, coordinate, solve problems, and provide resources.

Stuart was in charge of building the sets for the spring play at his school. After the designs were completed, he planned how he and the committee could accomplish the work in time. He prepared work schedules and called to remind people when to come to help. He made sure carpentry supplies and plenty of paint and brushes were available. When committee members

Leaders motivate others to get a job done. Often they pitch in and help, which can be motivating in itself.

without upsetting people. A diplomatic person, whether a leader or not, uses words in ways that don't offend. For example, saying something like, "We've only got one more day to get this done. What can I do to help you?" is much more diplomatic than saying, "Haven't you got that done yet?" Diplomatic people also learn to use qualifiers when they speak. In other words, they add phrases like "In my opinion," "To me," and "I think" to what they say. These lessen the judgmental sound of many statements. See for yourself. Which statement leaves some room for input from other people while still getting a point across: "Green isn't the right color for that backdrop" or "I don't think green is the right color for that backdrop"?

wanted to talk and eat rather than work, Stuart encouraged them to keep going. His job was to see that the sets got done by the deadline the play's director had set.

Promoting Good Group Relationships

The second task of a leader takes social skills. The leader needs to behave in ways that increase group member's self-esteem, personal worth, and group spirit. Building good group relationships makes people willing to put forth the effort to reach the group's goals. When people in a group do not get along or feel good about their participation, they are apt to leave the group.

At the same time that Stuart was pushing committee members to finish the sets on time, he had to make them feel important and essential to the effort. He praised their work and let them know how glad he was that they were helping. His appreciation and enthusiasm motivated the others to do their best.

A good leader cannot operate well without **diplomacy**, the ability to handle situations

Leadership Styles

Ways in which leaders use the skills they have to accomplish the tasks of leadership is called leadership style. There are three general styles of leadership: participatory, directive, and free rein.

With *participatory leadership*, the leader and group members work together to make plans and decisions about what the group will do. Under this type of leadership, group members tend to show interest in their work. Because they have input, they work whether the leader is there or not and are enthusiastic about the group. If followers are not responsible, this type of leadership style might not be effective.

A *directive leader* sets the group's goals and plans and controls all the activities of the group. Members in this type of group may be less motivated because of their lack of input. Directive leadership may be best in stressful times or in emergencies when people need to be told what to do. When a job needs to be done in a hurry, directive leadership tends to work best.

A leader using the *free-rein style* of leadership allows group members to work on their own in planning and organizing work.

The leader only participates when asked direct questions. Strong followers are needed in these groups. Free-rein leadership may be best when group members are trying to develop specific skills or when creative thinking is needed.

FOLLOWERS

Everyone — even a leader — is a follower at times. All groups have more followers than leaders. A leader in one group will probably be a follower in another. For example, the leader of the debate team may be a follower in the math club.

The success of a group depends as much or more on followers as it does on leaders. Without good followers, leaders accomplish little or nothing, or they have to do all the work themselves. Leading a group is time-consuming. When followers are willing workers, the leader can be more free to manage. The group will be more productive and more likely to survive as a group.

Many people prefer to be followers. That's okay. They can contribute to groups in their own way. To be successful, a group needs the participation of all members.

Some people join groups for social reasons only. When work needs doing, they flit around having fun but doing nothing.

These people are quickly recognized — and resented — by the rest of the group. When you join a group, plan to do your share of the work. When all work together, each person has less to do.

Another common problem for groups is those people who are quick to criticize the leaders although they would never accept a leadership role themselves. Some groups survive because volunteers are willing to lead them. Finding volunteers to spend time on leadership isn't easy. When you see people giving many hours without pay to an organization, appreciate what they do rather than criticize their efforts. If you want change, then volunteer your time and be part of the solution.

WHY WORK TOGETHER?

You've probably heard the saying, "Two heads are better than one." People work together for this reason. Like everyone else, you have special qualities, knowledge, and abilities to bring to a group. Pooling your personal resources with others means that you can accomplish more together than you could apart. Working together works.

Just as good leaders can earn the respect of others, good followers can, too. What qualities should a good follower have?

SECTION 2 REVIEW

1. Why do many groups have bylaws?
2. What is parliamentary procedure?
3. Define "leader."
4. Describe three types of leadership skills.
5. Identify the two major tasks of leaders.
6. What is diplomacy?
7. List three leadership styles.
8. Explain why followers are important in a group.

Chapter 15 Review

Chapter Summary

- To work well with others, a person needs a friendly attitude, respect for others, cooperation, and reciprocation.
- People with authority have the right to give orders, make decisions, and enforce rules.
- When faced with authority, some people try to do what the person in charge wants, while others tend to do the opposite. Perhaps the best course of action is to do some of each, depending on the situation.
- Appropriate behavior helps all students take advantage of the opportunities school has to offer.
- At work, good relationships with your boss and your co-workers can be just as important as good work skills.
- You can make your daily encounters with people more pleasant and rewarding by thinking about their feelings.
- Groups need order and structure in order to function well.
- Leaders guide or influence others. Technical skill, skill in working with people, and thinking and planning skills are very useful to leaders.
- Leaders choose a style of leadership in order to see that the work of the group is accomplished, while promoting good relationships among group members.
- The success of any group depends both on leaders and on followers.

Chapter Review

1. What is reciprocation?

2. Why do some people have authority over others?
3. Do all people respond to authority in the same way? Explain your answer.
4. Can a tendency toward rebelliousness be controlled? Explain your answer.
5. What can students do to get along well in school?
6. What two concerns do bosses have?
7. Why is getting along with co-workers important?
8. What are the benefits of making sure everyday encounters with others are pleasant?
9. How do groups make decisions?
10. List six qualities of a good leader.
11. What is meant by the term "motivate"?
12. Why might participatory leadership be more effective than the other two types?
13. Describe two types of problem followers in a group.

Critical Thinking

1. Discuss qualities that some people have that make them difficult to work with. What can be done to get along with people who have these qualities?
2. How should you react to people who misuse their authority?
3. Think of someone in authority whom you respect. How did that person earn your respect?
4. What do you think creates rebellion in some people?
5. How much of a role do you think popularity plays in leadership?

Chapter 15 Review

Activities

1. **Investigating a school rule.** Is there a rule in your school that you disagree with? Investigate the rule and write a report on your findings. Why was the rule put into force? Does it serve the purpose for which it was intended? What might happen if the rule were discontinued? How do others feel about the rule? Draw a conclusion. Should the rule stay in effect? Why or why not? (*Acquiring and evaluating information*)

2. **Skits on working relationships.** Working with a group, prepare short skits showing at least one good example of a working relationship and one bad example. (*Teamwork, creative thinking, communicating information*)

3. **Student groups.** Make a list of school and community groups that students join or could join. Discuss how each operates. (*Organizing information, communicating information*)

4. **Lessons from cartoons.** Collect cartoons that show working relationships. What lessons are learned through the humor? (*Acquiring and evaluating information*)

STRENGTHENING VALUES

Aim For Peace

Peace is a state of harmony. In peaceful settings people use their relationship skills to solve problems. They avoid verbal and physical attacks. By appreciating differences, peace comes more easily. Charlie promotes peace by:

- Telling what he would like his ecology club to do but also listening to other suggestions and going along with the group's decision.
- Following the rules that his parents have set at home.
- Letting minor complaints go at work.
- Helping two friends who are close to a fight settle their differences without violence.
- Getting to know people who are different from him, whether the difference is race, cultural background, or anything else.

Do you think some people dislike peace? Explain your answer. Some studies have pointed out that males tend to be more violent than females. Explain why you agree or disagree. What are the advantages of peace? How do you encourage peace in your relationships and community?

Relating to Older Adults

IMAGINE THAT ...

while heading home after an errand, you notice ahead an older woman walking and carrying two bags of groceries. In an instant a boy on a bicycle races past the woman, grabbing her purse from her shoulder and knocking her to the ground. You rush to help. The woman's groceries are scattered, but worse, you see the fear in her eyes. Thankfully, she is only bruised, so you help her get safely home. She doesn't stop shaking. As you leave, you realize that she feels much more than physical pain. She will no longer feel safe in her own neighborhood. The few dollars she lost was nothing compared to losing her sense of security and independence. She will never be the same. You wonder how someone can do that to another person.

THE AGING PROCESS

THINK AHEAD

About These Terms

ageism   *chronic diseases*
gerontology   *Alzheimer's*
disengagement   *disease*
osteoporosis

About These Objectives

After studying this section, you should be able to:

* Explain ageism.
* Explain two general theories on aging.
* Identify how older adults change physically, mentally, socially, and emotionally.

rowing older is a fact of life. In some societies, it is feared as the beginning of a decline in mental and physical abilities. In others, it is looked forward to eagerly as a time for reflection and for receiving respect from younger generations. Which of these attitudes do you see in society?

◆ ◆ ◆

ATTITUDES TOWARD AGING

All around you are signs that today's emphasis is on youth. Products that hide the gray, reduce wrinkles, and cover age spots all point to a preoccupation with staying young. Youth is desirable; old age is not.

Although progress is being made against this attitude, some people are still prejudiced against older adults. They feel that older people cannot be as alert, intelligent, and capable as younger people. This bias is called **ageism** (A-jiz-um). Like all prejudices, it is unfair. It views all people as alike, instead of as distinct, unique individuals. Ageism prevents older adults from living their lives to the fullest. It also denies others the opportunity to benefit from their talents and experience.

Beyond Stereotypes

In general, members of society are grouped by age. Most people spend the majority of their time with those in their age group. As a result, many young people have not had much contact with people over age sixty-five. Is this true for you?

If you don't know older adults very well, you might find it easy to believe many stereotypes about them. Most stereotypes about older adults are negative. For example, some people believe older people are sickly, forgetful, childish, and unable to adjust to new situations. Some stereotypes, on the other hand, are more positive. Warm and friendly, patient and wise are common ones. Older people may or may not have these qualities. Stereotypes never tell the whole story. Older adults are not all the same, just as teens are not all the same. You must look at individuals and understand what aging is all about in order to see the real people behind the myths.

THEORIES ON AGING

The aging process is a natural part of living. **Gerontology** (Jair-un-TAHL-uh-jee) is the study of the aging process. It has helped many people understand older adults and the problems and rewards of growing older.

Two general theories explain how the lives of older adults change as they age. These theories appear to contradict each other.

The first is the *activity* theory. This theory says, "Use it or lose it." In other words, active, involved people cope with aging

With people living to older ages, many find that they are adding happy, productive years to their lives.

Recognizing Stereotypes

Learning to recognize stereotypes helps you understand the difference between common beliefs and real facts.

ROBB *"After old Mr. Applegate moved into the Fraser house down the street, my friends and I knew after one look at him that he would be a grouch, and we were right. The first time he saw us skateboarding down his driveway, he started yelling out the window at us. No one likes him. He got mad at my friend Carl, who delivers the paper, too. The paper missed the porch a few times, and you think old Applegate could walk down three steps to pick it up? No way! Looks to me like he could use the exercise."*

MR. APPLEGATE *"Moving into the Fraser house hasn't been easy for me. I left my friends in the town where my wife and I lived. Living here I could be closer to my daughter, who can help me since my wife is gone now. I don't get around very well anymore because of my arthritis. I don't know people in the neighborhood, because I can't get out much. The kids in the neighborhood try to ride their skateboards on my driveway, but I can't have them getting hurt on my property. In my old neighborhood the kids used to come by and sit and talk to me. I miss that."*

CAN YOU RECOGNIZE STEREOTYPES?

When you recognize stereotypes, you are aware that a common belief about a group of people or things may not be true.

- Does Robb have a stereotypical idea about Mr. Applegate? What is it?
- Did Robb form his opinion *before* or *after* anything happened?
- Is Robb's opinion accurate? Explain.
- What can a person do to avoid believing stereotypical ideas?
- What could Robb and Mr. Applegate each do to improve the situation described above?

more easily than people who are less active. Physical, mental, and social skills remain strong when they are used often. Those who don't exercise soon can't. This theory suggests that older adults should stay as busy and active as possible.

The second theory is called *disengagement.* **Disengagement** means withdrawal from others and from activity. This theory states that in old age, it is normal and healthy for people to become more solitary and sedentary. Social activities and contacts are less frequent and important. Physical activity diminishes as the body ages. Older people often grow less concerned about others and focus more on themselves.

People who stay active and busy are more likely to cope well with the aging process.

Disengagement may seem like a logical progression for older people. Studies have shown, however, that disengaged people are less happy, healthy, and satisfied in almost every area of life than those who remain active and involved.

Given the broad age range of older adults — from sixty-five to ninety-five and older — it's possible that both theories are true. When people first retire, having outside interests and activities may be the healthiest, most fulfilling lifestyle. As they age and approach death, however, disengagement may be one way to prepare to leave family and friends.

Changes as People Age

Aging affects people in many ways. Changes occur physically, mentally, socially, and emotionally.

Physical Changes

The physical effects of aging are usually the most apparent ones. In general the body weakens and abilities decrease.

Physically, older adults become smaller, as the tissues connecting the bones flatten and compress. Because the body's cells die off and are not replaced as quickly as before, physical reactions and reflexes become slower. Many internal organs and systems work at a lower level. Muscles may become weaker, and bones may break more easily. The senses don't respond as they do in younger people. For example, some loss of hearing and vision usually occurs in older adults.

Some physical changes affect eating habits. A weakened sense of taste or smell can lead to a lack of interest in food. Because of this, some people do not eat enough. Others may try to improve taste by salting their food heavily, adding to problems of high blood pressure and heart disease. The loss of teeth can interfere with eating enjoyment. Older people often have small amounts of saliva, making chewing and swallowing difficult. Physical problems may make it hard for them to shop for and prepare nutritious foods.

Dietary needs change as people age. If people become less active, they need fewer calories than before. They may, however, need greater amounts of some nutrients. For example, a disease called **osteoporosis** (AHS-tee-oh-por-OH-sus) ("brittle bones") causes loss in bone mass. Bones become thin and weak and break easily. Osteoporosis affects many older adults, especially women. Increasing the amount of calcium in the diet can help prevent osteoporosis or make it less severe. (Calcium intake is important for young women in order to prevent this disease in later years.)

Chronic diseases, illnesses or conditions that occur repeatedly or never go away, are a fact of life for many older adults.

Examples are arthritis, rheumatism, high blood pressure, and heart conditions. These illnesses become more common as the body becomes less able to deal with the stress of disease.

Alzheimer's disease is another serious ailment associated with old age. The ability to reason, remember, and concentrate is gradually lost. In its severest form, it destroys the ability to use the mind. Researchers are learning more about its causes and treatment. So far, however, Alzheimer's has no cure.

Maintaining Physical Health

Some physical changes are unavoidable in older adults. Nevertheless, people can do a great deal to maintain their physical abilities. Exercise plays a part. If properly done, exercise is as beneficial and no more dangerous to older adults than to younger people. Good nutrition is also important. Many physical problems are made worse by poor eating habits. Finally, attitude can be a major factor in determining physical ability. Older people who realize that aging is not a disease and that sickness is not inevitable are more likely to work at maintaining their health.

Mental Changes

Some changes that older adults experience have to do with the mind. As the body slows, the mind often does, too.

Older adults sometimes have difficulty with memory. There are three parts to memory — receiving information into the brain, storing it in the short-term memory, and storing it in the long-term memory. To remember and use information, all three must function well and in an organized way. In younger people, the interaction among these three parts is fast and easy. In older adults, all three parts of memory usu-

ally still function, but moving information between them becomes more difficult. This is why older adults may have trouble calling up information quickly.

Problem solving can also be slower in older adults. To solve problems, people must remember, organize, and use facts. Older adults may have trouble concentrating on more than one thing at a time, which can interfere with problem-solving ability.

What older adults lose in speed, however, they often make up for in thoroughness. Their skills in logic and understanding are often improved. Brain cells are stimulated by use. Older adults who are students may have to work longer and harder to learn new material than they did when they were younger, yet they tend to learn it more thoroughly.

Thoroughness was an asset for seventy-three-year-old George Wysocki. Although he had retired from his job as an assembly line supervisor, he was often consulted when problems arose on the line or when a new method was needed to improve pro-

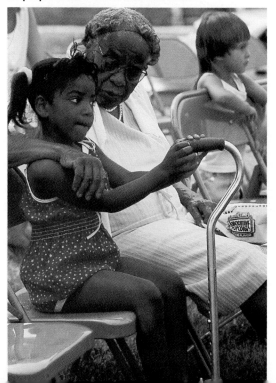

As people grow older, physical problems are more likely to occur. Some diseases affect mobility, making it difficult for people to take care of their own needs.

ductivity. It took George a while to understand all the aspects of the problem. Once he did, however, his experience on the line and his long-practiced reasoning ability enabled him to offer valuable suggestions. George enjoyed the mental challenge and the chance to be useful.

The loss of mental abilities is not a necessary part of aging. The greatest declines in thinking ability are probably due to outside factors. Depression, grief, poor health, poverty, and a lack of trying can all interfere with the ability to think clearly.

Staying Mentally Healthy

Mental stimulation is necessary to keep older adults thinking effectively. Their activities should require active, not passive, participation. Some older people join clubs or become politically active. Others take part-time jobs, continue their education, or serve as volunteers. Many community groups and activities offer discount rates to older adults to encourage their participation.

Social Changes

Older adults may see differences in their social roles and relationships. As some roles become less important, they often develop new ones.

The greatest role change for older adults is brought about by retirement, when the work role is let go. This loss can be particularly difficult if a person's sense of worth and self-esteem has been tied to work. Men especially can have a hard time adjusting.

When Marva's husband retired, it was almost as trying for her as for him. Clarence had been a food-processing plant manager for almost 30 years. Now he wanted to "manage" the household, which Marva considered her job. This caused resentment for Marva and frustration for Clarence. Then Clarence heard about a program to help young business owners by matching them with retired business managers. Participating in the program allowed Clarence to share his knowledge and experience with someone who could appreciate his help.

Older adults may also see changes in their gender roles. As people age, the differences between their roles as women and men lessen. The roles often blend, with each gender taking on qualities usually associated with the opposite gender. A woman who has always let her husband make decisions for the family may become more assertive. A man whose work kept him from spending as much time with his children as he would have liked, may now take an active part in caring for his grandchildren.

Friendships often become more important as people age. Older adults tend to have more friends than any other age group except teens and those in their twenties. One of the pleasures of being older is having more time for friends. Also, as other family members die and grown children move away, friendships can become especially rewarding and necessary.

Older adults often find mental stimulation in being around children. The benefits are mutual, as children have much to gain from spending time with older people.

Neugarten and Grandparenting

One of the first social scientists to study aging was Dr. Bernice L. Neugarten. She was a pioneer in research on the aging process and the psychological aspects of aging. Through her study of grandparenting, Neugarten identified five different grandparenting styles:

- *Formal Grandparent.* This style of grandparenting is the indulgent, gift-giving grandparent. The grandparent gives pleasure by doing things for the grandchildren. The grandparent is not interested in being a substitute parent. Formal grandparents are rarely concerned with discipline of grandchildren.
- *Fun-Seeking Grandparent.* The grandparent-grandchild relationship is based on having fun together. This type of grandparent acts like a playmate. Grandparents and children gain mutual satisfaction and pleasure from their shared activities. Older adults who find great meaning in life through children are most apt to be grandparents of this type.

- *Substitute-Parent Grandparent.* This type of grandparent cares for grandchildren and takes a parenting role. This role is almost always taken by a grandmother. The situation is most apt to occur if the grandmother cares for the children while parents work.
- *Wise Grandparent.* The grandparent in this style possesses special skills, resources, or authority. This type of grandparent often has control over children as well as grandchildren. The wise grandparent is most often a grandfather.
- *Distant Grandparent.* The grandparents in this style are distant and remote from grandchildren. They do not participate in the grandchildren's lives in any meaningful way.

The role of grandparent has become more important in today's world because more people live long enough to become grandparents. Four-generation families are now fairly common. Over half of all older adults have great-grandchildren.

Grandparents can play a major role in their grandchildren's lives. They can provide stability and help children feel safe, especially if divorce or other problems have upset the children's lives. Involved grandparents can give their grandchildren a sense of family roots. Most grandparents find pleasure, satisfaction, and comfort in the grandparent role.

Staying Socially Healthy

In general, older adults who are able to, keep the same types of social lives and interests that they did when they were younger. Active, outgoing people tend to remain that way throughout their lives. People who have lived quiet, less social lives continue in their patterns as well.

Many programs are available for older citizens. Centers and clubs for senior citizens offer companionships and sharing of all sorts of interests, everything from cards to dancing. Transportation can be a problem, one that younger friends and special busses for older people can help solve.

Emotional Changes

As they age, some people feel that life no longer has meaning for them. They may believe that no one needs or respects them. Sometimes this occurs in retirement due to the loss of the work role. Older adults may become depressed or discouraged about living. This can be a response to the death of a spouse or friends, or to increasing health problems. Childless men whose wives have died are most likely to lack the will to live. This feeling of despair also worsens the effects of other physical conditions and diseases.

When Lurleen's husband of 42 years died, she thought she would, too. Social activities seemed too frightening or painful without him to share them with. Finally, her daughter persuaded her to see a counselor. With help, Lurleen came to see that she still had much to live for. She found the courage to stand on her own and take control of her life again.

Staying Emotionally Healthy

Living in a way they find satisfying is important to older adults. Satisfaction with life appears to slow down the aging process. Older adults need to balance activity and involvement with the tendency toward disengagement.

An active interest in life helps older people; however, they also need opportunities to talk about the past. By reminiscing, they sort through their experiences and make sense of their lives.

Contact with friends and family members is one of the best ways to maintain emotional health. Younger people can encourage conversation, visit, and show appreciation for the wisdom and experience that older people have.

SECTION 1 REVIEW

1. What is ageism?
2. What is gerontology?
3. Describe two general theories about how the lives of older adults change as they age.
4. In what ways do older adults change physically?
5. In what way do many older adults improve mentally?
6. How can older adults maintain social health?
7. What causes some of the emotional changes that older adults experience?

SECTION 2

ISSUES AND CHALLENGES

THINK AHEAD

About These Terms
fixed income
sandwich generation
elder abuse

About These Objectives
After studying this section, you should be able to:
* Summarize the main concerns of older adults.
* Compare the housing options available to older adults.
* Recommend ways teens can relate better to older adults.

eople are in this world together. What affects one generation soon has impact on others. Every community can benefit by shared concerns for the problems that all people have, including those of older adults.

◆ ◆ ◆

Concerns of Older Adults

Have you ever thought seriously about what problems face the older people you know? If you do, you might think of ways to help someone who needs you. Even simple acts can make a difference in the lives of older citizens.

Financial Concerns

Many older adults commonly face financial difficulties. They may live on a **fixed income**. That is, they rely on monthly payments, such as Social Security or a pension, that do not change even when expenses increase. These payments may not provide a comfortable lifestyle. They are usually only a fraction of what a working person earns. People without an additional income or savings often have a hard time making ends meet.

Estimates say that about one-fourth of all older adults live in poverty. They do not have enough income to meet their basic needs. Women, members of minority groups, and those over age eighty-five are most likely to be poor.

Fears about the future can contribute to the problem. Since no one can predict when death will occur, some older adults live more frugally than necessary to save money for later years. They may endanger their health by skimping on such needs as food and heating. Lack of money can also be a major obstacle for older adults in receiving good health care.

Medical Care

Because of the aging process and chronic illnesses, many older adults need more medical care, which can be very expensive.

Coming at a time when income is apt to be decreased adds to the difficulties. Although government programs such as Medicare help pay the costs, many older adults do not have the funds for adequate health care.

Over-medication is another problem. Because of body changes, older adults may not be able to handle the same doses of medicine as they did when they were younger. Also, having several health problems can mean that different doctors are prescribing medicines. One study found that the average older patient takes 13 different kinds of medicine a year. Some drugs are dangerous when mixed. Older adults may have trouble remembering which medicine to take and the right dose. These hazards make it especially important that doctors be informed about all medications an older person is taking and any negative effects that resulted.

Living Arrangements

Most older adults want to remain independent as long as possible. Often they measure their self-worth by how well they can care for themselves. They may be able to spend many years in independent living, as long as the residence is safe and convenient.

The National Safety Council reports that preventable injuries are the sixth leading cause of death among people aged sixty-five and older, and many of these occur in the home. Steps can be taken to make housing safer for older people, especially those with disabilities. Some of the changes are simple, such as rearranging furniture to create clear and easy traffic patterns, or applying skid-resistant strips to bathtubs and the backs of rugs. Other changes require more effort. Railings may need to be installed on staircases and in bathrooms. Kitchens may need to be remodeled to allow people with wheelchairs and walkers to use sinks, cabinets, and large appliances. The height of cabinets and storage spaces may need to be lowered. What other changes can you think of?

Older people often have to change their living arrangements when their partner dies or when failing health prevents them from managing alone. The options open to them will depend on their resources, on their family, and on their needs.

Shared Housing

An increasing number of older people are renting out rooms in their homes to other people. This arrangement enables them to stay on in their own homes. Often, the renter is another retired person. A variation on shared housing is congregate housing—an arrangement whereby a group of people live in the same building and share meals and some living space while having their own room for privacy.

Shared and congregate housing have many advantages for older people. These arrangements are generally less expensive than living alone or in a retirement community. They also provide companionship and security while allowing a level of independence.

Moving in with Family

In many cases, older parents who can no longer manage on their own move in with the adult child's family. This arrangement calls for adjustments on all sides. The parent has to adapt to being dependent on the adult child. The adult child has to adapt to being responsible for the parent. All concerned in this arrangement experience a loss of freedom.

Generally, taking care of the older adult falls to the woman of the household. Many middle–aged people today are referred to as the **"sandwich generation."** These people have responsibilities related to the generations on each side of their own age group. They are raising children and, at the same time, fulfilling the role of caregiver for their aging parents, which can be difficult.

On the other hand, benefits are possible when an older adult joins the family. The older adult may be able to help out in the house and to contribute financially. Children and grandchildren have a chance to get to know the older person better. With a positive, loving attitude, relationships can deepen and grow.

Retirement Communities

Retirement communities consist of groups of housing units designed to meet the needs of older residents. The housing units are often arranged around a communal building where residents can meet for meals and social activities. Many retirement communities provide maintenance services and transportation to nearby health facilities and shopping centers.

Costs of retirement communities range from very expensive to modestly priced. Some communities offer subsidized rents for low–income residents.

A variation on the retirement community is the Continuing Care Retirement Community, or CCRC. CCRCs provide medical care as well as living accommodation. People who move into a CCRC generally live in independent units for as long as they are able to. When they begin to need nursing care they move into a nursing facility, often on the same premises.

Nursing Homes

Sometimes the only option for a frail elderly person who needs skilled nursing is a nursing home. The percentage of older people living in nursing homes is small but rising. This increase is a result of several factors including the longer life span of women, an increase in the number of older adults who have no one to care for them, and an increase in the number of older people who have chronic illnesses.

Nursing homes are an expensive option for families who need care for an aging person. All the services the home provides add to the cost of operation.

Nursing homes vary greatly. Some resemble dormitories, with residents sharing small rooms and eating, toilet, and entertainment facilities. Others offer residents, especially married couples, small cottages more similar to private homes. Some are designed for people needing a great deal of care and supervision. Others are small communities of basically self-reliant people. Still others may offer more than one type of service. The cost of living in a nursing home, regardless of services, can be very high.

The decision to place a family member in a nursing home is not an easy one for most families. The older adult may not wish to move. Family members may feel they aren't carrying out their responsibility. At some point, however, many families simply can't give the older adult the care that is needed. In these cases, a nursing home may be the answer.

Choosing a Nursing Home

Selecting the right nursing home for an older adult is not usually an easy task. Following are some suggestions and considerations that can help if you ever participate in making such a decision:

- Discuss possible homes with the older adult's primary care physician. Ask for recommendations.
- Talk to people who have relatives or friends living in specific homes.
- Consider location. The home you choose should be near enough to allow family and friends to visit.
- Meet with members of the administrative staff. What does their home have to offer? Ask questions. Find out costs and services provided.
- Is the building well-maintained? Are rooms clean and attractive? Are halls and other common areas clean and as odor-free as possible?
- Make a special check of the kitchen and eating areas. Are they clean and are sanitary practices followed as food is prepared and served? Are meals well planned? What arrangements are made for residents who have difficulty feeding themselves?
- Do residents appear to be clean and well cared for? Are they generally content with their circumstances?
- How do members of the staff treat the residents? Are they courteous, respectful, and kind?
- Are exercise and rehabilitation facilities available and professionally staffed?
- What recreational facilities are available? Is there a planned program of activities?
- Does your family member have special needs? Make certain that these can be adequately accommodated.

Elder Abuse

A growing concern in society today is the issue of **elder abuse**. Most often this is physical abuse directed at aging people by their adult children.

Caring for an aging parent — especially one who is ill — can be stressful. The stress has been known to trigger violent reactions in some people. Those who take care of older relatives need a network of people to help. All family members should share in the care, if at all possible. Community organizations that specifically address the needs of the elderly are another resource. Anyone who observes this type of abuse going on needs to take action to bring it to an end.

Crime

According to U.S. Justice Department statistics, people aged sixty-five and older are less likely than younger people to be victimized by crime. The effects of crime, however, can be far more destructive to their quality of life.

Crime is a major concern among older adults. That fear grows when someone they know becomes a victim of a crime. They may refuse to leave their homes. Some may move to a different neighborhood where they may feel more secure. Actually, being unfamiliar with their surroundings makes them less safe.

When older adults are victims of crime, they may feel the loss more sharply than other people. For a person on a fixed income, the theft of $50 is much more serious than it is to a working person. If a tele-vision set is stolen, a housebound older adult may lose his or her only link to the outside community. A physical injury received during a crime can sometimes be life-threatening. An older person's body does not heal itself as quickly as before.

RESOLVING THE ISSUES

The issues discussed here and many others facing older adults are in the process of resolution. As the older population increases, it is making its voice heard in government. Lawmakers are working to solve the problems of older adults. The issues are complicated, however, and the answers are not easy.

As with many problems in society, not all answers lie in government. Individuals need to take responsibility for each other. Even teens like you can take action that will improve the situation of the older people around you. Perhaps someday someone will do the same for you.

Elderly adults are often vulnerable. They need safe surroundings and support from caring people to live securely.

Teens and Older Adults

You may wonder why you should be concerned with the lives of older adults. After all, like other teens, you have your own challenges and problems. The bottom line is that people need each other. They have much to give and to gain from one another. Sharing enriches, and eases, the lives of all.

Older adults' age and experience give them a unique perspective on life. When older people talk about the past, teens can see how the world has changed and what caused these changes. They can decide whether it was for the better or the worse, and what they can do about it. By listening to older adults talk about the challenges they have faced, teens can find new ways of looking at their own situations and solving their own problems. Finally, teens can learn from the example of older people's lives that very few problems last forever and that life is a series of ups and downs. They can gain a different perspective on what is happening to them and feel good about themselves.

"As we grow old, the beauty steals inward."

◆

RALPH WALDO EMERSON

The Rites of Spring

FAMILIES

AROUND

THE

WORLD

In the northern part of what used to be called the Soviet Union, bears, wolves, and lynx still prowl. There, winter comes early and stays late. Farmers in the region, anxious to get their crops in the ground, still have celebrations designed to hurry winter on its way.

Most of these celebrations, which take place between New Year's Day and the month of March, date back thousands of years. The custom of holding the celebrations has remained intact despite government efforts to end it, because the older people in the communities have kept the celebrations alive.

In one community, older women work together with younger ones making costumes from fur and horns, paper and thread. These costumes are worn by many who take part in the celebration, especially the young men who race belled and ribboned sleighs between villages.

In the village squares, poles topped with disks encourage the sun to come farther north. Bonfires show the sun the path it should follow. Women cook lots of round pancakes to represent the sun. Music, laughter, and entertainment continue all day long in the squares.

The moment everyone enjoys the most, however, comes at sunset when the Snow Queen, the image of winter, is burned. The Snow Queen is a large, painted figure made from straw and paper. It is carried to the river where a huge bonfire is lit. The fire represents the rays of the sun that will melt winter away. With long poles, villagers lift the large doll onto the flames. Later, the ashes are dumped into the river, which will soon flow swiftly with the spring thaw. Winter is officially over.

Older people can also benefit from knowing you. Teens can provide a variety of services that some older adults can no longer perform for themselves. For example, teens can drive them to appointments, run errands, or mow the lawn. Probably the most important thing that teens can provide, however, is companionship. This is especially appreciated when older adults have lost friends through death or moving.

Young people can help older ones stay alert, active and in touch with the community. Regular visits can also give older adults a sense of security. They know they can count on someone in an emergency, especially if they are unable to use the telephone.

Teens can be an important resource for older adults. In return teens have much to gain from providing help and companionship.

Where Do You Start?

Teens have many opportunities to get involved in the lives of older adults. If you have older family members living with you or near you, spend time with them. Perhaps an older adult in your neighborhood would appreciate your help and companionship. You could also contact a local or regional Agency on Aging to see what needs exist in your community or inquire at a nursing home about volunteering.

Relating to Older Adults

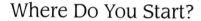

Some teens may find it difficult to relate to older adults. They may be affected by stereotypes about older people or uncomfortable around people with disabilities. The more time you spend with older adults, however, the easier it will be to relate. If you are unsure how to act around older adults, ask yourself how you would like to be treated if you were in that situation. You will soon discover that what older adults need as people is not that much different from what you need, too.

SECTION 2 REVIEW

1. Why is a fixed income often a problem for older adults?
2. Explain how over-medication can be a problem for older adults.
3. Describe possible disadvantages and advantages related to having an older family member move in with family.
4. What is elder abuse?
5. Why is crime directed at older citizens often more destructive than it is for younger ones?

Chapter 16 Review

Chapter Summary

- Because most people associate mainly with people about their own age, young people may not have much contact with older adults.
- One theory of aging suggests that people who remain or become active cope better with old age. Another theory, disengagement, suggests a withdrawal from others and from activity is a normal response.
- Aging affects people physically, mentally, socially, and emotionally.
- The physical effects of aging generally involve a weakening or lessening of ability.
- Older adults may have problems with their memory and with problem solving, but their thinking is usually more thorough.
- Older adults often live on a low income that makes meeting health and medical needs difficult.
- Many older people can live independently. Modifications may be needed, however, to make their homes safe and convenient.
- Housing options for older people include shared housing, moving in with grown children, and retirement communities. Nursing home care is sometimes needed.
- Elder abuse and crime are two serious problems faced by older adults.
- Older adults can help teens gain a different perspective on life. Teens can help older adults by providing help and companionship.
- Opportunities for teens to become involved in the lives of older adults may exist within their own families or neighborhoods.

Chapter Review

1. How would you describe society's attitude toward aging?
2. How can belief in stereotypes about older adults be avoided?
3. In what way are the two theories about aging contradictory?
4. List three physical changes that occur in older adults.
5. Explain what a chronic disease is and give three examples.
6. How does age affect thinking ability?
7. How can older adults stay mentally healthy?
8. Socially, what is the greatest role change for most older adults?
9. Why is depression a problem for some older adults?
10. What are some of the problems brought about by low income for older adults?
11. What are four modifications that can be made to make a home safer and more convenient for older adults?
12. What is the "sandwich generation"?
13. Why is the decision to place a family member in a nursing home difficult?
14. Why does theft often have a greater impact on older citizens than it does on younger ones?

Critical Thinking

1. Discuss what is meant by the statement, "Age is a state of mind."
2. When an older person moves in with the family, what can all family members do to promote adjustment to the change?

3. How do you think disengagement might affect the conversation of an elderly adult? Do you think understanding the principle of disengagement could make a younger person more patient when conversing with older people? Explain your answer.
4. Why do you think advertisers who are selling clothes for mature people often show the clothes on models who are in their thirties? What is the effect on the public?

Activities

1. **Older adults' accomplishments.** Collect newspaper and magazine articles about accomplishments of older adults and arrange them in a bulletin board display. (*Acquiring and evaluating information, communicating information*)
2. **Services for older adults.** Find out what programs and services are available to older adults in your community. You may wish to compile a list that can be duplicated and shared with older adults who may not be familiar with all of them. (*Acquiring and evaluating information, communicating information*)
3. **Overburdened.** Working with a group of classmates, try to solve this problem: Edna's elderly mother still lives in her own home, but she is increasingly less able to care for herself. Edna handles all the care for her mother, which is becoming a heavy responsibility. Edna has one brother and a sister, both living in other cities. They do little to help, and Edna feels that she is overburdened. (*Teamwork, problem solving*)

STRENGTHENING VALUES

Aim For Understanding

Understanding means seeing things from another person's point of view. Your feelings about others improve if you put yourself in their position and ask yourself how you would feel. Soo Kim shows understanding by:

- Phoning her grandfather regularly to see how he is doing.
- Listening sympathetically when her elderly aunt talks about some physical problems that are bothering her.
- Offering some advice to a friend who is having family problems.
- Taking her younger brother to a dental appointment when her mother is ill.

In what ways does Soo Kim put the needs of others before her own? What rewards can come to a person who is understanding? Why might a lack of understanding lead to conflict? Describe a situation in which you showed an ability to be understanding.

You and Your Friends

IMAGINE THAT ...

you have just received a package from the mail-order house. You have been eagerly waiting for it to arrive. Because of high demand, you had to wait several weeks until the backorders could be filled. Finally, it's here — your new friendship kit. It contains everything a person needs in order to make friends. At least, that's what it said in the catalog. The description, however, wasn't very complete. You don't really know what the package contains, although you are eager to find out. The contents just may change your life. You begin to tear the paper from the package.

FRIENDS IN YOUR LIFE

THINK AHEAD

About These Terms
reciprocity   *gossip*

About These Objectives
After studying this section, you should be able to:
* Explain what people gain from friendships.
* Describe the different kinds of friendships people can have.
* Suggest ways to make and keep friends.

side from family, what are the most important relationships you have? Most people will answer by saying, "friends." For this reason, it makes good sense to learn what it takes to develop and look after these relationships.

♦ ♦ ♦

WHAT FRIENDSHIP PROVIDES

If you were asked to explain why you are friends with a certain person, you might say, "We both like the outdoors," or "I can be myself with him," or "When I have a problem, she always helps me find an answer." These are all specific examples of what friendship provides people.

In a more general way, people gain three important things from friendships:

♦ *Emotional support.* Friends provide comfort, reassurance, acceptance, understanding, and many other emotional needs.

♦ *Models for imitation.* Friends teach useful social and physical skills. They learn from each other.

♦ *Opportunities to practice roles.* Friends may try out different roles with each other. The teen years are a time for new experiences and growth. Friends provide an audience and feedback as you work to establish your identity and separate from your parents.

ALL KINDS OF FRIENDS

When teens think of friends, they usually think first of people who are much like themselves. It feels comfortable to be around people who share your interests and outlooks. Satisfying friendships, however, can be had with all types of people.

"*Friendship is a single soul dwelling in two bodies.*"

♦

ARISTOTLE

Emotional support comes with friendship, as people spend pleasurable time together.

Friendships with Children

Friendships with children can be beneficial to children as well as to you. Many families today are very busy, especially when all the adults in a family are employed. Children often care for themselves at a very young age. As a result, many children need attention, help, and sometimes just companionship. You may know children in your neighborhood, or even your family, who fit this description. They need your friendship.

Young children tend to look up to teens. Because they are eager to grow older, they want to know about teen interests and activities and they try to join in. They even try to imitate teens. You can listen to children and you can teach them. Their lives will be richer because of your efforts.

What can you gain from showing friendship to children? For one thing, you learn responsibility. When you take care of someone else, you learn to understand their needs and meet them. The knowledge you gain about children may be helpful if you decide to become a parent someday. Because children admire teens, your contact with children can feel good. Setting a good example for children helps you do

Maori Family Ties

Friendships help provide people with what they need, but in most cultures families are the first providers. Belonging to a kinship group among the Maoris, the native people of New Zealand, means having very strong obligations to other family members. No matter how distant the kinship, Maoris can depend on their relatives.

Maoris like to keep in touch with their kin. They drop in whenever they can and have the right to expect a meal and a bed. In fact, when they travel, Maoris almost always stay with relatives rather than friends. They may stay for a few days or weeks.

Maoris are also raised to share freely with their kin. They give away possessions, lend money or belongings, and help with any kind of work

that must be done. They help with all kinds of family events. Weddings and coming-of-age parties may cost non-Maoris a lot of money. Maoris, however, get food, labor, and money for the events from their families.

Maoris believe they should be loyal to each other, no matter what. This has caused problems with Maori police officers who are unwilling to arrest kinfolk.

Most Maoris who get help from kinspeople are very willing to repay the debt. In modern times,

however, families are spread out. Not everyone knows his or her kinspeople well. As a result, some Maoris abuse their kinship rights. They drop in on family members they know only slightly and stay for extended periods of time. These people usually have no intention of repaying the obligation.

In spite of the fact that some people abuse family ties, however, most Maoris feel that to be abandoned or rejected by their kin would be a calamity.

what is right while providing a model for their behavior. Your self-esteem, and the child's, too, can build.

Most people have many opportunities to interact with children. You may have younger brothers and sisters or nieces and nephews. Perhaps there are children in your neighborhood. Many schools offer volunteer positions, such as tutors and playground monitors. Park districts and other civic groups also look for volunteers

for their children's programs. Your time commitment can be as large as you like.

Friendships with Adults

As you learned in the last chapter, friendships with older adults can also be rewarding. Older adults can help teens put their difficulties into perspective, and teens can give them much appreciated companionship.

TEAMING UP WITH TECHNOLOGY

SINCE

friends enjoy spending time together,

HOW

can they use technology as entertainment?

When you and a friend go bowling or see a movie, you take advantage of technology. These are two of the more common ways that technology can provide entertainment, but there are others. Computers have tremendous potential. In addition to playing games, some people use computers to communicate with others in many locations. A modem is a device used to hook the computer to tele-phone lines that allow linkage with computers all over the world. You may not be able to see a computer friend, but you can share ideas and interests with this type of technology.

JOINING THE TEAM

- Not everyone has a computer at home. If you wanted to learn more about computers and to use one, what could you do?
- What other kinds of technological entertainment can you name?
- Is entertainment related to technology always expensive? Explain your answer.
- How do you use technology for entertainment?

Older adults can also offer teens the benefit of their experience as well as personal friendship. For example, when Lori was a young child, Bernice, then a teenager, occasionally baby-sat with her. Now Lori is a teenager and she and Bernice are still friends. Bernice understands when Lori is excited or upset about something. She went through many of the same things herself a few years ago. She can often give Lori good advice about problems.

Friendship and Gender

Friendships between females tend to be different from those between males. Females like to share personal concerns and emotional and intimate feelings. Males tend to share interests and activities.

You may have friends of both genders. Besides the usual benefits of friendship, a friend of the opposite gender can often help you see issues from that gender's point of view.

Other Backgrounds

Getting to know people of all races, nationalities, and economic levels can help you grow as a person. Why would this be true? The more people you spend time with, the more opportunities you have to learn. People who are different from you can bring insights and information that you might not normally encounter. Many benefits are possible. You will understand all people better. You will be more aware of how people think and why. You will be a

Handling Rejection

One obstacle in forming any relationship is the fear of rejection. People see rejection as failure. This is especially true for teens, whose self-esteem is often closely tied to acceptance from peers. Like peer pressure, rejection is something teens must come to terms with. It is only as hurtful as you let it be.

To handle rejection, first look for opportunities to grow. Examine why you were rejected. If you need to change something about yourself, work for improvement. Don't be too hard on yourself. Sometimes rejection occurs for superficial reasons. When no significant reason exists for the rejection, put the experience aside and move on.

Above all, keep your spirits up. Think of the athlete who didn't make the high school team but went on to have an outstanding career in college and the pros. Think of the outstanding employee who went through many applications and interviews to get the job. Those who don't let rejection get them down can come out winners.

MAKING FRIENDS

Making friends is not easy for everyone. Shyness, low self-esteem, and lack of experience can make it difficult for some people to make the first move in becoming friends, but these can be overcome. To make friends, you must first realize that you are worthy of being a friend. You have qualities and abilities that people will appreciate and benefit from.

Like others, you may fear rejection when taking the first step, but you have to realize that nothing is lost by trying. You may have to stop worrying about what others will think. Just try, and keep trying until you discover what works for you.

What To Do

You can do things that will help you make friends. You can also develop qualities that make a difference.

Try:
- Smiling.
- Speaking first.
- Introducing yourself to people you don't know.
- Asking simple questions to start a conversation.
- Giving sincere compliments.
- Focusing on others instead of yourself.

Be:
- Friendly and cheerful.
- Courteous.
- Clean, neat, and well-groomed.

Show that you are:
- Interested in other people.
- A good listener.
- Easy to get along with.

Show that you have:
- A good sense of humor.

What other items can you add to this list?

more interesting person yourself because of your knowledge of others and your broader perspective.

In a world that is filled with so many diverse people, it pays to be receptive to all. Your ability to adapt to different kinds of people will come in handy as you work with others in school, on the job, and in the community. Society can benefit from each person's effort to reach out to others in friendship. Fewer problems occur in communities and neighborhoods when people like each other. Where there is more understanding, there is more liking.

Where to Look

Sometimes making friends is simply a matter of knowing where to look. The possibilities for friendship are extensive.

The worst thing you can do is isolate yourself. You need to be around people in order to make friends. Go where people are, whether it's a part-time job, a community center, a school function, or a community event. Join a team. Become a volunteer. Develop a new interest and join with others who share it.

Then give it time. Friendships don't normally develop immediately. A smile today may become "hello" tomorrow and light conversation the next day. That's enough to get anyone started toward friendship.

KEEPING FRIENDS

Often, friendships are easier to build than to maintain. In fact, the oldest and strongest friendships sometimes require the most work. This is because friends may begin to take each other for granted. Within the security of the relationship, they may become less kind and considerate.

Friendships are kept strong on a daily basis through small gestures. Loaning a book, helping clean a room, giving a small gift for no special reason — all these are acts that friends do for each other because they *want* to, not because they *have* to. Friendship is not all giving, however. For a friendship to remain strong, each friend must benefit from the relationship as well. An important quality of friendship is reciprocity. **Reciprocity** (reh-sih-PROSS-ih-tee) means mutual exchange. Each friend gives to and takes from the relationship. Benefits most people enjoy include spending time and doing things together and being praised, appreciated, and listened to.

Keeping Friendships Strong

Friendship is like a delicate plant. It needs attention and care to keep it growing. Here are some tips for making a friendship thrive:

- Accept your friends for what they are. Don't try to nag them into becoming something they don't want to be.
- Encourage your friends in their goals, and praise them when they accomplish them.
- Apologize when you hurt your friends, and forgive them when they hurt you.
- Be loyal to your friends. This means keeping secrets and not spreading **gossip**. Gossip is conversation that often includes rumors about people. Because gossip is often distorted and even untrue, it can be damaging to others.
- Work through problems together. Use the communication and conflict-resolution skills you have learned.
- Be reliable. Make sure your friends can count on you to do what you say you will do. Keep your promises.
- Be willing to share your friends with others. People grow through interaction with others.

Friendships thrive when people spend time together. Sometimes simple activities turn out to be the best.

Friends are there for each other in bad times as well as good. When one friend experiences problems or undergoes a crisis, the other is ready with support.

Being friends does not mean that you must always agree with each other. Honesty is important in a friendship. Good friends respect each other as individuals and are able to accept differences of opinion and outlook without allowing them to threaten the relationship.

Lasting friendships are a treasure. Occasionally they continue for a lifetime. When both sides are willing to make the effort, a friendship can survive the challenges that come along.

SECTION 1 REVIEW

1. List three things that friendships provide.
2. How can you benefit from having friendships with children?
3. Why is it a good idea to make friends with people who have different backgrounds from yours?
4. List five suggestions for making friends.
5. What does reciprocity mean as related to friendship?

SECTION 2

CHALLENGES OF FRIENDSHIP

THINK AHEAD

About These Terms
peer pressure   *cliques*

About These Objectives
After studying this section, you should be able to:
- Recommend ways of dealing with peer pressure.
- Suggest strategies for coping with competition and loneliness.
- Evaluate ways to deal with troubled friendships.

aving friendships would be easy if nothing ever got in the way. Unfortunately, that's not real life. Friendships are challenged every day. People who are equipped to meet the challenges can keep their friendships strong.

◆ ◆ ◆

PROBLEMS IN FRIENDSHIP

Handling friendships is not easy at any age, but during the teen years, the challenge can be greater. Teens have so many of their own personal concerns to deal with that trying to include the concerns of others can be difficult. Because the teen years are a time of change, what teens want from a friendship may change. The teen years are as much a testing ground for friendships as they are for the skills needed for the future.

Friendships are important to teens because they help bridge the gap to independence. Building relationships with others means a little less reliance on family, a little more ability to handle what comes along. Handling friendships is a learning experience, with many issues and problems to be approached and conquered.

Peer Pressure

One of the most challenging situations teens can face is peer pressure. How strong are you? Can you turn your back to your friends when you know they are in the wrong? It isn't easy, is it?

Peer pressure is an attempt to influence someone in a similar age group. You experience peer pressure when your friends want you to join in their activities, actions, or beliefs.

Peer pressure may be positive or negative. When people encourage others to improve themselves in some way or pressure them *not* to do something wrong, peer pressure is positive. Problems arise, however, when peer pressure is negative. Have you ever

known that you needed to study for a test but were tempted by your friends to do something else? Have you ever wanted to do something worthwhile but were afraid of what your friends might think? If so, you have felt negative peer pressure.

Peer pressure has no power in and of itself. No one can make you do something you don't want to do. Teens, however, are very sensitive to criticism and acceptance from their peers. This is because they have not yet formed a strong personal identity. They are often not sure exactly who they are and what they value. This uncertainty results in a lack of inner strength to resist if friends are pressuring for certain behavior. Thus, peer pressure convinces them that they *want* to do what others are doing even though deep down, this may not be true.

The danger of peer pressure is that it disguises itself as friendship. People who use peer pressure often know that their actions

Standing up to peer pressure is not easy. Are you strong enough to turn your back when it becomes necessary?

and what they are encouraging others to do is wrong. Getting friends to join them gives them moral and social support. It abuses one of the benefits of friendship. True friends do not ask each other to do something if either person feels it is wrong or unwise.

Handling Negative Peer Pressure

Learning to handle peer pressure is a major task of the teen years. It is never easy to say "no" to friends when you want to be part of the group. Those people with a strong sense of themselves and of what they want from life can do it. High self-esteem helps them put the importance of friendship in perspective. They join their friends when they want to but are not afraid to strike out on their own either.

Competition

People face competition all through life — in the family, at school, at work, and among friends. In competition, one person gains something at the expense of another. Therefore, competition creates winners and losers.

Healthy competition can be a good thing. It encourages people to strive for the best in themselves and others. When a friendship is strong, individuals take satisfaction in what each accomplishes. You may have watched two friends race across the finish line at a track meet. Only one is the winner, but if they walk away with arms across each other's shoulders, they show that friendship is still important to them.

When people let it, competition within friendship can create conflict. Uncomfortable feelings are best put aside through discussion. Learn how your friend feels and be sensitive. When you are the winner, take your win with humility. Look for ways to boost your friend's self-esteem. When you

How to Say "No"

Being with a group of friends and "going along with the crowd" can be fun. You may, for example, be persuaded to learn something new. There may be times, though, when you are pressured to do what you know is wrong. Here are some tips that will help you say "no."

- Remember, you have the right to say "no." You need not give reasons, make excuses, or apologize.
- Be assertive. You can be firm without offending others.
- Say "no" convincingly. Let people know by the tone of your voice that you mean it.
- Use facial expressions that indicate your seriousness. Look steadily at the person and don't smile.
- Use body language. Make no gestures that might indicate that you are less than sure of yourself.
- Suggest an alternative activity. This puts the pressure on the person or people who are pressuring you.
- If the pressure is too much, leave.

are the loser, be proud of your friend. In true friendship a friend's joy is also yours.

Loneliness

Everyone experiences loneliness. You don't have to be alone to feel lonely. You can be around many people and still feel lonely if you are not connected with someone.

Because teens are often still developing their relationship skills, they are especially prone to feelings of loneliness. Giving in to these feelings tends to increase them. Hung Nguyen, for example, came to the United States from Vietnam when he was fourteen. Because he couldn't speak English

Are you a good listener? Friendship thrives on knowing that someone hears and understands you, yet often in conversation it is easy to get caught up in what to say next rather than really focus on what the other is saying. Sound familiar?

Listening helps you get to know a person better. You can learn about your friend's birthday, family members, favorite foods and activities, and similar details. More importantly, however, good listening skills encourages your friend to reveal feelings and concerns. Try listening to your friend, not with the idea of "fixing" the problem, but with interest and support. Your friend isn't usually looking for your solution or judgment, just acceptance and patience.

well and didn't know American customs, he stayed by himself and didn't try to make friends. He was afraid that if he tried, he would do something wrong and be humiliated. Soon he and everyone else at school began to consider him as a "loner." This made it even harder for Hung to approach others. To make friends and overcome loneliness, he needed to stop thinking of himself as a lonely person.

Most lonely people feel afraid that others won't accept them. This fear causes them to withdraw, increasing their loneliness. They don't understand that friendship is based on sharing — weaknesses as well as strengths. They don't see that friends care about one another despite their flaws. They may try to make friends by telling others only about their good points, but this drives others away because it sounds like bragging.

Coping with Loneliness

Sometimes feelings of loneliness are not permanent. They come for no apparent reason and quickly leave. This is normal, especially among teens. True loneliness, however, will not go away by itself. It must be overcome with positive action. You must use your relationship skills to reach out to others. Practice good communication skills, especially listening. Ask others about their interests. As you build a connection with them, you'll have a chance to talk about your own concerns as well. Rapport and empathy will grow as you discover common bonds.

Sometimes, feelings of loneliness cannot be overcome, despite the best efforts. This can be a sign of a serious problem. A person with low self-esteem may be overly concerned about rejection. Other serious problems in life may prevent a person from reaching out and connecting with others. Talking to a trusted adult can help — a parent, an older sibling, a member of the clergy, or a school counselor. Covering up this kind of problem will not solve it. In fact, the longer it goes on, the worse it becomes.

Popularity

Popularity is an issue for many teens. What does popularity mean? A person who is truly popular is liked and accepted by many people. He or she has qualities that nearly

People who are truly popular share certain traits that are admired by all. What are some of these?

everyone admires. Popular people care about others regardless of who they are. They may have a particular set of close friends, but they are liked by many others as well.

A desire for popularity causes problems for many teens. Because they want to be liked and have friends, some strive for popularity in the wrong ways. In the struggle to "fit in," they bow to negative peer pressure. Sometimes they do gain a level of popularity within a certain group of people, but they often pay a price. People who give in to peer pressure and give up their values in an attempt to be popular often have regrets. Others see what they are willing to do and have no admiration for their actions.

People who place too much emphasis on popularity are usually the ones who make mistakes in trying to achieve it. A better approach is to forget about how high you are on the popularity scale. Realize that other people react to the combination of personal qualities that you have. Try to

Can Work and Friends Mix?

When Simone got her first job at a fast food restaurant, she suggested her friends visit her at work. She was sure they would be impressed. It never occurred to her that they would ask her for free food or hang around for hours. When Simone's boss pointed out that her friends were costing the business money, Simone realized the need to separate her work and her personal life.

How can you be both a valued employee and a valued friend? Here are some tips:

- *Stop the problem before it starts.* When beginning a job, you might say something like, "My boss had to fire someone who always talked to friends instead of working. I said my friends aren't like that."
- *Explain the situation.* Tell your friends you enjoy seeing them, but while at work your job comes first.
- *Make time for your friends.* Good friends are understanding, but no one likes to be ignored or forgotten.

Keeping friends while accepting work responsibilities is as important to your success as any skill you learn on the job.

develop positive personality traits and genuinely care about others, thereby increasing your opportunities for friendship. That's where true popularity begins.

Personality Traits

Most popular people share certain personality traits. These traits are often associated with happiness. Popular people are cheerful. They see the good in life. Because they are content with themselves, they can value others as well. They accept and appreciate other people for what they are. They are friendly and have good things to say about others.

Behavior

Behavior is also a key to popularity. People enjoy being with someone who shows concern and gets involved. Self-pity or constant complaining, on the other hand, drives them away. Think of the people you most enjoy being around. What do they say or do that makes you like them? You may be able to use similar techniques. For example, Brian always has a friendly smile and a kind word for everyone — especially those who often go unnoticed by others. He makes people feel special. Smiling and speaking may not come easily at first, but anyone can do it with a little effort.

Popularity feeds on itself. Teens who are liked feel good about themselves, and teens who feel good about themselves are generally well-liked. This allows them to be even more open and secure in their relationships.

Cliques

Throughout society people tend to divide themselves into groups. Because of background or things they have in common, many people form groups that are manageable for socializing. The people who come

Friendship is a fulfilling part of life. Making an effort to be the kind of friend that you want others to be for you is the key.

together feel close and comfortable with each other, and the association continues. It's no surprise that this happens with teens, too.

Teen friendship groups form routinely, but some can create problems. When they become exclusive, deliberately rejecting people, they are called **cliques** (CLICKS). People within a clique may scorn or ignore others on the outside, causing hurt feelings. Thoughtful people do not go along with this. They either set a better example for others in the clique or leave the group. People on the outside sometimes wish to be part of a clique, but they might think twice about the way the group operates. Forming other friendships could be a better answer.

DEALING WITH TROUBLED FRIENDSHIPS

Because people are constantly growing and changing, friendships change and often end. Usually this happens because there are fewer likenesses between the friends than there used to be.

Everyone has had the experience of hanging on to a relationship past the time when it brings much pleasure and satisfaction. When a friendship no longer brings benefits or has true meaning in your life, it may be time to end it. Some so-called friendships may even be causing you trouble, influencing your life in negative ways. Such friendships also call for an ending.

When dissatisfaction occurs, people respond in different ways. Sometimes people show loyalty to the friendship by trying to make things better. When specific problems occur, they may try to solve them. If the friendship cannot survive, the individuals may simply neglect the friendship, letting it die on its own. A more direct approach is taken when someone acts to end the friendship immediately.

Breaking off a friendship should be handled with tact and concern for the other person's feelings. This is easier if both people want to end the relationship. When you are ending a friendship, express your feelings without blaming or judging the other person. At the same time, don't allow yourself to be pressured into maintaining the relationship if you sincerely believe it is better to end it.

COPING WITH LOST FRIENDSHIP

When a friendship ends against your will, you are likely to feel any of several negative emotions. You may feel sadness or anger over the loss. You may even feel guilty or want to blame yourself or the other person. These feelings are to be expected and must be worked through. Time helps lessen the pain. Eventually, you can focus on the good times you had together rather than on the pain at the end. Soon, you can begin to look forward to new friendships and the rewards they will bring.

SECTION 2 REVIEW

1. What is peer pressure? Give five tips for resisting peer pressure.
2. Suppose your grades are consistently better than your friend's, which bothers your friend. What can you do?
3. If loneliness is a serious problem for someone, what should he or she do?
4. What does popularity mean?
5. What is a clique?
6. What is the best way to break off a friendship?
7. What attitude is best when a friendship ends against your will?

Chapter 17 Review

Chapter Summary

- Friendships have important contributions to make to people's lives.
- People of all ages and types can be friends with each other.
- Making friends may not be easy for everyone, but there are a number of things you can do, such as smile and speak first.
- You can find friends practically anyplace, but the best places to look are those where you know you will find people with whom you share things in common.
- Keeping friends requires effort.
- Friendship is a give-and-take relationship for the people involved.
- Teen friendships may face problems related to negative peer pressure, competition, loneliness, popularity, and cliques.
- The ending of a friendship may be painful for you emotionally. It will take time for you to work through these feelings, but you can look forward to new friendships.

Chapter Review

1. Give two examples of the emotional support that friendships provide.
2. Why can many children benefit from friendships with teens today?
3. How can society benefit when people make friends with all types of people?
4. What is one of the biggest fears people have when they think about trying to make friends with someone?
5. Should a friendship be expected to develop immediately after you meet someone? Explain your answer.
6. Describe three ideas for keeping a friendship going.
7. Can peer pressure be positive? Explain.
8. In what way can competition be good for people?
9. What communication skill is especially useful when reaching out to others in friendship?
10. What personality traits are usually associated with popular people?
11. In what way do cliques sometimes hurt people?
12. Why do some friendships end?
13. What effect does time have on a lost friendship?

Critical Thinking

1. Do you think a friendship group can operate without being exclusive? Explain your answer.
2. Sometimes people think simple questions like "Have you lived here long?" and "Do you have any brothers or sisters?" are not interesting enough; however, if someone you have just met asks you such a question, how do you feel? Why do conversation starters often have to be simple?
3. Suppose you moved to a new neighborhood? What are some things you could do to make new friends?
4. Have you ever had a friend from another country? If so, how did the friendship enrich your life?

5. Have you ever associated or worked with children? If so, in what ways did you find the experience rewarding?
6. Have you or has someone you know stood up to intense negative peer pressure? How did you or the other person deal with the situation?
7. Think of some people you like very much. What qualities do they have that make them likable?

Activities

1. **An enriching experience.** Write a description of an experience you and a friend shared together that enriched your friendship in some way. (*Evaluating, writing*)
2. **Television friendships.** In class, discuss television programs that depict friendships. In what ways are the friendships true–to–life and in what ways aren't they? (*Interpreting and communicating information*)
3. **Pictures of friends.** Collect pictures that you think show friendships. What expressions or actions shown in the pictures make you think the people are friends? (*Interpreting information*)
4. **Friendship skits.** Working in small groups, develop and present brief skits depicting the following situations:
   - A person handling negative peer pressure without giving in.
   - Two friends confronting a problem in their friendship.
   - One person breaking off a friendship with another.
   (*Teamwork, creative thinking, problem solving*)

STRENGTHENING VALUES

Aim For an Open Mind

Having an open mind means not judging something in advance, before you understand it. Open-minded people are willing to rethink their opinions about people and ideas. Josie keeps an open mind when she:

- Thinks of each new person she meets as a possible friend instead of finding fault with them right away.
- Doesn't let the opinions that others have prevent friendship with them.
- Gives someone who has hurt her another chance to be her friend.
- Gets the facts on all sides of an issue before reaching a decision.
- Samples different types of ethnic cooking.

What are the benefits of having an open mind? What happens when people are close-minded? How can you tell whether a person is open-minded or the opposite? Which type of person is more pleasant to be around? Which type are you?

Dating Relationships

IMAGINE THAT ...

you have just been on the television game show, "Dream Date" — and you won! You are about to go on the dream date of a lifetime. You have three people to choose from as a partner for the date. One is especially attractive. Another has a personality that grabs your attention. The third has interests that are similar to yours. Three plans are described for the date, all very different. One has an outdoor theme, with athletic activities planned. The second is quiet and elegant, including good food and entertainment. The basis for the third is sight-seeing. You will go interesting places where there is much to see. The decision is yours. How easy will it be?

SECTION 1

THE DATING PROCESS

THINK AHEAD

About These Terms
dating   *compatible*

About These Objectives
After studying this section, you should be able to:
* List the purposes of dating.
* Describe stages in dating.
* Explain how changes in society have affected dating patterns.
* List qualities that help make a dating relationship positive.

ating means different things to different people. Across cultures and generations, dating customs and patterns are not the same. Perhaps the common thread that runs through most dating situations is purpose. Through dating, people learn to relate to those of the opposite gender, sometimes leading to a lifelong relationship with one special person.

◆ ◆ ◆

DATING

Dating is shared social activity between people of opposite genders. For many people dating, especially in the early stages, is not easy. People don't always know what to say or do. The less a couple knows about each other, the more awkward it may be to get through those first dates.

Dating poses risks for people. You may be rejected. You may be embarrassed by making some mistake. You may be confused by dating rules that change. You may be disappointed when a relationship doesn't turn out to be what you had hoped it would. It takes courage and self-confidence to put yourself on the line with another person. Nevertheless, an interest in dating usually outweighs the risks for most people.

When to begin dating is a question that many teens think about. Family rules may control the timing. Once a teen begins to date, new issues arise. Families don't want teens to lose track of time needed for schoolwork and family responsibilities. They also don't want teens to have to deal with sexual pressures too soon. Teens who do date have to stay in touch with the other responsibilities they have.

Some people do not date or decide to delay dating until they are older. That's okay. People mature at different rates, so some are ready at an earlier age than others. Different maturity levels are especially noticeable during high school. Because females mature faster than males, more females than males may be interested in dating. This pattern tends to level off after high school as both genders reach full maturity.

The subject of dating often causes concerns for teens. Some want to date but don't have anyone to go out with. Some want to date but are reluctant to do the asking. Some feel different because they aren't interested in dating at all. What teens need to realize is that time takes care of most concerns. A change in focus can help. Teens who concentrate on their friends, activities, and schoolwork are spending their time well. Dating relationships can be part of life eventually.

As young people mature, many turn to dating as a way of learning how to relate to those of the opposite gender.

Purposes of Dating

As you know, dating includes a wide range of activities. Anything from going swimming or studying at the library to watching a movie or going to a lecture can be considered a date. A date may be formally arranged and conducted or casually agreed to, with no definite plans. Regardless of the form, however, dating everywhere serves certain basic purposes. Dating provides opportunities for:

◆ *Enjoyment.* A date usually includes entertainment and recreation. You and your partner can relax and enjoy yourselves.
◆ *Friendship and companionship.* Dating gives you the chance to share activities, events, and thoughts with others.

itself may not be focused on choosing a partner, most mate selection occurs through the dating process.

- *Preparing for marriage.* As a couple dates, the partners each gain a better understanding of the behavior and attitudes of the opposite gender. They can learn to solve problems together.

How time is spent on a date depends on the interests of the couple. Simple activities are often pleasant, and inexpensive as well.

"If men and women are to understand each other, to enter into each other's nature with mutual sympathy, and to become capable of genuine comradeship, the foundation must be laid in youth."

HAVELOCK ELLIS

- *Learning social skills.* Knowing how to act in social situations can help you gain poise and self-confidence. You learn to cooperate and be considerate of others.
- *Personal development.* You can learn about your own identity through your dating relationships. Dating helps you mature and develop self-esteem.
- *Learning gender roles.* What does it mean to be a woman or a man? How do women and men act toward each other? Dating can help you answer these questions.
- *Giving and receiving love and affection.* The need for love is met in intimate relationships, the kind that can develop through dating.
- *Selecting a mate.* As people mature and, perhaps, become more interested in marriage, dating provides a chance to meet a suitable person. Although dating

ATTRACTION

Dating begins with attraction. What makes you like some people and not like others? Because you are a unique individual, your personal preferences are unique also. In dating, you will be attracted to some people and not attracted to others.

At first you may be attracted to someone who is nice looking or who is held in high regard for something such as athletic ability or academic achievement. These factors may not be negative, but they don't necessarily make the person right for you. Personal qualities are more important in a dating relationship. If you are not treated well and you don't enjoy another person's company, even the nicest appearance counts for very little.

You may also be attracted to people your friends find attractive. This is okay, but you should not allow it to be a limiting factor. Remember, you are an individual, and the qualities you appreciate in a person will not be exactly the same as those of your friends.

People you find attractive for dating may have talents or skills you admire. You may like a certain personality and enjoy a sense of humor. Perhaps someone makes you feel important and valued as a person. More than likely, the individual shares some of your interests and likes to do many of the same activities. For what other reasons might a person be attractive to you?

THE DATING PATTERN

Dating tends to follow a pattern. In general, three stages can be seen in the process.

STAGE 1: CASUAL DATING Dating usually begins in group activities. During the preteen and early teen years, most people are involved in same gender peer groups. During puberty, interest in the opposite gender builds. The first boy/girl social interaction often occurs in such group activities as school parties or dances. The group gives protection and help in handling the attraction between the genders.

STAGE 2: PAIRING As each grows in maturity and confidence, male and female peer groups tend to merge, so the peer group includes both genders. Couples may pair off informally within the group to learn more about each other. Often no agreement exists, and the two people are free to see others. At some point, couples pair off more exclusively. There are fewer group and more couple activities. Couple relationships become more important and other friendships less so.

STAGE 3: DEVELOPING COMMITMENT The strength of commitment varies depending on the couple, their stage of life, and their purposes in the relationship. Younger couples may "commit" to one another for only a few months. This is natural for those in the early stages of maturity. Older couples may stop seeing others. They may begin considering a future together. This commitment may or may not lead to engagement and marriage.

SOCIAL CHANGES

Lydia was looking through her family's photo album. One picture of her mother was taken when Mrs. Gianos was Lydia's age. She wore a boy's high school jacket and a ring on a chain around her neck. "I was going steady with that boy," Mrs. Gianos explained. "We had decided not to date anyone else, and that was how I showed our commitment." Lydia thought it was odd. She knew couples who dated only each other, but it was simply something they had decided to do. They didn't make such a public display of it. Had Lydia talked to her grandparents about their dating customs, she would have been even more amused at how things have changed.

Lydia's reaction is a common one. Generational differences are often surprising. In her mother's era, roles and responsibilities were well-defined. The male asked for the date, planned and paid for the activity, picked up his date, and took her home. The female waited to be invited and generally went along with whatever plans her date had made. Relationships progressed step-by-step from casual dating to exclusive dating to engagement. Today, dating is much less formal than it used to be. A more casual approach is taken to dress as well as customs.

Changes in society have had an effect on dating. As gender roles evolve, women and

One Date Is All It Takes

One of the purposes of dating is to meet a marriage partner eventually. The Lapps are people who live above the Arctic Circle in parts of Norway, Sweden, Finland, and the former USSR. They have cut dating down to the bare essentials: boy meets girl, boy meets girl's parents, boy and girl get married.

Although less common than in the past, traditionally, the Lapps herd reindeer to make a living. Different groups of Lapps rarely meet each other. Once a year, however, they gather at a fair to trade with each other. Naturally, as young men meet young women from other groups at this time, they begin to think about choosing a bride.

The boys watch the girls at the fair as they help their families. If a boy decides he likes a particular girl, he speaks to her — very politely and respectfully. If she shares his interest, she can expect him to come to meet her parents.

Later, when the boy shows up at the family's reindeer-hide tent, he will compliment the girl in front of her parents to let them know he appreciates her. Then he sits down and waits. He will rarely be acknowledged. It is up to him to make the next move.

When he thinks the time is right, the boy asks to make coffee. The parents supply him with a pot and cups. If the girl's parents ignore the coffee, the boy takes the hint and leaves. He has been formally rejected. If the parents accept the coffee, however, it means they accept him, too. The wedding will take place within a few days. Once the fair breaks up, the bride and her new husband will begin to follow the reindeer again.

men relate to each other differently. One of the most important changes in terms of dating and relationships has been the expanded role of women in the workplace. Since many women now either work outside the home or expect to when they finish their education, they are more likely to pay their own way on a date or even pay for the whole date. They often accept more rights and responsibilities in dating, such as choosing the activity on a date and driving to and from it. Also, more women are postponing marriage to pursue careers, which lengthens the dating time frame.

As more people, especially young women, become involved in sports and concerned with physical fitness, more dates include physical activities. A date may consist of an early morning jog in the park and then breakfast, or a game of racquetball at a health club before dinner.

Dating A Coworker

The idea of dating a coworker may sound appealing at first. You would be able to see each other every day. You could have lunch together and go out straight from work. You might even be able to travel to and from work together.

In reality, dating a coworker is generally *not* a good idea, however. Working with someone you're dating can be stressful. Your roles as coworker and friend might come into conflict with each other. What if a dating partner tried to take advantage of your feelings by asking you to do some of his or her tasks or to "cover" for a mistake? What if your partner were promoted and became your boss? How awkward would it be for you both if you split up? These are possibilities to consider before becoming personally involved with a coworker.

Specifically in teen dating, more teens are working at part-time jobs, making the workplace a popular meeting place. Also, parents and other adults are getting more involved in teen activities. They are sponsoring more dances and other activities for young people. This is due largely to the increased dangers of drug and alcohol use by teens.

POSITIVE DATING RELATIONSHIPS

Not surprisingly, the qualities that characterize good friendships are also those that make a strong relationship between dating partners. These include:

- *Compatibility.* People who can exist together in harmony are **compatible**. They share interests, values, and atti-

tudes. As a couple, they "see eye to eye" on many things and spend their time together on activities they both enjoy.

- *Honesty.* People in a positive dating relationship are honest with themselves and with each other. They can be themselves and express their feelings openly. They don't fear rejection or ridicule by their partner simply for being who they are.

- *Respect.* When two people respect each other, they honor and esteem one another and accept and appreciate their individuality. They take a sincere interest in each other's activities and listen to their ideas and opinions.

- *Mutual Nurturing.* In any good relationship, the people involved must be supportive. They help each other grow by giving encouragement through success and failure.

- *Independence.* Partners enjoy time and activities away from one another as well as time spent together. Neither partner tries to limit the other's interests or relationships with family and friends.

Other traits that mark a healthy dating relationship include trust, the ability to resolve conflicts, and a similar degree of commitment to the relationship. Are there any others you would include in the list? Giving careful thought to all these qualities and putting them into action will help make any dating relationships you have more pleasing.

SECTION 1 REVIEW

1. Define "dating."
2. List six purposes of dating.
3. Describe the three general stages of dating.
4. How has the role of women in society affected dating customs?
5. List four qualities that help make a dating relationship successful.

SECTION 2

DATING CONCERNS

THINK AHEAD

About These Terms
rape   *date rape*

About These Objectives
After studying this section, you should
be able to:

- Describe the following dating concerns and suggest ways to deal with
  them: asking for a date; overcoming
  shyness; managing finances; considering parents; dealing with abuse
  and violence; and ending a dating
  relationship.
- Cite a guideline that is useful in
  dating relationships as well as
  all others.

ost people
want to make a good impression on
others. Most are concerned with acceptance by their peers. These desires can
make dating a cause of anxiety. As with
other forms of stress, dating concerns
can often be helped by knowledge,
understanding, and a positive attitude.

◆ ◆ ◆

ASKING FOR A DATE

In the past, it was the male's responsibility to ask for dates. Only in a stable, committed relationship was it acceptable for
the female to issue invitations. Today,
depending on the circumstances, either
gender may ask the other for a date.

Asking for a date is often a cause for
anxiety. Will the person you ask accept?
How will you feel if your invitation is
rejected? These kinds of concerns create
tension and stress.

Being turned down for a date can be a
blow to your self-esteem. It helps to realize
that the other person may have any number of reasons for saying "no," some of
which may have nothing to do with you.
Perhaps the person is shy or insecure. He
or she may have recently broken up with
someone and not feel ready to begin a new
relationship. The person may have made
other plans or have obligations that restrict
social life.

People sometimes reject invitations
because they simply aren't interested.
Daphne, for example, invited Arthur to a
musical production at her school. Arthur
didn't care for theater and knew he wouldn't
appreciate it as Daphne did. He thought it
would be unfair for her to spend money on
his ticket when he wouldn't enjoy the performance. He thanked Daphne but told her
how he felt. His honesty allowed Daphne to
find someone else who appreciated the
evening more and with whom she had an
enjoyable time.

Rejection should not be taken personally.
A person is no less worthy because of a
turn down. Brushing off any negative feelings can give the courage to try again with
someone else. More often than not, there
are many people just waiting to be asked.

When you are on the receiving end of an
invitation, remember that what you say and
do has impact. Compare these responses:
"Go out with you? No way!" and "Thanks

so much for asking, but I don't think we should go out. Your friendship is important to me, but I wouldn't be comfortable with anything more." A straightforward but kind response is usually best.

OVERCOMING SHYNESS

Shyness is particularly common in dating, even among people who are not ordinarily shy. Lack of experience with male/female relationships can add to the discomfort. The pressure to please may give feelings of insecurity. Feeling shy or uncomfortable is natural when you want to make a good impression.

One way to relieve anxiety is to go on dates with other couples. As part of a group, decisions of where to go and what to talk about can be shared.

Making good use of personal relationship skills is very helpful in overcoming shyness. If shyness is a problem for you, try focusing on the other person. Find out what interests your date and ask questions about that. Comment on things you have in common and ask for opinions. Remember that other people may also feel unsure of themselves. Your interest in them will help them feel more confident.

MANAGING FINANCES

Money is always a concern during dating. Going out can be expensive, and students may have little money to spend on recreation. Paying for a date can strain an already tight budget.

Not all dates are expensive, however. Browsing at a favorite store, splitting a pizza with friends, playing tennis at the YMCA — all can be considered a date by today's relaxed standards. What other enjoyable, low-cost activities can you think of?

If you're anxious or shy about dating, go out with another couple. In what ways would this make dating easier?

Many couples today share the cost of dating. In part, this is a reflection of the more casual nature of dating. It also shows the increased equality of the genders. People may have some uncertainty about sharing expenses, however. Generally, the person who asks for the date is expected to pay. It's a thoughtful gesture, though, to offer to help pay expenses. This can be done by simply saying, "You bought the tickets, so I'll buy the treats." Don't press the issue if your offer is rejected.

Never assume that your date has plenty of money to spend on you. When the other person is paying, a good rule of thumb is to take spending cues from him or her.

CONSIDERING PARENTS

Parents and other caregivers often have concerns about their children's safety and well-being as they begin to date. Most set restrictions to protect young people from situations they may not be able to handle.

Curfews, age limits, and rules about using the car are a few examples.

Dating restrictions often cause conflict within the family. Teens may believe they are old enough to be trusted. They may feel that their parents still see them as children. Parents may remember the difficulties and challenges they faced as young people. They may want to save their children from making the same mistakes they did.

As with all conflicts, resolving disagreements about dating rules requires understanding, communication, and compromise. Teens need to realize that, although they are maturing, many situations may still be difficult for them to deal with. They can learn from their parents' experience. Parents may be trying to get used to the idea that their children are growing up and learning how to make their own decisions. When both sides explain their views calmly and listen to the other view, compromises can be reached.

Handling finances on a date can be awkward. By thinking ahead about what you will do, you can avoid discomfort.

T A K I N G ACTION

Dating is about spending time together, not about creating financial hardships. How can you have fun on less money? Here are some suggestions to try:

• **Walk, hike, or bike on public trails or swim at public beaches.**

• **Do routine chores (walking the dog?) or creative projects (cooking?) together.**

• **Take advantage of the low admission costs of school- and town-sponsored events.**

• **Watch for bargain days or times for reduced admission to commercial sports or amusement centers, movies, or other entertainments.**

• **Enjoy special dining at noon when meals are less expensive and eating places are likely to have "specials."**

Talk with your date about what he or she would enjoy, making mutual decisions about activities.

Recognizing Inferences

When people make inferences, they draw mental conclusions based on reasoning from evidence they see, hear, or read. Making inferences helps a person develop reasoning skills. Just be sure you have enough information to form accurate opinions and ideas.

TIFFANY *"Of all my friends' parents, my Mom is the strictest when it comes to dating. When I ask her why, she just says something about the time not being right. Well, I keep wondering when the time will be right. Mom knows that a lot of my friends are dating now. I'm as old as they are. I think she thinks I'm not responsible enough, but that's not true. Even though I make a mistake here and there, I do try to follow the rules. Whatever I've done, I don't think it's enough to keep me from dating."*

MRS. TYRRELL *"It's a risky world out there for kids, and if I'm overprotective, it's because I don't want anything terrible to happen to Tiffany. The thought of her out in a car alone with some boy I hardly know scares me. She just doesn't realize the trouble that kids can get into. With drug abuse, bad drivers on the roads, and rapists out there, anything can happen. When Tiff is home, I feel safer. I know she wants to go out, but I have my reasons for making her wait."*

CAN YOU RECOGNIZE INFERENCES?

- What does Tiffany infer from her mother's reluctance to let her date? Is Tiffany's inference right or wrong?
- What does Mrs. Tyrrell infer from her observations about society? Does she have cause for concern?
- How could Tiffany and her mother avoid making incorrect inferences?
- Do you think information heard second-hand should be used to make inferences? Explain your answer.

DEALING WITH ABUSE AND VIOLENCE

Abuse and violence can occur in dating relationships. They are more likely to take place in committed relationships, but they do even happen on casual dates. Abuse and violence, of course, have no place in any relationship.

Physical Abuse

Physical abuse includes actions such as shoving, slapping, punching, or worse. Abusive people see violence as an acceptable way of solving problems. When there is tension in the dating relationship, they try to frighten their partners into compliance with violence or the threat of it. They often feel sincere sorrow after the abuse and may promise to never do it again. The abused partner forgives the abuser, and the cycle begins again.

Abusive relationships rarely improve on their own. Abusers needs professional help to understand and control their emotions. They need to learn nonviolent ways of resolving conflicts. Abused people need to understand that they do not deserve the abuse and that this is not how a healthy relationship functions.

Ending a dating relationship is the safest response when abuse surfaces. First, the risk of injury is eliminated. Second, the chance of becoming more emotionally involved in a destructive relationship is ended.

The Principle of Least Interest

Dating partners can be abused emotionally as well as physically. The "principle of least interest" states that the person who cares least about the relationship controls it. Lisann, for instance, knew that Mitchell cared very much for her, but she was only mildly interested in him. She took advantage of his feelings for her. She would forget to return his calls and cancel dates at the last minute, knowing he would forgive her and keep seeing her. She abused him verbally by thoughtlessly criticizing him and making fun of things he thought were important. Mitchell continued the relationship because he could not admit that some-

one he cared about so much could feel so little in return. Only when he accepted this fact could he end the relationship.

In another situation, Doug abused Tori's affection for him by taking her places she was not supposed to go and keeping her out past her curfew. This created many problems between Tori and her family before Tori finally realized how little Doug respected her feelings. She finally stopped going out with him.

Date Rape

Rape is an act of violence. **Rape** is forced sexual intercourse. It may occur between strangers or people who already know each other. **Date rape** is rape that takes place in a dating situation.

Avoiding Date Rape

To decrease the chances of date rape occurring, in dating situations you can:

* *Avoid risky situations.* Be careful about where you go, especially with people you don't know well.
* *Set limits for yourself.* Know before the date what behavior is acceptable and unacceptable, for both you and your partner.
* *Communicate.* Tell your partner about the limits you have set. Make sure your partner understands and accepts them.
* *Recognize disrespectful behavior.* Learn to identify signs that your partner is not taking your standards seriously. Be aware of pressure to do something that goes against your values.
* *Be assertive.* If a situation makes you uncomfortable, say so forcefully, verbally and nonverbally. If it continues, get away or call for help.

Date rape occurs more frequently than most people realize. It often isn't reported. Teens in particular are reluctant to report date rape. They may incorrectly feel that it was their fault. They may think they won't be believed or that it wasn't rape if they were on a date. They may be afraid of the publicity and attention that will follow an accusation of rape.

Rape is never acceptable behavior. Teens who feel they are in a threatening situation must be assertive and call for help. They must leave the situation as soon as possible. If rape occurs, whether on a date or not, they must report it. This will help others become more aware of the seriousness of the problem. It may also prevent the rapist from repeating the act.

ENDING A DATING RELATIONSHIP

Ending a dating relationship is very much like ending a friendship. It can be done cruelly and hurtfully. It can also be done kindly and gently, which hopefully lessens the pain.

Losing any relationship can be painful, even when you are the one who has decided to end it. When you are explaining why you want the relationship to end, be straightforward and focus on the differences between the two of you. Point out why you feel the two of you aren't right for each other. Avoid attacking the other person.

Sometimes when confrontations over breaking up occur, the discussion ends in an argument. You may believe there are good reasons to end the relationship. Your partner may feel there are equally good reasons to continue it. In this case, you may wish to write a letter outlining your position calmly and logically. Say that you are sorry about what has happened. Try to word your letter so that you don't damage the other's self-esteem. Then be firm in your refusal to meet or go out again. Giving someone false hope when you know the relationship is over is cruel.

Ending a dating relationship smoothly means doing so directly and with kindness.

Dealing with the Breakup

If it is your partner who decides to end the relationship, the breakup can be even more painful. Feelings of hurt, betrayal, and self-doubt are common. You may blame yourself — or your partner — for causing the breakup. You may even promise yourself that you will never get involved again. These feelings are all a natural reaction to loss. Working through them and coming to a healthy acceptance of the situation is necessary. The following suggestions can help:

• *Realize that most teen dating relationships are not permanent.* Teens are still growing and changing. As they develop new interests and values, some relationships will no longer be as satisfying as they once were.

- *Understand that sometimes a breakup is no one's fault.* It cannot be avoided by being "nicer" or "more attractive" or "a better person." Sometimes when people lose interest in a relationship, it has nothing to do with their partner. Changing yourself to please another is not the answer.
- *Remember that although this relationship did not work out, another one will.* Take the time you need to heal, but don't dwell on your hurt.
- *Re-evaluate the relationship.* If you see that you made mistakes, learn from them. Learn from the things that you did right as well.

The Road to Recovery

The end of a committed relationship can be a major blow, whether it is your choice or your partner's choice. Here are some suggestions to help you recover:

- *Put the experience down on paper.* Write about the relationship — its good times, its problems, why it ended, and what you can learn from it. Read what you have written regularly.
- *Prepare for memories.* Going to a meeting place that you and your ex-partner especially liked or seeing a movie you both enjoyed may be difficult at first. If necessary, avoid doing things that remind you of the relationship for a while, but don't let it affect your life.
- *Accept your ex-partner's new relationships.* After breaking up, people naturally look for new companions and commitment. Don't take it personally. Follow the example and get on with your own life also.
- *Rely on family and friends.* Family and friends can help fill the gap left by your ex-partner. Don't be afraid to let them know you hurt. Let them be there for you.

- *Be good to yourself.* When you are physically injured, you take extra care of yourself to speed the recovery. When you are emotionally hurt, do something to make you feel stronger inside. For example, try learning a new skill, reading a book by a favorite author, or doing volunteer work.

A Guideline to Follow

A few pages in a book cannot prepare you for every complication that comes along in dating. For example, what do you do when someone asks you to go to a special event, but you would prefer to go with another person who hasn't asked yet but just might? Although the answers aren't easy, one guideline will serve you well. Treat your dating friends as you would want to be treated. You will gain respect and admiration, which gives you a good feeling inside.

SECTION 2 REVIEW

1. Why is asking for a date often a cause for anxiety?
2. What can a person do to overcome shyness on a date?
3. What are some ways of dealing with the financial concerns of dating?
4. How can disagreements between teens and parents related to dating be resolved or avoided?
5. Why is it best to end a dating relationship that includes abusive behavior?
6. Give four suggestions for dealing with the end of a dating relationship.
7. What guideline is useful to follow when dating?

Chapter 18 Review

Chapter Summary

- Dating is shared social activity between people of opposite genders. Dating can be an important part of personal growth, but not everyone is ready to date at the same age.
- Dating serves certain basic purposes including providing opportunities for enjoyment, friendship and companionship, and learning social skills. It also helps in mate selection and preparation for marriage.
- In the past, dating customs were more formal than they are today.
- Changes in society — particularly the changes in the roles of females — have resulted in changes in dating practices.
- Qualities that characterize good friendships are also those that make a strong relationship between dating partners.
- Because people fear rejection, asking for a date is often a cause of anxiety.
- Shyness is common in dating relationships, but it can be overcome by making good use of personal relationship skills.
- Money is usually a concern during dating, but expenses can be kept down by participating in low-cost activities and sharing expenses.
- Parents and teens may have disagreements about dating rules, but these can be resolved through understanding, communication, and compromise.
- Abuse and violence, including rape, may occur in a dating relationship, but this type of behavior is never acceptable.
- The end of a dating relationship can be painful, but you must deal with the hurt and get on with your life.

Chapter Review

1. What are three risks that people often associate with dating?
2. Why are females often ready for dating before males of the same age are?
3. How does dating promote social skills?
4. How important is appearance as compared to personal qualities in a dating relationship?
5. Describe how casual dating begins.
6. Do women have more or less choice and responsibility in dating today than in the past? Explain your answer.
7. What is "compatibility"?
8. What role does respect have in dating relationships?
9. How should a person react when rejected after asking someone for a date?
10. How should a person respond when turning down a date offer?
11. Why do people often feel shy on a date?
12. When you don't know how much money your date has to spend, what can you do?
13. Why do parents set rules for dating?
14. What is the difference between rape and date rape?
15. List four ways to help yourself recover after a breakup.
16. What do you gain when your treatment of the people you date reflects the way you would like to be treated?

Critical Thinking

1. Describe dating customs from the past that you have observed on television or in the movies. Compare these to today.

2. Although many females do ask for dates today, some, particularly teens, feel uncomfortable asking. How is this custom handled in your community?
3. What effect do you think early dating might have on the high rate of teen pregnancy?
4. What are some ideas for low-cost dates in your area?
5. Suppose you were a parent and your teenage child repeatedly came in after curfew. What would you do?

Activities

1. **Foreign dating customs.** Find information on dating customs in other countries. Report to the class on the differences and similarities you find. (*Acquiring and evaluating information, communicating information*)
2. **The cost of a date.** Work with a group to estimate the cost of a particular kind of date in your area. Compare results with other groups. Each group should take a different type of date (for example, prom, movie and pizza, dinner and school dance, bowling, etc). (*Teamwork, mathematics, comparing*)
3. **Dating customs from the past.** Ask an older person you know about dating customs when he or she was a teen or young adult. Share your findings with the class. (*Interviewing, communicating information*)
4. **Handling problems.** In groups plan and perform skits that show how to handle specific problems presented in Section 2 of this chapter. (*Teamwork, problem solving*)

STRENGTHENING VALUES

Aim For Respect

Respect is consideration for another person's feelings, beliefs, and rights. It means seeing another person's needs and wants as equal to your own. Austin shows respect by:

- Abiding by the curfew his girlfriend's parents set when he and Tierney go out.
- Asking Tierney where she would like to go when they are on a date.
- Listening to his friend's opinions and trying to understand them.
- Talking to his parents with words and tone that show his regard for them.
- Knocking on closed doors before entering a room.
- Obeying the law.

Does Austin have to agree with his parents and his friend in order to respect them? Explain your answer. Respect can be shown for more than just people. How do people show respect for their country? How do you show that you respect others? How does this affect their respect for you?

Learning About Love

IMAGINE THAT ...

you are doing a study of love. To begin with, you look up the word "love" in the dictionary. The list of definitions is long. You decide to start listening and keep notes on how people use the word "love." The first entry comes soon, while you are in the lunch line in the cafeteria. Someone in front of you says, "Oh, great, it's pizza day. I *love* pizza." During the next few days, you fill your notebook with entries about love. People *love* their parents, their friends, and their pets. They would *love* to go somewhere with you. They *love* Ms. Sullivan's history class. They *love* a song, a movie, a book, an activity, a person. You begin to wonder about this word. Can there be a more overworked word in the English language?

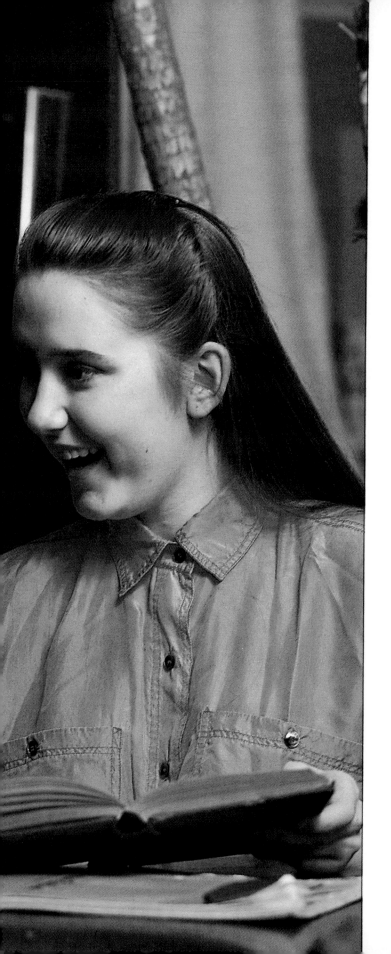

THINK AHEAD

About These Terms
infatuation
mature love

About These Objectives
After studying this section, you should
be able to:
* Explain the stages that people go
  through as they learn to love.
* Explain the difference between infatuation and mature love.

When people say
something like, "I love warm apple pie
with ice cream," you know what they
mean. You don't wonder how serious
they are or if their feelings will last.
Even though people throw the word
"love" around casually in everyday
conversation, they know that the real
impact and meaning of love is linked to
relationships between people. This is
when the word also causes the most
confusion.

♦ ♦ ♦

349

Although love between people is most common, love can also be felt in other ways.

Learning to Love

The idea of "learning" to love another person may seem strange. People usually think of love as something natural. It's true that the desire to love and to be loved is inborn in all individuals. You learn to love, however, as you learn to do other things — through experience and observation. You learn about love by receiving love from others and by observing the love relationships of others. Once you have received love, then you can give it back and spread it to others. In this way, love multiplies. A person who has never experienced love, however, cannot give it.

Learning to love is a lifelong process. It begins at birth and progresses through a series of stages. Each stage helps you build a stronger foundation for future love rela-

tionships. Each new stage builds on the previous one. If the love relationships at one stage or another are not satisfying, it is difficult to go on to the remaining stages successfully. With this is mind, take a look at the stages that people go through as they learn to love:

STAGE 1: SELF-LOVE A person's first love is love of self. Babies cry when they need something and smile when their needs are met. When babies' basic needs are met, that is, they are well-fed, diapered, kept comfortable and safe, and receive attention, they feel good about their world and about themselves. These are the first feelings of love.

STAGE 2: LOVE OF CAREGIVER As babies' needs are met and they receive love and attention, they gradually come to trust and love their caregivers. (This is usually the parents.) Babies learn to love by being loved. If babies' needs are not fully met, they may never develop the capacity to give and receive love.

STAGE 3: LOVE OF PEERS As children begin to interact with others their own age, they develop attachments to their playmates. They eventually develop a strong relationship with one or two best friends of the same gender. The feelings they have are one form of love. Friends become, and will continue to be, very important.

STAGE 4: HERO WORSHIP As children grow older, they develop a loving admiration for an older person — an older sibling or other relative, a close family friend, a sports coach, a teacher, or even a famous personality, such as a movie or TV star. They think they would like to be like this person. They imitate the talk, mannerisms, and dress of their chosen role model. This lets children try out several traits, which helps them decide what they really want to be like. It helps them develop their identity.

Fromm and Love

Erich Fromm, a noted psychoanalyst, is a leading theorist on love. His book, *The Art of Loving*, has been translated into many languages and has sold millions of copies.

Fromm notes that hardly any activity begins with such high hopes and expectations and fails as often as love. Fromm believes this failure is because most people do not understand the nature of love. He says that most people believe the problem with love lies not with the ability to love but instead with a person's loveableness. They link loveableness to being popular and sexually desirable. People think that loving is simple but that it is harder to find someone lovable.

Fromm, however, says that the main love problem is the ability to love. In spite of what most people think, Fromm says it is not easy to develop this ability. Love is primarily giving, not receiving.

Fromm says there are four basic components of love:

- *Care* is an active concern for the life and growth of another.
- *Responsibility* is actively responding to the emotional needs of another.
- *Respect* is awareness of the unique personality of the other and concern that the other should grow and develop as he or she is.
- *Knowledge* is an ability to see and understand the reality of the other person.

Fromm says that love is an activity. When people love, they are in a constant state of active concern with the loved person. This outward focus helps people overcome the natural inclination to think mostly of themselves.

STAGE 5: LOVE OF OPPOSITE GENDER

During the preteens or early teens, children become interested in the opposite gender. At first, this attraction is nonspecific, that is, they are attracted to the opposite gender in general. Children at this stage are often referred to as "boy crazy" or "girl crazy." When girls get together, they talk about boys. When boys get together, they talk about girls. They often hang pictures or posters of their favorite opposite-gender movie, TV, or music personalities. Later, they focus on one individual who has traits they admire. These relationships are usually short-lived and based on superficial qualities, such as appearance, popularity, or athletic ability. Young teens are excited about being in love. They develop a love of love. Some people never progress beyond this stage. They always focus on how love makes them feel. They are continually

When children are young, they learn to care about their friends. They often play with children of both genders. When they are a little older, their best friends are usually of the same gender.

searching for the ideal love, one that will fulfill their every need and make their life perfect.

STAGE 6: MATURE LOVE This is the stage that most people find the hardest to recognize and the most difficult to attain. It involves caring, sharing, respect, understanding, trust, and commitment. It develops over time. Over the next several pages, you will read more about this type of love and the love discussed in Stage 5, a love that is self-centered and sought only as a means of self-fulfillment. As people develop and mature at different rates, so do their needs, their values, their ideas about love, and their feelings toward others. Some people's experiences have helped prepare them for a mature love relationship at an earlier age than others. Some people never develop fully enough emotionally to be capable of a mature love relationship.

INFATUATION

Infatuation (in-FACH-uh-WAY-shun) is an intense emotional involvement that begins with a sudden, strong attraction based on physical appearance or other obvious traits, such as body language, voice quality, charm, or self-confidence. The feelings are very real and very powerful. Infatuation, however, is not a type of love that lasts.

An infatuated couple wants to spend all their time together. They want to share all their feelings — joys, sorrows, secrets, hopes, and fears — with each other. They are emotionally immersed in each other and are overwhelmed by their own emotions. They feel an elation and self-confidence that spills over into other aspects of life. While it lasts, it is very enjoyable and satisfying.

Infatuation is a "me-oriented" type of love. Partners focus more on how wonderful the relationship makes them feel and

TAKING ACTION

Are you lovable? Do you have qualities that someone would love in you? If you don't believe you have the qualities that make you worthy of someone's love, chances are that others will see you the same way — they won't think you are worthy of their love. How can you improve your self-image so you can feel more lovable?

First, give yourself a pat on the back now and then. Tell yourself, "Nice try!" "Not bad!" "Don't you look sharp!" Don't wait for perfection to use self-praise lavishly.

Second, be good to yourself. Remember, you are your own best friend! Give yourself the best possible food, rest, and healthful lifestyle. Also, give yourself an occasional special treat, such as a purchase or an enjoyable, relaxing outing. It doesn't have to be expensive.

Finally, don't take yourself too seriously. Learn to accept and laugh at your shortcomings!

emotions are not as new and strong, they no longer cloud judgment and reason. The partners may realize that the attraction was superficial, based only on surface traits rather than more meaningful and enduring inner traits. They may realize that the other person has inner traits or shortcomings they cannot accept, or that they have very little in common. The dream, complete with an idealized partner with whom one can "live happily ever after," is over.

What happened to Jeff and Audra shows how infatuation works. For six months, they were inseparable. They studied together, talked on the phone, and took long walks in the park. When they were together, no one and nothing else seemed to matter. They seemed to fulfill each other's every need, yet, within a few weeks, their feelings for each other cooled and then died completely. Without the intense emotion, they found they had little left. They had fallen out of love as quickly as they had fallen into it.

Infatuation is a natural type of love relationship. It can provide valuable experience when young people are learning what is involved in a truly loving relationship. In some cases, it can also be the beginning of a committed relationship, a stepping-stone on the way to mature love.

how it satisfies their own needs than on the feelings and needs of the other person. In fact, infatuated people are really more in love with the idea of love and the happiness they expect it to bring them than they are with their partner. It is a very self-centered kind of love.

Infatuation is also an unrealistic type of love. It is passion without reason. Their desire to be happy in the relationship can cause infatuated people to overlook basic important differences between them and their partner. Problems, undesirable traits, and shortcomings tend to be ignored or glossed over. Infatuated people see only what they want to see.

Reality Sets In

With time, as the intense emotional high of the relationship begins to die down, reality begins to set in. When the attraction and

MATURE LOVE

Mature love is what most people have in mind when they think of true, or real, love. As you read earlier, it is love that lasts.

As the name implies, people who share a mature love have reached a high degree of growth in their emotional development.

Beads of Love

FAMILIES

AROUND

THE

WORLD

For centuries, beads were used in trade among people in Africa. They were treasured and valued. Although money is now used by most African people, beads still indicate when something is valued. They have become symbols and signs of love.

The Samburu women of Kenya treasure their bead necklaces. A young woman may wear more than a hundred strands of beads. They pile up around her throat and spill down over her shoulders. These strands are gifts from admirers. Men of the Samburu give them to the women they think are beautiful. In turn, the beads make the women more beautiful in the men's eyes.

The more beads a woman has, the more desirable she is. The beads show that many men have thought her beautiful. She gains status among her friends and family. The man who finally marries her will be thought to be very lucky. The more beads a woman wears, the better her chances of getting a good marriage proposal.

The Zulus of South Africa also use beads to express their love. The women make beaded necklaces with beads of many colors and pat- terns. The colors, the combinations of colors, and the pattern in which they are woven make up secret messages. These messages may express love or sadness or loss. The message may be about wealth or poverty. Whatever the beads' message is, it usually remains secret. Its meaning is known only to the woman and her husband or the man courting her.

They are secure and comfortable enough with themselves to share themselves and commit to another person. They are able to put another person's feelings and needs above their own. Indeed, the most important aspect of mature love is that it is other-person-centered rather than self-centered, as with infatuation. In mature love, the happiness comes from the happiness of the other, not the happiness the relationship brings to one's self. In mature love, the health, happiness, and well-being of the loved person are just as important as your own — sometimes even more important. Caring and responding to the needs of the other person are very important elements of mature love.

Physical attraction remains a strong element of mature love, as it was in infatuation. Partners still enjoy being physically close. Mature love, however, is composed of so many other equally satisfying elements that physical attraction is not the main focus.

"*Love consists in this, that two solitudes protect and touch and greet each other.*"

—◆—

RAINER MARIA RILKE

How Love Develops

Mature love may begin like infatuation, with a sudden, strong attraction. The initial attraction may be purely physical or superficial, just as it is with infatuation. With mature love, however, the attraction deepens and grows as the couple explores each other's interests and values and find they have shared interests, beliefs, and goals. Mature love involves getting to know the real person, the one that lies beneath the surface. Sometimes, in fact, the attraction does not even occur until after the couple has gotten to know each other. They may have been friends for years and then suddenly realize they have a deeper attraction for each other — or they may be like Alita.

In Alita's words, "I didn't even like Rashid at first. He seemed kind of withdrawn. I thought he was stuck up. Since we were lab partners in chemistry, though, we had to work together. As we got to know each other, we became friends. We started meeting to do homework together, and that progressed to going out to eat once in a while.

We always seemed to have a good time together. Rashid was never a date in my mind, and our relationship was never romantic. Then when Rashid's family almost moved out of state, we were struck by the possibility of going separate ways. That's when we realized we cared much more about each other than we thought. I never dreamed this would happen."

In mature love, as the couple spends time together, they see each other in a variety of real-life situations. They see how they react to good experiences as well as such things as boredom, frustration, stress, and crisis. They learn about and come to love each other's good qualities. At the same time, they also learn about each other's faults and flaws. They do not ignore or overlook these undesirable traits, as infatuated couples do. Instead, they accept the imperfections as part of their loved one's unique personality. They realize no one is perfect. They are not in love with a dream.

The time they share together and the experiences and activities they share draw a couple closer together. Their emotional attachment deepens. They enjoy not only a physical closeness but also each other's companionship. Partners are happy and relaxed in each other's company. Unlike an infatuated couple, they are secure in their feelings for each other. They don't need constant reassurances that they are loved.

TELLING THE DIFFERENCE

Distinguishing between love and infatuation isn't always easy. How would you evaluate each of the following situations? Which ones sound more like love and which like infatuation?

- Greg began dating Marina because she was on the pom pom squad. He especially liked the envy he noticed from other males when he was out with Marina.

- When Cal's grades started to go down, Hailey was concerned. She suggested that they limit their time together so that he would have more time to study.
- Ma-Ling was moody for several weeks after her mother lost her job. Jun was supportive and realized that her moodiness was not directed at him.
- When Kenna was sick and had to be at home for a month, she wanted Frank to come over after school every day. Other-

wise she thought he might start spending time with someone else.

- Elisha liked going with Derrick because his parents had bought him a nice sports car. He always had plenty of money to spend on her.
- Collette cared for Barry so much that she tolerated the smell of cigarettes and smoke that was always with him. Although she never wanted to date a smoker before, Barry was an exception.
- Lemar and Jackie enjoyed doing simple things together. Even when there was no conversation, they felt comfortable.

Most couples in a serious relationship think at some point or another about love. Individually or together they may wonder if what they feel is real love. No formulas are available to help them. Instead, they must evaluate everything about the relationship in order to reach a conclusion. When doubt remains, the best approach is to give it time. Real love endures.

Is It Love or Infatuation?

WITH INFATUATION . . .

- Feelings are self-centered; each person is concerned only with his or her own happiness and fulfillment in the relationship.
- Physical attraction is a major part.
- Feelings are based on one or two qualities in the other person.
- Differences, undesirable traits, and shortcomings are ignored.
- It is short-lived.

WITH REAL LOVE . . .

- The feelings may begin suddenly but grow and deepen as the two people get to know each other.
- The focus is on the other person; each person is concerned with the happiness, needs, and well-being of the other.
- Physical attraction is only part of the relationship.
- Feelings are based on the total personality of the loved one.
- The approach is realistic; undesirable traits and shortcomings are recognized and accepted as part of the loved one's uniqueness.
- It is long-lasting.

SECTION 1 REVIEW

1. Is the ability to love an inborn quality? Explain.
2. Briefly describe each of the six stages of learning to love.
3. What happens if the love relationships in one stage or another are not satisfying?
4. Define infatuation. Describe the characteristics of infatuation.
5. What is the most important aspect of mature love? How does this compare to infatuation?
6. Why is time so important to the development of mature love?

THE DOWN SIDE OF LOVE

About These Terms
possessive
crushes
unrequited love

About These Objectives
After studying this section, you should be able to:
- Describe several problems associated with love.
- Identify ways to handle love-related problems.

ike anything else, love has its ups and downs. As people experience and evaluate love, they can encounter some difficulties. Understanding them helps people face and manage the situations and emotions.

• • •

PROBLEMS IN LOVE

The love that males and females feel for each other is complicated. As they look for "real" love, they find love relationships that bring all sorts of experiences. The problems that love sometimes creates need to be solved so that people can stay emotionally healthy.

Feeling Used

Whenever you show caring concern for, and a willingness to support, another person, you run the risk of being used. Some people take advantage of others in order to get what they need without giving support or caring in return. This is not a healthy situation.

While giving to, and sometimes sacrificing for, a loved one does feel good, it must also be mutual. It is unfair to expect one person to always give and never or rarely receive. It shows selfishness and lack of caring and concern by the one who benefits. It can also be a sign of low self-esteem and insecurity in the "giver." A person who has had limited exposure to love while growing up may feel a strong need for it but may not know how to give it in return.

Sometimes situations like these can be resolved with honest communication. Justin, for example, felt he was always doing things for Diana — driving her to work, helping her write term papers, buying her gifts. He enjoyed making her happy, but he was growing angry because he felt she did little in return. When he finally told her this, Diana was surprised. She had often wanted to do things for Justin. Because he never actually asked for help, however, she was afraid it would look as though she didn't think he could manage for himself. Honest communication cleared up their misunderstanding and strengthened their relationship.

Can the relationship between two people be too close? If one takes advantage of the other or is possessive of the other, there may be problems.

Love cannot thrive when one person feels used. If talking doesn't bring about change, then the relationship will probably end.

Possessiveness

In some relationships, the desire for closeness and commitment gets out of control. A partner may become **possessive**, with strong feelings that the two should spend all their time together. There is a desire to exclude the couple from all other relationships, including those with friends and family. Possessive partners expect total commitment and total devotion. They want to possess their beloved and be possessed in return. They want complete control of the other's life.

Possessive behavior is based on emotional insecurity. Possessive partners have a frantic need to know they are loved. Their sense of self-worth is bound up in their partner's devotion to them. They look for every indication that they are loved and for the smallest sign that their partner's love may be lessening.

When someone is very possessive, the other person becomes a victim. The situation is very stressful. Possessive behavior smothers and suffocates its victim and eventually smothers the love.

Crushes

Brooke always looked forward to going to English class. Her teacher was a young man who had been out of college for only a few years. He was vibrant and caring, and Brooke always felt as though he was speaking only to her. She often daydreamed about him and wrote poems that spoke of her feelings for him. Sometimes she would try to think of excuses to go to his room — for extra help or to have a question answered. Mr. Phelps was unaware that Brooke had a crush on him.

Crushes are common, particularly with teens. **Crushes** are intense, and usually passing, feelings of infatuation for another person. They are often directed at people with whom love is unattainable. The desired person may not even be aware of the feelings that the other has.

People who experience crushes can't let their feelings have a negative impact on their routine. Daydreams are okay when they don't interfere with more important activities. Crushes are temporary. When there is no likelihood of a relationship with the person, the feelings can be allowed to subside over time.

Having a crush is a common experience during the teen years. Sometimes people do or say things they later regret when they have a crush on someone. Can you think of some examples?

Unrequited Love

Real love is a two-way street. At one time or another, however, most people go through the experience of caring deeply for someone who doesn't care for them. In such cases, love is a one-way street.

In the search for love, people are always measuring who cares more for the other. Sometimes you can have loving feelings for a person who doesn't feel the same way about you. Love may have died or never existed. Feeling **unrequited love** (un-rih-KWYT-ud), love that is unreturned, hurts. Some people never give up when this happens. They fool themselves into thinking that the other person's mind will change. They may make every effort to win the other's love, all in vain. Facing the truth is necessary in situations like this. Time and energy is better spent focusing on new relationships and getting on with life.

When love is unreturned, people have to manage the emotions they feel. They have to realize that many opportunities for love still lie ahead.

Identifying Emotional Language

Emotions can easily get in the way of good communication. The messages you receive from others may not be accurate when people are in an emotional state. An appropriate reaction from you depends on your ability to understand the emotions behind the statements.

WHITNEY *"I'll never go out with another man for as long as I live. How could Nick do this to me? We've been going together for almost a year. He always said he loved me. And he wants to toss me aside for Erika? It's pretty obvious now that he never cared for me at all. He must be out of his mind. Erika's no good for him. Besides that, no one likes her. Now I know why she was always hanging around. She had a plan and it worked. I'm the loser. That sure is the truth — nothing I do ever turns out right."*

NICK *"Whitney was very special to me for the year that we went together. I'll never forget the good times we've had, but I'm not ready to stay with one person for life. Erika is on the school newspaper staff with Whitney and me, so it was just natural that Erika and I have gotten to know each other better. I like her, and I want to spend more time with her. Whitney's going to have to accept that I don't love her anymore. For a while I thought I did, but people change, and they have to get on with life."*

CAN YOU IDENTIFY EMOTIONAL LANGUAGE?

When you *identify emotional language*, you listen to tone, facial expressions, and body language. You look for the reasons behind what the person is saying.

- What statements does Whitney make that are factual?
- What statements does she make that are emotional? Are these statements true? Explain.
- If you were listening to Whitney, what would your response to her be?
- How can emotional expressions like Whitney's be helpful? How can they cause problems?

If Love Ends

Perhaps the greatest risk in loving another is knowing that it may not last and that the end of a relationship can bring a great deal of heartache and pain. No one can tell what the future will bring. People's goals, values, and attitudes can change. People who once believed they would always want the same things from life may see things

A love relationship that ends can cause pain for a while. Most people give themselves some time to recover and then get on with life.

differently. They find they need to take different paths in life and end their relationship. Other times, difficulties and challenges can produce strain in even the best of relationships. They can cause people to be selfish and hurtful. Sometimes the partners decide that the hurts cannot be forgiven or that the risk of hurting each other again is too great, so they end their relationship.

Frequently, after a love relationship has come to an end, either or both of the partners avoid future relationships because they don't want to risk being hurt again. This "solution," however, is not a solution at all. Risk is an unavoidable part of life. No one accomplishes anything without risking something. If you want to start a business, you must risk your money. If you want to win a race, you must risk losing. If you want love, you must risk being hurt.

Risk, however, can be managed. When you start a business, you make sure there is a market for what you want to produce. Before you run a race, you condition yourself physically. Likewise, when you enter a relationship, you prepare yourself for the

risks. You know that you may be hurt or that it may not work out. As you grow in experience, your judgment improves. You learn to make your love relationships satisfying ones, for yourself and others.

SECTION 2 REVIEW

1. What happens when only one member of a couple does all or most of the giving and caring in a relationship?
2. Describe a possessive love relationship. What is the eventual effect of possessive behavior on a relationship?
3. What is a crush?
4. What is a common reaction to unrequited love?
5. What is perhaps the greatest risk of loving?
6. How might ending a relationship affect a person's attitude toward future relationships?

Chapter 19 Review

Chapter Summary

- People learn to love through experience and observation.
- Learning about love is a lifelong process that progresses through a series of stages. Each stage helps build a stronger foundation for future love relationships.
- By understanding the characteristics of infatuation and mature love and how each develops, you can learn to tell the difference between the two.
- Some people take advantage of a love relationship to meet their own needs but do not or cannot reciprocate.
- An emotionally insecure person may want another to show total devotion.
- Crushes are common and normal as long as they do not cause problems.
- The end of a love relationship can be difficult, yet it can also be a learning experience.

Chapter Review

1. Give an example of casual use of the word "love."
2. What happens if a baby's needs are not fully met?
3. List the stages a person goes through in learning to love.
4. When a person continually searches for the perfect relationship, what stage of love is he or she stuck in?
5. How does infatuation often begin?
6. What does it mean to say that infatuation is "me-oriented"?
7. What do infatuated people tend to overlook?
8. Explain why mature love needs time to develop.
9. What happens when someone in a relationship feels used?
10. Why do some people become possessive in a love relationship?
11. What problem can occur with crushes?
12. What is unrequited love?
13. What attitude should be taken toward love that ends?

Critical Thinking

1. Do you think males and females handle love relationships differently? Explain your answer.
2. Do you believe in love at first sight? Why or why not?
3. With real love, romantic feelings may become less intense with time. Does this mean that love is dying? Explain your answer.
4. How old do you think a person needs to be to experience real love with someone of the opposite gender? Explain your reasoning.
5. Do you think real love can be experienced many times in life, or can real love occur only once? Explain your answer.

Activities

1. **What is love?** Complete this sentence in writing: "Love is . . ." (*Creative thinking, analyzing*)
2. **Giving advice.** Suppose you write an advice column. Respond to someone who writes to you, saying: "I am totally in love with Libby. I've sent her flowers, bought her presents, and told her how I feel. She never returns my calls, though, and sometimes she looks the other way when I see her at school. What else can I do to win her love?" (*Reasoning, problem solving*)
3. **Love poems.** Look up poems about love. Share these with the class and discuss how accurately they reflect real love. (*Acquiring and evaluating information, communicating information*)

STRENGTHENING VALUES

Aim For Patience

Patience is the ability to wait, despite pressures to do otherwise. Young children are often short on patience. Usually, as they grow older, they learn to delay gratification. Patience helps prevent stress that comes when desires can't be met. Roberto shows patience by:

- Not rushing into marriage when his feelings for Vicky seem like real love.
- Deciding to skip a couple short trips he would like to make in order to save for a bigger trip later to visit his relatives.
- Listening to tapes and mentally planning a remodeling project while he is stuck in heavy traffic.
- Reading a magazine during an especially long wait in the doctor's office.
- Listening carefully and without interruption to a friend who has a stuttering problem.

Do you think patience is a quality that can be developed? Explain. Do you think a person can be too patient? Explain. What advantages are linked to patience?

Understanding Sexuality

SECTION 1

SEXUAL IDENTITY

SECTION 2

SEXUAL BEHAVIOR

IMAGINE THAT ...

you are the parent of a son and a daughter. Your daughter has always loved the outdoors. Sliding in the mud, climbing trees, and catching insects are some of her favorite activities. She loves to play softball with children in the neighborhood, often participating in games on the vacant lot down the street. Your son is just the opposite. He prefers indoor activities. From an early age he showed an interest in music. Not only can he sing well, but he loves to go to the neighbor's house to create his own music on the piano in their basement. Your spouse worries about the children, saying that their interests are not right for them. Your spouse is starting to push the children to change, which is making everyone unhappy. You are getting concerned.

SEXUAL IDENTITY

THINK AHEAD

About These Terms
sexuality
sexual identity
gender role

About These Objectives
After studying this section, you should be able to:

+ Explain what sexuality is.
+ Explain how gender roles are learned.
+ Describe how sexual identity forms.

ew topics are more sensitive than that of sexuality. Some people are uncomfortable with such discussions, yet others are open with their thoughts. Most, however, have a desire to learn more about their characteristics and behavior as males and females.

◆ ◆ ◆

WHAT IS SEXUALITY?

When all the students in Ms. Soto's family living class wrote definitions for the term "sexuality," the results were interesting. The definitions were varied. Many linked the definition of sexuality to sexual behavior, specifically physical contact between individuals. The class soon learned that "sexuality" means much more.

How a person handles values and beliefs about sexual behavior is, of course, one part of **sexuality**, but that is not all. The way people see themselves as males and females, or **sexual identity**, is also part of sexuality. Sexual identity forms in many ways.

GENDER ROLES

As you develop an understanding of what you are as a male or female, you first observe how others define the genders. The behavior and characteristics expected of a male or female combine to make up a **gender role**. Whatever is thought to be more acceptable for each gender becomes part of that role.

Gender roles can be viewed at two different levels — societal and individual. In other words, what does society say a male or female should be like? On the other hand, what is each person's idea of male and female roles? Often gender roles in society are described in general terms, yet how each person lives and carries out a gender role can be different in many ways.

If you had to list words that describe females, what words would you put in the list? What would you list for males? The words you put in these lists would probably not all be the same as what your ancestors might have listed in their day.

In society the roles of men and women used to be more separate and distinct than they are today. Generally speaking, women were homemakers, passive, and caring. Men were wage earners, aggressive, and unemo-

tional. The lines of distinction are blurred today. Even though many expectations still exist about how men and women should behave, there is more overlap of gender roles than before.

The Problems

Gender roles can be a real source of confusion and conflict for people, especially as ideas about roles are changing. Some people don't want roles to be any different than they were years ago. Others have accepted certain role changes. You see examples of the problems that arise all the time. Should a female play football? Should a male do needlepoint? Who should stay home with children, males or females? Should certain jobs only be done by males or females? Can males and females serve equally well in the military? What should the appearance of males and females be like? This list could go on and on.

Gender roles describe what males and females should be like. What characteristics describe what you believe a male should be? Will your description be the same as others?

An Equal Opportunity Society

FAMILIES

AROUND

THE

WORLD

The Kalahari Desert is a vast expanse of sand covering much of Botswana in central southern Africa. It is a harsh place to live and a good place to have a steady marriage partner.

The Bushmen are a small, nomadic people who have made the Kalahari their home since long ago. Their society, including gender roles, is a practical and pragmatic one. That is, it is based on common sense and what works. Tasks are done by those who do them best. Those who are good hunters lead during hunts. Good storytellers are listened to at night. Women take an active part in decision making, and men and women share equally in their marriage.

Women are betrothed — promised in marriage — at age six or seven. They are married around age eleven. From then on, husband and wife share the work of gathering food, building shelters, and caring for their children. It is not unusual to see a man carrying a tired toddler, soothing a crying youngster, or laughing at the children's antics.

Children for the Bushmen are treasures. They are rarely scolded or punished. If a child is orphaned, someone else in the group will adopt, care for, and love the child. Adults enter easily and often into their children's games.

Mothers teach their daughters about edible desert plants and how to find them. Fathers teach their sons how to hunt, set snares, and find honey and water.

There is little anger among husbands and wives. The Bushmen have a sense of humor about almost everything. There is very little they cannot laugh about.

Divorce is rare among the Bushmen. When it does occur, it is accomplished by one partner picking up his or her belongings and sleeping somewhere else.

People tend to be more tolerant nowadays of those whose interests and actions are moving away from traditional gender roles. For example, when Thad first became a nurse ten years ago, he was one of just three males in his graduating class. Many of his patients felt uncomfortable being cared for by a male nurse. The attitude today, however, is much more accepting.

FORMING SEXUAL IDENTITY

Children learn about gender roles from birth. The most common question asked about a new baby is, "Is it a boy or girl?" People relate to an infant on the basis of its gender. In one study, some people were told a baby was a boy, others were told the same baby was a girl, and still others were told the sex of the baby was unknown. In each situation, the baby was treated differently. Those who did not know the gender of the baby were uneasy and uncomfortable. They didn't seem to know how to relate to the baby.

As children grow, they learn which feelings and actions are considered appropriate for their gender. They learn this just as they acquire other types of knowledge. They gain approval for certain behaviors and disapproval for others. They observe what other people are doing and imitate these behaviors. They learn from the way others treat them.

In school, for example, Seth did so well on his basic math assignment that his teacher praised him and found more for him to work on. She gave him some extra problems that were even more challenging. When Autumn did well with the same basic math assignment, the teacher allowed her to clean the chalk board and hang pictures on the bulletin board. What effect could this subtle difference in the handling of Seth and Autumn have on their attitudes and abilities with math? Ability and interest in mathematics

has been traditionally viewed as linked to males. Many believe, however, that females can be very successful in math, especially when they receive the same encouragement that males often get.

Most information about gender is taught indirectly. Children build a sense of themselves as males and females from informal contacts and experiences, such as the toys they are given and the games they play. Often the people who shape children's thinking are not even aware that they are doing so.

Influences

Of those who influence a person's sexual identity, one of the most important is the family. What it means to be a male or a female is first learned within the family setting. By the time children reach school age, they know a lot about gender differences.

During the grade school years, children continue to learn more about the roles of men and women. They become more aware of the differences between the sexes. They

Children form a sexual identity based on what they learn and see around them. How do young males learn what behavior is appropriate for them? Have attitudes changed over the years?

identify with and copy behaviors of their same-gender parent or another same-gender adult.

Peers are an important source of information as well. The activities that interest good friends are just naturally shared. Children of all ages want to be like their friends. Copying the behavior and adopting the attitudes of friends is quite common.

Television and movies are a major source of ideas about sexuality. Books, advertisements, and music videos all suggest what women and men should be like and how they should relate to one another. Unfortunately, much of what people see and read in the media is not realistic. Designed for entertainment, the portrayals of people are often exaggerated and superficial. People can easily absorb ideas that cause them problems in real life rather than help them.

Heredity or Environment?

Not all people agree on how gender characteristics are acquired. Certainly, all the influences you have just read about have an effect. These are all environmental influences. The question is, how much is already naturally present through genetic inheritance? For example, are males naturally more aggressive than females, or do they learn to be? Are females naturally more nurturing, or are they taught this characteristic?

Evidence for both possibilities exists. For centuries men have been protectors and providers. Men throughout history have fought to keep their families and their property safe, while females have been in charge of the home. Even among animals, the male of a species fights to protect, while the female takes care of the young. Psychologists, however, have noted that people also reinforce some behavior. Little boys are given fighting toys to play with, soldiers and war vehicles, for example.

Gender roles are not as distinct as they used to be. What changes have been seen in the last several decades in female roles?

Little girls have their dolls and play furniture. Little boys are encouraged to be tough and strong, yet little girls get sympathy, when there's a problem.

Which one has the greater influence, environment or heredity, is debatable. Although heredity may always be an ever-present force, environment in the form of attitudes and actions can bring about change. The increasing number of women in sports is an example. The strength and toughness it takes to play sports is much more commonly seen and encouraged among women than it used to be. Likewise, seeing men who spend time with their children and are openly affectionate with them is more common. Many of the traits that were once considered strongly male or female are shared traits today. Because people are recognizing the benefits of having a blend of traits, society is slowly altering the general picture of each gender role.

A COMFORTABLE IDENTITY

As you can see, sexual identity is complicated. With so many different images of maleness and femaleness around, feeling comfortable with yourself may not be easy. What you have to realize is that you don't have to fit any particular description. You don't have to let the television or a group of friends make you feel that you're not what you should be. The world has room for all kinds of people. You will find many who have qualities similar to yours. You will find many people who appreciate the qualities that you have as a male or female. A comfortable feeling comes when you discover and accept what you are, giving yourself more freedom to develop the talents and qualities that you have.

SECTION 1 REVIEW

1. What is sexuality?
2. What is a gender role?
3. On what two levels can gender roles be described?
4. Describe four influences on sexual identity.
5. Does society's view of gender roles always stay the same? Explain your answer.

SECTION 2

SEXUAL BEHAVIOR

THINK AHEAD

About These Terms
sexually transmitted disease (STD)
sterility
abstinence

About These Objectives
After studying this section, you should be able to:
- Characterize the sexual feelings that develop during adolescence.
- Describe the symptoms of, and treatments for, the main sexually transmitted diseases.
- Recommend ways of dealing with pressures to become sexually active.

o discussion of sexuality would be complete without a look at sexual behavior. How you handle this aspect of your sexuality has high impact on your life.

◆ ◆ ◆

As teens develop, they discover new feelings related to sexuality. How to handle these feelings becomes a challenge in light of the pressures around them to become sexually active.

EXPERIENCING CHANGE

With adolescence, physical and psychological changes signal the beginning of adult sexual development. Sexual characteristics develop as teens become physically able to produce children. Curiosity about sex and the opposite gender increases, as experienced through sexual daydreams and fantasies.

Sexual desires are experienced differently by males and females. Males tend to be more easily aroused sexually by thoughts, jokes, or visual images. These desires may not be associated with feelings of love for a particular female; however, this does not mean that adolescent males cannot feel affection or caring for a young woman. Sexual desires in females tend to be associated with feelings of love, romance, and tenderness.

These physical and emotional changes can be troubling to teens. If thoughts about values and goals aren't clearly in place, teens can have a difficult time knowing how to react to strong sexual feelings. Messages about sexual behavior can be confusing. Teens frequently feel pressure from within and from others to respond to what they feel.

People respond to sexual feelings in many ways. Choosing to become sexually active, however, poses problems for those who are not ready for this step in their lives.

THE DANGERS

Saying "yes" to sexual pressures can have serious consequences. When the time is right, a sexual relationship can bring much mutual pleasure. When not, it can have serious consequences. Two of the most important for teenagers are diseases spread through sex and pregnancy.

Sexually Transmitted Diseases

A **sexually transmitted disease (STD)** is an illness spread from one person to another through sexual contact. Over twenty STDs have been identified. STDs are an epidemic in the United States, with over twelve million cases a year. Three million of these occur in teenagers.

STDs are spread because when people have sex, they are having sex with everyone their partner has ever been with as well. Sometimes STDs are passed because a person is unaware that he or she is infected. In other cases, irresponsible people don't care about infecting others.

STDs tend to cause women more pain and suffering than men. In women, some STDs lead to a painful general infection in the pelvic area. This is known as pelvic inflammatory disease (PID). PID can damage the female reproductive organs. It can create problems that prevent childbearing. Some STDs affect the baby during pregnancy.

All STDs are preventable. Not becoming sexually active is the best prevention. Some STDs are easily cured. Others last a lifetime. A few are fatal. Some of the most widespread STDs are:

CHLAMYDIA Chlamydia (kluh-MID-ee-uh) is the most common STD. Four million cases occur each year. The most common symptom is painful urination. Sometimes women have a pain in the abdomen, nausea, or a low fever. Many people, however, show no symptoms. Chlamydia can lead to **sterility** (stuh-RILL-uh-tee), which is the inability to have children. This disease can be treated with antibiotics.

GENITAL HERPES Genital herpes (HUR-peas) causes open sores on the sex organs. These are like cold sores and heal in about three weeks. This STD cannot be cured. Anyone with an open sore can pass the disease to others. Women with actives herpes can infect their babies during delivery. This can cause brain damage or death in infants.

GENITAL WARTS These are small growths on the sex organs. They can cause discomfort and itching. There is no cure for genital warts, although they can be removed by a doctor. The warts can lead to cancer.

HEPATITIS B This disease attacks the liver and causes flu-like symptoms. There is no cure. Most people recover on their own; however, hepatitis B can lead to liver disease or cancer. A vaccine that prevents the disease is available.

GONORRHEA The germ that causes gonorrhea (gahn-uh-REE-uh) grows in warm, moist areas of the body. Symptoms include burning, itching, and discharges. In women, the disease can cause sterility. If a pregnant woman has the disease, her child's eyes will be affected at birth. Gonorrhea is treated with antibiotics.

SYPHILIS In early stages, the symptoms of syphilis (SIF-uh-lus) include sores on the sex organs, fevers, aches, rashes, and hair loss. At later stages, it affects the heart, eyes, and brain. It can lead to insanity and death. Syphilis can be cured with antibiotics.

The AIDS Epidemic

One of the most frightening of all STDs is AIDS — acquired immune deficiency syndrome. In this disease, a virus called the *human immunodeficiency virus* (HIV) invades and kills the cells of the immune system. The body is then unable to defend itself from any number of diseases. HIV can live in the body many years before developing into AIDS. Once a person has AIDS, however, he or she has only a 50 percent chance of living longer than three years. Death is often slow and painful, caused by pneumonia or cancer of the skin or glands.

HIV has been spreading rapidly among teens but it is difficult to know how many are infected. Because of the time lag between initial infection and the onset of AIDS, most infected teens will not show signs of AIDS until they are in their twenties. They can, however, pass the disease on to others.

AIDS is not spread through casual contact, such as holding hands or sitting next to someone. It is not spread through saliva or tears, through the air (as from coughing), or through insect bites.

AIDS is spread through intimate sexual contact. An infected male can pass the disease to a female partner when the HIV virus enters her blood through any tiny rips in the vaginal wall during sexual intercourse. If the female is infected, HIV can enter the male's blood through any tiny skin breaks in the penis. Neither the male nor the female would normally be aware of these tiny breaks.

Determining the Strength of an Argument

Learning to determine the strength of an argument develops your ability to analyze all the information you receive. The stronger the argument, the more likely you are to be convinced of its merit.

MRS. CARTON *"If there's one thing I can say about my students, it's that they listen. They don't always agree with everything we talk about in health class, but they are open to ideas. Our unit on sexuality was an eye-opener for many of them. They have read the facts and statistics that show the problems of teen pregnancy and the dangers of irresponsible sexual activity. What the book said and what I told them, however, came to life when they started talking about situations they are familiar with. Tia described what happened to a friend of her family who has AIDS. It was a pretty graphic description. They all know people who have had babies too young, and they've seen what they have to go through. My students know that abstinence isn't easy, but I see more and more of them making that choice."*

PATTI *"I can't believe a few of the people in my health class. They don't take anything seriously, even when all the evidence is right under their noses. The problem is some of them think that nothing will ever happen to them. My friend Tyra will tell you different — at least now. She has herpes, and it's made her life miserable. Mrs. Carton doesn't really tell us what to do, but a lot of people in my class **are** getting the point. What we have talked about may just change some lives — and maybe even save some."*

CAN YOU EVALUATE THE STRENGTH OF AN ARGUMENT?

- What is the issue here?
- What information gives strength to Mrs. Carton's argument?
- Why will students react in different ways to the argument?
- Which is more valid, statistics and facts or real-life examples? How would you describe the impact of these on an argument?

HIV can be transmitted in other ways as well. Blood transfusion is one. With blood testing, however, the incidence of transmission this way is now very low. HIV can also be transmitted when IV drug users share needles. Finally, an infected female can pass the virus to her baby if she becomes pregnant. This can happen through the exchange of blood with the embryo or fetus in the uterus, during childbirth as the baby passes through the mother's vagina, or through the mother's milk while nursing.

There is no known cure for AIDS. Some treatments do slow the progress of the disease, but they have serious, negative side effects. Saying "no" to all high-risk behaviors is the only way to be safe from AIDS.

Getting Help

Anyone who is sexually active is at risk for STDs. Younger teens and those with more than one partner are most at risk. Those who suspect they have a sexually transmitted disease should get medical help immediately. They will be required to give the names of their partners, so they can also be tested and treated if necessary. Most treatment, however, is confidential.

Getting treatment for any of these diseases takes courage. The consequences of avoiding treatment, however, can be disastrous, for oneself and one's partner.

The teen pregnancy rate is a problem for society. More importantly, it is a personal problem for the many teens whose lives are negatively affected.

Teen Pregnancy

Another negative consequence of teenage sex is teen pregnancy. One million teenagers get pregnant each year. About one-third of these pregnancies occur in the first three months of sexual activity. Becoming a teenage parent has negative results:

- *Education.* Many teen parents, both males and females, do not finish high school or go on for further education, decreasing their chances to get jobs that will support them and their children comfortably. Many teen mothers fall into poverty and stay there after their child's birth. Few get financial support from the baby's father.
- *Health Problems.* Childbirth complications are more common for teen mothers than for older mothers. Many teen mothers do not get medical care during pregnancy. They often have underdeveloped babies, some with physical and mental handicaps. Babies born to teens younger than sixteen are more apt to die in the first year of life than babies born to older women.
- *Emotional Costs.* Teens are usually not ready for the many responsibilities of parenting. They still need time for their own development. Children born to teens are more likely to be abused, abandoned, or require some type of foster care.

- *Child Development.* Children of teen parents are often slow to develop. They tend to get lower grades in school and have more misbehavior problems. Failing grades and lower levels of education are common. Children of teen parents tend to begin sexual activity early, marry at an early age, and divorce frequently.
- *Cost to Society.* Teen families are often dysfunctional. As you have learned, families that do not meet their members needs tend to result in people who cannot cope in or contribute to society. A weak family weakens society.

In some cases, teenage parenthood turns out well. Positive outcomes from teen parenting require sacrifices and great effort on the part of the teens and their families. Although some stories have happy endings, where teen pregnancy and parenting are concerned, however, the reality is that the negative possibilities far outweigh the positive.

SEXUAL PRESSURES

Pressure to become sexually active is greater for teens today than ever before. Studies show that more teens are having sex — and at a younger age — than in the past. Why? Why, when the risks are so great, do so many young people choose a path that can cause such serious problems? The reasons for one teen may not be the same as the reasons for another.

In the first place, you live in a society that sends sexual messages from every corner. Think about the movies people watch and the advertisements they see. The images are much more explicit than they used to be. What people see, they are likely to mimic and believe is acceptable. The more they see, the more acceptable the behavior seems. When people transfer the behavior to their own lives, however, they must deal with any consequences.

Sexual messages come from much more than the media. They are also sent by the people around you. Some teens live in situations where teen pregnancy is common. A cycle develops. A teen has babies, raises them in poverty, and eventually the babies grow and become teen parents who continue the cyle. Teens in these situations need to discover that they can break the cycle. Although it isn't easy, it is possible. The first step is not having babies too soon. Without the responsibility of children, a young person has the freedom to get an education, get a job, and have an income. Thinking about what you *can* do and *can* become is better than just letting parenthood happen and take control of your life.

Peers are a strong influence on sexual behavior. They may speak and act in ways that say having sex is not only okay, it's what everybody's doing. Should you believe this? You have good reason not to. The talk you hear comes from some who exaggerate and others who take risks. Why follow their example? Teens who think for themselves don't buy into the thinking and pressures of others. These teens are out there and there are many of them, although they may not be as vocal as the rest. In listening to certain people, you might feel "different" at times, but better to feel "different" for a little while than to do something that ruins your whole life.

Sometimes the pressure to have sex comes from inside. A teen who needs love, for example, may see sex as one way of fulfilling that need. A person might believe sex is a way to hold on to a relationship. Sex may even seem symbolic of becoming "adult." None of these is a good reason for having sex. A lasting relationship cannot be based on sex, and a poor relationship cannot be saved by it. A friend or a partner who makes you feel that you must do something you don't want to is acting selfishly. Having sex is no proof of adulthood. A truer test is waiting until you are ready for all the responsibilities of sexual behavior.

Of course, the most basic pressure to have sex is simply physical desire. Even teens who reject the outside pressures to become sexually active can have trouble resisting their own feelings. Sexual feelings are natural, and they can be strong. Your best defense against reacting without thought is to think before reacting.

Saying "No" to Sex

Many teens have difficulty standing up to sexual pressures. They become sexually active before they feel ready. The following reasons can help teens say "no" to sexual behavior:

- You don't want to be pregnant or get someone pregnant.
- You don't want to get an STD.
- Your parents would be upset if they found out.
- It goes against your values.
- It would hurt your reputation.
- You don't want a sexual relationship to push you into an early marriage.
- You need time to know yourself better.
- You want to learn to be more creative in expressing feelings of love and tenderness.

PLANNING AHEAD

Nearly any situation is more manageable when you plan ahead for it. You are more likely to do what is right for you when you are prepared.

Because they recognize the risks linked with sexual activity, many people today are choosing **abstinence** (AB-stuh-nunts), which is refraining from sexual intercourse. You can make this decision on your own. You may wish to write down your promise to yourself and keep it in a place where you can reread it later.

When you have a close relationship with someone, you can talk about your feelings before an intimate situation arises. Make sure your partner understands your point of view clearly. Find out what your partner's thinking is, too.

Then stay out of situations that could cause problems. Avoid being alone with your partner in empty houses, cars, or other private spots. Plan activities that involve others and that occur in public places. This will also help you focus on something besides sexual feelings. End evenings that you spend together when the planned activity is over. Intimacy tends to increase and willpower decrease as the night progresses.

Remember that you have the power to say "no" to any situation that doesn't feel right to you. It is your responsibility to yourself to refuse to participate in something that you believe is wrong.

When you say "no," be assertive. Don't send mixed messages. Sometimes one partner will try to say "no," while at the same time wanting to please the other. This double message often means the "no" is ignored.

If it is your partner who is uncertain about sexual behavior, respect his or her feelings. Pushing someone into activity that makes the person uncomfortable is a sign of selfishness and an immature relationship. Such a relationship is not the place for sex.

TAKING ACTION

The decision to share your body intimately with another should not be dictated by chance or pressure. Keep these four things in mind in your relationships:

1. You are a worthwhile person; your feelings and decisions count. You don't need to "give in" when saying "no" feels right.
2. Know how to say "no" before you need to by practicing and choosing convincing words that reflect your decision caringly without putting down your partner.
3. When intimacy feels "right," ask yourself this: "Is this a memory I want to be recalling 20 or 25 years from now?"
4. If you want to avoid sexual involvement with a partner, avoid the times and circumstances where you're likely to encounter intimacy. You even have the right to avoid the partner, if you want.

Finally, remember that building a loving relationship takes time. The partners need to get to know each other and to share experiences, thoughts, and feelings. Adding sex when it is not wanted often kills a growing relationship.

Expressing Sexual Feelings

No one can say that abstinence is an easy answer. People have sexual feelings that need expression. Many find that alternative ways of showing love for a person, however, can be very fulfilling.

Talking and joking, sharing dreams and interests — all can create a sense of intimacy and closeness. One young couple liked to go window shopping together as they planned for their future. Another couple used their lunch hour to have picnics together in a park near where they worked. They often wrote letters to each other and read them aloud during these outings. These couples showed their love and affection for their partners, yet the expressions did not involve sexual behavior.

Love and affection can be shown in other nonphysical ways. Making dinner, buying a small gift, offering to do an unpleasant job, and other small sacrifices can express caring more than sexual behavior does. Sexual feelings can be shown in the tenderness and consideration you give someone you love. Respecting your partner's needs and goals, as well as your own, and choosing ways of expressing sexual feelings that are appropriate for you both, may be the best — and safest — way to say "I love you."

THE RIGHT TIME

When is the right time to have sex? "Now" is the easy answer for anyone who thinks that he or she is in love. You have to remember, however, that love can come in many forms. Love can be experienced many times before it is real and deserving of commitment and marriage.

Most people want sex to be special. They want the strong feelings of desire to go along with the strong bond to a loved person. They are willing to wait, saving sex for the valued framework of marriage and family.

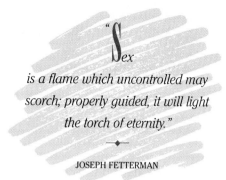

"*Sex* is a flame which uncontrolled may scorch; properly guided, it will light the torch of eternity."

— JOSEPH FETTERMAN

TAKING RESPONSIBILITY

Real-life stories point out what can happen to people who become sexually active too soon. They tell of lost self-esteem, of disease, of unplanned pregnancy, of abandoned hopes and dreams. Something is missing when these things happen — responsibility.

What does it mean to be sexually responsible? It means knowing the facts about sexuality. It means thinking about the consequences of your decisions and actions to you and others. It means reacting with your mind, not your body. It means knowing yourself and your values — and living by them.

SECTION 2 REVIEW

1. Do males and females experience sexual desires in the same way? Explain your answer.
2. List and briefly describe seven STDs.
3. List three reasons why teen pregnancy is a problem.
4. Describe three pressures to become sexually active.
5. What is abstinence?
6. What situations should you avoid in order to deal with sexual desires?
7. Explain how sexual feelings can be expressed in nonphysical ways?

Chapter 20 Review

Chapter Summary

- Sexuality includes an understanding of what a person is as a male or female as well as the handling of values and beliefs about sexual behavior.
- Gender roles can be a source of confusion and conflict for people.
- Information about gender is usually taught to children indirectly.
- Sexual identity is influenced in many ways. Some influences are hereditary and some are genetic.
- People need to become comfortable with their sexual identity.
- Saying "yes" to sexual pressures can have serious consequences.
- Sexually transmitted diseases are very dangerous, since some are uncurable and even fatal.
- Sexual contact is one way that AIDS is spread.
- Teen pregnancy causes problems for the mother, father, and society.
- The pressure to become sexually active is very heavy in society today.
- By planning ahead teens can do much to control their sexual behavior.

Chapter Review

1. What is sexual identity?
2. How do gender roles of the past compare to those of today?
3. Why are gender roles a source of disagreement at times?
4. Are children often handled differently on the basis of gender? Explain your answer.
5. Where are ideas about gender first learned?
6. Why are media images of sexuality often unreal?
7. Do people know whether environment or heredity has a greater influence on sexual identity? Explain.
8. List seven STDs.
9. How is AIDS transmitted?
10. How does teen pregnancy cost society?
11. Describe how peers provide pressure to become sexually active.
12. What right do you have if someone pressures you to become sexually active?
13. List three ways to express sexual feelings other than through sexual behavior.
14. What does it mean to be sexually responsible?

Critical Thinking

1. Do you think differences in the way men and women feel and behave is inborn or taught by society? Explain.
2. Give an example from your own experience that shows how gender roles are changing.
3. Does clothing send sexual messages? Explain your answer.
4. What methods of persuasion do some teens use to try to convince a partner to have sex? What are good responses to each?
5. Who has the responsibility to say "no" to sex, males or females? Explain your answer.

Chapter 20 Review

Activities

1. **Messages about sexuality.** View three popular television programs and three popular music videos. Decide what messages about sexuality they give and whether these are positive or negative. Relate your findings in a short report to the class. (*Interpreting and communicating information*)

2. **Changing sex roles.** View episodes of popular television shows portraying family life from each of the last three decades. Look for ways in which sex roles have changed over time, as portrayed in these shows. Share your findings with the class. (*Interpreting and communicating information*)

3. **People who influenced society.** Find information about a person who was influential in changing the way society regarded men and women, such as Susan B. Anthony or Amelia Earhart. Write a short biography of the person, highlighting the activities and the changes the person helped bring about. Explain how the person's life continues to affect people today. (*Acquiring and evaluating information, writing*)

4. **Difficult sexual situations.** Working in small groups, write and perform skits showing people involved in a difficult sexual situations and the ways they resolve them. (*Teamwork, creative thinking, problem solving*)

STRENGTHENING VALUES

Aim For Self-Control

Self-control means self-discipline. It means managing your emotions and thinking before acting. Tanica shows self-control when she:

- **Ends her date with her boyfriend Matthew at a reasonable time, although she'd like to stay later.**
- **Respects Matthew's uncertainty about a sexual relationship and doesn't push him to act against his values.**
- **Plans dates with Matthew so that they are not alone, such as studying in the library or listening to music in the family room.**
- **Delays sexual activity until she is more certain of her values and goals.**
- **Uses her head to make decisions rather than just reacting.**

How might Tanica practice self-control in aspects of her life other than sexual? In what ways have you shown self-control? How can self-control be strengthened? What do you do when you feel yourself losing self-control?

Growing as a Person

"When my friend Wilson, who lives next door, decided to run in the Special Olympics, I was as excited as he was. Every week I went with him to a vacant lot to practice his start and build up some running speed. On the day of the race, I was sure he could do it. Wilson ran hard, and he came in sixth. I was crushed, not for me but for him. After the race, the ribbons were awarded. I'll never forget the look on Wilson's face as he came rushing toward me, proudly holding his sixth-place ribbon. 'We did it!' he called out to me. 'I crossed the line!' I think that was the first time in my life that I realized what it means to be a winner."

CHARLES

381

Development Lasts a Lifetime

SECTION 1

DEVELOPING AS A TEEN

SECTION 2

LIFE-SPAN DEVELOPMENT

IMAGINE THAT ...

you are going on a whirlwind journey through the rest of your life. You will be able to see yourself at twenty. Then you will see the way things will be in your thirties, forties, and fifties. Eventually, you will pass through every decade that is ahead. What do you think you will see? What do you *want* to see?

SECTION 1

DEVELOPING AS A TEEN

THINK AHEAD

About These Terms

hormones   *temperament*
body image

About These Objectives

After studying this section, you should be able to:

♦ Identify the five areas of human development.
♦ Explain how teens change in each area of development.
♦ Describe the impact of developmental changes on teens.

evelopment is a process of growth and change over the course of life. In some ways you are what you will always be. In other ways, however, development will cause you to be different from what you are now. Although you cannot control certain aspects of your development, you can do much to become the person you want to be.

♦ ♦ ♦

AREAS OF DEVELOPMENT

What changes have you already seen in yourself as you have grown? As you begin to list your observations, you will see that they fall into certain categories. The most obvious changes have been physical ones. Other changes have been intellectual, emotional, social, and moral.

Physical Self

Your physical self is the combination of your outward body appearance and how your body functions. Your basic body type and its functions were inherited from your birth family. Often people can point to physical features that they recognize in relatives. Tallness, curly hair, and big feet, for example, can all be passed down through a family.

During the teen years, the physical self undergoes many changes. The most dramatic are the height and weight spurts in the early teen years. At the same time, teens begin to develop the traits of adults of their gender. Females usually mature and change one to two years before males.

Girls take on a womanly shape. Boys grow facial hair and their voices begin to deepen. These obvious changes are accompanied by changes in how the body functions. The body begins to produce chemical substances called **hormones**, which control reproduction. Hormones also have a major effect on moods and feelings.

Body Image

Reactions to body changes can be disturbing to teens. Many teens are uncomfortable with the changes in their bodies. A teen who develops faster or slower than most others may feel different.

Body image, or the way you see your physical self, can be a problem. Media images of people are distorted. Very few people look like the models and celebrities that appear in the media. Sometimes models don't even look like themselves. Skillful photographers and makeup artists work their wonders to make these people look better than life. Still, the rest of the world admires them and tries to measure up.

The pressure to live up to false images can cause teens to focus on so-called flaws. Overlooking their good points, they see only what is negative and magnify it. One teen feels too short. Another wants to lose weight. Still another focuses on a nose that is too large or hair that's too curly. Females are particularly prone to judging their own appearance. They are taught to please by looking good. Males are more often taught to please with their abilities.

Strangely enough, the features that people dislike in themselves are not usually that noticeable to others. When people look at you and get to know you well, they are much more likely to be drawn to your strong points.

Teens grow at different rates, with some maturing earlier than others. They need to become comfortable with their body image.

SINCE teens go through many physical and emotional changes, medical technology can monitor your health and provide help for those with particular problems.

HOW does technology affect their ability to handle these changes?

When your health is good, you are better able to handle the changes that your body is experiencing during adolescence. The availability of fast foods can encourage poor eating habits. On the other hand, through technology, many fresh, frozen, and convenient foods are available. Teens need to make the right choices. Exercise equipment can also be used to promote good health. Even

JOINING THE TEAM

- When you don't feel well, what happens to your emotions? What implications does this have for teens?
- Many parents and grandparents note that soft drinks were a rare treat in the past. Milk, juice, and water, were consumed instead. Was this true in your family? What is the effect on you?
- How physically fit do you think teens are today? Has technology helped or hindered?

A nice smile, a friendly personality, and caring ways can counteract the negatives. Think about the people you know. Which is more important to you — a physical feature that isn't perfect or the way the person treats you?

Despite what you know in your mind, you may still have some trouble with body image. What can you do? First, make the best of yourself physically. A person who is clean and follows the principles of good health and exercise is on the right track. Be realistic about what you can be and work toward that.

Second, learn to like what you see. Look in the mirror and find some good qualities. If your nose is the problem, focus on your hair color. If you don't like your teeth, think about your eyes. Use positive self-talk to tell yourself what is good. Compliment yourself. When you start to fall into the negatives again, pull out these positive thoughts and treat yourself to them. Eventually, you will boost your own body image.

Mental Self

Another way in which you develop is mental. The mental, or intellectual, self is the thinking self. You learn and use knowledge, logic, and reason. Understanding ideas and relationships is important, too. Your mental abilities affect how you do in school and the way you manage everyday life.

Sometimes people think that mental abilities are shown only through school achievement. This is not so. Mental abilities are also displayed in creative and artistic ways. One person may be able to memorize easily. Another person may have mechanical ability.

Aaron, for example, does all right in school, but he's known as a genius with cars. He can listen to an engine and know in a flash what kinds of repairs it needs. He even earns spending money by repairing cars while still in high school.

During the teen years, you develop a more adult way of thinking. You come to understand that behavior has consequences. Sometimes these consequences are positive and sometimes negative. As your thinking matures, you are better able to choose behavior that will bring you rewards and satisfaction.

You also learn the mental skill of planning ahead. Younger children tend to think only of the moment at hand. Being able to plan ahead means that you don't have to learn everything through experience. When you understand the possible outcomes of your actions, you can sometimes avoid or solve problems before they occur.

Lisa showed her increasing awareness of planning ahead when she said: "It took me a long time before I realized that my impatience was hurting me. I never had any money when I needed it because I'd always spent it — and usually on things that weren't important. I'd go out on a night when I should have been home studying for a test. I really have to work on it, but I'm starting to be able to look ahead, be more patient, and get what I really want."

Learning Styles

Understanding something about the way people learn can help you make the most of your mental development. People learn in different ways; that is, they have different learning styles. People learn through

People learn in different ways. A person could learn to play the piano by *watching* the teacher and then *doing* the fingering.

the use of their senses. Some learn best by listening, others by seeing, and still others by doing. Most people have a preferred way of learning but can learn through the other ways as well.

People who learn best by listening do well at lectures and with audiotapes or records. They are able to listen to another person talk, and they absorb what is said. One teen noticed how true this was for him. He could sit and read for hours with very little sinking in. When someone explained it to him, however, he caught on quite fast. Armed with this insight, he often taped classroom lectures and listened to them later for reinforcement. Doing so was much more effective than reading notes later on.

People who learn by seeing do well with reading. They are able to understand material they read. They work well with computer programs, charts, exhibits, flashcards, demonstrations, movies, and videos.

Colin, for example, learns best by reading and watching. When he was learning to play the piano, he had his teacher demonstrate fingering and hand movements. After watching a couple of times, Colin could do it himself.

Learning by doing usually involves physical actions of some type. The action might be writing, speaking, participating in skits, playing games, or doing experiments. Some people learn by creating something through sewing, needlework, woodworking, or metal work.

Shannon, for example, learns by doing. In her words, "I learn best by writing things. I copy my notes or take notes from my textbook when I study. If someone asks me how to spell a word, I can't do it unless I take my finger and 'write' the word out. I'm the same way with my Social Security number. When I'm asked for it, I have to do my 'finger writing' bit to remember what it is."

Most people learn best when there is more than one learning style involved. Teachers often want students to take notes as they listen to lectures, which involves both listening and doing. Watching movies or videos involves seeing and hearing. Working on the computer means seeing and doing.

Understanding how you learn best can help you develop your learning abilities. If you learn best by seeing, take advantage of this as you read or watch. Use your best learning style for learning the materials that will be most important for your future.

Emotional Self

Feelings and emotions are a normal part of life. They provide information that you can use in understanding yourself and others.

There are eight basic emotions. These are fear, surprise, sadness, disgust, anger, anticipation, joy, and acceptance. Emotions can vary in strength or intensity. Anger can be expressed as red-hot rage or mild irritation. The emotions can also be combined into other emotions. For example, disappointment is made up of sadness and surprise.

When you were very young, you were more self-focused. A young child's emotions are expressed freely, without much regard for the effect on other people. Part of growing up is learning to understand and manage emotions. You begin to see that getting along with others is linked to the way you handle your emotions.

As a teenager, handling emotions reaches some stumbling blocks. Not only do you feel a wide variety of emotions, but the hormonal changes in your body increase your mood swings. Some of your feelings may be weak ones. Others may be overwhelmingly strong. You may feel supremely happy at one moment or be flat in despair at another. Your feelings themselves aren't right or wrong. What can be right or wrong is how you handle your emotions. Being able to deal appropriately with your emotions is one sign of growing up, of being adult.

Controlling Emotions

The way you handle your emotions tells people a lot about you. Are you stuck in child mode because you get angry over every disappointment? Are you adultlike when you decide to try something new and challenging even though it scares you?

You can't stop the way you feel; however, you can channel your responses to feelings. Emotions need to be handled skillfully. Some need more management than others do. Any reaction that hurts you or others needs to be controlled. You will read more about controlling emotions in the next chapter.

Social Self

Your social self is the side of you that relates to other people. Each person has an inborn style of reacting to the world and relating to others. Called **temperament**, this style is shown very early in life. It is revealed in how active a baby is, how well it adapts to new people and experiences, how intensely it responds, and how persistent it is.

Some babies have an easygoing temperament. They are calm and take new experiences in stride. New people, places, and activities don't upset them. A baby with an easygoing temperament might rarely cry and not be bothered when needs are not immediately met. On the other hand, a baby with an excitable temperament cries more and might be easily upset by new experiences and faces.

Another type of temperament can be seen in babies that warm up to people slowly. They tend to withdraw and watch before they participate. They seem almost suspicious of new people and experiences. Once they are comfortable with a situation, however, they participate wholeheartedly.

A person's basic temperament is inherited. Its influence tends to persist throughout life. It affects the way people react to the world around them and their relationships to others.

Just because you inherit a certain type of temperament, however, does not mean that you are locked into certain social behavior. You can learn ways to deal with people more effectively. Excitable people can learn ways to control their reactions. Learning trust helps those who are slow to warm up. Someone with an easygoing temperament can be helped to be more assertive. These changes can be useful in dealing with the world and in relating to others.

Developing socially means learning to relate well to other people.

Moral Self

Another way that you develop is morally. When you were very young, you had no concept of right and wrong. Your actions were based primarily on your own self interests. Gradually, you learned that some behavior is not acceptable. You discovered that what you do has an effect on others, a very strong consideration when making decisions about appropriate behavior.

As you know, the moral principles people learn are first taught within the family. What a family values is impressed upon the younger members. Often religious teaching adds to the moral code a person develops. As children grow older, becoming teens and young adults, they develop their ability to evaluate situations and issues according to their moral principles.

Moral development is vital, not only to individuals but to society as well. What happens when people have no regard for others? What happens when they act on selfish impulses only? You know that the results can be destructive. Only when each person strives to follow rules that are morally sound can people be strong together as well as apart.

SECTION 1 REVIEW

1. What is body image?
2. What can a person do to be more comfortable with his or her body image?
3. What are the three learning styles? Give an example of each.
4. Why are emotions often a problem for teens?
5. What is temperament?
6. Why is the moral development of individuals so important to society?

SECTION 2

LIFE-SPAN DEVELOPMENT

THINK AHEAD

About These Terms
life-span development
life task
adolescence

About These Objectives
After studying this section, you should be able to:
- Explain the concept of life-span development.
- Describe the life tasks and changes of adolescence and adulthood.

eaching adulthood does not mean that you are through developing. Although development in adults is not as easily observed, it is continuing. Development is a lifelong process, one of continual learning and change.

◆ ◆ ◆

PERSONAL DEVELOPMENT

A person's personal growth and development can be compared to that of a tree. When a tree is chopped down, its life history is shown in the rings of a cross section of the tree. Each ring is a year in the tree's life. A tree's rings, however, are not always evenly shaped or equally spaced. There are often irregularities, discolored places, and scars. Each event, good or bad, that the tree experienced was imprinted in the tree itself. These events left a lasting mark on the tree and affected its growth and health.

In the same way, each of your experiences leaves a lasting impression on you. What you are today in personality and in attitudes about yourself stem from your past. Your previous experiences affect your current thoughts and actions.

Neither you nor the tree can erase the scars, blemishes, and discolorations from the past. They will be with you always. In spite of these experiences, however, the tree continued to develop, and so will you.

What does this mean to you? It means that despite adversity, there is always hope. Because development does not end, you can continue to work toward being the best you can be. Your development can continue throughout your life-span.

> "*Life* is not a having and a getting, but a being and becoming."
>
> ◆
>
> MATTHEW ARNOLD

The concept of **life-span development** recognizes that change occurs throughout a person's life. These changes involve growth and development in all aspects of life — physical, mental, emotional, social, and moral. People are not fully formed when they become adults. Instead, they are in a constant process of growing and changing.

STAGES OF LIFE

Each person, in living, passes through various stages. Generally speaking, these stages are infancy, childhood, adolescence, young adulthood, middle life, and late life. All people have similar patterns of development. The patterns can, however, be altered by personality and circumstances. Because each person is unique, the precise pattern of development is also unique.

Passing through the stages of life is an ongoing process. Each stage has its own potential, traits, and problems. The stages build on each other. Managing each stage successfully provides a solid base for the next. The stages are considered in terms of what has gone before and what is yet to come. People have within them aspects of the children and youth they were. They also have inside the forces that will take them into the later stages of life.

Looking at life stages is useful because the framework provides a way of examining and measuring growth. On the other hand, it may suggest a precision that does not exist. Stages are not always entered and exited at the same age. Therefore, the tasks of each stage may be met at different points in people's lives.

Life Tasks

A **life task** is a challenge to be met at each stage of growth. These challenges are faced by all those going through a stage.

Life tasks can be skills, habits, knowledge, or attitudes that are needed in a stage.

You feel competent and successful at each stage of life when you are able to accomplish your life tasks. Success at the tasks leads to happiness and success at later tasks. Those who are unsuccessful at their tasks find they feel inadequate. Such feelings of failure make it difficult to meet the tasks of the next stage successfully.

ADOLESCENCE

Adolescence (AD-ul-ES-unts) is the stage of life between childhood and adulthood, or the teen years. This is the stage of life you are in right now. Getting through adolescence successfully means accomplishing several tasks.

Finding Your Identity

Building a sense of identity is the main life task of adolescence. Before you can figure out what you want from life and how to get it, you must know who you are as a person. A secure sense of self gives you the confidence to deal with the demands made on you.

The search for identity involves all facets of your life. Growth can be uneven at times, with progress made in some aspects of life and not others. This can be frustrating. During these years, however, teens keep working, searching, learning, and growing. As they discover their unique goals, talents, and styles, they gradually begin to see who they are and where they fit in society.

Sloan described the way he felt as he searched for his identity when he said, "I've always been my parents' son and my older sister's brother. Somehow, I never seemed to be just me. Last year, I took chemistry and really loved it. I think I would like to work in a laboratory someday. I also ran

Erikson's Stages of Life

Psychologist Erik Erikson developed a well-known way of looking at life-span development. He proposed eight stages of life, from birth to death. He felt that in each stage a particular life task has to be handled well for the person to grow and develop. The life task, or problem, must be solved before personal development can continue. Erikson believed that no person is ever completely successful at the life tasks. Mistrust or fear of failure, for example, can occur in late life as well as childhood. Here are the life stages and tasks that Erikson identified:

1. **INFANCY: *Trust vs. Mistrust.*** In the first stage, the child must learn to trust others, to believe the world is a safe place. Through their love and care, parents play a vital role in helping babies learn trust.

2. **TODDLER: *Autonomy vs. Doubt.*** As children grow, they begin to see that they are separate from others. They develop a sense of autonomy, or self-will. They understand without doubt that they are people with minds of their own. They feel strongly independent.

3. **PRESCHOOL: *Purpose vs. Fear of Failure.*** When children are about age three to five, they begin to discover the joys of doing. They are active and full of energy and try many new skills. They learn to be purposeful and not to fear failure but to keep on trying.

4. **SCHOOL AGE: *Accomplishment vs. Inferiority.*** School-age children learn to be proud of their accomplishments.

They avoid a feeling of inferiority by developing their talents through hard work and industry. They learn to work together.

5. **ADOLESCENCE: *Identity vs. Role Confusion.*** Adolescents must come to a sense of self. Teens develop their identities or the sense of knowing who they are. Confusion results if they don't, and if they are unsure of who they are and what they want from life.

6. **YOUNG ADULTHOOD: *Love vs. Avoidance.*** Young adults, once they have established their identities, begin to look for love and intimacy. Those who are unsure of themselves may avoid close relationships.

7. **MIDDLE LIFE: *Involvement vs. Boredom.*** Involved people are willing to take care of others and make a lasting contribution to the world. Some people do this through their families, while others are involved in community and civic activities. Those who are unable to become involved tend to feel bored and to believe that their lives are meaningless.

8. **LATE LIFE: *Integrity vs. Despair.*** Erikson considered integrity as a sense of wholeness and fulfillment. Those who are successful in this stage can look back on life and feel that they were successful. They accept that life will soon be over. People who feel depressed or despair about their lives are often unable to face the thought of death.

for junior class rep on student council and won. A couple of ideas that I've taken to the council have been put into action. I am beginning to understand who I am and what I can accomplish on my own. It's a good feeling!"

One part of finding your identity is to integrate your personality — that is, to put in place the pieces that make you special. You will gradually learn what topics and interests you want to pursue as an adult.

One of the life tasks of adolescence is discovering who you are and what is important to you. Why do you need to do this?

Your emotions will stabilize and form a pattern for dealing with life. You will make a cohesive whole from your roles, talents, abilities, likes and dislikes, values, and attitudes. You will begin to plan for the future and move toward adult responsibilities.

Most people begin the teen years with a confused sense of who they are. They are unsure about the roles they want to play in the future. As they grow and develop, they are able to form a solid understanding about themselves that will carry them through life. This is called finding your identity.

Becoming Independent

Another task of adolescence is becoming independent. At some point, most people separate themselves from their parents. They live on their own, earn their own money, and control their own lives. Both parents and child see the child as a separate, independent adult. Some people struggle eagerly for independence. They may hardly be able to wait until they can be out on their own. Others, however, are in no hurry to break free.

To become independent, you need decision-making and management skills. As teens learn these skills, they are able to become less dependent on parents. Leaving home symbolizes the end of childhood and the beginning of a new stage in life.

Planning for Employment

Still another task of adolescence is planning your life's work. Most years of adult life are spent earning a living, often in more than one job. In general, people who plan what they want to do and who prepare for a career are happier. Those who just take whatever job comes along tend to be less satisfied with their lives.

Jobs that pay more and offer more challenge and satisfaction usually require preparation. During the teen years, people begin this preparation. Some jobs require college attendance, so students take courses to prepare themselves for college. They study to earn grades that will be high enough for admission to the college they choose.

Some people are able to get on-the-job training for the careers they seek. They become apprentices or enter company training programs. Technical training is required for other jobs. A community college or trade school may be the best choice to prepare for these jobs.

To choose the right career, you need to know what your talents and interests are. Some people are good at working with machines, others with people. Some people like indoor detail work, while others prefer manual labor outside. Planning for employment that builds on your interests and abilities is one of the life tasks of the teen years.

Preparing for that career puts you on the right track as you move to adulthood. You will read more about this preparation in a later chapter.

Moving Through Adolescence

People move through adolescence at their own speeds and paces. Some are able to work through their life tasks with ease. Others find them more difficult. One route through adolescence is not better than another, just different.

Many people believe that the teen years are a time of turmoil and stress. The stereotype is that teens are involved in constant battles with parents, siblings, teachers, friends, employers, and others.

Granted, some teens do find adolescence very stressful. The rapid change and development can bring problems in relating to others. As teens move toward independence, they are bound to have clashes with parents, who may wish to hold them close.

Life structure includes the roles, relationships, and the physical environment you live in. How would you describe the life structure of this young woman?

The majority of teens, however, handle adolescence well. For them it is an exciting and satisfying time of life, a time of normal growth and development. They are able to build good relationships with others. They have strong ties to both family and friends. Most teens accept their parents' views on religious, political, and social issues. They have found ways to work toward independence without the conflict that some expect during this time.

ADULT DEVELOPMENT

Adult development is not based on age alone. People differ in the ages at which they marry, become parents, and make career choices. How people develop as human beings is based on how they solve the series of life tasks that they face.

As people leave their teens, they establish a structure for their lives. A life structure is based on three things. First are the *roles* a person fills, such as spouse, parent, or teacher. The second aspect of life structure involves *relationships* with others, including family members, friends, and co-workers.

As a child, you had dreams about what you wanted to be when you grow up. During adolescence, it is time to think more seriously about this question.

Life Structure Changes

FAMILIES

AROUND

THE

WORLD

A change in physical surroundings can affect a family for generations. Take, for example, the simple matter of custom and tradition. If parents move to a different country, children will learn the customs of their adopted home.

A family in Scotland, for instance, observes some New Year's customs that are very different from those followed in the United States. New Year's Eve is called hogmanay by the Scots, and one of the traditions is the thorough cleaning of the family's home. It is considered bad luck to begin the new year with a dirty home. It is also thought bad luck to begin a New Year's party before the stroke of midnight. Compare this to typical New Year's celebrations in the United States, which usually

begin before midnight so friends and family can start the new year together.

Another Scottish New Year's superstition is that a family will have good luck all year if the first person to cross their threshold is a tall, dark man. Some families with tall, dark-haired sons, nephews, or husbands will send the men outside a few minutes before midnight. They

are then the first to step into the home as midnight strikes.

Children of Scottish parents who are raised in the United States may not observe these traditions. They may forget or modify them to make them more "American." This may result in a new family tradition that may change again to suit the changing aspects of their own children's life structure.

The final aspect of life structure includes the *physical world* in which the person lives. This includes the community, neighborhood, and residence.

Adult life proceeds through times of stability and times of change. During stable periods, a person's life structure is established and maintained. During times of change, the life structure shifts and changes also. Sometimes these changes are minor, while sometimes

they are major. Changes in life structure can include adding or subtracting roles, building new relationships or ending old ones, and changing the physical setting.

The periods of change in a person's life can come from without or within. Some changes are external. These include new jobs, getting married or divorced, or becoming a parent. Other changes may come from within the person. These often result as pleasure or dissatisfaction with the life structure that is in place.

Personal growth and development comes from coping with and working through the life tasks that accompany these changes in life structure. As you have read, some of these changes can cause crises, bringing stress or disruption. Other changes are low-key and occur with little adjustment needed.

Most people who study adult development look at each decade of life individually. They find many similarities in the changes and life tasks that occur. Even so, they stress that these are overall trends. Each person is unique in how he or she approaches and deals with the following life tasks of the adult years:

DEVELOPING INTIMACY   During a person's twenties, life is centered around the task of building intimacy. The prime thrust of this decade is to build strong relationships with others. Many people marry and form families. Those who do not still build strong caring relationships with people to prevent feelings of loneliness and isolation.

BUILDING A STYLE OF LIVING   A second life task of the twenties is to build a life structure and establish a style of living. Many people are able to choose where they live and visit, the kinds of clothes they wear, how they spend their time, activities to pursue, and whether they marry and have children. Some people choose a busy, hectic way of life. Others live in a more leisurely way. Some styles of living include a few very intense relationships, while others have a wide variety of contacts and activities. The way you choose to live will reflect what is important to you. Finding a way of life that makes you comfortable and confident and includes people to share it with will be a major life task when you reach your twenties.

ESTABLISHING ROOTS   During people's thirties, the main life task is establishing roots. People settle down and find stability and a sense of place. Many people fulfill this need through their children. They believe the next generation gives life continuity. They feel connected to the past through their parents and attached to the future through their children. Many couples who were not interested earlier in having children find they have a strong urge to have them now. Interest in career and community may also be strong at this time.

REEVALUATING LIFE   During the decade of the forties, many people reevaluate their lives. They may ask, "Is this all there is?" The choices they made earlier are questioned and looked at again. This is the time of life when people first begin to realize their own mortality. They start to feel that time is getting short. Often they find new interests and want to take advantage of opportunities before it is too late. Some are satisfied with their lives. Others may look for change — perhaps more education, a new career, or a focus on the family.

FINDING STABILITY AND PEACE   The fifties usually bring stability and peace. People are through the turmoil of whatever life changes they made in their forties. Their children, if they have them, are usually out on their own. Workers are at the peak of their earning power. For many families, there are fewer money problems than at any other stage of life. Couples may have a greater sense of freedom when their children have left home. This freedom often brings more contact with friends. Friendships may become more important than they were earlier. Marriages in this life stage tend to be happy and satisfying.

COMING TO TERMS   From the sixties decade and on people look forward to retirement and anticipate life's end. People face the task of coming to terms with how they've lived their lives. They look back on their years and find meaning in their activities and relationships. Reliving the past helps them master the present and keep a sense of self. Those who are unable to come to terms with the passage of years and what they have done are often unhappy, even despairing. Others are able to look forward to their last years with satisfaction about the past and zest for the future. They don't worry about how many years are left but what they are going to do with them. Their lives have purpose and meaning.

UNDERSTANDING YOUR DEVELOPMENT

Understanding life-span development and its different stages helps you see the way your life may unfold in the future. At the same time, you will meet life's challenges and tasks in your own way at your own time. Because you are unique, your pattern of adult development will differ from that of others.

During the retirement years, many people come to terms with life and find time to enjoy life in ways they never could before.

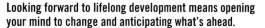
Looking forward to lifelong development means opening your mind to change and anticipating what's ahead.

The stages of life described in this chapter are only a guide to what may occur. They are not a plan for life. For example, most people become parents in their twenties, when the major life task is building intimacy. Some, however, have children at other ages.

Development and growth for most people is a continuous process. Stress and crisis can occur to disrupt the normal flow of events. Even crises, however, are a source of possible growth and development. At every age, life brings change, pleasure, and sadness. Dealing with these is part of the challenge of lifelong development.

LIFELONG DEVELOPMENT

The idea of lifelong development is an exciting one. It says to you that you need never stop learning and improving as a person. The lifelong development that people experience is spurred on by change.

When people resist change, they can easily become bored and stagnant. When they accept change, however, and master it, they discover challenges and stimulation. Life becomes more personally satisfying.

You can open your mind to change. You can welcome it rather than fear it. You will see changes in society. You will have new experiences and new demands upon you. You will learn new skills. All of these forces push people to grow and develop. For balance in life, however, change must be accompanied by some stability. What supplies that ongoing feeling of continuity throughout life? Certain qualities that you have as well as your early training and experiences supply a foundation for living.

Despite what you may think, it's not too soon to think about the way your life will go. Too often people look back with regrets. Having some idea about what lies ahead can help you be prepared. You can make decisions and plans that will give direction and purpose to your life. You can aim for lifelong development that allows you to be what you truly want to be.

SECTION 2 REVIEW

1. What is life-span development?
2. In general, what are the stages that people go through in life?
3. What is a life task?
4. Briefly describe the three main life tasks of adolescence.
5. List six life tasks of adulthood.
6. Do all people experience life-span development in the same way? Explain your answer.

Chapter 21 Review

Chapter Summary

- Physical changes in the teen years can be dramatic and disturbing.
- Mental growth in the teen years includes the ability to think of the consequences of actions and to plan ahead.
- Emotional growth requires controlling and dealing with emotions appropriately.
- Teens grow socially when they learn to relate to people effectively.
- Teens grow morally as they develop a sense of right and wrong. Moral growth is vital to individuals and society.
- Personal development is ongoing. People continue to grow in all areas throughout life.
- Life tasks of adolescence include finding an identity, becoming independent, and planning for employment.
- As adults develop, they establish a life structure based on their roles, relationships, and physical world. These aspects change over time.
- During their twenties and thirties, people focus their energies on forming bonds and establishing roots.
- As they get older, people often question the direction of their lives. They may decide they are happy with themselves, or work to change their situation.
- In the final stage of life, people must be able to come to terms with the past and look forward to their last years.

Chapter Review

1. Name the five categories of human development.

2. How can media images of people make it difficult for teens to develop a positive body image?
3. Do all people learn in the same way? Explain.
4. What are the eight basic emotions?
5. How does temperament affect social behavior?
6. Where do people first learn moral principles?
7. Is your development complete when you reach adulthood? Explain your answer.
8. List three life tasks of adolescence.
9. What are the two main life tasks during a person's twenties?
10. What often makes the decade of the forties difficult?
11. What is the final life task?
12. What is exciting about the idea of life-long development?

Critical Thinking

1. How might a person help others develop a positive body image?
2. Where might young people learn morals if they are not taught by the family? What might be the positive and negative consequences of this?
3. Why do you think people who don't control their emotions well are said to be "acting like children"?
4. How can understanding the life tasks of each stage of life help you relate better to adults?
5. Which stage of life do you think is, or will be, most difficult? Explain your answer.

Activities

1. **Areas of development.** Write a short paragraph describing development in one of the areas discussed in this chapter. Do not name the area. Read your description to the class and have classmates identify the area you are describing. (*Writing, communicating information*)

2. **Comparing human development.** Review the comparison made between a person and a tree at the beginning of Section 2 of this chapter. Write a paragraph, a short essay, or a poem comparing human development to another type of growth or progress. (*Comparing, creative thinking, writing*)

3. **Beauty in other cultures.** Research and write a report on ideas of beauty in other cultures. Describe physical features that are thought attractive and explain why they are valued. Compare them with ideas of beauty in the United States. (*Acquiring and evaluating information, comparing*)

STRENGTHENING VALUES

Aim For Honesty

Honesty is truthfulness. It means more than simply not lying. It means giving your best effort and being true to your feelings and beliefs. Nils has developed a sense of honesty over his lifetime as shown in these ways:

- As a young child, he learned not to take candy from store shelves.
- In grade school, he did his best to understand his courses and complete his assignments.
- In high school, he refused to go along with the popular group of students when they did something he thought was wrong.
- As a young, working adult, he doesn't try to impress his boss by taking credit for other people's work.

Do you think more honesty is needed in the world? Explain your answer. Is it more difficult to be honest with yourself or with others? What might be the long-term consequences of dishonesty? In what ways have you shown honesty?

A Close Look at You

SECTION 1

YOUR PERSONALITY

SECTION 2

YOUR SELF-ESTEEM

IMAGINE THAT ...

you have just worked out the prototype for a new invention. You call the device an emotion barometer. It measures when the negative emotion, anger, moves into the danger zone. When wearing the barometer, a person is alerted by a soft beeping noise if the emotion could start causing trouble. You reason that at this point, the individual can take action to get control. Now you need to do some testing to see how well the system works. Who might you get to help? There's a coach at school who would be a good test case. A couple of your friends are especially good candidates. Of course, you'll try it out, too. Will the barometer work? You hope so, because you think there's a real market for it in the world.

SECTION 1

YOUR PERSONALITY

THINK AHEAD

About These Terms
phobia   *extroverted*
introverted

About These Objectives
After studying this section, you should be able to:

- Describe how heredity and environment help shape personality.
- Explain three types of traits that combine to make up each individual's personality.
- List steps you can follow to help you control your emotions.
- Explain the social differences between extroverted and introverted people.
- Describe what you can do to develop the type of personality you want to have.

side from physical features, what makes all the people you know so different? Could it be personality? Each person has a special blend of characteristics that is like no other. That's what makes people so interesting.

♦ ♦ ♦

Roots of Personality

Have you ever thought about what has made you the type of person you are today? The answer is twofold and complicated. Both heredity and environment have shaped your personality, sometimes in ways that you are not even aware of.

You may recall from an earlier chapter that heredity and environment influence your sexual identity. The same is true of personality. No one can say for sure where the influence of heredity ends and the impact of environment begins. It is more accurate to think of the two working hand in hand. Environment molds and affects the raw material of heredity.

Georgette, for example, had always been high-strung and impatient. These were inherited traits. As she grew, however, she learned the value of calmness and patience from experience, an environmental factor. Her intelligence and ability to change — part of her inborn makeup — allowed her to work to acquire these new traits. The support of family and friends, another aspect of her environment, also helped her succeed.

Although heredity and environment are important in shaping personality, they cannot be used as an excuse for failure or a reason for success. People have the ability to mold their personalities, to change them to some degree, and to become more the individuals they want to be.

"*Remember, no one can make you feel inferior without your consent.*"

ELEANOR ROOSEVELT

Personality is complex. Many influences shape the behavior and attitudes people have.

Elements of Personality

Many different traits combine to make up an individual's personality. In general, there are three types of traits: emotional, social, and intellectual. As you read, remember that all are continually affected by heredity and environment.

Emotional Traits

If you were to make a list of emotions, you could probably name many. The eight basic ones you read about in the last chapter are fear, surprise, sadness, disgust, anger, anticipation, joy, and acceptance. The degree to which you experience each one, and how easily and often they occur, are part of your personality makeup. Some people, for example, seem to find humor in almost any situation. For them, joy seems to be a more common emotional response than does sorrow or anger.

Don't Be Afraid of Fear

Fear is one of the eight basic emotions. Healthy fear alerts you to possibly dangerous situations. A **phobia** (FOE-be-uh), however, is a strong, irrational fear for no obvious reason. Phobias not only serve no purpose, they can interfere with a person's day-to-day life.

The object of a phobia may be a thing, an event, or an act. Some of the most common phobias include acrophobia (the fear of heights), arachnophobia (the fear of spiders), and agoraphobia (the fear of threatening situations). Some people even suffer from phobophobia — the fear of fear.

No one is certain what causes phobias to develop. Phobic people are often very sensitive and imaginative. They may not have been taught in the family setting to see the difference between real and imagined fears. Some experts believe that the object of a phobia is a symbol of some other fear from a person's early childhood. The person has forgotten the fear but has never come to terms with it.

The fear may be unwarranted, but the reaction is very real. Symptoms of a phobic reaction include dizziness, shortness of breath, increased heart rate, and nausea — in other words, all the reactions to a truly dangerous situation.

There are two basic types of treatment for phobias. One is exposure therapy. Here the patient learns to confront the object of the fear, in gradually larger doses. A person with arachnophobia, for example, may first look at a picture of a spider and then, later, look at the real thing. The other treatment consists of a patient's recalling his or her childhood, even seemingly insignificant events, until the event that triggered the fear is discovered. The person can then deal with the fear and get past it.

Sometimes phobias are slight enough to cause only minor problems. You may even be able to overcome them by yourself with some encouraging self-talk and by confronting the problem head-on.

Emotions are often the most obvious elements of your personality. They strongly affect how others see you. Clyde, for example, had a fearful nature. He hesitated to meet new people. Many people who didn't know him well thought he was arrogant. Their impression of him was wrong.

Controlling Emotions

Like other elements of personality, you have some control over your emotions. You may not be able to stop your initial response, but how you handle the reaction is largely up to you.

Negative emotions, such as anger and frustration, are often the most difficult to control. Unfortunately, they can also do the most damage when you let them take charge.

It is normal to feel all kinds of emotions. Learning to understand and manage them is the key.

The following steps can help you meet the challenge of controlling your emotions:

1. *Identify the emotion that is causing the problem.* Try to pinpoint exactly what you are feeling. You may be experiencing one emotion or a combination of several. You may feel angry because you are disappointed. You may feel hatred for something that frightens you.

2. *Identify the cause of the emotion.* This could be a person, an event, or a job that you find unpleasant. Once you have identified the cause, ask yourself what aspect of it you are reacting to.

3. *List what you can do to overcome the emotion.* What steps can you take to change your reaction? What tools do you need?

If you feel disgust with another person's actions, perhaps getting to know the individual better will change your opinion. If you are anxious about an upcoming event, learning about the event and how it will affect you can help you prepare for it and put you more at ease.

4. *Take the necessary steps.* Once you have decided what needs to be done, take action. Talk to the person, rehearse the event, or do whatever else is necessary. You may want to seek help from others, such as a friend who has faced the same situation or a trained professional.

Dealing with negative emotions in this way gives you more control over your personality. It teaches you to turn negative emotions

Defeating Depression

All people have ups and downs. Normal people feel lower at some times than at others. Depression, however, is more than this. It is a long-lasting feeling of helplessness, hopelessness, or worthlessness. Often it has no apparent cause. It can strike anyone, but women are twice as likely as men to suffer from depression. About five percent of all teens experience depression every year. People may express depression with statements like these: "I can't seem to care about anything," "I don't have any energy these days," and, "What's the point?" Other signs include:

+ Eating too much or too little.
+ Sleeping too much or too little.
+ Difficulty in concentrating.
+ Unexplained physical ailments, such as headache or upset stomach.
+ Lack of concern about physical appearance.
+ Talk or thoughts of suicide.

Researchers think depression may be caused by a number of different factors. Certain personality traits, such as low self-

esteem and lack of self-confidence, can make a person prone to depression. Stressful events, such as death and divorce, can bring about depression. Genetic factors may make some people more likely than others to become depressed. An imbalance of chemicals in the brain may also contribute to the problem.

There is help for depression. Eating right and exercising regularly can give you a good physical and mental base to fight off depression. Talking about your feelings when you are low can also prevent the feelings from growing worse. For more serious depression, the advice and care of trained professionals is needed. Guidance counselors, doctors, members of the clergy, and community mental health clinics are all good sources of help and information.

Depression is nothing to be ashamed of or embarrassed about. It is not a sign of weakness or mental instability. Like a fever or a stomachache, it is a symptom of a deeper problem, a sign that something is not right and needs attention.

into opportunities for growth and improvement. Anger at an injustice, for example, can motivate you to work to make the situation more fair. Sorrow at another person's loss can be the first step in making life better for others.

Of course, there are some negative emotional responses you cannot change. Some things will always be sources of irritation or anxiety. Then the stress management skills that you have learned can be helpful.

On the other hand, there are some emotional responses that you may not want to change. Feeling joy at a friend's success, experiencing delight at a beautiful sunrise — these are things that bind people together and add pleasure to life.

Social Traits

Social traits are those that affect how you relate to others. All people show certain social personality traits. They may be polite or rude, obedient or rebellious, accepting or judgmental. Most people behave somewhere between extremes. It's also natural to express different traits in different situations. For example, you may tend to be more judgmental of strangers, whom you don't know, than of your friends, whom you know and like.

Everyone relates to other people in his or her own way. When social aspects are considered, however, personalities can generally be described as introverted or extroverted.

Introverts and Extroverts

Introverted means focused inward or on oneself. Introverts tend to prefer activities that allow them to concentrate on what might be called the "inner" life. They enjoy activities like reading, listening to music, sketching a landscape — those that encourage self-examination and self-knowledge. This does not mean that they do not enjoy the company of others. They simply have a greater appreciation of time spent without others present. Also, introverts are not necessarily shy people. They may relate quite well to others.

At the opposite end are the extroverts. **Extroverted** means focused outward or on others. Extroverts prefer the company of groups to being alone. They enjoy such activities as playing team sports, performing before an audience, and participating in a discussion. They are open with their feelings and opinions. Of course, they may also enjoy and appreciate quieter activities as well.

Most mental health experts agree that a balance of introverted and extroverted qualities is desirable. People who are unable to enjoy either time spent with others or time spent in quiet reflection are not fully developed socially.

Controlling Social Aspects

Like emotions, social aspects of your personality can be partially controlled and changed. Forrest, for example, was naturally extroverted and outgoing. He spent most of his free time involved with others. When a teacher talked one day about knowing one's values and priorities, he realized he hadn't thought much about them. After that, Forrest made it a point to find opportunities

The way you relate to others is part of your personality.

for reflection. When he read something or heard people talking, he asked himself whether he agreed or disagreed or how it made him feel. When he came across something that raised his curiosity, he learned more about it.

Forrest began to understand why he felt and acted as he did. He felt more capable of deciding whether he was developing into the person he wanted to become. Forrest still enjoyed activities with his friends but found it satisfying to know that he could take time out for reflection as well.

Intellectual Traits

Intellectual traits deal with the mind and mental abilities. These skills include logical processes, such as making deductions and predicting consequences. Your critical thinking skills are included — evaluating arguments, recognizing ambiguous statements, and recognizing bias, for example. The intellect is also the source of the imagination, which expresses itself in any number of creative processes, from writing poetry to discovering a new way of accomplishing a task. Your intellectual traits are in continuous use — when you read a book, decide what to eat for lunch, or understand a friend's joke.

There is much you can do to develop the intellectual aspect of your personality. School provides a ready opportunity for intellectual growth. Almost any situation, however, can be a learning experience. What possibilities for learning can you find in these everyday situations:

- An older shopper in the checkout line comments to you on how prices have risen.
- Your car needs an oil change.
- You spot an unusual rock while walking to school.
- You see a painting that you admire in a friend's home.

Your intellect is part of your personality, too. In what ways can you control this part of your personality?

You can develop your personality and raise your self-esteem by improving your personal strengths. First, however, you must know what those strong points are. Sometimes other people see this more clearly than you do.

Choose two or three people who know you well and see you in a positive light. You might approach them with words such as, "I'm trying to work on improving my skills. You know me pretty well. Tell me, what strengths do you see in me?"

Watch for patterns in their responses. Were you surprised when they identified a strength that you hadn't considered? How did their image of you compare with your own?

Now look for opportunities to highlight others' strengths sincerely to them — not just obvious talents, such as sports or music, but also traits and skills that make them special to you. You have the power to help them develop their own personalities.

Not everyone has the same capacity for mental growth. All people, however, can develop their mental abilities to their fullest.

YOUR PERSONALITY AND YOU

Personality is not static. Its emotional, social, and intellectual elements are always responding to internal and external influences. It grows and changes as a person does, intentionally or unintentionally. By being aware of this fact, you can work to develop the personality you want to have.

How you deal with your personality affects where you go from here. It is not a contradiction to accept yourself as you are and still work to improve yourself. Improvement is always possible. Trying to improve yourself will keep you learning and growing over the years. Taking a closer look at your personality can help you understand how you got where you are. Then you can plan what you want for your future.

SECTION 1 REVIEW

1. Name the two major influences that shape personality.
2. What three types of traits combine to make up each individual's personality?
3. List four steps you can follow to help you control your emotions.
4. What does it mean when a person is described as introverted? Extroverted?
5. Give examples of intellectual traits of a person's personality.
6. Can a person improve his or her personality? Explain your answer.

YOUR SELF-ESTEEM

About This Term
ideal self

About These Objectives
After studying this section, you should
be able to:
- Explain this formula:
  $$\text{Self-esteem} = \frac{\text{Successes}}{\text{Ideal self}}$$
- Identify traits of people with low and
  high self-esteem.
- Name the basic needs that must be
  met in order for a person to have
  high self-esteem.
- Describe ways in which you can
  improve your self-esteem.

When you feel good about yourself, your self-esteem is high. Do you think your self-esteem can fluctuate from day to day?

ften when people are asked to describe their strong points, they can think of few. When asked to list their weaknesses, however, they readily come up with a long list. How you feel about your strengths and weaknesses has a great deal to do with how you feel about yourself. How you feel about yourself affects all areas of your life.

◆ ◆ ◆

WHAT IS SELF-ESTEEM?

As you know, self-esteem is how you feel about yourself. Your self-esteem started developing when you were an infant. It has grown and changed as you have grown and changed and will continue to do so all your life. Self-esteem may be high or low or somewhere in between.

Success and the Ideal Self

Harvard psychologist William James was especially interested in self-esteem. He thought that it could be considered in terms of a formula:

$$\text{Self-esteem} = \frac{\text{Successes}}{\text{Ideal self}}$$

In this formula, your successes are your accomplishments in life. What do you do well? Are you a good student, a skilled athlete, a talented artist or musician, a hard worker, a caring person, a valuable family member, or looked up to by your friends? The activities and qualities you show in your everyday life are a measure of your successes.

Your **ideal self** is a mental image you have of who you would like to be. It is related to your goals and dreams. What do you want to be or do? Are you working toward these goals? The formula says that your self-esteem depends on how well you feel your successes meet your goals and dreams.

Self-esteem is based on individual attitudes about what is ideal. If a person has modest goals, it doesn't take many successes to reach the ideal. Therefore, someone who has what looks like limited amounts of actual achievement to outsiders could still have high self-esteem. This does not mean, however, that you should always set easy goals for yourself. Goals can be challenging, yet realistic.

On the other hand, a person who has many accomplishments may have low self-esteem because these successes don't measure up to the person's perception of ideal. People who are admired by others because of popularity or athletic skill may actually have low self-esteem. Their self-esteem is low because they expect too much of themselves.

Delores, for example, was the youngest of three daughters in her family. Her two older sisters were cheerleaders and were each elected homecoming queen when they were seniors. Delores was not. Although she served on the student council and was editor of the school newspaper, she still felt like she wasn't quite the person she should be. Her successes did not match with what she thought was ideal.

Low Self-Esteem

People with low self-esteem generally put down their talents and achievements. Success to them is only a matter of luck, and failure just proves how inadequate they really are.

They avoid new situations or become very anxious when they must face them. They believe that they cannot achieve anything through their own efforts and feel that there is nothing they can do about it. They are generally defensive and often blame others or make excuses when things don't go well. They feel they are powerless and not in control of their lives.

Causes of Low Self-Esteem

Feelings of low self-esteem may begin in infancy. Babies who are cuddled and well cared for tend to feel secure and confident about the world around them. Babies who are neglected or not treated in loving ways tend to be fearful and unsure of themselves.

Analyzing Behavior

The ability to analyze behavior helps you become aware of how and why people act as they do. Then you are more understanding and better able to respond correctly.

LENNY *"When I was in fourth grade, my teachers found out I was dyslexic. I didn't see letters and words the way everyone else did. Some were reversed and backwards. I couldn't read like the rest of the kids. It hurt me that everyone else could read better and got better grades than I did, but no matter how hard I tried, I just couldn't. The worst part was when some kids made fun of me. I would get so mad that I'd say anything to get them off my back. A few years ago I had to move in with my older sister. She's been trying to help me, but I think it's hopeless. She says I should have some of my friends come over and watch videos or something. What she doesn't know is that I'm kind of between friends right now. I want to have friends, but it's just hard for me. Nothing ever lasts."*

OSCAR *"I met Lenny a few months ago. We were friends for a while, but I got to where I just couldn't take him anymore. He's so negative, always criticizing everybody and everything. Nothing is ever his fault; it's always somebody else's. Well, I'm sorry, but that's just not the way it works. Lenny gets angry over the least little thing. He always wants to have everything his way, and when it goes the opposite, he takes off. With Lenny you do a lot of listening and hardly any talking. He kind of clings when you're his friend, and that kind of friendship is hard to manage."*

CAN YOU ANALYZE BEHAVIOR?

When you analyze someone's behavior, you try to find reasons for what he or she is doing.

- How would you describe Lenny's self-esteem?
- What possible reasons can you give that might help explain Lenny's behavior?
- Would Oscar's attitude toward Lenny be any different if he knew more about Lenny's background?
- How can the ability to analyze a person's behavior be helpful to you?

As children grow, adults and even the children themselves may dwell too much on negatives. Parents may continually point out mistakes, thinking children will try to be perfect next time. Instead, children may begin to feel that they can't do anything right and stop trying altogether.

Have you ever heard a person give someone else a negative label? For example, a parent might say, "I'm afraid Blake is simply uncoordinated and probably always will be." Chances are, Blake will try to avoid doing physical activities thereafter, knowing in advance that his efforts will probably fail or he will look clumsy. Maybe Blake will never be a gymnast, but he may be very good at track or wrestling, if he tries. It could also be that he is simply growing and will become more coordinated as he matures. Negative labels can be very damaging to self-esteem.

Although families have a great impact on self-esteem, blame cannot automatically be placed there when self-esteem is low. A person who becomes too focused on ideals that are impossible to reach may create his or her own problems with self-esteem.

Results of Low Self-Esteem

People with low self-esteem often have trouble making friends. Because they don't think much of themselves, they can't imagine that others could like them. What friends they do have, they tend to hang on to. If the friends want to do something wrong, people with low self-esteem tend to give in to peer pressure and go along with it. They are afraid their friends will drop them otherwise.

Research shows that those with very low self-esteem are more likely to have trouble academically and are more apt to drop out of school. They may become depressed and turn to alcohol or other drugs. Delinquent behavior is often related to low self-esteem.

High Self-Esteem

People with high self-esteem accept themselves and others. They get along well with a variety of people and tend to make friends more easily than those with low self-esteem. They set goals, take risks, and accept challenges. They are justifiably proud of successes and don't dwell on failures. They accept responsibility for their actions.

BALANCING WORK AND FAMILY

Work and Self-Esteem

Part of the value of work is that it gives you opportunities to accomplish something. Whether you are decorating a cake, helping a customer, or simply making the workplace more pleasant, demonstrating your ability increases your feelings of self-worth.

Success on the job, in turn, can make you more confident and active in your family life. A positive experience with a customer, for example, might encourage you to help a sibling with a problem or to tolerate some annoyance more cheerfully. You have shown to yourself at work that you are skilled at dealing with people. Now you carry this positive self-image into your personal life.

The principle also works in reverse. People who feel positive about family relationships and about their role in managing the home often take a more confident approach toward the challenges of work. Knowing that in one evening, for example, you can prepare a meal for your family, study for an exam, and go to a club meeting gives you confidence in your ability to manage a variety of responsibilities at your place of work.

IMPROVING SELF-ESTEEM

You don't have to settle for low self-esteem. You can make improvements. A high level of self-esteem can be achieved by meeting these basic needs: identity, belonging or acceptance, security, purpose, and self-worth.

Your *identity* is who you are. It's partly your self-concept but more than that. It is accepting yourself as a unique individual with both strengths and weaknesses. You allow yourself to have feelings and express them, too.

People with a high self-esteem feel good about what they are able to accomplish.

Belonging, or acceptance, is a feeling of being a part of a larger whole. It is a feeling of connection to others. You get a sense of belonging through your family, friends, classes, and other groups.

The need for *security* is the need to feel safe. You tend to feel safe in situations in which you know what is expected of you and are confident that you can accomplish it. You feel safe when you know you are accepted for yourself and respected even if you are not perfect.

Having a sense of *purpose* means that you know what you want to be or what you want to achieve. You set goals and work toward achieving those goals. Your life takes on more meaning as you see the significance of what you are doing now as it relates to your future. Sometimes you will need to take risks and sometimes you will fail. What's important, though, is that you learn from your experiences and keep working.

A good sense of *self-worth* means you feel worthy of love and respect. You have confidence in your ability to achieve what you set out to do. You feel that who you are and what you do are important.

A Growing Identity

Development of personality and self-esteem are usually linked to physical growth. As people grow older, they become more aware of how they see themselves and how others see them. At some point, they see themselves as adults.

In Central and South America and in the Caribbean islands, a young woman's passage into adulthood is called a *quinceanera*. This is a 500-year-old tradition that celebrates a girl's fifteenth birthday.

This is an important event for the entire family. Many families begin planning the celebration from the day a daughter is born. A mother may pass down to her daughters articles of clothing that she wore at her own quinceanera. Other family members are often asked to help out, especially if it is to be an expensive, extravagant affair. They may supply the girl's dress, her flowers, the food, or the band.

The quinceanera is a feast marked with symbolism. It begins with a church service during which the young woman wears a long gown similar to a wedding dress. This signifies that she is growing closer to the age of marriage. The ceremony is usually followed by a large birthday party. One of the traditional gifts is a doll dressed in a gown much like the girl's own. It is to be the last doll she will receive and also reminds her that she has left childhood behind. A girl's first dance with a boy also is traditionally delayed until her quinceanera — another sign that she is ready for the joys and responsibilities of adulthood.

What You Can Do for Yourself

In general, is your self-esteem relatively high or low? How you feel about yourself can vary from time to time depending on circumstances. There are several things you can do to help develop and maintain high self-esteem.

- *Accept yourself.* Know your strengths, but accept the fact that you also have weaknesses. Forgive yourself when you make mistakes. After all, you are a human being, and all human beings make mistakes. Learn from them. Set reasonable goals for yourself and be proud of yourself when you reach them. Learn to stop comparing yourself to others, whether siblings or friends, and be what *you* can be.

- *Be open to learning.* No one knows everything. No one knows how to do everything. Try new things. Learn new skills. Accomplishment increases self-esteem.
- *Reach out to others.* Develop good relationships with a variety of people. Worthy friends come in all shapes, sizes, and ages and have various ethnic backgrounds. Look for good role models. Remember that people are not perfect, but some can provide good examples for you to follow.

Remember, too, that you will not be exactly like them, and that's okay. Help others. Try volunteering. Doing good deeds for others helps you feel good about yourself.

- *Be positive.* Talk to yourself in a positive way. Instead of putting yourself down for the dumb things you did today, remind yourself of the good things and look forward to tomorrow. Dare to be optimistic. Expect things to turn out well, and they probably will. If they don't, then believe that they will the next time, and use your efforts to make it so. Instead of frowning at yourself in the mirror, smile. Recognize your good points.
- *Be assertive.* You can speak up for yourself without offending others. Don't be afraid to express your feelings and opinions. You have a right to stand up for what you believe and to act accordingly.

What You Can Do for Others

During the teen years, your peers have a major impact on how you think and feel about yourself. In return, your actions and behaviors can affect what others think and feel about themselves.

By accepting people as they are, you contribute to their self-esteem. Speak to them, smile at them, pay attention to what they are saying, and give them positive input. Raising their self-esteem will improve yours as well.

Self-esteem is likely to be higher when you reach out to others in friendship and support. When you build the esteem of others, your self-esteem builds as well.

Self-esteem is important. Each individual must work to build a self-esteem that is enabling.

FEEL GOOD ABOUT YOURSELF

Self-esteem plays an important role in all parts of your life. How you feel about yourself influences the decisions you make and helps shape the type of life you live now and will live in the future. What will that be? It's up to you.

SECTION 2 REVIEW

1. What is self-esteem?
2. What is psychologist William James' formula for self-esteem? Explain briefly what it means.
3. Describe in general a person with low self-esteem.
4. Describe in general a person with high self-esteem.
5. List the basic needs that must be met in order for a person to have high self-esteem.
6. List five things you can do to improve your self-esteem.

Chapter 22 Review

Chapter Summary

- Heredity and environment are the two major influences that shape personality.
- The three types of traits that combine to make up each individual's personality are emotional, social, and intellectual traits.
- Negative emotions need to be controlled. A step-by-step process can help a person do this.
- Personalities may be introverted or extroverted. Introverted means focused inward or on oneself. Extroverted means focused outward or on others.
- Intellectual traits deal with the mind and mental abilities.
- Personality grows and changes as a person does. You have the ability to shape and change your personality.
- Your self-esteem — how you feel about yourself — will grow and change all your life. It may be high or low or in between, depending on how well you feel your successes meet your expectations.
- To achieve a high level of self-esteem, these basic needs must be met: identity, belonging, security, purpose, and self-worth.
- To develop and maintain high self-esteem, accept yourself, be open to learning, reach out to others, be positive, and be assertive.

Chapter Review

1. Describe how heredity and environment help shape personality.

2. What steps can be taken to help a person control emotions?
3. Can a person have qualities of both an introvert and an extrovert? Explain your answer.
4. What type of trait is imagination?
5. Why is it important for you to analyze and understand your personality?
6. What is an "ideal self"?
7. Why can some people have a minimal number of successes in life and still have a high self-esteem?
8. What do success and failure mean to a person with low self-esteem?
9. What may cause low self-esteem?
10. Are families totally responsible for a person's level of self-esteem? Explain your answer.
11. Why is having a sense of purpose important to self-esteem?
12. How does a positive attitude help build self-esteem?
13. Are people with a high self-esteem assertive? Explain your answer.
14. How can you help others with self-esteem?
15. Why is self-esteem important?

Critical Thinking

1. Do you think some people need to control their positive emotions? Explain your answer.
2. Do you think you are more introverted or extroverted? Why? Compare with your classmates how you see each other in this area.
3. What do you think would be the ideal personality?

4. Do you think a person's self-esteem could be so low that improvement is impossible? Explain your answer.
5. Discuss the relationship between personality and self-esteem.

Activities

1. **Personality analysis.** For your own use, make a list of what you consider to be the strong points and weak points of your personality. Write down some things you can do to improve your personality. Look at these every day and try to do at least one thing that you feel would improve yourself. (*Self–management, personal responsibility*)
2. **Positive feedback.** For three days, write down the negative things you hear people say about themselves, including things you say about yourself. Discuss findings in class. What can be done to encourage people to be more positive? (*Listening, self–esteem, problem solving*)
3. **Discovering clues.** In a magazine or newspaper, find an interview of a famous person. Go through the article and identify responses that indicate aspects of the person's personality and the level of his or her self–esteem. Share your findings with the class. (*Acquiring and evaluating information, communicating information*)
4. **Building self–esteem.** Working with other members of your class, make a list of things each person can do to build someone else's self-esteem. (*Teamwork, organizing information*)

STRENGTHENING VALUES

Aim For Self-Respect

Self-respect means valuing yourself as a person. It means caring enough about yourself to make the most of your personality traits, to be your very best. It also means avoiding what could hurt you. People with self-respect have high self-esteem. Antonia shows she has self-respect by:

- Exercising daily to take care of herself physically.
- Taking a walk or cleaning her room to control her feelings of anger.
- Joining the photography club to help overcome her shyness.
- Practicing the piano daily to develop her musical talent.
- Making a decision to not use drugs.

In what ways does each of the above show Antonia's respect for herself. How do you think a person develops self-respect? How do you show that you respect yourself?

Developing Character

SECTION 1

MORAL DEVELOPMENT

SECTION 2

MOVING TOWARD MATURITY

IMAGINE THAT ...

a special award is to be given to one student in your school at the end of the year. It is the *Character Award*. You have been asked to head a committee that will choose the student to receive this award. Your committee must come up with criteria for making the decision. At your first meeting, you begin to talk about what real character is. As you talk, many opinions are brought forth. Sorting through the thoughts and suggestions will be complicated. You begin to record the committee's ideas.

✦

THINK AHEAD

About These Terms
morality   *code of ethics*
conscience

About These Objectives
After studying this section, you should
be able to:
♦ Explain why morality is important.
♦ Describe the stages of moral devel-
  opment.
♦ Explain the role of values in moral
  development.
♦ Explain what a code of ethics is.

✦

hat would the
world be like without morality? Some
people might argue that morality *is* lacking in many ways. Morality contributes
order and benevolence, or goodness, to
the world. The morality of each individual contributes to the moral strength of
the larger group. Only when each person learns and practices moral principles can order and benevolence thrive.

✦ ✦ ✦

419

WHY MORALITY?

When you teach a younger sibling not to hit a playmate, when you write your *own* research paper in school, when you return the extra dollar you got in change, you are practicing morality. **Morality** is a system of conduct based on what is right and wrong. Most people have a good sense of what is right and wrong, but do they live by it? Do you?

People are quick to notice and resent the immorality in others. Some complain about corrupt politicians. They don't like it when certain business people take advantage of them. In nearly every walk of life, be it education, law enforcement, or government, examples of immorality abound. People are frustrated and angry when others don't do what is fair and right, yet some don't follow the principles themselves.

Morality thrives or dies by example. Families teach children their earliest lessons about what is right and wrong. Later influences include friends and educators. If people choose not to teach morality and be good moral examples, children won't grow up as moral beings. They will become adults who act inappropriately, and they will raise more children who do the same. The more this happens, the greater problem a community has with the ways people treat each other.

High standards of morality are important to a community, but they are also important to individuals. How others treat you depends on how you treat them. You will feel better about yourself and gain respect and cooperation when you practice high moral standards.

MORAL DEVELOPMENT

People don't just automatically know what is right or wrong. They learn as they grow. As the moral self develops, three broad levels are reached. Each level has two smaller stages, for a total of six stages.

Morality can be influenced in many ways. When you know that what you are doing is right, you can have a better feeling about yourself.

Preconventional Level

The first level of moral reasoning is called the preconventional level. At this level, children's basis for moral thinking focuses on the outcomes of behavior. The rules have been established by parents, teachers, or other authority figures. Children obey because of what will happen if they don't.

Most children have entered the preconventional level by the time they are age six, when their consciences begin to form. A **conscience** (KAHN-chuntz) is an inner sense of what is right and wrong in one's own behavior or motives. In healthy moral growth, the conscience develops as the person's experiences and ability to understand new concepts increase. An eight-year-old's con-

Courage of Their Beliefs

FAMILIES

AROUND

THE

WORLD

The Religious Society of Friends, or Quakers, is a denomination known for its strong moral beliefs. Quakers hold to their values, even in the face of strong social opposition.

Quakers promote peace, tolerance, and equality among all peoples. Quaker families teach these values to their children while still young. Anger and quarreling are discouraged. Thoughtfulness and unselfishness are praised. Children learn to resolve conflicts by working creatively with one another. They learn to speak their minds without aggression, to listen to the ideas of others, and to be open to other points of view.

As adults, Quakers act on their beliefs in the larger society. In America, Quakers opposed slavery and helped runaway slaves through the Underground Railroad. In Germany before World War II, Quakers went to the Nazi authorities to try to stop their persecution of the Jews. Although they are pacifists and refuse to fight in a war, they have often volunteered to take relief supplies to war victims, even passing unarmed through enemy territory.

The Quakers' beliefs are often in conflict with those of government and society; however, they do not believe in using protest or violence to promote their views. Instead, they work to resolve conflict with positive solutions.

science is far different from an eighteen-year-old's.

In the first stage of this level, children obey rules to avoid punishment. They have learned some notion of what is right or wrong, but they don't understand why the rules exist. They only know what will happen if they disobey. For example, a child might decide not to taste the frosting on a cake baked for company because of a fear of punishment.

At the second stage of the preconventional level, children obey to obtain rewards or to have favors returned. Again, children don't understand the "whys" of right and wrong, but they know what behavior is desired by others. Five-year-old Jared, for example, decided to share his toys with a playmate because he knew his mother would praise him, which is a form of reward for him.

Conventional Level

The next general level in the development of the moral self is the conventional level, which includes stages three and four. At this level, people focus on the rules and expectations of the group. The group may be family, friends, a school class, or units of government. Children accept whatever the group says is right. Most people have reached this level by the age of thirteen.

In stage three, people obey to avoid disapproval or dislike from others. Good behavior is whatever pleases other people. People who participate in activities they know are wrong because of peer pressure are at this level of moral development.

Obeying rules because they represent authority is stage four. Laws are upheld, not questioned. People in stage four are willing to accept laws because they know that laws and rules are needed for an orderly society.

Tammy obeys traffic laws because she is afraid of what people would think if she got tickets and lost her license. Kit always obeys the laws when he rides his moped. He believes it is important to follow them. Both Tammy and Kit are at the conventional level of development.

Postconventional Level

In the last level moral development is based on moral principles. People begin to evaluate customs, rules, and laws in terms of their own personal standards of behavior.

In stage five, people may feel that not all laws are good ones. They often work within the system to change laws they believe are not fair. In this stage, emphasis is on the importance of personal agreements with others. Decisions are made based on a personal ideal of what is fair and just.

As a Halloween prank, Karl and A.J. dumped several sacks of garbage in a teacher's back yard. A.J. was picked up by the police for trespassing and littering. When Karl found out, he turned himself in. He said, "It wasn't fair for A.J. to be the only one punished. We dreamed up the idea together and we did it together. It's only right that we be punished together." Karl went to the police because of what he believed about fairness and justice.

Stage six of moral development is based on universal moral principles, such as the sacredness of life, the equality of all people, and the golden rule. People who are in this stage have adopted these principles as their own and act to carry them out. People who reach the highest point of this level are those who devote their lives to others, such as Mother Teresa or Martin Luther King, Jr.

Like other aspects of personality, moral growth is not always consistent. Even people who have reached the higher stages may occasionally behave inappropriately. A person's attitudes and actions overall reflect true moral growth.

MORAL REASONING

As you read early in this text, it isn't always easy to tell right from wrong. You may be unsure. Even when you feel certain, someone may disagree with you. How can you both be right? Controversy about some moral issues is bound to exist. People are not all raised the same. They don't all learn the same principles and adopt exactly the same values.

A person's morality shows in many ways. Whether at home, in school, or on the job, people face decisions that require moral judgment.

CRITICAL THINKING SKILL

Recognizing Values

People sometimes give little thought to their values. They may even ignore them. Recognizing and living by values is a key to moral growth and character development.

JOBETH *"Layla and I have been friends since third grade, so what happened in high school was very difficult for me. When we were sophomores, she started going places with a senior girl on our volleyball team. We have a team curfew, but Layla and her older friend ignore them. If our coach finds out, they could be kicked off the team. Layla changed in other ways, too. She was always fun-loving, but now it's getting out of control. Ever since she got her driver's license, she drives like a maniac. I quit riding with her. In fact, our whole friendship is just falling apart. I had hoped Layla and I would be friends for life, but I just can't live in her world anymore, and she can't live in mine.*

LAYLA *"JoBeth probably thinks I walked out on our friendship, but she could have come along with me. My parents don't understand why JoBeth and I never do anything together anymore. I think they want me to be more like her. They got real upset after my second speeding ticket. I didn't think it was such a big deal. I'm thinking of quitting the volleyball team, and they're upset about that, too. It's just that I have better things to do. JoBeth will never quit. Once we both hoped to go to college on athletic scholarships in volleyball. JoBeth still wants that more than anything. That's fine for her, but I'm a different person now, not the one that JoBeth knew in grade school.*

CAN YOU RECOGNIZE VALUES?

- Describe JoBeth's values.
- Have Layla's values changed, or is she ignoring them?
- Are family values important to Layla? Explain.
- Will these girls' values grow or change in the future? How?
- How can having a strong sense of positive values help you in life?

Some situations are confusing. Take honesty, for example. People believe in honesty as a moral value; however, might there be any exceptions? What about the newspaper reporter who refuses to reveal a source? What about the terminally ill person who chooses not to tell people about his condition? What about the starving person who steals food? These questions, and others like them, are not easily answered.

Throughout life, you will always be faced with moral dilemmas. You can develop the ability to deal with them by using your reasoning skills. First, ask yourself questions to get at answers. Consider how anyone might be hurt. Choose actions that do not harm

Just as your code of ethics guides your behavior in your personal life, so it will also shape the way you deal with others in the workplace. Usually this presents no difficulty. Employers want employees who act responsibly, who are honest with customers, and who avoid illegal activities—the same principles that most individuals hold also.

Problems arise, however, when an individual's ideas of right and wrong clash with the employer's. Suppose a supervisor tells you to overcharge an account to make up for a bookkeeping error? What if your employer uses company money to support a political cause that you strongly oppose? What if you are required to do something you find unethical, even though it is a standard industry practice?

The decision-making process described in Chapter 8 can help on such occasions. As you work through it, you need to pay special attention to the possible consequences of each option. Work-related decisions often have an impact on a wider range of people than do personal decisions. You need to balance the good you might accomplish with the harm—especially to others—you might cause.

others. Think about your own well-being but not in a selfish way. Second, turn to principles and values that you know are right. Values are the guiding force in moral behavior. Third, gather factual information. Talk to those who can help you. Finally, think for yourself. Moral principles can fall too easily to pressure. Strong moral convictions will help you act with confidence.

ESTABLISHING A CODE OF ETHICS

One of your greatest allies when you must make moral decisions is your code of ethics. A **code of ethics** (ETH-iks) is a clear set of rules or principles that guide actions and decisions. It is the real-life application of a person's values. It takes your welfare as well as the welfare of others into consideration. When you value honesty, then part of your code of ethics is, "It is wrong to lie."

A code of ethics is not created overnight. Rather, it takes shape as you confront the issues and problems of daily life. It develops as you think about what is right and what is wrong. As you make these decisions, you build a code of ethics. This code then guides you when you face similar situations. A strong code of ethics is a mark of true moral development.

SECTION 1 REVIEW

1. What is morality?
2. What is a conscience?
3. For what reason do children obey at the second stage of the preconventional level?
4. Describe the conventional level of moral development.
5. What happens at the postconventional level of moral development?
6. Explain how to use moral reasoning skills.
7. Explain what a code of ethics is.

MOVING TOWARD MATURITY

THINK AHEAD

About These Terms

maturity
conform
self-discipline
egocentrism

prejudice
philosophy of life
character

About These Objectives

After studying this section, you should be able to:

- ◆ Explain what maturity is.
- ◆ Describe qualities of mature people.
- ◆ Explain what a philosophy of life is.
- ◆ Define character.

o one wants to be labeled as "immature." Behavior that seems childlike in some way often earns such a response. People would much rather be called "mature," but how is that distinction earned?

◆ ◆ ◆

WHAT IS MATURITY?

Maturity (muh-TUR-uht-ee) is to be fully developed. People show maturity in their physical, mental, emotional, social, and moral selves. True maturity is never really achieved, because personal development never stops. As you have learned, it continues over the life span.

The level of maturity people achieve varies. People may have completed their physical growth but are at low levels of emotional or moral maturity. Bill, for example, stopped growing a couple of years ago, so he's reached an adult level of physical maturity. He still has trouble getting along with others and controlling his temper. This shows that he hasn't yet reached high levels of emotional and social maturity.

The term maturity is sometimes used to mean grown up or adult. In this sense, certain qualities and traits represent the maturity needed for adult life. Some of these qualities are described here.

Independence

As people grow and mature, they move from dependence on others to independence.

Maturity is not just how you look; it is also how you act. What signs of maturity do you see here?

Mature people have established their identities and become independent. Not only do they earn their own livings and live apart from their parents, but they also make their own decisions. Many people find independent decision making difficult. They may be afraid to make mistakes.

Alise really wanted to work in a women's clothing store but she applied at several different types of stores. When an ice cream shop offered her a job, Alise had mixed feelings. Should she take the ice cream store job or wait in the hope that she would be offered a job in a clothing store? Alise had trouble making a decision because this was important to her, and she didn't want to make a mistake.

It is seldom possible to know exactly what results a decision will bring. Using the decision-making process helps you make thoughtful decisions. In addition, you can evaluate your decisions on the basis of the following four items before you carry them out. A good decision for you will:

- Fill your needs and wants, not those of someone else.
- Not hurt you or anyone else emotionally or physically.
- Be realistic and based on fact, rather than on hope, wishes, or fantasy.
- Have acceptable short- and long-term results.

Another aspect of independence is knowing when to express your individuality and when to conform. To **conform** is to follow the customs, rules, or standards of a group. Some amount of conformity is needed for life and society to run smoothly. At other times individuality is all right. Gaining independence means using your own judgment about whether or not to conform.

Kerri, for example, works in the mail room at the Federal Building. The dress code says "No Denim," so Kerri can't wear jeans to work. Although she gets dirty hauling mail sacks around, she hasn't broken the dress code. Jeans would be practical for her, but she values her job enough to conform to the rules.

Self-Discipline

Self-discipline is the ability to direct your own behavior in a responsible way. Young children generally have little self-discipline, which is why they need the guidance of adults. Developing self-discipline is one sign of growth toward personal maturity.

Responsibility is a part of self-discipline. When you are responsible, you are able to see the relationship between what you do now and the results your actions will have in the future. Responsibility means recognizing those results and handling any related duties. Taking on and carrying through an obligation is being dependable and reliable.

Gerard broke the strings on his stepdad's tennis racket when he borrowed it for a tennis match. He took it to be restrung the next day. Since he was using it when the strings broke, he felt it was his responsibility to get the strings replaced.

Self-discipline is needed to work toward long-term goals. It isn't always easy to give up today's pleasures for something that may not happen for months and years, yet self-discipline today can be the cause of greater freedom in the future. You can see self-discipline in the teen who sticks to school work even when social activities could distract. The teen's freedom to choose a good career in the future depends on self-discipline today.

Good Work Habits

Good work habits are part of self-discipline. It isn't necessary to be perfect, just to work effectively for success. You can develop a system to help you work well in this way:

- *Decide what you want to get done or accomplish.* Set meaningful goals.
- *Make time to get things done.* Don't say, "I'd like to do this, but I just don't have time."
- *Set up a deal or a trick to motivate yourself.* Instead of avoiding what you dislike doing, you might say, "I'll do my least favorite

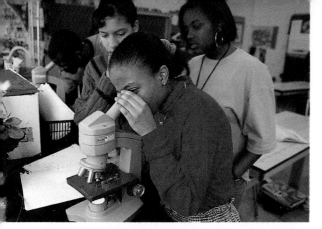
People with good work habits don't let distractions get in the way of what they have to do.

thing first, then two things I really like, then one thing I don't like, and I'll save the best till last." Perhaps you could make a date with someone to do something you don't like to do. You might decide to reward yourself with a treat when you finish a particularly unpleasant task.

- *Make lists.* Write down your plan, the steps you will take to accomplish it, and the deals you've made to motivate yourself.

Another step in building good work habits is to do each task as if it were the most important one you have. Not all jobs are equally important. With good work habits, you do all jobs to the best of your ability.

Respect for Others

One mark of maturity is that a person can respect, appreciate, and consider the needs and feelings of others. First, a person must overcome egocentrism. **Egocentrism** is the inability to see life from anyone's viewpoint but your own. Egocentric people place themselves in the center of life's concerns.

Most children view the world as revolving around them. Learning to see the world through the eyes and feelings of others is overcoming egocentrism. Teens who begin to be sensitive to others show they are developing social maturity.

Prejudice

Respect for others cannot be limited by unfair judgments. **Prejudice** (PREJ-ud-us) is an unfair or biased opinion, often about certain religious, political, racial, or ethnic groups. People who are prejudiced do not base their opinions on knowledge or facts. They look at labels rather than looking at the people involved.

Prejudice hurts people. It is a problem in society. People are ignored, challenged, injured, and denied fair treatment because of prejudicial attitudes. Prejudice is learned, but it can be unlearned. You can confront your own feelings of prejudice in several ways:

- Work to see people as individuals with unique qualities.
- Reject name-calling and conversations that make fun of or speak negatively about people.
- Take an active role in combating discrimination.

Knowledge

Human babies are born in a state of what could be considered complete ignorance. They rapidly begin to learn information about the world. People continue to learn and gain knowledge throughout life.

Mature people have or know how to get the information they need to manage their lives. They have prepared themselves for a job. They also acquire practical knowledge. Shopping skills, where to license your car, how to apply for a loan, or how to fill in a tax return are all examples of practical knowledge needed for everyday living.

Competence

Ability and skill are part of competence. Mature people have mental, emotional, and social skills that they use in dealing with everyday life. Competent adults use their skills successfully in all aspects of life. Competence is related to knowledge. You need to know how to use the knowledge you have to solve problems, make decisions, and manage your resources.

A person's level of competence has to do with whether that person succeeds or fails. Knowing how to deal with success and failure is a mark of maturity. People react to mistakes and failure in different ways. Some quit. Some withdraw into themselves and don't give a full effort. Others bounce back and work even harder.

Here's how Hollis reacted after what he viewed as a failure. In his words, "When I didn't make the football team, I just gave up. I quit working out and playing other sports. I thought that I'd failed. After the season was over, I saw the football coach one day and he asked if I was going out for soccer. I said no and he suggested that I try. He said I really wasn't big enough for football, but with my speed, I should be good at soccer. I thought about it for a while and then started working out again. I ended up making the soccer squad and found out I really like the game more than football."

A huge difference exists between failing at a particular task and being a failure. In this competitive world, everyone fails at something. Failures and mistakes are nothing to be ashamed of. They only mean that what you did was not effective. What counts is how you react. If you can accept what happened and learn from it, you can use mistakes and failures as a means to grow and develop. Actually, failure can help you by:

- Giving you new information. You discover what doesn't work.
- Pushing you in new directions. You may work to learn new skills.
- Making you more realistic about what you can and can't achieve.
- Giving you freedom. You've survived one failure, so you feel more free to risk another. You know you'll be all right.
- Making you more human to other people. It can make you seem warm and vulnerable to others.

People combat failure by trying and trying again.

Are You Mature?

- Do you accept responsibility for your mistakes rather than make excuses for them?
- Do you accept what cannot be changed?
- Do you work to change what needs changing?
- Do you control strong emotions?
- Are you open to other points of view?
- Are you willing to do jobs that are difficult or unpleasant?
- Can you work without reward?
- Can you wait for what you want when necessary?
- Are you determined to overcome stumbling blocks?
- Do you keep promises?
- Do you think for yourself?
- Can you put the needs of others ahead of your own?

Thinking about your philosophy of life and even putting it into words helps you have a better understanding of yourself.

Success can make you self-confident and increase your self-esteem. While success is to be desired, it can also have unexpected results. It can make you overconfident or lazy, which can lead to future failure. Success can make you overly afraid of failing. This takes much of the joy and pleasure out of life.

A PHILOSOPHY OF LIFE

As you become a mature person, you will begin to develop a **philosophy of life**, the sum of your beliefs, attitudes, values, and priorities. This philosophy affects the goals you work toward, the personal traits you cultivate, and the way you treat others.

You may already have a philosophy of life without realizing it. Examine your thinking to see. Try listing your values and ask yourself which are most important. Write down your goals, short- and long-range. Are they consistent with your values? Think about what principles you follow. What would you or wouldn't you do? When you can get in touch with this kind of information, you will be well on your way to developing and understanding your philosophy of life. You can then work to live by it.

"*Make the most of yourself, for that is all there is of you.*"

RALPH WALDO EMERSON

DEVELOPING CHARACTER

Perhaps one of the most complimentary things you can say about a person goes like this, "Terry has real character." People with **character** are morally strong. They have the ability to think, judge, and act with maturity. A code of ethics enables them to face the challenges of life. Their personal philosophy guides them. Because of all this, they are admired. Do people see character in you? They will if you make it happen.

SECTION 2 REVIEW

1. What is maturity?
2. Upon what four principles is a good decision based?
3. Define self-discipline.
4. What can you do to develop good work habits?
5. Why is prejudice a problem?
6. What is the best approach to failure?
7. Explain what a philosophy of life is.

Chapter 23 Review

Chapter Summary

- Morality is important to individuals and to society.
- Moral development occurs in stages. The stages are organized into three levels.
- The moral development of children at the preconventional stage lasts until about age thirteen.
- The influence of the group comes into play at the middle level of moral development.
- During the final level of moral development, people turn to principles as a basis for morality.
- Values help people make moral decisions.
- People form a code of ethics based on values.
- Certain qualities show a person's maturity level. These are independence, self-discipline, good work habits, respect for others, knowledge, and competence.
- A philosophy of life gives a person a framework for living.
- Character comes with moral development and maturity.

Chapter Review

1. How do people learn morality?
2. List the three levels of moral development.
3. When does the preconventional level of moral development begin?
4. What are children avoiding at the first stage of moral development?
5. What are people avoiding at stage three of moral development?
6. What is moral development based on in stage six?
7. How can a person handle moral dilemmas?
8. How does a code of ethics develop?
9. Do all people reach the same level of maturity? Explain your answer.
10. What happens when people conform?
11. How is patience related to self-discipline?
12. When you have good work habits, how do you evaluate the importance of jobs that you need to do?
13. What is egocentrism?
14. List three ways to confront your own feelings of prejudice.
15. List five positive aspects of failure.
16. What can you do to get in touch with your philosophy of life?

Critical Thinking

1. What do you think the condition of morality is in society?
2. Royce complained about a congressman's misuse of campaign money. Then he took home several boxes of blank computer disks from work for personal use. What is the contradiction here?
3. Why don't people have identical values? Should certain values be shared by all?
4. Are all adults mature? Explain your answer.
5. How do you think people become prejudiced?

Chapter 23 Review

Activities

1. **Most important points.** Working with a partner, decide what you think are the two most important points in this chapter. Compare your conclusion with the rest of the class. (*Teamwork, analyzing, comparing*)
2. **Values for all.** As a class, make a list of values that you believe all people should share. (*Teamwork, organizing information*)
3. **Immature behavior.** For three days, keep a log of the immature behavior you see. Share your observations with the class. Explain why the behavior seemed immature and what a more mature approach would have been. (*Organizing information, communicating information*)

STRENGTHENING VALUES

Aim For Modesty

Modesty is humility. It is the ability to appreciate yourself and your qualities without bragging. Modesty shows that you have confidence in yourself. You don't need to make yourself feel important by making others feel inferior. Eugene shows modesty when he:

- Points out how others on his committee contributed to the success of their project.
- Accepts a compliment with a simple "thank you."
- Knows he did a job well, but he doesn't advertise it.
- Gives a sincere compliment rather than thinking he should get one.
- Focuses on others, not just himself.

What are the benefits of being modest? Do you think a person can be too modest? Explain your answer. Would you describe yourself as modest? What examples can you cite in your own life that point out your modesty?

The Meaning of Citizenship

SECTION 1

YOUR ROLE IN SOCIETY

SECTION 2

VOLUNTEERISM

IMAGINE THAT ...

you have been asked to create a video about citizenship. It will be used to show children and teens what good citizenship is all about. You decide to use the video for a visual tour of your neighborhood and community, showing examples of good citizens in action. You will also show the problems that need attention. As you are drawn into this project, you begin to see that there are both good and bad things going on in your neighborhood. You want to raise awareness. You want to inspire people through your video to care enough to make things better. What will you show them and how?

YOUR ROLE IN SOCIETY

THINK AHEAD

About These Terms

citizenship   pollutants
press conferences

About These Objectives

After studying this section, you should be able to:

* Identify rights and responsibilities of citizens.
* Describe ways of staying informed about and participating in your community.
* Give specific ways of preventing crime and caring for the environment.
* Explain how respecting property and promoting understanding help your community.

s you approach the end of your teen years and look forward to adulthood, you begin to look at the larger world and see what your place in it might be. You become more aware of your rights and responsibilities as a citizen.

◆ ◆ ◆

WHAT IS CITIZENSHIP?

Citizenship is membership in a community that guarantees certain rights and expects certain responsibilities. Citizenship usually refers to a person's position in a nation or other large community. Although you are not normally considered a "citizen" of your school, you can still practice good citizenship attitudes and skills there.

Citizens' Rights

Being a citizen provides you with certain rights. In the United States, these are listed in the Bill of Rights, the first ten amendments to the U.S. Constitution, as well as in later amendments. These include the right to:

- Vote for government representatives.
- Express your opinion freely and publicly.
- Receive an education.
- Travel freely within the country.
- Receive a fair and speedy trial.
- Not be denied any other right because of race, gender, or ethnicity.

Citizens' Responsibilities

The advantages of citizenship are balanced by its responsibilities. In fact, assuming the responsibilities of citizenship is the only way of assuring rights, for yourself and for others.

Participation

Perhaps the most important duty of citizenship is participating in community events and government. Citizens who do not get involved in their community are often less satisfied with it. They are also less likely to know how to work for solutions when problems arise.

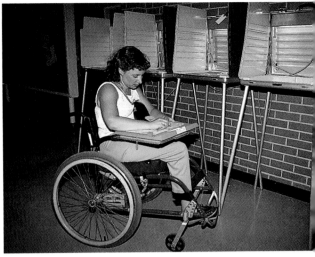

Participating in government is an important duty of every citizen. How else besides voting can you do this?

When people think of citizen participation, they often think of voting. This is a very important duty, as well as a right. Government officials affect many aspects of daily life, including how much you pay in taxes, how often garbage is picked up, and the availability of community resources, such as parks and museums. What others can you think of? Neglecting your right to vote can hurt the quality of life of the entire community.

To choose good leaders, citizens must stay informed. They must be aware of issues that affect their community. They must learn about problems and possible solutions. They must understand their leaders' ideas for solving these problems and improving the community.

Most communities provide a number of sources of information that citizens need to make responsible choices. The media, through newspapers and television and radio news programs, report on issues and on government leaders' positions on them. Political leaders often hold **press conferences**, where they answer questions from news media representatives. Government agencies hold public hearings on issues that they will be acting on. These hearings are opportunities for citizens to ask questions and voice concerns. Libraries can help citizens learn more about issues and about how their political leaders have handled them in the past.

Another way of staying informed is through education. Schools teach the basic skills needed to make intelligent choices, such as history, economics, and resource management. They offer students the chance to get involved in their community. Natasha's high school band, for example, marches in many local and statewide parades and celebrations. Student government gives young people an idea of what is involved in making fair and workable laws for a community. A community relies on well-educated citizens to meet the needs of its people.

Sometimes keeping informed about issues and choosing representatives still does not result in satisfactory leadership. Then individuals have the duty to become more involved. Jonah's father, for example, thought his son's school should place more emphasis on writing and communication skills. He presented this idea to the school board but got no satisfaction. As a result, he decided to run for a seat on the school board himself. There he was able to work for changes that he believed would improve education and make the community stronger.

Not everyone has the time or expertise to sit on a board, of course, but anyone can learn what such boards are doing. You can attend board meetings, read their written materials, write to them, and talk to board members. These people are greatly influenced by people in the community, but if they don't know what you think, they cannot take your view into consideration.

RESPECTING PROPERTY

As a teen, you may own relatively little property. Books and sports equipment are some things teens own. Think about how you feel toward your possessions. Some cost you hard-earned money. Others have sentimental value. You want to be able to enjoy them and get the best possible use from them.

Just as your possessions are important to you, the same is true for other people. Good citizens understand this and work to ensure everyone's right to enjoy their property. They know that they don't want their own property harmed, so they won't cause that kind of pain for anyone else. How would you rank these examples as signs of respect for property:

Schools encourage people to stay informed about the changing world and its needs.

- Mac cuts through his neighbors' yard when he is late for school.
- Becky borrows sweaters and jewelry from friends and then forgets to return them.
- Tyrone saves chewing gum and candy bar wrappers until he finds a trash can.
- Carla asks her sister's permission before borrowing her car.
- Eva takes small items from work for her own use.
- Warren hangs many items on the walls of his apartment even though the owner has asked him to limit the number of nail holes.
- Santiago organized a group of friends to clean up the graffiti, writing and drawings, that others had painted on a fence in his neighborhood.

Respecting community, or public, property is a duty of citizenship also. This can be as simple as returning library books on time and in good condition. It can be more active, as when Herschel and his friends spent one Saturday morning picking up trash from the courthouse grounds. What other ways of showing concern for others' enjoyment of public property can you think of?

Finally, owning property is not something good citizens take lightly for themselves. They respect their possessions enough to take good care of them. They want them to last and to be an asset to the community. The Higueras, for example, own a large home in an older section of town. They keep the house well-painted. They mow the lawn and plant flowers along the driveway. They make sure the fence is in good repair. By caring for their own property, the Higueras make others feel positive about their community.

PREVENTING CRIME

Good citizens understand the importance of obeying laws. They realize laws are necessary to protect the rights of everyone in the community. Not breaking the law is the most basic way of controlling crime, yet it is only a start.

You can discourage crime in your own home. Keep entrances well-lighted at night. Lock doors and windows, especially when no one is at home. Do not leave expensive items within easy access of criminals.

You can help keep your neighborhood safe as well. Get to know your neighbors and their habits. Keep alert for unusual activities, such as unfamiliar cars driving about or strangers who don't seem to know the neighborhood. You may want to organize a formal or informal neighborhood watch, where neighbors promise to look out for possible criminal activity and help each other through emergencies. Jamal, for instance, knew his elderly neighbor Mrs. Meyers liked to walk her dog every afternoon. When he hadn't seen her in several days, he called her home and discovered she was very ill with pneumonia. He called another neighbor, who drove Mrs. Meyers to the hospital.

Preventing crime is not the only benefit of knowing your neighbors. What others can you name?

Caring For Their Community

FAMILIES

AROUND

THE

WORLD

The people of Denmark are raised with a sense of tolerance and respect for others. Their sense of responsibility extends not only to family and friends but also to members of the community. This was dramatically demonstrated by the Nazi occupation of World War II.

When the Nazis invaded Denmark in 1940, they met with strong resisitence. In other Nazi-occupied countries, for example, Jewish people were required to wear a yellow Star of David. However, Denmark's King Christian X announced that if Jewish people had to wear the Star, he would be the first to put one on. He refused to allow the persecution of his people, regardless of religious or ethnic differences.

In 1943, the Nazis took over the Danish government. The Danes immediately went to work. Within twenty-four hours they had contacted all the Jewish families living in Denmark—some 8,000 people in all—and smuggled them into Sweden, a neutral country. That was not all. The fleeing Jewish people left behind all their possessions, their homes, and their businesses. In other countries, these might have disappeared. The Danish people, however, took care of their fellow citizens' belongings.

They stored their possessions. They continued to run Jewish-owned businesses. They hid Jewish religious articles.

At the war's end in 1945, the Danish Jews returned from Sweden. They were warmly welcomed by their friends, their government, even their business competitors. They found their possessions, their homes, and their businesses waiting for them. Their fellow Danes, with their true family spirit of caring and respect, had shown them they were truly valued members of the community.

You can also help prevent crime in your community. Report crime when you see it happen. Cooperate with police officials. Write or call the appropriate elected officials to tell them you support their efforts to prevent crime and prosecute criminals.

The key to crime prevention is involvement. When people don't care about their neighbors, when they become afraid to get involved, crime grows. Criminal acts hurt everyone — in higher taxes to hire more police, in higher prices to pay for stolen goods, in less trust and more suspicion among neighbors and strangers alike. Good citizens do what they can to prevent these damaging consequences.

A very puzzling phenomenon occurs sometimes when people witness a crime in action. Some people, especially when they are with others, will stand by and do nothing. Groups of people have been known to watch someone being attacked without interfering or seeking help. Personal safety is, of course, a concern, but what excuse can there be for not even calling the authorities? People need help when crimes occur. Those around them must react with compassion and a sense of responsibility. Assuming that others will take action doesn't work. A good citizen doesn't ignore a need.

PROMOTING UNDERSTANDING

Samuel's Aunt Rebecca can remember when she knew every family in her neighborhood. Young couples moved into houses or apartments, raised their children, and spent the rest of their lives in the same home. Now the Changs, who emigrated from Taiwan, live next door. The house on the corner of her street has just been rented by Salim Vemuri, a schoolteacher from Pakistan.

The growing international aspect of business and education means that today you have a greater chance of coming into contact with a wider variety of people than ever before. Your school, workplace, and community are made up of a number of different racial, ethnic, and social groups. Some individuals are American-born. Others were born in — and may be citizens of — other countries. This situation provides opportunity for greater respect for, and understanding of, the beliefs and lifestyles of other people.

Respect and understanding, however, don't just happen, especially when differences are great. Many people are uncomfortable with others of a different culture. They are afraid of offending them through ignorance, so they remain distant.

Sylvia saw this happening in her neighborhood when the Petrovic family from Russia moved in. She found her neighbors avoided the newcomers, saying they couldn't understand their speech and didn't know what to say to them. Sylvia went to the library and read some recent articles on Russia. She tried to learn a few words of the language. When she visited the Petrovics, she greeted them in Russian, brought them some homemade brownies, and asked them about the things she had read. By showing an interest in the Petrovics and a desire to understand them, Sylvia made them feel more accepted and confident. She also set an example that her neighbors soon followed.

Good citizens don't let differences isolate people. What barriers are these individuals overcoming? What lessons about citizenship are being learned?

CARING FOR THE ENVIRONMENT

Every year, Americans throw out over 150 million pounds of garbage. It is estimated that up to 110 million Americans breathe unhealthful air. Good citizens realize that statistics like these are a direct result of individual actions. They act responsibly to protect their environment — their home environment and the world environment both.

Like preventing crime, protecting the environment begins by not making the situation worse. Good citizens help preserve the environment by not contributing to the garbage and pollution problem. They buy products with a minimum of packaging. They use reusable — rather than disposable — items, such as cloth napkins and glass jars. They reuse disposal items, such as grocery sacks, as long as possible.

Good citizens also protect the environment by conserving energy. Energy production usually results in the production of **pollutants**, or impurities in the environment. Using cold water instead of hot, turning off appliances when not in use, and walking instead of driving a car are all ways of conserving energy.

Because air and water know no boundaries, good citizens also work to improve the environment on a global scale. They donate skills, money, and other resources to international environmental groups. They write letters to the heads of companies whose practices may be damaging to the environment. Even where they cannot change a practice directly, they join with others to support those people who can.

COMMUNITY PRIDE

A strong and happy community only exists when the people make it so. The more people there are who spend their time tearing down, the harder it is for the rest to build. People want to be able to walk the streets safely. They want a clean and healthful environment. They want to be friends, not enemies. A good feeling comes to those who practice good citizenship as they contribute to the solutions instead of the problems.

SECTION 1 REVIEW

1. List three rights of United States citizens.
2. Why is voting an important responsibility of citizenship?
3. How can feelings about your possessions guide your attitude toward the property of others?
4. Why is it important to obey laws?
5. What opportunity is provided by the great variety of racial, social, and ethnic groups living in a community?
6. What are pollutants?

SECTION 2

VOLUNTEERISM

THINK AHEAD

About These Terms
volunteerism   *altruistic*

About These Objectives
After studying this section, you should be able to:
- Explain how you can benefit by volunteering.
- Identify qualities needed by volunteers.
- Name specific volunteer opportunities.
- Explain how to choose a volunteer opportunity that is right for you.

ave you ever been helped by a volunteer? Chances are, you have. Volunteers are all around you. They help plan and carry out many events in schools. They tutor children and put away books in libraries. They coach and raise money. They listen to people who need help. The spirit of **volunteerism**, or willingness to give service to others, is alive and well in many corners of your community.

◆ ◆ ◆

VOLUNTEERS ARE NEEDED

Although volunteers are everywhere, the need for more still exists. The ranks of volunteers used to be heavily filled by women. When fewer women had jobs outside the home, they were more available to do volunteer work. That picture has changed. As more women have entered the work force, the need for volunteers has grown.

Volunteers are also needed because agencies and organizations have fewer funds available today to do what needs doing. Public and private social service agency funds can rarely be stretched far enough. When economic times are tight, programs are cut because people cannot be paid. The answer? Find people who will help by donating their time.

Teens are an excellent volunteer resource. Often they have a little time they can spare. They may wish to do something useful with that time rather than spend it in front of the television or just "hang out." Teens have high energy levels, plenty of enthusiasm, and spirit. They are needed in the world of volunteers.

Retired people have also become an important volunteer resource. Many older adults find that volunteer work gives purpose and meaning to their lives after they retire. Longer life spans and better health enables an increasing number of retired people to contribute to their communities through volunteerism.

Doing volunteer work is one of the best ways for good citizens to show they care about their community. Every community has needs that are not met and jobs that are not done. People who volunteer their services help fill these needs and discover that the rewards are many.

TAKING ACTION

Did you ever notice how easy it is to not notice? No, this is not double-talk. What it means is that often people walk through life never seeing what needs doing around them.

Does your community need you? You could pick up the fast food container that's on the ground and throw it away — even though you didn't put it there. You could fix the broken swing that children play on in the park. You could plant flowers where they will add beauty in your neighborhood. You could call city officials about the lights that are out or the sign that is down. What else could you do? When your eyes and heart are open, you will have answers.

You will enjoy volunteer work more and do a better job if you choose activities that interest you.

WHAT CAN YOU GAIN?

Most people see the value of volunteers to the organizations they help. Fewer people, however, realize how giving of one's time and talents enriches the life of the individual.

Doing volunteer work allows you to use your present skills and learn new ones.

Choosing volunteer work in the fields you feel confident in helps you enjoy the work more and do a better job. It also gives you the chance to expand your skills and knowledge into related areas. This not only gives a feeling of personal satisfaction, but it can help you achieve future goals as well. Samantha, for example, is a talented artist. When she offered to help design an advertising campaign for a charity's fund-raising drive, she learned how to use a graphics program on the group's computer. This was a skill she found valuable as she later worked toward her goal of becoming an architect. People who are uncertain about their choice of a career can learn what jobs they might be good at by exploring their skills through volunteer work.

Volunteering gives you the opportunity to meet a wide variety of people. Making new acquaintances can be personally as well as professionally beneficial.They can result in friendships that make life more pleasant and interesting. They can also be sources of help and information about job openings, career opportunities, and workplace skills. Often people who volunteer are able to use the people they work for as references for future education and job applications.

Volunteering can also help strengthen personal relationship skills. You learn to work with others and follow directions. You develop communication skills. You increase your ability to empathize with others.

Donating resources now can also save other resources in the future. Randall learned that many convicted criminals return to prison because they lack the reading and writing skills needed to get jobs. He became a tutor for a literacy program at a state prison. He felt this not only helped the inmates but would also help reduce the amount of tax money spent on prisons.

Volunteering can teach valuable career and personal relationship skills.

Helping Others Balance the Load

If you've ever struggled with balancing personal, school, and family responsibilities, you can appreciate the value of volunteers who help others accomplish just that feat. Opportunities to volunteer in this area are as limitless as families' needs.

Child care, as you know, is a major concern of working families. You can help by volunteering at a child care facility or a library, in an after-school or summer recreational program. If you need to be at home, you can still help—by telephone. Some community groups have "homework hotlines" to assist children with school subjects. Others have set up telephone networks that connect children who are home alone with a reassuring voice when problems or loneliness arise.

Care for older relatives is also a concern for more and more families. Organizations that help meet this need, such as senior centers, meal delivery services, and nursing homes are often looking for volunteers to help them expand their programs.

Even if you don't take part in a formal volunteer activity, you can show the volunteer spirit. At home, you might do extra tasks for a family member or help a neighbor with a home repair. You may be able to help family members in their work as well by volunteering to take care of some filing or copying. Every responsibility you assume is one less thing for someone else to factor into the effort to balance work and family life.

A Special Feeling

Perhaps the most important benefit to volunteers is the rewarding feeling of improving life for someone else. Volunteers often get to see the effects of their work on others. Visiting the elderly in a nursing home, helping children at a child care center, delivering meals to homebound people — all let volunteers know that they have made life better for someone. Most volunteers agree that this feeling alone makes what they do worthwhile.

"*Light tomorrow with today!*"

ELIZABETH BARRETT BROWNING

THE QUALITIES YOU NEED

In many ways volunteering is like having a job. Although you are not paid for your work, you are still responsible for doing what you say you will. People who volunteer make a commitment. Others count on them to be present and on time according to any agreement. When you volunteer, you need to follow through and work hard. People put their trust in you to do an important job. Letting them down hurts the organizers, the job that needs doing, and your reputation.

Many personal qualities come in handy when you volunteer. Good relationship skills can be practiced and also learned on many jobs. You can lead and you can follow. You can also use specific skills, such as knowledge about a sport or experience with a computer. It's interesting that the qualities you have can be used when you volunteer, but they can also be developed.

Volunteers can have a positive impact on others. How have you benefitted from the volunteer activities of other people?

Often people who have a volunteering spirit are called **altruistic** (AL-true-ISS-tick). That is, they have an unselfish concern for the welfare of others. They are willing to step in and help when there is a need. You may be able to think of well-known people who exhibit this quality. It is one that is universally admired.

WHERE TO VOLUNTEER

The opportunities for volunteering are too numerous to include them all. Anywhere there are people helping people, there is probably a need for volunteers. Here are a few ideas:

- Children's sports leagues
- Hospitals
- Retirement homes
- Animal shelters
- Church organizations
- Music and theatre groups
- Schools
- Libraries
- Environmental groups
- Parks and zoos

Who Needs Your Help?

The opportunities for volunteering are all around you. Here are just a few organizations that use volunteers:

Special Olympics
Suite 500
1350 New York Avenue NW,
Washington, DC 20005
An international sports program for people with mental disabilities.

The Sierra Club
730 Polk Street
San Fransisco, CA 94109
Promotes ecological awareness and preservation.

Habitiat For Humanity International
Habitat and Church Streets
Americus, GA 31709-3498
Helps provide housing for working, lower-income families.

Second Harvest
343 South Dearborn
Chicago, IL 60604
Collects donated food for distribution to soup kitchens.

What Can You Do?

Sometimes you just need some ideas to get your own ideas flowing. What can you do as a volunteer? Start with these and then add to the list:

- Recycle one aluminum can every day.
- Plant a tree.
- Write an environmental column for your school newspaper.
- Write to a company about their overuse of packaging materials.
- Tutor a child who needs help in your school or neighborhood.
- Organize a drive to get coats, mittens, and scarves for needy children in the winter.
- Take a busy parent's child for a couple hours of entertainment to give the parent some free time.
- Hand out pamphlets during a political campaign.
- Get training to work a teen hotline.
- Adopt a park or neighborhood area that needs cleaning.

In addition, many national charitable groups may have local branches in your community. The American Red Cross offers a broad variety of services to people, from free blood-pressure screenings to food and shelter for natural disaster victims. They have branches in most major cities. Big Brothers/Big Sisters pairs up children from single-parent homes with adults who act as friends and role models. Habitat for Humanity helps low-income families find decent housing by building new houses or rehabilitating older ones. The Salvation Army provides numerous services for the homeless, elderly, and others in need of aid.

To offer your services as a volunteer, first consider your interests, abilities, and the time you are able to invest. Then learn about the different organizations. Libraries often carry informational material supplied by these groups. You can also call each group directly. Look in the Yellow Pages under "Social Service Organizations." Newspapers often have regular columns devoted to volunteering opportunities. Some larger communities have volunteer coordination centers where you can learn what service groups exist and what kind of help they need. When you volunteer, consider persuading a friend to join also. This can benefit you, your friend, and the organization.

What's Right for You?

Sometimes people think of volunteering as a huge commitment. That need not be so. Volunteering comes in all sizes. When you develop a volunteering spirit, you find little ways in everyday life to do things for people. You might volunteer at home. You might do something for a neighbor occasionally as the need arises. If you have the time, you can get involved in an activity that takes a regular commitment of hours and energy. You can find the level that fits your life the best when you say to yourself and others, "Yes, I'd like to help."

SECTION 2 REVIEW

1. Give two reasons for the increased need for volunteers.
2. How can meeting people through volunteering be professionally beneficial?
3. What may be the most important benefit to volunteers?
4. How is volunteering like having a job?
5. What does "altruistic" mean?
6. List five places that might possibly need volunteers.

Chapter 24 Review

Chapter Summary

- Citizenship includes both rights and responsibilities. The rights cannot be enjoyed unless the responsibilities are assumed.
- Good citizens stay informed about the issues that affect their community. They participate in meeting the community's needs.
- Good citizens are actively involved in preventing crime and in bringing criminals to justice.
- Good citizens strengthen their community by promoting understanding among different groups of people.
- Good citizens work to protect the environment and keep their community clean.
- By volunteering, you help both yourself and others. You improve people's lives while learning skills and developing talents.
- Volunteer opportunities abound, in both formal organizations and individual situations. You can find opportunities that suit your abilities and interests.

Chapter Review

1. Identify five responsibilities of citizens.
2. Explain how the following help citizens stay informed: the media; public hearings; libraries; education.
3. What is a press conference?
4. How does respecting your own and others' property help the community?
5. Identify six ways of controlling and preventing crime.
6. Name five things good citizens do to help protect the environment.
7. Identify five ways in which you can benefit by volunteering.
8. List four qualities needed by volunteers.
9. Where could you find information about places that need volunteers?
10. Does volunteering always require regular commitments of time and energy? Explain.

Critical Thinking

1. When people destroy public property, who pays?
2. What reasons do people sometimes give for not assuming their responsibilities as citizens? Are these reasons valid?
3. People often fail to care for the environment because they feel that the actions of one person don't make a difference. How would you respond to this argument?
4. What false ideas or expectations do people sometimes have about volunteering? How do these ideas discourage people from volunteering? How might unrealistic expectations leave people disappointed when they do volunteer?

Chapter 24 Review

Activities

1. **Citizens' rights.** Using a copy of the Constitution of the United States and of your own state, identify the rights they guarantee to citizens. Present your findings in a brief oral report to the class. (*Acquiring and evaluating information, summarizing, speaking*)

2. **Foreign citizens' rights.** Find information about the rights and responsibilities of citizens in other countries. Compare and contrast these with those of United States citizens in a written report. (*Acquiring and evaluating information, comparing and contrasting*)

3. **Local government.** In newspapers, find information about upcoming meetings of community government bodies. Attend one of these meetings. Make a brief written or oral report on how it was conducted, what was discussed, and what was accomplished. (*Acquiring information, communicating information*)

4. **A problem for government.** Write a letter to a government representative about a problem that you believe this person can help solve. Identify the problem and explain what you think this person should do to solve it. (*Communicating information, problem solving, writing*)

5. **Volunteer opportunities.** Interview a representative of a volunteer organization. Learn about the group's function and its opportunities for teens. Share this information with the class. As a class, compile a comprehensive list of volunteer opportunities in your community. (*Interviewing, communicating information, organizing information*)

STRENGTHENING VALUES

Aim For Generosity

Generosity means giving of your time, talents, and other resources without expecting to be paid back. Chelsea is known for her generosity. She:

- Volunteers once a week at the local chapter of the American Red Cross.
- Donates older but wearable clothing to her church's clothing drive for the homeless.
- Helps register voters before national and local elections.
- Includes an elderly neighbor on many of her trips to the grocery store, shopping mall, and library.

Must a person have many resources in order to be generous? Explain your answer. Is generosity contagious? Explain. Do generous people expect something in return? How can you use your talents and skills to help others? Give an example of how you have shown generosity.

Moving Toward Independence

"My first day on the job was a disaster. To begin with I dropped an order on the floor. I was trying to balance three plates, and the sandwich just slid off. By the end of the day, I had totaled two checks wrong and broken a glass. I guess I thought I wasn't cut out for the work world. That was six months ago. Now I can balance a tray with the best of them, and I'm quick, too. My boss says he doesn't know what he'd do without me. I've learned a lot in the past few months — not just about working but also about me. I'm starting to think about my future more seriously than ever before."

AIMEE

On Your Own

IMAGINE THAT ...

you have just moved into your first apartment. With your family's help, you have gathered the supplies and furnishings you need to get started. After arranging the furniture and unpacking several boxes, you are tired, hungry, and ready to relax. For your first meal in the apartment, you bake a frozen pizza, and round out your meal with an apple and a glass of milk. How exciting to be on your own at last! As you eat, however, you notice how quiet it is. For a few moments, a feeling of loneliness surrounds you. Then you notice the bareness of your living room walls, and you begin to think of ways to make the apartment feel like home — your home.

MAKING THE MOVE

THINK AHEAD

About These Terms

security deposit *lease*

About These Objectives

After studying this section, you should be able to:

- Identify factors that may affect the decision to leave home.
- Give examples of questions that should be considered when apartment-hunting.
- Describe various housing options.

t some time, usually at the end of the teen years, people move away from their families and begin living on their own. Living independently is an important step in growth towards maturity. It gives you a chance to learn more about yourself and to prove that you are able to handle the decisions and responsibilities of adulthood. Knowing that you can live alone and take care of yourself is a good feeling.

◆ ◆ ◆

451

DECIDING TO LEAVE HOME

Young adults today are waiting longer to leave home than they used to. In fact, there are more eighteen- to twenty-year-olds living at home today than at any time in the past fifty years. This is due in part to the high cost of living independently and to the fact that people are waiting longer to marry.

There is no single "right" time or reason for moving out on your own. Each individual is different. You may leave home temporarily to attend college or get other training. Some people leave home when they get married or join the armed forces. Usually people do not leave home until they are financially self-supporting and feel ready to handle the many responsibilities of adult living.

One of the first decisions you will face when you move away from home is where to live. People who go on to school often choose group living, such as a dormitory.

"*The most important thing is to learn to rule oneself.*"

JOHANN WOLFGANG VON GOETHE

SELECTING HOUSING

Choosing a place to live is one of the first decisions to make when leaving home. What type of housing will you choose? You may have several options.

For some, the first step in moving out on their own involves group housing. Students who attend college, for example, may live in a dormitory. Those entering the military live in barracks. Most others, however, will need to explore other possibilities, such as living in an apartment.

Apartment Living

Many young adults first experience independent living by moving into an *apartment*. Newspaper classified ads usually carry apartment listings. Rental agencies and some real estate companies locate apartments for people. Family, friends, and co-workers may also provide leads on available apartments.

Finding the right apartment is not as simple as you might think. You may be disappointed with your choice if you don't do some careful checking. Questions you should consider when apartment hunting include:

- *Can you afford the rent?* Most rental agreements also require a **security deposit**, a one-time payment usually equal to one month's rent. The deposit is returned to you when you move out if you have not damaged the apartment. Otherwise, it is used to pay for any necessary repairs.

Coming of Age in the Ituri Forest

FAMILIES

AROUND THE WORLD

Among the Efe people of the Ituri Forest in Zaire, a young girl's coming of age is an important event. The celebration of the event is called an *ima*.

An ima can be expensive. Food and drink are supplied for the whole community during the several days of feasting. The girls are housed, fed, and cared for in a special hut until it is judged that they have reached womanhood. Imas today are rare unless families with girls about the same age share the expense.

Families of the girls prepare special ornaments and clothing for them. Woven head-dresses of straw and feathers and braided armbands and breast-bands of grasses and plants are made and dyed. The dyes are made from shaved wood, roots, and fruit juices.

The most important piece of the girls' com-ing-of-age costume is often a carefully deco-rated piece of bark cloth. This was once the tradi-tional cloth of the Efe. Most Efe today wear cot-tons they trade for in the villages.

On the morning of the ima, all the girls in the camp wash in the river. Those who are celebrat-ing the ima are rubbed with palm oil and dressed in their finery. They may wear wrist-watches and carry paper money as signs of their wealth. The other girls in the camp dust and paint themselves. They orna-ment themselves with leaves and beads and other jewelry. When the girls finally emerge from their ima hut, they are the center of attention.

- *Must you sign a **lease**?* This is a written agreement between the landlord and the tenant spelling out the rights and responsibilities of each.
- *Does the rent include utilities?* If not, ask what the average cost of utilities is for the apartment.
- *Does the apartment look and smell clean?*
- *Is everything in good repair?* Any needed repairs should be made before you sign a lease.

- *What furnishings are provided?* Many apartments are equipped with larger appliances, such as a refrigerator and range. They may or may not include such furniture as tables and chairs.
- *Is the apartment safe?* What sort of locks are on the doors and windows? Is any additional security provided? How safe is the neighborhood in general?
- *Is the location convenient to work, school, and other places you go frequently?*

Often a lease obligates you to pay rent on an apartment for a specified length of time. What might happen if you don't ask the right questions and get the information you need before you sign?

Other factors may be important to you as well. For example, do you have pets? These may or may not be allowed. What parking is available? Are laundry facilities provided? Before you begin to look, you may wish to make a checklist of features that you would like in an apartment.

Even with plenty of looking, you may not find exactly what you want. Most apartment dwellers adjust. They may have to deal with noisy neighbors or with less space than they might like. Making an effort to find the most suitable apartment available is time well spent.

Furnishing Your Apartment

Have you ever stopped to think about all the furnishings in your home that you rely on — not only larger pieces of furniture, but even smaller items like drapes and light bulbs? One of the challenges of moving into your own apartment is furnishing it to suit your needs and wants, usually on a limited budget.

Few young adults moving into their first apartment have everything they would like. Instead, they gather furnishings from a number of different sources. Older items, such as tables, lamps, and cooking utensils, may be donated by friends and family members, or bought inexpensively at thrift stores, rummage sales, or through the classified ads. Other items, such as a bed, may be bought new. Some furnishings can be constructed easily from existing materials. For example, basic sewing skills could turn an old pair of pillowcases into curtains. Wooden and plastic crates make interesting storage containers.

When furnishing your apartment, choose according to needs. If you are a student, a sturdy desk and a good lamp for studying will take priority over a plant stand.

Furnishing your apartment as you want it will take time. Let it be an opportunity to show your creativity and resourcefulness.

Other Housing Options

An apartment is not the only housing possibility available. A person may rent a *room in a private home*, often in exchange for performing certain jobs. A roomer might care for the family's children or do lawn work.

Renting a room can be helpful to both parties, especially when the homeowner is an older person. LaKeeta, for example, lives with Mrs. Beisser, who is eighty-two years old, in Mrs. Beisser's house. In exchange for her housing and meals, LaKeeta does some housekeeping and runs errands for Mrs. Beisser, who can no longer drive.

As LaKeeta explained it, "It's a great arrangement for us both. Mrs. Beisser has a nice older house, and it really 'feels' like home. I have my own job and my own social life, but I also like to spend time with Mrs. Beisser. I think she feels safer with someone around the house, too."

Renting a *sleeping room* is a variation of home sharing. A sleeping room is a single room, usually in a private home. This arrangement may or may not include kitchen privileges.

Housesitting is another possibility for independent living. Housesitters live in people's homes while the owners are away for extended periods. They are allowed to live there rent-free in exchange for watching and maintaining the property while the owners are gone. Housesitting can give you a taste of independence before you decide if you are ready for it.

MOVING BACK AGAIN

Many young adults decide to move back home after living on their own for awhile. The high cost of living may make them decide that they can save more money by living with parents. Some people move home after a divorce. A period of time with family can help them recover from the stress and hurts of the divorce and decide where they want to go from there. Sometimes a person with health problems or an injury may need help during the recovery period.

Renting a room in a home is a housing option that can be economical. Someone who owns a large, older home may have rooms to rent.

Sharing Your Space

Sharing an apartment or a house with a roommate offers many advantages. It is usually less expensive than living alone. Many people enjoy the companionship of a roommate, especially if they are close friends. It is also helpful to have someone to share household jobs. As with any relationship, however, conflicts can develop if people fail to communicate and cooperate with each other. Here are some tips for successfully sharing your space with a roommate:

- Decide beforehand how you will divide expenses and household responsibilities.
- If you buy items jointly for the apartment, decide who gets them if one of you moves out.
- Agree on a code of conduct. Decide what behavior will and will not be acceptable in your home.
- Respect each other's privacy. Sharing space does not mean giving up all personal possessions. Do not borrow clothing without asking. Do not read your roommate's mail.
- Be considerate. Think of each other's needs, wants, and responsibilities before acting. Ask for input before making a decision that affects a roommate. Respect the other's wishes.
- Keep a sense of humor. Problems are bound to arise, even between the best of friends. Most of them are not worth staying angry about. Make them opportunities for personal and mutual growth, not conflict.

When young people move back in with a parent or parents, the family may need to work out an agreement about the arrangement. What might happen if they don't?

They were three adults with equal rights and responsibilities in the household. Alex saw that some of his responsibilities included letting his parents know his schedule so they would not be inconvenienced. His parents realized that, although Alex was still their son, he was also an independent adult, who needed to be treated as such.

Very few people live permanently with parents. Usually, moving back home is a temporary arrangement, often for financial reasons. Later, the young person again moves out on his or her own.

TAKING THE STEP

Moving out of the family home is a major milestone in a young person's life. It can be full of pitfalls and challenges. When approached thoughtfully and confidently, however, it can also be an adventure packed with learning experiences.

Moving back home can create some problems. When Alex returned home after a year of living alone, it was difficult. He had been used to coming and going as he pleased. His parents wanted him to call them when he was out late. On the other hand, they expected him to pay rent and do his own laundry. Even though he was an adult, he felt like a child. Can you see how different assumptions about behavior caused conflict?

Alex and his parents needed to look at their relationship in a new light. When they sat down and talked about their expectations, they came to a better understanding.

SECTION 1 REVIEW

1. List two reasons why young adults today are waiting longer to leave home.
2. What are two major factors that affect the decision to move out on your own?
3. Name at least three sources you might use to locate available apartments.
4. Why do most rental agreements require a security deposit?
5. What is a lease?
6. Renting an apartment is one housing option. Name and describe one other housing option.

SECTION 2

MANAGING ON YOUR OWN

THINK AHEAD

About These Terms

investing   *autonomy*

About These Objectives

After studying this section, you should be able to:

• List and describe the concerns that single people have when they are on their own.

ingle people who live independently have the same basic concerns as others — food, shelter, work, friendships — but with an added dimension. Single people must make all their own decisions, everything from what brand of toothpaste to buy to how they will invest their money. Living on your own means managing life in ways that work well for you.

◆ ◆ ◆

When you are on your own, responsibility for yourself means making more decisions than you ever have before, including large and small ones.

FINANCES

Single people don't usually have financial support from other people. They rely on their own income and make financial decisions themselves.

Single people are their own money managers. They must make sure all bills are paid and decide whether remaining money is saved or spent. They must rely on their own values and priorities to make decisions about money.

Singles need to plan for the future. About ten percent of all single people will remain unmarried for life. Also, many people who are now married will become single due to the high divorce rate and an increased life span. For whatever reason, many people will spend at least some part of life as singles. They must make decisions about:

- *Insurance*, for themselves and their possessions. Renters in particular may overlook insuring their property, because they do not purchase homeowners' insurance, which provides that coverage.
- *Savings*. These can include regular savings accounts, savings bonds, and certificates of deposit. They are important for emergencies and luxuries alike.
- *Investments*. **Investing** is using money to make more money. Many young people just starting out don't think about starting early to make money work for them. They may not have money to invest, or they may think of investing as something for older, more financially stable people. It is never too early, however, to plan for long-term financial security. Professional investment counselors can help single people invest their money to provide them with a better living in later years, whether they remain single or marry.

NUTRITION AND HEALTH

Often young people are accustomed to having someone else take care of their health and nutrition needs. Living on your own, however, means that you are responsible for that, too. Whatever the need — for exercise, medical appointments, or healthful food choices — the decisions are yours.

Brenda, for example, had never thought much about choosing nutritious foods. When she moved out on her own, she had to do all of her own shopping. She began to read labels more carefully. Single-serving sizes of frozen dinners and soups from the supermarket were expensive. A family friend, who was a home economist, sug-

gested that Brenda make recipes in large quantities and freeze individual portions for later use. The home economist also gave Brenda a list of ideas for quick, healthful meals and snacks, like macaroni and cheese with tuna and fresh fruits in low-fat yogurt. Now when she shops, Brenda looks for inexpensive foods that can be quickly mixed with others for convenient, nutritious eating.

Living alone, Brenda also found that she had a tendency to skip meals at times or rush through them. Not having someone to eat with on a regular basis brought about this habit. Setting up a meal schedule and making the mealtimes special helped Brenda solve the problem. For her, watching the birds and squirrels out the window while she ate made the difference. She

When you live on your own you have to learn to eat alone. Planning ahead and making mealtimes special will help you eat well.

bought a bird feeder and began to set out food. Eventually mealtimes became relaxing moments to look forward to.

SAFETY

Personal safety is another responsibility of adulthood. You probably already follow many safety rules, sometimes without even thinking about it. As a single, independent adult, however, you will want to give extra consideration to your personal safety. Here are some guidelines for keeping yourself safe:

- Make sure the doors and windows of your home have reliable, working locks, and use them.
- Keep a list of emergency numbers near your telephone.
- Know your neighbors. This will not only help you identify strangers, but will give you someone to turn to if you need help.
- If you suspect someone has broken into your home, leave immediately. Call the police from a neighbor's phone.
- Be aware of your surroundings. Notice anyone or anything that seems unusual or out of place.
- If you are out after dark, don't walk or park your car in poorly lit areas.
- Lock your car when you leave it, and have your keys ready when you return.
- Always check the back seat of your car before getting in.

Can you think of other precautions you might take to ensure personal safety? Police and fire departments can provide more information.

TRANSPORTATION

Many young adults who live at home have access to an automobile. They can either use a family car or share rides with

There was a time when people had no fear of leaving their doors unlocked. Do you think this is true in any communities today?

friends to get to school, work, and other activities. When they move out, however, they may need other means of transportation. A single person may have to buy a car, use public transportation, ride a bicycle, or walk. Finding transportation can be a test of resourcefulness.

Single people who are fortunate enough to own a car soon learn that upkeep is expensive. Gasoline, insurance, and maintenance all add to the cost of owning an automobile. Learning to do regular maintenance tasks and make minor repairs yourself can help cut costs. Sometimes community colleges, or even service stations, offer courses on simple auto care and maintenance.

When Julio moved out, his parents gave him the older family car he'd been driving to use as his own. Although he felt lucky to have the car, Julio had never realized all the effort and money involved in its upkeep. In addition to gasoline and insurance, Julio paid for oil changes and new spark plugs, a new tire to replace a flat, and a new taillight after someone hit his car in a parking lot. He soon decided that the television he had been hoping to buy would have to wait until he had enough money left over after regular and unexpected expenses.

Magazines often give lists of preparation steps for planning such things as weddings. What would a list look like for a single person planning to move out of his or her parents' home to a first apartment?

Make a list of what you would need to do or consider in preparation for independent living. Think about the areas of employment, transportation, meal preparation, insurance, furnishings, kitchen and personal care appliances, and utilities.

Some people don't earn enough to meet their expenses. As you have learned, many young people learn to do without things they thought they needed. Others find roomates to share living expenses. Still others move back home if independent living is too expensive. What would you do if you were living on your own and money became tight?

ENRICHMENT

Life as a single is full of opportunities for personal growth. Some singles have more time and energy for their careers. If they have fewer family responsibilities, they may be able to spend more time on interests or volunteering. They may have more opportunities to travel and to have a variety of experiences. Singles can change some aspects of their lives with less worry about how it will affect others.

Everyone can benefit from time spent alone. Quiet activities, such as reading, listening to music, and reflection, can enrich a person's life. Single people often have more opportunities for enjoying quiet time.

Singles can also know the satisfaction of **autonomy**, the ability to direct your own life independently. Many singles enjoy knowing they are responsible for their own personal and financial well-being.

Time to yourself can be an advantage of single living.

Finding the Right Balance

When single people leave home they need to establish their own routines and their own way of living. One of their first challenges is to find the balance between work, family, and social activities that is right for them.

Some singles, keen to advance in their careers, put all their energy into their work. They work hard, bring work home, take work-related courses in the evenings—and they don't set aside time for family and friends. Treating family and friends in this way is hurtful. The individual who acts in this way risks losing the family support that can ease the transition to independence as well as the friendships that help make life enjoyable.

At the opposite end of the spectrum are those newly independent singles who overdo the socializing at the expense of their work. Caught up in the excitement of their new independence they go out night after night, and then wonder why they don't have enough energy to do their work. In doing so, they risk losing the independence that they so value. Few unemployed people can support themselves.

Fortunately most singles eventually find a formula that works for them. They manage to balance work, family, friends, and community in a way that agrees with their values and priorities.

RELATIONSHIPS

Singles may face extra challenges in building satisfying relationships, especially if they live alone. There are, however, many ways of fulfilling this need.

Toby, for example, had moved to a different town and was working at a new job. He had trouble getting to know people at work and in his apartment building. Eventually he decided to use his love of football to meet others. He volunteered to be a coach for a youth football league. Toby not only met people who shared his interest in the game, but he also helped others at the same time.

Clarisse solved the same problem in a different way. She first organized a card-playing club among her co-workers. When she discovered that several others shared her enthusiasm for art, she suggested that they sign up for an evening art class. Later one of her classmates asked her to go sight-seeing in a nearby city.

Both Clarisse and Toby overcame their loneliness by reaching out to others. They used their interests and talents to build relationships. Both recognized the importance of involvement.

Being involved in activities can be beneficial in other ways as well. For example, teaching children might give Toby an idea about whether he would like to have some of his own someday. What Clarisse learns in art class could turn her interest in painting into a rewarding, perhaps profitable, hobby.

The methods that Clarisse and Toby used to connect with others are only a few. Here are several others:

- Presentations and lectures on topics of interest at libraries and universities.
- Groups and activities sponsored by religious organizations.
- Volunteer groups, such as Big Brothers/Big Sisters or the American Red Cross.
- Parents Without Partners, a group for single persons with children.
- Groups related to occupations.

Comparing and Contrasting

Comparing and contrasting people, ideas, and things helps you make up your mind about your likes and dislikes. In turn, you learn to be more selective, whether you are choosing a friend or buying a consumer product.

LEW *"Ten years from now, I see myself married and starting a family. I'll have finished college and hopefully have a good job in some field of engineering. I also like being around kids and think I'd make a good father. I wouldn't be surprised if I found myself a father of four one day. I often imagine myself teaching my kids how to read or play basketball or ride bikes. A lot of people — my parents included — see me as mature for my age. I sure hope I am."*

ROY *"When I think about the future, I can't imagine making commitments until I'm a lot older. I think I'd be content being a teen forever — dating around, playing basketball with my brother Lew, working in Mrs. Wilson's garden. Lew is the serious one in the family. I like taking life easy and not making plans that can't be changed. Having fun is important. I plan to enjoy myself, and then I'll settle down."*

CAN YOU COMPARE AND CONTRAST?

Comparing and contrasting means evaluating similar and different traits or qualities in a person, idea, or thing.

■ In what ways are Lew and Roy similar? In what ways are they different?

■ What qualities do you admire and reject about each brother? Which of the two brothers is most like you?

■ Think of two siblings you know personally. Consider their traits and qualities. In what ways are the two alike? How are they different? Are differences necessarily right or wrong?

■ Think about the last time you chose between two items or products and purchased one of them. Compare and contrast the two items or products.

◆ Music groups.
◆ Community theatre.
◆ Sports activities, such as playing on a softball team.
◆ Hobby groups.

What other places or activities can you think of where singles can meet and make friends?

DEVELOPING A WAY OF LIFE

As you move out on your own, you will develop a way of life that suits you. You will make decisions about the way you want to live your life. The kind of life you choose will be based on your values and your heritage. The experiences you've had with your family and others will influence your choices. You can bring all aspects of your life together to form a pattern that pleases you. Where you live and visit, the kinds of clothes you wear, how you spend your time, and the activities you pursue all say something about you.

When Lauren got her first job, she knew what kind of life she wanted. She saved her money until she could afford a nice apartment in a complex with a fitness center and a swimming pool. She enjoys having a nice car and taking trips with her friends.

Harland lives a very different life. He and a friend share an apartment in an older building. He is very active in his church and spends much of his spare time working on church-related activities. He also enjoys quiet evenings at home listening to music and reading. Harland regularly sends money home to help his family.

Some people choose a busy, hectic way of life. Others live at a more leisurely pace. Some people prefer a few very close relationships, while others enjoy a wide variety of contacts and activities. The way of life you choose will reflect what is important to you. Finding a way of living that makes you comfortable and confident — and finding people to share it with — will be important when you are on your own.

SKILLS FOR INDEPENDENCE

Successful single living depends on learning and using skills that can help you. Knowing that you need to maintain good health is one thing. How to do so is another. You will need to know many details about managing your life: how to manage money in order to make the best use of it; how to be a good consumer; and how to get and keep a job.

In the rest of this unit you will learn about all of these subjects. As you go out on your own, remember that much more information exists than can be provided here. You can learn from books, magazines, newspapers, classes, and people you know. The more you know, the better equipped you will be to manage your life successfully.

The skills you need to be independent can be learned in many places. Families can provide much of what you need to know if you are willing to ask and listen.

SECTION 2 REVIEW

1. Name three things singles need to make decisions about when planning for their futures.
2. What is investing?
3. Explain why some single people fall in the habit of not eating nutritiously.
4. What are five things a person can do to be safe at home?
5. What does autonomy mean?
6. Name four places or activities where singles can meet people and make new friends.

Chapter 25 Review

Chapter Summary

- There is no single "right" time or reason for moving out on your own.
- A decision about housing is one of the first and most important decisions you must make after deciding to leave home.
- Moving back home after a period of being on their own is common for people today.
- Most single people are responsible for their own finances.
- Single people must make sure they take steps to stay healthy.
- Personal safety is a responsibility of adulthood.
- Owning a car is a convenience, but it is also a responsibility.
- Life as a single can be full, rich, and personally satisfying. Although singles may face extra challenges in building relationships, they can use their interests and talents to meet people and make friends.
- To develop a way of life that suits you, you will make decisions based on your values, your heritage, and your experiences.

Chapter Review

1. Why are young adults today waiting longer to leave home than they used to?
2. Name two factors that influence the decision of a young person to move out on his or her own.
3. What are five basic questions to consider when looking for an apartment?
4. What information should you obtain about an apartment when considering it for rental?
5. What is a security deposit? Why do most rental agreements require a security deposit?
6. Suppose you are trying to furnish an apartment on a limited budget. From what sources might you obtain furnishings?
7. Name and describe two housing options other than apartment living.
8. Why do single people need to make financial plans for the future?
9. List five precautions you should take to ensure personal safety.
10. What can a person who lives alone do to prevent loneliness?

Critical Thinking

1. How well do you think you would deal with living independently? What personal traits do you have that would make it easier or more difficult for you?
2. List some advantages and disadvantages of living alone compared to sharing a home with others.
3. Do you think employers make judgments based on marital status when hiring and promoting employees? Are they justified in doing so?
4. Some people think those who choose to remain single are selfish or trying to avoid responsibility. Do you agree or disagree? Explain your answer.
5. Identify television shows or movies with single characters. How realistic is their portrayal of single life?

Chapter 25 Review

Activities

1. **Ready for responsibility?** On a sheet of paper, make a list of responsibilities involved in living independently. After each item, rate yourself on a scale of one (the lowest) to ten (the highest) on how completely you handle that responsibility now. Then write a short paragraph explaining whether or not you feel ready for independence, based on your ratings. (*Self–management, writing*)

2. **Steps toward independence.** Make a list of five things you can do this week to grow toward independence and take responsibility for yourself. (*Self–management, personal responsibility*)

3. **Personal expressions.** As a class, make a list of ways in which people express their way of life. Include such things as personal habits, activities, type of purchases, and attitudes. (*Teamwork, organizing information*)

4. **Ad analysis.** Find ads in magazines and newspapers showing some aspect of single living. What products seem aimed at single people? How are their lives depicted? Describe for your class the image of living as a single that you found in advertisements. (*Acquiring and evaluating information, communicating information*)

STRENGTHENING VALUES

Aim For Independence

Independence means taking responsibility for yourself. It means meeting your own needs, wants, and duties without a lot of help from others. Sylvia shows her independence by:

- Buying her own clothes with money from her part-time job.
- Making decisions based on her own values and beliefs, not those of her friends.
- Doing her schoolwork on time and without pressure from others.
- Eating right and getting enough sleep without being told.

Within the family, do you think independence in a privilege that must be earned? Explain your answer. How do you show your independence?

Health and Wellness

SECTION 1

INFLUENCES ON HEALTH

SECTION 2

LEADING THE HEALTHY LIFE

IMAGINE THAT ...

it is 6:45 a.m. and your alarm clock rings. You struggle up through the fog of sleep to shut off the noise. After staying up until 3:00 a.m. watching television, you can hardly make it out of bed. You don't feel like eating breakfast, but you grab a soft drink that contains caffeine. Maybe that will help you wake up in time for school. You go through your first-hour class in a daze. You can't remember a thing the teacher said. In the cafeteria at lunch, nothing looks good. You are tired of feeling rotten all the time and wonder why you feel this way.

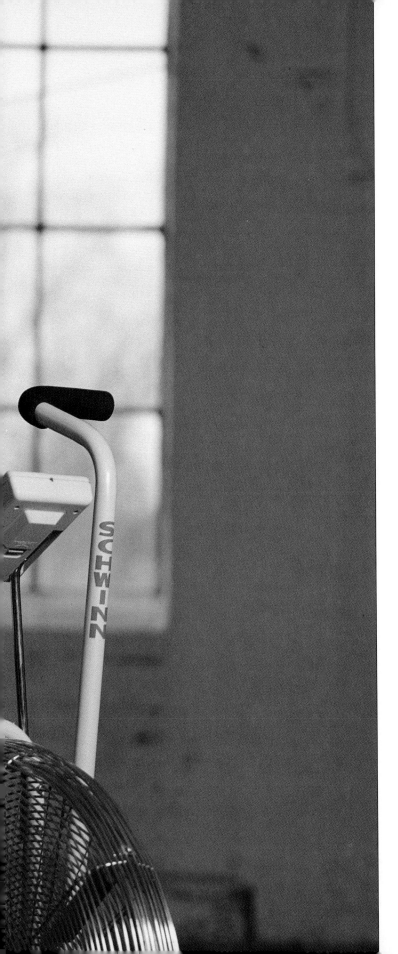

INFLUENCES ON HEALTH

THINK AHEAD

About These Terms

vaccines   deductible
antibiotics   wellness

About These Objectives

After studying this section, you should be able to:

- Give reasons for improved health among people today.
- Explain how poor living habits can contribute to disease.
- Explain what is meant by wellness and tell what influences it.

Many of the actions you take each day have an effect on your health. The amount of sleep you get, what you eat and drink, and whether you exercise are all related to the way you look and feel. Once you are independent, you become responsible for your own health. With some work and effort, you can enjoy the rewards of good health.

◆ ◆ ◆

467

IMPROVEMENTS IN HEALTH

People today are healthier than they have been in the past. **Vaccines**, chemicals developed to protect against specific diseases, have helped reduce the rate of many illnesses. Whooping cough, diphtheria, polio, and measles are all diseases that were common in the past but have been controlled by the widespread use of vaccines.

Antibiotics, special medicines that destroy disease-causing germs, have contributed greatly to treating many diseases. Tuberculosis and meningitis are two diseases that used to be almost incurable. Today these are treated successfully with antibiotics.

MULTICULTURAL PERSPECTIVES

FAMILIES AROUND THE WORLD

Pharmacy in the Forest

In your country, when families need medicine, someone probably visits a pharmacy. In South America, the Tirio Indians of Suriname go into the rainforest.

The Amazonian rainforest is made up of thousands of plants, most of which are unknown to outsiders. The Tirio, however, can name them all. (In Suriname they have a saying: "In the forest the Indian knows everything.") They use approximately 300 different plants for medicine. Plants supply remedies for insect stings, fevers, lice, colds, burns, and skin rashes. This medical knowledge is extended to families by village shamans, or wise men.

Modern civilization, however, is reaching into the rainforest. Tirio Indians sport wristwatches and wear Walkman tape players. The young people had begun to look on the shamans as relics of the past. The wise men, in their late 50s and 60s, had no apprentices to learn from them.

Then the ethnobotanists came. These scientists, who study the ways tribal people use plants, have taken an interest in the Tirio's plants. They know these plants might be turned into new medicinal drugs or cures for diseases.

Because the scientists respect the knowledge of the shamans, the younger generation of Tirio have begun to respect it as well. They have begun to take an interest in the plants and are now working with the shamans to record their knowledge before it disappears. In this way, a new generation of healers is in training.

Finally, the standard of living today has improved health. Better housing and better sanitation help keep people healthy. Today, people have more money to spend on health care, including health insurance. In 1940, less than ten percent of the population had health insurance. Today, more than eighty-five percent do.

Felix has health insurance through the company he works for. He has to pay the **deductible**, an amount of money that a person must pay before insurance begins to pay. For Felix the deductible is the first $200 of his medical bills. Then the company pays for eighty percent of the rest. Insurance protects him from financial losses in case of serious medical problems. Having insurance makes him more likely to seek medical care when he needs it.

DISEASES RELATED TO LIVING HABITS

The general overall level of health today is better than it was in the past, but this does not mean that all people are in a state of good health. Serious illnesses today include heart and liver disease, cancer, and strokes. These diseases can be caused or affected by personal habits and behavior.

Dustin learned this lesson the hard way. As a manager at a large business firm, he worked at his desk most of the day and didn't have much time for exercise. Sometimes he even worked through his lunch hour, so he grabbed a hamburger and french fries from a nearby fast-food restaurant. He smoked cigarettes, supposedly to relieve the stress of his job. Some nights he had trouble getting to sleep, so he took sleeping pills. Although Dustin was able to get along for a number of years

TEAMING UP WITH TECHNOLOGY

SINCE

more teens are health conscious today,

HOW

does technology help them maintain wellness?

Advances in health-care technology have an impact on people in many ways. Nutritionists, for example, use computers to help analyze dietary needs. Doctors use such procedures as *magnetic resonance imaging* and laser surgery to diagnose and treat health problems. By learning

about new medical advances, you can get more involved in your own health care.

JOINING THE TEAM

- Have you ever used technology to help you stay physically fit? If so, what did you use?
- How do you use technology to help maintain your health in other ways?
- Do research on a specific health-care field. What kind of training and skills are necessary to work in that field? What new technology is used in the field?

with poor habits, eventually he began to have health problems. Finally, a heart attack slowed him down and caused him to take a close look at his habits. He was lucky to have a second chance.

WELLNESS

Wellness is a positive state of physical and mental health. It is more than just the absence of disease or sickness. Wellness is a decision and a commitment. It means taking responsibility to live in a way that promotes good health.

A person's attitude toward wellness is critical in influencing behaviors that affect health. Working toward wellness is, in many ways, preventive medicine. Developing personal habits that lead to wellness can help prevent illnesses.

Wellness pays. Not only do you look and feel good — and feel good about yourself — when you are healthy, but you also save money. Health care is expensive. A serious illness can create thousands of dollars in medical bills. Behaviors that promote wellness may be able to save some of these costs.

It took something serious for Dustin to learn the importance of wellness. With his doctor's help, Dustin learned new health habits. He gave up smoking. He started bringing his own lunch to work — lean meats on whole-grain bread with fruit or vegetable salad. He started walking every evening and playing racquetball twice a week. To relieve stress, Dustin turned to music or reading a book. He has learned to take his work less seriously. He feels happier now and has more energy. Dustin never realized how much he was damaging his own health until he started taking care of it.

Mental and Physical Wellness

Wellness involves both the body and the mind. Mental health is just as important to well-being as physical health.

In terms of physical health and wellness, the mind and body work together. Stress, crisis, and other mental strains can affect how the body functions. They can cause physical as well as mental illnesses. Some researchers estimate that about half of those who seek medical treatment suffer from physical illnesses directly related to emotional stress.

Ned lived in a neighborhood where the crime rate was high. Drive-by shootings and other violent acts were frequent. The pressure of living in such conditions caused him to feel tense and stressed all of the time. He developed a bleeding ulcer. Ned's emotional state affected his physical health.

Athletes are particularly aware of how good health habits affect the body. Many eat nutritious foods, stay in condition, and get enough rest in order to give their best performance.

Working Toward Wellness

Your wellness is, to some extent, under your control. You can control your physical habits. You can control many of the experiences you have. For example, only you can say "no" when someone offers you a cigarette or a drink.

To some extent, you can control the environment you are in. If people you know have poor habits, you don't have to imitate them. You can choose to be with people who have the same attitude toward wellness as you do. Can you think of some people and places that encourage a positive attitude toward wellness?

Controlling Other Factors

Certain factors that affect your health you cannot control. Many health-related factors are inherited. For example, if several people in your family have heart problems, you may be at risk to develop them, too. Also, certain diseases seem to be more common in one gender than the other.

People with lower incomes tend to have more health problems than those with more money. This may be because they don't eat as well or because they lack necessary health care.

You can't control heredity, your gender, or your family's income level. You can, however, work to control their influence on your health. For example, you can:

- Become aware of your family's medical history, including any diseases that have affected other family members. Do nothing that might make getting the disease more likely.
- Get regular medical checkups to identify problems early.
- If a medical problem occurs, learn about your options and the advantages and disadvantages of each.

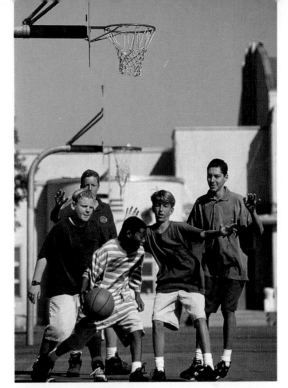

Associating with people who share your interest in wellness can help you. Practicing good health habits, such as exercising, can be easier and more fun when you do it together.

Chloris's family doesn't have much money. She knows they can't afford medical care for illnesses. She exercises regularly, eats nutritious foods, and gets enough sleep. These habits help her control her health, despite her family's financial situation.

Whatever your financial situation, you can follow Chloris's example. When it comes to wellness, prevention is much better than looking for a cure.

SECTION 1 REVIEW

1. List four diseases that are controlled by the use of vaccines.
2. How is wellness preventive medicine?
3. Name three aspects of your life that you can control to help achieve wellness.

People who are in good health have the energy and alertness they need for daily living. Sometimes people with poor health habits don't even realize what wellness feels like.

LEADING THE HEALTHY LIFE

THINK AHEAD

About These Terms

anorexia nervosa   aerobic exercise
bulimia   hallucinations
compulsive eating   paranoia

About These Objectives
After studying this section, you should be able to:
- Identify and explain six factors in achieving and maintaining wellness.
- Identify personal and community resources that can help you stay healthy.

s you have seen, your health is in many ways your own responsibility. How you lead your life greatly influences your mental and physical well-being.

♦ ♦ ♦

HEALTHFUL HABITS

The personal habits you develop as a young person are important to your health. If you have learned habits that are not healthful while growing up, you may find it hard to develop better ones. Replacing poor habits with good ones is the key to wellness.

"The first wealth is health."

—

RALPH WALDO EMERSON

Eating Right

Food choices have a major impact on your health. A good diet while you're young helps you grow and develop normally. A poor diet can lead to a number of problems, including illness, tooth decay, difficulty in concentrating, and irritability. A poorly nourished body has a lower resistance to disease and takes longer to heal itself when injured.

As you get older, good nutrition remains important to wellness. Eating right can help fight heart disease, weight problems, diabetes, and some types of cancer.

More information about nutrition is available now than ever before. It can be found in books and magazines and learned from health-care professionals, such as doctors, nutritionists, and family and consumer scientists. Here are some basic nutrition guidelines to follow:

- Eat the recommended number of servings of foods from each of the five groups in the Food Guide Pyramid every day.

Food Guide Pyramid
A Guide to Daily Food Choices

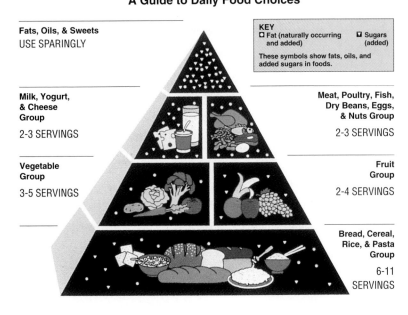

Fats, Oils, & Sweets
USE SPARINGLY

KEY
☐ Fat (naturally occurring and added) ☑ Sugars (added)
These symbols show fats, oils, and added sugars in foods.

Milk, Yogurt, & Cheese Group
2-3 SERVINGS

Meat, Poultry, Fish, Dry Beans, Eggs, & Nuts Group
2-3 SERVINGS

Vegetable Group
3-5 SERVINGS

Fruit Group
2-4 SERVINGS

Bread, Cereal, Rice, & Pasta Group
6-11 SERVINGS

The food guide pyramid gives you guidelines for eating nutritiously. When figuring serving sizes, use these equivalents for one serving:
- 1 cup milk
- 8 ounces of yogurt
- 1½ ounces natural cheese
- 2 ounces process cheese
- ½ cup cooked or raw vegetables
- 2-3 ounces of meat, poultry, fish, eggs, dry beans and peas, nuts, and seeds
- 1 whole fruit
- ½ cup canned fruit
- 1 slice of bread
- 1 roll
- 1 ounce of ready-to-eat cereal

- Don't fill up on the "empty" calories of sugary foods and soft drinks.
- Limit your intake of sodium and fats by eating fewer fried foods and fatty meats. Many fast-food restaurant offerings are high in both fat and salt and should be eaten in moderation.
- Eat regular meals instead of snacking at odd hours.
- Read labels on packages of processed foods for nutritional information.
- Learn about good nutrition. Find out your nutrient and calorie needs.

Maintaining a Desirable Weight

Excess weight is a common cause of many diseases. High blood pressure, arthritis, heart disease, and diabetes are more apt to strike those who are overweight. Being underweight may not be healthy either. It can weaken the body and make it harder to fight off illness. For the best health, your weight should fall within the range shown for your sex and height in standard weight tables. Remember to consult your physician before trying to gain or lose large amounts of weight.

Eating Disorders

Eating disorders are psychological problems related to food and eating. They result in abnormal eating behaviors. Stress and crisis are sometimes linked to eating disorders. These disorders are related to issues of power and control. The teen years are a time of high risk for these problems. In most cases, professional help is needed to overcome eating disorders.

Anorexia nervosa (an-uh-REX-ee-uh ner-VOH-suh) is a mental disorder that shows itself in a fear of being fat. The patient, usually a female, refuses to eat enough to maintain a healthy body weight.

In anorexia nervosa, the patient is over-controlling the body. This mental illness can cause death because of malnutrition and the strain put on the body. Patients must often be hospitalized for treatment.

Patricia was twenty pounds overweight in the eighth grade. Her weight made her self-conscious and lowered her self-esteem. She decided to lose the extra weight before high school. When she did, Patricia felt so much more confident and successful that she didn't want to stop. Soon she was dieting simply to feel in control. Even though she had become extremely thin, she did not see herself that way.

Then Patricia caught a bad cold that developed into pneumonia. She spent a week in the hospital recovering. Patricia's physicians and family were very concerned about her. They helped her get counseling in order to deal with the problem. Patricia needed to find ways of feeling successful and improving her self-esteem without destroying her health.

Bulimia (buh-LIM-ee-uh) is an eating disorder involving "binge" eating. A person who has bulimia eats huge amounts of food in a short period of time. Often vomiting or laxative use follows the eating binge. As with anorexia nervosa, persons with bulimia are usually female. Unlike anorexia nervosa, bulimia is not usually life-threatening. It can, however, create health problems related to weight gain and loss and frequent vomiting.

A third type of eating disorder is **compulsive eating**. Sufferers are unable to resist food and cannot stop eating. Like bulimia, compulsive eating is a lack of control over eating habits. It is usually a response to emotional distress, such as depression, anger, or anxiety. Compulsive eating plays a major role in obesity.

The body needs recovery time in the form of sleep. Work is easier and play more enjoyable when you feel rested.

Getting Enough Sleep

Getting enough sleep at night is very important. Most people need seven to eight hours to feel their best the next day. The range, however, is quite wide. Some people need only five hours of sleep, while others require ten each night. The amount of sleep you need is determined by heredity and health. The right amount of sleep is the number of hours that helps you feel rested and alert.

Sometimes healthy sleep can be interrupted by depression, stress, and tension. If you can't sleep, it's better to get up and do something that relaxes you until you feel sleepy. Tossing and turning in bed makes falling asleep again less likely.

There are a number of personal habits that will help you sleep well. Some scientists who study sleep and sleep habits make the following suggestions:

Parents have traditionally settled children down with a bedtime story at night. Teens and adults often use the same technique to relax before going to sleep.

- Exercise regularly in the morning or late afternoon, but not just before going to bed.
- Go to bed and get up about the same time every day.
- Sleep only enough to feel alert and rested.
- Skip caffeine (as in soft drinks) after 4:00 p.m.
- Don't take sleeping pills unless they are prescribed by a doctor. Then take them only as ordered.

- If you feel hungry at bedtime, eat only a light snack. Don't go to bed hungry or directly after eating a big meal.
- Use your bed and bedroom only for sleep, not for reading, watching TV, or working.
- Just before going to bed, do something that you know relaxes you.
- Keep your bedroom at a temperature that helps you sleep best.

Dealing With Stress

As you learned earlier, too much stress can interfere with your daily activities. It can also lead to medical problems. Fortunately, there is much you can do to reduce the amount and intensity of stress in your life.

Sometimes you can control stress by simply accepting that life is full of ups and downs. Recognize that things do go wrong, but life will get better. Attitudes like these will help you stay physically and mentally healthy. What others can you think of?

Being able to relax helps you control stress. Know what activities you enjoy and take time to do them. For example, Dean enjoys music. In his words, "I can relax just by putting on my headphones and listening to my favorite music. When I'm tense, I let myself go with the music. I can feel myself breathing slower and more deeply. Listening to music always makes me feel much better."

Physical activity is another good way of dealing with stress. It relieves you of tension and nervous energy and improves your physical condition as well.

Some simple methods can be used to get exercise. Taking the stairs instead of the escalator is one example. Can you think of others?

Exercising

Exercise helps keep your muscles toned, your lungs working well, and your blood circulating smoothly. Nutrients and oxygen can move more easily to all parts of your body.

If you exercise regularly, you are apt to feel better and have more energy. Without exercise, your muscles, including your heart, will weaken. Your breathing will become shallow.

One of the most important types of activity is aerobic (uh-ROE-bik) exercise. **Aerobic exercise** is strenuous activity that raises the heart rate and increases the amount of oxygen taken into the lungs. Such activities as walking, swimming, jogging, and cycling are good aerobic exercises.

Experts suggest at least thirty minutes of aerobic exercise three to four times a week. This time should include about five minutes at an easy pace to warm up, twenty minutes of fairly strenuous exercise, and five minutes at an easy pace to cool down.

You should see your doctor before beginning a serious exercise program. Simply adding more exercise to everyday activities, however, is usually safe and helpful. For example, you could:

- Use the stairs instead of an elevator or escalator.
- Walk instead of drive short distances.
- Park your car in the far corner of a parking lot rather than looking for a space close to the door.

Where in your daily schedule can you include exercise?

Not Using Harmful Drugs

Staying away from harmful drugs is your right as well as your responsibility. It is an important part of wellness.

Tobacco

Tobacco use is a leading cause of illness. Smoking is the most common preventable cause of death in the United States. Smoking can lead to lung cancer. It is also related to cancers of the throat, mouth, esophagus, pancreas, and bladder. Heart disease, emphysema, chronic bronchitis, and strokes are also related to smoking. Cancer of the lip and mouth has been linked to pipe smoking and the use of smokeless tobacco.

Smoking is dangerous to your health in other ways as well. Smoking:

- Speeds up your heart beat and narrows blood vessels, putting extra strain on the heart.
- Causes shortness of breath.
- Irritates the throat.
- Puts foreign materials into the lungs.

Over time, any of these factors can cause disease.

When Ralph's father had a stroke, the doctor said it was a combination of high blood pressure (increased heart rate) and narrow blood vessels, which were related to his smoking habits. The long term effects of tobacco on the body led to his stroke.

Alcohol

Alcohol is a threat to good health. Serious problems, such as brain damage, heart disease, liver damage, cancers, ulcers, and gastritis, have been linked to alcohol use. In addition to physical diseases, alcohol use is also linked to poor mental health for drinkers as well as their families.

Alcohol consumption can be a serious threat to the safety of others, too. About half of all fatal car accidents in the United States are related to alcohol use. This is because alcohol affects the brain, slowing reflexes and causing poor judgment.

Working Wellness into the Balance

BALANCING WORK AND FAMILY

When juggling the demands of family, school, and work, family members also need to build time for wellness into their schedules. Here are some tips for making sure that good health practices are part of the family routine:

- Keep nutritious, easily prepared foods on hand. Teach family members healthful ways of preparing foods.
- Exercise regularly as a family activity. Walking or biking together can build strong bodies and strong families.
- Reserve regular times to discuss personal and family-related problems. Unresolved conflicts can lead to stress. Just knowing you will have the chance to talk them over can make them more manageable.
- Discuss the dangers of using alcohol, tobacco, and other harmful drugs.
- Insist that family members use safety belts in cars, and encourage them to wear the appropriate helmets and protective gear when taking part in risky activities.

Other Harmful Drugs

Drugs typically affect the mind and influence behavior by changing feelings, mood, and how the user sees the world. They can lead to addiction and can have destructive effects on the lives of those who take them.

A person's health can be damaged the first time a drug is taken. Drugs can affect the brain so that wrong signals are sent to the body. A person may stop breathing, go into a coma, or have a heart attack.

Long-term damage from drug use depends on which drugs are involved. Permanent liver, heart, kidney, lung, and brain damage are common physical effects. Drugs also affect mental functions. Several drugs cause **hallucinations** (huh-loo-sih-NAY-shuns), seeing things that aren't there.

Depression and severe mood changes are common. Even **paranoia** (pare-uh-NOY-uh), the excessive fear of people and things, can result.

Anyone concerned with health and wellness will not use drugs. Harmful drugs can cause permanent damage that may prevent you from ever being healthy again.

RESOURCES

Good health and wellness are not conditions you can take for granted. They require commitment, effort, and a variety of resources to achieve. You can use personal and community resources to help you reach your goal of wellness.

Personal Resources

Knowledge is a personal resource that is needed for good health. You need to know which behaviors will improve your health and which will damage it. Of course, understanding which behaviors are healthful is not useful if you aren't willing to behave in these ways.

Emmy Lou is typical of the person who sometimes has trouble putting her knowledge into action. Here's how she put it: "I can tell you all the important facts about nutrition and how you should eat, but sometimes it's hard for me to make good choices. Still, it's easier to pass up the jelly donut for the fresh fruit when you know how your choices affect your health."

Planning ahead for health care is also important. For example, having health insurance is one way to protect yourself financially from bills in case of an injury or illness.

When Justine fell and broke her leg, the medical bills quickly added up. There was one for the emergency room, one for the lab technician who took X-rays of the leg,

TAKING ACTION

One way to lessen stress in life is to have a support system in place before you need it. Can you name a specific person or group for each of the following situations?

- Who would you see if you had a leg injury?

- Who would you go to for a toothache?

- Who could help you deal with overwhelming stress?

- Who would you be able to talk to if you thought you might have an eating disorder?

- Who could help you if you needed to give up smoking?

Getting to know your local health-care providers is an important step in your move toward independence.

and another for the X-rays themselves. There was a bill for the doctor who set the leg, and even one for renting the crutches Justine used while recovering. Fortunately, her family's health insurance covered most of the costs. Can you imagine the consequences if they had not had insurance?

Community Resources

Communities offer resources related to health and wellness. Health care services are very important. Doctors, nurses, hospitals, and clinics help when you are physically ill. Some clinics even offer free or low-cost services. Facilities and professional staffs can help those with mental problems, such as eating disorders or addictions to drugs. Other professionals help people learn to cope with stress.

Communities offer public and private facilities that can help you stay well. Parks, tennis courts, and swimming pools provide opportunities for exercise. Belonging to a health club and participating in an organized recreational program are other ways to enjoy exercise.

The government offers health programs. Most counties have public health departments that provide health-related services. Two of the major federal government health programs are Medicare, for older adults, and Medicaid, a program to help low-income people with medical bills. Other federal programs are offered through the Department of Health and Human Services. These cover many areas of health care, such as research on diseases and their cures, mother and child health services, and programs to prevent and control the spread of disease.

Many nonprofit organizations are devoted to health issues and concerns. Most of these are volunteer organizations. The American Red Cross, the Kidney Foundation, and the American Heart Association are examples of this type of group.

Much health-related information is available as well. Books and magazines can teach you about health issues. The public library is a good source of this kind of information. Many educational programs on radio and television deal with health concerns.

Many organizations provide help with health problems. They can offer information and support.

Making full use of your resources — personal and community — is important for maintaining good health. Only you can act and behave in ways that make wellness an important part of your life.

SECTION 2 REVIEW

1. Name six things you can do to maintain wellness.
2. Why is eating a variety of foods important for good nutrition?
3. To what are eating disorders related?
4. Give three suggestions for controlling stress.
5. What is the leading preventable cause of death in the United States today?
6. How can drugs affect mental functions?

Chapter 26 Review

Chapter Summary

- Many of your daily actions affect your health. Once you are independent enough to control these actions, you become responsible for your own health.
- Medical advances have controlled the spread of many diseases, but diseases related to poor living habits are becoming more common.
- Wellness is a decision to work at maintaining physical and mental well-being. There is much you can do to achieve wellness.
- Personal and community resources can assist you in achieving and maintaining good physical and mental health.

Chapter Review

1. Identify three factors that have contributed to an improved state of health today.
2. Explain how you can control your chances of being affected by a disease.
3. What is meant by wellness? What are its benefits?
4. Give four suggestions to follow for good nutrition.
5. You have read in this chapter, "In terms of physical health and wellness, the mind and body work together." How is this true in the case of eating disorders?
6. List six habits that can help you sleep better.
7. What is aerobic exercise? How often should you do it? What should be included in that time?
8. Explain how alcohol use can threaten the physical and mental health of people who drink. How does it affect their families and others?
9. How is knowledge a helpful resource for staying healthy?
10. Identify four general types of community resources that can help you achieve and maintain good health.

Critical Thinking

1. Name three things you can do to encourage healthful habits in your family.
2. How can places of business promote wellness among their employees?
3. How are good safety practices a part of wellness?
4. Why do you think some people use tobacco, alcohol, and other harmful drugs? How can the conditions that lead to drug abuse be eliminated?
5. Do you think that, as medical science finds more cures and treatments for diseases, people become more careless about their health? Explain your answer.

Activities

1. **Health resources.** As a class, make a lists of resources that provide information in the following areas: nutrition; exercise; drug use; stress and mental health; health insurance. (*Teamwork, organizing information*)

2. **Promoting health.** Make a poster that promotes a healthful habit or discourages one that is not healthful. (*Creative thinking, communicating information*)

3. **An irresponsible attitude.** Write a creative, humorous essay entitled "An Unhealthy Day in the Life of . . ." In it, describe the daily routine of a person with an irresponsible attitude toward health and wellness. (*Creative thinking, writing*)

4. **Overuse of antibiotics.** Interview a pharmacist or physician to find out what happens when people overuse antibiotics. Do antibiotics work on viral infections? Should a physician prescribe an antibiotic over the phone? Report your findings to the class. (*Interviewing, communicating information*)

STRENGTHENING VALUES

Aim For Wellness

As you have learned, wellness is the overall result of a variety of healthful habits. Carlo practices wellness by:

- Working to develop a taste for certain fruits and vegetables that he did not like when he was younger.
- Playing basketball with friends several times a week.
- Getting regular medical and dental examinations.
- Reading and listening to music to relieve stress.
- Talking about problems with someone who can help.

How does the quotation, "An ounce of prevention is worth a pound of cure," relate to wellness? How do you practice wellness? How can you include more healthful habits in your daily life?

CHAPTER 21

Managing Money

SECTION 1

SPENDING AND SAVING MONEY

SECTION 2

LIVING ON A BUDGET

IMAGINE THAT ...
you have just been hired for a part–time job at a movie theater. Just think — a paycheck every week! You daydream about all the things you'll be able to buy now — the designer jeans, the sports equipment, the CDs — but, wait. You decided to get a job to help pay for your own expenses. What about the supplies you need for art class? You'll need books for next term, too. Then you think about the birthday present you want to buy for a friend. Your savings account for attending community college isn't growing very fast either. You begin to wonder just how far those paychecks will really go.

SPENDING AND SAVING MONEY

---◆---

THINK AHEAD

About These Terms
joint account   *loan*
credit   *down payment*
interest   *balance*

About These Objectives
After studying this section, you should
be able to:
* Explain what money means to
  people.
* Identify and describe the two basic
  approaches to spending money.
* Identify and explain different credit
  options.
* Explain why saving money is
  important.

---◆---

ike a financial
fingerprint, each person's approach to
money is different. Everyone has a different attitude about money, different
spending habits, and different expectations of how to use money in the future.

◆ ◆ ◆

The Meaning of Money

What does money mean to you? Is it simply a resource for purchasing goods and services, or does it also serve other purposes in your life? What money means to you is tied closely to your values and goals.

How you spend money tells others a lot about you. What you buy shows what you think is important. Your priorities are revealed.

To some people money is simply a means of managing life. It gives them the ability to have and do what they need and want to in life. For others, money provides a sense of achievement and status. These people may view the money they have as a measure of their own worth. Some people use money to buy things that they hope will impress others. They may use money to try to buy respect, love, or affection. Money may also be used to manipulate or force others to do something.

Dawn is always spending money on her friends. She buys them gifts and treats them to movies. In her friend Jeri's words, "For some reason, Dawn feels she has to spend money on me. It's as though she thinks I won't be her friend unless she does. The truth is I'm her friend because I like her, not because of how much money she has. I keep telling her that she doesn't have to buy people's friendship."

Spending Styles

What you value also affects your spending style. There are two basic approaches to spending money, the *present-oriented* and *future-oriented* styles. Each differs greatly from the other. Very few people are purely one style or the other. Instead they are a mixture, with one style more predominant.

Present-oriented people buy what they want *now*, rather than waiting. They frequently want the best product there is. They do very little financial planning or saving. They often do not consider how their spending habits affect other members of their families.

People who are more focused on the future are able to put off purchases today so they can buy other items later. They are able to foresee the effects of the decisions that they make about spending. They ask other family members to participate in financial decision making. This type of spender is goal-oriented and willing to be flexible about purchases to reach these goals.

How you view money affects what you do with it. Remember this as you read on about money management. Ask yourself how your attitude toward money affects your ability to manage money.

Money means different things to different people. What would you say it means to these people?

Potlatch — Giving Until It Hurts

FAMILIES

AROUND

THE

WORLD

Many Native American groups along the Pacific Northwest coast of America have held the belief in their culture that all social and political cal events must be public. All witnesses to such events had to be repaid and, of course, well fed. The celebration that accompanied such events was called a potlatch.

The meaning of "potlatch" originally comes from the Chinook word meaning "to give." At a potlatch, northwestern Native Americans have given away property at great feasts. Potlatchs were given when young people reached puberty, at naming ceremonies, at initiations of boys into secret societies, and at marriages. The most important potlatch was given at death. Responsibility for the

potlatch fell on the family of the father of the deceased.

All family members were expected to help provide the gifts—slaves, clothing, or skins in the early days. Later blankets were often the primary gift. The gifts were displayed in public on the beach. Permanent posts were set up marking the ends of the long line of presents so that everyone would remember how much was given. The family also supplied huge amounts of food, by fishing and gathering or buying food with wages.

The potlatch advanced the host family in rank and in standing in the community. The bigger the display, the more invitations given, and the bigger the feast, the greater was the respect given to the family and the longer people remembered the event.

Providing a memorable potlatch, however, often put a family deeply in debt. Many families were bankrupt by the process.

HANDLING EVERYDAY EXPENSES

Most teens are financially responsible for only part of their needs and wants. Housing, food, and other needs are taken care of by adults. For which of your expenses are you responsible?

As you become more independent, you start to assume more financial responsibility. At some point, you will discover that it is not always safe or convenient to keep enough cash on hand to pay all your bills. Two alternatives to this are checking accounts and automatic teller machines (ATMs).

Using a Checking Account

With a checking account, you deposit money in a bank, savings and loan association, or credit union. You are then able to write checks for your purchases. With a credit union account, checks are called *share drafts*. The financial institution holds your money safely until you are ready to use it by withdrawing it or writing a check or draft.

Checking accounts can be opened so that one or more people can write checks on the account. If you open an account in your name, you are the only person who can use the money in the account. A **joint account** is in more than one person's name. All the people listed can write checks or withdraw funds. Some teens have a parent or other adult listed on the account, too. This way another person could have access to the account in an emergency.

While checking accounts are very convenient, checking privileges can be abused. Sometimes people write checks for more money than is in their accounts. When that

A checking account provides a convenient way to pay for items and pay bills. Often stores will not cash a check unless you provide one or more forms of identification (driver's license; credit card). Some people have their name, address, phone number, and driver's license number printed on checks for ease of identification.

happens, the check is said to "bounce." If you write a check for something without enough money in the bank, you will still have to pay for the item. In addition, most businesses charge a fee for bad checks to help cover the costs of collecting their money.

Writing bad checks is illegal. If it happens regularly or frequently, the person writing them can be arrested.

ATMs

Some financial institutions have automatic teller machines (ATMs). These machines are convenient because they allow you access to your account when the institution isn't open. Some ATMs are available 24 hours a day. You can withdraw cash from your account or make deposits.

USING CREDIT WISELY

Credit means borrowing or using someone else's money and paying it back later. Larger purchases, such as houses and automobiles, are most often bought this way. Credit allows you to buy goods and services today and delay payment for them.

Credit is "rented" money. Any time you rent something, there is a rental fee involved. **Interest** is what is paid to use someone else's money. Credit is more expensive than paying cash because of the interest you pay. The three main types of credit are credit cards, loans, and installment buying.

Credit Cards

Credit cards are plastic cards that people can use to buy goods and services on credit. They are very convenient and easy

SINCE more teens work today,

HOW does technology help them manage money?

Many teens have checking accounts and many use automatic teller machines. Some use credit cards and receive computerized printouts of financial transactions. Having easier access to money and credit requires the mature responsibility of living within a budget.

JOINING THE TEAM
- Name other ways technology helps teens manage money.
- Make a list of careers in finance. Choose one of the careers listed and investigate to find out ways in which technology is used in that type of work.

---

to use. Because they make spending simple, however, credit cards are also easy to misuse. People may charge more than they can comfortably pay for out of their current income.

Many different credit cards are available. Cards like American Express, Visa, Mastercard, or Discover can be used in a variety of places to buy many types of goods and services. Single-use cards are issued by companies for use only in their businesses. Department stores and gasoline companies often issue single-use cards.

How you pay for the privilege of having a credit card varies. Many credit cards have annual fees. Some cards start collecting interest when you make a purchase. Other cards do not charge interest if you pay the full amount due each month. The amount of interest charged on credit card debt varies among cards. Rates are often high. Information about interest and interest rates is included in the material sent out with each card and should be read carefully.

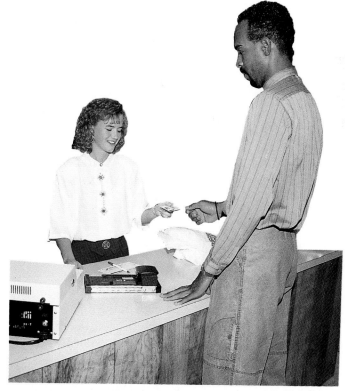

Credit cards offer convenience in paying for purchases. What problems can they cause for people?

If you get a credit card, be sure to write down the number of the card and the telephone number of the company. Keep these numbers in a safe place where you can find them. If your credit card is lost or stolen, call the company immediately. Someone there will take steps to prevent anyone else from charging items on your card.

Loans

A **loan** is money lent out at interest. The cost of loans varies a great deal. Loans also vary in their terms, such as how long the loan is for and whether it is to be repaid in installments or a lump sum. Because of this variety, it is important to shop carefully for a loan.

There are many possible places to borrow money. Banks and credit unions are common sources of low-cost loans. Some people are able to borrow from family or friends at good rates. Expensive sources of cash include small loan companies, cash advances on credit cards, and pawnbrokers.

There are federal laws that control the information given to you when you borrow money. This helps you compare costs and terms of various loans. Before signing papers for a loan, be sure that you understand what is expected of you. Find out what the consequences would be if you were not able to meet those expectations.

Installment Buying

Installment buying is often used to purchase large items like cars, furniture, and appliances. In installment buying, you make a partial cash payment, called a **down payment**. You then pay the **balance**, or remaining amount, in monthly installments. Getting installment credit from the dealer who sells the product is often expensive compared to the cost of other types of credit. Check carefully before making a commitment.

If you buy an item on the installment plan, be sure you understand the contract you sign. If you miss a payment, the whole amount can come due. If you cannot pay, the dealer may be able to take back the item. If that happens you will probably lose all the money you have already paid. Also, if more than one item has been purchased on credit from the same place, the dealer may be able to take back *all* the items.

Many people judge installment plans by how much their monthly payments will be, which can be misleading. If payments are low, the interest charges may be high. A low payment may be convenient, but for how many months will you have to make it? Look instead at the total amount of interest you will have to pay. Then decide whether buying on the installment plan is worth it.

Applying for Credit

To get credit, you must apply for it. People who loan money or allow you to buy items on credit want to know that you will be able to pay what you owe.

A credit application typically asks about employment, including how long you have been on the job. Other questions may concern how many people are in your family, what other sources of credit you have, whether you rent or own a home, and how much money you already owe.

The company that you have asked for credit then does a credit check. It may consult with a credit bureau that has records of how you have handled credit in the past. Some companies contact individuals or companies that you've done business with before. Based on your history of using credit and the information you provide, the company then decides whether to extend you credit.

Large items, such as refrigerators and automobiles, are usually purchased on an installment plan when credit is used.

LeRoy was doubtful when he applied for a car loan at his credit union. He had a credit card that he used regularly and responsibly, but he had never made a major purchase on credit. He was afraid the loan officer would think he didn't have enough experience with repaying borrowed money; however, the loan officer checked with LeRoy's boss, his landlord, and the companies that provided him service. When she learned that he was a conscientious, reliable worker and that he always paid his rent and other bills on time, she authorized the loan.

Having a good credit record is important. If you are denied credit, you must be told why by law. If the decision was based on incorrect information provided by a credit bureau, you have the right to get the error corrected.

Credit Tips

Credit is easy to use and misuse. You need to manage your use of credit just as you manage your use of cash. To use credit wisely, do the following:

- Use credit only when necessary. Make sure that the benefits outweigh the costs and risks.
- Shop for the best credit bargain. Compare terms and interest rates.
- Go to a bank or credit union first. Their rates should be lower than most other sources of credit.
- Pay off installment loans and credit card debts quickly. These are both expensive sources of credit.

- Assume no more credit than you can repay out of your current income. Experts advise that you limit credit payments to no more than 20 percent of your take-home pay.

It is easy to "overdo it" when using credit. Because you do not actually see the money you are spending, you may forget that these expenses are as real as those paid in cash. Sometimes people get into serious credit trouble. When this happens, a professional credit counselor may be helpful. He or she can show them how to pay off their bills and how to keep from making the same mistakes in the future.

"*When reason rules, money is a blessing.*"

PUBLILIUS SYRUS

SAVING YOUR MONEY

Most people agree that the main reason for earning money is to be able to spend it on what they need and want. They would also agree, however, that *saving* money is as important as earning it.

Saving money for use in the future is not easy. It requires giving up things you might like to have or do today. Nevertheless, saving is important if you want to make your money count.

Saving money is one way to earn extra money. If you put your money in some type of savings account, it will earn interest. Some people add the interest to their savings. Others sometimes use it for special purchases.

Savings are essential for emergencies. You can't predict what will happen in the future. Illness, accidents, and unemployment can all bring about a need for savings. Experts suggest that you try to keep at least three times your monthly salary in an emergency fund.

The temptation to pay later is always there. When the amounts add up, however, the ability to pay later may not exist.

Having money in a savings account can give you a feeling of security. You know that if something unexpected happens, you have the means to take care of it.

Regular savings accounts are convenient. Most banks, savings and loans, and credit unions allow unlimited access to these accounts. With a few restrictions, you can deposit and withdraw money as you like.

Interest rates on regular savings accounts are usually relatively low. If you are willing to tie up your money for longer periods of time, you can earn higher rates. Certificates of deposit (CDs) and government savings bonds offer higher rates of interest. Your money, however, is not available to you for a specific period of time without some penalty. Find out more about accounts available to you at your bank, savings and loan, or credit union.

MANAGING FINANCES IN A MATURE WAY

As you can see, financial independence carries with it many options. The possibilities are exciting but can be risky as well. True financial maturity means learning to manage well, making the most of what you have.

Tips for Saving

Saving your money takes self-discipline. This is especially true if you are a present-oriented spender. Listed below are some tips that can help:

- Put money in savings at the beginning of the month *before* you begin paying bills. If you wait to save "what's left over" at the end of the month, you may never save anything.
- If the place where you work offers one, use the payroll savings plan. The money you want to save will be deducted before you get your check.
- After you've paid off an installment debt, keep on making the payments. Put the money in your savings account.
- Save tax refunds, raises, and expense account reimbursements.

SECTION 1 REVIEW

1. Name the two basic approaches toward spending money.
2. What are two alternatives to keeping cash on hand to pay your bills?
3. Define credit.
4. Explain installment buying.
5. Why is it important to save money for the future?

A budget can be a handy money managment tool when you learn how to use it.

SECTION 2

LIVING ON A BUDGET

THINK AHEAD

About These Terms
budget
fixed expenses
flexible expenses

About These Objectives
After studying this section, you should be able to:
* Explain what a budget is.
* Identify and describe the four basic steps in creating a budget.
* Explain specific concerns when working out a family budget.

or most peo-
ple, good money management involves living on a budget. A **budget** is a plan for spending. It is one tool for money management. A budget can help you manage your money so you have it to spend on what you need and want most.

◆ ◆ ◆

CREATING A BUDGET

There are four basic steps in creating a budget: (1) estimating your income; (2) recording your expenses; (3) analyzing your spending; and (4) planning for your needs and goals. Each step requires some effort and honesty if the budget is to work. It is also important to keep in mind your values and priorities as you look at where your money goes and how you would like to spend it.

Estimating Your Income

The first step in creating a budget is to estimate the amount of income you have available to spend. It is better to estimate conservatively. Remember that money for taxes, Social Security, and company benefits is taken from your paycheck before you get it. Base your income on your actual take-home pay rather than on your hourly wage or salary. Add in your allowance, if you receive one, and any other regular income.

Recording Your Expenses

Secondly, you need to determine exactly what your expenses are. Expenses vary from person to person. Teens usually need money for school supplies, clothing, transportation, and entertainment. What other expenses might you have?

Figuring your expenses requires some record-keeping. Try carrying a small notebook to jot down amounts and what you buy when you spend money. Keeping accurate records will help you be more effective in making your budget.

For Howard, keeping records was difficult. He didn't think he would ever get into the habit of writing down what he spent. In time, however, he began to see how useful even his partial records were, and he made more of an effort to write down his expenses. Soon, keeping records was easy for him.

Analyzing Your Spending

Third, analyze your spending records. You will probably be surprised at how much money you spend on items that aren't actually important to you. Without realizing it, people often have many small spending "leaks." For example, how much do you think you spend each month on:

- Snacks, candy, and chewing gum
- Magazines
- Makeup and hair care
- Small clothing accessories
- Greeting cards and gifts

When you start analyzing your spending records, you'll probably be amazed at how much you spend on small unimportant items.

Once you are aware of the leaks in your budget, you can decide what to do about them. Some may be important enough to figure into your expenses. You may want to eliminate or cut back on others.

As you look at your records, you will notice that you have certain expenses that you pay regularly. These are called **fixed expenses**. These might include car payments, school activities fees, or tuition. If you are still living at home, you may not have as many fixed expenses as you will when you live on your own.

In addition, there are **flexible expenses**. These are expenses that do not occur regularly. They may be nonessentials, such as a birthday gift, or necessities, such as a textbook for school. Flexible expenses can be adjusted. For example, you may want to buy a new pair of shoes this week, but if there is no money for them in your budget, you will probably have to wait until next month.

Planning for Your Needs and Goals

The final step in making a budget is planning how you want to spend your money. List and total your fixed expenses, and subtract the total from income. Then you can decide how to distribute the remaining money for flexible expenses. Set spending limits for each category of flexible spending.

In this stage, you need to know your financial aims. This includes both short- and long-term goals. What do you want to do with your money? What expenses are necessary? Which are luxuries? You should also consider your spending style. If you have a present orientation, you may need to allow for some impulse spending.

Jana knew she was a "have it/spend it" kind of person. She found that the hardest thing about making a budget was deciding

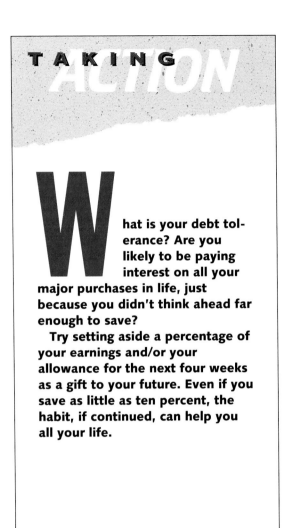

What is your debt tolerance? Are you likely to be paying interest on all your major purchases in life, just because you didn't think ahead far enough to save?

Try setting aside a percentage of your earnings and/or your allowance for the next four weeks as a gift to your future. Even if you save as little as ten percent, the habit, if continued, can help you all your life.

what she really wanted to accomplish with her money. That meant thinking about her goals. She knew she wasn't going to college right away but thought she might someday. Although her plans weren't definite, she started saving. She still enjoys spending her money but makes a serious effort to save some as well.

If you have done a good job of making your budget, you will be able to live with it. Periodic checks will help you see whether it is working. Remember that a budget is a personal thing. To work, it must suit your needs, wants, and priorities. If you are able to meet your financial goals, your budget is a success.

THE FAMILY BUDGET

Many of the principles of personal budgeting can be applied to making a family budget as well. Like an individual, each family has an income and expenses. Although some expenses are common to all families, each one must decide which are most important, based on *family* goals and priorities.

Perhaps the greatest difference in budgeting for an individual and budgeting for a family is that the family budget must take into consideration the needs, wants, and goals of the entire family. After the basic family needs of shelter, food, and clothing have been met, decisions must be made about which of the many wants any remaining money will satisfy.

Personal relationship skills are essential to preventing conflict about money matters. Communication and cooperation are especially important, but you should also have patience, understanding, and loyalty. Try looking at a situation objectively, with the long-term outcome in mind. For example, is it more important to buy a new car or to save the money for education? Like personal budgeting, successful family budgeting requires the ability to decide what needs are most important and the willingness to work to meet them.

ACHIEVING FINANCIAL GOALS

For the individual and the family alike, making money count is hard work. It requires thought, planning, and self-discipline. It is the only way, however, to achieve your short- and long-term financial goals.

Financial Danger Signals

Part of effective money management involves knowing when problems are developing. You can then get help or take action to get your finances back on track before things get out of hand. Some financial danger signals include:

- Paying only the minimum amount on credit card bills and other monthly credit accounts.
- Paying regular monthly bills with loans or savings.
- Using credit to pay for items like food and entertainment that are normally paid for in cash.
- Not knowing how much your total debt is and how much interest you are paying on the debt.
- Depending on irregular income, such as overtime or tax refunds, to keep up with the bills.

If any of these situations occur, it's time to take a hard look at your spending habits. Perhaps your use of credit has gotten out of hand. Spending may need to be cut to levels more realistic for your current income. A budget can help you with this process.

SECTION 2 REVIEW

1. What is a budget?
2. List the four basic steps in creating a budget.
3. How does budgeting as an individual differ from family budgeting?
4. What personal relationship skills are essential to preventing conflict when dealing with family finances?

Chapter Summary

- Money means different things to different people. For some, it is tied to feelings of self-esteem, power, and control.
- Checking accounts offer safe, convenient alternatives to paying some expenses in cash, but they must be used responsibly.
- Buying goods with credit allows you to enjoy items now and pay for them later. Using credit is almost always more expensive than paying with cash.
- Different types of credit include credit cards, loans, and installment plans. They vary in interest rates and in time allowed to pay them off.
- Savings are an important part of money management, especially for emergencies.
- A budget is a plan for future spending based on income, expenses, and priorities.

Chapter Review

1. Explain what money means to different people.
2. Describe the two different spending styles.
3. When is a check said to "bounce"? What are the consequences of writing bad checks?
4. What safety precaution should be taken in case your credit card is lost or stolen? What protection does this offer?
5. Describe three possible consequences of missing an installment payment.
6. Give three tips for managing credit use.
7. Give three advantages of keeping money in a savings account.
8. List three tips for saving money.
9. How do fixed and flexible expenses relate to budgeting?
10. Why are personal relationship skills helpful when planning a family budget?
11. List three financial danger signals.

Critical Thinking

1. Can people be happy with very little money? Explain your answer.
2. How can past experiences, including those of other family members, affect a person's attitude toward spending money?
3. Do you think it is a good idea for teens to have their own credit cards? What potential benefits and risks are involved?
4. What personal traits are necessary for — and can be strengthened by — making and following a budget?

Activities

1. **The importance of money.** Interview three people about what money means to them and its importance in their lives. Share your findings with the class. (*Interviewing, communicating information*)

2. **Money from other countries.** Bring to class examples of money used in other countries. Compare their relative worth to each other and to American dollars. (*Acquiring information, mathematics*)

3. **Comparing credit.** Collect information on different credit cards. Compare their interest rates and how the interest is figured. (*Acquiring and evaluating information, mathematics*)

4. **Budgeting.** Create a monthly budget, using the steps outlined in this chapter. Explain how your values and goals influenced your spending and saving decisions. (*Money management, self–management, mathematics*)

5. **Calculating costs.** Maureen bought new bedroom furniture on the installment plan. The price of the furniture was $1500. She paid 10% down and must pay the remainder in monthly installments of $100. The interest rate of the plan is 17%. How long will it take Maureen to pay off the debt? What will her monthly payments be? How much total interest will she pay? (*Interpreting information, mathematics*)

STRENGTHENING VALUES

Aim For Resourcefulness

Resourcefulness is skill in using what you have to get what you need and want. It means using resources creatively. Gretchen shows resourcefulness by:

- Finding a way to earn extra money to pay for her dance lessons.
- Making a gift for her grandmother instead of buying one.
- Offering to tutor Lionel in math in exchange for his help in painting her room.
- Asking her history teacher to recommend some sources for a research paper.
- Planning tomorrow night's dinner menu while waiting in line at the store.

What resources are available to you? How can you share or exchange resources with others to benefit everyone?

Consumer Skills

IMAGINE THAT ...

you have saved enough money to buy a stereo system. You go to an electronics store, thinking you know exactly what you want. You soon discover, however, that you are faced with a complicated decision. There are more brands of sound systems than you knew existed. Some are small and basic. Others look as though they need a room all to themselves. The salesperson cheerfully explains all the different features of each one, plus their warranties, prices, and the special credit rates available for one week only. You leave the store with more questions than you had when you went in — and without the stereo system. Getting just what you want at a reasonable price is not as simple as it seemed.

BEING A GOOD CONSUMER

THINK AHEAD

About These Terms

bargain	*impulse buying*
consumer	*unit price*
comparison	*fraud*
shopping	*direct advertising*
warranty	*indirect advertising*

About These Objectives

After studying this section, you should be able to:

* Explain how good consumers judge quality and price.
* Tell how to comparison shop.
* Explain impulse buying.
* Give tips for saving money.
* Recognize and explain advertising techniques.

 **consumer** is a person who purchases goods and services to fill needs and wants. Businesses encourage you to buy in many ways — clever advertising, attractive packaging, and skilled salespersons. Remember, however, that *you* make the final decision about buying.

♦ ♦ ♦

499

A good consumer learns as much as possible about a product before buying it. The larger the purchase, the more important it is to be well informed.

TRAITS OF GOOD CONSUMERS

Being a good consumer is not always easy. To be a good consumer, you must:

- Take time to become familiar with available products, prices, and standards of quality.
- Read and do research to learn what features to look for or avoid in products.
- Use self-discipline to resist society's message to consume.

If you become a wise, educated consumer, you are most apt to be satisfied with the goods and services you purchase.

Several skills can help you be a practical consumer. The first step, however, is *wanting* to be a good consumer. Getting the most for your money must be a personal value of yours before you will take the time and energy to work at it.

JUDGING QUALITY AND PRICE

The goal of a good consumer is to get top quality at a fair price. To reach this goal, you have to understand what makes good quality in the item you are buying. You also have to know what a low or high price is for the item.

What Is Quality?

To learn about quality, you can find out how products are judged by independent groups. You can discover how engineers and other professionals rate products. Consumers Union, which publishes *Consumer Reports*, and Consumers Research are two groups that test products in laboratories and report to readers. Their reports give you an idea of what features show good quality.

Consumer information is available at all public libraries. Ask the reference librarian to help you find what you need.

Experience is often a good teacher in evaluating quality. For example, Twila bought a new kind of shampoo. When she used it, she found that it had an unpleasant smell, didn't rinse out easily, and left her hair oily and limp. Twila's response was,"I'll never buy that brand again!" Have you ever had an experience similar to Twila's?

Time or Money?

Different families have different attitudes toward material possessions. Some families think it is important to spend money on things that the family can use and enjoy. Others prefer to keep possessions to a minimum. Still others have little choice: they simply cannot afford to spend money on anything except essentials.

Families who feel that family life is most rewarding when it includes many material possessions need to take stock from time to time. To make the money to buy things, they may work long hours. Indeed, there's a danger that people may spend so much time working to afford their possessions that they have little time or energy to enjoy them together.

Families who do not want to buy many items may believe that family members should be able to enjoy life and one another's company with a minimum of possessions. They may want to teach younger members that possessions don't bring happiness, and that time spent together as a family is more important.

Families who are struggling to get by don't need possessions to encourage family unity. They can seek out low-cost activities, such as family picnics or community–sponsored programs, as a way of combining quality time together with financial responsibility.

A Fair Price

Price is also important when making a buying decision. You don't want to pay more than you should for an item, yet you want the best quality for the price. Sometimes the item with the lowest price is not the best buy.

Ramona was shopping and found panty hose at a very cheap price. Since she needed them for work, she bought several packages. The first time she wore the new hose, she found that they snagged and ran quickly. Her "bargain" hose were no bargain.

Four conditions make a purchase a true **bargain**:

- The product is one you need, want, and will use.
- The item's quality meets your needs.
- The product sells at a price you are willing to pay.
- The item is sold by a reliable dealer.

Comparison Shopping

One of the best ways to find good quality at the lowest price is to comparison shop. **Comparison shopping** means looking in several stores to compare quality and price before buying.

Before you begin to shop, write down your standards for the item you are going to buy. Then look for the features you want and avoid those you don't need. For example, what features would you look for in a new pair of shoes?

Sometimes you can put the telephone to good use. If you are looking for a specific item, call several stores. You may be able to find out which stores have the item and the price you will have to pay. Calling first can save you time. The preliminary price information gives you a general idea of what you can expect to pay. You will have a better idea of what is a bargain and what is overpriced.

When you compare the prices of competing brands, be sure that the comparisons are equal. Read the labels carefully so you can tell whether the products are comparable. For example, don't compare prices for silk shirts with prices for cotton shirts.

Many products come with a warranty. A **warranty** is a written guarantee. You may wish to check competing products to see whether or not they have warranties. Then check what is covered by the warranties of the products that have them. A warranty may cover parts. Check to see *which* parts. Labor for repairing the product may be covered. Also, check the length of time the warranty is in effect. Other items may be included, depending on the product and the company that makes it.

If you are buying on credit, consider and compare credit terms. As you learned in the last chapter, costs can vary greatly among different types of credit.

Be sure to find out whether the store or company backs its products. Ask about the store's return and delivery policies.

Can you do comparison shopping every time you make a purchase? Under what circumstances might the practice *not* be useful?

When you decide to comparison shop, be sure that the time and effort you spend will be worthwhile. Comparison shopping is most effective when the item you are buying is expensive or a major purchase. It is also important if credit is involved. For smaller items, when the amount of money to be saved is small, comparison shopping may not be reasonable.

Some comparision shopping, on the other hand, can be done simply. You might be looking at different brands of detergent on the grocery shelf, for example. By comparing quantities and prices, you might save a little money with very little effort.

IMPULSE BUYING

Impulse buying is purchasing items without previous consideration or thought. You see something you like so you buy it. Impulse buying is typical of present-oriented spenders. When they see something they want, they rarely stop to consider the consequences of buying the item.

Retailers promote impulse buying by the layout of their stores. Impulse items are often close to the front of the store, so everyone sees them as they enter. Such items are also placed near checkout aisles or stations. People waiting to be helped can see them and be tempted to buy them.

Controlling Impulse Buying

To control impulse buying, you must know your needs and wants. Before making any purchase, you should consider whether it fits into the needs and wants you've outlined. Is the purchase really necessary?

A shopping list can also help you control impulse buying. Because it helps you focus only on what you really need and want, you will tend to ignore other items.

Determining the Credibility of a Source

When you learn to determine the credibility of a source, you are better able to see where to place your trust. You can make more responsible decisions.

DAWN *"I needed a dress for the prom, so my cousin Kerry and I went to Jax, my favorite store in the mall to shop. The clerks there really go out of their way to help you. The clerk who helped us brought out dress after dress for me to try on. She thought I looked good in all of them. The clerk said she had heard that none of the other stores in the mall had a good selection of dresses anymore. I finally settled on the blue one even though it cost a little more than the rest. The clerk said it brought out the blue in my eyes."*

KERRY *"When my cousin Dawn needed a dress for prom, I went with her to help pick one. We sure looked at a lot of dresses at Jax. I was disappointed when Dawn picked the blue one. It was too pale for her. The red one looked so much nicer on her with her fair skin. The style was better for her, too. The red one didn't even cost as much either. I wanted to go look at some other stores, but Dawn said she thought she should get this dress now before someone else buys it."*

CAN YOU DETERMINE THE CREDIBILITY OF A SOURCE?

When you determine the *credibility of a source,* you decide whether the traits and qualities of a person, idea, or thing have merit.

- What was the primary source that influenced Dawn's decision?
- How would you evaluate the credibility of that source?
- Did Dawn make any mistakes? If so, what were they?
- What would you have done in Dawn's place?
- Think of two friends. If each were to tell you the same piece of news, who would you be more likely to believe? Why?

Taking only as much money as is needed for what you've planned to buy may also help. Impulse shoppers find it easy to spend "extra" money they are carrying.

Experience taught Keith a lesson about impulse buying. His friends liked to play video games at the arcade after school. Keith knew he had to study before going to work at night, but if he had a few dollars with him, he couldn't resist going with them. Finally, his grades and his savings fell so low that he knew he had to stop. Now he carries only about as much money as he thinks he'll need for lunch and bus fare. Not only have his grades improved and his savings increased, but the experience has taught him to think twice whenever he is tempted to buy something.

A garage sale is a fantastic place to study buying mistakes. The next time you visit a garage sale (even one that your family has) try to determine why you think the family is selling the merchandise.

Can you find evidence of impulse purchases; "cute," but useless items; books that were read once and discarded; fashions that went out of style; or one-use items that aren't worth storing? What lessons can be learned from these items?

Notice, also, the quality of children's clothing and toys that outlasted the child's growth, the home furnishings that weren't worn out at redecorating time, and the sturdy tools that Grandpa doesn't need in his new apartment. There are bargains at garage sales — if you are a wise consumer.

ANALYZING ADVERTISING

Advertising can be very helpful to consumers. It lets you know about new products. It helps you keep up-to-date about existing products, especially if they have been changed or improved. Advertising gives you price information, and informs you when sales occur. It tells you where to find products and services. Being a good shopper would be much harder without advertising.

A wise consumer, however, is also cautious about ads. Since the purpose of advertising is to get you to buy more goods and services, businesses use it to create needs and wants that didn't exist before.

Advertising is everywhere — on television, radio, billboards, posters in buses or subways, calendars, and articles of clothing. It is in newspapers and magazines. You must be careful that you use advertising and not allow it to use you.

Advertising is designed to get your attention. What types of advertisements attract your interest the most?

Shopping Savvy

To save money when you go shopping, think about the different ways you can buy what you need. Shopping tips include:

- Take advantage of sales, advertised specials, and markdowns on needed items.
- Try private brands, lesser known brands, house labels, or discontinued models. They often provide better value for the money than new-model, brand-name items.
- Shop at discount stores rather than neighborhood or convenience stores.
- Buy basic quality; avoid deluxe models.
- Shop at garage sales, thrift stores, and through the want ads for items whose quality you can judge.
- Pay cash. Using credit is always more expensive.
- Use coupons. Be sure, however, that a name brand item with a coupon discount is cheaper than the same quality house brand item.
- Buy staples in quantity or larger sizes to get lower costs. Use **unit price**, a measure of the cost per unit of weight or volume, to compare prices on different sized packages.
- Don't be fooled by eye-catching, convenient packaging. Items like small cans of pudding with pull-top tabs are convenient but costly.

Remember that small sums add up. A dollar saved here or there may not seem like much. Those dollars, however, can be the means for getting the extra things you need and want.

Consumer Alerts

Not a day goes by that someone somewhere is not taken in by some form of consumer **fraud**, attempts to cheat you. Your best defense against fraud is to become knowledgeable. Learn to recognize and reject or investigate situations like these that have the potential for fraud:

- A telephone solicitor who calls you (you haven't placed the call) and offers to sell you an item at a good price. He wants your credit card number as a means of paying for the item.
- A person at your door who is "taking a survey" and wants to come in for a moment.
- A television plea to send money to help people who are in need.
- A telephone caller who wants you to donate money to a charity or give money for any purpose that you are not sure about.
- A mail solicitation that looks too good to be true. You may have won a "prize" or you get something "free."

Can you think of other fraudulent schemes that you have heard about? Share some specifics with your class.

Advertising Techniques

Companies may advertise directly or indirectly. **Direct advertising** appeals directly to you. It may try to appeal to your values in trying to convince you to buy a particular product. One common approach is to appeal to glamour. You are supposed to think that you can be as glamorous as the model in the ad if only you use the advertised shampoo. Health, happiness, success, good looks, and love are other values that advertising tries to promote.

Indirect advertising is more subtle. For example, celebrities are often associated with products without trying to sell them. The hero of a movie is seen drinking a can of a well-known soft drink. You see the star in a television series getting on an airplane from a major airlines. Companies pay to have their products featured in this way.

Another form of indirect advertising is the printing of company or product names on *clothing*. If you have a sweatshirt with the name of a brand of athletic shoes on it, you are advertising the shoes every time you wear the shirt. Can you think of other examples of indirect advertising?

A Critical Eye

To use advertising successfully, you must be able to analyze it with a critical eye. Then you will be in a better position to decide whether the product advertised is one you'd like to buy.

- Learn to recognize fact and fiction. Advertising is not always a reliable source of information. An ad for calcium pills that claims to have the highest amount of calcium of all pills tested, for example, may refer to a test that included only two other brands of pills.
- Recognize "no-promise" promises. Beware of conditional words in ads such as "can" and "often." If your cold medicine promises to "relieve symptoms for up to 12 hours," does that guarantee you will feel better for 12 full hours?
- Watch out for advertisements that say, "Price is less than our cost!" Stores must sell a product at a profit to stay in business. Are they really selling at less than cost? If so, why? If you have comparison shopped, you will be able to tell if the price is really a low one or not.
- Be careful of percent-off ads. If a store raises its prices, then advertises, "30 percent off selected items," you may pay

Advertising can be a help or a hindrance depending on the creator's intention. Can you tell the difference?

more for items "on sale" than you would otherwise.

- Get the whole story. Advertised prices sometimes don't include other fees or the cost of other items that must be purchased to make the advertised item function. For example, Mitzi was interested in a computer. When she saw one advertised at an incredibly low price, she went to look at it. It turned out that only the computer itself came for the advertised price. When she figured in the price of the screen, keyboard, cables, and programs needed to make the computer run, the advertised price was no bargain.

If you are able to analyze advertisements carefully, they can help you to be a practical consumer. Knowing what you want and recognizing value is important in being able to resist the lures of advertising.

SECTION 1 REVIEW

1. What are three traits of a good consumer?
2. List the four conditions that make a purchase a bargain.
3. When is comparison shopping most effective?
4. What is a warranty?
5. How can a person control impulse buying?
6. Describe two types of advertising techniques.

SECTION 2

CONSUMER RIGHTS AND RESPONSIBILITIES

THINK AHEAD

About These Terms
Better Business Bureaus
Consumer Action and Advisory Panels
small claims court

About These Objectives
After reading this section, you should be able to:

* Describe the four major rights of consumers.
* Explain responsibilities consumers have.
* Describe effective ways of making a consumer complaint.
* List resources consumers can use.

onsumer rights and responsibilities in the marketplace must be considered together. Consumers' interests (rights) are protected by state and federal law. At the same time, however, consumers also have responsibilities.

* * *

People expect businesses to treat them fairly. The opposite is also true. Can you think of ways that consumers sometimes treat businesses unfairly? Motels, for example, often bolt furnishings down in order to prevent people from taking them.

CONSUMER RIGHTS

Consumers have four major rights:

* The right to safety.
* The right to be informed.
* The right to choose.
* The right to be heard.

Consumers have a right to products that are *safe*. Some goods that are hazardous to health or life may be banned by law. In other cases, labels provide warnings that the product *can* be dangerous. Specific directions are given for the safest possible use. If you buy the product, you are aware that it can be dangerous if misused. What common household products can you name that carry this type of information?

The Mark of a Good Consumer

In Germany, families who are concerned about the environment look for the Blue Angel label. The label, used on products that are potentially harmful to the environment, does not mean that the product is perfectly safe. It only means that it is less damaging than other similar products on the market.

Blue Angel labeling began in 1978. By the early 1990s, more than 3500 products in 60 categories bore the mark. Some of the products approved for Blue Angel marking are aerosols with CFCs (chemicals that damage the ozone layer), oil burners that produce low levels of carbon dioxide (a greenhouse gas), wallpapers and flower pots made from recycled materials, recycled tires, brake linings and floor tiles that are free of cancer-causing asbestos, and trucks and buses that produce little soot and little noise.

Products proposed for the label must go through stiff evaluation and testing. Three government agencies, an independent jury, experts in various fields and special interest groups oversee the selection and testing process. The public nominates more than 100 products a year for the Blue Angel mark. Only three or four, however, earn the coveted label.

The mark carries weight among German consumers, eight percent of whom belong to the environmental party, the Greens. These families buy Blue Angel labeled products, so manufacturers are motivated to improve the quality of their products. In the early 1980s, only two percent of the oil burners produced in Germany met Blue Angel standards. Within two years, eighty percent qualified.

The labeling works, too. Estimates are that the amount of toxic solvents in German waters has dropped by about 40,000 tons since the mid-1980s. In an era when families feel threatened about their environmental safety, this is a significant contribution to such problems.

Consumers have the right to be *informed*. Several federal agencies work to be sure that companies provide accurate information about products, both in advertising and in labeling. Lars, for example, is allergic to some dairy products. He reads the list of ingredients on food packaging to help him select products that fit his special dietary needs.

Consumers have the right to *choose*. This means that there must be a variety of products and services from which to select. Having options helps keep prices competitive. Suppose there are seven businesses in your community that offer copying services, and only one in a community nearby. How do you think this will affect prices?

Finally, consumers have a right to be *heard*. If they are not satisfied with a product or service, they should receive a full hearing and fair treatment. Also, the government must consider consumers' interests when making decisions that affect them. Consumers must make their views known to their representatives and to government agencies.

CONSUMER RESPONSIBILITIES

Consumers have responsibilities as well as rights. They must be *careful, considerate shoppers*. They should treat merchandise as carefully as if they owned it.

Theresa was grocery shopping. On a shelf among loaves of bread, she saw a package of "frozen" beans sitting in a puddle of water. Can you see how someone's lack of consideration cost the store — and eventually its shoppers — money?

Consumers have the responsibility to *pay* for all merchandise. They should not tolerate shoplifting. This also results in losses for the store and higher prices for shoppers. Shoplifting is illegal. Someone who decides to shoplift may pay a high price in having such a blight on his or her permanent record.

A simple act of laziness costs a grocery store money. Think of the cost involved if many people were this thoughtless.

The consumer is responsible for *saving sales records and receipts*. Then records will be available if a product needs to be returned or exchanged.

Talia had a radio for nine months. Suddenly it stopped working. Although she had purchased it so long ago, Talia returned it to the store and asked for a replacement. She showed the customer service representative her receipt and the radio's warranty, which guaranteed the product for one year. She had little trouble getting a replacement.

Consumers are responsible for *following product instructions*. Otherwise, products may not perform as promised.

Vernon was very disappointed with the wax he bought for his car. The wax was hard to put on and buff off. It left streaks he couldn't rub off. When he complained at the store where he got the wax, he was asked if he'd waxed the car in the sun. The clerk said that the brand of wax he used only worked when used indoors or in complete shade. If Vernon had read the directions more carefully, he could have avoided wasting much time and energy.

CONSUMER COMPLAINTS

Filing a consumer complaint when you have a problem with goods or services is both a right and a responsibility. You have the right to be treated fairly and honestly, and you have the responsibility to others to save them from unfair treatment if you can.

Refunds and Replacements

Returning unsatisfactory merchandise for a refund or replacement is a common consumer problem. Handled correctly, however, many of these situations can be resolved successfully.

Most stores are cooperative about refunds and exchanges if you have the necessary receipts.

As with any consumer problem, the first step is to write, call, or visit the place of business involved. You will probably have the best success if you go in person with the product and your receipts. State your problem and tell what you want done. Be polite but firm. Repeat what you want done as often as you need to do so.

Alvin bought a pair of pants. The seams came apart the first time he washed them. He returned them to the store, saying politely, "I wore these pants only once. The seams came apart when I washed them. I'd like to return them for a refund." The clerk asked if he would prefer to exchange them for another pair. Would you accept another pair of the same kind of pants?

Alvin did not. He asked to talk to the store manager. Again he was polite but firm about what he wanted. When she, too, pushed for an exchange, Alvin complained to the vice president for consumer affairs of the company that made the pants. He wanted to give the firm every chance to satisfy him before turning to other options. Ten days later, he received a check for the price of the pants.

Remember that often two points of view exist on an issue. Many stores have had to deal with irresponsible shoppers. A person who buys a dress, intending to wear it once and then return it to the store, for example, is dishonest. Stores do not want to sell garments that have been worn or perhaps even damaged. They may not even be able to, which costs them money. The loss is then passed along to the consumer with higher prices. Returning an item is fine, as long as the reason is a good one. Stores that have to deal regularly with deception may seem strict with their policies, but the cause may be the consumers themselves.

Writing a Letter of Complaint

Sometimes writing a letter of complaint is the most practical approach when you have a problem. Information you receive when you buy a product may tell you where to send such a letter. Most of the time, the letter should be written and sent to the head of the consumer relations department. If you don't have an address, check at the public library. Most libraries have a government publication that lists the names as well as the addresses of the heads of consumer relations departments for hundreds of companies. Type or write carefully and clearly, and make certain your spelling is correct.

Be sure the letter is as businesslike as possible. Be reasonable and logical without attacking the company. State the problem and what you want the company to do. Include copies of your receipts and any other information that would support your case. Keep a copy of the letter.

Billing Problems

Almost everyone who uses credit or has monthly bills has a billing problem sooner or later. People may be billed for items they didn't buy. Payments that were made may not have been credited to the right account. The combination of human error and the widespread use of computers sometimes makes these problems difficult to solve. Be sure, however, that the problem is corrected as soon as possible. As you know, incorrect information can be given to credit reporting companies, and you may have trouble getting credit later.

Merle was billed on his credit card for a purchase made by someone in a town 2000 miles away. He'd never even been there! Merle didn't pay the charge but wrote to the company explaining the situation. In the meantime, the credit card company charged him interest on the unpaid amount. It took him three months to get the charge taken off the bill. Then another two months went by before the interest expense was removed. By contacting the company, however, Merle avoided paying for something he had not purchased. Also, if he had not explained the situation, the unpaid bill would have caused problems with that company and could have affected his credit record.

When you report, in writing, that there is a mistake on your bill, the company is required by law to investigate your complaint. It must reply within 90 days of the date your letter was received. If you are right, the billing will be corrected and any interest charges removed. If you are wrong, you are expected to pay the disputed bill within ten days.

A consumer problem can often be settled when you write a letter of complaint. What guidelines should you follow when writing such letters?

RESOURCES FOR CONSUMERS

As a consumer, you have many resources to help you when there is a problem. Some are operated by the government, others by businesses and industries.

Government Agencies

The United States Government and all state governments have consumer affairs offices, although they may have slightly different names in each state. Many county or city governments also have agencies that deal with consumer problems. These agencies are more concerned with the serious problems of fraud and misrepresented goods and services than they are with such problems as shoddy merchandise and poor service. They are, however, available to every citizen and may be able to help with your problem. The attorney general of each state is involved in enforcing consumer protection laws.

Better Business Bureaus

Better Business Bureaus are independent organizations sponsored by businesses in a community. They monitor advertising and keep files on local companies. The information on file may include how long a company has been in business, how often complaints have been made against a company, and how a company handles complaints.

Better Business Bureaus do not give advice to consumers but will share information with them. Citizens can make a complaint or get information by making a telephone call. Sometimes a Better Business Bureau will help a consumer with complaints that involve faulty service or misleading information.

CAPs

Consumer Action and Advisory Panels (CAPs) are organizations formed by specific industries to help solve consumer problems. The appliance, automobile, funeral, moving, travel, magazine publishing, and direct marketing and selling industries all have some type of CAP. If you have a problem with one of these businesses, a CAP may be able to help you.

Specific procedures must be followed before a CAP will become involved with a case. The complaint must first be taken to the retailer, dealer, and manufacturer. Then, if the problem is still not resolved, a CAP will consider it. All information must be presented in writing. If the evidence for the consumer is considered strong enough, the CAP can put pressure on the manufacturer.

If you are ever unsure about doing business with a company, a call to the Better Business Bureau may give you information that is helpful.

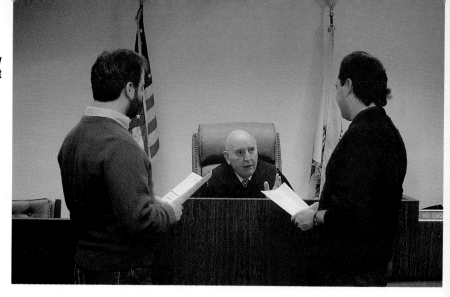

Some consumer disputes are settled in small claims court. The amount of money involved is limited, and an attorney is not required.

Small Claims Court

Sometimes consumer disputes must be resolved through **small claims court**. These courts handle cases that do not exceed certain money limits that are set by each state. In addition, you cannot sue for more than the actual cost of the items or services lost.

To use the small claims court, you must file a complaint and pay a filing fee. There may be other fees as well. The clerk of the court will help you understand the procedures used in your state and tell you what you will be expected to do. You may wish to visit the small claims court and watch a few cases before your own comes up.

Lawyers are not required in small claims court. In some states, they are not allowed. The judge works to bring out the facts of the case and to understand the issues. You will need to have all the evidence concerning your case. The decision will either be announced immediately or mailed to you.

Enforcement of judgments is not always good in cases tried in small claims court. The judge may order the person being sued to pay, but he or she may refuse. You may have to spend more time and effort in order to collect what you are owed. For these and other reasons, small claims court should be used as a last resort.

A Consumer in a Consumer Society

Living in a consumer society has many advantages. You have a wide selection of products and services to make life easier and more enjoyable. Competition helps keep prices reasonable and quality high. The final responsibility for getting good quality and fair prices, however, remains with you, the consumer.

SECTION 2 REVIEW

1. List the four major consumer rights.
2. Identify four consumer responsibilities.
3. What is the first step to successfully handling a complaint involving a refund or replacement?
4. Why is it important to have billing errors corrected?
5. What are the main concerns of government consumer agencies?
6. Why should small claims court be used as a last resort?

Chapter 28 Review

Chapter Summary

- A consumer is a person who purchases goods and services. As a consumer, you must make responsible, informed shopping decisions.
- To be a good consumer, you must know how to determine the quality of a product and the fairness of the price.
- Comparison shopping is a good way of getting the best quality for the best price.
- Advertising has both advantages and disadvantages for consumers. Claims for products must be carefully evaluated.
- Many consumers' rights are protected by state or federal law.
- Consumers are responsibile for acting in ways that protect businesses and other consumers from loss.
- Filing a consumer complaint is a right and a responsibility that helps ensure fair treatment for all. Many government and private agencies exist to help consumers who believe they have been treated unfairly.

Chapter Review

1. What is a consumer?
2. Identify two resources for learning about product quality.
3. Can price alone determine whether an item is a good buy? Explain your answer.
4. List four suggestions for effective comparison shopping.
5. What is impulse buying?
6. Explain the advantages and disadvantages of advertising.
7. Give four tips for analyzing advertising critically.
8. What information on product labels helps ensure a consumer's right to safety?
9. Why doesn't a responsible consumer tolerate shoplifting?
10. Describe the qualities of an effective letter of complaint.
11. What are Better Business Bureaus? How can they help consumers?

Critical Thinking

1. According to the text: "The message (in a consumer society) often seems to be that happiness comes through possessions." Do you agree or disagree with that statement? Use specific examples to support your answer.
2. Name three products that you and your family buy regularly. What advertising techniques are used to sell them? How do they affect your decision to buy the products?
3. What can consumers do, individually and as a group, to ensure the quality of goods in the marketplace?
4. Should the government play a role in determining fair prices and honest advertising, or should it be the consumer's responsibility to find the best price and to detect false or misleading ads? Give reasons for your answer.

Chapter 28 Review

Activities

1. **Comparing products.** Find a product comparison in an issue of *Consumer Reports.* Using the magazine's findings, decide which product you would purchase. Explain your reasons to the class. (*Acquiring and evaluating information, communicating information*)

2. **Indirect advertising.** Look for examples of indirect advertising. Make a list and share it with the class. (*Acquiring and evaluating information, organizing information, communicating information*)

3. **Advertising techniques.** Find advertisements in newspapers and magazines. Try to recognize the various techniques and appeals. (*Acquiring and evaluating information*)

4. **A letter of complaint.** Imagine that you have purchased a defective product. Write an effective letter of complaint, using the tips suggested in the chapter. (*Creative thinking, writing*)

5. **Consumer problems.** In small groups, write and perform two skits. In the first, show a consumer successfully handling a complaint. In the second, show the consumer handling it poorly. Have the rest of the class identify what the consumer did right or wrong in each case. (*Teamwork, creative thinking, communicating information*)

STRENGTHENING VALUES

Aim For Ecological Awareness

Ecological awareness means thinking about how your actions affect the environment. It means taking responsibility for keeping the environment clean and safe. As a consumer, Mark shows ecological awareness by:

- Talking with others about his environmental concerns.
- Finding ways to cut down on what he throws away. For example, Mark wrapped Christmas gifts in old boxes he found around the house rather than asking for new ones at the store.
- Buying products that are made and used without damaging the environment.
- Recycling glass, aluminum, and paper products.
- Staying informed on environmental issues.

How ecologically aware are you? How can you encourage others to buy products that cause no harm to the environment? How can you spread ecological awareness in your community?

Thinking About a Career

IMAGINE THAT ...

it is the first day of a new school year. Some of your friends are talking about how they spent their summer. One worked with children in a neighborhood program that offered games, crafts, and field trips. Another volunteered at a senior citizens' center. Still another helped her uncle by working as a receptionist in his real estate office. You listen with interest as each person talks about the experiences that went along with the jobs. Some of your classmates are even thinking about related careers. You start to wonder about your own plans for the future. You ask yourself: What do I want to do with my life? Where will I be in five years, or ten? You realize that it's time to start thinking — now.

PREPARING FOR A CAREER

♦

THINK AHEAD

About These Terms
career
aptitude
career counseling

About These Objectives
After studying this section, you should be able to:
- Describe the different kinds of tests for evaluating interests and skills.
- Identify the services offered by career counselors.
- Explain how vocational schools and universities prepare students for careers.
- Identify family-related careers.

♦

our teen years are the time to begin thinking about the work you would like to do in the future. The kind of work that you will do over a period of years will be your **career**. The decisions you make about your career will be important ones.

♦ ♦ ♦

PLANNING FOR THE FUTURE

What do you want for your future? What are your goals for the next thirty years? What are you doing now to help make those goals a reality? If you don't plan, you could drift.

Someday you may have a family of your own. The well-being of that family depends on you. A job provides the income that families need to survive. It gives a family the opportunity to make choices in life — about where and how to live. It gives them power and control. It gives them strength.

Planning for the future can be difficult. You don't know what will happen to you. While some things in life are unpredictable, you do have control over others. You can take steps to find the career that you need, a key to your future. Think and act. If you don't, you may find that time and circumstances make it more and more difficult to achieve your goals.

TAKING ACTION

Look through the classified ads in your newspaper and find the car you would like to be driving and the house or apartment you would like to be living in five or ten years from now. What kind of income would you need?

Now look at the "Help Wanted" ads. Do you find employment advertised that matches your interests and abilities? Will a career in this field provide the income to support the living standard represented by the car and house you found?

If there is too big a difference between the lifestyle and the career you chose, you may need to do some rethinking. Committing to more education or training in preparation for a better-paying job or lowering your living standard somewhat are two possibilities.

When should you begin to plan for the future? Even if you cannot make definite decisions at this point, now is the time to start thinking.

EVALUATING YOUR INTERESTS AND ABILITIES

The first step in thinking about a career for your future is to consider your interests and abilities. What do you like to do? What are you good at? Are there jobs available that will take advantage of your interests and skills?

A variety of resources are available to help you learn more about the skills you possess and the occupations for which you may be suited. Which of these would be a good career? Many different types of tests have been developed to help people determine which occupations might be right for them. You may wish to take one or more of those. You can learn about careers by talking with adult members of your family, friends, neighbors, employers, and counselors.

Tests

You have probably taken intelligence and aptitude tests during your school years. *Intelligence tests* rate your mental skills. *Aptitude tests* measure your **aptitude**, or natural talent and capacity for learning, in certain areas. Aptitude tests can cover many areas, such as mechanical aptitude or physical coordination. Intelligence and aptitude tests give broad guidelines about types of careers that may be right for you.

Sarah is interested in medicine and wants to be a surgeon. Her intelligence tests showed her to be above average, but her eye-hand coordination was not good. What advice would you give Sarah concerning her career choice?

Another type of test often used is an *activities preference test* or *interest test*. This type of test helps you translate your likes and dislikes into specific work preferences.

Tests have been created to help people see where their real interests and abilities lie. These can help point you in the right direction as you pursue a career. Ask your school counselor about how, when, and where you could take such tests.

No right or wrong answers exist on this test. Instead, there are lists of activities, and you select your preferences from the lists. Test results show patterns of interests and activities. You can then compare these patterns to work requirements to discover occupations that require activities you like to do.

Finally, there are *job preference tests*. These tests list two jobs and ask you to choose between them. When the test is scored, you are given a list of jobs that should suit your interests.

One important question to ask yourself as you consider a particular career is "How will it affect my family life?"

Career choice has a great impact on family. It helps determine how well you can provide for a family financially. It affects how much time you can spend with family members. Job choice often influences where you will live and whether you will move frequently. The type of work you do can even shape the values of younger family members.

To decide how much weight to give these and related issues, you must determine how you feel about each one. For example, how important is financial security to you? How important is time spent with family members? How do you feel about moving to a new location? Do you find change refreshing or disruptive? What values do you hold? How might your values influence your job choice?

To answer any of these questions requires some serious thinking about even more basic family issues. When you consider financial aspects, for example, you must think about whether you expect to marry; whether you want children and if so, how many; and whether you will need to support parents or other members of your present family.

All of these issues may seem overwhelming. Every question seems to lead only to more. You can't predict how you will feel in the future or what circumstances you may find yourself in. However, you <u>can</u> play an active role in shaping your life. Giving careful thought to choosing a career that helps you meet your expectations for family life is well worth the effort.

The usefulness of these tests is limited. Tests can't tell you specifically what job to search for. They also can't predict how successful or happy you will be with a certain job. They will, however, give you ideas about the careers in which you will have the best chance for success.

Career Counseling

Career counselors are another source of assistance in pinpointing your interests and skills. **Career counseling** helps people choose and be successful in their work. Many guidance counselors in schools also serve as career counselors. Counselors are also found in employment agencies and in private firms.

Career counselors talk with clients about their interests, talents, and career goals. They work to match people's skills with occupations. Counselors are skilled in giving tests, such as those previously described, which reveal people's work strengths and interests.

Career counselors are good sources of information about jobs as well. They are aware of the current job market, both locally and nationally. They know which career fields are apt to grow and expand and which are likely to disappear.

If you have questions about the education and or training needed for specific jobs, career counselors can answer them. Also, they can often suggest schools where training can be obtained. If you wish to research particular careers, counselors can provide reading and reference lists.

Private career counseling can be costly. The fee may be worthwhile, however, if you want personal advice and support. The International Association of Counseling Services prints lists of approved services. Your library should have or be able to get these lists.

Decisions About Education and Training

What do you plan to do after completing high school? If you plan to "get a job" and you find one you like that suits you, you're all set. Good workers are needed and appreciated in all jobs. Sometimes, though, people can't find jobs they like that will support them. Other times they "outgrow" their jobs and look for something that will be more interesting to them and, perhaps, pay more. Often, people find that they need more education or training to qualify for the jobs they'd *really* like to have. Perhaps you already have an idea of the kind of career you want and know you will have to prepare for it. You can obtain further education or training in several ways.

Vocational or Technical Schools

Vocational or technical schools provide career training. These schools prepare you for specific occupations, such as mechanic, beautician, or electronics repairperson. You receive specialized training for the work you've chosen. To get the most out of this type of training, you need to know the occupation you want and be eager to prepare for it.

Colleges and Universities

Two-year community colleges and four-year colleges and universities also train people for careers. Sometimes people attend college without knowing exactly what kind of job they want. After studying for a while and learning about the options available, they are able to make a choice.

Because college is expensive, however, they usually want to reach a decision within a year or two. Otherwise they may spend money on unnecessary courses. Other people know what they want to do and choose college because that is the only way they can accomplish their goals.

Maria wanted to be a teacher from the time she played school with her friends when she was four years old. To become a good teacher, she needed to know how children learn, different theories of education, and effective discipline techniques. For her, a university degree was a must.

Education/Training Costs

Going to college or to a vocational or technical school requires money. Tuition, fees, and books are expensive. If you live away from home, you will have living expenses as well. These expenses, however, are investments in the future. Often, the more education and training you have, the more money you are likely to earn over the course of your lifetime. Additional education and training can give you an edge in the job market as well. They may help you be more employable and promotable.

Lindsey was just promoted to supervisor of medical records at the hospital where she works. She hasn't been there very long and is the youngest person in the department. She was promoted because she has specific training in medical records and in using the computer to manage them. The money she spent on her training has already paid off.

The Winds of Change in South Africa

FAMILIES

AROUND
THE
WORLD

As white settlers began to arrive in South Africa in the early 1800s, life for the black families, who already lived there, became more difficult.

With their opportunities to make a living limited, most blacks could not get ahead. Laws were passed that restricted what they could do. Blacks had to have permission to enter and work in certain areas. To pay their taxes, they had to find work with whites. They were not allowed to have their own businesses.

For many years black South African workers had to travel several hours a day to jobs that paid very little. Those who could not commute, lived close to their jobs in "hostels." Only a third of these workers had their families with them. The rest visited their families only once every few months, or even less.

Many South Africans, both black and white, have long recognized that this situation could not go on. Since the 1970s many of the laws that separated the people have been repealed. Black unions, which have the right to bargain for higher wages, have developed. There are programs for black workers to receive technical and vocational training. Many companies are training black workers to move into management positions. Black South Africans can now own their own small businesses.

These changes have been a long time coming, and there are many changes that must yet be made. Slowly, however, job opportunities for blacks in South Africa are improving, bringing expectations for a better life to the many black families who live there.

Apprenticeship

For many occupations, you can receive on-the-job training through an apprenticeship. Trade occupations such as plumbing, painting, and carpentry offer apprenticeships. As an apprentice in a particular trade, you receive training from a skilled worker in that trade. You learn as you gain experience, and you can earn money at the same time.

In most apprenticeship programs, you must register with the state or federal government. Then you work as an apprentice for a set length of time, usually four to six years. At the end of that time, you may have to take written and practical tests to prove your knowledge and skills. You will then receive a certificate or license. Apprenticeship programs vary, however.

You can learn some job skills through apprenticeship programs. You earn as you learn from people who are already knowledgeable.

The career counselor in your school can help you find out more about programs in your area.

Considering Education and Training

Whether you plan to be educated or trained past high school depends in part on your interests, your work goals, your financial situation, what your family expects of you, and what you expect of yourself. Be sure you have considered all the aspects of your choice when you make decisions about this issue.

FAMILY LIVING CAREERS

Since you are studying about families — and careers, too, you might like to think about how the two go together. Many people make careers of working with and serving families. In general, people who work with families need good communication skills. They are patient people, who have a calm approach to life. Most of all, they care and want to help others.

Higher Education: How Will You Pay?

The cost of attending a college, university, or vocational school is high — and getting higher. This is a problem for many students. Some even decide they cannot afford higher education.

There are some things you can do now to help make higher education more affordable:

- Ask your school guidance counselor about taking Advanced Placement courses. You can earn college credit without taking college courses.
- Keep up your grades and be active in extracurricular activities. Many college and university scholarships are awarded based on good grades and school and community involvement.
- Try to decide what general course of study you will follow. Many schools and departments within a college and some professional groups offer scholarships for those studying in that field.
- Learn what type of financial aid is available from the government. Federal and state governments offer grants and student loans to those who are eligible.
- If you have a particular school in mind, ask about tuition discounts. For example, tuition may be lower for weekend and summer classes.
- Attend a community college. Two-year colleges prepare students for occupations or further education. They are less expensive than four-year universities.
- Work and save your money. Also, get information from the college Office of Student Employment about on-campus jobs.

Some family related jobs are briefly described below. This list is by no means complete. You might like to do some investigating to find more information about these and other similar careers.

Minimal Training

You don't need a college education to work with families. You may be able to get training for some jobs through a vocational program. Sometimes you can learn what you need to know with on-the-job training and experience. The pay is not usually very high for such jobs, but, if you like helping people, the rewards can compensate. A few job possibilities of this type are described here.

CHILD CARE WORKERS   Some people love children and decide to work in the child care field. You might work in a center

Qualified child care workers should have no difficulty finding a job since opportunities in this field are increasing constantly. Why do you think this is so?

or become licensed to care for children in your own home. A nanny lives and cares for children in their home. With the ever increasing need for child care, opportunities in this field are increasing all the time.

SOCIAL SERVICE AIDES   Many social service agencies need people to work in their offices. Social service aides, for example, link social workers to the clients who come into an agency. They may help people fill out applications for financial help and offer other assistance.

Holly works in a welfare office. As clients come in, she interviews them to see whether they are eligible for benefits. Then she shows them how to fill out forms and makes them feel at ease.

GERIATRIC WORKERS   If you would like to work with elderly people and their families, you might look for a job in a nursing home or retirement complex. Aides and office workers are needed to take care of many of the routine needs that older people have.

George has a sense of humor that works well for him in his job. As a nursing home aide, he transports elderly people around the home and runs many errands. He thinks of the residents as his family. Because many of them are lonely and some in poor health, they love the attention and the teasing that George offers.

College Training

Many of the careers in which you work with families require some college training, with a major in sociology, psychology, social work, or other related subjects. Depending on the job, a two- or four-year degree may be needed. Some require even further schooling. Such positions typically pay more than those for which college is not required, but salaries for these jobs cover a wide range. A physician, for example, makes much more than a social worker. When the pay is not particularly high, job satisfaction is more likely to come from the opportunity to help improve life for others.

COUNSELORS Several kinds of counselors work with families and their members. Marriage counselors help couples whose marriages are in trouble or who are considering divorce. Family counselors treat the whole family when relationships are strained and family members need help getting along with each other. Financial counselors help families with their money concerns and problems.

Jody is a marriage counselor. She sees many couples who have fallen into destructive, hurtful habits without realizing it. She listens to their problems and offers an outside, objective viewpoint. She helps people identify the source of the conflict and resolve the situation in ways they can live with. With her experience and empathy, she can help save relationships when both people are willing to work at it.

Some relationships have deteriorated so much that separation is the only workable option. Then Jody helps couples behave civilly and reasonably to make the breakup as painless as possible. She helps them deal with their feelings and begin to rebuild their lives.

RELIGIOUS LEADERS Religious leaders, such as ministers, pastors, and rabbis, frequently deal with families and their problems. They often serve as marriage or family counselors.

SOCIAL WORKERS Social workers have contact with families in many of their jobs. Those who work with foster families or in adoption cases have special interests in families.

Scott works for a private adoption agency. He helps match children with couples who want to adopt. He also does follow-up counseling to help them deal with the problems and make the adjustments involved with bringing a new child into the family. Scott takes great satisfaction in bringing together children without parents and couples longing for children to help create new, loving families.

POLICE OFFICERS Some police officers are specially prepared to serve families. They may be called in to settle family disputes and deal with all sorts of family problems. Because an officer's safety is sometimes on the line, a person must be willing to take risks in this job.

TEACHERS People teach family life on both the high school and college levels. Home economics and sociology are two subject areas that deal with family life.

HEALTH CARE WORKERS The health care field offers many chances to work with families. As a physician or a nurse, you might work with the elderly or with infants in the obstetric area. Since all families need health care, many professionals are needed in this area.

SETTING CAREER GOALS

Family-related careers are, of course, only a few of the possibilities out there for you. You will want to use knowledge about your interests and skills to help you narrow down the options. Then you can set some work-related goals for yourself.

In deciding on a career and career goals, you should realize that you will probably have at least six to eight jobs during your lifetime. Changes in the job market, in family situation, and in personal interests cause people to switch jobs and even careers several times in their lives.

Chet has always enjoyed selling real estate. He likes the challenges of getting to know people and matching them with a house that fits their personalities and lifestyles. However, the real estate market is often uncertain. With three young children to provide for, Chet is now looking for something more steady. He is training to become an insurance agent. What aptitudes and skills that helped Chet succeed in real estate will help him in his new career?

To prepare for a career that may change over the years requires flexibility. You need to think about how one job or career might lead to another.

The path that your career takes may not be a straight one. At this point in your life, however, it is important that you make some plans. Goals for your career will give you focus over the next few years. As the years unfold, you can adapt or change your goals to match your changing interests and circumstances.

SECTION 1 REVIEW

1. Name three types of tests that can help you focus on a job that is right for you.
2. What valuable information can career counselors give you about the job market?
3. Identify the two main types of educational institutions that provide career training..
4. About how many jobs will the average person have over a lifetime? What causes people to change jobs?
5. List five professions that deal directly with family living.

GETTING A JOB

THINK AHEAD

About These Terms
resumé   *interview*
application form   *professionalism*
references

About These Objectives
After studying this chapter, you should be able to:
- Identify ways to learn about job possibilities.
- Explain how to fill out a job application form.
- Recommend ways to prepare for an interview.
- Define and explain the importance of professionalism.

electing and preparing for a career is only a start. The next step is actually finding a job. This can be a frustrating and discouraging process. You need to know how to get hired as well as how to do the job. Enthusiasm, self-confidence, and energy can help you convince others that you have a positive contribution to make.

◆ ◆ ◆

Just imagine all the job possibilities that are out there. How will you go about finding and getting the one that is right for you?

LOCATING JOB POSSIBILITIES

Finding a job today is not always easy. You will probably spend much time and effort in your search, but there are many ways of locating job possibilities.

Ask Others

One of the best ways of learning about job possibilities is through friends, family members, neighbors, and acquaintances. If you are looking for a job, tell others. Tell them the kind of work you are looking for and ask them to let you know if they hear about such a job.

Visit Businesses

Another good way of learning about jobs is to visit various places of business and ask what they have available. Doing this is hard work. It takes courage to walk in off the street and ask about possible job open-

ings. Often there are none. The more contacts you make, however, the better chance you have of finding one. You may also impress a possible employer with your interest and initiative.

Placement Offices

School placement offices can be a source of information about jobs. Job openings are usually posted. Counselors may be able to help you make a list of firms to approach for the type of job you are seeking. Community colleges often have active placement offices. Even if you aren't attending the college, it may be helpful to visit the placement office and see what information is available.

Employment Agencies

State employment agencies have job listings as well as counseling and testing; however, they are able to place only about one-third of the people who apply there.

SINCE many teens look for part-time jobs,

HOW does technology help them find work?

Employers may target potential teen employees through ads on local cable-television programs. Some community centers or libraries offer data-based job-listing services. Some people send resumés by fax to respond quickly to job leads. Taking advantage of high-tech developments can put you closer to finding the job you want.

JOINING THE TEAM
- Some people ignore technology that could help them. Why is it important that you not do this when job hunting?
- Where in your community could you go to find technological help as you explore career possibilities?

Private employment agencies charge a fee for helping you find a job. Their placement rate is even lower than that of the state agencies. If you decide to go to a private agency, be sure you understand what the fees are, who pays, and the conditions of the contract before you sign.

Derek found a job through a private employment agency. He paid half the fee and his employer paid the other half. The job didn't work out. Since he had worked only one month, he hoped he could get his money back from the agency. He didn't realize that once he accepted a job, he owed the agency its fee, regardless of the outcome.

Some people and organizations make it their business to know where available jobs exist. Enlisting the help of a job placement office can put you much closer to finding a good job.

Want Ads

Often when people are thinking about looking for a new or different job, they start by reading the newspaper want ads. Unfortunately, the want ads are usually a poor source of jobs and information about jobs. You must follow up to find out whether a job interests you or if you have the qualifications for it. One study found that in a year in a typical city, only one-fourth of all employers hired anyone as a result of a want ad.

Sending Resumés

Sometimes job seekers develop a list of companies for whom they'd like to work. They send a letter asking about jobs and a resumé to each of these companies. A **resumé** is a written account of qualifications, including education or training and experience. Generally, sending out unrequested resumés is not an efficient means of finding a job. Companies receive hundreds of resumés for every job offer they make. Many have a policy of not responding to unsolicited letters.

Other Sources

Other possible sources of information include the Chamber of Commerce and the telephone book Yellow Pages. These sources can give you an overview of the businesses in your community. You can then follow up to see whether any of them have jobs available.

APPLYING FOR A JOB

When you find a company that has a job available, you are likely to be asked to fill out an **application form**. This form gives the company basic information about you. It lets them compare candidates for the job.

The application form may be the only chance you have to make a "first impression" on the person who is hiring. You want to be sure it represents your best work. Read the instructions carefully and follow them exactly. Use a pen that doesn't leak and write neatly and clearly. Answer all the questions. If a question does not apply to you, write "not applicable" in the space for the answer. Be sure you have all the information with you that you need, such as your Social Security number and your employment record.

Most application forms ask for references. **References** are people who have agreed to discuss your ability and character with a potential employer. Be sure to ask these people for permission before including their names as references. Take their names, addresses, and telephone numbers with you for the application form.

John will always remember his first experience filling out a job application. First, he had to borrow a pen from the clerk. Then he had trouble understanding a question. He became tense and frustrated and began hurrying and writing sloppily. For one question, he scratched through his first answer and wrote another in the margin of the paper. Then he had to ask for a phone book because he had forgotten the list of his references' addresses and phone numbers. Needless to say, he did not get the job. How do you think he prepared himself when he applied for his next job?

One of the first things you do when applying for a job is fill out an application form. How well you handle this step can mean the difference between getting an interview or not.

INTERVIEWING

An **interview** is a face-to-face meeting between an employer and a potential employee. Many people seeking a job approach the interview with anxiety. They know that what they say and how they act can make the difference between acceptance and rejection. It's no wonder that job interviews create stress. You can reduce your nervousness if you prepare carefully and have some idea of what to expect.

First Impressions

First impressions in an interview are important. The way you dress and act will say much about you before the first question is asked.

Lane kept this in mind as he prepared for his first job interview. He wore clean dress pants and a dress shirt borrowed from his dad. He polished his shoes and wore a tie. He made sure his hair was clean and neatly groomed. He arrived fifteen minutes early so he wouldn't have to rush finding the room. If you were interviewing Lane, what impression would his preparations make on you?

The Interview

The purpose of the interview is to find out if you are capable of handling the job that is available and if you will be a good worker. The questions that you will be asked help the interviewer discover these facts. Everything you say and do should convince the interviewer that you can or will learn to handle the job and that you are eager to prove that you can work hard and well.

The more you know about your talents, abilities, and skills, the better chance you will have of explaining them to others. Before the interview, plan ways to explain what you have to offer. Do not memorize a "speech," but have a general idea of the points you'd like to get across.

LaDonna's father coached her on what to say to the interviewer. He told her the interviewer might begin by saying, "Tell me about yourself." In answer to this question, LaDonna should explain two or three experiences she's had in the past that show why she would make a good employee. Her father also told her to expect a question or two about her strengths and weaknesses. He said she should make the point that she has certain strengths that could help the company. He also gave her tips for answering other questions. When the first thing the interviewer said was, "Tell me about yourself," LaDonna was able to relax a bit and answer naturally about her previous experiences.

It doesn't matter if you are somewhat anxious; the interviewer will expect that. Try to avoid nervous habits, such as twisting your hair or cracking your knuckles. Smile and maintain good eye contact with the interviewer. Answer questions as clearly

An interview can be challenging. Learn what to do before you go and be prepared to put your knowledge into action.

and concisely as possible. Concentrate on your abilities and strengths and how you can tell the interviewer about them.

Ask any questions that you have about the job. Do not be hesitant to ask about wages or salary, but avoid making it appear as if that is the only thing about the job that appeals to you.

Ending the Interview

When you leave, thank the person for the interview. In some cases, it is appropriate to leave a resume. It is a nice gesture to write a thank-you note to the interviewer later that day.

PROFESSIONALISM

After you have found a job, you must show that you take it seriously and want to keep it. One way in which you demonstrate this is your attitude. This is one of the most important qualities for being a successful worker. How you think and feel about your job shows in your behavior and your job performance.

Employers want to hire people who will work hard, make a commitment to the job, and enjoy their work. They want people with high moral standards who will behave ethically on the job. Self-discipline, being able to work without direct supervision, and a sense of responsibility are valued qualities.

Professionalism is showing a positive attitude toward, commitment to, and ethical behavior on the job. You will be a valued employee if you can develop the attitude of professionalism.

When Kadar began working in a restaurant kitchen, he was dismayed at the unprofessional behavior of some employees. They arrived late, were rude to customers, and careless about cleanliness.

Kadar thought about how he'd feel if he were eating at this restaurant. If the restaurant lost customers, its owner would lose money, and that would hurt them all. Kadar understood the importance of professionalism to himself and to others.

"*Every calling is great when greatly pursued.*"

OLIVER WENDELL HOLMES

LOOKING FORWARD TO THE FUTURE

It is never too early to start thinking about your career and goals for the future. The opportunities are many, varied, and exciting. Skills and interests you have now could lead to a rewarding career, if only you are willing to work for it.

SECTION 2 REVIEW

1. List four ways of learning about job openings.
2. Why is it important that your job application represent your best work?
3. What is the purpose of a job interview?
4. What does the term "professionalism" mean?

Chapter 29 Review

Chapter Summary

- Your decisions about work are some of the most important in your life. Now is the time to begin thinking about a future job or career.
- Various types of tests can help you select a career by showing your aptitudes and interests. Career counselors can advise you about job possibilities in different fields.
- Vocational schools, colleges, and universities are places that offer advanced career training. Apprenticeship programs offer on-the-job training to become a skilled worker in the trades.
- Flexibility is an important job skill because you may want to change jobs or careers.
- Many careers deal directly with family living. People go into these professions because they want to help others.
- There are a number of sources of information about job openings. Friends, family, and places of business are among the best.
- Applying for a job usually includes filling out a job application form and being interviewed. Both should represent your best work.
- Professionalism shows in your commitment to a job and in your ethical behavior. It is highly valued.

Chapter Review

1. What is the difference between intelligence and aptitude tests?
2. How can career counselors help you choose a career?
3. How can attending college help people who aren't sure about what kind of job they want?
4. Explain the importance of flexibility to your future work life.
5. Identify three types of family living counselors and explain how each one helps families.
6. What is the difference between a state employment agency and a private one?
7. Give four suggestions for filling out a job application form.
8. When interviewing for a job, how should you respond to questions about your strengths and weaknesses?
9. What qualities show a sense of professionalism?

Critical Thinking

1. How can you decide if your present interests are ones you would like to base a career on?
2. What might be the advantages of working for a few years after high school before pursuing further education? What are the possible disadvantages?
3. What is your definition of a satisfying career? What are important factors in deciding on a career?
4. Give examples of specific actions that show a sense of professionalism.
5. Name five common first jobs for teens. What valuable experiences do first jobs offer?

Chapter 29 Review

Activities

1. **Interests and abilities.** On a sheet of paper, make a list of ten personal interests and abilities that you have. Then list five jobs or careers that would allow you to combine two or more of your interests and abilities. (*Self–management, organizing information*)

2. **Job applications.** Bring job applications from at least two different places of employment to class and fill them out. Use the suggestions given in the chapter. (*Self–management, organizing information*)

3. **Interview skills.** Working in pairs, conduct mock interviews before the class. (You may use the application forms you filled out above.) Have the rest of the class evaluate the strengths and weaknesses of each job–seeker's responses. (*Teamwork, interviewing, evaluating*)

4. **Researching a job.** Choose a job or career in which you might be interested. Research the training or education needed for it. (*Self–management, acquiring and evaluating information*)

5. **Career goals.** Write a short essay on your career goals. (*Self–management, writing*)

Forming Your Own Family

534

"Until I met Herschel, I'd never had any serious thoughts about marriage, but now I do, and we both talk about it. Herschel's parents have been married for nineteen years. He says they're just as happy as when they started out. He wants to have a marriage like theirs, so he says he's going to be careful about choosing someone to marry. My parents have been divorced for several years. That makes me want to be careful, too. It's funny how we both have the same concerns, but for different reasons. Herschel and I have a lot to find out about each other, and we're not in a hurry."

LEESA

Selecting A Partner

SECTION 1

UNDERSTANDING ATTRACTION

SECTION 2

POSITIONING FOR SUCCESS

IMAGINE THAT ...

you have the opportunity to design the right mate for you. The person will be made to order according to your specifications. There's a catch, however. You may only choose ten qualities that you want. You begin to think about the people you know and have known, mentally listing the characteristics that you liked best. At first you think about what the person will look like, but then you move on to other more important qualities. The list grows long. As you begin to narrow the possibilities down, you realize that this isn't going to be as easy as you thought it would be.

UNDERSTANDING ATTRACTION

THINK AHEAD

About These Terms
homogamy
complementary needs
propinquity

About These Objectives
After studying this section, you should be able to:
- Describe theories of mate attraction.
- Explain the value of knowing what traits you find attractive and desire in a spouse.

People have always been interested in why partners select each other. Why are some couples drawn together and others not? In theory, you have freedom of choice in selecting a partner. In reality, your choices are limited by where you live, the people you know, and other influences that may not be apparent.

♦ ♦ ♦

537

THEORIES OF ATTRACTION

Several different theories explain how people select their mates. People who develop theories of mate selection try to understand just what it is that causes a friendly relationship to develop into a long-term commitment. None of the following theories explains all relationships. Each, however, gives some insight into what causes people to choose each other.

Homogamy Theory

Scientists who have studied dating and marriage partners have found over and over that such couples are similar to each other. This is called the theory of **homogamy** (huh-MAH-guh-mee), which means sameness. The theory says that people who choose each other are more alike than different from one another.

Some scientists have suggested that people desire three levels of homogamy in possible mates: in outer qualities; in goals and values; and in ideas about roles.

Outer Qualities

First, people are attracted to those with the same outer qualities as they have. Some of the traits that many couples share are race, age, religion, education, and family background. Of course, you may know couples who have striking differences. Still, most are similar in these and other traits.

Gimel's experience illustrates the impact of shared outer traits. Gimel lives in an extended family with strong family ties among the members. His parents are immigrants, who both work in a truck manufacturing factory. They speak little English. Gimel usually dates women who live in his neighborhood and whose families are like

his. Once, however, he spent the evening with a student whose father was a lawyer. Gimel found himself uncomfortable all evening as Mara talked about trips she'd taken to places Gimel had never even heard of. Also, she described how much trouble she was having getting along with her father's third wife. Although Gimel thought Mara was attractive, he never asked her out again. What differences in family background made it hard for him to relate to her?

That people tend to choose someone like themselves as partners makes sense. Similarities create comfort, rapport, and ease in beginning relationships.

Goals, Interests, and Values

Couples who share outer qualities will next look for homogamy in goals, interests, and values. When two people like the same things and believe in similar ideas and ideals, they are more apt to develop positive feelings for one another. Agreeing with another's values shows acceptance of the other as a person.

Homogamous goals and values are more common among people with similar outer traits. For example, two people raised in the same religious faith are more likely to

The theory of homogamy says that people who are similar will choose each other as partners. What similarities does this couple have?

hold the same values regarding the use of money or of leisure time. People who have received the same type of education may be more likely to share views about politics or economics.

Roles

As couples become more serious about each other, homogamy in ideas about roles becomes more important. The expectations people have about their responsibilities as future partners and parents affect their goals for and attitudes about marriage. The more similar these are, the more apt the relationship is to progress further.

Roles were a problem for Cody and Pamela. They had been seeing each other for quite a while and were starting to think seriously. They began to talk about what they wanted for the future. Pamela dreamed of having children, the sooner the better. She wanted to have several and thought it was important that she stay at home while they were young. Cody, on the other hand, thought that if he and his future wife both had careers, they could travel and enjoy the benefits of two incomes. If they had children, he hoped that would be later in their marriage. These differences led to the breakup of their relationship.

Complementary Needs Theory

The theory of **complementary needs** suggests that people select others who complement (complete) and meet their personality needs. Each partner's psychological strengths help balance the traits of the other. For instance, a person who is outgoing and lively may be attracted to someone who is calm and serene. A strong leader may choose a mate who is a follower.

On the surface, the theories of homogamy and complementary needs appear to

BALANCING WORK AND FAMILY

Beliefs About Balance

A relationship stands a better chance of lasting if a couple agrees on the issues concerned with balancing work and family life.

As you might imagine, and as the theory of homogamy states, people who hold similar views on these issues may have fewer disagreements. However, their similarity of views may result in a "doubling up" on some issues. What if both partners value time with family over career, for example? What if both want jobs that involve travel?

On the other hand, the theory of complementary needs suggests that a relationship may benefit from diversity. A partner who values home life might assume more of the family responsibilities than the person who puts greater importance on work, and vice versa. When a conflict arises, however, these opposing values could present problems.

When the time comes, you may need to determine which theory applies to you and your partner and then discuss the problems that you might have in the future.

contradict each other. Actually, they work together. At a basic level, people are drawn to those like themselves. After this first level of selection occurs, they seek people who can help them meet their psychological and emotional needs. Ideally, both types of attraction lead to the selection of a partner who affirms and reinforces a person's sense of self and basic philosophy about life.

Social Exchange Theory

Many researchers believe that selecting a mate is based on the social exchange theory. This means that people consider the qualities they want in a mate and what they have to offer in return. Desired qualities may be personal and material resources, appearance, behaviors, intelligence, and services. According to this theory, you will tend to choose someone who brings you the best "package" of practical and emotional rewards at the smallest cost to you. You select and develop those relationships in which you feel most rewarded. Since people, in general, tend to get together with others who offer qualities equal to what they have to offer, the exchange theory goes along with homogamy.

You may have seen this theory at work in the relationships of people you know. A successful businessman, who can provide a family with a comfortable living, may look for a wife who enjoys entertaining clients. A professional musician, who spends much time traveling and practicing, may choose for a husband a man who can manage her career and organize her schedule.

Propinquity Theory

Libby and Bryan met and became close in high school. After graduation, however, Bryan enrolled in a local community college, while Libby went to a university in another state. They found that long-distance phone calls and weekend visits were expensive, time-consuming, and not enough to keep their relationship going. Without regular close contact, they grew apart. Eventually they decided that continuing the relationship with so much distance between them was not worth the effort.

Libby and Bryan's relationship illustrates the propinquity theory. **Propinquity** (pro-PIN-kwit-ee) is nearness in time or place. This theory states that people are more apt to meet, get to know, and stay with others who are physically nearby. Propinquity theory is related to social exchange theory in that relationships with those who are nearby are less costly. Costs of a relationship lacking propinquity include time and money spent on phone calls and travel, and emotional costs such as loneliness. A more convenient relationship brings rewards without these types of expenses.

Ideal Mate Theory

Another theory about how people choose a partner is called the ideal mate theory. Most people have an image in their minds of an ideal mate, based on physical appearance, character, or various other traits. For some people, this image is very clear; they can see how the ideal mate would look and act. Others, however, have a more vague idea of some ideal traits a partner would have.

Closeness, or propinquity, can lead to partnership. Why is this true?

Arranging a Marriage in Southern India

FAMILIES

AROUND

THE

WORLD

In southern India, the theories of attraction do not apply exactly as they do in the United States. The culture is very different. Most marriages are arranged.

There are many complex steps in arranging a marriage. The process may take several months or even years. Often it involves a great number of people.

In rural areas, marriage arrangements may begin when a girl is about twelve to fourteen years old. Her parents invite the parents of eligible young men — who may be much older than the girl — to a feast. There they have a chance to meet the girl and judge her character.

After the feast, those parents who are interested in the girl as a wife for their son send representatives to her par-

ents. The agents and the girl's parents discuss terms of the marriage. At this time, the groom may visit the bride's house to discuss her education, her skills, and her family's wealth.

When the families believe that they have made the best possible match for their children, a date is chosen for the wedding.

During these arrangements, the girl may see her intended bridegroom only once or twice. She may not see him at all. She usually has little say in her parents' choice. She must trust them to find a husband who will treat her well and provide her with a good life.

People who have an ideal mate in mind measure their dating partners against this idea. They are more attracted to those who seem like their ideal mate.

Often the image of an ideal mate is based on parents. A person may idealize the parent of the opposite gender — or their exact opposite, depending on whether or not the parent is admired.

UNDERSTANDING THEORIES

Obviously, the theories of attraction do not neatly describe every situation. They do offer "food for thought," however.

Typically, people find themselves in serious relationships without ever having considered what traits or values are important to them. Knowing what attracts you to a potential mate and why helps you to see the "magic" of relationships more realistically. Also, thinking about the characteristics you seek in a life partner encourages you to consider what assets you can bring to a marriage.

People often choose partners who have qualities that are similar to a loved family member. A daughter, for example, might be drawn to someone who is like her father.

SECTION 1 REVIEW

1. What is homogamy?
2. Name the three levels of attraction according to the theory of homogamy.
3. According to social exchange theory, how do people select mates?
4. What is propinquity?
5. On what is the image of an ideal mate often based?

POSITIONING FOR SUCCESS

THINK AHEAD

About These Terms
readiness
institution of marriage

About These Objectives
After studying this section, you should be able to:
- Summarize the readiness factors associated with successful marriages.
- Evaluate attitudes toward marriage.
- Identify danger signals in a relationship.

heories of attraction can help explain why you are drawn to a certain person. After the initial attraction, however, you must still ask yourself if you are ready to take on the challenges of marriage. This is not a simple question to answer, and it can only be answered by you.

♦ ♦ ♦

READINESS FACTORS

No formula guarantees whether a marriage will be a happy one. Does that mean you should rush in to marriage without giving any thought to whether you are ready? Of course, it doesn't. You can put yourself much closer to success by thinking ahead. Certain qualities and conditions help show that a person is prepared, or positioned, for marriage. This is **readiness**. The more conditions and qualities that partners have or take time to acquire, the more apt they are to find themselves in a marriage that brings them satisfaction in life.

A couple's age when they marry can affect the success of their marriage. People in their middle to late twenties are more mature and ready to settle down.

Age

The older a couple is at the time of their wedding, the more likely the marriage is to be stable. This effect levels off at about age twenty-seven for men and twenty-five for women. A thirty-year-old woman, for example, is no more apt to be successful than a twenty-five-year-old one.

Older people are more apt to be emotionally mature, to have better jobs and income, and to have more social experiences. All of these contribute to better marriages.

Independence

People cannot be ready for marriage unless they are able to stand on their own. When examining your own level of independence in preparation for marriage, you might ask questions like: Do I make good decisions? Do I have the practical knowledge that I need to survive on my own? Am I able to make decisions without always turning to family for help? Do I feel comfortable with the idea of living apart from the family that raised me? Can I support

myself and a family? If the answers to these questions are "yes," chances are you are well on the way to independence.

Before you choose a partner, ask the same questions about him or her. If you are independent and your partner isn't, you may not like what happens after marriage. Too much reliance on you could be one result. Another possibility is too much dependence on family.

Although the link to parents and other family members will always be present — and should be — marriage means that a new family is forming. If you or a potential partner is not ready to transfer your first priority to a spouse, you are not ready for marriage.

Friendships

Friendships offer good clues as to what might happen to a person in marriage. The more friends of both genders a person has, the more apt he or she is to have a successful marriage. Why might this be true? The answer is a simple one. The same relationship skills that are used to build friendships are also needed to build strong marriage relationships. Those who are not able to build and maintain good relationships before or outside of marriage will likely have the same problem in marriage.

Oliver, for example, was first attracted to Chauncy because she was such a good listener. When he talked about his problems, she could see his situation and offer solutions. When he had good news, she shared in his happiness. He soon realized that this trait was also one reason that Chauncy had so many friends. If so many people like Chauncy, Oliver reasoned, there must be many reasons why. She began to look more and more attractive to him as a potential marriage partner.

Having siblings can also increase a person's chances of having a good marriage. Learning to get along with brothers and sisters provides valuable training for sharing life with a spouse.

Parental Approval

Parental disapproval is a warning sign that a relationship deserves a second look. Secretive meetings by couples only make matters worse.

Parents may disapprove of a potential partner for different reasons. They may see troublesome qualities in the person that their son or daughter does not see. They may think the timing is not right. In most cases, postponing the marriage is a good reaction to parental disapproval. Time allows situations to be resolved. It also gives you a chance to learn more.

Sometimes parents come to support their child's choice of partner and a decision to marry. By the same token, many

couples eventually see their parents' reasons for objecting, and they decide not to marry. When the issue is a partnership for life, taking a little extra time to make the decision is a small price to pay. Marrying against the wishes of parents, even when those wishes seem unfair or unreasonable, can cause couples great stress.

Knowledge of Each Other

In one study of 1000 marriages, researchers found that partners who had known each other at least five years before marriage were the happiest. Although many couples marry sooner, it is essential to success to take the time to know each other well before pledging a lifetime to your partner.

Couples who marry after a very short time together may not have had time to learn about each other and to talk out the important issues facing them. Likewise, couples who are separated from each other prior to marriage often have problems adjusting. You can be more sure that your relationship will last if you have more experiences in facing life's challenges together.

One way to learn more about each other is to go over prepared checklists that are designed for this purpose. They can be obtained from counselors, religious leaders, library books, and magazines. Going over such checklists together brings up important issues for discussion and decision making. Greater understanding and confidence in the relationship often results.

"There can be little liking where there is no likeness."

AESOP

A Sense of Responsibility

Along with marriage comes new roles and responsibilities. People who are unwilling or unable to take these on do not make

---

Getting to Know You

The better a couple knows one another, the greater their chances for enjoying a happy marriage. Partners need to consider questions like these as they begin to think seriously about each other:

- *What was your childhood like?* Studies have shown that people who had happy childhoods are most likely to make happy marriages as well.
- *What role does religion play in your life?* Couples who share religious beliefs have an obvious advantage of compatability. The strength of those convictions is also a factor. For example, two persons who were raised in different faiths but who do not feel strongly about religion will not feel the differences as much as people who are active in different faiths.
- *Will age make a difference?* Too great an age difference can present a problem in later life when one partner is considerably older than the other. Age may also affect each partner's attitude toward having children.
- *Can any race or ethnic differences be handled?* Marriages between people of different races or ethnic backgrounds are becoming more accepted. Any disapproval from family, friends, and society, however, can cause stress. Race and ethnic background can also be major factors in how a person is raised, and therefore can cause serious differences in attitudes, values, and expectations. As with any relationship, however, two people who are aware of the challenges and committed to the marriage can overcome these possible problems.

good marriage partners. Think about all the responsibilities that the adults in your family have. They provide a place to live and food to eat, as well as other basic needs. They take care of all family members, including each other.

When thinking about a marriage partner and your own readiness for marriage, you need to decide whether you are equipped to meet responsibilities. Financial readiness is very important. Low income often contributes to instability in a marriage. People should be able to earn enough money to meet their financial obligations before they decide to marry. If education is unfinished, that may need to come first.

Married couples have other important responsibilities to one another, too. On a practical level, they must be willing to help take care of routine household tasks, such as cooking and bill paying. On an emotional level, they must want to support each other.

A Belief in Marriage

To be ready for marriage, a person must have a deep desire to marry and build a life with a partner. A belief in the **institution of marriage**, or marriage as a way of living, is important. In other words, the thought that marriage itself is worth preserving in society is part of a person's value system.

People who believe in marriage are ready to settle down and do what is necessary to make the marriage work. Family life itself must be an important value. People who are mature are willing to put the needs of others before their own. They are willing to work and sacrifice to build a family life. Without these attitudes, readiness for marriage is not possible.

People who believe in marriage as a way of living are more likely to make an effort to stay together.

A Realistic Attitude

All of the qualities and conditions that you have read about help determine readiness. Having them is good positioning for a fulfilling marriage. Many people who have these qualities, however, may still have an unrealistic attitude about the future. They may expect too much from the relationship, from their partners, or from themselves. They may not realize that choosing the right partner is only the beginning of making a successful, long-term relationship.

The following points can help you develop a realistic attitude as you think about readiness for marriage and what a potential marriage partner should be like:

- *Love is not enough for a successful marriage.* You and your potential partner need to appreciate each other as friends and workmates, too. Love alone will not enable you to solve problems and tackle all the situations that life has to offer.
- *Love is different from and more than sexual attraction.* Some couples with a strong physical attraction to each other get so focused on their sensual relationship that they fail to talk about the things that are important to them. Sexual attraction tends to lessen with time. Then their differences and problems create conflicts that drive them apart.
- *Marriage is not a cure-all.* Some people want to marry for the wrong reasons. They may be anxious to get away from a destructive home environment, to seek

CRITICAL THINKING SKILL

Identifying Contradictions

A contradiction occurs when ideas or actions stand in opposition to each other. Contradictory statements, for example, send opposing messages.

Manual Mirror

CHUCK *"I've been dating Marcie for a year, ever since Homecoming in our junior year. I'm sure she's the one for me, although I'm not ready to make a real commitment. I love her, but she's so possessive. When I took Marcie's friend Tina out last week, Marcie wasn't very happy. We fought about it, but I told Marcie that she's the only one I really care about, so she shouldn't worry. My older sister Wanda puts in her two cents worth, too. Her advice is always good. She keeps reminding me about what happened to her. Right after high school she married her high school sweetheart and got divorced a year later. I know the same thing wouldn't happen to Marcie and me, so whatever Wanda's trying to tell me, she's wrong this time."*

MARCIE *"Chuck and I need each other. I know that. Everyone says we're too young to be so sure, but sometimes you just know. It didn't really bother me that he went out with Tina. He just had some things to figure out. He always comes back to me anyway. When we talk about getting married, he keeps bringing up what happened to his sister Wanda. Okay, so her relationship failed, but that has nothing to do with us. Wanda was too young to know what she really wanted anyway."*

CAN YOU IDENTIFY CONTRADICTIONS?

To identify contradictions, you must look for ideas in statements and/or actions that are the opposite in meaning.

- In what ways do Chuck and Marcie contradict themselves?
- Do they ever contradict each other? Explain your answer.
- What do you think the contradictions made by Chuck and Marcie indicate about them?
- Has anyone ever said something like this to you: "Now wait; just a minute ago you said . . . ." What might this have been a sign of?
- How can contradictions get in the way of good communication?

social status or financial security, to give in to family pressure to marry, to seek the stability of a permanent partner, or to have children. In most cases, these reasons will not lead to strong marriages. They are unlikely to promote the selection of a partner to whom you can make an honest and true commitment.

- *What you see is what you get.* Don't plan to change your partner after marriage. If a person cannot or will not change before marriage, why should he or she change afterward? It is better to find someone whose traits you already find appealing than to try to change a person's habits later on.

- *Don't expect a perfect partner.* You aren't going to be one, and you aren't going to get one.

Being in love can easily blind a couple to what is going on in their relationship. You might not see what you don't want to see. You might overlook the signs of readiness. The smart person realizes that this can happen and takes steps to prevent it.

DANGER SIGNALS

Charlotte and Foster had been dating for over a year. They seemed to get along well together, and most people thought they made a good match. Charlotte, however, knew that Foster had a habit of being very critical of her. She believed that as their relationship became a closer, more caring one, he would stop. Instead, it only grew worse over time. Every day he found something to complain about, some way of trying to make her feel incompetent or inferior. Finally Charlotte realized that this was Foster's problem. It had nothing to do with her. Although it was difficult, she broke off the relationship.

Like Charlotte, some people encounter danger signals as they move toward establishing a long-term relationship. These signals should warn partners that the relationship may not be a healthy or successful one.

Abuse

As you read earlier, abuse can be both physical and emotional. It comes from an inability to handle problems in a mature way and has no place in a loving relationship. Without outside help, abusive relationships rarely improve and usually worsen.

The occurrence of any type of abuse in a relationship is a danger signal. If abuse occurs, the partners should stop seeing each other. They should seek help in dealing with the situation and deciding how or if the relationship should continue.

Substance Abuse

The abuse of alcohol, drugs, or other substances is also a sign that a relationship will be a difficult one. Substance abusers often have emotional problems that make it hard for them to stay in involved, committed relationships. Also, because substance abuse decreases self-control, it makes the abuser more prone to acts of physical or emotional abuse.

Getting out of a relationship with a substance abuser can be difficult. The partner may feel that he or she is abandoning the other person just when the greatest need for support exists. Abusers must solve the problem themselves, however. A partner can be a supportive friend while making it clear that a long-term relationship can be considered only when the abuser has control over the problem.

Jealousy

Jealousy is another danger signal. It is a sign of insecurity in a relationship. The jealous partner is afraid of losing or being abandoned by the other. The person wants to narrow the world down to just the two of them. Jealous people try to eliminate the partner's friends and activities. When jealousy seeks control of the other, it can be a form of emotional abuse.

To some degree, these feelings are normal in a relationship's early stages. Partners are not yet sure of each other's feelings. In a mature, committed relationship, however, feelings of jealousy and uncertainty should rarely occur. Loving partners want to be with each other and share each others' lives, but they also

A jealous partner makes it difficult for the other to have friends. How do people show jealous feelings?

and can be hurtful. It can even lead to physical abuse. Discussion leads to compromise and the resolution of problems. An argument does not solve a problem. It becomes one.

Watching for Signals

Paying attention to danger signals can save couples from destructive, mismatched relationships. Acting on danger signals, however, can be difficult. Postponing the marriage may be necessary. Breaking off a relationship that is threatening is also a possibility. Either way, danger signals must be recognized and resolved before the wedding. They will not disappear later on.

THE RIGHT CHOICE

Choosing to marry — and whom to marry — are among the most important decisions you will ever make. Having realistic ideas about marriage and married life and a real understanding of your possible spouse gives you an advantage in making your marriage a happy one.

understand that they have the right to other friends and activities that may not always be shared. They accept and appreciate these differences.

Arguments

No relationship is without disagreements. If a couple spends much of their time together arguing, however, they should seriously reconsider their relationship. One or both partners may not have learned the qualities needed for a successful, mature relationship, such as communication and compromise. They may not be as compatible as they thought.

Argument is different from discussion. Discussion is honest, thoughtful, and sticks to the subject. Argument is poorly reasoned

SECTION 2 REVIEW

1. List seven factors that help make a person ready for marriage.
2. Why are people with many friends more likely to have happy marriages?
3. What can couples use to get to know each other better?
4. Why is financial readiness important in marriage?
5. Give five points that are part of a realistic attitude about marriage.
6. List four danger signals in a relationship.

Chapter 30 Review

Chapter Summary

- Most experts agree that homogamy is important to long-term relationships. People desire homogamy in both outer and inner traits.
- The theories of complementary needs and social exchange state that couples choose one another because each one fills certain needs for the other person.
- Other theories state that being physically nearby and resembling a person's ideal mate are important factors in choosing a mate.
- Certain factors affect the likelihood of a successful marriage. Mature, independent couples who are willing to accept responsibility are more apt to have happy marriages.
- A strong marriage also requires knowledge of one's partner, a desire to be married, and realistic attitudes.
- Danger signs in a relationship, such as abuse and jealousy, should warn couples that the relationship needs help and perhaps should be ended.

Chapter Review

1. Name the three levels of homogamy. Explain how each level is related to the preceding one.
2. How do the theories of homogamy and complementary needs work together?
3. How are the theories of social exchange and propinquity related?
4. Why is it valuable to understand and think about what attracts you to a potential partner?
5. How is age a factor in readiness for marriage?
6. List three questions that could be asked in order to help determine if a person is independent enough for marriage.
7. How can friendships show readiness for marriage?
8. For what reasons might a parent disapprove of a potential marriage partner and the marriage itself?
9. What did one study show about how long people should know each other before marriage?
10. What do people believe when they believe in the institution of marriage?
11. Can a marriage survive on love alone? Explain your answer.
12. Why can it be difficult to end a relationship with a substance abuser? On what terms might the relationship continue?

Critical Thinking

1. You may know of relationships in which "opposites attract." How do you explain successful relationships between people who seem to have little in common?
2. How have the changing roles of men and women affected people's attitudes about marriage roles?
3. Can a marriage succeed if only one partner is committed to it? Explain.
4. According to this chapter, independence from parents is important for a successful marriage, yet so is parental approval. How do you explain these seemingly contradictory statements?

Chapter 30 Review

Activities

1. **The first date.** Make a list of questions that are commonly asked on a first date. Explain why the information sought is important, according to different theories of attraction. (*Organizing information, communicating information*)

2. **Desirable traits.** Write down the five traits you find most desirable in a partner, numbered according to importance. Combine your list with others in the class, making separate piles for male and female students. On the blackboard, list the five most popular traits for each gender. Discuss their similarities and differences and the effects on relationships. (*Organizing information, comparing and contrasting*)

3. **Mobility and mate selection.** Society is very mobile. Write a short essay on how this trend toward movement and travel affects mate selection. Include reference to the theories of homogamy and propinquity. (*Interpreting and communicating information, writing*)

4. **Marriage through the ages.** Interview married people of both genders from different generations—your own, your parents', and your grandparents', if possible—about the traits they looked for in a spouse and their expectations of marriage. Compare and contrast these in a short report to the class. Identify any changes or trends you may have noticed. (*Interviewing, comparing and contrasting, interpreting information*)

STRENGTHENING VALUES

Aim For Good Judgment

Good judgment means making wise decisions. It is based on looking at a situation objectively and realistically. It means balancing immediate desires with long-term gains. Demitri showed good judgment when:

- He decided to postpone marriage until he is financially able to support himself.
- He asked his girlfriend Melinda questions about herself in order to see how similar they are in their goals, values, and ambitions.
- He made an effort to get to know and appreciate Melinda's family and friends.
- He signed up for a family living class at school.

How might Demitri have shown poor judgment in each of those situations? How does a person learn good judgment? Why is it sometimes difficult to know what is the best decision? Do you believe that you typically use good judgment? Give an example of your use of good judgment.

Choosing Marriage

SECTION 1

THE ENGAGEMENT

SECTION 2

THE WEDDING

IMAGINE THAT ...

you are about to be married. Today you are single. Tomorrow you will be half of a partnership. Today you have independence. Tomorrow you become linked to someone who will be a permanent part of your life. You are very busy with last-minute details, but your mind races with thoughts about the life-altering event that is about to take place. You feel a bit jittery as the questions keep coming: Will you miss your freedom? Have you spent enough time making sure that this is right? Do you want to spend the rest of your life with the person you have chosen? Is what you want now the same thing you will want in the future? At last a calm feeling takes over within you. You know exactly what you want to do.

THE
ENGAGEMENT

THINK AHEAD

About These Terms
engagement
premarital counseling

About These Objectives
After studying this section, you should
be able to:
* Describe the purposes of an engagement period.
* Explain why breaking an engagement may be necessary.

he first official
step on the way to saying "I do" is the
engagement. An **engagement** is a
promise or intention to marry. It says
that you and your partner are ready to
accept the commitment and responsibilities of marriage.

♦ ♦ ♦

Purposes of Engagements

The engagement is a time of planning for the wedding ceremony. Even more important, however, it is a time to prepare for marriage. Through various ways, it allows the couple to address the many issues that will affect the success of their marriage.

Learn About Each Other

The engagement period is a time of learning more about each other. As they spend time together, couples will begin to accept "the little things" about one another. Each must be comfortable with the other's spending patterns, cleanliness habits, food preferences, and hobbies. Couples who are well acquainted in this way before marriage may find fewer surprises and problems during marriage.

This discovery process allows a couple to identify and deal with differences. They can then decide if these differences will enhance their relationship or undermine it. What effect do you think these differences might have on a marriage:

- Tia loves Chinese food. Scott's favorite is Mexican.

- Glen would like to have two children once he and Martha are more financially and emotionally secure. Martha wants to start a family right away and have four or five children.
- Tanya and Barry have strong, opposing political views.
- Marcus and Tabitha are of different religions.

Only the couple themselves can decide whether the differences between them are serious enough to threaten the success of their marriage. This is easier when each partner is sure about his or her values and expectations for the relationship.

Generally, problems caused by differences are more easily solved before rather than after marriage. Working together to deal with the issues strengthens the relationship and sets a pattern for the future. In this sense, engagement is a testing ground for marriage. It allows couples to work together on the problem-solving techniques that they will use in married life.

Many couples believe that living together before marriage is the way to find out if they are truly compatible. This seems to make sense; however, recent studies have shown that couples who live together before marriage are less satisfied with their marriage than those who do not.

Creative people often find unique ways to begin an engagement.

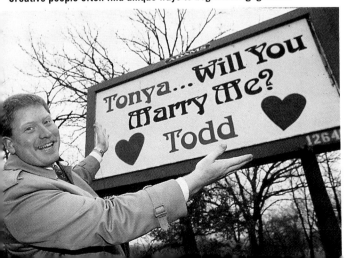

Develop Teamwork

Engagement is also an opportunity for the couple to develop teamwork. This means the couple starts to think as "we" rather than "I" when making plans and setting goals.

A couple need not be exactly alike to make a good team. In fact, a combination of the partners' different strengths and qualities can make an effective working partnership. You can see the same principle on a sports team, where the players'

The engagement period is one of excitement and anticipation. On the serious side it is also a time of careful checking to be sure that the relationship is a strong one.

different talents all contribute to the success of the group.

Trust is important to developing teamwork. Engaged couples must be able to discuss meaningful issues without the fear that seriousness will scare the other away. They confide in each other so that a deeper understanding can develop. They begin to rely on each other to hold up both ends of the partnership.

Good communication skills are also necessary. Couples need to talk about many areas: household management; parental roles; earning and managing their money; and the importance of religion, volunteer work and charity in their lives, for instance. They must clearly express their own views on these subjects and fully understand their partner's.

Finally, compromise is essential to teamwork. As the couple plans for the future, they must be thinking about what is best for *both* of them, as well as for any children they may have. Reaching agreement includes some giving in on each side. A willingness to do so enables a couple to make better decisions that keep both of them content.

Create New Relationships

During the engagement period, families and friends develop a new relationship with the couple. The prospective spouse is seen as a future family member and is often included in family activities to help family and friends adjust to the upcoming marriage.

A growing number of engagements today are between partners who have been married before and may have children. These situations are more challenging. They are often more complex because they involve more family members than first marriages. Children may be directly affected by the engagement and marriage. Ex-spouses and grandparents may have an interest because of concerns for the children. In these cases, the engagement time for a couple can be valuable for dealing with everyone's personal concerns.

When Eugene and Jolene told his son T.J. that they were getting married, T.J. didn't seem pleased. Although they saw evidence that he liked Jolene, T.J. just didn't want a stepmother. Eugene and Jolene used the time during their engagement to help T.J. become used to the idea that the three of them would be a family after the wedding.

Seek Advice

Some couples value the advice of trained professionals and seek counsel prior to their marriage. In fact, some religions require such **premarital counseling** before couples can be married in the faith.

Good premarital counseling helps couples focus on their reasons for marrying by addressing questions about their relationship. For example, they might be asked:

- How or why did you fall in love? Was it quick and unexplainable, or did it occur slowly, for reasons you both understand?
- What, right now, is your partner's most endearing trait? Is it a long-lasting quality? Will it still seem as appealing in the future?
- Do you "put your best foot forward" with your partner? Do you act in ways that show respect and consideration?
- Do you and your partner reveal your inner selves to each other? Are you accepting of and accepted by your partner?

Other questions focus on how well the couple has considered more practical issues of married life, such as:

- Where will you live? Will one of you move into the other's home? Will you rent an apartment or buy a house?
- Do you agree on financial matters, including a budget, your spending priorities, and who will be responsible for buying and bill paying?
- Do you want children? If so, when? How many? Who will be the primary caregiver?
- Will you both have careers outside the home? If so, will one be more important than the other? Whose?
- Do you get along with one another's families?

Counseling usually helps couples learn about potential trouble spots. If couples know what types of disagreements are apt to arise, they can better handle them. In many cases, this allows them to resolve these issues before marriage.

Some engaged couples take advantage of community resources to learn more about marriage and each other. Community

Sometimes during premarital counseling, couples go over checklists of questions that help them find out more about each other. What happens if they learn that important issues are a problem?

education, social service agencies, and religious organizations may offer classes or information on marriage issues.

The engagement period is an important time of transition and work, leading to the exchanging of vows and the joining of two lives into one future. This time can be crucial in helping couples build a relationship that will last, the backbone of an enduring marriage. Well spent, this period can contribute to the success of the marriage.

BROKEN ENGAGEMENTS

When couples become engaged, they usually see marriage as the only outcome. About one-third of all engagements, however, are broken before marriage. There are four major reasons for this.

Many couples find, as their engagement proceeds, that they don't love each other enough for marriage. The strength of their feelings for one another does not outweigh the necessary sacrifices and compromises.

Separation can also make it hard to maintain a relationship. Annessa and Lamar, for example, were engaged just

TAKING ACTION

magine that you do premarital counseling. List five areas of concern that you would find most important to "get out in the open" through discussion with the couple. Now rank these areas in order of importance. Compare your list with those of your classmates. You might try acting out some of the common issues.

Would you discourage the marriage if the couple disagreed on some of these issues? If so, how would you tell them?

Check out the issues you identified by inviting a premarital counselor to speak to your class.

Sometimes couples have too many problems meshing their personalities. Although they care for one another, their conflicting personality traits leave them unable to develop the give-and-take needed for a successful relationship.

A broken engagement is far better than marriage followed by divorce. Breaking an engagement, however, is a very painful experience. Both partners grieve for the loss of an important relationship. Returning gifts may feel awkward. So can giving explanations to family and friends. Nevertheless, the difficulties are less than what would be experienced if the marriage were a mistake. If the couple can treat each other with respect and dignity, breaking the ties between them is likely to be easier.

> "In matrimony, to hesitate is sometimes to be saved."
>
> — SAMUEL BUTLER

before Annessa enlisted in the Navy. She was away for six months. When she came home on her first leave, her experiences had changed her so much that she seemed like a stranger to Lamar. He, too, had made new friends and found new interests. With so little left in common, they broke the engagement.

Parental opposition often ends engagements. The conflict with parents may cause too much strain on the couple, or the couple may become convinced the parents are correct.

SECTION 1 REVIEW

1. List four functions of the engagement period.
2. List three things a couple can learn about each other during the engagement period.
3. Does a couple need to be exactly alike in order to make a good team? Explain your answer.
4. What is the purpose of premarital counseling?
5. List four reasons why engagements sometimes end.

A wedding can be as simple or elaborate as people wish, depending on customs, preferences, and finances. Often partners tailor the wedding to their own special needs and personalities.

THINK AHEAD

About These Terms
contract
prenuptial agreements

About These Objectives
After studying this section, you should be able to:
- Describe the types of contracts people make when they marry.
- Explain customs and requirements connected to weddings.
- Explain why weddings can be stressful and suggest ways to cope.

hen the engagement period ends and all goes well, the wedding follows. Few ceremonies in people's lives are treasured as much as this one.

♦ ♦ ♦

MAKING PLANS

Over the years, many cultures around the world have created and carried out ceremonies that mark the union of a man and woman in marriage. Weddings are as varied as the people who have them. If you have attended many wedding ceremonies, you know how different they can be. Something as simple as a gathering of the couple and a few friends may be right for some. Other weddings are huge, elaborate events involving hundreds of people.

Because weddings are important to people, much effort is likely to go into the planning. A bride and groom talk about what will be pleasing to them, often tailoring the ceremony and other festivities to their own wishes. The beliefs and customs of the family also dictate some of the decisions that are made. Cost can make a difference, too, as wedding plans are made.

Whatever plans are carried out, the result is still the same. Weddings mark the beginning of a new family. They are the formal expression of a commitment made by a woman and a man as they look forward to a life together.

CONTRACTS

When a couple marries, they enter into one or more contracts with each other. A **contract** is a binding agreement that is made between two people. The marriage itself is a contract overseen by the laws of the state and made official with a marriage license. Other contracts can be made by a couple on their own before marriage.

The Marriage License

The marriage license makes a marriage contract between two people legal. Once a license is obtained and signed, the couple is bound to the laws that cover marriage in their state. These laws differ from state to state.

The state controls who is allowed to marry by issuing licenses to those who meet its standards. These standards often include restrictions about persons of unsound mind, who have certain diseases, or who do not meet minimum ages. In some states, people with certain close blood ties, such as cousins, may not be issued a license. States often have laws regarding privileges and obligations in marriage and inheritance rights.

Also to satisfy the law, a marriage ceremony must be performed by an authorized person and must be witnessed. The license becomes valid when it is signed by the witnesses and the person who marries the couple.

Prenuptial Agreements

While a state's marital laws spell out certain requirements, procedures, and protections in marriage, many couples want to do more. Before the wedding, some couples make agreements regarding special concerns that they have. Marriage agreements that precede the wedding are called **prenuptial agreements** (pre-NUP-shull). Sometimes couples have lawyers draw up prenuptial contracts.

Prenuptial agreements typically deal with three major issues between the partners: protecting property from outsiders; establishing ownership in case of a marriage breakup; and defining the roles, duties and freedoms of each partner. Partners, of course, can write agreements on any topic they wish.

Protecting property from outsiders through a prenuptial agreement is a contract most often used in remarriages.

Property or money from a first marriage can be protected for children from that marriage. Caitlin used a prenuptial agreement in this way. As she explained it, "When I got remarried, I set aside the life insurance proceeds from my first husband for our two children. I'd been saving it for their educations. I wanted it very clear to the man I was going to marry that I considered the money my children's, not mine."

Sometimes prenuptial agreements provide preparation for a breakup. Such an agreement usually states, "If this relationship ends, this is how we will handle it." These types of agreements are ordinarily used only when the couple has many assets.

To many people, providing for the end of a relationship when it is just beginning seems "cold" and "unloving." They may see it as signaling a lack of commitment to the relationship. On the other hand, a practical agreement that provides protection can give a sense of security.

Finally, a prenuptial agreement can cover the duties, freedoms, and roles that partners foresee in marriage. The agreement may also say who will take time off from work to raise children, who will manage the money, how major decisions will be made, or how much freedom each partner will have. This type of agreement is less apt to be a legal contract.

For the majority of couples without unusual circumstances, the biggest advantage of developing a prenuptial agreement is discussing important issues and coming to some decisions. Writing an agreement makes clear the personal views and responsibilities of each partner.

CUSTOMS

In addition to its legal aspect, a wedding is also a couple's opportunity to express their commitment in a way that is uniquely their own. They may write their own wedding vows or choose a special place for the ceremony.

The couple may also express themselves through customs and rituals with widely accepted meanings. These have both symbolic and practical values.

The exchange of rings is a traditional symbol of marriage and sometimes engagement. Because it has no beginning and no end, the ring represents trust, unity, and timelessness. Gold is often used for wedding rings because of its great value, strength, and enduring quality. Sometimes, however, the man or woman chooses not to wear a ring for safety or personal reasons.

Traditionally, a party of celebration called a shower was given for the bride. Showers were usually all-female events. Today, organized by close friends or relatives, showers or engagement parties are often given for the couple with friends of both partners involved. The couple's friends and their parents' friends celebrate the engagement and upcoming wedding together. Typical gifts are items the couple will need to set up a household.

Writing a prenuptial agreement may seem a bit formal, but doing so can clarify expectations and also provide protection. If you were to write one with a future mate, what would you want to include?

Many older wedding customs are no longer followed. For example, it was once considered bad luck for the partners to see each other before the ceremony on the day of the wedding. Today, photographs — including those of the couple together — are frequently taken before the wedding so everyone is free to enjoy the entire reception. The giving of a dowry — the possessions and money a bride's family gave to the groom as a condition of the marriage — is another tradition that is no longer practiced in American society.

CEREMONIES

Wedding ceremonies have been performed since ancient times. They are usually a combination of legal requirement and personal preference.

Wedding ceremonies are either civil or religious. The choice is determined by the couple's preferences, religious beliefs, and family circumstances.

Civil ceremonies are performed by a judge, justice of the peace, or other appropriate official. They may take place in a home, on a beach, in a courthouse, or anywhere the couple chooses. This type of wedding is usually less formal than a religious ceremony. Often it is personalized to suit the couple.

Many people choose to be married in religious ceremonies, which often take place in a house of worship. A religious official performs the ceremony. Because strong families are the basis of most faiths, marriage is an important religious ceremony. Religious readings, music, and vows all reflect the couple's beliefs. These ceremonies are usually less flexible than civil ceremonies; however, partners may be allowed to write their own vows and include poems and songs that they find meaningful.

Weddings are often followed by some type of reception. Here the bride and groom are "received" and honored by family and friends. Like the ceremony, receptions can be kept simple or made very elaborate.

WEDDING STRESS

Weddings can be times of great stress as well as joy. Arranging activities and making decisions can be complicated and time consuming. Because it is the joining of two families, the wishes of many different people must be considered. The participants want everything to go smoothly. In fact, they often feel the event must be picture perfect. All this can create stress.

Financial Stress

Financial stresses are common, as weddings are usually very expensive. At any income level, a wedding can strain the budget. Traditionally, the bride's family paid for the costs of the wedding ceremony and reception, and the groom's family paid for the rehearsal dinner. Today, the groom's family may contribute more to the cost of the wedding. With couples being older when they marry, many pay part or all of their own wedding expenses.

The costs of a wedding when parents are divorced may be divided in nontraditional ways. Again, communication to prevent misunderstandings is extremely important. Usually, a parent who is not paying toward wedding costs is not involved in the planning. The parent can still be included as a guest, of course.

Reaching Agreement

Conflicting wishes and ideas about the ceremony can also cause stress. Sometimes planning a ceremony that is satisfac-

One-Sided Wedding

Americans are used to weddings at which bride and groom both enjoy the celebration. In Arab countries, however, the bride does not attend the festivities.

A young man's bride is usually chosen by the women in his family — grandmother, mother, aunts, and sisters. He does not see her. The young woman often does not know she is to be married until her family brings her out to meet these strangers. The groom's family chooses his wife based on her beauty and character.

At the wedding ceremony, the groom, his father and the bride's father meet to confirm the contract. The groom's family pays half of the agreed bride price; the other half will be paid to the bride's family in the event of a divorce. The bride's family agrees to pay as much, and often more, than the groom's family. This money is the bride's. She keeps it even if the marriage is terminated.

For the wedding the bride is dressed in red with a black veil. Her hands and feet are painted with elaborate patterns in henna, a red dye. She wears much jewelry. The jewelry may be hers, or it may be borrowed for the occasion from relatives.

The wedding is a time of feasting — for male relatives. For three days, they celebrate the nuptials. The bride and her female relatives remain secluded. On the third day, the bride is finally escorted to her husband.

The day after the wedding night the bride is unveiled in front of the groom's female relatives. (Young Arab girls are veiled from the time they are ten or eleven.) She then goes with the family to her husband's home.

tory to parents as well as the couple, given the financial situation, can be a problem. Couples and parents should remember that a wedding is meant to be an expression of the couple's tastes, attitudes, and values. Couples may have to be assertive about making decisions and planning the ceremony. Still, they must also consider the wishes of parents and other family members, especially when others are paying for some or all of the wedding.

Stress can also arise from complications involving divorced or deceased parents. Good communication is essential in creating a smooth wedding. Engagement announcements and wedding invitations must be carefully worded. Photographs and seating arrangements must be carefully planned. The advice of experienced wedding planners and photographers may be needed to avoid offending family members. Planning ahead can avert problems.

SINCE planning a wedding involves many responsibilities,

HOW does technology make the event easier?

Today even traditional weddings are affected by everyday technology. A bride may register a list of desired gifts at stores on computer. Invitations to guests can be sent by overnight mail. Information and instructions to wedding planners and participants could be transferred by fax or cellular phones.

Technology makes even traditional customs more modern and efficient.

JOINING THE TEAM

• Can you think of other ways technology might play a role in handling these aspects of a wedding: record keeping, photographs, music, and honeymoon?
• Do you think using technology would add to the expense of a wedding? What less expensive alternatives are available for the methods identified above?

On the other hand, family members should put differences aside at times like this. Sometimes solutions don't suit everyone. A cooperative spirit helps make the occasion the happy one that it should be.

When relatives don't cooperate, the couple cannot let the problems of others become their own. The best approach is to make decisions thoughtfully and then stand by them. Explain your plans calmly and let others react as they will. Don't worry about trying to please everyone.

Couples can reduce stress with realistic plans and expectations. They can keep a wedding within the budget. They can understand that, no matter how carefully they rehearse, something may go wrong. Most important, they can keep a sense of humor. No bride wants to trip while walking down the aisle and no groom wants to pass out at the altar, but often the unexpected things that happen are sources of amusement and story-telling for a lifetime.

Most people look back on their wedding day as a high point of their lives. If they have selected the right partner and used the time during their engagement wisely, their wedding day can be the beginning of a long and happy married life together.

SECTION 2 REVIEW

1. What makes a marriage contract legal?
2. List three reasons for writing prenuptial agreements.
3. What does a wedding ring symbolize?
4. What are the differences between civil and religious wedding ceremonies?
5. What are some of the common stresses of a wedding?

Chapter 31 Review

Chapter Summary

- The engagement period can be a very useful time for a couple.
- Working out problems before marriage is a good idea.
- When couples learn to work as a team, they think in terms of "we" rather than "I."
- The family and friends should be included in a couple's efforts to prepare for marriage.
- Many couples seek counseling before marriage as further insurance that they are making the right decision.
- If necessary, wedding plans can be called off during the engagement period.
- Weddings are important ceremonies in many societies of the world.
- Upon marriage couples become bound by the marriage laws in their state. On their own they may also make agreements that cover other issues.
- Wedding customs have changed over the years.
- Couples have choices to make when planning a wedding ceremony.
- The stress associated with weddings can be handled if people plan carefully and cooperate.

Chapter Review

1. What are the two main purposes of an engagement period?
2. In what way is the engagement period a testing ground for marriage?
3. How does compromise help a couple develop as a team?
4. What makes relationships with families more complicated today than in the past?
5. Explain how premarital counseling can help a couple.
6. What can breaking an engagement prevent?
7. What is a contract?
8. When a marriage license is signed, how is a couple protected?
9. What is a prenuptial agreement?
10. How has the custom of having showers changed over the years?
11. Who can perform a civil ceremony?
12. Who pays for the cost of a wedding?
13. How can trying to please everyone cause stress when planning a wedding?

Critical Thinking

1. How long do you think the engagement period should be? Why? (Note that some experts recommend 6-12 months.)
2. Do you think people treat each other differently before marriage than they do afterwards? How might a person guard against surprises?
3. Which do you think is better, a simple wedding or an elaborate one? Explain.
4. What customs would you follow if you were planning a wedding?
5. How can assertiveness, confidence, and high self-esteem help a bride and groom who are planning a wedding?
6. Describe any unusual wedding ceremonies that you have seen or heard about (under water; on horseback; in a cave). Why do you think people choose such ceremonies?

Activities

1. **Wedding costs.** Research the costs of weddings. Make a list of possible costs, such as cake, organist, flowers, photographer, location, reception, clothes, invitations, rings, and refreshments (catering). Plan a wedding that includes a certain number of people and estimate the total cost. (*Acquiring and evaluating information, mathematics*)

2. **A thank you note.** Assume that you have just been married and must send thank you notes for gifts. Write a note thanking someone for a particular gift. Share these with the class, looking for examples of those that might be well received. (*Creative thinking, writing, evaluating*)

STRENGTHENING VALUES

Aim For Commitment

Commitment means dedication and obligation. It means giving something high priority and following through as expected and planned. Helen shows commitment:

- To getting good grades, by planning some time for study each night.
- To her friends, when she agrees to plans they make and then follows through.
- To helping the environment, by recycling.
- To a strong family, by treating the people in her family the way she wants them to treat her.
- To her future family, by deciding that when she marries, she will choose a partner carefully and then work hard to make the marriage a success.

Some people fear making commitments. They may not have the confidence in themselves that they can carry out what they commit to. How do you handle commitments? Describe a commitment that you have seen through. How could learning to handle small commitments help you handle larger ones?

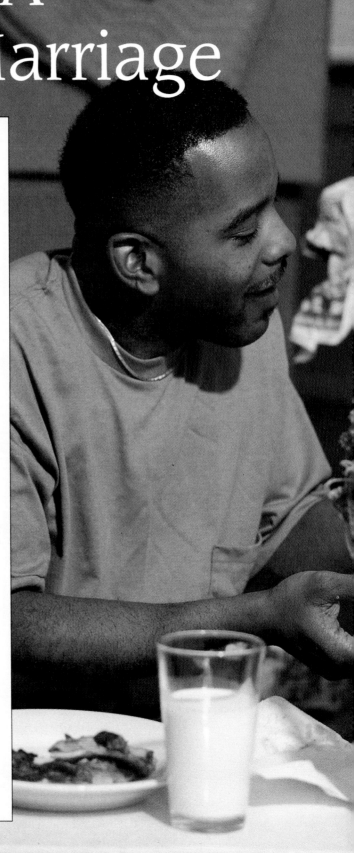

Building A Strong Marriage

IMAGINE THAT ...

you have been married for several years. The "honeymoon" was over long ago. In fact, sometimes you fondly remember what those early months were like. Although you had adjustments to make, the newness of it all was exciting. Now, two children later, life has settled into a routine. Nothing is bad, but you sense that something is missing. With jobs, children, and busy schedules, the closeness you and you spouse once had has dwindled. You want to feel some of the old feelings, but, just as you did last week, you push this thought aside in order to get on with the responsibilities at hand. You wonder if your spouse feels the same way, but by the time evening rolls around, you have forgotten to ask.

THINK AHEAD

About These Terms
marriage commitment
U-shaped curve

About These Objectives
After studying this section, you should be able to:
- Identify and explain attitudes and qualities of a strong marriage.
- Describe the marriage satisfaction cycle.

A good marriage relationship does not automatically follow the wedding ceremony. Instead, it is built through the efforts of the couple. Both partners must work and sacrifice to maintain a strong couple relationship over the years.

◆ ◆ ◆

567

TRAITS OF STRENGTH

In a strong marriage, both partners have a high level of personal satisfaction. What creates this satisfaction varies from couple to couple. Partners create and develop their own ways of interacting. There are, however, some common traits of strong, happy marriages.

Realistic Expectations

The single most important factor in whether you have a happy marriage is what you expect of it. Most people come to marriage with higher expectations than can be met. Each partner has ideas about how the other is supposed to be and act. There are expectations about *what* should be done as well as *how* it should be done. When a partner, for whatever reasons, doesn't behave as expected, the first strains in the relationship occur. With romance so difficult to sustain, many people are disappointed when marriage settles into what is seen as routine.

Erik and Bethany had some problems with expectations after they had been married for a while. Erik had always been a hard worker, but Bethany didn't think this would get in the way of their marriage. Erik spent many hours on the job. She thought that he would want to be with her rather than working so much. He thought she understood that he had a high-pressure job, and in order to get ahead, he had to put in his time. They never really talked about this issue until it became a serious one between them.

Like Erik and Bethany, many couples with unmet expectations fail to communicate their dissatisfaction. Resentment then builds. Each may think the other should automatically know what is expected without being told. Mind reading, however, is not possible.

Couples who know each other well are more apt to have realistic expectations about what married life will be like. They are, therefore, less apt to be disappointed. Their satisfaction with each other helps make their relationship stronger.

Matching expectations with reality is sometimes difficult for couples. A stronger marriage will result if you talk about roles and responsibilities. The understanding that results can lead to cooperation and compromise, both important qualities in any relationship.

Commitment

Couples differ in their levels of **marriage commitment**, the desire to make a marriage work. Partners who are truly committed to the relationship will want and expect it to last, despite any troubles that occur. They know that they will have to work together to solve the problems they face, and they want to. Sometimes a firm commitment can help prevent problems, as well.

A strong commitment to marriage means that partners put each other first. In general, the partner comes before children, work, or extended family members. This

If partners don't put each other first some of the time, they have a tendancy to grow apart. A sense of commitment to each other and the marriage is a strong force in holding people together.

type of commitment to each other is one thing that helps a marriage remain strong even when stress and crises occur.

Making the commitment a high priority isn't always easy, as you can see by what Lynette says. In her words, "Our son Mitchell has a learning disability, so I have to work with him every evening to help him keep up in school. Sometimes it's hard for me to remember that my first loyalty is to my husband. When Roy asks me to go for a walk with him, I try not to say, 'I can't. I have to help Mitchell.' I realize Roy's time, love and support are important to me. Not only does our time together keep our marriage strong, but it also keeps me better for Mitchell."

Marital satisfaction tends to be lower while children are raised. Love and appreciation of family still exist, but the couple may be too busy and pressured to enjoy each other as much.

The Marriage Satisfaction Cycle

Many newlywed couples believe that the excitement and intimacy of their engagement and wedding will last. Very few marriages maintain that level of happiness, leaving people disappointed.

Many family scientists have studied happiness and satisfaction in marriage. Looking at marriage over the life cycle, they identified a pattern called the U-shaped curve. A **U-shaped curve** describes something that starts at a high level, drops as time progresses, and then rises again, forming the letter "U."

The first years of marriage are usually happy ones. The couple starts at a high level of satisfaction. They establish their daily patterns of living — activities, decision-making procedures, and way of adjusting to each other's needs, habits, and personalities. Because many people "put their best foot forward" during dating and engagement, there may be some surprises during this time. In general, however, the newly formed union is a happy one.

Typically, when the couple has its first child, marital satisfaction begins to decline. As resources such as time and money become scarce, the parents usually participate in fewer activities together.

The stress of parenting, however, does not cause overall life satisfaction to drop. The satisfaction gained from parenthood and children may more than offset the decline in marriage satisfaction. Nevertheless, children generally decrease parents' happiness in the marriage relationship. The physical and emotional demands of parenthood can interfere with the closeness the couple previously enjoyed.

The overall low point of the U curve occurs when children are of school age. The two lowest points tend to be as children enter school and when they are teens.

Marital satisfaction begins to rise again when children start to leave home. Resources such as time, energy, and money become more plentiful. The middle-age couple's satisfaction with marriage rises until it is high or higher than the satisfaction felt by newly married couples.

Couples who understand the U-shaped curve of marriage satisfaction will be better able to cope when happiness declines. Those who are committed to their relationship will work to make the decline as small as possible. They will realize that the current struggles will pass and that better times are ahead again.

Acceptance

Acceptance is an important quality for dealing with any aspect of life. In marriage, this means accepting yourself and your partner for who you are. Both of you have strengths and weaknesses; both of you have attractive and unattractive personality traits. Focusing on the positive traits and lovingly accepting the less desirable parts leads to a stronger relationship.

Married couples sometimes make the mistake of trying to "redo" or improve their partners. As you read earlier, some even enter the marriage with this idea. This approach rarely works. People will change only if *they* want to, not because someone else tells them they should. Attempts to make them into something different often cause feelings of resentment or disappointment. They may be hurt that their partner no longer finds them "good enough."

Of course, advice and even criticism have their place in a marriage also. This is especially true when one person sees the other engaging in damaging or dangerous behavior. Loving partners, however, think of the other's feelings when expressing dissatisfaction.They first ask themselves whether the issue is important enough to risk offending their spouse. They practice tolerance, allowing for the differences in the relationship. They realize that tolerance is a two-way street, because both partners probably have qualities that can be overlooked. To some, these differences sometimes even become endearing traits.

Flexibility

Flexibility regarding change is another part of building a strong bond. Neither you, nor your partner, nor the marriage itself will stay the same. Changes in jobs, values, and ways of living can make it hard for a couple to stay together over the years. If you can accept change and learn to make the most of the opportunities it offers, you will have a better chance of maintaining a strong relationship.

Changing circumstances created challenges for Kyle and Della. When Della's company asked her to transfer to a new position in a different city, Kyle was very unhappy. He felt secure in his home, job, and lifestyle. He worried about how a move would change their lives. Eventually, though, he began to see it as a chance to make a fresh start. His acceptance of the change and his support for Della strengthened their relationship. A different reaction could have seriously damaged it.

Thoughtfulness

Another quality that helps build and maintain a strong marriage is thoughtfulness toward you partner. During dating and engagement, a couple usually works hard to please each other. They buy small gifts or do unexpected favors. Often these gestures cease sometime after the couple marries, yet they may still be needed to show a caring attitude.

Thoughtfulness, of course, is more than just buying things for each other. It involves showing empathy and caring when your partner has a problem. It means taking the extra effort to support your partner. Think of how thoughtfulness is shown in these examples:

• Brenda calls Philip when she finds she won't be home until later than she expected.

Thoughtfulness can be shown in many ways between partners. Sometimes something little, such as a call to let the other person know about a change in plans, means a lot.

- Colin slips a note of support and encouragement into Anne Marie's coat pocket on her first day at a new job.
- While Felice studies for a final exam, Alejandro occupies their young son by coloring pictures with him.

"*It takes two to make a marriage a success and only one to make it a failure.*"

HERBERT SAMUEL

THE COMBINATION

All the qualities you have just read about show strength in a marriage. Each is necessary. Each requires effort to cultivate. A couple that is willing to develop these qualities can look forward to a happy married life and someday look back on their time together with satisfaction.

SECTION 1 REVIEW

1. How can unrealistic expectations cause problems in a marriage?
2. What is a marriage commitment?
3. Describe the U-shaped curve of the marriage satisfaction cycle.
4. Should married couples try to improve their spouses? Explain your answer.
5. How can flexibility be helpful in a marriage?
6. How can thoughtfulness be demonstrated to a mate?

SECTION 2

SKILLS AND RESOURCES

THINK AHEAD

About These Terms
mutual   estranged
intimacy

About These Objectives
After studying this section, you should be able to:
- Summarize the relationship skills that contribute to a strong marriage.
- Recommend resources for married couples who need help with problems.

ualities for success in marriage do not come about automatically. They are built with the help of skills and resources.

◆ ◆ ◆

SKILLS

In Units Two and Three of this text you learned about skills for strengthening relationships. Communication, resolving conflicts, managing resources, and making decisions all help you build good relationships with others. These skills are the basis of a strong marriage, as well. Marriage, at its best, is a lifelong relationship that uses all these skills.

Communicating

Communication is the most important relationship skill needed in marriage. Couples need to communicate to exchange information, coordinate schedules, and make life run smoothly. Good communication in marriage, however, is much more than this. Couples must feel free to express goals, values, and expectations, and feel comfortable listening when a partner does the same. They must be able to share successes, failures, and concerns, without fear of judgment or ridicule. This kind of communication allows partners to praise and affirm one another and build each other up.

Ideally, communication in marriage occurs in an atmosphere of complete trust. Partners know that private discussions will be kept private, and that information will not be used to hurt one another or someone else. To do so would be a betrayal — a violation of trust — and damaging to the relationship.

Good communication is constantly challenged in marriage — by the needs of children, the demands of work, the necessity of household chores. Communication skills can easily be forgotten and lost. Couples may need to set aside specific times to talk to each other, such as in the morning or evening when children, neighbors, and television are not distractions. Doing so shows their commitment to keeping their marriage strong.

When one partner tunes the other out, good communication cannot take place. In a strong marriage, couples make sure they find time regularly to give each other undivided attention. Why would recognizing when a partner especially needs this be very helpful?

Resolving Conflicts

Good communication skills are perhaps never as useful as when used to resolve conflicts. Conflicts occur in every relationship. Being able to resolve them in a positive way is a key to building a strong marriage.

Couples have different ways of dealing with conflict. Some people believe that truly happy couples never have disagreements. They see any conflict as a sign of trouble in the marriage. As a result, they avoid disagreement of any kind. What are the possible consequences of this attitude?

At the opposite end are couples who seem to argue constantly. They turn every disagreement into a conflict. As you learned in Chapter 30, excessive arguing can be a sign of trouble in a relationship. It can signal basic incompatability. It can be a symptom of deeper, more serious dissatisfaction. Part of conflict resolution is deciding which differences must be resolved and which can be tolerated.

A healthy relationship avoids both extremes. Couples deal with problems as they occur, whether they involve money, child-rearing, or division of household chores. They try to be sensitive to each other's needs and expectations. They use reason, compromise, and the other conflict resolution skills to come to a decision they both can live with.

When partners in a happy marriage resolve conflicts, they balance giving and taking in the relationship so that each partner gets needs met. Marriages where one partner does most of the receiving and the other does most of the giving are seldom satisfying. On the other hand, couples who "keep score" and only give as much as they perceive they are receiving are probably not satisfied with their marriages either.

Conflicts About Work

A demanding job can be a source of conflict for many couples. If one partner frequently has to put in extra hours or bring work home, the other may feel resentful at being neglected. If both partners are overworked, the marriage may not get the attention it needs.

Couples need to talk about situations like this. They need to decide if the extra hours are really necessary and, if they are, how they can still find time for each other. They need to agree on compromises that will make their home life easier. Perhaps the partner who has less work can take on more of the responsibilities around the home for a while.

The important thing is that the partners communicate, understand the situation, and agree on ways to handle it.

As with other conflicts, successful resolution depends on putting the relationship first.

Managing Resources

As with many marriages, lack of resources was a problem for David and Anya. They never seemed to have enough money to do or have what they wanted. Both Anya and David, however, were committed to managing the resources they did have. They used David's skill at carpentry to repair second-hand items they bought at garage sales. Anya used her organizational talents to clip and use coupons to save money on their food bill. They both took advantage of free community programs for entertainment. They not only saved money, but they also developed a sense of unity and togetherness in working for a common goal. Rather than let lack of resources cause stress between them, they forged closer bonds through shared sacrifice.

An Unequal Arrangement

FAMILIES AROUND THE WORLD

Switzerland is a small country with a large impact on the world. Its neutrality in times of war is legendary. It has three official languages (German, French, and Italian) and is tolerant toward people of many nationalities. It offers equality to those of different religions. Until recently, however, that same offer of equality did not extend to women.

For most of Switzerland's history, women have taken second place to men. Since 1907, by Swiss law, men have had all the authority in a marriage. Men were the only ones allowed to provide for their families. A woman who wanted to work had to get her husband's permission. If a woman wanted to open a bank account, she had to have her husband's signature authorizing her to do so.

A woman's sole role, according to the law, was to "stand alongside her husband with her advice and assistance and support him, as she is able, in his care for the partnership." Wives were, however, allowed to manage their households on their own.

In 1971, Swiss women finally got the right to vote in federal elections. (They had been trying to achieve that right since 1884. In some areas, Swiss women are still not allowed to vote in local elections.) It took another 14 years for Swiss women to change the marriage laws. In 1985, 61 percent of the women in Switzerland voted to repeal the laws that required wives to get their husband's permission for so many activities. Only 48 percent of the men were in favor of making such a change, however.

Spending Time Together

Money is not the only resource to manage in a marriage. Time is another. It's hard to build a strong relationship if you don't spend time with your spouse. Doing activities together, whether work or play, can build closeness and help express love.

As with communicating, couples face many barriers to spending time together. Many find ways of turning mutual responsibilities into pleasant, shared experiences.

Sam and Rebecca, for example, spent one Saturday cleaning out their garage. Rebecca found an old dress that reminded them of many happy times. Sam's unused tools got them talking about the playhouse they had once built and decorated for their children. The couple turned a household job into an opportunity for sharing and closeness.

Managing Family Finances

Disagreements over money are a leading cause of marital breakup today. Here are some ideas on managing this resource for a happy marriage:

- *Talk about money.* Before marriage, discuss spending habits and attitudes about money. After marriage, communicate about financial matters. Is one partner spending too much? Can you afford to "splurge" on something or to make a major purchase?
- *Make a budget and stick to it.* Determine how much money is available for family expenses, and how much — if any — will be kept for individual use. Make sure both partners feel they are contributing equally. Don't forget the importance of unpaid work.
- *Establish priorities.* Distinguish between needs and wants. Compromise about what is essential and what is a luxury. Decide on long-term financial goals as well.
- *Assign financial responsibility to the partner who handles it better.* This could mean that one person makes all the financial decisions. It could mean division of money management responsibilities. For example, one partner might set the budget amounts, while the other decides on individual purchases.
- *Always save something.* Even a small amount set aside regularly is useful. More important, it gives a feeling of shared sacrifice and commitment that strengthens a marriage.

Of course, there must be room for individuality in marriage as well. As you learned earlier, the desire to spend all of one's time with a partner can be a sign of jealousy and insecurity. Happy, satisfied couples know they can spend some time apart without threatening their relationship. They can appreciate those talents that their partners develop and express while pursuing interests that are not shared.

Sharing Decisions

As partners in marriage, couples have many decisions to make together, such as where to live, how to manage resources, and issues concerning child-rearing. Sharing decisions together lets a couple know that they are working toward the same goal in their marriage. Discussing the advantages and disadvantages of several options helps couples see what is the best choice for them. **Mutual** (MYOO-choo-al) decisions, or decisions which both partners agree to, also increase the likelihood of follow-through by both husband and wife.

Couples may have different styles of decision making. Some may share most decisions equally. Others may divide decision-making responsibilities between the husband and wife. Sometimes the two styles are combined. Because Collette buys most of the family's clothes, for example, she decides how much to spend. When the family needed a new car, however, both Collette and Patrick decided on what model to buy.

As couples make decisions about what is best for themselves and their family, they must try to make the outcome as fair as possible. This does not mean that both partners will feel equally satisfied with every decision. Individual decisions are often more favorable to one person than to the other. On the balance, however, partners should feel that they are being treated fairly, that neither one is sacrificing or receiving more than the other.

Intimacy is an important part of a loving relationship. Both partners should initiate hugs, hand holding, and gentle touches at times so that the other feels loved.

Sharing Intimacy

Karl tells Melissa about problems that he wouldn't share with anyone else. Philip and Geraldine have a favorite song that they listen to together. Shannon and Ian go for long walks, holding hands and saying nothing.

All these couples are showing **intimacy** — closeness that develops from long friendship. Marriage partners need to express intimacy, but not just through sexual relations. Sexual activity may be one expression of intimacy, but intimacy is also expressed each day in many other ways that are also important. A conversation may be intimate when it is warm and loving and includes deep feelings. A look that says "I care" can be a moment of intimacy. A touch or hug can give the same message. Intimacy of this type is vital in a marriage. It builds a warmth that helps sustain the relationship.

Partners may have different levels of need for intimacy. If so, they should talk about their needs and find ways to meet them. Sometimes one partner needs to learn ways to express feelings. Another may need to step back at times and give the partner some space. Finding a level of intimacy that satisfies both can do much to preserve a marital relationship.

When intimacy is expressed in many small ways within a marriage, sexual intimacy can follow more easily. Partners feel an emotional closeness that prepares them for sexual expression. In a healthy marriage, sexual attraction can continue into old age.

Intimate expression in a marriage can break down for many reasons. When people stop making an effort to be close, problems can begin. One person may simply forget that the other needs to feel loved in obvious ways. Another person might let day-to-day life interfere with closeness. Still another may lose trust or a sense of commitment to the marriage. When emotional closeness breaks down in a marriage, couples begin to feel **estranged**, or alienated. Expressions of intimacy decrease. Sexual relations can also be strained.

As you can see, what couples think and feel affects how they act, and how they act affects what they think and feel. Emotional support leads to intimacy, yet intimacy provides emotional support. The wise couple knows this principle and makes it work for them, not against them.

RESOURCES

Marriage, like other areas of life, is challenged by predictable and unpredictable change. Even lack of change can challenge a marriage with boredom. Where does a couple turn for direction and support during these times?

Values

The most accessible source of direction in a marriage is a person's values. Values determine how you will handle what life gives you. As you know, they guide you in making decisions under difficult circumstances. Some values that help support a marriage are faithfulness, honesty, and respect for oneself and others. What others can you name?

Family

Families can help with a couple's marital problems in a variety of ways. Parents can offer advice based on their own years of experience. Siblings may be eager to help provide child care, on a regular or temporary basis. Extended family members may be willing to provide financial assistance. These acts of support and sharing can benefit both the couple and their families.

On the other hand, couples must not rely too much on their families. This can cause resentment on the part of family members and strain the ties between partners. Married people have accepted the responsibility of building a life for themselves, and this includes dealing with problems on their own.

When a couple marries, they must work out the relationships with members of their extended families, too. Why is a balance of closeness and independence best?

How complex and important is your network of friends and family? Considering your own situation, try outlining a social calendar for a year that includes your important holidays and celebrations and the people usually involved; regular sports events, such as a bowling league; employment expectations, such as a company party; and other predictable events or reunions.

In light of the complexity of your own valued associations, imagine adding all the people and events of your mate's situation, if married. With whom would you spend major holidays? Would a weekly meal with inlaws be an expectation?

Couples find answers to such difficult choices by talking things over and creative problem solving and showing love and respect for each other.

Friends

Friendships often become less important after marriage. This is because partners are wrapped up in each other as they are establishing their marriage relationship. They may believe that they can be everything to each other.

Spouses, however, are usually not able to meet all the emotional needs of the other. Friendships can take that pressure from the couple. Relationships with friends can be resources for a married couple by providing help, people to confide in, and others to share interests that may not be shared by the spouse. Most often, friendships after marriage are same-gender friendships or friendships between couples.

Marriage Enrichment

A variety of marriage enrichment programs are available to couples. Their purpose is not to "fix" broken marriages but to make average or good ones even better.

Many marriage enrichment programs are sponsored by religious groups. Others may be sponsored by mental health centers or colleges. Couples attend a series of sessions over several weeks or intensive full-day weekend sessions. Program content often includes communication skills, solving conflict, and building intimacy and closeness between the partners.

Marriage Counseling

Sometimes the relationship between marriage partners goes bad. The couple may have lost their close, loving feelings, or they may have conflict they are unable to resolve. Their commitment to the marriage is threatened because they don't know how to improve the relationship.

Identifying Relevant and Irrelevant Information

Relevant information is necessary; irrelevant information is not. When you are evaluating a situation, you need to decide which information falls into each category. Then you can make decisions and take action.

RIDLEY *"My wife and I were headed for divorce when we decided to see a marriage counselor. The counselor wanted us to talk about the problems we were having. I told her that Louisa has quite a few habits that bother me. For one thing she always cracks her gum. I've never liked it when people do that, ever since I was a kid. Another thing is Louisa won't admit that she has any bad habits, like spending too much money. At least I admit that I'm not good about calling home when I'm going to be late. She hates that, but I think I'm doing better. When we first started counseling, Louisa didn't admit to her drinking problem, but I talked about mine in the second session. She also didn't think our yelling sessions were worth talking about, but I do. She says all couples argue, and we're not any different."*

LOUISA *"Counseling is letting Ridley and I get things out in the open. Ridley says I care too much about what other people think, but I just want to look good. I like nice clothes, and I wish he could understand that. It's not like he's perfect. Anyone who squeezes the toothpaste tube in the middle can drive a person crazy. Besides that, he's always making plans at the last minute and expecting me to be ready for anything. We go round and round about this all the time. Ridley told the counselor that I have a drinking problem. Why does he just keep looking for one more thing to find wrong with me?"*

CAN YOU IDENTIFY RELEVANT AND IRRELEVANT INFORMATION?

To find information that is relevant, you need to identify the facts and choose those that have impact on the situation.

- What issues do you think the counselor would consider as more relevant than others in the comments that Louisa and Ridley make? Explain your reasoning.
- Have Louisa and Ridley focused on what is relevant and what is not? Explain.
- What happens when people focus too heavily on that which is irrelevant?
- In a court of law, information is often thrown out when an attorney claims it is irrelevant. Why do you think this is important courtroom procedure?

These couples often seek marriage counseling. Marriage counseling is most successful when both partners want to improve their relationship and are willing to work at it.

A marriage counselor helps couples learn to solve their own problems by serving as a fair, objective referee for the partners. Since most marriage problems involve the breakdown of communication, this is often the area counselors work on first. Couples may also need help in understanding and overcoming their anger and guilt toward each other.

Most state laws do not regulate who can be called a "marriage counselor." As a

Couples should not feel embarrassed about seeking the help of a counselor. An unbiased, third party, who is trained in marital problems, can make a difference in their lives.

result, some who call themselves marriage counselors are not competent. Couples may need to make some effort to find a skilled counselor.

Local health care agencies and family service agencies, such as family service bureaus and mental health groups, may be able to help locate a qualified counselor. Sometimes these groups provide counseling at a low cost.

Marriage counseling does not work for everyone. Sometimes counseling convinces a couple a divorce would be best. Couples who go through counseling, however, have the satisfaction of knowing they made an extra effort to save their marriage.

THE BUILDING PROCESS

Building a strong marriage is a challenging and continuing process. Compromise and negotiation will be necessary as a couple seeks to meet each others' wants and needs and to live together in harmony. Their commitment to each other, the relationship skills they possess, their ability to share their lives fully with each other, and the support they receive will work together to make their marriage a nurturing one.

SECTION 2 REVIEW

1. What is the most important relationship skill in a marriage? Why?
2. Is conflict handled the same way by all couples? Explain your answer.
3. Should time spent together to strengthen a relationship always involve an entertainment activity? Explain your answer.
4. Why is it important for married couples to make mutual decisions?
5. Why are intimate expressions like hugs and private conversations important in a marriage?
6. What are five resources that can give help and direction to a married couple?

Chapter 32 Review

Chapter Summary

- When people have unrealistic expectations about a spouse, they may face disappointments in the marriage.
- People who are committed to marriage are willing to work to make it last.
- The idea that you can change a partner after marriage is not a good one.
- Flexibility allows people to adapt to new situations in a marriage.
- As in any relationship, marriages survive better with good communication and thoughtfulness.
- Conflicts in marriage can be resolved when couples focus on the problems and use the appropriate skills.
- Married couples must manage resources, both money and time, in order to have a happy marriage.
- A system for managing decision making must be established in marriage.
- Expressions of intimacy are important to married couples.
- To improve a marriage or solve problems, couples can turn to several possible resources.

Chapter Review

1. How can a realistic attitude help a person in marriage?
2. How do people show that they are committed to marriage?
3. How could a knowledge of the marriage satisfaction cycle strengthen a marriage?
4. What can happen if a person tries to make a spouse change in certain ways?
5. What quality helps a married couple deal with change?
6. Can thoughtfulness be shown to a marriage partner in ways other than buying gifts? Explain.
7. List three things that can get in the way of a couple's communication.
8. Should a couple strive to have no arguments at all? Explain your answer.
9. Give four money management tips that a couple should follow.
10. In decision making what does fairness mean?
11. Can intimacy be expressed on different levels? Explain your answer.
12. When is marriage counseling most successful?

Critical Thinking

1. Some people say that "little things mean a lot." How does this relate to a successful marriage?
2. What are some ways a couple could counteract the routineness in their married life? Is there a positive side to routineness? Explain your answer.
3. What do you think makes some couples grow apart and others come together?
4. Without giving names, describe a marriage that you believe is successful. Explain your reasoning.
5. What do you think is the most important point made in the chapter about building a strong marriage?

Activities

1. **Marital problems.** Working with a group, plan and present a skit that shows the right way and the wrong way to handle a particular situation in a marriage. (*Teamwork, creative thinking, problem solving*)
2. **Communicating love.** Debate this statement: Since "actions speak louder than words," a marriage partner should not have to be told that he or she is loved. (*Reasoning, debating*)
3. **Showing thoughtfulness.** Working with a partner, make a list of ways that partners in a marriage can show thoughtfulness toward each other. Compare your list with those of others in the class. (*Teamwork, creative thinking, organizing information, comparing*)
4. **A successful marriage.** Write a few paragraphs describing what you would do to make your marriage successful if you decide to marry. (*Self–management, writing*)

STRENGTHENING VALUES

Aim For Support

When people give support, they are encouraging and concerned. They praise other people's accomplishments and help them overcome obstacles. They are there when they are needed. Janine and Malcolm are a married couple. They show support when:

- Malcolm listens to Janine after she has a difficult day at work, and she does the same.
- Malcolm encourages Janine to try for a new position at work, saying that he believes in her.
- Janine fixes dinner alone so that Malcolm can study for a test in a class he is taking.
- Malcolm calls Janine from work to make sure she is okay after her grandmother's death.

How do you think people feel when they are given support? Does giving support to someone ever mean taking risks? Explain. Do you like to give support as much as receive it? In what ways are both giving and receiving support a part of your life? Give some specific examples.

The Parenting Question

IMAGINE THAT ...

you are standing in one of several lines that weave back from a long counter. Several clerks are interviewing people at the head of each line. You are applying for parenting credentials. In your hand is the application you just filled out and the test you completed. The test was hard, but you knew it would be. You feel nervous about all the questions you had to answer. You hope that all the courses you have taken on children and parenting will convince the clerk that you now know enough to raise a child. After passing in-service training with a master parent, you believe that you are ready to take on the task yourself. Will the clerk grant you parenting credentials? In a few minutes, you will know.

ABOUT PARENTING

THINK AHEAD

About These Terms

parenting	*adoption*
genetic diseases	*closed adoption*
infertility	*open adoption*
fertility	

About These Objectives

After studying this section, you should be able to:

♦ Discuss the challenges and the rewards of parenthood.
♦ Describe pressures to have children and reasons for remaining childless.
♦ Define infertility and discuss its effects on a couple.
♦ Identify reasons for adoption and describe adoption procedures.

any jobs and responsibilities in society require training, skills, and knowledge. In order to operate a vehicle, for example, you must prove that you are capable. You can bring a baby into the world, however, without any preparation at all.

♦ ♦ ♦

CHOOSING PARENTHOOD

Few would say that people should pass tests and fill out applications in order to qualify for parenting, but many believe that something needs to be done to prepare them for the job. The solution is two-fold. One, people need to view parenting as a choice. Two, people need to seek, absorb, and use the parenting information that is available to them. These are the themes for the two parenting chapters in this text.

For many people parenthood just happens. They give little or no thought to whether having a child is the right thing to do. The high pregnancy rate among teens is evidence that many children are brought into this world without forethought. What some people forget to consider is that having a child has a high impact on your life.

People who make a conscious decision to have children are more likely to want them and be prepared to take care of them.

Parenthood can't be undone. Marriages are broken through divorce, people change jobs every day, and moving to a new home is common. Parenthood is permanent, however. Once you have a child, your life is different forever.

The impact on the child is equally important. When people are not prepared to love and care for a child properly, they make mistakes. Whatever goes wrong, the child pays a price that could last a lifetime.

By making parenthood a conscious decision, you do something special for yourself and your child. Everything will not always be perfect, but you and your child have a better chance in life. You say, "I want a child and I'm prepared to raise one. I know how to help my child become a happy, well-adjusted person in society." When you exercise choice, you give yourself power and control over your life.

In the past, married couples were expected to have children unless they were physically unable to do so. Today, however, modern methods of birth planning allow choices about if and when to have children. The fact that parenthood can be a choice places a heavy burden on people to think carefully. As in all decision making, the best choices are made when all the options and consequences are weighed. What values do you hold that would lead you to have children or to choose not to have them? What external pressures do you feel to have or not have children? What beliefs or circumstances might cause you to remain childless? Answers to questions like these can help you make decisions about parenting that are right for you.

CHALLENGES OF PARENTING

Before you can make choices about parenting, you need to have a full understanding of what it means to parent. **Parenting** is the process of caring for children and helping them grow and learn. Good parents use skills, plus lots of time, energy, patience, and understanding, to raise children who are healthy and well-adjusted.

Having children can be a challenge to even the most dedicated and loving parents. Parents must provide for *all* their children's needs. This means not only their physical needs of food, water, clothing, shelter, and safety but also their intellectual, emotional, social, and moral needs. You will read more about how parents handle these needs in the next chapter.

Providing for children's needs is a big responsibility, financially as well as personally. Raising a child is expensive. Babies and children grow rapidly, which means food and clothing expenses increase. Costs for medical care, child care, education, and recreational activities cannot be overlooked either. Having a child frequently means that a family needs more room, which can also add expense. Conservative estimates say that the cost of raising a child is two and one-half to three times the family's yearly income at the time the child is born. Of course, some families will spend less and some more.

The personal costs of having a child include the time and energy it takes to provide all the care that babies and children need. At times, parents feel they have no time or energy left for themselves or for each other. The financial costs may mean that parents have to lower their standard of living — going out less, buying fewer and less expensive clothes, and finding cheaper and less time-consuming forms of recreation. The drain on parents' time and the financial effects often make parents feel they have lost their freedom. One parent expressed this thought when she said: "I didn't realize how much having a baby was going to tie me down. Somehow, I just imagined I'd live like I did before, except I'd take Lila with me. I never dreamed how much trouble it is taking a tiny baby places.

Raising a child is a big responsibility that lasts for eighteen years. What are the costs to a parent, both financial and otherwise?

Besides, I had to quit work when I lost my baby-sitter and couldn't find another. That means I don't have the money to do a lot of the things I enjoy most anyway."

Men are less apt than women to see the disadvantages of having children, perhaps because the "costs" to women of having children are usually greater than to men. Since women tend to take on most child-rearing duties, they must expend more time and energy and often feel more tied down by having children. They may also have to make career sacrifices or modifications. They may, therefore, see more advantages in not having children than men do. Sharing parenting roles helps spread the personal costs of child-rearing more evenly between men and women.

FAMILIES

AROUND

THE

WORLD

Strong Mothers

Among the nomadic Tuareg people of the Sahara Desert, women are much respected. No man would risk the loss of honor that would occur if he were to beat or assault a woman.

Unlike women in other Muslim cultures, Tuareg women do not cover their faces with a veil and are not kept separate from the men. Tuareg women voice their opinions openly and take part in discussions. They take part in organizing special celebrations.

Tuareg women are very strong. They are the ones responsible for digging postholes for the family's tent, setting up the tent and taking it down, and loading and unpacking the camels and donkeys. Their hands are large from milking the goats and

from using a huge and heavy wooden pestle to grind the grain that is their staple food. Their heavy work goes on even while they are pregnant.

Tuareg women also participate in what, in other parts of the world, is considered a masculine sport — wrestling. Wrestling takes place on special occasions, such as the naming ceremony for a baby. It takes place between women, often between cross-cousins — the daughters of a brother and sister. Visitors who come to the

naming ceremony, however, may be caught up in the events, too. Soon all the women are wrestling. The wrestling is all good natured, with jokes and friendly insults exchanged.

Mothers have an especially honored place in Tuareg society. They hold knowledge about group customs and the use of herbs. Group members seek them out to ask for advice. Women believe that their skill as strong wrestlers shows that they are strong enough for their role as mothers.

REWARDS OF PARENTING

On the other hand, children bring many rewards. Parents say the main benefits of having children are shared love and affection and the feeling of being a family. Some couples feel a need to have children to make their family complete.

To many, parenthood brings a sense of fulfillment. A feeling of satisfaction and pride comes with providing for all the needs of children and watching them gradually grow and develop into healthy, happy, well-adjusted, responsible, and successful adults.

Another reward of parenthood is the stimulation children provide. Playing and learning with a child can be great fun for both parent and child. Seeing and rediscovering the world — from tiny, scurrying insects to huge, roaring oceans teeming with life forms — through a child's eyes can be both entertaining and enlightening. Parents may find a new appreciation of all the wonders of the world and of life itself.

PRESSURES TO HAVE CHILDREN

In many ways society promotes the idea of having children. Everything from tax deductions for children, to restaurants that allow children to eat free, supports society's expectation that people will have children.

In general, children grow up assuming they will become parents. Small children practice parenting when they "play house." Children hear others say, "When you have kids of your own …" Such comments give the impression that parenthood is automatic. For example, Belinda always knew she'd have children. When she was small, she pretended her dolls were babies and

One of the pleasures of parenting is seeing the world again through a child's eyes. The simple things that an adult might take for granted, like flowers, offer special delight to a child.

spent hours caring for them. Her family belonged to a church that had a strong emphasis on large families. Belinda was taught that motherhood is the basis of fulfillment for women.

When couples reach childbearing age, pressures to parent may be more personal. The couples' parents often look forward to grandchildren and make frequent comments — sometimes subtle, other times very direct — that they are anxious to be made grandparents.

Peer pressure can also be very strong to encourage a couple to begin a family. Friends with children might make such comments as: "When are you going to grow up and have kids of your own?" or "You two would make such good parents." Statements like these can make a couple feel strange and out of step with the rest of the world if they don't have children.

Some pressures to bear children are more obvious and convincing than others. Couples need to be aware of the many pressures that can push them toward parenthood. Of course, children should be valued in society, but valuing them means more than just having them. Children should be born because parents honestly want them and are willing to make a commitment to their upbringing. People are not fair to themselves or their children when they have children because "it's the thing to do" or because of outside pressures. Children are a source of joy and fulfillment for many people but not for all.

PRESSURES TO REMAIN CHILDLESS

Because of the widespread belief that people should have children, most pressures to remain childless come from within the couple themselves. About ten percent of people of childbearing age choose to have no children.

CRITICAL THINKING SKILL

Recognizing Propaganda

Propaganda is information and ideas spread deliberately to further one's cause or to damage an opposing cause. Propaganda often shows only one side of a situation or only a very narrow view of a situation.

By recognizing propaganda, you learn to weigh the information and ideas you receive and then make choices based on your personal knowledge and ideas or opinions.

MRS. MORENO (LUISA'S MOTHER)

"Luisa's been married for five years now, and she and her husband still don't have any children. Some of my friends keep asking when I'm going to become a grandmother. That's what I'd like to know, too. It's been a long time since we've had babies in the house. I've told Luisa and Julian that a family's not complete until there are children, but I don't think they listen. I tell them that I just want them to be happy, and that takes children."

LUISA *"I'm the oldest of six children in my family and the first one to marry. My mother and Julian's father keep talking about grandchildren. Julian's father says we must have a son to carry on the family name. He says that Julian must prove his manhood by having sons. Even our friends want us to start a family. They all have children, so they think we should, too. Julian and I have a good life together. We're not against having children, but I don't think we should have to keep explaining our feelings to people."*

CAN YOU RECOGNIZE PROPAGANDA?

- Is there any propaganda in the comments that Mrs. Moreno makes? If so, what is it?
- Is there any propaganda in what Julian's father has said to the couple? If so, explain.
- If Luisa and Julian take propaganda seriously, what might they do?
- Upon what should Luisa and Julian base their decision to have or not have children?
- Propaganda is often used in the political arena to sway the public on issues and candidates. How can a person guard against believing propaganda?

Some couples take a broad overview of the issue. They may be concerned with overpopulation in this country and around the world. Some believe the world has only a limited number of resources and too many people will deplete these. A few people worry about nuclear war and whether they want to bring a child into a world that has problems. Those who are worried about such worldwide issues tend to have few, if any, children.

Some people have other values more important to them than children. People who are ambitious and want successful careers may decide children would interfere with their career goals. Many people enjoy travel or other activities that are more difficult to do with children.

Some people just do not care for children. Martha is one of these. She grew up in a big family, so she had plenty of experience with children. Even though her mother says she'll be lonely in her old age if she doesn't have children, Martha sees it differently. She says, "That may be true, but I see no point in spending twenty years I won't enjoy raising a child just so I won't be lonely fifty years from now!"

Some people avoid having children because of diseases that run in the family. Such **genetic diseases** are passed from parent to child, although all children may not have the disease. Some inherited diseases are diabetes, hemophilia, sickle cell anemia, cystic fibrosis, and Tay-Sachs disease. Couples who have such diseases in their families can have genetic testing or counseling. This will help them learn their chances of having a child with the disease.

Germaine's brother died from sickle cell anemia. Now Germaine says, "Because I'm a carrier for sickle cell, I've decided not to have children. I can remember the pain and misery everyone in my family went through when my brother died. It's the one time I remember most clearly from my childhood. I'm not willing to take the chance of having my kids die like that." Germaine's choice might not be the same that others would make, but he felt it was right for him.

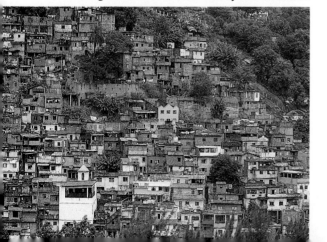

Some people have deep concerns about the condition and future of people in a heavily populated world. Thoughts about having children can be influenced by these concerns.

Only you can decide whether you want to parent. Your choice, however, has broad implications for your future and that of your children. Making the right choice for you is important in how happy and satisfying your life and the lives of any children you might have will be.

INABILITY TO HAVE CHILDREN

Sometimes couples find that the choice of whether or not to have children has already been made for them. They try to have a child, but they are unable to do so. **Infertility**, or the inability to have children, affects about one in five married couples. A couple is said to be infertile if they are not able to achieve a pregnancy after a year of intercourse without using birth control.

Since **fertility**, or the ability to have children, peaks in a person's twenties, the longer a couple puts off having a child, the greater the chance of infertility. Couples in their thirties and forties have the most problems with fertility.

About half the couples who have fertility problems can have children with medical help. Complete medical histories and a series of special tests can find out whether the problem is with the man or the woman. Once the source of the problem has been found, treatments can be started to try to overcome the problem.

Being treated for infertility means medical people ask about details of the most private part of a couple's life together. Treatment for infertility can take several years and cost thousands of dollars and still not yield successful results. Couples who go through the process must have a firm commitment to having a child and a willingness to accept what happens in the end.

CHOOSING ADOPTION

Adoption is the legal process of taking a child of other parents as one's own, thus binding the parents and child in every legal way. The adoptive parents are responsible for the child until the age of eighteen. After adoption, birth parents no longer have any of the rights or duties of parenthood.

The decision to adopt is made for many reasons. Couples with fertility problems may not have success with medical treatment or may not wish to wait the long time it can take for medical treatment to help. They may not believe that fertility treatment is right for them. Sometimes single people adopt children to fill their need to parent. People who fear passing on serious genetic diseases to their offspring may choose to adopt. Sometimes people who can safely have children of their own prefer to adopt because they are concerned with overpopulation or feel the need to help a child who might otherwise not have a home. Such couples often adopt children who are called "hard to place." These children may be older or have severe health problems or disabilities.

Many couples wish to adopt babies. They want to enjoy all the pleasures of raising a child from infancy. The number of infants available for adoption, however, cannot meet the demand. A couple waits an average of five years for a healthy infant or toddler, and the wait can run as long as ten years. Because of this, some people choose to take an older child, since the demand for older children is not so high and, thus, the wait is not nearly as long. Raising a child adopted at an older age can present special difficulties. Such a child may have emotional scars from losing birth parents or from lack of stable, loving care.

When Abe and LaJean first got four-year-old Craig, he was in poor shape. He was malnourished and had been physically abused. When anyone came close, he

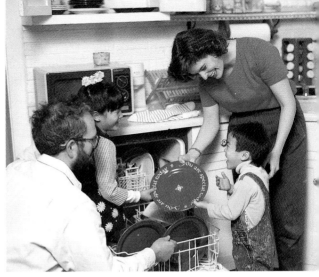

Families grow through adoption as well as birth. What special concerns do families with adopted children have?

kicked and screamed. It took a long time before he began to trust Abe and LaJean. The couple almost gave up dozens of times. Although Craig desperately needed their love, he couldn't accept it. It took four years before they all settled into what might be called "normal" family life. Craig did eventually blossom into a loving son, but there were many times when Abe and LaJean were sure the pain and problems would never be worth it.

Age and disabilities do not necessarily mean problems. Many families have happy experiences with children who are labeled "hard to place." A realistic viewpoint recognizes that the family may be challenged to meet the child's needs but that a loving, knowledgeable family can be successful.

Infants who are placed for adoption have been given up by the birth parents for any of a variety of reasons. Often the birth parents have realized that they cannot give the child the kind of home and upbringing that is needed. Giving up a child is not an easy decision. It can be a generous and loving one, however. Families, as well as social and religious agencies, offer help with such decisions.

Arranging Adoptions

About three-fourths of all adoptions are arranged through public agencies. These state-approved agencies are concerned with serving the child, the birth parents, and the adoptive parents. Birth parents are often given counseling to be sure they have considered all options before giving up the child. Social and medical information is collected to give to adoptive parents.

The agency is also concerned about whether the adoptive parents will be able to care for the child. There is often pre-adoption counseling. Once parents are approved, the agency tries to match the traits of the child to those of the parents. When a suitable child is found, it comes to the parents for a trial period. Permanent custody is awarded by the court if both the parents and agency are satisfied at the end of the trial period.

The issue of identity is a sensitive one in adoptions. In a **closed adoption**, identities are not revealed. The advantage is privacy for the birth parents. With an **open adoption** identities are known. Specific information may be contained in files. The birth mother may even meet the adoptive parents and remain in contact over time. Open adoption is more commonly chosen today than it used to be. It offers the advantage of allowing birth parents and child to know about each other instead of always wondering. Disadvantages include any confusion or problems that might occur when multiple parents are involved.

Adoptions can also be arranged through private placements. Such placements are often quicker than going through a public agency. These adoptions may be arranged by clergy, doctors, or lawyers. Couples adopting in this way often pay the medical, hospital, legal, and, in some cases, living expenses of the child's birth mother. It is illegal, however, to "buy" the child itself.

There are potential dangers in private adoption. Legal advice can help protect the rights of all involved. The rights of birth parents are not ended until the adoption decree is signed. The adopting parents should have the written consent of the birth parents obtained after the child is born. Without this consent, there are many pitfalls in the private adoption process.

Steve and Becky, for example, decided to adopt a child through their physician. He located a baby for them and everything seemed to be going smoothly. When the baby was five months old, Steve and Becky learned that the baby's birth father was seeking custody. Two days before the baby's first birthday, they had to give him up. They were heartbroken over their loss, but without the consent of both birth parents, they had no legal right to the child.

Adoption is an emotional process. It can bring joy to parents who are adopting a child. It can also bring heartache to birth parents who feel unable to keep and care for the child. In the end, adoption is simply another way of choosing parenthood and building families.

SECTION 1 REVIEW

1. List the five areas of need that parents must provide for children. Give an example of each.
2. Identify two financial costs and two personal costs of having children.
3. Briefly describe three rewards of parenthood.
4. Why do children generally grow up with the expectation that they will be parents?
5. What are three reasons people may choose to remain childless?
6. Define infertility. When is a couple said to be infertile? What are some of the disadvantages of being treated for infertility?
7. Compare adoption through public agencies and private placement.

PREPARING FOR PARENTHOOD

You can learn much about children by observing them. A happy, healthy child doesn't get that way automatically. It takes faithful, hard work by loving parents.

THINK AHEAD

About These Terms
parenting readiness
child development

About These Objectives
After studying this section, you should be able to:
◆ Identify factors that couples should examine to determine when they are ready for parenthood.
◆ Describe the effects on mother, father, and baby if a child is born before parents are ready.
◆ Explain how parents can learn about children and parenting in order to prepare for the demanding and rewarding role of parenthood.

nce people decide they want to become parents, whether through childbirth or adoption, they must decide *when* they will be ready to have a child. They must then prepare themselves as much as possible for their new role — parenthood.

◆ ◆ ◆

TIMING

Studies in life span development show that the timing of an event is just as important as the event itself. If a baby is unplanned, it can bring many, often unwanted, changes to the lives of both mother and father. Responsibilities increase and goals may have to be postponed or given up. An unplanned pregnancy often creates stress and crisis — for mother, father, and often, for the baby. A couple should plan to have a child only after they have examined their own **parenting readiness**, the degree of preparation they have for parenting. Are they ready for all the changes and responsibilities a child brings? Their decision should be based on factors like these:

• *Emotional Maturity.* As you read earlier in this chapter, having a child is a heavy responsibility and takes a major commitment of time and resources. Parents must make sure that they are emotionally mature enough to handle the responsibilities and stresses of having a child. This is especially important for teens to consider, since they are still developing emotionally. They may not be ready to take on the care of another person when they are still learning to be responsible for themselves. Emotional maturity brings the patience, self-control, flexibility, self-confidence, and sense of responsibility that are so important to good parenting.

• *Financial Readiness.* You read earlier in this chapter that raising children can cost a lot of money. Would-be parents need to look ahead to future expenses and income. Careful financial planning before children enter the family can help ease the financial burden and related stresses often felt by young families.

• *Goals and Expectations.* The timing of having children also affects goals parents have set for themselves and their lives. Since children can cause plans to change, deciding when to have them is the best insurance against having to alter important goals.

• *Age.* Age of the parents can affect all the factors above — and more — so it is very important to consider age when determining readiness for parenthood. With age, usually comes emotional maturity, or at least a greater degree of it; some people are never emotionally mature enough for the responsibilities of parenthood. With age also comes the experience and wisdom that can help parents better deal with any problems parenthood might bring them. The age factor also affects income level and career goals. Very young parents tend to have less education and training, which limits their job choices to low-paying, unskilled

One baby is lots of work, so imagine what it means to have two. The responsibilities are doubled.

jobs. Therefore, they may be plagued with constant financial problems and may not be able to achieve their career or lifestyle goals. In addition to all of this, with age also comes physical maturity. The physical maturity of the mother can affect both the mother and the baby. You will learn more about the effects of age as you read on.

Having a baby without planning ahead and considering all the factors that indicate readiness for parenthood can have serious lifelong effects on everyone — mother, father, and baby.

Effects on Mothers

Not considering the age and physical maturity of the mother when determining readiness for having children can have very serious consequences. Teens who are pregnant are twice as likely to die from a miscarriage or from excessive bleeding as older women. The risk of complications in pregnancy and delivery are greater for teen mothers. Women over thirty-five also face risks during pregnancy.

Having a child tends to end a young mother's current education. Those who have a baby while in high school or college are less apt to graduate than those who wait. Child care needs and financial pressures are the most common causes of mothers dropping out of school.

April, for example, had intended to stay in school after her baby was born, but she soon found that this was not possible. She needed more money than her part-time job could provide. Trying to keep up at school and work, while still taking care of her baby, was just too much. She finally decided to drop out of school to work and care for herself and her child.

Women who have children at young ages are apt to have low incomes. Lack of education is often the problem. If mothers

drop out of school, they don't have the training and experience needed to get good jobs.

As you read earlier, having a baby usually restricts the personal freedom of the mother. Her work and social life are limited because of the demands of the baby. Older mothers often cope with these demands more easily than younger ones. A mother who has had a chance to earn and spend her own money and who has done some of the things she wants to do is apt to accept restrictions more easily. Maxine, for example, waited until she was twenty-eight before she had her first baby. Having finished college and worked in a bank for six years, she was ready to have a baby. She and her husband had traveled and done interesting things. They were ready to settle down and put the responsibilities of children first.

The earlier a woman has a baby, the more apt she will be to have other children soon after. Both the babies' and mothers' health suffer in these cases. In addition, demands increase when people are supporting and caring for several children. Teen mothers have been found to have very high levels of stress compared to other teens.

Effects on Fathers

Fatherhood creates a legal obligation for a man to support a child until the child reaches age eighteen. When a man fathers a child too early, he may have to interrupt his education. Unplanned babies have caused many young men to drop out of school to earn a living. These men may be able to return to their educations later, but this usually means a double burden of work and study.

Men who marry and become fathers in their teens are more apt to have low-paying, unskilled jobs. These provide less job

A man who is prepared for fatherhood has the time, patience, and financial means to care for a child. Children need fathers as much as they need mothers.

security and chance for advancement. Money problems may then become a life-long concern.

Some young fathers do not marry the mothers of their babies. They must still contribute financial support. The father of a child has a legal duty to support his child — regardless of his age or whether or not he is married to the child's mother or lives with the child. Fathers as young as age fourteen have been sued for child support.

Men who father children while still in their teens find they may not fit into either the teen world or the adult world. Their responsibilities make them different from their more carefree peers. They are not yet fully adult, however, and do not have adult interests. They often feel alone and confused about their roles in life.

Effects on Babies

The age of parents makes a big difference to babies, too. Babies born to teen mothers face greater health hazards than those born to older mothers. A teen mother is not apt to be physically mature yet. Teens also tend to have poorer diets and get less prenatal care than older women. These factors affect the health of the baby. Babies of teen mothers are likely to be premature, with low birth weights. The younger a mother is, the more likely her baby is to die before its first birthday.

What happened to Verna happens to many teen mothers who face pregnancy alone and don't have the maturity to handle it. Her baby weighed only three pounds when it was born. She had eaten very little during her pregnancy because she tried to hide it from her friends and classmates. What she did eat was junk food, rather than well-balanced meals. When she finally saw the doctor for the first time after she was about six months into her pregnancy, he was very concerned about the health of the unborn child. Verna's poor health and malnutrition led to early childbirth and a small, sickly baby.

Studies have shown that babies born to older mothers tend to be smarter than those born to younger ones. Psychologists don't know for sure why this happens. They think that it is because a child born to a teen parent often lives in a home where adults have lower income and educational levels. Poor nutrition before and after birth and lack of medical care can also limit a child's intellectual potential.

Finally, researchers have found babies born to young parents are more apt to be abused. Teen parents often expect too much too soon of their babies. They do not have a good understanding of a baby's needs or abilities. They tend to have a low tolerance for crying. The stresses and strains of coping with parenthood before the parents have fully reached adulthood themselves can lead to child abuse.

LEARNING ABOUT CHILDREN

Very few people fully realize what parenthood will be like. For many, becoming a parent is a time of stress and crisis. This is especially true if the pregnancy is unplanned or unwanted. Even babies who are planned and wanted create disruption and strain in parents' lives. A baby changes the parents' lives forever.

"*Parenthood remains the greatest single preserve of the amateur.*"

———◆———

ALVIN TOFFLER

Couples move into parenthood most easily when both partners have had a chance to prepare themselves by learning about children and parental roles before they become parents. Knowledge about child development is helpful. Classes and books on **child development** describe what children are like at every stage from birth through the teen years. Knowing what children are capable of at different ages helps parents respond to them correctly. Parents can be more understanding and self-confident. They will know what they need to provide and will feel less stress. They will find greater satisfaction and success in their parenting role.

Learning about children means knowing what a child needs and can do at all ages of development. What signs are there that this baby's parents are concerned and knowledgeable about the child's development?

Gaining Experience

One of the best and simplest ways to prepare for parenting is to have experience with children. People from large families grow up around babies and children. The trend toward smaller families, however, means fewer people have a chance to learn to care for children in this way.

If you are growing up in a small family, you can find ways to gain experience in caring for children. Many teens baby-sit to earn money. The practice you get in caring for children may be more valuable than the money you earn.

Some people do volunteer work with children. Activities, such as the Big Brothers/Big Sisters program, teaching a Sunday School class, or coaching a sports team, help future parents learn about children. Loy, for example, also spends time at a community center where neighborhood children go for recreation. By leading some of their activities, he has learned a great deal about children.

Watching children and parents in public places can be both interesting and informative. Some children behave poorly, yet others behave well. Observing how parents handle these behaviors can give you ideas about good parenting.

TAKING ACTION

Would you make a good parent? How can you get an answer before you commit to raising a child for 18 years?

Pilots use computer flight simulators to practice flying skills before taking the real plane up. Try creating practice parenting situations for testing your own skills and interests. You might baby-sit or:

• Invite children into your classroom for a play school experience.

• Volunteer to help with an after-school activity at an elementary school.

• Work with young children at a library, religious organization, or child care facility.

• Reach out to a youngster in your neighborhood.

Don't base your parenting decision on a single experience. Even the best of pilots have had their "crashes" in simulation!

Classes and Other Resources

Many people take courses to learn more about parenting. Taking classes before having children is a good way to prepare, especially since time may be more available. Many high schools have classes in child development and parenting. Most communities offer adult education classes in parenting. You can also find classes sponsored by many community colleges, social or mental health agencies, religious organizations, and hospitals.

Books and magazines also give information on having and handling children. The card catalog at the library will, no doubt, offer more books on child development and parenting than you can read. They can help you prepare well for parenthood if that is the choice you make someday.

SECTION 2 REVIEW

1. What needed qualities does emotional maturity bring to a parent?
2. Briefly describe three other factors, besides emotional maturity, that a couple should examine when determining when they will be ready for parenthood.
3. Identify serious physical risks associated with teen pregnancy
4. How can having a baby affect a teen mother's education, career, and income?
5. What effects can becoming a parent have on a teen father?
6. What physical effects are likely for a baby born to a teen mother? What are two other possible effects on the baby of teen parents?
7. How can learning about children help prepare a couple for parenting? What are three ways to learn more about children and parenting?

Chapter 33 Review

Chapter Summary

- Once chosen, parenthood is permanent and changes parents' lives forever, so all options and consequences must be considered when deciding whether to have a child or remain childless.
- Parenthood is a very big responsibility that brings both financial and personal costs, but it also brings many rewards.
- Society, families, and friends offer many pressures to have children.
- Some couples have very good reasons for choosing to have children.
- Sometimes couples who want children find they are unable to have them.
- Couples and sometimes singles may become parents through adoption.
- The timing of having a child can have long-lasting effects on mother, father, and child. There are several factors that should be examined to determine readiness for parenthood.
- Learning about children, child development, and parenting can help prepare a person for parenthood.

Chapter Review

1. What are the responsibilities of a parent?
2. Explain why raising a child is expensive.
3. How does a person's personal life change when he or she has a child?
4. Give two reasons why people choose to become parents.
5. Is peer pressure ever part of the pressure to have children? Explain.
6. List and briefly discuss four reasons that people may choose to remain childless.
7. Give four reasons why people might choose to adopt a child.
8. Why do some people choose to adopt an older child instead of a baby? What special difficulties might there be when an older child is adopted?
9. Discuss the advantages and disadvantages of private adoption.
10. List the four factors parents should consider as they decide when they will be ready to have a child.
11. Explain why teen parents are more likely to have financial problems than parents who wait until they are older to have children.
12. Must a teen father support his child when he is not married to the mother?
13. Why are babies born to young parents at greater risk for abuse?
14. How can the study of child development be helpful to parents?
15. How can watching children and their families in public places be helpful?

Critical Thinking

1. Why might having a child strengthen an already strong marriage but weaken an already weak marriage?
2. How can the attitude that all couples should have children be harmful to society's children?
3. Parenting is fulfilling for many people. How could a person's lack of parenting knowledge and skills make the role unfulfilling and even difficult?

4. What would happen if one member of a couple wants to have a child while the other member is strongly against it? Can you think of any ways to prevent this problem?
5. Do you think your feelings about having children and parenting will be the same in five, ten, or even fifteen years from now? What might happen to affect your feelings and attitudes?
6. Do you think an adopted child should have access to the identity of birth parents? Explain your answer.

Activities

1. **Overcoming infertility.** In your library, research the methods used to help infertile couples. What methods are used? What are their success rates? Are there negative consequences? Report your findings to the class. (*Acquiring and evaluating information, communicating information*)
2. **Preparing for birth.** Write a pledge to any future children you might have, explaining what you will do to be prepared for their birth. (*Creative thinking, self–management, writing*)
3. **Child care costs.** Interview the parent of an infant to find out the costs involved in caring for the child. Make a list of all expenses and compute average monthly cost of care. Compare results with others in the class. (*Interviewing, mathematics, comparing*)

STRENGTHENING VALUES

Aim For Realism

Realism means seeing life as it is, not as you'd like it to be. It means facing the facts and making the best of them. Salina has a realistic attitude when she:

- Observes that babies are sweet, but they are work, too.
- Plans to be emotionally and financially ready before she has children.
- Only makes commitments that she knows she can keep.
- Brushes off the negative feelings that come after a poor performance in a soccer match.
- Saves some of her money for unexpected expenses.

How will Salina's realistic attitude help her avoid problems in her life? Do you have to be able to see the negatives in order to be realistic? Explain your answer. Will a realistic attitude help or hinder as you set goals for yourself? Explain. Do you think you view life realistically or not? Cite some examples to support your answer.

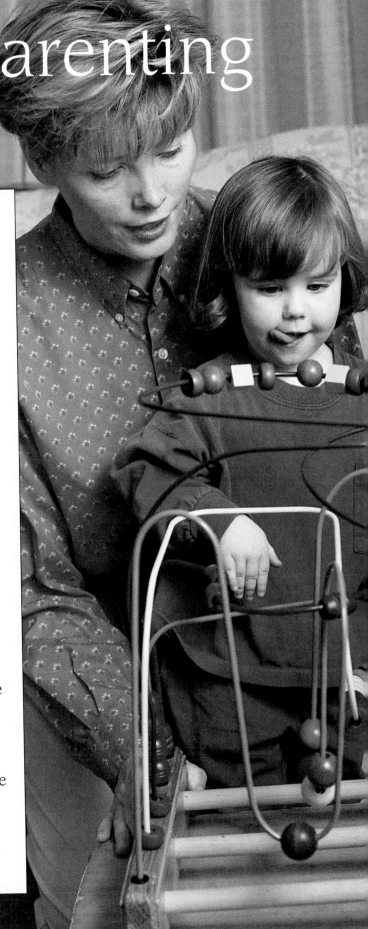

Skillful Parenting

SECTION 1

PROMOTING DEVELOPMENT

SECTION 2

GUIDING BEHAVIOR

IMAGINE THAT ...

while sitting in a park, you notice several preschoolers playing in the sand. One child attracts your attention. While the rest are sharing sand toys, he grabs buckets and utensils from the hands of others. His father looks up now and then from his newspaper and yells at the boy to stop but takes no action. The children are getting annoyed with the boy. Finally, the boy starts to throw sand at the other children. The father jumps up and yanks the boy from the sand. He says some nasty things as he drags the screaming child away and swats him repeatedly. Although you were irritated with the child, you now wonder who the victim is here — the other children or the little boy.

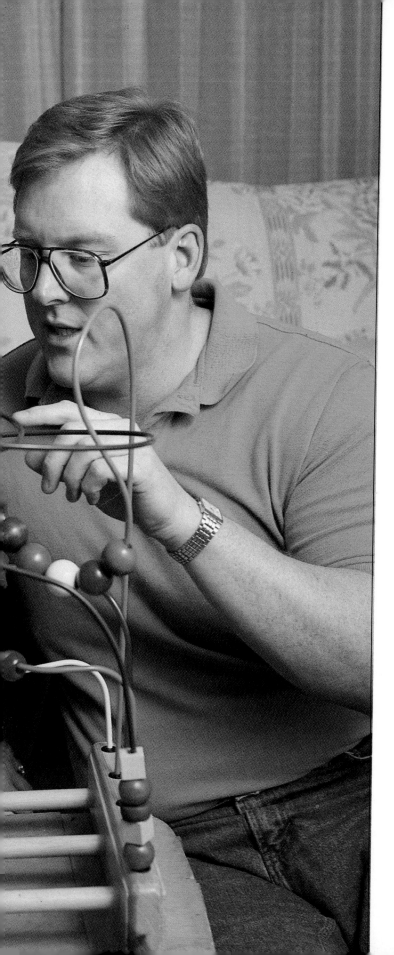

PROMOTING DEVELOPMENT

THINK AHEAD

About These Terms
motor skills
monitoring

About These Objectives
After studying this section, you should be able to:

• Explain the roles of mothers and fathers in parenting.
• Describe how children develop in each of these areas: physical, intellectual, emotional, social, and moral.
• Give suggestions for promoting children's development.
• Describe concerns in caring for children with special needs.

ne day you may decide to become a parent, but if you don't know something about children, you could have problems. Although you can take whole courses on child development, you can begin to build a foundation in this chapter.

◆ ◆ ◆

Ideally, raising a child is a partnership. Both parents share in the responsibilities — and the rewards.

Parenting was considered mostly the responsibility of the mother. The father worked to earn the money that provided the physical needs of food, shelter, clothing, and medical care. The mother provided everything else.

As you have read, however, mothers and fathers today are more apt to be equally involved with their children. Recent studies in child development have shown that both mothers and fathers are important to children. Children have needs that are not easily met by one parent alone. Fathers can be just as competent and involved as mothers in rearing children. Each parent brings strengths and weaknesses to the parenting role. Each has different personalities, interests, and skills. When both parents are involved with children, each can help make up for what the other lacks. They can both take responsibility for helping children develop.

AREAS OF DEVELOPMENT

When you studied your own development, you looked at several areas in which growth and change can be observed. Children develop in these same areas — physical, mental, emotional, social, and moral. They need adult attention all along the way in order to make the best of their development.

Physical Development

Parenting begins with physical care. Children need food, clothing, exercise, rest, medical care, and protection from harm. As parents provide these needs, children become aware that their parents care about them.

PARENTING ROLES

Your role as a parent, if you choose it, will actually be multiple roles. A parent is a nurturer, provider, protector, teacher, booster of self-esteem and confidence, counselor, and behavioral guide, to name just a few. When two parents are present in a family, who plays these roles? Ideally, the roles are shared.

An Equal Partnership

In the past, parenting roles were separate and distinct. Each role of mother and father had its own responsibilities.

Trying Times for Girls

FAMILIES

AROUND

THE

WORLD

Being a good parent means loving and taking care of a child regardless of what gender it is. Parents in many Asian countries, such as China, however, have shown a preference for boys, although the picture is changing.

Traditionally, Chinese boys helped on the farm. They took care of their elderly parents. On the other hand, girls worked at home only until they got married. Then they worked for their husband's family. Girls also had to have a dowry (money or property a bride brings to her husband when they marry), so Chinese families often looked on girls as a needless expense.

Over the years, the prejudice against girls has been changing. One government policy, however, has hampered the process. Overpopulation has forced the Chinese government to recommend strongly that couples have only one child. The vast majority of couples feel that if they can only have one child, they still want a boy. A man may even divorce the mother of a girl so he can remarry and have another child. The man's parents may encourage him because they, too, want a boy.

The favoritism toward males can be seen in several other ways. If there is a shortage of food, girls may be given less to eat than boys. Some parents do not carry daughters' baby pictures or boast about their daughters. Some grandmothers ignore granddaughters but lavish attention on grandsons.

Prejudice against girls creates other problems, too. In one province, the 50,000 bachelors outnumber women in their age group by ten to one. Many of them will never marry.

Fortunately, among young people in Asian countries the attitude is changing. Many among the new generations feel that a child is precious whether male or female.

Good Nutrition

Because children haven't the means or the knowledge to know what makes up a nutritious, well-balanced diet, parents have to provide the right foods. Children are growing at a rapid rate and need plenty of nutritious foods to help them grow and develop strong, healthy bodies. Providing children with all their nutritional needs is not always an easy task, so parents must take special care to plan children's meals and snacks. This is especially true of small children who frequently do not eat much at one sitting and therefore need to eat often.

Sasha, for example, gives her children juice and nutritious snacks to eat at mid-morning and mid-afternoon. Their favorite snacks are raisins, peanut-butter-filled celery sticks, and fresh fruit. At meals she also gives them a variety of nutritious foods.

When they decide they don't like something, she encourages them to try just a little. Sasha has decided that forcing them to eat could make them dislike mealtimes and certain foods forever. She believes they will eventually learn to like foods that they see other people enjoying.

Clothing

Parents must see that young children are dressed appropriately for the weather. Garments should allow for freedom of movement but not be so large that they interfere with play, get caught on play equipment, or cause the child to trip and fall. When parents provide young children with clothing that the children can put on and take off themselves, such as pull-on pants and tops and clothing with snaps or Velcro® fasteners, they help their children be independent at an early age. This sense of independence and the resulting pride the children feel from doing something by themselves is important to their emotional development.

Exercise

Children need plenty of opportunities for exercise so they can release pent-up energy, develop strong bones and muscles, and develop motor skills. **Motor skills** are the abilities that depend on the use and control of muscles, especially those in the arms, legs, hands, and feet. Picking a flower, throwing a ball, and pedaling a tricycle are examples of motor skills.

Katrina helps her son get the exercise he needs when she takes Mikail to the park each afternoon to let him run and play. They live in an apartment that is too small for active play indoors and has no outdoor play area where Mikail can romp in the fresh air. Mikail's older sister Anna takes swimming lessons and also plays T-ball in the summer.

Parents should promote regular physical activity so that children develop properly. Starting such habits early can make exercise a lifetime habit.

Rest

Parents are also responsible for seeing that children get adequate rest. Children are very active, and they grow rapidly. Therefore, their bodies need plenty of rest to replenish energy supplies. Good sleep habits promote health and well-being. Without enough sleep and rest, children often do not learn as well, are irritable, and may be more likely to become ill.

Medical Care

Making sure children receive good medical and dental care is another way parents provide physical care for their children.

Regular physical and dental checkups help keep children's bodies and teeth healthy. Infants and children undergo a series of vaccinations to protect them from getting certain diseases, such as polio, measles, and mumps. Public health clinics can help families who cannot afford these vaccinations. Parents also see that their children get prompt medical attention when they are ill or injured.

Self-Care

Parents also help children gradually learn to take over some of their own physical care. You already read how parents provide easy-on and -off clothes so children can dress themselves. When children are old enough, parents help them learn how to keep their teeth and gums healthy by brushing and flossing regularly. They help children learn to wash their hands before eating and after toileting to prevent the spread of germs. This type of learning not only helps children develop healthy personal care practices, it also gives them a sense of independence.

A Safe Environment

Safety is vital for children, who are often described as "accidents waiting to happen." Parents are the primary protectors. For younger children, this means monitoring children and their activities and taking steps to keep the home safe.

Monitoring means supervising children and being aware of where they are and what they are doing. Young children need constant monitoring. A toddler who is not carefully watched can get into a dangerous situation in minutes in spite of all efforts to keep the home safe. As children get older, they need less monitoring. It is still important, however, for parents to know where

their children are and what they are doing, even after children have reached their teens. Higher levels of parental monitoring of teens is related to lower rates of drug and alcohol abuse, running away, and delinquency.

Of course, all homes, no matter what the age of the inhabitants, must be kept safe from such dangers as fires and intruders. Parents of young children must take several additional measures to keep their children safe. One of the first things one parent did when his son started to crawl was put plastic plugs in the unused electrical outlets. He was concerned that the child might poke something in an outlet and get shocked. The father also put child-proof locks on all kitchen and laundry room cabinets. Cleaning products can be very dangerous and may cause poisoning or chemical burns.

What better way to find out what might be a problem for young children than getting down on the floor and crawling about in order to see things at a child's level. Doing this can help you spot possible dangers that adults might not normally notice but that children could easily see and get into.

As children grow older, parents help them learn about dangerous substances and situations, about how to avoid dangers, and what to do if an emergency occurs.

Intellectual Development

Children come into the world helpless and without knowledge and skills. Parents take pride in helping children learn and develop thinking and language skills. Children learn from parents, but they also learn through experiences and play. By providing learning experiences and opportunities for play both in and outside the home, parents give their children the best chance to develop intellectually.

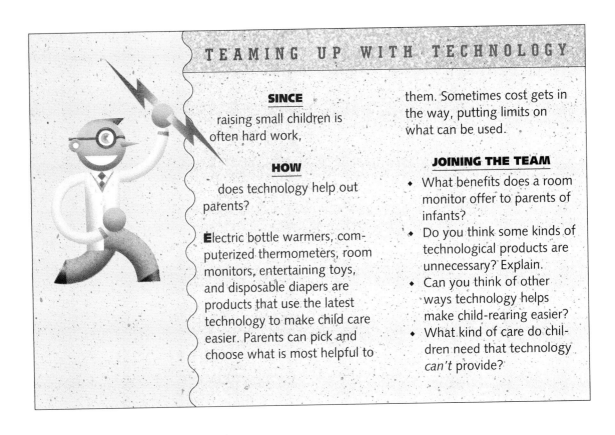

Providing Learning Experiences

When they know how children learn, parents can offer their children a variety of experiences that help them learn and develop intellectually. According to the Swiss psychologist Jean Piaget, intelligence in children develops as a series of stages:

- *Sensorimotor Stage.* This stage lasts from birth through about age two. During this stage, children learn through their senses and actions. Children explore things that are bright-colored, make noise, have a smell, or have different shapes or textures they can feel (soft, smooth, rough, sticky, slippery). As they explore and investigate through their senses, children discover how things work.
- *Preoperational Stage.* This stage lasts from ages two through six. Children at this age still learn through the senses and direct experiences. They are also beginning to learn that objects and words can be symbols, that is, that they can be used to represent something else. Children begin to develop language and learn to pretend. They can now create make-believe situations that imitate real life so they can learn more about the world around them.
- *Concrete Operations Stage.* This stage lasts from ages seven to eleven. Children this age still learn best through direct experience. They also begin to think logically. They begin to classify objects into categories. Developing collections of anything from rocks to trading cards to figurines is an enjoyable learning experience for children of this age.
- *Formal Operations Stage.* This stage begins about age eleven or twelve and continues throughout adulthood. Upon entering this stage, children begin to be able to use abstract thinking. This means they are capable of thinking about what

might happen or what might have caused something to happen even though they have not actually experienced it. Now children can solve problems just by thinking.

The new intellectual abilities children acquire at each stage outlined by Piaget determine the limits of what a child can learn at that stage. By understanding how their child can best learn and what limitations are on their child's ability to learn, parents can provide learning experiences and activities appropriate to their child's level of development.

Learning Language

The ability to use and understand language opens up a whole new world of learning experiences for children. Throughout life, people learn through communication. Social skills develop along with communication skills.

Nurturing parents encourage language development from the day a child is born. They talk to babies as they are providing their physical care. As babies grow older, parents point out objects, animals, and familiar people and identify them by name. They sing and read stories to children. As they take strolls or run errands, they talk about what they see and what is happening. When children are old enough, parents ask children questions about what they see or about what is happening to help children think about and reflect upon what they see.

When Jorge was a baby, for example, his parents sang and talked to him often — as they fed him, bathed him, diapered and dressed him, and as they cuddled him. Later they told him the names of toys and other objects as they handed them to him or pointed at them. They read him storybooks and pointed out characters and objects from the story in the book's illustra-

Help from Employers

Enlightened employers know that it's in their interest to keep their employees happy. One way to do this is to provide ways of helping parents balance their work and family commitments.

On–site child care is one example of benefits designed to help parents. Employees who can bring their children to work with them don't have to make an extra journey to drop the children off, and don't have to worry if they need to work a little late.

Flex time, which allows employees to work flexible hours, is a great benefit for parents. It enables them to tailor their work hours around their children's needs. A parent may choose, for example, to work from 7 A.M. to 3 P.M. so as to be home with the children after school.

Job sharing, an arrangement in which two people share one job, is also attractive to parents. In some cases, two parents who share a job may also share child care.

tions. They taught him simple songs and rhymes. Wherever they took him, to the store, to a park, for a walk, or for a ride, they pointed out all the new objects, animals, and people there were to see and talked about what was happening.

Emotional Development

Emotional well-being is deeply rooted in how well parents provide for the emotional needs of children. Parents can do so much to build children's self-concept, self-esteem, and sense of independence. Nurturing (providing love, attention, support, and encouragement) is especially important for good emotional development.

Parents can help children build self-esteem, confidence, and a sense of independence by offering them plenty of opportunities for success. As you learned earlier, clothes that are easy for children to put on and take off are one way of making children feel successful.

Parents should praise children's successes, even the small ones. Doing so helps children feel good about themselves and encourages them to take on new tasks and challenges. When parents praise children's successes and stress their strong points, children develop good self-concepts. They feel good about themselves and gain confidence. Children whose parents belittle them and focus on poor behavior or weaknesses tend to have poor self-concepts. Children with poor self-concepts have little confidence in themselves and are afraid to try new things.

Sometimes parents need to add some extra encouragement and support to help boost the self-concept. Jacob's mother did just that. When Jacob was having trouble learning to ride his two-wheel bicycle, his mother wouldn't let him give up. She said, "I know you can do this. We'll just keep trying." She helped him until he mastered the skill. The effort was worth it when Jacob proudly pedaled down the street for the first time, shouting, "Look at me, I'm doing it! I'm riding by myself!"

Offering children chances for success by teaching them self-help skills promotes independence. Helping children learn decision-making skills does too. One mother promoted independence by encouraging her children to do activities on their own. She also gave the children choices in what they wore and what nutritious foods they could eat for snacks. She let them make as many decisions as possible. When they made poor decisions, she helped them live with the consequences.

Social Development

The parent-child relationship is a child's earliest social relationship. Social development actually begins at birth. Infants are calmed by a soothing voice and by being picked up and held. Giving them attention in the early weeks of life does not spoil them. Babies thrive on the love and attention they receive from parents and other family members. By the time they are two or three months old, they show how much they enjoy the love and attention by offering smiles, coos, and gurgles in return. (Those same smiles will be an important part of social relationships for a lifetime.) As with emotional development, nurturing is essential for good social development. When a baby is left alone most of the time, except when physical care is provided, the infant actually begins to fail to respond to people or familiar objects.

You read earlier in this chapter how parents talk to infants as they provide care. This not only encourages language development but also contributes to social development. Babies come to enjoy the company of others and, in learning language, they gain the social skill of communication.

Another way parents promote babies' social development is by playing games like "peek-a-boo" and "pat-a-cake" with the infant. The interaction is fun for parent and child.

All the positive exchanges that take place within the family are good for social development. Children learn what to do and what to say in order to get along with and relate to others by watching and interacting with parents and other family members. The family acts as a sort of training ground for developing social skills. The skills then transfer to relationships outside the family and can be used throughout life. As you know, this process of learning to relate and get along with others is called socialization.

When children are socialized, they learn to behave in acceptable ways. The behavior learned depends mainly on the expectations and attitudes of those who provide care, usually the parents. As they mature, babies learn that certain behavior is rewarded with a smile or praise. They begin to repeat the behavior that brings approval. Babies also learn that some behavior results in a negative response, such as a frown or scolding. Negative responses like these are among the earliest efforts to shape a child's behavior.

Moral Development

The seeds of moral development are sown earlier in life. Children learn to base their behavior on what they believe is right and wrong from the family, most often parents.

Moral development shows in behavior, in how children treat others. As toddlers, children begin to learn the rules that parents and other caregivers set. They may not understand the reasons, but they know what behavior will meet with disapproval. Hitting a playmate, for example, makes parents unhappy.

Between the ages of five and seven, children begin to develop a conscience. Doing something wrong triggers guilt because they know what they should be doing.

At this age, the difference between truth and lies becomes more apparent. Because children are very imaginative, they may sometimes confuse fantasy with reality. Parents need to recognize that tall tales are not lies. Children need help, not punishment, in separating fact from fiction.

From about ages seven to ten, children accept the authority of their parents, teachers, and other caregivers. They may not like all the rules, but they usually follow them to avoid punishment. They are not quite ready to do what is right because of their own beliefs. As they develop, children make

TAKING ACTION

To experience some of the responsibilities of parenthood, offer to take care of the child of a close friend or relative on a weekend, from Friday afternoon until Sunday night. If this is not possible, imagine that you will be caring for an active three-year-old over the same period. Now ask yourself the following questions in order to plan for the responsibilities you are taking on and then compare your answers with those of your classmates:

- **What planned activities will have to be changed?**

- **What will you enjoy doing with the child?**

- **How will you pay for the child's expenses?**

- **How will your meals or sleeping habits be affected?**

- **What effect, if any, will this have on your friendships?**

Compare your answers with those of your classmates.

mistakes. While they are learning to monitor their own behavior, they aren't fully able to do so yet. For this reason, children need love and guidance as they develop morally. You will read more about this later in the chapter.

CHILDREN WITH SPECIAL NEEDS

Some children have special needs because of physical impairments, emotional problems, or learning disabilities. These children have the same basic needs that other children do. Because of the extra challenges they face, however, they need special attention as they grow and develop so that they can reach their fullest potential. As a result, parents of special needs children have extra challenges, too.

Attention, patience, time, and energy are useful when caring for children with special needs. Some of these children require extra physical care and companionship. Many have to work much harder to achieve goals for learning or for physical mobility. Parents may have to work with doctors, therapists, and educators to develop and carry out plans to help children meet desired developmental goals.

One big problem facing families of children with special needs is financial. The medical care, special equipment, and/or schooling that such a child needs may strain the family's budget. Sometimes children remain economically dependent on parents for their entire lives.

The attitude of the child's parents toward the disability or other problem makes a big difference in the child's future. Parents should praise their child's accomplishments and show they are proud of what the child has worked to accomplish. They should teach the child to be as independent as possible. For example, assigning the child certain household tasks that fit his or her abilities helps the child feel needed and worthwhile. Parents who pity, resent, coddle, or overprotect a child with special needs hinder the child's emotional development. The child may become self-pitying or angry and may not work to accomplish attainable goals. As a result, the child is likely to have difficulty functioning in society and may not achieve full potential. A child with a positive attitude will have a happier and more productive life.

Parents who manage best with a child who has special needs are those who have a positive attitude, are strong and secure personally, are patient and understanding, and can handle any extra expenses. The rewards of caring for a child with special needs can be great. Like any other child, they need love, but they give it, too.

SECTION 1 REVIEW

1. Compare the roles of mothers and fathers in parenting today.
2. Briefly describe what parents can do to promote physical development.
3. Why is monitoring especially important with very young children?
4. Briefly discuss Piaget's four stages of development. Explain how understanding these stages can help promote a child's intellectual development.
5. Give three examples of ways parents can promote language development.
6. What does praise have to do with good emotional development?
7. Define the term "socialization."
8. When a six-year-old tells a "tall tale," is this a lie? Explain your answer.
9. Describe two challenges that face a parent whose child has special needs.

GUIDING BEHAVIOR

THINK AHEAD

About These Terms

authoritarian style   *discipline*
authoritative style   *time-out*
permissive style

About These Objectives

After studying this section, you should be able to:

* Describe the three basic parenting styles.
* Explain techniques and rules for effective discipline.

ne of the greatest challenges a parent faces in raising children is guiding their behavior. A lack of attention to this effort when children are young can result in problems as children grow older.

◆   ◆   ◆

THE CHALLENGE

Even the most skilled parent is challenged by efforts to guide a child's behavior. Authorities do not always agree on what approach is best. Children are different in how they respond to parents' actions. Some parents feel unsure about the approach to take, so they either let problem behavior go or react incorrectly. Despite all of this, parents need to develop and use a solid approach to guiding behavior.

PARENTING STYLES

Parents have different styles of handling behavior. The style they use is based on the parents' ideas of what the parent-child relationship should be. Parents develop their parenting styles from their own experiences during childhood, their personalities, societal influences, and the parents' basic attitudes toward children and child-rearing. There are three basic styles of parenting:

Parents need to spend time with children, giving them love and talking to them in positive ways. Good behavior follows more naturally when this is done.

- *Authoritarian Parenting.* The **authoritarian style** of parenting is based on the belief that children should obey their parents without question or hesitation. Parents set rules to control or restrict children's behavior. They may also set goals they expect children to achieve, such as high grades in school or award-winning athletic performances. Rules and goals are made firmly clear to children, usually with little or no further discussion. Failure to meet goals or obey rules is dealt with swiftly and firmly.
- *Authoritative Parenting.* In the **authoritative style**, parents set limits and standards and goals but base their expectations on children's abilities and stage of development. Parents explain to children the reasons behind the limits that are set and the decisions that are made. In addition, they listen to children's input and ideas. In this style, children are allowed a certain amount of independence and decision making within the established limits.
- *Permissive Style.* In the **permissive style**, parents tend to let children set their own goals, rules, and limits. Parents provide little or no structure or discipline. Children are given all the freedom they can handle. Parents are accepting of children's impulses, feelings, and behavior.

Frequently, parenting styles involve different blends of these basic styles. What works for one situation may not work as well for another. A child's age, personality, and sense of responsibility also affect what style is used. Many different parenting styles can be successful as long as children's different needs are met. More important than the specific style of parenting is the love, attention, support, and security that the parents provide.

"Give a little love to a child, and you get a great deal back."

JOHN RUSKIN

DISCIPLINE

Discipline is the process of helping children learn to behave in acceptable ways. It helps children conform to the expectations of the family and society and gradually learn to control their own behavior. This ability to control one's own behavior is called self-discipline.

Many people confuse discipline with punishment. In fact, punishment is only a small part of discipline and is used only when necessary. Actually, another word for discipline is *guidance*. Discipline is used to guide children to control their actions and behave acceptably. Disciplining effectively is not easy.

Three key principles are part of effective discipline. They are encouraging good behavior, setting and enforcing limits, and dealing with misbehavior.

Encouraging Good Behavior

One of the best ways for parents to encourage good behavior is to set a good example for their children. Much of children's learning comes from watching others. Children are great imitators. They adopt many of the beliefs, feelings, and behavior patterns of those around them.

As Chen's comments show, parents who expect one behavior but display another will not get desired results. Chen describes his friend's situation this way: "I have a friend who lies a lot. His father gets mad when he does and tells him not to. The funny thing is his parents will lie to the school counselor to cover for him if he skips school. What do they expect?"

When children do behave in a desired manner, parents should offer praise that specifically identifies the good behavior. Praise helps children feel good about themselves and makes them want to continue the desired behavior.

Setting and Enforcing Limits and Rules

Limits range from physical restrictions, such as not being able to go out of the yard, to rules for behavior. Limits help children know what is acceptable, appropriate, and safe to do. Limits and rules should not be so extensive that a child feels hemmed-in and becomes frustrated. Limits should be reasonable and appropriate for the child's age. As children grow older, they need fewer restrictions, especially when they show they follow the rules. Limits and rules should also be simple and clearly stated, so the child understands exactly what the desired behavior is.

Dealing with Misbehavior

No matter how hard parents try to encourage good behavior and to set reasonable limits, all children misbehave at times. Sometimes a simple warning or reminder of the rule is enough to keep a child from repeating an undesired behavior. Other times, letting the child suffer the natural consequences of a misbehavior is punishment enough. For example, if a child does not come to the dinner table after being called repeatedly, the child can eat the dinner cold or miss the meal. Another method is to remove the child from the presence of others or from the center of

Children learn how to behave by watching others. Learning to follow the rules of a game, for example, can come as family members play together.

activity for a short time. This is called **time out**. Another common disciplinary method is removal of privileges. Some parents "ground" children, not letting them go anywhere for a period of time. In all cases, the punishment should be in proportion to the seriousness of the misbehavior.

A parent may need to cool off for a while before setting a punishment in order to prevent overreacting. For example, Mrs. Paxton "grounded" her daughter for a month in the heat of the moment. Later, she realized that a week would have been more appropriate. Changing her mind would take some of the impact out of the punishment. On the other hand, trying to enforce a month's grounding under the circumstances would be difficult. Either way Mrs. Paxton had a dilemma that would never have occurred had she thought before she reacted.

Frequently, it takes a combination of disciplinary methods to bring about the desired behavior, as you can see in this example. The Kimborough family is trying to teach Shawnell to share. He's at the stage where he grabs whatever he wants.

They talk to him about sharing and praise him when he shares his toys or asks for something he wants. They punish him by removing him from the situation when he grabs without asking or refuses to share. They coach him in what to say to get another child to share toys.

Issues in Discipline

Experts vary in their opinions on spanking. Some feel strongly that spanking should be avoided. They point out that spanking does not help children learn desirable behavior and may teach them that hitting is acceptable. Other experts believe that in certain situations, appropriate use of spanking can produce effective results without causing harm to the child.

Whatever their views, experts generally agree on two points. First, caregivers should never use spanking to vent their own anger or frustration. Second, in most situations, there are effective, positive guidance techniques that can be used instead of spanking.

SUMMING UP

Without a doubt, parents want children who behave well. Life goes more smoothly for the family and for the children when behavior is under control. Parents can have good results if they are prepared with clear thinking about guidance techniques. Turning to these basic, hard-and-fast rules is a good place to start:

* *Begin early.* Shaping behavior when children are very young is much easier than when they are older. Letting inappropriate behavior go uncorrected in a preschooler may mean that the behavior will be locked in and much more difficult to change when the child is older.

Many parents use the time-out method of discipline. When misbehavior occurs, the child is required to sit alone for a specified number of minutes. The time can be lengthened as the child grows older.

The behavior that children learn when they are very young carries on as they grow older. A parent who knows this makes the effort to shape appropriate behavior from an early age.

- *Take action.* Always be prepared to follow through. Demands and threats are meaningless unless something is actually done to change a child's incorrect behavior. In other words, don't say, "Stop that," unless you plan to make sure in some appropriate way that the behavior ceases.
- *Be consistent.* Children are confused and don't know what you really want from them when you react differently to the same behavior. In other words, decide what behavior is unacceptable and handle misbehavior the same way each time it occurs. You can't let something go one time and then punish for it the next.
- *Be united.* When more than one person disciplines children, they need to get together on their thinking. Otherwise confusion may result. Children are quick to manipulate parents who do not present a united front.

Much has been written about guiding children's behavior. You will do a much better job with any children you might have in the future, if you do some reading, observing, and thinking today.

SECTION 2 REVIEW

1. Briefly describe the three basic styles of parenting.
2. Compare discipline and punishment.
3. How can parents encourage good behavior in children?
4. Can parents have too many limits and rules? Explain.
5. Explain "time out."
6. What are three problems related to physical punishment?
7. List four basic rules for guiding children's behavior.

Chapter 34 Review

Chapter Summary

- Good parenting means taking care of needs in all areas of development.
- As parents provide for children's physical needs, children become aware that their parents care about them and about their health and safety.
- By providing a variety of experiences with materials, people, and new situations, parents enable children to develop their minds.
- Parents stimulate both learning and social skills when they encourage language development.
- Parents play an important role in promoting their children's emotional and moral development.
- Through parent/child and other family relationships, children learn to relate to and get along with others.
- Children with special needs can develop to their fullest potential in the right environment.
- Discipline helps children get along with others.
- Parenting styles can vary.
- To guide children's behavior, parents need to become knowledgeable about discipline techniques.

Chapter Review

1. Which role is more important in the family, the mother's or father's? Explain your answer.
2. Why is a nutritious diet so important to young children? How can parents help children develop good eating habits?
3. Define the term "monitoring" and explain why it is important to a young child's safety. What are some other things parents can do to keep their child safe from harm?
4. List the four stages of intellectual development according to Piaget.
5. Explain the importance of language to learning.
6. Describe two ways parents can help their children develop emotional well-being.
7. How does giving an infant attention promote social development?
8. List three qualities that can help parents of children with special needs.
9. Why do parents generally use a combination of parenting styles?
10. Define discipline.
11. List three key principles that are a part of effective discipline.
12. Why should a parent think carefully before setting a punishment?
13. What might the results be from hitting a child as a consistent form of punishment?
14. Why is consistency important when guiding a child's behavior?

Critical Thinking

1. What should a parent do if the telephone or doorbell rings while the parent is bathing a toddler?
2. Do you think adults should use baby talk when talking to infants and young children? Explain your answer.
3. If you have children someday, what parenting style would you use most often and why?

4. When guiding children's behavior, what effect will the "do as I say, not as I do" attitude have?
5. In a family with two parents, do you think only one parent should be in charge of discipline? Explain your answer.

Activities

1. **Healthful snacks for children.** Develop a recipe book of healthful snacks for children. Try to include all food groups. (*Acquiring and evaluating information, organizing information*)
2. **A special needs child.** Choose one type of special needs child and do research to learn more about the condition. Learn about possible causes and about various ways children with this special need can be helped to reach their fullest potential. Find out about the most recent advances in combating causes of the problem or overcoming the problem. Learn about sources of help for both the children and their parents in your area. Report your findings to the class. (*Acquiring and evaluating information, communicating information*)
3. **Parent–child interaction.** In a public place, such as a mall or grocery store, observe parent–child interaction in three to five situations. Describe and evaluate how behavior was handled. Report your observations to the class. (*Observing, evaluating, communicating information*)

STRENGTHENING VALUES

Aim For Patience

Patience is the ability to tolerate delay and trouble. It is understanding that goals take time and effort to achieve. Patient people are willing to move slowly and with repetition if need be. Hans shows patience when he:

- Lets his four-year-old sister button her own coat even though he could do it faster.
- Reads his sister her same favorite story over and over.
- Stays cheerful and understanding while waiting to be served at a busy restaurant.
- Waits in heavy traffic without getting upset.
- Demonstates several times how to saddle a horse to a friend who has trouble getting it right.

People who are impatient often have physical reactions. What might these be? Do you think people are more often impatient over small things or big ones? Explain your answer. Are you patient? What might a person do to become more patient? Describe a situation in which you were patient.

Looking Forward

Your study of families has now reached an ending and a beginning. What have you learned and how can you apply it to your life?

During your journey through this text, all kinds of families and situations have greeted you. You have discovered how diverse families are. They come in all shapes and sizes, each with its own attributes and problems. Like every other, your family has a place in the picture.

You now have a better understanding of the importance of families, to individuals and society. Not only do families provide in many ways for their members' needs, but they also serve as a foundation for every community. Families need support and preservation.

You have also learned new skills and polished old ones. Think about what you can do. You have the capability to communicate well and resolve conflicts. You can make good decisions. You can be a manager. These are tools that help make family life and relationships with others rewarding. By practicing and perfecting them, you can make them a standard and useful part of your life.

As you leave your study of families behind, you will take understanding with you. If you hadn't thought about it before, you should now realize that you have a better understanding of people of all ages, of people who are different from you, of people who are close to you and those who are not. Your ability to understand helps create bridges that unite people.

Families Today has given you the opportunity to develop insight. Hard times can come to anyone. Individuals and families face crises everyday. They have adjustments to make and struggles to meet. Insight gives you the vision to see your way through a situation and help others do the same. You can survive because you know what to do.

There is one person you have probably thought about more than any other during your study — you. You have been the focal point in many discussions and in much of what you have read. How do *you* get along with family members? How do *you* strengthen relationships? How do *you* fit into the world? What you have learned about yourself can serve you well if you let it. Leave this course with self-discovery, and you leave with something special.

Your study of families and the people around you has ended, but your experiences with them have only begun. Where are you headed with your new knowledge?

First, open your eyes — wide. See what is worrying people about society. Many families are troubled. You've read about it — drugs, alcohol, abuse, crime, poverty, hunger, and pain as families pull apart. Many who study what goes on in society paint a bleak picture of what they see. Can there be a light at the end of the tunnel?

The answer is "yes," and the solution is you. United with others of your generation and bonded by a desire to make a better world, you can make a difference. Begin at home. Make yourself the best that you can be. You have that power. Then make your family today and the family of your future the best that they can be, for that is where everything begins.

Throughout this text you have imagined. Now imagine one more time. Close your eyes — tight — and visualize a brighter world. Then make it happen.

Glossary

A

abstinence. (AB-stuh-nunts). Refraining from sexual intercourse. (20)

active listening. Trying to understand what the speaker is feeling or what the message really means. (5)

adaptation. (ADD-ap-TAY-shun). Making changes that are practical and appropriate. (13)

addiction. (uh-DICK-shun). Dependence on a particular substance or action. (13)

adjustment. A period of working to change routines and feelings until everything feels normal. (12)

adolescence. (AD-uh-LES-unts). The stage of life between childhood and adulthood. (21)

adoption. The legal process of taking a child of other parents as one's own, binding the parents and child in every legal way. (33)

adversarial divorce. (add-ver-SAIR-ee-uhl). A divorce where the spouses become legal opponents. (12)

aerobic exercise. Strenuous activity that raises the heart rate and increases the amount of oxygen taken into the lungs. (26)

affirmation. (AF-ur-MAY-shun). Providing positive input that helps others feel appreciated and supported. (7)

ageism. A prejudice against older people. (16)

alcoholism. An addiction to alcohol. (13)

alimony. (al-uh-MOH-nee). Financial support of an ex-spouse. (12)

altruistic. (Al-true-ISS-tick). An unselfish concern for the welfare of others. (24)

Alzheimer's disease. A disease that affects older people causing loss of the ability to reason, remember, and concentrate, and eventually, the ability to use the mind. (16)

annulment. (uh-NULL-ment). A decree that states that a legal marriage never took place because of some prior condition at the time of the marriage. (12)

anorexia nervosa. (an-uh-REX-ee-uh ner-VOH-suh). A mental disorder that shows itself in a fear of being fat. (26)

antibiotics. Special medicines that destroy disease-causing germs. (26)

anticipatory grief. The beginning and slow progression of the grieving process before death caused by prior knowledge of the death due to terminal illness or old age. (14)

application form. A form that gives the company basic information about you. (29)

aptitude. Natural talent and capacity for learning in certain areas. (29)

assertive. Communicating ideas and feelings firmly and positively. (5)

assimilation. (uh-SIM-uh-LAY-shun). After a person moves from one culture to live in another, many of the habits, customs, and patterns that they knew before are put aside. (1)

authoritarian style. A parenting style based on the belief that children should obey their parents without hesitation or question. (34)

authoritative style. A parenting style where parents set limits, standards, and goals but base their expectations on children's abilities and stage of development. (34)

authority. The right to give orders, make decisions, and enforce rules. (15)

autocratic style. The responsibility for major decisions is in one person's hands. (2)

autonomy. The ability to direct your own life independently. (25)

B

balance. Remaining amount. (27)

bankruptcy. (BANK-rupt-SEE). A legal process that declares a person unable to pay debts. (11)

bargain. A product that is needed, wanted and will be used; good quality; sells at a price you are willing to pay; and the product is sold by a reliable dealer. (28)

Better Business Bureaus. Independent organizations sponsored by businesses in a community. (28)

body image. The way you see your physical self. (21)

budget. A plan for spending. (27)

bulimia. (buh-LIM-ee-uh). An eating disorder involving "binge" eating. (26)

bylaws. A set of rules established by a group. (15)

C

career counseling. Counseling that helps people choose and be successful in their work. (29)

career. The kind of work that you will do over a period of years. (29)

character. Being morally strong; having the ability to think, judge, and act with maturity. (23)

child development. A description of what children are like at each stage of growth. (33)

chosen role. A role that is deliberately selected. (4)

chronic diseases. Illnesses or conditions that occur repeatedly or never go away. (16)

citizenship. Membership in a community that guarantees certain rights and expects certain responsibilities. (24)

cliques. (CLICKS). Exclusive groups of friends. (17)

closed adoption. An adoption procedure where the identities of the birth parents is not revealed to the adoptive parents. (33)

co-dependency. A condition developed by the family members of a person who has a compulsive disorder. (13)

code of ethics. A clear set of rules or principles that guide actions and decisions. (23)

commitment. A pledge to support something of value. (7)

communication channel. The way in which a message is passed. (5)

communication. An ongoing process of creating and sharing messages with others. (5)

comparison shopping. Looking in several stores to compare quality and price before buying. (28)

compatible. Existing in harmony with another person. (18)

competition. A struggle for superiority or victory. (6)

complementary needs. A theory that suggests that people select partners who complete and meet their personality needs. (30)

compromise. Giving in on some points of disagreement and having your way on others. (6)

compulsive eating. An eating disorder in which sufferers are unable to resist food and cannot stop eating. (26)

conflict resolution. An approach to solving disagreements. (1)

conflict. A disagreement or struggle between two or more people. (6)

conform. To follow the customs, rules, or standards of a group. (23)

conscience. (KAHN-chuntz). An inner sense of what is right and wrong in one's own behavior or motives. (23)

consequences. (KAHN-suh-KWEN-sez). The results of decisions. (8)

Consumer Action and Advisory Panels. Organizations formed by specific industries to help solve consumer problems. (28)

consumer. A person who purchases goods and services to fill needs and wants. (28)

contract. A binding agreement made between two people. (31)

control. Directing the behavior of another person. (6)

cooperation. The ability to work with others. (15)

credit. Borrowing or using someone else's money and paying it back later. (27)

cremation (kree-MAY-shun). The reduction of a body to ashes through intense heat. (14)

crisis. (CRY-suss). When a situation is so unstable or critical that the outcome will make a decisive difference for better or worse. (13)

crushes. Intense, and usually passing, feelings of infatuation for another person. (19)

cultural heritage. Information taught to young members of families about the beliefs, customs, and traits that have been important to their ancestors and continue to be for them. (1)

culture shock. The difficulties and feelings of uneasiness that people have when they are exposed to another culture. (1)

culture. Everything about the way a group of people live. (1)

custody. A legal decision about who has the right to make decisions that affect children and who has the physical responsibility of caring for them. (12)

D

date rape. Rape that takes place in a dating situation. (18)

dating. Shared social activity between people of opposite genders. (18)

decision-making process. A series of steps that are followed in order to make effective decisions. (8)

decisions. Choices. (8)

deductible. An amount of money that a person must pay before insurance begins to pay. (26)

delegating. Assigning responsibilities to others. (10)

democratic style. Decisions are made by more than one person. (2)

denial. (dih-NEYE-uhl). Refusing to believe the facts, and thinking and acting as if those facts do not exist. (14)

dependent. Relying greatly on others. (2)

diplomacy. The ability to handle situations without upsetting people. (15)

direct advertising. Advertising that appeals directly to you. (28)

discipline. The process of helping children learn to behave in acceptable ways. (34)

disengagement. Withdrawal from others and from activity. (16)

divorce. A legal action that ends a marriage. (12)

down payment. Partial cash payment. (27)

drugs. Chemical substances, other than food, that change the way the body or mind functions. (13)

E

egocentrism. The inability to see life from anyone else's viewpoint. (23)

elder abuse. Physical abuse of older adults. (16)

emotional support. Everything that families do to help meet the emotional needs of each member. (1)

emotions. The feelings you have in response to thoughts, remarks, and events. (1)

empathy. (EM-puh-thee). The ability to put yourself in another person's situation. (4)

empty nest. The home with children gone. (2)

enculturation. (in-KUHL-chur-A-shun). Each generation passes along what it has learned to the next as the culture carries on. (1)

engagement. A promise or intention to marry. (31)

environment. (in-VY-run-munt). Experiences. (7)

estranged. Alienated. (32)

ethnic identity. (ETH-nick). A group of people who share a common set of traits and customs, or culture. (1)

ethnocentrism. (eth-no-SEN-triz-um). Thinking that your culture is the best or most natural. (1)

evaluating. Studying the results of your decision in order to determine how effective it was. (8)

exploitation. Using another person unfairly for personal benefit. (4)

extroverted. Focused outward or on others. (22)

F

facilities. Places designed for a particular purpose, such as schools, libraries, museums, and parks. (9)

family life cycle. A basic family pattern in society. (2)

family management system. A method of operating that distributes the household work fairly. (10)

family system. Family members acting together with their different roles and personalities. (7)

feedback. A response to a message that indicates whether the message was understood correctly. (5)

fertility. The ability to have children. (33)

fixed expenses. Expenses that you pay regularly. (27)

fixed income. A steady income of the same amount per month, which does not change when expenses increase. (16)

flexible expenses. Expenses that do not occur regularly. (27)

fraud. Attempts to cheat you. (28)

functions. Purposes. (1)

G

gender role. The behavior and characteristics expected of a male or female. (20)

genetic diseases. Diseases that run in the family; such diseases are passed from parent to child. (33)

gerontology. (Jair-un-TAHL-uh-jee). The study of the aging process. (16)

given role. A role that is automatically acquired. (4)

goal setting. The act of establishing a goal for yourself or your family. (9)

goal. Something you plan to be, do, or have, and you are willing to work for it. (2)

gossip. Conversation that often includes rumors about people. (17)

grief. Painful emotional and physical feelings caused by a loss through death. (14)

grounds. A marital crime such as mental or physical cruelty, desertion, adultery, and insanity. (12)

H

hallucinations. (huh-loo-sih-NAY-shuns). Seeing things that aren't there. (26)

heredity. (huh-RED-uht-ee). Traits received from parents at birth. (7)

homogamy. (huh-MAH-guh-mee). Couples who are similar to their partners. (30)

hormones. Chemical substances in the body which control reproduction. (21)

hospice programs. Provide support and care for people who face death. (14)

household work. Work a family does in the home in order to keep up with day-to-day living. (10)

human resources. Qualities people have, such as knowledge, skills, talents, and energy. (9)

I

ideal self. A mental image a person has of who they would like to be. (22)

ideal. Perfect. (2)

identity. A view of yourself as a person. (11)

images. Mental pictures of what you believe something is like. (2)

impact. Effect. (8)

impulse buying. Purchasing items without previous consideration or thought. (28)

impulse decisions. Decisions made quickly, without thought. (8)

incest. Sexual activity between people who are closely related. (13)

income-producing work. Work that provides money for needs. (10)

independence. The ability to take care of yourself. (1)

indirect advertising. Advertising that is more subtle. (28)

infatuation. (in-FACH-uh-WAY-shun). Intense emotional involvement that begins with a sudden, strong attraction based on physical appearance or other obvious traits. (19)

infertility. The inability to have children. (33)

institution of marriage. Marriage as a way of living. (30)

interdependence. A feeling of mutual reliance. (2)

interest. What is paid to use someone else's money. (27)

intervention. Taking direct action to cause change when someone else is in a crisis state. (13)

interview. A face-to-face meeting between an employer and a potential employee. (29)

intimacy. Closeness that develops from long friendships. (32)

introverted. Focused inward or on oneself. (22)

intrusive. (in-TROO-siv). Something that enters your life without your invitation or willingness. (3)

invalidation. (in-val-uh-DAY-shun). When partners respond negatively to each other, accusing and belittling each other. (12)

investing. Using money to make more money. (25)

isolation. (EYE-suh-LAY-shun). The feeling of being set apart from others and completely alone. (14)

J

joint account. An account in more than one person's name. (27)

L

launching. A process which sends children out on their own. (2)

leader. Someone who guides or influences others. (15)

lease. A written agreement between the landlord and the tenant spelling out the rights and responsibilities of each. (25)

leave of absence. Time off from work to use for some purpose. (10)

legal guardian. One who has financial and legal responsibility for taking care of a child. (2)

life task. A challenge to be met at each stage of growth. (21)

life-span development. Changes involving growth and development in all aspects of life, including physical, mental, emotional, social, and moral. (21)

loan. Money lent out at interest. (27)

long-term goals. Goals that require much time to be achieved. (9)

M

management process. A system for managing goals and resources to get what you want in life. (9)

marriage commitment. The desire to make a marriage work. (32)

material resources. Money and possessions. (9)

mature love. True or real love. (19)

maturity. (muh-TUR-uht-ee). Development of the physical, mental, emotional, social, and moral self. (23)

mediator. An unbiased person in the middle who leads others in conflicts to solutions. (6)

monitoring. Supervising children and being aware of where they are and what they are doing. (34)

moral code. The principles of right and wrong that you live by. (1)

moral decisions. Decisions that deal with matters of right and wrong. (8)

morality. A system of conduct based on what is right and wrong. (23)

motivate. Cause people to act. (9)

motor skills. The abilities that depend on the use and control of muscles, especially those in the arms, legs, hands, and feet. (34)

mutual. (MYOO-choo-al). When two people agree. (32)

mutuality. (myoo-chu-WAL-ut-ee). Two people contributing to the feelings and actions that support a relationship. (4)

N

needs. Requirements for a person's survival and proper development. (1)

negotiate. To deal or bargain with another. (6)

no-fault divorce. Allows partners to claim that the marriage relationship has broken down, with no one to blame. (12)

nonverbal communication. Communication without words. (5)

O

open adoption. An adoption procedure where the identities of the birth parents is made known to the adoptive parents. (33)

optimist. Someone with a positive point of view. (3)

options. Possible courses of action. (8)

osteoporosis. (AHS-tee-oh-por-OH-sis). A disease caused by lack of certain nutrients resulting in loss of bone mass. (16)

P

paranoia. (pare-uh-NOY-uh). The excessive fear of people and things. (26)

parenting readiness. The degree of preparation a couple has for parenting. (33)

parenting. The process of caring for children and helping them grow and learn. (33)

parliamentary procedure. Rules of order that describe how a meeting should be run so that everything goes smoothly and all points of view are heard. (15)

passive listening. Provides responses that invite the speaker to share feelings and ideas. (5)

peer pressure. An attempt to influence someone in a similar age group. (17)

permissive style. A parenting style in which parents tend to let children set their own goals, rules, and limits. (34)

personality. The characteristics that make a person unique. (1)

pessimist. Someone with a negative point of view. (3)

philosophy of life. The sum of one's beliefs, attitudes, values, and priorities. (23)

phobia. (FOE-be-uh). A strong, irrational fear for no obvious reason. (22)

pollutants. Impurities in the environment. (24)

possessive. A feeling of wanting to exclude all other relationships from the relationship of a couple. (19)

power. The ability to influence another person. (6)

prejudice. (PREJ-ud-us). An unfair or biased opinion, often about religious, political, racial, or ethnic groups. (23)

premarital counseling. Couples seeking the advice of trained professionals and counsel prior to marriage. (31)

prenuptial agreement. Marriage agreements that precede a wedding regarding special concerns of couples. (31)

press conference. Meetings held by political leaders where they answer questions from news media representatives. (24)

prioritize. (pry-OR-uh-tize). To rank something according to its importance. (9)

procrastination. (pruh-KRASS-tuh-NAY-shun). Putting off. (8)

professionalism. Showing a positive attitude toward, commitment to, and ethical behavior on the job. (29)

propinquity. (pro-PIN-kwit-ee). Nearness in time or place. (30)

R

rape. Forced sexual intercourse. (18)

rapport. (ra-POR). A feeling of ease and harmony with another person. (4)

readiness. Certain qualities and conditions to help show that a person is prepared, or positioned for marriage. (30)

reasoning. Thinking logically in order to reach a conclusion. (8)

reciprocation. (ri-SIP-ruh-KAY-shun). Giving and getting in return. (15)

reciprocity. (reh-sih-PROSS-ih-tee). Mutual exchange. (17)

references. People who have agreed to discuss your ability and character with a potential employer. (29)

reimbursements. (re-im-BERS-ments). Money paid back to families so they can afford child care of their own choosing. (10)

relationship. A connection made with another person. (4)

resourceful. Recognizing and making good use of resources. (9)

resources. Everything available to you for use in managing your life. (8)

respect. To hold someone in high regard. (6)

resumé. A written account of qualifications, including education or training and experience. (29)

risk. The possibility of loss or injury. (8)

role conflict. A disagreement over role expectations. (4)

role expectation. Anticipated behavior. (4)

role model. People you learn behavior from by shaping your thinking and giving you examples of behavior to copy. (4)

role. An expected pattern of behavior associated with a person's position in society. (4)

S

"sandwich generation." Refers to middle-aged adults who have responsibilities related to the generations on each side of their own age group. (16)

security deposit. A one-time payment paid when you move into a leased space. (25)

self-concept. The picture you have of yourself. (1)

self-discipline. The ability to direct your own behavior in a responsible way. (23)

self-disclosure. Telling about yourself. (4)

self-esteem. The way you feel about yourself. (1)

service industries. Jobs which involve processing information with the aid of computers and providing services to others. (3)

sexual identity. The way people see themselves as males and females. (20)

sexuality. How a person handles values and beliefs about sexual behavior. (20)

sexually transmitted disease (STD). An illness spread from one person to another through sexual contact. (20)

shelters. Offer a safe place to go in the event of physical violence or sexual abuse. (13)

short-term goals. Goals that require short periods to achieve. (9)

sibling rivalry. Competition between brothers and sisters. (7)

siblings. Brothers and sisters. (7)

small claims court. Courts that handle cases that do not exceed certain money limits that are set by each state. (28)

social exchange theory. The idea that people trade rewards and costs in relationships. (4)

socialization. The process of learning to relate and get along with others. (1)

stability. Having few changes in your life. (12)

stereotype. A standardized idea about the qualities or behavior of a particular category of people. (4)

sterility. The inability to have children. (20)

strategy. (STRAT-uh-jee). Basic plan. (10)

stress management. Techniques that help to cope responsibly and comfortably with the pressures of daily life. (11)

stress. Physical, mental, or emotional strain or tension. (11)

subculture. A culture shared by a group of people who live within a larger, different culture. (1)

support system. A group of resources that provide help when a family needs it. (10)

T

technology. Using scientific knowledge for practical purposes. (3)

temperament. The way a person reacts to the world and relates to others. (21)

time out. A disciplinary method involving removal of a child from the presence of others or from the center of activity for a short time. (34)

tolerance. (TAHL-uh-runts). The ability to accept people and situations as they are. (6)

traditions. Customs that are followed over time and often passed from one generation to another. (7)

trend. General direction of change over a period of time. (3)

trust. The belief that others will not reject, betray, or harm you. (4)

U

U-shaped curve. Describes something that starts at a high level, drops as time progresses, and then rises again, forming the letter "U." (32)

unemployment. Not having a job. (11)

unit price. A measure of the cost per unit of weight or volume. (28)

unrequited love. (un-rih-KWYT-ud). Love that is unreturned. (19)

V

vaccines. Chemicals developed to protect against specific diseases. (26)

value system. The set of values that you have. (1)

values. Beliefs and feelings about what is important. (1)

verbal communication. Spoken words. (5)

violence. Physical force used to harm someone or something. (13)

volunteerism. Willingness to give service to others. (24)

W

wants. Things desired but not essential. (1)

warranty. A written guarantee. (28)

wellness. A positive state of physical and mental health. (26)

will. A legal document that states how a person's property is to be distributed after death. (14)

work ethic. An attitude toward work. (10)

Index

Credits

Arnold & Brown, 18, 23, 24, 27, 33, 43, 60, 61, 66, 74, 83, 103, 109, 122, 132, 134, 146, 171, 172, 173, 176, 206, 207, 209, 219, 221, 234, 235, 238, 240, 258, 260, 274, 295, 301, 342, 360, 366, 373, 374, 384, 393, 397, 423, 425, 428, 439, 454, 457, 459, 462, 479, 490, 492, 503, 506, 509, 512, 547, 549, 556, 568, 573, 580, 590, 615, 616, 621

Roger B. Bean, 173, 273, 294, 487

Keith Berry, 59, 127, 137, 138, 149, 152, 182, 188, 193, 200, 203, 257, 287, 291, 363, 436, 452, 486, 513, 518, 533, 581, 586, 592, 595

The Bettmann Archive, 73

CLEO Freelance Photography, 116, 220, 251, 270, 303, 313, 327, 350, 358, 359, 431, 594, 598

James Carlson, 221, 470

Leo de Wys, Inc.
  Bill Bachmann, 35, 148, 604
  Bob Krist, 98

Pam Francis, 418-419

David R. Frazier Photolibrary, Inc., 36, 37, 88, 89, 199, 211, 265, 434, 558, 591

FPG
  Ron Chapple, 21(T)
  Steve Joester, 256
  Bill Losh, 268
  Michael Simpson, 33

Ann Garvin, 52

General Motors Corporation, 79

Grand Illusions, 8

Linda K. Henson, 521

Image Bank,
  Adeo, 58
  Werner Bokelberg, 458
  David Brownell, 177
  Britt Erlanson, 239
  Don Klumpp, 75
  Elyse Lewin, 493
  Kevin Rose, 81
  Michael R. Shneps, 82
  Elaine Sulle, 511

Mary Jones, 17, 22, 28, 35, 40, 49, 57, 62, 71, 78, 87, 97, 105, 113, 118, 129, 135, 145, 152, 165, 171, 181, 187, 195, 202, 215, 224, 233, 240, 249, 254, 267, 272, 283, 291, 299, 306, 317, 323, 333, 339, 349, 357, 365, 370, 383, 389, 401, 408, 419, 425, 433, 440, 451, 457, 467, 472, 483, 492, 499, 507, 517, 526, 537, 542, 553, 558, 567, 572, 585, 594, 603, 613

Tom Lindfors, 14-15, 94-95, 162-163, 212-213, 280-281, 380-381, 448-449, 534-535

Troy Maben/David R. Frazier Photolibrary, Inc., 223

Ted Mishima, 16-17, 20, 28, 48-49, 62, 70-71, 96-97, 100, 106, 112-113, 128-129, 143, 144-145, 151, 159, 164-165, 180-181, 194-195, 197, 214-215, 232-233, 248-249, 252, 266-267, 282-283, 298-299, 316-317, 324, 332-333, 348-349, 351, 364-365, 382-383, 388, 393, 396, 400-401, 432-433, 450-451, 466-467, 482-483, 498-499, 516-517, 527, 536-537, 552-553, 566-567, 571, 583, 584-585, 589, 602-603, 620

Cristin Nestor, 18, 39, 460, 475, 530

North Wind Picture Archives, 72

Peoria Journal Star/Fred Zwicky, 554

Photo Edit
  Michelle Bridwell, 359
  Mary Kate Denny, 130
  Richard Hutchings, 318

Elena Rooraid, 529

David Young-Wolff, 471

Liz Purcell, 38, 55, 77, 108, 121, 139, 150, 169, 190, 199, 217, 242, 262, 269, 285, 312, 319, 337, 354, 360, 367, 394, 410, 413, 421, 437, 453, 468, 485, 508, 522, 541, 562, 575, 588, 605

Jeff Stoecker, 44, 63

Tony Stone Images, 2-3

Lori Adamski Peek, 191

Bruce Ayres, 131

Peter Correz, 40, 244, 340

Robert E. Daemmrich, 50

Ken Fisher, 91

John Fortunato, 56

Chip Henderson, 491

Frank Orel, 23

Steven Peters, 204

Don Smetzer, 275

Steve Weber, 524

David Young-Wolff, 115, 392

Ken Trevarthan, 76, 222, 455, 504, 507

USDA, 473

Uniphoto Picture Agency

Rick Brady, 276, 420

Paul Conklin, 427

Bob Daemmrich, 406, 412, 414, 415

Ed Elberfeld, 402, 435, 438

Charles Gupton, 284, 286

Henley & Savage, 216, 228, 300, 546

B. Metta, 255

Jeffry W. Myers, 226, 405

Frank Siteman, 309, 371, 399

Joe Sohm, 617

Bruce Waters, 369

Washington, DC Convention and Visitors Association, 31

West Light

Adamsmith Productions, 543

Annie Griffith Belt, 565

Comnet, 328

Dennis Degnan, 606

Fotographia Productions, 597

Walter Hodges, 1, 302, 304

Julie Houck, 322, 538

Brian Leng, 613

Julie Marcotti, 577

Jim Pickerell, 118

Jim Richardson, 310

Ken Rogers, 587

Mark Stephenson, 403

Lee White, 555

Mike Yamashita, 620

Jim Zuckerman, 353

Dana C. White, Dana White Productions, 5, 6, 7, 9, 10, 11, 13, 21(B), 29, 33, 34, 41, 42, 52, 53, 57, 64, 84, 87, 90, 99, 101, 102, 103, 119, 120, 125, 132, 133, 136, 141, 154, 158, 166, 167, 173, 175, 183, 196, 198, 202, 221, 229, 236, 238, 259, 272, 292, 297, 301, 334, 335, 341, 342, 344, 360, 368, 373, 386, 408, 410, 422, 423, 429, 441, 442, 444, 462, 463, 472, 475, 476, 481, 484, 489, 500, 502, 503, 510, 519, 523, 528, 540, 542, 547, 560, 569, 578, 580, 590

Duane R. Zehr, 361, 456

Special thanks to the following individuals, schools, business, and organizations for their assistance with photographs in this book. **In Peoria, Illinois:** The Greater Peoria Family YMCA Childcare Center, Woodruff High School. **In Chicago, Illinois:** Chicago Academy for the Arts, Esperanza Community Services, Facets Multimedia Theatre, Jones Metropolitan High School, Murray Language Academy, Oak Park River Forest High School, University of Illinois at Chicago Police Department, West Suburban Hospital. **In Southern California:** John Adams Middle School, Asian Youth Center, Mt. Olive Pre-School, The Manuel & Charlotte Myers Family, Santa Monica Community College, Santa Monica High School, Will Rogers Elementary School, Venice Family Clinic, Westside Women's Health Center, Windward School.

Models and fictional names have been used to portray characters in stories and examples in this text.